A Library of Literary Criticism

Leonard S. Klein

General Editor

The Editors

Martin Tucker, the general editor, is well known for his editorship of *Modern British Literature* and *Moulton's Library of Literary Criticism of English and American Authors*, as well as several literary studies. He has contributed the Old English section in this work. Other leading scholars:

Robert Raymo (Medieval)
Kenneth Friedenreich (Elizabethan and Jacobean)
Harold Kollmeier (Shakespeare)
John T. Shawcross (Milton and Neoclassical)
Betty T. Bennett (Romantic)
Wendell Stacy Johnson (Victorian)
Ray C. Longtin (American)

A Library of Literary Criticism

Frederick Ungar Publishing Co.
New York

A Survey of Modern Criticism
on English and American Literature
from the Beginnings
to the Twentieth Century

MARTIN TUCKER

General Editor

Volume IV: Supplement

Printed in the United States of America

Library of Congress Cataloging in Publication Data (Revised)

Main entry under title:

The Critical temper.

(A Library of literary criticism)
Includes bibliographical references and index.
CONTENTS.—v. 1. From Old English to Shakespeare. v. 2. From Milton to Romantic literature. v. 3. Victorian literature and American literature.—v. 4. Supplement.
1. English literature—History and criticism. 2. American literature—History and criticism. 3. American literature—History and criticism.
I. Tucker, Martin, ed. II. Series.
PR85.C77 820′.9 68-8116

ISBN 0-8044-3307-0

CONTRIBUTING EDITORS

General Editor, Martin Tucker

OLD ENGLISH LITERATURE

Martin Tucker
Long Island University

MEDIEVAL LITERATURE

Robert Raymo
New York University

ELIZABETHAN AND JACOBEAN LITERATURE

Kenneth Friedenreich
University of Texas at San Antonio

SHAKESPEARE

Harold Kollmeier
Temple University

MILTON, AND NEOCLASSICAL LITERATURE

John T. Shawcross
Graduate Center of the City University of New York

ROMANTIC LITERATURE

Betty T. Bennett
State University of New York at Stony Brook

VICTORIAN LITERATURE

Wendell Stacy Johnson
Hunter College of the City University of New York

AMERICAN LITERATURE

Ray C. Longtin
Long Island University

CONTENTS

FOREWORD TO THE SUPPLEMENT

This Supplement to *The Critical Temper*, published in 1969, expands and updates the survey of twentieth-century criticism on English and American literature from the beginnings to 1900. Like the three-volume original, the focus is on major authors and—in the case of earlier literature—anonymous works, those most likely to be studied in college courses covering the various periods.

The arrangement and approach remain the same as in the original *Critical Temper*. The work is arranged by periods, each under a different editorship. Within each period, authors are presented alphabetically and the criticism chronologically within each author section. While the criticism on many of the most important authors in the original set was arranged by genres or specific works, in the Supplement only those authors updated by twelve or more selections are so divided. Although a certain overall unity was sought, it was left to each individual editor to decide which authors would be included and, of course, which critical excerpts would be chosen. Thus, for example, John T. Shawcross, editor of the section "Milton, and Neoclassical Literature," found that the drama of the period has in recent years evoked less attention than in the past and felt further that criticism in periodicals was not as important as that in books.

Not every author from the original *Critical Temper* has been updated. Among the many who have, the coverage is not necessarily in proportion to their original treatment or general esteem. The emphasis has rather been on new critical approaches and insights during the past ten years. Thus, some major authors who have continued to evoke interest and criticism but no major shifts or departures may be absent from the Supplement or updated with only one or two selections. On the other hand, some authors and anonymous works not accorded separate sections in the original *Critical Temper* have been so treated in the Supplement because of a marked increase in critical attention. These are: *Deor, The Dream of the Rood, The Wanderer* and *The Seafarer*, John Clare, Mary Shelley, Mary Wollstonecraft, Charles W. Chesnutt, and Kate Chopin. Criticism has not been restricted to the last ten years for these authors and works.

Headnotes have been provided for the new authors and anonymous works, following the format of those given in the first three volumes. For authors being updated, new standard editions and biographies are noted, preceding the criticism; in a few instances, new bibliographic sources are given for authors not updated. The reader will also find that the Supplement contains a Cross-Reference Index to Authors and an Index to Critics, as was the case in the earlier volumes.

The editors extend their appreciation to the many publishers, periodicals, authors, and agents who have granted permission to reproduce the selections in this volume. Only in a very few instances was a worthy selection reluctantly omitted because permission was denied or a copyright holder's stipulations were unreasonable. The editors also wish to thank their respective universities and colleagues for encouragement on this project.

M.T.

PERIODICALS USED

Listed below are titles, their abbreviations, if any, and place of publication.

AL	American Literature (Durham, N.C.)
ATQ	American Transcendental Quarterly (Hartford, Conn.)
ASE	Anglo-Saxon England (Cambridge)
AnM	Annuale Mediaevali (Pittsburgh)
	The Arnoldian (Annapolis, Md.)
	Blake Studies (Normal, Ill.; later Memphis, Tenn.)
	The Chaucer Review (University Park, Pa.)
EAL	Early American Literature (Amherst, Mass.)
ELH	English Literary History (Baltimore)
ELR	English Literary Renaissance (Amherst, Mass.)
ES	English Studies (Lisse, Netherlands)
EIC	Essays in Criticism (Oxford)
HQ	The Hopkins Quarterly (Guelph, Ont.)
JEGP	Journal of English and Germanic Philology (Urbana, Ill.)
K–SJ	Keats–Shelley Journal (Cambridge, Mass.)
	Louisiana Studies (later Southern Studies; Natchitoches, La.)
	Medium Aevum (Cambridge)
MissQ	The Mississippi Quarterly (Mississippi State, Miss.)
MLQ	Modern Language Quarterly (Seattle)

MLR	The Modern Language Review (Cambridge)
MP	Modern Philology (Chicago)
	Moreana (Angers, France)
	Mosaic (Winnipeg, Manitoba)
Neophil	Neophilologus (Amsterdam)
NM	Neuphilologische Mitteilungen (Helsinki)
NYR	The New York Review of Books (New York)
NMS	Nottingham Mediaeval Studies (Nottingham)
PLL	Papers on Language & Literature (Edwardsville, Ill.)
PQ	Philological Quarterly (Iowa City, Ia.)
	PMLA (New York)
	The Psychoanalytic Review (New York)
	Proceedings of the British Academy (London)
SQ	Shakespeare Quarterly (Washington, D.C.)
SS	Shakespeare Survey (Cambridge)
SLJ	The Southern Literary Journal (Chapel Hill, N.C.)
Sp	Speculum (Cambridge, Mass.)
SEL	Studies in English Literature (New Orleans; later Houston)
SP	Studies in Philology (Chapel Hill, N.C.)
SIR	Studies in Romanticism (Boston)
SSL	Studies in Scottish Literature (Columbia, S.C.)
SLitI	Studies in the Literary Imagination (Atlanta)
	Studies in the Renaissance (New York)
TSLL	Texas Studies in Literature and Language (Austin, Tex.)
TLS	TLS: The Times Literary Supplement (London)
	Traditio (Bronx, N.Y.)

	The Victorian Newsletter (New York; later Gainesville, Fla.)
	Victorian Poetry (Morgantown, W. Va.)
	Victorian Studies (Bloomington, Ind.)
WAL	Western American Literature (Logan, Utah)
WHR	The Western Humanities Review (Salt Lake City, Utah)
	The Wordsworth Circle (Philadelphia)

OLD ENGLISH LITERATURE

Martin Tucker, editor

ALFRED THE GREAT

849–899

Thomas A. Carnicelli, ed., *King Alfred's Version of St. Augustine's Soliloquies* (1969)

An investigation of the themes of the Old English *Consolation* reveals integrity, intelligence, and even profundity. Alfred has managed to adapt with a great degree of skill the dominant ideas that Boethius brings forward. Freedom consistently and on many levels takes the place of Boethian order as the primary condition of human existence; Wyrd [fate] takes the place of fortune as the major secondary condition; and Wisdom takes the place of Philosophy as the means by which man endures and at least occasionally triumphs over what is allotted to him after he chooses. Yet, in spite of the coherence the Old English adaptation has in themes and ideas, it is not a complete stylistic success.

It has sometimes been said that this obscurity (so called here for lack of a better term) of the Old English text is caused by Alfred's insufficient knowledge of Latin and the shortcomings of Old English. (See W. J. Sedgefield, *King Alfred's Version of the Consolations of Boethius; Done into Modern English*, Oxford, 1900.) But the absence of translation errors and the full-scale consistent alterations that extend in some cases from the opening pages of the Old English work to its conclusion indicate clearly that Alfred was aware both of Boethius' beliefs and of the difference in his own. Old English also is uselessly blamed; E. K. Rand points out that Latin itself was not a philosophical language until Boethius, who wished to make completely accurate translations of Greek philosophy, adapted it for this purpose. Had Alfred had the training and the intents of Boethius, there is no reason, as far as his language was concerned, why he could not have made a translation. Old English, with the rich coining power of the Germanic languages, would certainly have proved adequate for the purpose.

The fault of the style of Alfred's work lies in a rather more complex sphere than that described by ignorance or an inadequate language; it lies in a discrepancy between thought and style, between Alfred's ideas and the form in which they are presented. Style is the structure of the work, of its arguments, of its sentences, of the assumptions behind its words—a structure that arises in, and in its complexity mirrors, a writer's conception of the universe. When all is in harmony, there is a perfect correlation between thought and style, as there is in Boethius' text and as there is to a greater extent in Alfred's. . . .

The conception of the universe that Alfred had evolved by the last years of his life compelled him to make many changes in the Latin text, and these changes in turn altered the style, but when he considered the whole work, he was probably aware that the Latin argument provided him with a structure that he could rely on while he explained the insecurity in his world. In borrowing this form, Alfred tacitly admitted that Boethius was the greater thinker, and for himself surrendered an undisputed claim to originality. But because of the power of his determination to express his beliefs, his book is not to be reckoned a failure. He succeeded in giving each page the imprint of his own mind, its honesty, strength, stubbornness; in spite of his self-imposed restriction, his ideas emerge with their own beauty and validity, which, it seems to me, in the final accounting transcend the partial irrelevance of his means of developing them.

F. Anne Payne
King Alfred and Boethius (Madison: Univ. Wisconsin Pr., 1968), pp. 135–36, 147

On the whole, English royalty has not been noted for devotion to the arts. So Alfred's combination of military prowess with scholarship may seem at first to be a little incongruous. It is certainly remarkable for a layman to have done so much in an age when the clergy were the chief authors, scribes and teachers. Yet his literary work is all of a piece with his military; in both he was seeking the welfare of his people. . . .

Exciting is not really the right word for Alfred's translations. They are workmanlike attempts to use the language to express more than a bare recital of facts, and when he was writing, English was an untried medium at this level. As he says himself, he sometimes translates word for word and sometimes paraphrases. He is governed by his originals but not so slavishly that he cannot break away from the Latin periodic sentence (which despite its later skilful employment by Dr. Johnson sits unnaturally in English), or add his own comments and glosses to the text he is translating. The most extended of these are the passages he added to Orosius, in which he retells the voyages of the Norwegian Ohthere along the outer coast of Scandinavia round past the North Cape to the White Sea, and of another traveller, Wulfstan, in Baltic waters from Slesvig to the mouth of the Vistula. Both these travels reappear in [Richard] Hakluyt's *Voyages,* and there are those who say Alfred's version is finer than the Elizabethan. But perhaps more typical are the shorter interjections and illustrations from daily life which he uses to explain and expand on his texts. In fact many will find that it is the passages where he is speaking with his own voice that are the ones which most come to life. In this he is rather like Malory six centuries later. Malory, too, is extending the range of English prose at the very beginning of modern English by working from foreign sources to produce his Arthurian romance. But his *Morte d'Arthur* is less of a translation and more of an original work. Even so the strain of working in an untried medium shows from time to time, and the passages where he turns to the reader in his own voice can clearly be seen to be less constrained. The same is true of Alfred; the difference for us is that we find Malory's subject-matter intrinsically more interesting. What is exciting about Alfred is that he was tackling the problems of vernacular prose writing so early; what is sad is that the course of history undid his work.

M. W. Grose and Deidre McKenna
Old English Literature (London: Evans, 1973), pp. 34, 37–38

F. Anne Payne, in *King Alfred and Boethius*, has analyzed Alfred's text as an expression of Christian Existentialism. . . . By Christian Existentialism she means that the dialogue between *Mod* and *Wisdom* takes place in a world lacking in Order and a sense of God's all-knowing eternity—a world in which there is an overpowering "sense of absurd disparity between the strength of man and the naked strength of Wyrd." Her view can be well summed up in the contrast that she finds in the dominant parts of speech used by the two authors: "Being for Boethius; Becoming for Alfred."

My disagreements with Payne center particularly in her discussions of order and eternity. She has captured, however admirably, only one-half of Alfred's vision. To say that one of Alfred's most important alterations of the Boethian text is his substitution of a theory which is based on the idea of freedom for one which is based on the idea of order is to ignore significant portions of the work. I do not believe it is possible to say, as Payne does, that Alfred never uses the natural world as a symbol of order, that for Alfred only present time exists and never a vision of eternity as a contrasting state of being. Alfred describes the natural order as the embodiment of change, as well as of cycle and order. I agree that for long stretches of his version it seems as if there is only the struggle of this present life, but then there are also very definite pictures of eternity as a state beyond this life and only by equivocation can one argue that Alfred does not present the vision of an orderly realm above the storms of this earth as well as the eternity of the second death.

Katherine Proppe
NM (December, 1973), pp. 635–36

ANGLO-SAXON CHRONICLE

891

The Anglo-Saxon Chronicle, if not actually a product of Alfred's educational programme, was compiled in his reign and most likely in the period when the translations were being made. The early part (it begins with Caesar's invasion of Britain in 54 B.C.) must come from secondary sources and is thus of less interest, but from 449 onwards it draws upon early traditions in its annalistic account of the coming of the English and their subsequent history, becoming fuller in its treatment of events as it approaches the date of compilation and can use living memory. Such a history would certainly fit in with Alfred's programme of education, and help to strengthen feelings of nationhood in his subjects. Copies were made and distributed to important centres, where some were continued. Seven manuscripts survive, but their relationships with these copies and with each other is a complicated and confused question. One called the *Parker Chronicle* because it once belonged to Matthew Parker, the Elizabethan archbishop and collector, came originally from Winchester. It was written around 900—from the beginning to 891 it is in one hand—and was continued in a variety of contemporary hands until 1070. Another, the *Peterborough Chronicle*, is written in one hand up to 1121 from a text originating at Canterbury and was continued at Peterborough until 1154, the last of the Chronicles to be kept up. The dates and coverage of the other five manuscripts fall between these two.

The *Chronicle* has been compared to a diary with entries for years instead of days, and the analogy has a lot of truth in it, for it is not a connected, coherent history, though in places the story does run on from year to year. It is patchy like a diary; there are many years without an entry, and many entries are obviously written up later to fill gaps. Some entries are so brief as to give almost a surrealist view of events, just as the notes in an old diary often show that the preoccupations of the moment are not always with what is going to have long-term importance. But it says what it has to say plainly and not without a touch of poetic imagination. . . .

M. W. Grose and Deidre McKenna
Old English Literature (London: Evans, 1973), pp. 38–39

BEDE

671–735

W. F. Bolton, *A History of Anglo-Latin Literature 597–1066*, Vol. I: 597–740 (1967)

Bede laboured faithfully to transmit what was true, and made every effort to verify facts and name his sources. This is to be expected of an honest historian, and so it sometimes surprises people to find that at the same time he includes in the *History* so many stories of strange wonders and incredible happenings. Not only does he relate how holy men saw visions and performed miracles but he also calmly states that at the moment when the head of Alban the martyr fell to the ground the eyes of his executioner dropped out, and that the scrapings of leaves from books out of Ireland and chips from the wooden beam on which Aidan leant when he died "being put into water" cured many of snake-bite and disease. We should not expect to find such stories now in a history book, but it must be remembered that Bede set out not only to record historical facts but also to preserve the stories and legends which were current in his day, and by doing so he has added enormously to our knowledge of those far-off times. We realize, for instance, on reading the stories of miraculous happenings how primitive in outlook and how credulous people were. They had no knowledge of the unchanging scientific laws that govern the universe but lived in a world where, it seemed to them, "every bush had its demon and every grove of trees its god." Their feeling of helplessness before unseen forces was profound and they longed for marvellous powers and events to come between them and an often malignant fate. For a long time after Christianity came to Britain men's faith was a strange mixture of Christian belief and pagan superstition, and this is illustrated by Bede's story of the sons of King Sabert of the East Saxons who refused baptism but clamoured to be allowed to go to Mass. . . .

Bede was essentially a man of his time. What marks him as something more is that he took such care to check when he could the truth of the stories he includes, not simply accepting a picturesque legend but patiently inquiring of those in a position to know the truth.

Mary R. Price
Bede and Dunstan (London: Oxford Univ. Pr., 1968), pp. 28–29

It must be admitted that Bede's Biblical commentaries are not nowadays read save by those concerned with his theology or with tracing the different sources which he used and the particular methods which he employed. Passionate in his support of orthodoxy and in his condemnation of heresy, he was a traditionalist whose prime concern was with the diffusion of the accepted beliefs of the catholic church, as they had reached him through the works of the fathers, among people who, as we can all too easily forget, were still emerging from paganism. We may recall an occasion when some monks were caught by wind and tide and carried out to sea beyond the mouth of the Tyne, while rustics on the bank jeered at them. "Let no man pray for them," they said, "for they have robbed men of their old ways of worship, and how the new worship is to be conducted, nobody knows."

It was towards the conduct of the new worship and to spreading a knowledge of its Scriptures that Bede devoted the greater part of his intellectual life. This was the achievement by which he himself, his contemporaries and the posterity of the European Middle Ages set the greatest store. The measure of that achievement is not easily gauged but we can appreciate something of its magnitude by merely learning that, apart from all his other writings, his Biblical commentaries on both the Old and the New Testament comprise about 45 books, some relatively short, others of considerable length. The influence of these books on the civilisation of western Europe is strikingly indicated by the fact that they can still be read in substantially more than 950 manuscripts scattered across every part of western Europe. Not all of his works achieved equal popularity. For example the four books of his commentary on Samuel are known in only eight manuscripts, perhaps because his extreme use of the allegorical method in this commentary proved distasteful. But his commentary on St Mark's Gospel is known in 95 manuscripts, on St Luke's Gospel in 90 and on the Catholic Epistles in more than 110. Bede's Biblical commentaries, already beginning to circulate in England during his lifetime, spread across Germany and France within a few years of his death. Many of them were still being copied in the twelfth and thirteenth centuries.

Peter Hunter Blair
The World of Bede (London: Secker & Warburg, 1970),
pp. 298–99

If one looks at the titles of the works available to Bede, one is struck by the absence of books of philosophical theology or of a metaphysical content. Bede did not, apparently, have access to Augustine's early philosophical writings, the *Contra Academicos*, the *De Beata Vita* or the *De Ordine*, nor did he have the *De Trinitate*, perhaps the greatest of Augustine's theological works, nor any of the treatises of the fourth-century Latin Christian Platonist Marius Victorinus. Again, he did not have a copy of Chalcidius's commentary on part of the *Timaeus*, one of the very few platonic sources available in the Latin west in the early Middle Ages, or of a work like that of Apuleius, *De Deo Socratis*. One can understand the absence of such works from a monastic library; but what is surprising is the lack of any work of Boethius, either the *Consolatio*—an omission so remarkable as to cause [Max L. W.] Laistner to remark upon it in his article on Bede's library—or of the theological tractates and translations.

The implications of this deficiency in his library are clear: Bede was deprived, through no fault of his own, of precisely the sort of works needed by a Latin divine to whom the writings of the Greek Fathers were not available, if he aspired to be in any sense of the term a dogmatic theologian. To suggest that, had such works been available, Bede would have produced great works on dogmatic theology would be wholly unwarranted; and in any case such an achievement, however admirable and desirable in itself, would have been of less value to the church of his day in England or on the continent of Europe than what he actually achieved. The process by which the barbarian kingdoms, established after the ending of Roman rule in the west, were turned into the civilized states of the Middle Ages was a gradual one, requiring several centuries of diligent scholarship to prepare the way for the renaissance of the twelfth century. To that renaissance Bede contributed much; but there are some things—its philosophy and its humanism—in which he had no share. The cultural achievement of Northumbria was a limited one, the work of a small élite of monks and clerics and a few cultured laymen within a restricted field, and it was within that field that Bede made his great contribution to medieval civilization. Bede was, without question, a great intellect, a great teacher, and a great Christian; but it is important in any evaluation of his work to maintain a sense of proportion. Bede served later generations as a commentator, a grammarian, an historiographer and a computist. This is his achievement, and it is enough to establish his greatness.

Gerald Bonner
ASE, Vol. 2 (1973), pp. 89–90

BEOWULF

650–750?

George N. Garmonsway and Jacqueline Simpson, trs., *"Beowulf" and Its Analogues* (1968) (prose)

The anonymous author of *Beowulf* was a master craftsman in the techniques available to every poet in any era. He clearly understood the need for structure and unity, both in the poem as a whole and in its individual parts. His descriptive passages reveal a knack for the telling detail, while his characterizations depend more on revelation than narration. His narrative technique is primarily dramatic, the product of both acute juxtapositions and gradual accumulation of detail. The pace is slow, befitting the sombre tone and theme. In the use of those particular advantages afforded the traditional formulaic poet (of Homeric Greece, Anglo-Saxon England, and modern Yugoslavia), he is unexcelled in English. His art never depends on the transcendence of tradition and the modern fetish for originality; rather he displays his mastery in exploiting to the full the potentials of inherited materials (plots and characters) and techniques (formulaic diction, themes and type-scenes). . . .

Lately, some scholars have returned to the nineteenth-century notion of a multiplicity of shorter poems bound together into a poorly unified whole, with the corollary of multiple authorship. The poem does divide neatly at line 1998 (with Beowulf's account to Hygelac of his adventures) and at 2200 (when events leading to Beowulf's coronation are described), and Beowulf's report in lines 2069a–2199 does differ in some details from the facts presented by the earlier narrator. But perhaps the poet is using a technique best known in the novels of Lawrence Durrell's *Alexandria Quartet*, by which the same events are described in variant terms by persons with entirely different points of view. The narrator's emphases for his audience would naturally differ from those of Beowulf reporting to his king, who would need details of the Danish political situation and justification for the loss of his retainer Hondscioh. The result of the report is unity, by summation of the events in Part I. He uses the same technique in the dual narration of the Breca episode and the repeated oblique references to Hygelac and Heremod.

Donald K. Fry
Introd., in *The "Beowulf" Poet: A Collection of Critical Essays*
(Englewood Cliffs, N.J.: Prentice-Hall, 1968), pp. 1–3

Even though in important ways Beowulf is set apart from other men, he shares the traditional values of Germanic society. When we concentrate on examining his battles with the monsters, we are necessarily stressing his uniqueness; most men are not qualified even to meet monsters, let alone defeat them. But when we see him in the scenes at court, or with his uncle King Hygelac or his young kinsman Wiglaf, we are conscious of the ways in which he not only accepts but asserts to the fullest extent the values of the world he lives in. In the long run, of course, both his detachment from the ordinary activities and capabilities of men and his involvement in them are needed for the developing of that stereoscopic effect of reality which this poem (like all major poems) creates. . . .

Consistently Beowulf's energies are directed outward and away from the world of human violence and warfare, directed outward with the purpose of preserving human community by fending off threats from the outside. All through the poem Beowulf's is the embodiment of a moral discipline so perfect as to seem instinctive and effortless. His tremendous strength, both physical and spiritual, is applied to precise objectives for the good of other men: it is never wasted, never turned on itself, never beyond the control of his calm heroic will.

Ravenswood is Beowulf's absence. It is what the world is like without him and without the almost superhuman values he asserts. It is ironic that for the Geats the story of the battle is superficially one of rescue and salvation. Their experience of being helpless and lordless during the battle is acute and frightening, but brief: Hygelac rides melodramatically over the hill to save them. But they were saved then only by the arrival of Hygelac, and saved later from the dragon's attacks only by the courage of Beowulf. But the Messenger's speech was prefaced by an elaborate reminder of the deaths of these two kings. That was the last rescue; there will never be another.

Ravenswood, as a vision of the perpetual violence which is man's lot, moves out of history into a timeless world. That battle of the far past is now, and it is the future for the Geatish nation. The scene suddenly and vividly fuses *wen*, the expectation of the probable future, with *geo*, the distant but inescapable past, and both with the insistent verbs of driving action in the present. The startling sense of life and reality of the narrative of the battle, its greater vividness and concreteness of detail in a poem where so much is half-veiled in misty hints, its exposure of basic universals of human experience in a scene that is both specific and half-allegorical—all these go far to give the Messenger's later prophecy of unending warfare and ultimate extinction for Beowulf's people the solid impact of fact, not fantasy. We know that it was, and if it was it will be.

Edward B. Irving, Jr.
A Reading of "Beowulf" (New Haven, Conn.: Yale Univ. Pr., 1968), pp. 129, 190–91

The whole episode [the battle between Beowulf and Grendel] is presented strongly in terms of God's power. Fundamentally it is His victory, although He acts through His chosen instrument, Beowulf. More than the Christian commonplace of God's omnipotence seems, however, to be implied in the description of the action. A much more technical notion, that of the *judicium Dei*, the judgment of God, as it was known, appears to lie behind the episode. This term is used by those who participated in or discussed trial by combat to refer to an organized attempt to call upon God to direct the justice of a claim or an action, and very often in the early Middle Ages to decide the truth of an accusation of treason. The language of the description and above all the barehanded approach of Beowulf so that equality will reign between the combatants argue for such an interpretation. Even the phrase *judicium Dei* (Dryhtnes dom) is used, and the power of God is continually stressed. . . .

Strictly speaking, of course, the battle with Grendel could not be a trial by combat because only one combatant appeals to God. Perhaps Beowulf by this very move not only claimed God's help by judiciary duel procedure but, by making quite clear to all that Grendel as an accursed descendant of Cain could not call upon God as he had done, emphasized and underlined Grendel's evil nature. On the other hand, perhaps, the Lord's injunction in Genesis not to raise one's hand against Cain might have been in his mind. Only with God's support can one hear the divine command. However, to settle this one would have to go into the whole tradition of Cain to determine whether the prohibition applied to Cain's descendants. [Robert David] Stevick has recently pointed out that although Grendel is quite clearly evil, there is "no implication [before Beowulf arrives] that Grendel's depredations in Denmark represent strife against God—or that his monster predecessors stray against God by means of attacks on earlier inhabitants of Denmark." The uncertainty of psychological motives in the first battle of the poem is indeed very great, and only speculation seems possible. The trial by combat element does, however, demand a new looking into it all.

With Byrhtnoth [in *The Battle of Maldon*], there is even more uncertainty. It is certainly not a duel *stricto sensu* because the other side does not appeal to God and besides it is not a battle of champions, but of armies against each other. The poet's attitude towards his hero may be condemnatory although there is an ambiguity of mood perhaps reflected in the word *ofermōd*. Tempting God by the judicial combat is not as far as I know alluded to in tenth-century England or earlier, but the notion of tempting God, as *Solomon and Saturn* shows, was not unknown. Perhaps the poet feels that Byrhtnoth has no right to call upon God to decide the battle; perhaps not. In any case, the hero calls upon God and allows his enemies to approach on even terms. He at least wants to make it a trial by combat to that extent even if all the conditions cannot be filled.

The two suggestions offered here, then, force us to rethink our interpretations of *Beowulf* and *Maldon* and raise again the question of trial by combat in England before the Norman Conquest. Whether we can accept the latter in England then or not, it is clear that Old English literature affords at least two examples of something very close to it. As [R.] Selden says, it may not be "easy to prove this custom" then, but this lack has always occasioned surprise. Perhaps we can now look at the matter differently.

Morton W. Bloomfield
Sp (October, 1969), pp. 546–47, 558–59

I believe that the Christian poet's purpose was to examine the values of the heroic world as they appear when set against the whole history of mankind from Genesis to the Apocalypse.

Beowulf had not customarily been looked at in this way in modern times, before I published my theory of the Christian theme of *Beowulf* in 1960, though Professor J. R. R. Tolkien had gone a long way in that direction in his highly influential essay, "*Beowulf*: The Monsters and The Critics." The reasons for the origin and persistence of other ideas about the nature of the poem require mention, as does Tolkien's own halt in a mid-way position.

Like all *Beowulf* students of the last thirty years, I owe a great debt to Tolkien, who taught us to read the poem with imagination, as he had done. He gave us the key to understanding in his recognition of two special elements in the work: the "fusion-point of imagination" which lies in the references to Cain, and "the memories viewed in a different perspective" which give the poem its depth. The first part of his now classic essay indicated some of the preoccupations which had blinded *Beowulf* scholars to the essential unity of the poem, and to these I need not revert. Another impediment *not* discussed by him was, I am sure, the belief that the hero of the poem was created as an ideal exemplar. Since Beowulf did not speak and behave at all points like a Christian prince, it was difficult to escape the conclusion that his creator had a somewhat limited or confused idea of Christian living. This conclusion did not accord with the unmistakably Christian language and thought of Hrothgar's long speech of admonition to Beowulf in lines 1700–84, and most critics, Tolkien included, agreed that at least part of the speech must have been added to the composition by a later hand.

Finding this view unsatisfactory, I began to work with the assumptions that Tolkien was right about the poet's historical perspective (which implied that Beowulf was a noble pagan) and about the importance of the references to Cain (which led me into research concerning the traditional relationship of "Cain's kin" and the Dragon) and that Tolkien was wrong to exclude Hrothgar's admonition from his consideration of the fusion-points between the heroic and the Christian worlds (which led to a study of the evolution of the figure of the heroic spiritual warrior). These researches disclosed that Hrothgar's admonition could itself be used as a key to unlock the symbolic meaning of Beowulf's life, involving as it does the right use of kingly power and wealth, which seemed to me to be a central concern of the poet, largely disregarded in Tolkien's interpretation. When I had satisfied myself that my original assumptions had been justified, in that I could now provide self-consistent answers to the critical questions raised by the text, I proceeded to draw inferences concerning the possible existence of different kinds of hidden meaning latent in the poem. . . .

Margaret E. Goldsmith
The Mode and Meaning of "Beowulf" (London: Athlone, 1970), pp. 2–3

guages to which English is related. Had it somewhere in its manuscript history succumbed to those perils of age, neglect, and fire to which we know it has been exposed, we should be left to speculate whether in fact the poets of any branch of the Germanic people were capable of composing a long sustained poem on a theme drawn from the world of pre-Christian Germanic tradition. In the light of such phenomena as the Sigurd lays of the Poetic Edda, the Latin *Waltharius*, the upturned horn of story which is Saxo's Danish History, and the Christian witness of the Old English *Andreas*, we might assume that they were, yet always be uneasy in the assumption. So the manuscript in which *Beowulf* is preserved, British Museum, Cotton Vitellius A 15, is a primary document not only for the English, but for the Germans, the Scandinavians, and their descendants in the New World as in the Old, with its proof that their ancestors had mastered the art of prolonged verse narrative and attempted that elevated mode of poetry which for the moment we may be content to describe as epic.

Moreover, this is a poem with claims on our regard far beyond its power of manuscript survival. It is most easily described as a poem of an epical and heroic nature, and in respect of its incident and action provides a notable synthesis of Germanic heroic legend and international wondertale as this latter was viewed in a Germanic context. . . . Structurally, to a modern eye, it is less than perfect; even so its story of a young hero is compelling, of an old hero moving. It offers a noble picture of an age, its assumptions and behaviour, its hierarchical bases, and the gold-decked splendour of its warrior class. It conducts its protagonist through diverse settings and episodes, by land and sea, at court and in battle, in contests with monsters and courtesies with his peers. And our poet has time for much more than adventures and monster-riddings. He was conscious, like other Anglo-Saxon poets, of the world's lack of duration. Life, he knows, is fleeting; all things are hastening to their end. . . .

Beowulf is a poem of multiple source and episode, which combines the attractions of a brave tale with high moral seriousness, and offers a reading of life and experience. And finally, it is by any standards a good, even a fine poem; and there have been many to think it a great one—less for its movement and action, or fable, than because they find it a statement about human life and values by an artist who—by virtue of his technical ability, his command of words and metre, his power to present narrative, argument, reflection, mood, and feeling in verse—has given lasting significance to the thing he wrote. . . .

Gwyn Jones
Kings, Beasts and Heroes (London: Oxford Univ. Pr., 1972), pp. 3–4

What makes Beowulf a tragic figure is his superabundance, his capacity for superhuman acts, his strength of thirty men, his exalted sense of social obligation, and his generosity—all these being characteristics that place him above ordinary human experience, to the point where, finally, he is destroyed by a dragon. It is this heroic energy, first visible in the sea passage from Geatland to Heorot and in his account of the swimming contest with Breca, and continued in the fights with Grendel and his mother, that is the basis of the poem's romance. Heaven's plenitude has extended in extraordinary measure to this greatest of men between the seas, and his experiences show him as constantly bursting the confines of normal earthly life. His energy is directed to the protection of the most ideal form of heroic life and society in middle-earth—Heorot in its unfallen aspect. In contrast to Beowulf, his king Hygelac, though reputed in Germanic historical monuments to have been almost a giant, falls dead in the land of the Franks while Beowulf swims away, carrying the armor of thirty men.

But Beowulf, like Heorot, becomes simply a memory. The close alignment of aged hero and dragon in Part 2 is the poem's decisive reminder that in the tragic vision even the most heroic form, perhaps most especially the heroic form, is defeated by the elemental facts of existence in time. The world that remains after Beowulf has died contains two sorts of people, cowards and outlaws, on the one hand, and those faithful to dryht loyalties (Wiglaf, the weeping woman, and the circling horsemen), on the other. By this point we have been shown the impact of heroic energy on the world of the fallen dryht and have been shown also that in such a world it is heroic energy that is destroyed while the fallen creation continues in time. The golden dryht of middle-earth and the youthful Beowulf are poetic images of the kind of joy and reality the *hæleð* want, but the irony of the tragic vision decrees that life is not shaped according to human desires. The poet, with the quiet assurance of great artistry, follows his account of the roaring flames and raging winds of Beowulf's cremation with a description of the disposal of physical things: the hero's ashes are sealed in a great barrow; the rings, necklaces, and armor of the ancient treasure are returned to the earth, hidden again and useless to men. Twelve riders circle the mound, ritually containing the grief of the Geats: they eulogize the greatness and glory of their dead king, and they mourn his passing. The closing scene expresses a pronounced tragic sense of confinement, of the putting into dark places of all that is splendid in this world. It shows the stilling of heroic energy.

Alvin A. Lee
The Guest-Hall of Eden: Four Essays on the Design of Old English Poetry (New Haven, Conn.: Yale Univ. Pr., 1972), pp. 222–23

If Old English poetry has any distinctive subject, it is that of courage, of honour or the heroic life. Yet while Hamlet's apparent paradox is only a part of the debate about honour conducted, in Shakespeare, by Iago and Falstaff as well as by Fortinbras and Hotspur, one defect of Old English poems seems to be that in them no such debate is possible. In *Maldon* there are good retainers and bad retainers; the only choice open is to die honourably or live shamefully. In *Beowulf* those who have made the wrong choice are rebuked . . . and to this there is no answer. Not even those who run away are allowed to disagree with the ethic of honour; so, though the Old English philosophy may be admirable, it hardly seems in any way complex.

Are matters really so simple? At one extreme the historian Arnold Toynbee could call *Beowulf* a poem of "barbarism on the warpath." But at the other, the considerable literature of explanation which has grown up around the poem over the last fifty years is in almost total agreement about the work's extraordinary delicacy and sophistication; it is seen as allusive, elegiac, ironic. Nor is this merely critical over-refinement. The highly educated response to the poem which most scholars would now accept has become established because external facts give it firm support—for one, the identification of Beowulf's king and uncle Hygelac with the historical pirate "Chochilaicus," for another, the later Latin and Norse references to the Scylding family and King Hrothgar at whose court Beowulf carries out his first adventures. The conclusions drawn need not be set out here. What is important is that the *Beowulf*-poet seems to rely consistently on allusions to (presumably well-known) legends, and that he uses this material in what is almost an anti-heroic way, to prove that "the wages of heroism is death." He is not satirising, and maybe not even criticising; the emotions aroused are intricate. But clearly something which could be called a philosophy of the honourable life is present. . . .

Given the help of established scholarship and criticism, a modern reader can see irony in *Beowulf* practically everywhere. But is that likely to have been intended under Dark Age conditions, when such a poem could hardly be studied, and when most people would never read it, but only hear it, and perhaps only once? If it was, we must conclude either that Anglo-Saxons were abnormally intelligent, or that they had some assistance in responding which is denied to us, but which compensated for the modern reader's learned apparatus. The first possibility must regretfully be ruled out. Indeed Kenneth Sisam, the most notable sceptic among modern critics, has expressed justifiable doubt about the sensitivity or simple knowledge to be expected from the men who might listen to heroic poetry, the military nobility and their companions . . . men, as he drily reminds us, "not chosen primarily for their intellectual qualities." . . . But the second possibility, that the original audiences had some guide to response which we do not, remains, and is almost certainly to some extent valid.

T. A. Shippey
Old English Verse (London: Hutchinson, 1972), pp. 17–19

We have seen that the headstrong hero motif in the first part of the action serves to magnify Grendel and thereby the hero who overcomes him. But Hygelac's speech brings out, besides, the narrowness of his nationalism: since it was the Danish hall that Grendel was haunting, the Geatish king thought it should be left to the Danes to deal with the troll. Again, the speech brings up Hygelac's love for his nephew, a love that made him unwilling to have the dear kinsman risk his life in a needless cause. In virtue of these traits the poet characterizes not only Hygelac but (indirectly) Beowulf as well. . . .

Beowulf's speech [his first after the dragon fight] and that of the messenger make a consistent pattern on the principle of contrast which the poet follows, composing after the event: under Beowulf the Geats lived in peace and freedom; after his death the Geatish state fell, victim of attacks from abroad. The contrast serves, of course, to exalt the hero, whose greatness alone upheld the fortunes of his people. But this contrast can hardly be historical, and in any case it would hold good whether Beowulf died of a dragon's bite a little earlier or old age a little later. The effect of the aged king's death on the international situation is one thing; the manner of his death, something else again.

Many great men have died in bed but for heroic story Beowulf's way of dying is as it should be: fighting to the utmost against an evil foe of his people, a foe stronger than he. And the help of his faithful retainer brings it about that the hero can slay the foe even though taking a wound that proves mortal. Beowulf dies as he had lived, a *folces weard* indeed.

Kemp Malone
ASE, Vol. 1 (1972), pp. 144–45

The story of the Swedish king Ongentheow, murdered by Geats, and the story of Beowulf's dragon have odd similarities: both the king and the dragon are "old and terrible" and "crafty"; both retreat to caves which they mistakenly put their trust in, and die there defending their treasure hoards, the dragon defending his hoard of gold, Ongentheow defending a different kind of treasure (*hord forstandan, bearn and bryde*, 2955b–56a)—his children and wife; both the king and the dragon are wounded in the forehead, strike back ferociously, and are later finished off; and both are killed not by one man alone but by two kinsmen working together. In a poem as carefully constructed as *Beowulf*, a parallel so close can hardly be accidental. But what does it mean?

Beowulf bristles from end to end with curious echoes and parallels, repeated or pointedly juxtaposed details of language, imagery, or thought which bind the poem together and establish its assumptions and values—if we can figure the equations. The parallels show up in many forms and serve a variety of purposes, from textural interest to allegorical patterning. We hear repeatedly, for instance, of the sleep that follows the feast, the sorrow or joy which comes in the morning (Ongentheow claims he will hang his Geatish attackers in the morning), the great difference between words and works, the troubles brought on by drunkenness or by gold, and God's payment of his friends (the repetitions of *frofor*) and grim repayment of his enemies (e.g., of Cain, *he him ðæs lean forgeald*, 114b). We also hear key words repeated and occasionally echoed by related words, *bearm*, for instance, and its near-relation, *fæþm*, words used throughout in many senses, from the bosom of the family or the bosom of the death-ship to God's embrace or Grendel's hug.

Whether or not the poem was composed orally, the theory of oral-formulaic composition comes nowhere near accounting for this patterning. . . .

I suggest . . . that though Beowulf is not guilty of sinful irascibility or concupiscence, he is nevertheless guilty. His errors, in the warrior world he inhabits, are as inescapable as, say, original sin. And that, I think, may be the poet's point. Beowulf had nothing to do, directly, with the murder of Ongentheow; if he bears any guilt at all, it is strictly guilt by association. But the parallel between the old Swedish king and the flame-spewing dragon suggests that in some way it is Ongentheow's ghost that kills him.

John Gardner
in *Anglo-Saxon Poetry: Essays in Appreciation*, ed. Lewis E. Nicholson and Dolores Warwick Frese (Notre Dame, Ind.: Univ. Notre Dame Pr., 1975), pp. 14–15, 22

Did the Anglo-Saxon audience appreciate *Beowulf*? Probably yes! Of course some may have preferred another poem celebrating the same or other events. But its very creation presupposes an audience at least willing to hear it and make comments about it. None of these opinions are recorded, and the lack of references to the poem anywhere in the writings of the Anglo-Saxon period has to some been a matter of surprise. It is a matter more worthy of surprise, however, that the first reviews were not to appear until a thousand years later.

Why is *Beowulf* important? The answer that has been most generally given, and possibly the only answer agreed upon, is the following: "It is very old and it gives many glimpses of the life of our distant ancestors." One cannot help wondering what those ancestors—the first audience of *Beowulf*—would do with an answer like that. Moving it back towards Anglo-Saxon times it loses all meaning—or at least all the meaning now attached to it. To anyone but the scholar who has his own investigations to make, to anyone who wants to appreciate it in its own right, it is the wrong answer. And in making *Beowulf* a scholarly problem—how old?, what glimpses?, what ancestors? etc. *ad infinitum*—it proved a bad answer. The history of more than a century of *Beowulf* criticism shows how, with some exceptions, belief in the problem was stronger than the belief that the poem may have been worth creating. . . .

The focus in *Beowulf* is on man's experience of the man-monster predicament. The monster is man's existential problem which has to be solved again and again.

As will appear a long series of concepts from the sphere of existentialist philosophy may be found applicable to *Beowulf*. An analysis of the relationship between the two spheres of thought might be interesting in itself, but would perhaps add little to what has already been said as far as the poem is concerned. Philosophy and art are different categories. With a work of art existentialism as such can have no place except as integrated beyond recognition; but a successful work of art, if it is another embodiment of the existentialist search for reality, will add to, and—by being a formulation which through no definition can have a parallel—modify, the abstract concept of existentialism within the world of ideas.

Andreas Harder
"Beowulf": The Appeal of a Poem (Trykt, Norway: Akademisk Forlag, 1975), pp. 13, 278

The ideals, divine and human, of paganism and Christianity exist side by side in *Beowulf*. The poem contains concepts both of a blind and whimsical force whose dealings with men are unrelated to their merit, and of a benevolent Christian deity who affords grace and guidance to the worthy. Similarly, Beowulf himself is presented both as the pagan heroic ideal of the mighty and renowned warrior and as the Christian ideal of the virtuous hero who rightly attributes his special powers, and the deeds arising from those powers, to the grace of God. . . .

Charles W. Kennedy [in *The Earliest English Poetry*] notes in his discussion of *Beowulf* "a parallelism of reference to the blind and inexorable power of *Wyrd* and to the omnipotence of a divine Ruler Who governs all things well," and points out, in addition, that sometimes "God and *Wyrd* are brought into juxtaposition in such a manner as to imply control of Fate by the superior power of Christian divinity." Kennedy's arguments are taken over by Miss [Marie Padgett] Hamilton in support of the view that the *Beowulf*-poet's concept of *Wyrd* is similar to that which appears in King Alfred's paraphrase of Boethius. . . . However, textual evidence which serves to indicate that fate in *Beowulf* is subject to God is limited to two passages. . . .

In *Beowulf*, the pagan ideals of personal prowess and earthly fame are far from being referable to the sin of pride and therefore at odds with God's grace, as the case might be in a poem with a more orthodox Christian world view. Rather, personal strength is a gift of God, and if it is properly used men are rewarded with victory in battle and as a consequence gain earthly renown. It is therefore not out of keeping with the Christian aspects of the poem that, in mourning Beowulf's death, the Geats . . . affirm that he was the *lofgeornost* of all the kings of the world. Beowulf's deeds of valour and his achievement of earthly fame are the proof that his activities have been blessed with the grace and guidance of God.

Mary C. Wilson Tietjen
JEGP (April, 1975), pp. 161, 170–71

What criticism can do is to illumine truth, but creative vision extends truth, shapes the archetype in its own image, commenting imaginatively (and hence more than logically) upon its archetypal mother. This happens all too rarely, but happen it does in John Gardner's *Grendel*, which illustrates the perfect rapport possible between two workings of a single myth. That it can stand beside the epic *Beowulf* is no small judgment on the achievement of the novel. . . .

To the hero's will to victory and the king's will to order, but above all to the poet's will to artistic reordering, Gardner's Grendel opposes his own absolute, "I knew what I knew, the mindless mechanical bruteness of things." Even as Grendel in the poem is stirred to violence by the tale of divine creation, Gardner's monster opposes the vision of human and historical continuity of which the Shaper sings. He endorses the law of violence which a rustic urges upon Hrothgar. He half grasps the Dragon's affirmation of an absolute law of entropy, random ordering and necessary dissolution. As the monster of *Beowulf* wreaks violence in reaction against the harper's tale of creation, so Gardner's monster opposes destruction to the Shaper's tale of order and to Hrothgar's vision of purposeful society. . . .

Grendel ignores—perforce must ignore—that man can interact and transcend his origins, while he, the monster *qua* monster, cannot. In this he defines monster. Beowulf knows the nature of courage, man's mortality and immortality as fame. Thus he defines the nature of the hero. The Shaper knows one truth beyond the truth of time: that vision which orders things and makes new truths. . . .

But vision extends truth, because it extends insight itself, as in this novel [*Grendel*], which bears witness to the power of the poem, which is the power and the will of myth to create.

Norma L. Hutman
Mosaic (Fall, 1975), pp. 19, 21, 31

CAEDMON

ca. 657–680

Accounts of the poet Caedmon and his acquisition of the gift of poetry have, over the years, tended to include references to analogous stories throughout the world. . . .

The ultimate value of assembling and analysing the analogues will depend upon the help they give in resolving some of the disputes which have arisen over the interpretation of Caedmon's contribution to English poetry and in elucidating some of the common assumptions about him.

The existence of Caedmon and the validity of his experience is not usually doubted by present-day writers. Whatever reservations they may have about the literal truth of the details, they usually accept the dream as the explanation of a remarkable event in Caedmon's life. R. M. Wilson expresses a commonly held point of view when he writes that "Bede was a trained and conscientious historian, living not far from Caedmon's monastery of Whitby, and we may therefore take it for granted that the poet actually did compose verses [on the creation of the world, and so forth]." Further, the authorship of the poem known as Caedmon's *Hymn*, paraphrased by Bede in Latin and surviving also in Old English versions, is no longer generally in dispute. . . .

F. P. Magoun Jnr., for instance, does not believe that Caedmon was completely without experience in versification before the time when he began seriously to compose. From the traditional entertainments at the feast, it would seem that he was in the habit of listening to Anglo-Saxon songs, and this may have given him knowledge of the metre and diction necessary for his compositions. . . .

Magoun's point of view comes largely from the belief that oral formulae like those in Caedmon's *Hymn* are only created slowly and that no one singer ever invents many, usually finding the available supply of traditional formulae quite adequate for his needs. But this in turn has been challenged on the grounds that the outstanding poet is the exception to the rule, the one who makes a break with tradition, as Caedmon supposedly did in choosing Christian themes. On a disputed subject such as this, the analogues may be considered admissible evidence, even if the conclusions to which they point are not clear. On the question of priority, for example, it is interesting to note that few of the analogues insist that their subject was the first to compose poetry of any particular kind; few insist that he produced verses in his own language.

G. A. Lester
Neophil (April, 1974), pp. 225, 233–34

The central problem for the critic dealing with Caedmonic (or "Caedmonian") poetry has been that of sorting out native Teutonic elements from Christian and discovering the relationship between the two. For some critics, it is the fusing of the two traditions that makes the miracle Bede felt to be present in Caedmon's *Hymn*. If one deals with the *Hymn* alone —the only authentic work of Caedmon—the problem takes these forms: Did Caedmon create new vocabulary and new formulas or did he (as Magoun thinks) use formulas which had slowly developed and had been used in Caedmon's presence many times? Did his vocabulary and formulas come from the psalms, not from native tradition at all? Does the *Hymn* show knowledge of sophisticated Latin rhetorical theory? The answers to all these questions is a doubtful "perhaps." The poem is structurally, as well as metrically, brilliant, as B. F. Huppé has shown most convincingly. But the poem is only nine lines long, which means that no cumulative structural or textural proofs are possible, and it is connected with a legend of an untutored cowherd. It can be shown that the hymn lacks the padding and occasional clumsiness of, say, the metrical Psalms, but its positive virtues, especially its seemingly sophisticated structure, must be left to individual assessment.

Longer poems in the Caedmonic school—even those which are strikingly inferior to Caedmon's *Hymn*—provide a better basis for analysis of Caedmonic style. The poems, one finds, are remarkably similar in rhetorical method. . . .

Christ and Satan, whether it was actually written early or late, is stylistically transitional. It is vaguely Cynewulfian in structure, the poet having abandoned chronology for a thematic principle of progression; but it is solidly Caedmonic in its premises—that God and Satan are opposing treasure givers, one true, one false (cf. *brytan*, 23, 123, etc.), and that hell is a place of exile (cf. 120, 187, 257, etc.).

These premises are the root of Caedmonic style. It may be that they originated when an extraordinary cowherd turned Teutonic concepts of the protector, fighter, hall-builder to a new purpose: *heofonrices weard; meotodes meahte; heofon to hrofe; moncynnes weard; frea ælmihtig* (Caedmon's *Hymn*, 1b, 2a, 6a, 7b, 9b). But in any event, the metaphoric premises that God is a chieftain, heaven a secure kingdom, hell a place of exile—these are the gift of the Caedmonic school to later religious poetry in Old English. The characteristic development of these premises in Caedmonic verse is an application of exegetical principles of *translatio*, wherein the source is curtailed, amplified, interpreted, and so forth for focus on particular themes, and wherein key words, images, and concepts are rhythmically encoded into the poetic texture for linear allegory. Later religious poetry in Old English generally maintains the Caedmonic premises but shifts to more complex forms of development (from biblical subject matter to pagan, as in *Beowulf*; from relatively simple linear allegory to more complicated allegory, as in *Beowulf* and *Elene*) and from narrative to lyrical meditation, as in *Christ and Satan* or *Guthlac*.

John Gardner
The Construction of Christian Poetry in Old English (Carbondale, Southern Illinois Univ. Pr., 1975), pp. 17–18, 38–39

CYNEWULF

ca. 8th Century

Albert S. Cook, ed., *The Christ of Cynewulf: A Poem in Three Parts* (2nd ed., 1909, repr. with a new preface by John C. Pope, 1964)

Robert B. Burlin, *The Old English Advent: A Typological Commentary* (1968), includes text and trans.

An editor who set up a text of [Milton's] *Paradise Regained* or [Wordsworth's] *The Prelude* without observing that a leaf was missing from his basic authority would not soon hear the last of it. With an Old English poem, however, such an oversight is more excusable and the chances of its occurring are much greater, not only because we are less familiar with the language, the metrical conventions, and the mode of thought, but because there is generally only one manuscript authority and its imperfections are not necessarily obvious. Thus it has come about that a series of highly responsible editors have overlooked the loss of a leaf from the Exeter Book in the midst of Cynewulf's *Ascension*, and two efforts to correct the error have met with less general approval than they deserve. . . .

This finely dramatic speech, with its perfect adaptation of the heroic conventions, is a magnificent climax to Cynewulf's presentation of the story of the ascension and its chief meaning for mankind. Occurring a little before the middle of his poem, it is succeeded by lyric and reflective passages as they arise in series out of the brief suggestions of Gregory's homily. In the end it is balanced by the powerful description of the judgment in which the runic passage is embedded, until the whole poem is brought to a beautifully quiet close by the simile of the voyage.

Cynewulf's powers have been more sharply defined and his reputation somewhat lessened by the general agreement to credit him with no more than the four signed poems. It seems only fair to do what justice we can to these, and especially to *The Ascension*. There are brilliant passages in the *Elene* that rank high among his achievements, but *The Ascension* has always impressed me as the best sustained, most original, and most moving of the four.

John C. Pope
in *Studies in Language, Literature, and Culture of the Middle Ages and Later*, ed. Elmer Bagby Atwood and Archibald A. Hill (Austin: Univ. Texas Pr., 1969), pp. 210, 218–19

If primary evidence is inconclusive, secondary evidence in other ways is equally so. The involved problems of archaeology, contemporary accounts, the history of writing, and the critical value of analogy are far beyond the scope of this book; yet it is necessary to consider a few matters of secondary pertinence here because of the nature of the evidence used in oral-formulaic analyses. These matters may be said to have one problematical center, Cynewulf; and it is in relation to Cynewulf and scholarly treatment of Cynewulf that they will be discussed. . . .

Cynewulf . . . aside from an apparent Latinity, certainly knew how to spell and certainly made his poems of traditional phraseology. This potential dilemma for criticism was first attacked by [Francis P.] Magoun, and his solution has been both confronted and reiterated by all who accept his theory, and even by some mild dissenters. Only [T. E.] Lord has spoken out against Magoun's solution. According to the bare possibilities of the textual evolution of poems, (1) either a poet writes his own poem, or (2) he dictates it to a machine, or (3) he dictates it to a scribe. If a poem was orally composed many centuries ago, then the first two possibilities are presumed closed. Indeed the whole argument of [Millman] Parry and Lord and some other classical scholars has favored the third possibility for the "first text" of the Homeric poems. The argument is based both upon historical study and upon, one may say, a psychology of composition. Archaeological and paleontological evidence, as it is understood at the present time, would place Homer and the first "classical" Greek writing in the same century—the eighth B.C. Then too, it seems by proof of analogy that an oral poet (that is, a singer brought up within and proficient in the oral tradition of poetic composition), once he has learned letters not only loses his skill in rapid oral composition but never attains a literary skill of any dependability. Homer is thought too fine and developed to be the beginning of a written tradition rather than the end, and apex, of an oral one. . . .

Robert Diamond has demonstrated that the four runic passages in Cynewulf's poems are as a whole just as formulaic (even slightly more so) as the narrative parts of the same poems. The narratives of at least two of the signed poems are variously liberal and close translations of Latin prose; the runic signatures represent not only an act of literacy in themselves but are one with a literary Continental tradition of acrostic signature and request for prayer; Cynewulf's poetry, according to the sample reconsidered analyses above, has a formulaic content roughly comparable to the formulaic content of *Beowulf*. These statements are based if not entirely then to a persuasive extent upon demonstrable facts. The likely conclusion to be drawn from them is that Cynewulf, a literate poet, composed a highly conventionalized poetry; or, to put it negatively, that the poetry to which Cynewulf's name is attached was not composed by an oral-formulaic method such as that described by Parry, Lord, and Magoun.

Ann Chalmers Watts
The Lyre and the Harp (New Haven, Conn.: Yale Univ. Pr., 1969), pp. 182–84

What we have . . . in the *Elene* is not a collection of heroic martial and sea passages surrounding a middle section composed of "rather tedious dialectic," but a complex and sophisticated poem which is unified in theme and structured around a repeated series of verbal motifs. The theme is a simple, yet fundamental one concerning the power of the cross, and through the cross, of Christ to effect the reconciliation of the two realms of darkness and light and the movement, through the revelation of the cross, from one condition to the other. The poem exists to reveal to the Anglo-Saxon audience the dual nature of Christ and His cross; they are the bridge between the worlds of darkness and light. . . .

We have been speaking of Cynewulf as the initiator of these themes and verbal motifs, when it has been accepted for a long time that the *Elene* is basically a translation of a version of the *Acta Cyriaci*. Yet it is noteworthy that, although "there is little in *Elene* which can be shown to be original" except for "poetic circumlocution" [P.O.E. Gradon], the circumlocutions are, by and large, elaborations of the action which become the verbal motifs we have been discussing. . . .

In conclusion then, we have a poem in which Cynewulf took a few hints from his Latin source and turned the bare narrative into a theological reflection on the nature of Christianity and the meaning of Christ and His symbolic representative, the cross. A Christian, according to Cynewulf, is one who gives up the darkness, the blindness of heart (modblinde) of the pagan and enters into the light where he can see God.

The conversion takes place through the agency of Christ and the cross which, in the duality of their existence, have bridged the two worlds, been hidden in darkness and made manifest in the light and, by their revelation to man, they enable him to transform himself.

Robert Stepsis and Richard Rand
NM (June, 1969), pp. 280–82

The "Jewish question" is not an important one for Anglo-Saxon England. But the question of the relationship of church to state, and especially the question of the proper action of a Christian ruler, is undoubtedly an important one. Cynewulf [in *Elene*] has chosen a narrative that raises this question at almost the earliest point in history it can be raised: immediately after the conversion of Constantine, when the Church (and Elene its representative) gained the power of the state (and Elene *its* representative, too). And the ambiguous position of Elene, saint and queen, with her different and probably irreconcilable models, is the position of the Christian in power ever since.

James Doubleday
in *Anglo-Saxon Poetry: Essays in Appreciation*, ed. Lewis E. Nicholson and Dolores Warwick Frese (Notre Dame, Ind.: Univ. Notre Dame Pr., 1975), p. 123

Both Caedmonic poetry and that stylistic strain represented by *Beowulf*, the *Wanderer*, and the *Seafarer*, use allegorizing devices, Caedmonic poetry in a way that simultaneously underlines the harmony of scripture and adapts it to Germanic culture, the second strain in a way that gives Christian interpretation to pagan or secular material. The Caedmonic strain brings scripture to Germania; the Beowulfian brings Germania to church. The poetry of Cynewulf, probably influenced by both Caedmonic and Beowulfian methods, marks a breakthrough in stylistic evolution: Cynewulf makes moral allegory of saints' lives, meditations, and the like. (The same method was an Irish commonplace.) Whereas the *Beowulf*-poet finds Christian topological content in the life of a pagan hero, Cynewulf reads the life of a saint in eschatological terms. Whereas the *Physiologus*-poet and the *Phoenix*-poet (the latter conceivably Cynewulf himself) find moral lessons through an allegorical view of creatures, Cynewulf finds moral instruction in the experience of the cross. Like Caedmonic poetry, the poetry of Cynewulf assumes a direct analogy of pagan experience and Christian, and explores each in terms of the other. Rightly understood, Cynewulfian style is not a sorry decline from classical Old English poetic style (except in terms of meter) but a change, a shift in emphasis—in rhetorical terms, a shift from the Ciceronian and Augustinian rhetoric of logic and rational persuasion to a Christianized sophistic rhetoric of intricacy and decoration.

John Gardner
The Construction of Christian Poetry in Old English
(Carbondale: Southern Illinois Univ. Pr., 1975), p. 85

DEOR

650–700?

Deor is one of the poems in the *Exeter Book*, an eleventh-century poetic miscellany given by Leofric, Bishop of Devon and Cornwall, to Exeter Cathedral; the copy is extant there. A printed version of the book first appeared in 1842. *Deor* has been variously classified as lyric, heroic, consolation, and begging poem. It contains a refrain found only in one other Old English poem, *Wulf and Eadwacer*, and a number of references to stories and incidents known in historical commentaries but not otherwise celebrated in English poems. A typical wandering-singer lament, it concerns a minstrel who consoles himself after losing primacy in his lord's favor to a rival singer. The poem was probably written down in its extant version in the seventh century but composed and sung in the sixth, and may be a Germanic/English variant of earlier Norse oral verse.

Kemp Malone, ed., *Deor* (4th ed., 1966)

Robert K. Gordon, ed. and tr., *Anglo-Saxon Poetry* (rev., 1954) (prose)

In a paper entitled "Two Old English Scop Poems," [*PMLA*, June, 1966, pp. 185–92] I advanced the view that *Deor*, as well as *Widsith*, gains strength from the comparison I there made of the two poems, which share certain features suggesting that the purpose of both is the same. For *Widsith* a plausible case can be made out that begging is its purpose. For *Deor* the case is trickier. . . . What is there in *Deor* that suggests it is a begging poem? What is gained by construing it thus? . . .

The view that *Deor* is a consolation poem is also an assumption, taking its cue from the way the poem begins and succeeding well enough for thirteen lines but then failing because thereafter the poem falls apart. The assumption that it is a begging poem accounts for all of it, enabling us to see how everything there fits together in a conscious and artful design. *Deor*, it seems to me, is either a very bad consolation poem or a remarkably adroit begging poem.

Its most remarkable feature is not its felicitous and unique refrain but the design of the poem, which is craftily contrived so that the scop can conceal his purpose at first, teasing us along to the end, where it is finally revealed. The scop is not a craven beggar but a clever one, indirect in his approach and employing wit and impudence rather than whining humility.

In the wit and impudence, in the refrain, and especially in the artfully contrived design qualities are displayed rarely found in Old English poetry and nowhere else there so effectively combined. This is not surprising. Qualities such as these were evidently confined to scop poetry, of which very little survives, perhaps only *Deor* and *Widsith*. These two poems, the source of most of our information about scops, have been wrongly interpreted, I think, and as a consequence we have in the past greatly overrated the professional status of scops and underrated their skill. On both scores

Deor helps to set us right, for, if forced to beg, the scop can hardly be credited with a highly honoured or esteemed calling and, if capable of begging so cleverly, his skill was considerable.

If *Deor* is a begging poem we not only need to revise our conception of Old English scops but to this particular scop we ought to grant his proper due, for though his is not the first such poem in the English language—an honour that belongs to *Widsith*—it is, I believe, the best.

Norman E. Eliason
in *Medieval Literature and Civilization: Studies in Memory of G. N. Garmonsway*, ed. D. A. Pearsall and R. A. Waldron
(London: Athlone, 1969), pp. 55, 60–61

In a recent review of problems in the Old English poem *Deor*, Frederick Norman has revived the notion that the poet was following a definite plan or scheme in the assemblage and arrangement of his heroic material. In what follows I seek to reinforce this notion by setting out evidence that the poet also worked to a set pattern in his handling of the underlying theme of misfortune and in the philosophy he applies to it, to show that the philosophical attitudes involved may be paralleled in detail from Boethius' *Consolation of Philosophy*, and to examine the possibility that the similarities between *Deor* and other Old English so-called elegies may point to a planned series of experimental treatments of Boethian themes. . . .

Brief and allusive though the poet's citations from heroic story may be in [*Deor*], I think it possible to detect in each of them an emphasis on three basic paradoxes or antitheses which all come down firmly on the side of optimism:

1. Misfortune tends to be long-lasting and cumulative, and while it lasts seems to the victim endless and insurmountable; but it does end and it can be surmounted.

2. Misfortune is intimate and personal; but it cannot long be hidden from others, and is indeed something all men must share.

3. Misfortune is a mental state; but it has external and physical causation, and can therefore be best faced by a positive mental attitude, both individual and collective, which will lead to positive successful action. . . .

Between these various poems [from *The Exeter Book*] the degree of possible Boethian influence obviously varies very considerably, from what seems to me to be a precise and thoroughgoing parallelism in *Deor* to the less precise resemblances in more scattered passages and details elsewhere; in all cases, clearly, other elements and influences are involved. Further investigation into their themes, attitudes, imagery and allegory is needed before one can pronounce too confidently on the possibility of such a synthesis as I have in mind. My first view is that the presence of these poems in a reasonably compact group in *The Exeter Book* anthology, which elsewhere shows signs of some deliberate arrangement of items, in itself suggests much more than a casual relationship, and that to reconsider them in the somewhat neglected context of Boethius may supply one missing link: they have been transmitted from the pens of literate poets without serious corruption.

L. Whitbread
Neophil (April, 1970), pp. 167, 180

THE DREAM OF THE ROOD

675–750?

This dream-vision poem, with its representation of Christ and its celebration of the Redemption, was composed later than *Beowulf* and earlier than the poems of Cynewulf. It is found on the sides of a sculptured monumental stone cross of the late seventh or early eighth century at Ruthwell in Dumfriesshire, and in the tenth-century Vercelli Book of manuscripts. In the poem, which has been called representative of the golden age of Anglo-Saxon culture, the cross becomes a dual symbol of pain and death and eternal life and triumph over adversity; the poet is stirred by his vision of Christ and the Cross and the Tree of Life to move from passivity to active faith, from weariness to hope. At various times the poem has been ascribed to Caedmon and Cynewulf, but scholars today believe it the work of another, unidentified poet.

Michael Swanton, ed. *The Dream of the Rood* (1970)

Robert K. Gordon, ed. and tr., *Anglo-Saxon Poetry* (rev. ed., 1954) (prose)

The highly individual style of the [*Dream of the Rood*] poet merely complements his fresh and original form. It is quite without parallel; no model is to be found among any of the large number of contemporary Latin cross panegyrics. And it has not proved possible to identify a convincing source for any large part of its material. While the poet of the *Dream* shows himself familiar with both contemporary liturgy and current exegetics, this amounts to little more than common phraseology or allusion; it cannot be shown that there lies behind the *Dream* a series of Easter antiphons, like the Advent antiphons which lie behind the probably ninth-century *Christ I*, or that it derives directly from patristic theology like Cynewulf's *Christ II*. The remoteness of apparent analogues to any part merely confirms the originality of the poet. We are obliged to consider the poem entirely in its own terms as an easy and natural development out of the religious concerns of its day.

The question as to whether or not an actual dream occasioned the poet's work, which so exercised those scholars who chose to attribute it to Cynewulf, is irrelevant. The church of Bede was thoroughly acquainted with the dream or vision as vehicle of prophecy or universal truths, often vouchsafed through the medium of a heavenly messenger or guide. Such visions may well have been considered appropriate to the religious poet at this time. The dream which occasioned Cædmon's Hymn affords a convenient parallel. Both require the poet to celebrate a particular theme—Cædmon the Creation and the *Dream* poet the Redemption. The dream convention must in any case have been recognised as particularly appropriate to a cross cult poem. After all, the Constantinian tradition as it was received in England attributed the very origins of the cult to such a dream. . . .

The cross is more than simply a symbol of individual salvation. As anticipated from the beginning in the bleeding tree image, it will reappear set up in the sky as a sign of sovereignty to herald Christ's second coming and to summon all men into the presence of their creator. We are thus provided with the rationale of an otherwise arbitrary vision. Only a brief and oblique allusion to the harrowing of hell is necessary to complete the doctrinal scheme, for unlike later Crucifixion poems, Christ's victory is already implicit in the battle on the cross. As common to contemporary Ascension poems, there is allowed no delay between the harrowing of hell and the entry into heaven. The two are brought into dramatic juxtaposition to maintain the impetus of the poem. The theological structure is therefore brought to a rapid and triumphal conclusion as Christ together with the visionary and the whole company of saints ascend to their heavenly *eðel* in a final great eschatological vision.

Michael Swanton
Introd., in *The Dream of the Rood*, ed. Michael Swanton
(New York: Barnes & Noble, 1970), pp. 62–64

Criticism of *The Dream of the Rood* has tended to ignore the modern, but nevertheless apt, title of the poem, and to treat it as a kind of early lyric on the crucifixion. This has resulted in a concentration of interest on the central account by the personalized cross of the events on Calvary, and a corresponding neglect of the rest of the poem, especially its latter part. There has been a tacit, and possibly correct, assumption by those who have studied the poem, from the unknown sculptors of the Ruthwell Cross to the latest commentator, that the lines on the crucifixion are supremely memorable and effective, and that nothing in the rest of the poem quite compares with them. Most critics have liked the second half of the poem much less: apart from a conventional, but attractive "elegiac" passage on the visionary in his waking state, the literary sugar on the doctrinal pill seems to wear a little thin from line 78 onward, after some suspiciously defective lines. Until quite recently, it was normal to voice doubts about the authenticity of this section, and the view that the Vercelli text of the poem represents a late, interpolated or expanded version of a hypothetical "original" is by no means an untenable one. It is, however, difficult to apply in practice, and it has had the unfortunate effect of making critics dismiss up to half the poem from their consideration. It is a particularly damaging criticism in an intellectual climate like our own which, despite tendencies in recent literature, continues to demand unity and coherence in a work. The metaphor of an "organic" unity has never been applied with any great success to a medieval poem, and might seem to be more than usually inappropriate in the case of a dream poem where strange connections and abrupt transitions are to be expected; nevertheless, a poem which has actually been recomposed over a long period by several different authors flouts some of our most cherished preconceptions about literature.

My own view is, in fact, the alternative one, that the Vercelli text preserves what is essentially the "original" poem, of which excerpts are to be found in abbreviated form in the mid-eighth century Ruthwell Cross inscription. At all events, it is the only complete version that we have, and, when correctly interpreted, it reveals a satisfying shape and coherence which becomes plainer when the traditional nature of the poet's material is understood. The purpose of the present article is to argue the case for the unity of *The Dream of the Rood* more thoroughly than has yet been done and also to provide a justification of the neglected second half of the poem. My initial assumption is that, since the crucifixion takes up only a minority of the verse-lines, it is not the main subject of the poem, which is, of course, the symbol of the cross itself and its role in the spiritual life; a contemporary, not merely an historical phenomenon.

N. A. Lee
Neophil (October, 1972), p. 469

The sufficiency of Christ as redeemer; the sacrifice to which nevertheless he deems it proper to submit in order to redeem; his unfailing promptness, willingness, eagerness for the sacrifice of himself—this mystery of acceptance of the Christian religion is given substance by his two garments, always distinct and yet the same.

Surely it is this traditional combination of thought and language that the poet of *The Dream of the Rood* adopts in investing the cross-Christ with garments that change without changing. The "tree of glory," he says in 14b–15a, is honoured by a garment, and then, in the following line, begins to show its metaphorical quality: a parallel phrase informs the reader that the cross is "clothed with gold." It is "covered in jewels" (16b–17a) and the jewels cover it "honourably," just as the garment itself (15a) is "honourable." It would be difficult for the poet to express himself more clearly —or indeed, more carefully; for, as though to guard against any suspicion that by choice of metaphor he intended the outside to suffer degradation, he inserts (15b) between mentions of the garment and the gold the phrase *wynnum scinan*: the cross "shines joyfully" in the full sense of the words, shines with things that are the cause of joy and, as such a cause, are the best of their kind. Having taken such measures, the poet may wait with confidence for the inside to reveal itself. It reveals itself as blood; and once revealed, this in turn becomes the outside of the cross. It must therefore rank as a garment; and accordingly, in 22–23, the poet places it alongside the garment of magnificence, dismissing the latter—already extensively described—in a single phrase and summing up its constituents, gold and jewels, in a single word "treasure." The squalid garment, on the other hand, is described twice over: it is constituted by a "drenching with moisture," by a "swilling with a flow of blood." No poet has used the metaphor more subtly, more tellingly. It is integral to the partnership between Christ and the cross which is at the heart of the poem.

James Smith
ASE, Vol. 4 (1975), p. 34

RIDDLES AND GNOMIC VERSE

The Old English Riddles of the Exeter Book present many problems, and though the riddles themselves have for the most part been solved, the problems they present have not. This is particularly true of the problem of style. The fact that the riddles make use of the conventions of Old English poetry is generally remarked on; yet it is not adequately accounted for by the recognition that the Old English riddles are literary, rather than oral, examples of the genre. Though preceded by the Latin riddles of Aldhem and Tatwine and Eusebius as well as those of Symphosius, the riddles of the Exeter Book mark the first literary appearance of the form in the Germanic languages. Scholars who have discussed them at some length as a literary form have taken them perfectly seriously; no attempt has been made to deal with them as at once poetry and play—that is, as a marriage of two forms that are to some extent incongruent, inviting parody. There remains also the question why some of the riddles depart greatly from the form usually taken by the Old English riddles and, indeed, from the form usually taken by the literary riddle in general. That it is possible to establish a formula for the genre in Old English is implicit in discussions of it. A closer look at the elements of such a formula will show that it is much less easily delimited than is generally supposed. In any case, departures from it are nowhere attributed to the openness of the literary riddle to stylistic parody.

Recognizing them as a literary form is not sufficient to explain the Old

English riddles—their diversity, their complexity, their often elegant poetry. I suggest that the Old English poet regarded the riddle form as no more than a vehicle—an excuse or occasion for a poem—and that the riddle form constituted a very loose, very wide structure within which parody could be constructed.

Ann Harleman Stewart
PLL (Summer, 1975), pp. 227–28

THE WANDERER AND THE SEAFARER

dates unknown, ascribed to 7th to 9th centuries

These two elegiac poems, extant in the eleventh-century *Exeter Book* of manuscripts, where they are separated by two leaves, present similar themes and employ similar poetic conventions. Scholars cannot ascribe any absolute date of composition, but speculate they belong to the period of the seventh to ninth centuries and that parts may have been written by the same author or composite authors. Both poems comment on earthly misery and God's mercy; in each is found a description of a winter storm, which the hero must endure; references to the terrors and joyous adventures of marine travel; and reminiscences of earlier splendors which have passed from view. Dominating both poems is a pervasive sense of exile and longing, and the mutability of fortune. Both poems also reflect the addition of Christian moralism to tales of worldly adventure. In *The Wanderer* the first section relates the wanderings of an upper-class man who has lost his lord; the second section is a sermon on the transitoriness of earthly fortune and the permanence of Christian grace. In *The Seafarer* early emphasis is placed on the dangers and adventures of the seaman's life; from line 64, the poem becomes a tract on the blessings of Christian belief in the face of adversity. For these reasons, most scholars believe these poems originated in Teutonic or Norse oral verse and were later written down by Christian scribes and zealots.

Thomas P. Dunning and Alan J. Bliss, eds., *The Wanderer* (1969)

Ida L. Gordon, ed., *The Seafarer* (1960)

Ezra Pound, *The Seafarer* in *The Translations of Ezra Pound* (1963)

The Seafarer has several specific references to the Christian God, many general evocations of Christian belief, and very few specific references to Germanic society or tradition (of which the only two extended ones are problematical, 97–102 and 112–115).

The conclusions are inescapable. Assuming that his poem is what is extant (the only possible assumption from which a critical analysis can proceed), one must see the *Wanderer*-poet as primarily concerned with the traditional details of Germanic society; and though there is an explicitly Christian framework within which the details of the poem operate (and toward which they may ultimately turn), both the dramatic situation to be seen and the heralded voices to be heard are clearly and loudly involved in traditions of Germanic heroic—pagan—society.

The insight of James L. Rosier is this: "Among Anglo-Saxon poems of whatever kind or tradition *The Wanderer* is particularly difficult to discuss pointedly because it is intrinsically a mirror of a mind in its several states and faculties, of memory and revery, of reason and imagination, of perception and conception." Aside from the obvious virtues of treating the poem by and for itself and of demonstrating the necessity for such treatment, Rosier's analysis has looked at the language of the poem and counted thirty-five occurrences of words referring directly to the mind. In the light of such weighty evidence, one must agree that the poem is significantly concerned with mind (though whether "*a* mind" is, as has been seen, quite another and not so easily demonstrated matter). But unfortunately Rosier's analysis does not proceed from his perceptive point of departure to an illumination of the poem; it becomes involved in terminology, confusing in procedure and purpose, and at times even incomprehensible, at least to this reader. His insight might have led him to clarify some of the major issues of the poem, but it did not, I think, partly because of his insistence on a novel approach with jargon to match, and partly because he ignores (as does nearly everyone else since 1958) the insight of Ralph W. V. Elliott.

Elliott's title, "The Wanderer's Conscience," should have been enough to put Rosier on the track: he might have been able to integrate the idea of conscience with the idea of mind.

Neil D. Isaacs
Structural Principles in Old English Poetry (Knoxville: Univ. Tennessee Pr., 1968), pp. 46–47

The Old English companion pieces, *The Wanderer* and *The Seafarer* . . . are built round three type figures, an exile, a sage and a seafarer. The latest editors of the former poem, T. P. Dunning and A. J. Bliss, compare *The Wanderer* to a musical piece in binary form, and refer to the two parts as "movements." That is to say, the structure of the poem is thematic, and consists of the juxtaposition of thematic elements, in this case the monologue of an exile, and the reflections of a sage, both parts dealing with the transitoriness of human life. Confusion as to the poem's meaning has arisen because critics assumed that in a poem which appeared to be a narrative, there must be a plot; but this is not the case. The exile's narrative is merely exemplary. The second part of the poem is not so easy to define and critics have differed as to where the division should come. In my view, the second part begins at line 73 with the introduction of the sage. But it differs from the first part in being reflective rather than narrative, and the dominant image, the ruined building, has no narrative context. Nevertheless, the two sections are structurally parallel. Each part has a section introducing the type figure and the dominant image; the exile awaits God's mercy as he rows across the sea, the sage looking upon the ruined building reflects upon the end of the world. In these two parts we have mutations of a common theme; the exile and the sea as symbols of loneliness, and the building, a symbol of security, as so often in Anglo-Saxon poetry, when ruined becomes a symbol of desolation. . . .

When we turn to *The Seafarer* we find a similar use of paratactic structure to express the theme. The apparent shifts of tone and theme in the poem led early commentators to think that the poem was a dialogue. In fact, it seems probable that the speaker, like the speaker in the poem *Resignation*, is turning away from earthly sorrow and, *longunge fus*, turns his thoughts to a voyage across the sea. He describes vividly his hardship on the sea. His kinsmen cannot comfort him, for those who dwell on land know not the hardships endured by those who voyage on the sea. Yet he longs to return to it, even though he knows not what God will decree for him on that tempestuous element. He is, I believe, the type of those who suffer in this world. It is not unnatural, therefore, that in the second part of the poem his thoughts should turn from this mortal life, transitory on earth, to heaven and the joys of the Lord.

Pamela Gradon
Form and Style in Early English Literature (London: Methuen, 1971), pp. 115–16

Why, after all, does one re-read *The Seafarer*? It is not because it teaches us that the world is transient, nor because it expresses medieval, penitential modes of thought; one values it primarily neither as a didactic nor as an historical object. Neither its message nor its interest as an example of medieval Latin themes passing into English is at the center of its nature as a poem, but only of its nature as a document. The reason the modern reader, as opposed to the modern professional scholar, goes back to it is that it gives evocative, lyrical expression to a state of mind which is communicated across a chasm of time. This is not to say that other aspects do not matter, nor that it is unnecessary to try to identify the traditional ideas on which the poem may draw, but its ideas, its traditions, even its sources are all framework. Its interest to the reader lies in the qualities which distinguish *The Seafarer* from other homiletic expressions of penitential themes—that is, in its flesh. The rhetoric and imagery of the poem are not decorative additions to the theme; in a sense, they are the poem.

The Seafarer begins with appeals to the reader's response to fiction and to sensuous imagery, by means of the use of the first person and of physical description. The opening lines, even if an accepted formula in Old

English moral, lyric verse, indicate that the poet wishes to explore his theme through an individual persona and to engage the reader in a familiar one-to-one relationship which focuses his attention on actual experience. However much the speaker may be a device to present a moral theme, the effect of the opening is to make one think in literal terms of the life and times of an individual man. . . .

By its mimetic and romantic manner, the first half of *The Seafarer*, asking the reader to live through the speaker's own confusions and to move with him towards perception of spiritual truth, is designed to elicit his sympathies. The second half calls for detached judgment. But the poem's own rhetoric, its shift in mode from confessional to moral, its ambiguities and antitheses, mean that at first the sympathies of the reader are limited by an ironic sense of the unsympathetic elements in the speaker's state of mind; in the later part the reader's judgment refuses to yield completely to the speaker because the poet's language continues to elicit his sympathy for the victim, mortal man. . . . The structures of the poem are so repeatedly antithetical, ironic and double, that the meaning of the poem as a whole is inevitably itself antithetical, ironic and double. This is the "message secreted in the structure." The poem ends, as it began, in dichotomy. Its rhetoric modifies the meaning of themes found elsewhere so that the experience the poem offers is very different from that of its putative sources. It is a poem in two minds, which a homily could hardly afford to be. At the end, the voice of the transfigured mariner is on one side while the moving images of the lost and bereaved, the weak and the dead are on the other. We watch the dramatic monologuist escape into abstraction, but remain ourselves standing by an open grave.

W. A. Davenport
PLL (Summer, 1974), pp. 228–29, 239–40

WIDSITH

650–700?

I have noted elsewhere that two poets that I take to be traditional, Homer and the *Beowulf* poet, sing in their songs of counterpart singers on the distant scene they sing of. Homer and the *Beowulf* poet thus let us draw the conclusion that they, the present poets, derive their story from those distant poets who were with the heroes of the past. The trick is to get us to believe in the connection between the very present poet and the past one in the tale and thus to verify the tale we are listening to. Now it seems to me that the *Widsith* poet might be up to something similar. There *was* a poet at the court of Ermanaric two and a half or more centuries before there was a poet singing or perhaps writing about him. If there had been no earlier poet at Ermanaric's court there would be no oral tradition about him: Ermanaric's *lof* [his praise], as well as his *leoht ond lif somod* [light and life together], would have perished from, or indeed never appeared in Germanic song, however alive his *history* was in the pages of Ammianus Marcellinus and Jordanes. . . .

There was a singer at Ermanaric's court. There was also one at Alboin's court two centuries later. There was also the one whose song we have in the Exeter Book. All were indeed wide-ranging. And all were, in a way, *one*, because each was, while he lived, the living voice of Germanic oral tradition. There are no disembodied voices in an oral tradition as there are in a society that learns and lives by books. I do not believe that "Widsith's" character is a fiction in our sense of the word. The poet who sang the prologue and epilogue became himself Ermanaric's Widsith even as he sang in Anglo-Saxon England centuries after Ermanaric's death.

Donald K. Fry argues in a paper in progress that the *Widsith* poet gently mocks the character "Widsith" he allows to speak in the body of his poem. The *Widsith* poet is a Christian trying to put into Christian perspective—and thus put down—"Widsith's" exuberant affection for earthly rulers. Perhaps. But I find more of a sense of the poignancy of the fate of wandering gleeman than Christian mockery, however gentle, in *Widsith*'s final lines. . . .

I think the whole *Widsith* performance is a tantalizing, sophisticated, and profound sort of riddle. If it is a riddle, the answer to the question "Say what am I called" is not only "Widsith," but also . . . the singer singing within an oral tradition. In order to answer that riddle you must listen carefully to what the song really says: "I have translated through men's traditionally-trained memories where the courts of Ermanaric and Alboin exist side-by-side—right here and now. But I know that sort of magic can exist only so long as the tradition lives." The very awareness of the magic marks the beginning of the end.

Robert P. Creed
in *Anglo-Saxon Poetry: Essays in Appreciation*, ed. Lewis E. Nicholson and Dolores Warwick Frese (Notre Dame, Ind.: Notre Dame Univ. Pr., 1975), pp. 382, 384, 387

GENERAL CRITICISM OF OLD ENGLISH LITERATURE

The application of the oral-formulaic theories of [Millman] Parry and [T. E.] Lord to Old English poetry has thrown much light on the texture of the verse, and the technique of composition, and on those elements which are common to Old English poetry and to the poetry of other old

Germanic dialects. On the other hand, the work of [G. B.] Smithers, [James E.] Cross, and others has shown that a number of ideas and themes in Old English poetry, for example, exile, journeys, and the decay of the world, derive from Latin patristic literature. Apparently, then, an unlettered native tradition and an exotic lettered tradition both had their influence, and the importance of the two traditions and their relationships with one another are being explored and evaluated. In the meantime, however, it is clear that Old English poets habitually used formulaic and thematic techniques which were devised in pre-literate times, and it is also clear that some of them at least had a sound knowledge of the learned literature of the Church. Now if some Old English poets were familiar with patristic literature, it is likely enough that some were also familiar with other Latin literature of the kind commonly studied in the monastic schools, and the aim of this paper is to consider what light such familiarity may throw on certain aspects of Old English poetic diction, formulas and themes. . . .

There are signs . . . that the echoes of classical antiquity which can be heard in Old English poetry are more than a mere scattering of allusions. Some of them, at least, seem rather to indicate a well-established and continuing tradition, the tradition of the school-master teaching the Roman classics, rhetoric, and conventional poetic diction, and imitative writing based on conventional themes and topics. This tradition had manuscript texts as its foundation, but perpetuated itself by the master's *viva voce* instruction of his pupils and was hence, also, in its own way, partly oral and collective. Latin learning in (say) the eighth and ninth centuries was certainly not a matter of silent reading in private, and in the best periods of the best schools pupils may have learned to declaim and dispute in Latin, and to cap and improvise verses. Alcuin at least did not omit to treat memory and delivery in his treatise—or rather dialogue—on rhetoric. Latin literary technique itself made use of something like themes and formulas in its rhetorical topics and conventional diction, and this technique may well have made its influence felt in Old English verse. Primitivism of one kind or another has beset Anglo-Saxon studies long enough, and some caution recommends itself in speculation about an oral tradition going back into the remote depths of the Germanic (or Indo-European?) past. Some Old English poetic themes and formulas may indeed be of high oral antiquity, but others are probably not.

B. K. Martin
JEGP (July, 1969), pp. 375–76, 390

Among the most unjustly neglected areas of Old English literature are the anonymous pre-Aelfrician homilies of the ninth and tenth centuries. Long dismissed as containing little literary merit, they nevertheless constitute an important body of Anglo-Saxon religious prose before the magnificent achievements of Aelfric and Wulfstan. And they are not necessarily as theologically and rhetorically unsophisticated as some critics would have us believe; very often the rhetorical techniques of these anonymous homilists represent highly skilled evocations of ideas and emotions.

Among the most important of these groups of anonymous sermons are the Blickling homilies, a collection that represents a wide range of popular sermon types, from conservative adaptations of standard exegetical interpretations to collections of colorful apocryphal materials. Its eclectic nature suggests the work of several authors; yet its probable organization as a once-complete homiliary and its characteristic hortatory tone suggest a deliberate attempt by the unknown collector to compile a homiliary consistent at all times with his doctrinal beliefs and parenetic techniques.

The most striking characteristic of the hortatory passages in the Blickling collection as a whole is their almost universal tone of benevolence. This is especially important in view of the constant eschatological emphasis in the homilies. No other subject affords such an opportunity for inspiring fear and trembling; yet the homilists do their best to ameliorate this effect, stressing God's mercy as well as His judgment, holding open to each member of the congregation the opportunity for salvation and carefully delineating the kinds of behavior leading to heavenly rewards. This tendency to move through loving inspiration rather than through fearsome threats occurs so consistently throughout the collection that one is convinced the unknown compiler must have deliberately chosen his homilies with this in mind. In this respect, the tone of the collection is much different from that of, for example, the Vercelli homilies, most of which are stern, often harsh, presenting vivid pictures of damnation meant undoubtedly to frighten the congregation into good behavior. In their relatively gentle, mild tone, the Blickling homilies more frequently resemble those of Aelfric in which the love of the shepherd for his people frequently ameliorates the sternness of his eschatological warnings. The Blickling homilies are not as learned, as intellectually vigorous as Aelfric's, and the anonymous authors have not his rhetorical skill. But they do show a deliberate, often highly effective attempt to lead their congregations by loving exhortation into the paths of good Christian behavior and belief.

Marcia A. Dalbey
NM (December, 1969), pp. 641–42

In spite of all that is today known about Old English verse that which is most fundamental and most interesting still remains a mystery. I speak of the way in which Old English poetry was composed, the methods employed by the vernacular poets and the rules governing their verse. There has been of course much speculation about the mode of composition, particularly in the past two decades by the "oral formulaists." But the "oral formulaic" theory has been sorely tested at both ends of the theory, both its "oral" and "formulaic" implications. As Stevick has pointed out (R. D. Stevick in *Speculum*, 1962), "oral" is clearly not a simple term, yet it has been used indiscriminately and often in a confused manner. For instance, the creative process elucidated in Creed's "slow motion enactment" of composition in *Beowulf* (R. P. Creed in *ELH*, 1959), which starts with a given formula and rarely looks beyond the B-line, hardly seems suited to account for the structural complexities of a major work; and it is vitally different from that encountered in musical improvisation, where the performer will employ anticipation, contrapuntal movements and so forth. Then again, "oral transmission" is different from "oral creation"; and since it is never clear in the oral tradition when one leaves off and the other begins, the distinction seems to have been conveniently overlooked.

The meaning of "formula" is also difficult. Scholars have become increasingly dissatisfied with Millman Parry's definition (in *Studies in Classical Philology*, 1930)—"a group of words which is regularly employed under the same metrical conditions to express a given essential idea": this is neither precise enough (too much a certainty exists in the ascription of formulas), nor inclusive enough; in some cases a single word would seem to be entitled to the same description, and yet it is unnecessarily exclusive (the metrical restriction seems arbitrary, because the metrical patterns of the half-lines, themselves lacking consistency, apparently combine unrestrictively to form full metric line). More fatal even has been the rejection of Parry's basic assumption that oral literature alone is characterized by a high percentage of formulas; considerable evidence can be mustered to show that at least some Old English texts which are formulaic can be attributed to literary artists and shown to be derived from literary sources. Riddles 35 and 40 . . . and the *Meters of Boethius* are cases in point.

That Old English verse was composed orally by formulas is thus . . . a theory, and a tenuous one at that; but that some Old English verse is both literary and formulaic cannot be denied.

F. H. Whitman
NM (December, 1975), pp. 529–30

MEDIEVAL LITERATURE

Robert Raymo, editor

JOHN BARBOUR

ca. 1320–1395

In Bruce [in *Bruce*] Barbour embodied a group of qualities desirable in a hero symbolizing the *natio* as he would like it to be, and as an individual his warrior does not exist above and beyond these. No medieval historian, Barbour included, tried to probe below the surface and analyse individual motives or moral attributes. A hero's heroism could be summed up in a half-dozen adjectives, taken from rhetorical models such as that of Matthew of Vendôme:

> All men lufyt him for his bounte;
> For he wes off full fayr effer,
> Wyss, curtaiss, and deboner;
> Larg and luffand als wes he,
> And our all thing luffyt lawte . . .

followed by a short physical description, brings Sir James of Douglas to life—a more sustained definition than is ever given of Bruce himself "that hardy wes off hart and hand" who betrays a few primary emotions such as anger and sorrow at the actions of the English and the plight of the Scots.

Loyalty to such a champion is loyalty to the *natio*. To create such a symbol Barbour needed no second-hand knowledge of the intimacies of Bruce's character and personal life. His virtues, prowess and the goals to which he aspires are constructed according to a formula, that of the *chanson de geste*, and Barbour gave the work unity by summing up in his hero popular sentiments associated with success in war, and particularly with resistance against a foreign oppressor. His audience must have included descendants of the named personages in *Bruce*, many of the latter sharing in the heroism of their leader, and Barbour's appeal was for this reason direct. The common people, as a group, are of one accord with their officers and "traitors" stand out as despicable enemies of Scotland. Just as Arthur of Albion was the type of a successful British king so did Bruce become his Scottish counterpart, a general heroic figure suited to Barbour's purpose in coupling his "suchfast story."

A. M. Kinghorn
SSL (January, 1969), pp. 144–45

In the figure of Bruce, Barbour creates a model of the good king or ruler. As the narrative unfolds, Bruce exhibits by turn the many qualities essential to his position—strength and courage in battle, wisdom and prudence in the maintenance of the realm, generosity, courtesy, and compassion toward his subjects, and personal honor, integrity, and devoutness. More important than any single aspect of his character, as Barbour repeatedly emphasizes, is Bruce's ideal combination or balance of virtues. He is not only valiant, but he is also prudent. As the narrator observes ". . . hardyment, gouernit with vit,/That he all tym vald sammyn knyt,/Gert him of vorschip haf the priss . . ." (VI, 369–71). Bruce can defeat a formidable number of his enemies single-handed as seen in his encounter with the men of Galloway (VI, 1–372), but he also knows when to retreat and save the lives of his men as evidenced by his actions at Methven and Dalry (II, 426–40; III, 31–60). He combines firmness and justice in his rule with compassion for his people. Thus to the admiration of many critics, Bruce even pauses in the middle of a dangerous march in Ireland to comfort a poor launder-woman in the throes of childbirth. As the narrator emphasizes after describing the incident:

> This wes a full gret curtasy,
> That sic a kyng and swa mychty
> Gert his men duell on this maner
> Bot for a full pouir laynder. (XVI, 289–92)

Above all, Bruce's actions are infused by a sense of honor befitting a ruler. As king and leader of the Scots, he is uncompromising in his loyalty to his subjects and the principles for which they struggle.

Lois A. Eben
SSL (April, 1972), p. 222

WILLIAM CAXTON

ca. 1421–1491

[Caxton's] patrons are all English and, apart from Margaret of Burgundy, they are all associated with the court or the City of London; and

thoroughly moral reasons. Now in the last book of the *House of Fame*, in a rush of lavish *descriptio*, satiric, even gay as it is, Fame is shown up for the total infirmity she is. The moral environment here, if it were not so funny, would be vicious.

The *House of Fame* and *Troilus and Criseyde* alone among Chaucer's poems end in a morally flawed poetic world; and again unlike the other poems, they use an ending self who is aggressive enough to criticize his environment. In the Epilogue the criticism is explicit and ends in prayer; in the *House of Fame* the criticism is less direct and ends in confusion. Yet in both we fancy we hear the author's "own voice," emotional, morally convinced, closing up artistic distances so that they virtually disappear. We almost seem to intrude, since what we momentarily hear is Chaucer striving toward atonement while he prays, Chaucer striving toward a poet's *gloria* while he scorns the goddess Fame and all her works.

Ann Chalmers Watts
The Chaucer Review, Vol. 4, No. 4 (1970), pp. 240–41

Troilus and Criseyde

Complex, complex. I began with that overworked word, and I find I must end with it. *Troilus and Criseyde* is the most complex medieval English poem on love that we possess. This complexity is the consequence in large part of the technique of amplification which Chaucer applied to his original. Idealized courtly love is examined in *Troilus* with an intensity of feeling and a range of attitudes which exhaust the topic. The method itself has been used with a boldness and an imaginative freedom seldom equaled. There can be few readers of the poem who come away with a sense of possibilities unrealized. No one wishes Chaucer had done more, not out of a sense of tedium, but out of a sense of completeness and fulfillment. Amplification can go no further.

Indeed, the question is, did it not go too far? Is the poem not overloaded, have not too many conflicting attitudes been folded in, does the poem not finally become dropsical and collapse? Is the predestination passage, for example, really necessary? The questions can hardly expect absolute answers, completely independent of individual taste. It does remind us of how far the process of amplification has been carried here. Chaucer's decision to experiment with abbreviation in his next several poems may suggest on his part a suspicion that, for the moment, with this method he had gone far enough. The danger of the method is loss of control, mere decorative elaboration or excessive inflation of an original. Its greatest utility is in the realization of the possibilities of a theme. It is to this method that in large part we owe the poem we have; there can hardly be any question that the method has been brilliantly employed.

The experience of romantic, passionate love, as it is developed by the amplification in *Troilus and Criseyde*, is presented as it is conventionally, though much more simply, in much of the love poetry of the period and by Chaucer in other of his poems of love. It is presented as a contradictory experience. These contradictions are only faintly present in Boccaccio's poem. The trope or figure for expressing this contradictory character of love in the poetry is the *contentio*, oxymoron. The pattern of *Troilus and Criseyde* is of an elaborate oxymoron in which the widest range of contradictory emotions, experiences, attitudes, and value systems is contained within the poem to express and dramatize this oxymoronic character of the experience: joy and sorrow, prudence and folly, passion and reticence, wisdom and half-wisdom, love as comedy and love as tragedy, society as spur and society as bridle, the illusion of freedom and the conviction of fate, philosophy that supports and philosophy that condemns.

Robert W. Frank, Jr.
in *Medieval and Folklore Studies*, ed. Jerome Mandel and Bruce A. Rosenberg (New Brunswick, N.J.: Rutgers Univ. Pr., 1970), pp. 169–70

Even as Troilus is no Dante in epic attainment of the heavens, so is he no Aeneas or Mark Antony in heroic love. He is not the model lover that Antigone describes, just as Criseyde is not a paragon like the *dames* of [Guillaume de] Machaut's lyrics. As compared with the stories of Boethius in the *Consolation of Philosophy*, and of Milton's Adam and Samson, this narrative of Troilus treats of providence quite unsatisfactorily. At every step Chaucer undermines with irony the language and conventions of epic, love romance, and theodicy. The total effect, however, is not that of mock epic as in the *Nun's Priest's Tale*, or of comic romance as in the *Wife of Bath's Tale*, or of philosophical slapstick as in a good part of Erasmus' *Praise of Folly*. The pervasive artistry of realism restores a significance to the narrative that the irony takes from it. The final effect is a simultaneous assertion of the vanity of the world *and* the intrinsic value of life in it.

In terms of the analysis presented here, the most interesting and revealing contrast to *Troilus* is provided by the story with which it is most often bracketed, the *Knight's Tale*. That both works utilize in important ways both the machinery of epic and the conventions of romance is a commonplace observation; that these are treated in the *Knight's Tale* much as in *Troilus*—undercut with irony wherever they appear—is perhaps obvious. At the same time it seems clear that the elements of realism found in Chaucer's narrative of Troy are absent from his tale of Thebes; characterization, action, and setting in the *Knight's Tale* are exaggerated and stylized in the extreme. The significance that is pointed to in the *Knight's Tale* has nothing to do with its location of the typically human in the specific events related. The meaning there instead is the product of another frame of reference that is negated in *Troilus*. Boethian affirmation is embodied in the story of Palamon and Arcite and explicitly formulated by Theseus in his "chain of love" speech. . . . In the *Knight's Tale* the application of reason in a Boethian frame leads to an ultimate affirmation of providence, while in *Troilus* a similar process repeatedly aborts.

The affinities of the *Knight's Tale* to the novel as that form has been developed by Fielding and Thackeray, Balzac and Flaubert, Hardy and James are virtually nonexistent. But in the case of *Troilus and Criseyde* the old comparison of Chaucer to such writers as these has at least some validity, probably a great deal. Like all important medieval works *Troilus* is profoundly medieval, yet like all major works some of its most significant affinities are with good literature regardless of time and place. The presentation of a concrete universal—the embodiment of the general in the specific—has been an aim of writers and a standard of critics of all ages, but the systematic and successful application of the techniques of realism to that end is most characteristic of novelists like those named and, before them, of Chaucer in *Troilus*.

James I. Wimsatt
PMLA (March, 1977), p. 214

The Legend of Good Women

The first weakness in the *Legend*'s structure lies in its lack of developmental capability. The *legenda* type of collection allows for no genesis of a "middle" in an Aristotelian narrative sequence. Every episode can achieve only the status of a repetition or a variation. Second, all the actual and potential unifying factors tend to be collected into the "Prologue," leaving the work seriously unbalanced in terms of the relation of parts to whole. Third, the fiction of an author selecting *legendae* from a wide, necessarily disconnected classical past allows for little development of crossing and connecting interests, personages or places. How well Virgil manages this in creating a community of interests within the *Eclogues*, and how poor Spenser is in understanding what is required for the *Shepheardes Calendar*. Chaucer attempts a few connections in the persons of Jason and Theseus but the result is not distinguishable from any of the other *vitae* in terms of sustained development. The main benefit which Chaucer derived from attempting serial composition in the *Legend* was to learn what sort of problems arise for the writer in this kind of additive, episodic patterning. The *Legend* was an excellent training-ground for the poet of the *Canterbury Tales*—a work which shows a clear and comprehensive appreciation of the potential uses of unity of place (as suggested by a title such as *Gesta Romanorum*) and unity of activity.

John Norton-Smith
Geoffrey Chaucer (London: Routledge & Kegan Paul, 1974), p. 77

The Canterbury Tales

The device of the Pilgrim poet subordinated by his characters in the *Canterbury Tales* is the brilliant outcome of Chaucer's earlier experiments with conventions: comic identity, suppressed power, and the denial of art. In the earlier dream visions, the poem evolves suddenly, through the agency of fantasies called up by the power of a pivotal book. In *Troilus and Criseyde*, the narrator serves as mediator between the *historial* narrative and the audience, both of which are greater than he—the book for its assumed veracity, the audience for its creation of the meaning received through his agency. The meaning is what "ye loveres" learn. In the *Canterbury Tales*, Chaucer plays the game of storyteller of his thirty storytellers, in a more complicated set of fictional perspectives than he had hitherto attempted. His speakers are all also listeners.

Each poem envisages its own readers, who, ideally, would be under the poet's perfect power to control, alert to his cues and sympathetic but unable to anticipate him or to consider alternatives. The ideal audience, be it reader or listener, is wholly subservient to the poet's authority. The Pardoner, for example, conjures up for himself such an audience for his sample sermon, in the imagined congregation he induces to buy his wares by the charisma of his imagery of the damned. The Pardoner describes how he masters his audiences—"them"—by playing on their guilt and fear of exposure, their vulnerability to judgment, and need to protect themselves; "they" always easily yield, comply with the ritual, the acceptance of which protects him. In exposing the fraudulent Pardoner to his humiliation at the hands of the secondary audience, the fictional pilgrims, Chaucer addresses his third audience, inviting them to appreciate their superiority to both of the audiences within the fiction, the credulous and the cruel, and to witness the defeat of the Pardoner's mysterious power to enslave. Each invites the reader to see the illusion of power broken, and in so doing, exerts his own power over the reader's response. These are continuing tensions in the *Canterbury Tales*, within the field of illusion where the poet, narrator, pilgrims, and reader contend in the task of interpretation.

•

Alice S. Miskimin
The Renaissance Chaucer (New Haven, Conn.: Yale Univ. Pr., 1968), pp. 107–8

Chaucer has so imagined and dramatically portrayed the Canon's Yeoman that the yeoman remains within a safe framework, religiously, theoretically, and experimentally, and by the same token repudiates the positive side of alchemical experimentation. From the vantage point of the era of modern science we know that the yeoman chose the losing side in the dispute over alchemy. For the experimenting and theorizing did continue in its haphazard and, as has been known since the late seventeenth century, wrongly based way. *But* these same experimentings and theorizings were an actual step (as events have proved) in giving birth to modern chemistry, and modern chemistry on its own very different principles has proved transmutation possible—in the countless ways it has manipulated nature to bring gold where there was not gold before: in industrial chemistry, in medicine, in all the alleviations that chemistry has brought to man's lot on earth. The "truth" has been revealed; the alchemists' faith has been justified; the philosopher's stone has been achieved. We depend on it daily in a thousand ways. It may prove our undoing. But whatever its future, an actual (and therefore in retrospect, necessary) step in its realization was the continuing of alchemical theorizing and the fires of alchemical experiment rather than their cessation. The Walters of Odington did not cease their labors in spite of the Pope's edict and the *Canon's Yeoman's Tale*.

Edgar H. Duncan
Sp (October, 1968), p. 655

The Prioress's Tale is . . . in face of the portrait of its teller given in the *General Prologue* perhaps a little surprising. It is not in the least a mannered narration; it is not in the least a sentimental story. Whatever the apparent ambiguousness of her behaviour and attitudes as represented by the *General Prologue*, whatever the apparent tepidity of her dedication to the rigours of the religious life, the tale that the Prioress tells would seem to show that her spirituality, even if not necessarily deep and highly developed, is neither feeble nor histrionic, and it would seem to suggest further that some of his commentators have far outstripped Chaucer in pointing up the Nun's weaknesses.

Her election to relate a Miracle of the Virgin is, for a nun, a natural enough decision, and the miracle that she chooses to recount is, in its kind, restrained, tasteful and moderate. It contains nothing of the exaggerations and absurdities which so often disfigure this *genre* in its medieval forms. The Prioress reveals herself as a person who, while having little of the obvious strength of the central ecclesiastical members of the pilgrimage, is yet capable of relating a story which, while participating in a tradition that so often displays a naïve and crude spirituality, is able to avoid its pitfalls and turn it to distinguished artistic account. It is a performance which must lead us to think that her critics have read into her portrait too much that is unflattering. This decisively sensitive rejoinder to the Shipman leaves an impression of quiet and assured maturity.

Her assurance is displayed in the economy and skill with which the fiction is organized and in the easy mastery of the verse of a mature tradition handled with unusual sensitivity. Its basic mode is tempered, gentle and unemphatic. As such it bears the narrative along without strain and without display. As befits its story, its staple vocabulary is apparently simple and undemonstrative; it is, in fact, the assured language of a tradition of Christian writing that is venerable and rich. . . .

Chaucer has given to the Prioress a verse which, in his best manner, is deceptively easy and simple, with a total control over a demanding rime scheme and a rhythmical pattern attuned to respond sensitively to the needs of the narration. Its use of language is unaffected and unobtrusive, deriving its hidden strength from the command of a series of words that are resonantly strong and evocative in his hands—*blisful, deere, sely, reverence*. Words like these recur through the poem and serve to remind us of the depth and the density of the verbal complex that the best late-fourteenth-century religious poetry in England has achieved. It embodies a mature management of language which enables the fullness and richness of a series of recurring words and phrases to suggest the depth and mystery which underlie this simple and otherwise merely pathetic story. Its success is intimately involved with this coexistence in its language of the apparently simple and that which is conceptually and emotionally rich and dense.

G. H. Russell
in *Medieval Literature and Civilization*, ed. D. A. Pearsall and R. A. Waldron (London: Athlone, 1969), pp. 225–26

[The] unusual combination of realistic and abstractly separate actions in the *Shipman's Tale* clearly suggests that a double purpose underlies Chaucer's composition. If the poem's multi-action plot configuration indicates Chaucer's concern that literature exemplify an idea, its psychological verisimilitude reflects, simultaneously, his feeling that literature has a mimetic function. Such a double attitude toward artistic purpose is generally thought to be characteristic of that cultural period labeled "high Gothic." This period is commonly described as occupying a transitional position in the gradual alteration of the medieval attitude toward the natural world. Because it had neither abandoned the supernaturalism of the earlier Middle Ages nor completely accepted the new naturalism, the high Gothic culture perceived and expressed a dual conception of reality. Truth was believed to reside not only in absolute, supramundane ideas, but also within the temporal movement of natural life. Consequently, the artist of this period was faced with an objective unknown to the allegorists of earlier centuries; he regarded it as his function to represent the ceaselessly mutating character of actual sense experience, as well as the inalterable, metaphysical reality of ideas.

As illustrative of this double artistic impetus, one can point to the naturalistic individuation of symbolic human form in cathedral statuary. The cycle drama also evidences a dual emphasis, as it communicates, often naturalistically, biblical ideas in a movement of continuous presentation suggestive of organic process. Arnold Hauser has observed a similar dynamic vitalism in the spiritually symbolic Gothic church: "A Gothic church . . . seems to be in the process of development, as if it were rising up before our very eyes; it expresses a process, not a result. The resolution of the whole mass into a number of forces, the dissolution of all that is rigid and at rest by means of a dialectic of functions and subordinations, this ebb and flood, circulation and transformation of energy, gives us the impression of a dramatic conflict working up to a decision before our eyes."

It seems that this view of the Gothic cathedral as the simultaneous expression of transcendent idea and vital process (or that of the cycle drama as both the ideological design of Christian reality and the "drama of movement," "dynamic life," and "changing and transitory particulars") brings us very close to the kind of thing Chaucer is about in the persuasive passages of his Tale. As we have seen, there is a sense in which these passages are exemplary forms, closed and separate from the mainstream of temporal life. Taken collectively as a series of triumphant moments, they represent life selectively ordered (in the manner of an allegorical structure). Only in this way is Chaucer able to isolate and define his idea of creativity. This idea has reality for Chaucer, even as the transcendent idea has reality for the cathedral builder, and yet ultimately it is inseparable from the things of sense experience. The idea is perceived within life and communicated in terms of the vital, psychological process of creative persuasion. Like the Gothic cathedral, the persuasion of the *Shipman's Tale* is both form and process; it exemplifies idealogical reality while it represents life. Chaucer abstracts and reincarnates for our perception the idea of creative triumph.

A. Booker Thro
The Chaucer Review (Fall, 1970), pp. 110–11

The *Knight's Tale* exists in a pagan world that has an ultimately tragic view of man. Arcite's dying cry, "What is this world? what asketh men to have?" (2777), is never satisfactorily answered and qualifies the joy of the marriage at the poem's end. The poem raises more questions about the meaning of human life than it is capable of solving; its ideal of chivalry is not begun but fulfilled by Christianity. The First Mover speech does not itself transcend the poem's pagan, tragic view of life, yet it points in the direction from which this change is to come. The nobility of Theseus' attempt to create order and purpose in the wretched world is not undercut by its limitations, only put in a proper perspective. Theseus' failures as an earthly First Mover should not blind us to his successes. Although a heathen, Theseus represents secular knighthood at its best and prefigures the ideals of Christian chivalry and even, on a human scale, the divine First Mover and the universal Chain of Love that will be revealed by Christ.

C. David Benson
The Chaucer Review (Fall, 1970), p. 123

The narrative manner of these romances, which Chaucer must have learned both from hearing minstrels in London and Westminster and from reading books, especially anthologies such as the Auchinleck MS., formed an important part of his native poetic inheritance. He received it with mixed feelings; and these mixed feelings find expression in *Sir Thopas*. This remarkable piece is more than simply a burlesque on the hack-work of tail-rhymers such as Thomas Chestre, though it is that. In some respects it may stand as an image, or cartoon, of Ricardian poetry itself, representing many of the weaknesses and some of the strengths not merely of the hacks but also of the true poets of the age, including Chaucer himself. Stylistically, the poem represents what Chaucer and his contemporaries accepted, as well as what they rejected, of native traditions. It should, therefore, repay consideration in the present context.

The most obvious part of the joke in *Thopas* is that Geoffrey Chaucer should be capable, in the way of a tale on the road to Canterbury, of nothing better than this "drasty" bit of tail-rhyme. Even if we do not agree with critics like E. T. Donaldson who hold that the pilgrim Chaucer is represented as genuinely incapable of anything better and genuinely indignant at the Host's interruption, the facts remain that the pilgrim does not introduce his tale as a burlesque, and that Harry Bailey seems to speak for everyone when he says he has heard enough. Chaucer the pilgrim may not be as incapable as Donaldson thinks; but at least he wants to tease his companions into thinking him incapable. On either reading, tail-rhyme represents a most degraded form of narrative verse, the very opposite of the polished performance which we would have expected from the one poet on the pilgrimage. But when we come to compare *Thopas* in some detail with the rest of Chaucer's work, we begin to see that the familiar self-depreciating joke has a second stage to it. For the poem, where it is bad, is often bad in a strikingly Chaucerian way. Certainly it does exhibit, as critics and editors have pointed out, many features (forms, words, rhymes, compounds, phrases, collocations) which are recorded nowhere else in Chaucer's work; and where these unique features figure in the hack-work of the age one may suspect that they are positively un-Chaucerian. In such cases we suppose, reasonably enough, that Chaucer, as a fastidious man of letters with a good ear for niceties of language, is enjoying a straightforward joke at the expense of Thomas Chestre and the rest. But many other similar features, at which we laugh with equal readiness, prove on investigation to occur also in Chaucer's unparodic verse, and even to be characteristic of it. The parody in *Thopas*, as Dieter Mehl says in his book on the romances, "often makes fun of conventions which Chaucer himself used at other times in all seriousness." The evidence of the concordance supports this conclusion. It suggests that the relationship between *Thopas* and the rest of Chaucer's work is more equivocal, and much more interesting, than appears at first sight.

J. A. Burrow
Ricardian Style (London: Routledge & Kegan Paul, 1971),
pp. 14–15

It is perhaps impossible to assess the Wife of Bath without consciously setting her in her time. It was a time in which wife-beating was still a common practice and was even regarded by many as the Christian duty of a husband. It was a time in which women were regarded (in the tradition of the early Church fathers) on the one hand as corruptors of men and on the other as little more than chattels, as a great deal less than human beings capable of fine intellectual and spiritual attainments. Whether consciously or unconsciously, Dame Alice reacts powerfully against the idea of women presented not only in the anti-feminist literature but in the society out of which the literature grew. She is perhaps the first feminist striking her blow for women's rights by refusing to conform to the inferior position (in marriage) that convention ascribes to her. Her style is that of a partial rebel, and it conflicts with her willingness and her desire to accept the authority of God. She cannot be the wholehearted rebel because she believes too many of the lies (about women) she is rebelling against. She has within herself the emotional revolutionary at war with the platitudinous conservative.

In the total picture, Dame Alice emerges as a woman who is loudly but superficially vulgar. She is vivacious and positive, yet somehow insecure. She is full of gusto and of bluster, yet capable of fineness and of delicacy. She has a mind potentially sharp but largely undeveloped. She is aggressively assertive, and yet she is almost pathologically concerned lest she present herself as virtuous. She purports to be gay, but we suspect much of her gaiety is mere noise. She has a strong resentment against men—hence her talk of requiting her husbands—but she has not the heart and she is too positive to transfer that generalized resentment to particular husbands. She is garrulous and self-sufficient, and she is frank to the point of innocence. Yet she is sophisticated in her lower-middle-class way. Her love of life is perhaps symbolized by her interest in sex, but she is interested in everything that is vital and alive. For reasons we can perhaps suppose but cannot with security define, she is a woman ashamed of (or reticent to show) the perceptions of fineness and the appreciation of purity—sexual and otherwise—that she feels.

Dame Alice is romantic in her ideals of love and of religion, but she tries mightily to conceal her romanticism. Her efforts at concealment are so prodigious that she (as if she were a she and not a fiction) has succeeded in large measure. There is an eventual point at which a consistent masker becomes his mask, and Dame Alice has gone far in that direction. Yet she has not arrived. There is still intact, waiting for readers to see it and to wonder at it, an appreciation of and a love for the essential Christian message that makes Chaucer's Wife of Bath far more convincing as a Christian than Chaucer's Prioress. Dame Alice's religious conviction is real, and it is an important part of her. The degree to which she is religious will inevitably be variously construed by various readers, but surely the time has come for us to recognize in her the authentic religious passion and to see her thereby—though of course only partially—beatified.

Gloria K. Shapiro
The Chaucer Review (Fall, 1971), pp. 140–41

The philosophical Clerk has transmuted the marriage moral of the Marriage Group to a universal Christian and cosmic moral, and his reserves of humor open us then to his ironic envoy, a defense of women which is the mirror image of the Wife's own confessions. Dioneo's cynicism in Boccaccio, which probably hides ambivalence on the part of his author, who has chosen for the tale the noblest place of all in his hundred tales, is tempered in Chaucer by gentilesse, and the Clerk's irony is a far cry from the sensual charges of the *Decameron*. Though the *Clerk's Tale* is true to its dramatic function in the Marriage Group, it holds consistently to the moral truth of the Griselda story. We need not press the fourfold allegories in the tale, since they have almost from the beginnings of Scriptural interpretation seemed to be the creation more of the epigonal critic than of the author. Yet it would be negligent not to speak of the realism of the domestic and literal level, the tropological exemplum, the allegorical or figural level of Abraham, Job, and the Blessed Virgin, and the anagogy of the Christian soul desiring God and obeying him in perfect charity.

Quite as important is the hierarchy of genres: the remote fairy tale with its deep psychological roots and its spectres of man and woman in monstrous conflict; the novella which imports realism to the story and provides a domestic element to the drama; the exemplum which follows from the reality and which provides new overtones to patience, beyond the marital, the social and the political to the justification of man to God; the symbolism of the Blessed Virgin and the whole aura of the Bible which provide transcendence to the Christian souls on this dramatic pilgrimage and to their counterparts, the reading and the hearing audience, an audience ripe to the specific but not obtruded icons of the poem; and at last the often touched drama which encircles the tale and makes it appropriate to the shy, keen, oral and humorous Clerk, friend both of Petrarchan humanism and of medieval ethos and religious order. To overstress or omit any one of these would be to reduce the poem's significance. Even these words reduce a great poem. Finally we must assert that the simple language of the poem, a truly "high style" though perhaps not in the Ciceronian or even in the Petrarchan tradition, belies the complex literary structure and purpose. Our Clerk is a philosopher, sober in intention and reverent to his Canterbury master of ceremonies and to the orders of gentilesse and nobility; yet he is not without knowledge of the mortal noble's power both of abuse and of restitution. He is also something I have always held more profound than a philosopher, a humorist who knows how to reinforce his sobriety by the saving touch that makes the chthonic, the real, the dramatic, the moral and the heavenly all part of God's order. If this be organicism, let us make the most of it.

Francis Lee Utley
The Chaucer Review (Winter, 1972), pp. 227–28

Chaucer's pairing of pilgrim and tale has far-reaching implications for a proper appreciation of the work. First, it is a completely *new* way of disposing of a variety of stories within a larger narrative frame such as a pilgrimage. Then it leads to the more important question of the appropriateness of the teller to the tale, a concern that has always fascinated students and critics, particularly because it calls into play a dynamic interaction between the pilgrims' descriptions in the *General Prologue*, and further characterizations elsewhere in the poem with the various factors in, and ultimately the effects of, their tales. To take one example, the Pardoner's portrait in the *General Prologue*, his interruption of the Wife of Bath in her prologue, his own prologue (a kind of confessional monologue) and his tale (a kind of sermon), and his kind of quarrel with the Host at the end of his tale, all must be reckoned with if one is going to develop a full understanding of the pilgrim-tale relationship.

And thus, the pilgrim-tale relationship, in turn, forces the consideration of the implications of the exchanges among pilgrims along the way. In other words, we must admit the possibility of a level of interpretation that views the various parts and passages of the poem as the elements of a whole that works dramatically, just as we admit the possibility of a level that works allegorically. This fundamental dramatic principle of the *Tales*, which is fairly commonly accepted, allows us to react to each tale as if it were the speech of a fictional character at the same time as we read it as an individual narrative poem or prose piece. This double perspective is made possible by the invention of Chaucer the pilgrim-narrator who "reports" the entire Canterbury event as the persona of Chaucer the poet who has "created" the entire poetic structure and the various narrative elements it contains. Chaucer the poet, thus, must be heard through his narrator, a persona he had been developing since the *Book of the Duchess*, but this narrator expands rather than limits the possibilities of the poem.

Taken separately and compared with its sources and literary type, any Canterbury tale reveals that Chaucer has probed the genre for new possibilities, has experimented with its conventions, and sometimes has utterly transformed it. Naturally, the Chaucerian touch affects individual poems in different ways, but the basic dramatic conception of the *Canterbury Tales* immediately transforms each tale by virtue of casting it as a speech delivered by a particular pilgrim with particular characteristics and motives. Chaucer fulfills the part of the great poet not by inventing new genres but by altering them to suit his singular purposes. When I describe him to my classes as "Chaucer, the destroyer of genres," I am saying that he is that extremely rare kind of artist who knows how to destroy so that he might build something that is uniquely and forever his own.

George D. Economou
in *Geoffrey Chaucer*, ed. George D. Economou (New York: McGraw-Hill, 1975), pp. 10–11

Of the twenty-odd tales, all contain religious language, and analysis will, I believe, show that all are structured so as to support a religious or moral position. One might then ask why Chaucer at the end of his work found it necessary to revoke "the tales of Caunterbury, thilke sownen into synne" (1085). The answer, I think, is that many of the religious references, especially in the fabliaux, occur in contexts that may seem blasphemous. And there is no doubt that as an artist Chaucer was not deeply engaged in his virtuous figures but was, and knew that he was, deeply involved in creating the challengers to orthodoxy, like the Wife of Bath, and the hilarious impieties of his grosser characters. Although Chaucer did not finally support the view that sexy and tricky people will prevail, he did create for them and vicariously share with them their moments of glory.

Throughout the *Canterbury Tales* Chaucer balances religious and profane elements: piety and impiety, reverence and irreverence, sincere religious devotion and the satirical use of religious forms. In varying combinations he juxtaposes and blends pagan and Christian language and values, contrasting and weighing possibilities and consequences. There are the limited good of the *Knight's Tale*, the ugly vision of the *Merchant's Tale*, the bright world of the *Franklin's Tale*.

The continuous use of religious references serves as a reminder that the pilgrimage is not merely a social or literary venture; these references function as reminders of the spiritual possibilities of pilgrimage. Chaucer moves toward the end of the *Canterbury Tales* closer to exclusively Christian concerns. In placing the *Parson's Tale* and his own *Retraction* last, he sets the whole work in a Christian perspective.

Chaucer is not primarily a religious poet, as Dante and Langland are. But he is a great and original poet whose viewpoint is essentially Christian. For many of his richest and most characteristic effects he uses religious language, and throughout the *Canterbury Tales* he uses religious structures —in the tales and in the pilgrimage itself. In the end, the language and the structure are Chaucer's.

Esther C. Quinn
in *Geoffrey Chaucer*, ed. George D. Economou (New York: McGraw-Hill, 1975), pp. 70–71

A writer who vindicates or defends piously held beliefs is writing comedies of a limited range; but they are not to be dispraised for being so. For the Christian poet, stripping off the disguises and masks of villainy precisely in terms of religiously defined norms and writing comedies about damnation demonstrates that comedy may derive its materials from anywhere; attitude and tone are all. And obviously comedy does not exclude suffering; it makes capital of it but uses it for its own ends and with the right tone and attitude.

These two broad types of comedic structures in Chaucer thus confirm that double perspective which is implicit in comedy generally. One cannot know the merely existing without testing it against essence, the factual without the ideal, the life of instinct without the life of reason, body without soul. The norms which are vindicated in Chaucer's comedies about adultery are clearly those of nature; in the others, the tension is clearer in terms of good and evil men and women. Chaucer does not pretend that his protagonists are not bad men and women; they are shown to be so, and one has the feeling that their predictable destruction has been part of a larger justification of law.

Chance, trickery, and improbable possibilities may be the laws of the best kind of comedies; from the perspective of the other type, these laws dwindle before an inexorable law. In the first type, things work out well for the agents; in the second, for the audience.

I do not know whether Chaucer's comic structures can be placed on any scale. Irony of various sorts invests them all. But of the tales of license and the "adultery" tales, the *Miller's Tale* is the "happiest," the *Reeve's Tale* less so, because the somewhat morose and dispeptic disposition of the miller of the tale tends to cast a large shadow over the action; and he has something of the humor about him. The *Shipman's Tale* even less so, perhaps because of the age of the persons involved: they should not behave so lightheartedly, or perhaps we feel that in the tale nothing is held sacred. They are lightweight alongside the *Merchant's Tale*'s somewhat more grandiose style and manner. Essentially, in formal ways they are the same; but they are all different in tone, in characterization, in kind of structure, and in the amount of the serious that has been added to the plot.

The others are ironic-comedies, built around the basic theme of unmasking. In these it is society at large that has profited from the unmasking. If the villains will not mend their ways, then they must go. And their going is justified when we consider the demonic values which they had hoped to impose upon the world. In the outer frame, the Pardoner and the Yeoman stay, the Canon goes; in the tales, the friar is carried off to hell; the rioters die.

Chaucer's range is considerable in its effects: there are tales in which considerations of moral responsibility are totally absent; others in which the question of rightness and wrongness somehow springs into our minds (*Shipman's Tale*—at least it disturbed earlier generations of scholars); still others in which the agents are frankly described as bad persons and so are calculated to rouse feelings of indignation in us.

Paul G. Ruggiers
in *Medieval Studies in Honor of Lillian Herlands Hornstein*,
ed. Jess B. Bessinger and Robert Raymo (New York:
New York Univ. Pr., 1976), pp. 197–98

General

Few readers would want to deny that Chaucer's verse conveys more of a sense of the speaking voice (and speaking voices) than Gower's; and the basic reason is that he works like the alliterative poets with "pieces of language." Yet Chaucer's verse is, to bring in a different quotation, "speech heightened," very unlike the naturalistic prose by which a modern novelist might attain some comparable end. One heightening agent is the metre, the compound of pentameter with half-line movement. This compound of balanced pentameter is evidence of an accomplished technique; but the intention triumphantly fulfilled in the best of Chaucer is the concealment of technique—the simulation of speech by a heightening of speech which can yet seem fresh and natural. If Chaucer had wanted real speech he could have taken his tablets out into the street and written it out in prose; but for the lively simulation of speech he needed verse and that complex metre. The metre justifies itself by a concentration of expressiveness, a significance not found so consistently in real conversation. The life of Chaucer's verse is that of the spoken language, but it is a life quite unlike chunks of liveliness.

If Chaucer's poetry is speech heightened, it is speech in its basic rhythmic shaping. The half-line movement is the final sign that the metre in Chaucer cannot be at war with speech-rhythm, on which it is built and with which it co-operates. . . .

Critics are always remarking, truly enough, on the paradox of Chaucer's learned spontaneity. Sometimes one half of the paradox predominates, sometimes the other. Chaucer the wayward genius unaffected by his time is an obviously incomplete picture, but when Blake says in the Prospectus for his engraving of the Canterbury Pilgrims, "Let the Philosopher always be the Servant and Scholar of Inspiration and all will be happy," he is certainly stating one side of the truth about Chaucer's greatness. Nowadays, of course, we have come full circle to Lydgate's view, and it is more fashionable to emphasize the other side of the paradox, Chaucer's professional expertise—which is equally incomplete. Chaucer is learned and spontaneous: the Wife of Bath is a mixture of quotations from antifeminist literature; she is also an uncomfortably convincing real person. It does seem to me that the metre I have outlined fits the paradox better than the metrical models of [Paul] Baum or [James] Southworth. Chaucer's rhythms too are learned, skilled, artificial, spontaneous and fresh—which is part of what I mean by Hopkin's phrase "speech heightened."

Ian Robinson
Chaucer's Prosody: A Study of the Middle English Verse Tradition (Cambridge: Cambridge Univ. Pr., 1971), pp. 172–73

We are ready for a new "marriage" in Chaucer studies: the old, the new, the borrowed, and (of course) the blue. With the *OED* and the *MED*; with [Eric] Partridge's example to guide us; with the new awareness and information from the rhetoricians; and with something borrowed from the exegetical critics—we are ready to begin our examination of Chaucer's "harlotrye." Our contemporary literature has been "liberated" legally for about a generation, since Judge Woolsey found *Ulysses* an acceptable import. We can now read without a blush Molly Bloom's soliloquy, with its reference to Stephen Dedalus' cock. We no longer need to ship copies of Henry Miller's schoolboy fantasies home from Europe in false-bottomed trunks. John Barth and John Updike and Allen Ginsberg and LeRoi Jones can publish four-letter words as part of their natural artistic vocabulary, using the blunt terms for comic or, more often, for emetic purposes.

Chaucer views copulation with healthy and effervescent good humor. The "swyvynge" that goes on in the *Miller's* or the *Reeve's Tales* is supremely good fun for those involved directly. In the latter narrative, the daughter and the wife enjoy immensely their (respective) fornication and adultery. We readers, the indirect participants, enjoy the comic ribaldry too.

Where there is adultery, there must be cuckolds. In Chaucer, they deserve their fates: they are stupid, suspicious, jealous, dishonest, and anti-intellectual. Only in Chaucer, perhaps, is the last of these shortcomings grounds for cuckoldry.

On the morning after his delicate young wife has betrayed him, the carpenter-cuckold in the *Miller's Tale* falls from the ceiling and breaks his arm. Sentimental readers feel a twinge of pity for the victim of this gratuitous violence, but the sympathy does not endure. John's arm will mend, we know, just as we are sure that the "hurt gags" in movie cartoons will not result in permanent injuries to Sylvester the cat.

When Nicholas' scorched "toute" heals, he and the inventive Alisoun will find another occasion to repeat their lovemaking. They will hoodwink the stupid husband again and again, but from us he will never elicit any lasting sense of outrage or pity. Chaucer keeps their whole affair good-humoured and comic.

Thomas Ross
Chaucer's Bawdy (New York: E. P. Dutton, 1972), pp. 15–16

Chaucer's achievement in his major works has been to hold in balance the two sides of the Boethian dichotomy: man is free to choose, but the choices are foreseen and foreknown. By throwing a larger emphasis upon human moral choice, Chaucer does more than merely mitigate the fortunal explanation of human experience. He does not shirk that extreme pole of the tragic mode, the pole of an inescapable destiny; he accepts that possibility, but he also admits that other equally tempting possibility: human responsibility is a factor in that destiny. In his mature work the two views are held in a delicate equilibrium in much the same way that fate and human defect are delicately balanced in the finest Greek tragedies.

Embraced between these two poles of thought, then, lies the whole question of Chaucer's serious art. The Providence of God is seen as sustaining the order which, in his own Adamic way, man has upset or shattered; or which, in the bleakest possible formulation, man's presence in the world has disturbed. Thus, as in Theseus' speech at the close of the *Knight's Tale*, a rational design is defined as Law to which each man must accommodate himself; and in the more ironical tales, like that of the Pardoner and that of the Friar, an ineluctable force leads the agents as if by predestined steps to their ruin. In each, however, the agents choose their destiny.

From this vantage point, the fortunal aspects of the *Monk's Tale* constitute a naïve level for the Christian poet whose later complex art depicts the fortunal as merely provisional or partial. Diametrically opposite to the fortunal view are the saintly tales like the *Second Nun's Tale* in which acceptance of and surrender to Providence are total. Between them, however, lies the more interesting bulk of Chaucer's work which offers an answer to the question of the limits of Fortune. This answer, which has to do with the role of prudence in an unstable world, is implicit in the sequence in which the *Monk's Tale* appears, bracketed between the *Tale of Melibee* and the *Nun's Priest's Tale.*

In the *Tale of Melibee*, Chaucer's Prudence urges upon her husband rational self-control and Christian resignation to a Providence that works out its own justice. The *Nun's Priest's Tale* declines all large questions of Providence in favor of a rule of expedience. Chaucer's irony forces us as usual to look both ways: towards the prudence of trust in God and His justice and towards the prudence of rational self-control in this world. Each is in its way a counterbalance to a merely fortunal view; each in its way informs the structure of the *Canterbury Tales.* Between the statements of two kinds of expedience, each offered as a way of life, the *Monk's Tale* offers its own terrible statement. Whether deserved or undeserved, the "unwar strook" of Fortune is a fact of existence. It exists, not to be rejected out of hand, but to be savored as a chastening reminder of the primal choice by Adam which has made all ensuing life perilous and unstable. In any event, man must choose; and if he is wise, he will weigh the choices offered by prudence carefully.

Paul G. Ruggiers
The Chaucer Review (Fall, 1973), pp. 96–97

Geoffrey Chaucer was a moral man and a skeptical man. He saw great sorrow in the world; sorrow, chaos, and error. He senses our aloneness and isolation. In the beginning, he perfected his role of the writer as listener and insisted that there was comfort in our confessions of grief. Later he understood there was another need to speak, a need to confess, and that words themselves could reveal more than the speaker might want to reveal, a truth Chaucer found long before Freud. Through words, through the selection of narrative, Chaucer found a way to portray character and to judge it at the same time. Above all, Chaucer found a way to express his own need to speak. Chaucer, once the listener, became the speaker who assumed various identities. Speaking was the act of writing, and the act of writing became the perfection of a moral art.

For myself as a writer what I learn as I look for Chaucer's identity in his work is how the writer's self may, out of its pain and uncertainty, draw toward an art which uses that self without the abrasive and unrelenting exhibition of the self which we have come to expect from our contemporary writers; an art out of the self, of the self, in which the self of the creator dies into the new and separate life of the creation.

Christopher Brookhouse
in *The Learned and the Lewed: Studies in Chaucer and Medieval Literature*, ed. Larry D. Benson (Cambridge, Mass.: Harvard Univ. Pr., 1974), pp. 79–80

Love is "joye of this world," and good as it may sometimes appear, it must obviously be bound inextricably to the world and to mutability. Although the lover may see himself and his condition to be tragic, from a broader perspective, *sub specie aeternitatis*, he must appear ludicrous and his situation comic. The lover who cannot see beyond his immediate condition cannot be taken seriously, and this is the courtly lover, the adherent of "fyn lovynge," that Chaucer consistently presents. The ideal love is doubtless that found in the oft-quoted passage at the end of *Troilus and Criseyde*, when the narrator addresses the "yonge, fresshe folkes" and advises them to leave their "feynede loves" and turn to God (V.1835–48). And in terms of this passage the ideal lover in all of Chaucer's writings would probably be St. Cecelia in the *Second Nun's Tale*. With such a love, however, we are out of the realm of both passion and courtly love. If we are to remain in this realm, we must expect to see love as the main ingredient in the human comedy. It may seem for a while to be something worthy and noble, but finally its inadequacies will be discernible and it will appear at best laughable and at worst destructive. Even when, as in the *Book of the Duchess*, the *Knight's Tale*, and the *Troilus*, Chaucer seems most sincerely to be presenting love and lover as noble and good, his final and real attitude seems to be one of ironic scorn. Like what may be seen in such significant writings as the *Art of Honest Loving* of Andreas Capellanus and the *Romance of the Rose* of Jean de Meun, Chaucer's method is to present earthly love as both good and bad. But, also as in these writings, his narratives bring out the ultimate destructiveness and folly of this love.

Edmund Reiss
in *The Learned and the Lewed: Studies in Chaucer and Medieval Literature*, ed. Larry D. Benson (Cambridge, Mass.: Harvard Univ. Pr., 1974), pp. 110–11

Considerable success is achieved in translating some given observation about speech or character or both into recognizably individual utterance. Chaucer's aim, we may assume, was to *suggest* such individuality rather than attempt anything "as round as gooth a belle," hence he had to start from the commonly shared basis in any given register of English, whether vulgar or polite, colloquial or courtly, from which more individualized speech habits, patterns of diction, choice and range of vocabulary, syntactical preferences, linguistic idiosyncrasies, and the like, could be developed. The result is the first appearance in English literature of a number of individual voices: they not only attempt to make their words "cosynes to the thiṅges of whiche thei speken," but their English confirms to varying degree the personalities and linguistic propensities which their maker has bestowed upon them: "By the fruyt of hem shul ye knowen hem."

Ralph W. V. Elliot
Chaucer's English (London: André Deutsch, 1974), pp. 421–22

If the controlling feature of Chaucer's work is comic irony, then the central force of that irony is the Chaucerian pose. The comedy is intensified throughout the Chaucer canon as the poet lowers the perceptive qualities of the narrator toward ever greater caricature. The ingenuous quality of this humor, the humility yet assured self-respect of character that it represents, and the wise awareness that self-satire can blunt the darts of an envious and fickle world, these are incontrovertible facts about Chaucer's character which we can glean by analyzing the evolution of his "persona." Hopefully, then, we are done, once and for all, with the complete separation of narrator and poet, for we thereby debase a brilliant, most personal stylistic device. Chaucer has done the work already; for our lasting amusement he has degraded his own pose. Certainly he needs no more help from us.

Thomas J. Garbaty
PMLA (January, 1974), pp. 103–4

GAVIN DOUGLAS

1474–1522

Douglas clearly has a cultural and historical importance. From him we can learn much of the literary tastes and attitudes not only of Scotsmen in the reign of James IV but of many educated men at his time. Scholars have made surmises, not always well-founded, about the nature of Henryson's reading; but we can be precise and definite about many of the books that Douglas read and admired. Douglas gives us an insight into the way in which readers of the early sixteenth century approached a great Latin poet. He illustrates very vividly what they valued in Virgil, and also how they read and studied the text of his poems. In the *Eneados* we can sometimes get close to Douglas as a translator, and examine the degree of consistency between his theories and his actual practice. This is possible, partly because he voices some of his ideas in the Prologues, partly because we know, fairly definitely, what edition of Virgil he used. Douglas's *Eneados* sometimes sheds light on the practice of later sixteenth-century translators, such as Surrey, [Arthur] Golding, or Chapman. The explanatory technique that he adopted (termed by H. B. Lathrop "the expanded method of translation") had its critics, such as Nicholas Grimald; but it continued to be used long after Douglas's time, in [George] Colville's Boethius

(1556), [Thomas] Phaer's Virgil, and Marlowe's First Book of Lucan. Even Dryden in the late seventeenth century did not disdain to incorporate notes and explanatory glosses in his translation of Virgil.

Priscilla Bawcutt
Gavin Douglas: A Critical Study (Edinburgh: Edinburgh Univ. Pr., 1976), pp. 205–6

The courtly setting of Douglas's life needs to be kept in mind. His acquaintance included such men as Cardinal Wolsey and Polydore Vergil: his sympathies were European, even English.

The broad cultural inheritance appears nowhere more clearly then in the *Palice of Honour*. It is a work with many European analogues, which form a highly developed genre of subtle conventions. Over these, Douglas shows the power of analectic command. Yet the *Palice of Honour* reads, as Priscilla Bawcutt remarks, like a young man's work: dazzlingly clever, intellectually brilliant, overdemanding, uneven. Its descriptive contrasts are sharp, but its catalogues too exactingly erudite and formal for modern readers. The subject—nothing less than right honour and fame and the spiritual goals of life—was ambitious even by medieval standards. If the *Palice of Honour* touches the theme of the *House of Fame*, it is nevertheless much more than a response to Chaucer, or an attempt to overgo. Douglas reviews the scope of poetry and history, true and feigned, in a series of visions moving between solemnity, philosophy and pure fun. Ironically, its most solemn visions, being written as literature, will be dismissed as mere dreams "quhilks ar not worth ane mite." Yet the types of true honour and fame survive through poetry—even when the poet is a figure of fun. These are topics of the master; but Douglas always seems to have heard other fames than Chaucer's rumoured.

Alastair Fowler
TLS (July 22, 1977), p. 882

WILLIAM DUNBAR

ca. 1460–1515

Dunbar was writing at a time, when imitation along with invention was regarded as perhaps the highest type of literary composition. In the "Goldyn Targe" he uses Lydgate's "Reson and Sensuallyte" as his basic model. It provides the framework of the psychomachia, parts of the introduction, perhaps the hint for the ship, certainly the list of goddesses and the two pieces of musical description. In conjunction with Chaucer's *Romaunt of the Rose*, it fills in the dramatis personae for the battlefield and identifies the arrows of Cupid. Dunbar's invention as always lies primarily in his art of selection, for example in accepting the fine description of harmony, but rejecting the chess metaphor. It is even possible that his substitution (the targe) may in this instance have been suggested by Lydgate. It will be remembered that in *The Pilgrimage of the Life of Man*, Grace Dieu explains the nature of the Christian's armour to the pilgrim. He culminates with the targe, which is identified as "prudence" and linked with "ryhtful jugement." Moreover the pilgrim is advised to defend himself with it against the powers of sin, thus anticipating the major conceit in Dunbar's "Targe":

Wherfor, whil thow art at large
Looke thow haue up-on, thys targe
Whereso thyn Emnyes the assaylle,
To force thy quarel and a-mende.

While this suggestion could not be proved, the *Pilgrimage* would certainly be known to a disciple like Dunbar. Moreover the passage beginning at l. 14290 ("Lat ech man -in especyal-") seems to have influenced "Of Manis Mortalitie."

Ronald D. S. Jack
SSL (April, 1971), pp. 226–27

Dunbar's primary aim in ["The Golden Targe"] seems to me to be to explore and enlarge upon a traditional theme in the graceful and witty language of the tradition, striving for as compact, complex, beautiful, and forceful a poem as possible. A reading which seems a parodic relationship with earlier dream visions has to ignore or regret the literary appeals in the poem, a reading which sees the poem as an idealization of love has to ignore much of the poem's matter and the tone entirely, and a reading which purports to be able to divorce the language or surface from the meaning seems to me to simply refuse to engage the poem at all. The poem has been accorded all these readings in print.

In the envoi, Dunbar calls on his "lytill quair" to be "symple of entent" (that is, clear in its meaning), but he also implies that a reader to whom the meaning will be clear will be an alert reader:

be . . . symple of entent
Before the face of eviry connyng wicht:
I knaw quhat thou of rethhorike hes spent . . . (272–74)

There is a real danger, almost a scholarly occupational hazard, of being more "connyng" (i.e. "knowledgeable, wise") than the poet intended or the poetry warrants, and thus of achieving a misreading of the poem and promoting a misconception of the literary past. However, there is no virtue in ignoring coherencies in a poem merely to preserve one's preconceptions of the poem and the poet. I believe, and I hope that I have demonstrated, that "The Golden Targe" is something more than a linguistic confection, that it deals with weighty questions in a manner both complex and coherent.

The *Roman de la rose* and its successors present a fairly consistent tradition. "The Golden Targe" enacts its tradition as a complex way of treating man's relationship to nature and the possibilities of perverting that relationship through the debasement of reason by a yielding to the appetites. Dunbar is asserting his place in a literary elite which has the sensibility to treat such a theme in such a light, witty, and sensuous way.

E. Allen Tilley
SSL (April, 1973), pp. 230–31

By its willful juxtaposition of brilliance and incompetence—by, in other words, its inconsistency—"The Golden Targe" reflects and calls attention to the inconsistency of genre of allegorical love-vision poetry which it nominally represents. But throughout, Dunbar is concerned with style as well as with substance. [J. J.] Speirs's comment that the poem is concerned with language is based in large measure upon Dunbar's numerous references to rhetoric. Homer and Cicero are cited specifically for their rhetorical ability (69–71), Mercury is associated with rhetoric (116–17), Chaucer is called "rose of rethoris all" (253), and in a most revealing statement, the poet says of his poem: "I knaw quhat thou of rethorike hes spent" (274). Dunbar explicitly associates rhetoric with style (70–72; 257–61) and especially with what he calls "termes," by which he means not only diction but rhetorical figures as well. Rhetoric, as Dunbar tells us, is metaphorical illumination (e.g., 258, 266): language illuminates thought, literally enables one to see what would otherwise be inchoate. But if rhetoric makes the mental landscape visible, that landscape itself must be rational to be comprehended. In "The Golden Targe" Dunbar describes an aureate landscape such as no one has ever seen, but it is comprehensible because of the rhetorical ability with which it is depicted. This landscape, however, does not in the world of love-vision exist for its own sake; rather it provides the setting for the allegorical vision to follow.

Throughout "The Golden Targe," it is not Dunbar's rhetoric that is deficient, but rather the vision which that rhetoric illuminates. Dunbar presents himself as struggling against the restrictions imposed upon him by the love-vision form. Into the aureate landscape intrude such formal necessities as the awakening and almost immediate falling asleep of the narrator despite the noise made by the clamorous birds. If Dunbar must include these elements he will nevertheless force the reader to see both their inherent irrationality and the absurdity of a facile and unquestioning acceptance of them. In the dream itself, Dunbar uses the rhetorical device of *synathroismus*, the apparently random catalogue, in order to call into question the dreamer's reliability, and provides the spectacle of Resoun's fighting valiantly, if unsuccessfully, in an attempt to turn back the allegorical personages who seem as numerous as the "stanneris" on the bed of Dunbar's aureate river. Resoun must ultimately fail, because Dunbar has after all written the poem, and after the blinding of Resoun the dreamer is surrounded by a host of allegorical figures who take him into custody. Throughout the poem there is a lack of balance between causes and effects; the battle itself, for example, is joined only because the dreamer is caught observing the courts of Venus and Cupid. But if the dreamer cannot observe them, he will not be able to describe them, and of what then can the poem consist? Similarly, the dreamer laments his capture in such heartfelt and despairing terms that it is difficult to remember that all that has happened to him in the context of the allegory is that he has succumbed to the attractions of Beauty. The rhetoric is grave, the subject trivial, and what the former illuminates is the mindlessness of the latter.

Walter Sheps
PLL (Fall, 1975), pp. 353–54

THE GAWAIN-POET

fl. 1375–1400

As we have seen from *Purity, Patience* and *Pearl*, there was for the *Gawain*-poet something *essentially* comic in the condition of "our own conscious kind"—a comedy that lay above all in the seeming impossibility for human beings of achieving a full consciousness of their status in the face of the divine. The Green Knight has certain similarities to the representations of God in *Patience* and *Purity*: he shares their omniscience with regard to the motives of his human antagonist, and his cool explanation that events too are under his control—

> Now know I wel thy cosses, and thy costes als,
> And the wowyng of my wyf: I wroght hit myselven (2360–61)

is strongly reminiscent of the emphasis on God's creative power in the earlier poems. But the Green Knight is given no hint of a place in any theological scheme, and we cannot say that man in *Sir Gawain and the Green Knight* is confronted, directly, or indirectly, with the divine. But, equally, the world of *Sir Gawain and the Green Knight* is certainly not one from which the divine is excluded: it has many references, as we have seen, to God, the Blessed Virgin, and other saints. We may surmise that for the poet the world of this poem, more than that of any of his others, was the everyday modern world, though of course heightened and idealized. It was not that of Biblical times, in which God spoke directly to man, nor even that of *Pearl*, in which man could at least approach God. It must therefore be a world in which it was at least possible to see the hero as comic, and yet not necessary to do so. The conception of the poem seems to require that we should perceptively *watch* Gawain being entangled in the situation to which his acceptance of the Green Knight's challenge leads him, and that we should see more clearly than he does the nature of his strengths and weaknesses (which means, too, those of Camelot and, by an easy extension, those of any civilized society); and yet we must also ourselves be entangled in and rebuked by the mystery he has to face.

If this is so, it has consequences for the treatment both of Gawain and of his antagonist.

A. C. Spearing
The Gawain Poet: A Critical Study (Cambridge: Cambridge Univ. Pr., 1970), p. 234

In spite . . . of the alliterative conventions in which he was working, the *Gawain*-poet's language must have had for his own audience a strong ring of everyday life. A similar realism would also have invested the many technical terms he uses, of arms and armour, of fortification, of the chase; for in the fourteenth century such terms were as familiar as those of cricket or of internal combustion are at the present day, so that the elaborate precision with which they are used would have been both delightful and realistic. The hunting terms are the ordinary ones used in treatises such as most medieval gentlemen would have studied, *The Master of Game* and *The Book of St. Albans*; and, moreover, the descriptions here are by no means as stiffly technical as they might have been. For the architectural intricacies of Bertilak's castle, contemporary reactions are suggested by the delight in fine detail of the same kind shown in the miniature painting of the time. To take a celebrated example, the calendar in *Les Très Riches Heures du Duc de Berry*: the background of many of these miniatures shows a castle of the Duke's—Dourdan, Étampes, Lusignan (with Melusine flying overhead in the form of a golden serpent), and, most of all to our purpose, Poitiers and Saumur. These are all depicted in the finest detail, and, indeed, if we sought an illustration of Bertilak's castle, "þe comlokest þat euer knyȝt aȝte," Saumur would serve well, for it is a cluster of turrets dotted with "chalkwhyt chymnees" and topped by "fayre fylyolez . . . ferlyly long" (like the similar ones at Poitiers), the whole encircled by crocketted, loopholed, and machicolated battlements, so that it too might have been "pared out of papure." Our poet, then, is using architectural terms not as in a technical treatise but to paint a miniature like those in the *Très Riches Heures*, and, far from being put off by the precise detail, his audience would no doubt have delighted in it as much as Jean de Berry must have done in that of the Limbourg brothers.

Cecily Clark
Medium Aevum, Vol. 40 (1971), pp. 12–13

The two contrastive games in the center of [*Sir Gawain and the Green Knight*] serve at once as a microcosmic reflection of the poet's world of play and as a thematic commentary upon it. The hunt, with its emphasis on the outward form, on protocol, and on achievement, looks back to the exterior setting of Arthur's festive court, and, tonally, it recapitulates the opening scene. The courtship emphasizes restraint and privacy. It inverts the rules of *amour courtois* and reminds us of the limitations of the world of play. In the process, it redefines the stature of the romance hero and thus points away from the reckless, anarchic games of the past to the constructive world of play that will follow. The courtship game, which is at the very core of this romance, is paradoxically anti-ludic. To prevail in it, as well as in the Exchange of Gifts, to which it is subordinate, Gawain is forced ultimately to refrain from playing.

Johan Huizinga, at one point in his discussion of Roman decorative art, observes that the play-element in it, though prominent, "has no organic connection with the structure of society and is no longer fecund of true culture." The same point, I think, can be made about courtly love in the late Middle Ages, and particularly as it is reflected in the literary reputation of the hero in *Sir Gawain and the Green Knight*. Indeed, there is good reason to believe, as one historian [John F. Benton] has put it, that the courts of love even in the time of Andreas Capellanus were mere "humorous figments of his imagination." That is to say, the rules of the game of love never really did reflect the conditions of feudal life in the mediaeval manor house. There was a time, no doubt, when *amour courtois* was an important literary game, which gave new significance and beauty to love. But by the end of the fourteenth century the code had become stale. As Chaucer's Squire—a man who should know—tells us, Gawain is of the "olde courteisye," and Lancelot, ". . . he is deed" (*CT*. V.95, 287). Therefore, when the Gawain-poet inverts the courtly love cliché, he parodies and destroys a literary game that had lost its vigor and significance, as all clichés must by their very nature. It is a stroke of genius, that he pairs the unproductive and perverse temptation game with another, the hunt, which pulsates with the ferocious intensity of real play. The contrast tells us where the poet's sentiment lay.

Martin Stevens
Sp (January, 1972), pp. 74–75

The poet's style, which dwells in minute detail on the profusion of things that make up Gawain's world, challenges our ability to read and to comprehend it all. It requires an act of almost devotional intensity on the reader's part to distinguish between significant and gratuitous detail, between the shimmer of jewelry and the aura of sanctity. As in the real world, a fine line divides the perception of transcendence in all things and a hedonistic obsession with their surfaces. Such a style teases us with our own imperfection, for we cannot read the poem from the vantage of Gawain, who vacillates between naïveté and paranoia, or Bercilak, who enjoys his complicity in making the obvious devious and the devious obvious, without taking into account the vantage of the poet, who, like Morgan le Fay, may or may not have intended it all.

We must choose between stirring panorama and significant clue. We must comb and be lost among the manic proliferation of things that make up the body of the narrative, and be caught, as Gawain is, between the significant and the insignificant, the necessary and the contingent. The loving description of each detail, however much it parallels the love of detail in some contemporary visual arts, also creates almost a mystical, totemic aura around each thing. Meaning glows from every detail. For the *Gawain* poet was writing for a class and a civilization that perceived all the elements of the natural world as symbols or images, an audience to whom the representation of physical reality seemed now increasingly gratuitous and now increasingly metaphoric, pointing always to a meaning beyond itself. The poet's most notable scenes are intrusions from another world, impositions upon an already created scene, like the entrance of the Green Knight.The action must stop to allow the intruder to be constructed, piece by piece, in minute detail. The element of surprise, the sudden appearance of an unexpected and surreal alien form, throws upon the scene we have already accepted an aura of the otherworldly, the magical, the supernatural, so that nothing can be as it once was and all the elements of the phenomenal world are suddenly open to question. The task of the *Gawain* poet is to redeem his audience, as he does his hero, from such abstraction and to reassert the limits and the worth both of human values and of the earthly world.

John M. Ganim
PMLA (May, 1976), pp. 383–84

Pearl

All the details which go to make up the description of the blissful country in *Pearl* are . . . associated with descriptions of the surroundings of the Earthly Paradise, rather than with the Garden of Love. Moreover, this part of the earth emerges as something which is, again and again, described not only for its own sake—through it is one of the wonders of the world—but because it is a point at which earth touches the boundaries of heaven, and this life the life hereafter. We have seen that in early epic the hero is sent to this land to learn the lesson of his humanity, and to gain a treasure which can never be put to use in the world. Even in the latest versions, the twin themes of self-knowledge and mortality are still firmly linked to accounts of the Earthly Paradise. The Garden of Love, although it may be an offshoot of the same tradition, could never serve a purpose like that of the *Pearl*-poet, but the journey to the Earthly Paradise is, by long use, perfectly adapted to his needs.

P. M. Kean
The "Pearl": An Interpretation (New York: Barnes & Noble, 1967), p. 113

In its treatment of grief, *Pearl* may be in some ways related to the *consolatio*, a form of late Classical and early medieval literature that, like Boethius' famous *Consolation of Philosophy,* attempted to instruct the grief-stricken and to offer solace to the bereaved by justifying to man the apparent whimsicality of Fortune. Originally conceived of as instructional discourses, these *consolationes* dealt generally, as does *Pearl,* with what John Conley calls "the sovereign theme of the Christian tradition, as of life itself: the nature of happiness, specifically true [heavenly] and false [earthly] happiness"; and it is apparent that in the course of the poem, the dreamer comes, however slowly and unwillingly, to accept the finality of the gulf between these two systems of values as a part of his heritage as fallen man. The poem thus ends with the narrator's lamenting, not, as before, the death of his daughter and the corruption of her body, but the corruptness of his own soul which has kept him from her, and with his prayer that he may himself eventually be counted among the lowly servants and "precious pearls" of God.

The theme of *Pearl* is that of most elegies: the acceptance, through suffering and revelation, of death as a part of the universal plan. In *Pearl,* the parts of the dream-vision become the stages of redemption. The narrator learns, through a series of trials, to accept his place among the living.

Charles Moorman
The Pearl-Poet (New York: Twayne, 1968), p. 63

The narrative structure of *Pearl* consists of an "erber" frame (stanza-groups 1 and 20), which records the spiritual change wrought in the dreamer, and a three-part dream—a ghostly adventure composed of a vision of the earthly Paradise (stanza-groups 2–4), a theological dialogue in which a celestial mentor instructs the dreamer (stanza-groups 5–16), and a vision of the heavenly City (stanza-groups 17–19). The triple division of the dream corresponds to the theologian's traditional division of the soul's ascent to God into three stages (from *without* to *within* to *above*), which may be roughly equated to man's three sources of knowledge (sense, intellect, and inspiration); or, to use Hugh of St. Victor's classification, the three modes of cognition: cognitation, meditation, contemplation. The relationship of the divisions of the dream to the modes of cognition is suggested by the manner of presentation of each. The initial *visio* of the marvelous land, itself an extended image, is perceived and described by the dreamer in terms of sense impressions but is not explained except for the solitary hint.

> Forþy I þoȝt þat Paradyse
> Watȝ þer ouer gayn þo bonkeȝ brade (137–38)
>
> [And so I thought that Paradise
> was over there opposite those broad banks.]

The dialogue, the discursive heart of the poem, consists essentially of the heavenly maiden's informing the intellect of the dreamer so that he may ultimately understand the reasonableness of the divine Will. The final *visio* of the heavenly City—mystical contemplation *per se*—is presented wholly in terms of inspired revelation, and is a remarkably close paraphrase of the vision of "þe apostel John" recorded in the Apocalypse.

The contemplative experience asserts the possibility of man's attaining to the eternal word of God, however momentarily, even while remaining in this transitory world of the flesh; it is the soul's ascent from the things that are made, to the Creator. Such an ascent is suggested by the parallels between *Pearl* and other medieval works using the same major forms, and it accounts for the juxtaposition of secular and theological elements in the poem. The narrator's experience is presented in terms which reveal a markedly consistent progression from the worldly to the religious point of view. In the dream proper, the details of the initial *visio* suggest details from the lands of both secular courtly-love poetry and accounts of the earthly Paradise; the chief affinities of the dialogue are with overtly didactic literature, especially the "vertical" debate in which one of the participants has supernatural superiority, and the final *visio* has as its sole source the Apocalypse and scriptural commentary. The progressively religious character of the dream is borne out by the poet's use of biblical allusions, which reveal a progressive increase with each successive section of the dream proper. Even more striking is the nature of the literary parallels found in the "erber" frame. The opening scene, with its panegyric on the lost pearl and its description of the garden, clearly belongs to the tradition of the love vision as exemplified by *The Romance of the Rose*; the closing scene, recording the spirit's return to the body, offers a remarkable number of parallels to the writings of contemplatives. The opening scene presents the worldly view of a lost transitory good, the earthly pearl-rose, in the terms of secular poetry; the closing scene presents the religious view of an anticipated eternal good, the pearl of great price which is the bliss of heaven, in the terms of a religious treatise.

Louis Blenkner
Traditio, Vol. 24 (1968), pp. 71–73

Through his artistic employment of color symbolism, the author of *Pearl* suggests the dreamer's need for various virtues in order to attain spiritual enlightenment and consolation. Although color symbolism in each stage of contemplation in *Pearl*—the "erber," the external world of creation; the Edenic jewel-garden, the internal world of the mind; and the New Jerusalem, the eternal world of God—underscores the nature of each realm, the poet's use of color symbolism in the descriptions of the "erber" and the earthly paradise prefigures the dreamer's vision of transcendence, the supernal brightness of *visio pacis*. Color symbolism in *Pearl*, one trace of God's handiwork, finally enables the dreamer and the reader to illuminate the dark mysteries of God by piercing the veil of the supernatural and to recognize the need for Christ's saving blood, "þat in þe forme of bred and wyn/ Þe preste vus schewez vch a daye" (XX, 1209–10), in order to gain spiritual peace.

Robert J. Blanch
NMS, Vol. 17 (1973), p. 77

Patience

Much of the poetic energy in the story is spent on the world in which Jonah moves. The effect is to exaggerate his smallness and helplessness, his "poverty," because it is a huge and terrifying place. But this world, including the tempests, further isolates Jonah by being instantly obedient to God. This combines with the repeated thwarting of the man's will to show all his purposes entirely contained by God's. The narrative pattern presents three parallel attempts by Jonah to provide comfort for himself, in the boat, in the whale, and in the "lefsel" (the first two are explicitly compared in lines 291–92)—all unsuccessful: "Nihil Deo adversante securum est."

What Jonah is doing in these attempts is seeking refuge from the tribulations of living in the world. His human singlemindedness about this is perfectly conveyed by the poet's added detail that the prophet is not quite content even in the shade of his woodbine. It would be fine, he says, if only it were back home. "On heȝe vpon Effraym oþer Ermonnes hilleȝ" (lines

462–63). The climax comes when Jonah, exasperated as much by mercy as misery, wishes to escape altogether in death—although ironically of even the heathen sailors it had been said: "be monnes lode neuer so luþer, þe lyf is ay swete" (line 156). As always he is concerned with himself and not the innocent Ninevites or the woodbine, but he is implicitly calling in question the entire plan of God's justice.

The resolution is in several layers. God's closing speech silences Jonah with an explanation of the essential patience of the divine plan, of the relation between evil or destruction and the merciful purpose behind it. As in the Bible the story ends here. Jonah as recalcitrant humanity is not reformed and God's speech cannot be answered. But the poem is not over. God's words are confirming the suggestions and hints of the prologue where the beatitudes stood for God's mercy. But just as there the homilist, while quoting the beatitudes, concentrated on the less comfortable truth that to resist is in any case useless, so his closing summary is equally reserved, making no appeal to God's promise of grace. There is a calculated discrepancy between the truth expressed by the homilist in his appropriate humility and that revealed by the narrative and God's part in it. Although the actual perspectives may be quite different, the situation is not unlike that in vision poems, where the dreamer's views are of course narrower than that of the poet and his audience. Here the audience watches Jonah's protracted dialogue with God, with the homilist as a guide, but they see more than he does. The point of *Patience* as a whole is more impressive than anything the homilist seems able to state in his own person.

David Williams
MP (November, 1970), pp. 135–36

Lines 417–20 [of *Patience*] may create the impression that if Jonah did not understand God's mercy at the time of his flight to Tarshish, he at least understands it now. But the subtle, carefully prepared lie in lines 421–23 argues that his praise is utter sarcasm. His self-aggrandizement minimizes not only God's role in the conversion of the Ninevites, but in the world at large: this, his most persistent error, leads to a complete misunderstanding of the nature of mercy. It is to Jonah's mind a casual gratuity, easily gotten and easily lost. . . .

It should be clear from this reading that the story of Jonah in *Patience* is not simply a "negative *exemplum*," and that its homiletic effect does not lie in the foolishness of Jonah's errors. The poem rests on a conception of the way God works in the world and of how men find themselves turned to his will. Jonah's errors serve to define God's comprehensive role, but his power, justice, and mercy are not simply necessary backdrops to the action; they are the poem's most fundamental theme. Men must submit blindly to him who shapes their history, but without an understanding of the just proportion in his mercy and *ryȝt*, human patience dissolves in adversity to Jonah's fretful, childish rebellion.

J. Schleusener
PMLA (October, 1971), p. 964

JOHN GOWER

ca. 1330–1408

If Gower's first patrons were in the court circle his public was far wider than the court. There are forty-nine manuscripts of the *Confessio Amantis,* and it was translated into Portuguese and Castilian.

The attraction of the *Confessio Amantis* may have lain in its novelty of architecture and style. It should I think be read as an autobiography. John Gower, then about fifty, is the lover who is becoming old. He remembers the time when he danced as lightly as a roe, the futile jealousies of other lovers, the moments of envy and malice, the hours he had spent with his lady, reading her Troilus, or playing dice or watching her dance. He knows that he has been unfaithful to others but not to her. Cupid has left him wounded and Venus tells him to make confession to her priest of the sins against her law. There follows, through question and answer, an exposition of the Seven Deadly Sins, their servants and their remedies, illustrated by many stories and broken by many digressions. And in the end Gower is shriven and, looking at a mirror, sees his wrinkled skin and his bleared eyes. He knows that Cupid has passed him by because he is too old. The Green Tree has withered. There is chill ointment for his wounded heart and Venus gives him a rosary of black and gold inscribed "To Rest" (*"Por Reposer"*).

The framework is novel precisely because the *Confessio Amantis* is not an allegory and since it is more than a sustained metaphor. It is a recital of facts to be understood in their literal sense and illustrated by allegorical figures and the use of symbol. It is odd how far away it is from either version of the *Romaunt of the Rose.* Its contents were novel since they were a great sequence of stories forming part of a single plot and possessing an over-riding unity. The stories often branch into disquisitions, but this provided the instruction which so many medieval publics appreciated.

The style had no precedent and no immediate succession. It may represent court English but if so it is court English as it was spoken not as it was sung. Dante would have recognized it as a *volgare illustre* for it is a polished, too polished, vernacular; but it is antithetic to the "aureate" golden lines that Lydgate learned from Chaucer. If Thomas Usk foreshadowed the Euphuists, John Gower foreshadowed the Augustans—and at times, much more surprisingly, Jane Austen.

Gervase Mathew
The Court of Richard II (London: John Murray, 1968), pp. 77–78

Some of Gower's success [in the *Confessio Amantis*] with the classical stories is due to his ruthlessness, his readiness to throw overboard the many-storied richnesses of antiquity in favour of a finite moral pattern, which in turn is reinforced by a uniformity of social setting. Ambiguities, fruitful or otherwise, are removed, and a clear story-line emerges, often with complete redirection of the original material to a new purpose. The stories of Jason and Medea, and of Paris and Helen, are examples of Gower's skill in cutting the antique moorings and isolating the tellable tale, akin to Malory's technique in handling the polyphonic or interwoven Arthurian narratives. Sometimes, of course, the classical material is intractable to Gower's purposes: there was not much, for instance, that the Christian moralist could make of the story of Orestes (Book III). Sometimes, too, the overt moral runs counter to the inner sense of the story. "Pyramus and Thisbe," for instance, is ostensibly an exemplum against irrational haste, and at one point the story of Troilus and Criseyde is referred to as proof that no good can come of flirting in church (V. 7,599). What we can assume is that Gower would have come to some less trivial conclusion in actually *telling* the tale.

Derek Pearsall
Gower and Lydgate (London: Longman, 1969), p. 20

From [the] pretentious pose of the narrator to be one of those *others* whom love fetters—of course, he wants us to understand that in actual fact a person of his serious concerns would not be caught dead in such a situation—there unfolds with growing brilliance the great joke of the entire *Confessio*, the comic frame story of Amans, the would-be dirty old man, frustrated and bewildered by an emotional commitment of embarrassing purity, and Genius, the affable Confessor forever in a muddle over which god he serves, too garrulous to listen with understanding, too obtuse to grasp any of the realities which lie behind the moral platitudes with which his prosaic mind is plentifully furnished. Both figures are creatures of the narrator's deficient imagination, the one a projection of his fantasies (not always impure) about "love" and "lust," the other of his beliefs (not always foolish) about "wisdom" and "lore." The joke is however without malice, for it is in didactic earnest: only by laughter can we come to recognize our moral beliefs and intellectual assumptions for what they are.

Life yields no easy harvest of either morality or truth, and the wisdom of age may be the knowledge that what we once believed could be thrashed out only with a flail, must in the end be winnowed by hearty and plentiful laughter.

Such I take to be the lesson of the *Confessio Amantis,* addressed not solely to Richard II or to Henry IV, but to every person, of royal station or not, who must eventually learn to rule the kingdom which is himself and must therefore be brought to understand the true meaning of Love. The poem is indeed the confession of a lover, of a poet who loved men and language and life, of a great wielder of words and a passionate believer in moral truth, who tried in his earliest work to hold up a mirror in which men might see the outrageous sinfulness of their daily existence, who cried out publicly in his middle years at the moral wilderness he saw around him, yet who had hope in his neighbor and faith in his God enough to end his life's work in jest at himself and his own best efforts. It would be entirely characteristic of John Gower that we should last see him with a twinkle in his eye and a solemn set to his lips. . . .

Anthony E. Farnham
in *The Learned and the Lewed: Studies in Chaucer and Medieval Literature*, ed. Larry D. Benson (Cambidge, Mass.: Harvard Univ. Pr., 1974), pp. 172–73

ROBERT HENRYSON

fl. 1450–1500

The most obvious fact about the *Testament* [*of Cresseid*] is that it is a continuation of Chaucer's *Troilus and Criseyde*, and a companion-piece to the fifth book of that poem. In lines 40–60 Henryson's narrator takes up a *quair*, a small book, and, telling us what he finds in it, gives an accurate summary of the contents of Chaucer's fifth book, the final sorrows of Troilus. Then the narrator takes another *quair*, presumably an imaginary one, and describes its contents: in short, "the fatall destenie/Of fair Cresseid, that endit wretchitlie"; in full, the rest of the *Testament*. The parallel between the two *quairs* is stressed by the parallelism of the wording: "I tuik ane quair . . . And thair I fand . . ." (40, 43); "ane vther quair I tuik,/In quhilk I fand . . ." (61–62).

There is nothing very unusual about a fifteenth-century poet writing a continuation of another man's poem—there were three different continuations of the *Aeneid* written during the century, for instance. But there is no reason to assume that Henryson was making any simple-minded attempt to provide the next instalment of an interesting story, or that he was being compulsively tidy about the loose ends which he thought Chaucer had left. The *Testament* stands, I think, in a complex relationship to Chaucer's poem. To begin with, it is a *tour de force*, an imitation of "worthie Chaucer glorious," and one not without irony—"Quha wait gif all that Chauceir wrait was trew?" The poem is filled with Chaucerian echoes, many of them coming from the fifth book of *Troilus,* and has an extremely Chaucerian narrator. It is literary, witty, and sophisticated, like Henryson's other major poems: the *Fables*, which are in part rhetorical exercises, clever reworkings of common school texts; and *Orpheus and Eurydice*, an ingenious and humorous retelling of one of the most familiar of all myths. But the *Testament* is also *about* Chaucer's poem, in the sense that a critical essay is about a piece of literature, or in the sense that the *moralitas* of one of Henryson's *Fables* is about the fable. It offers, by implication, a remarkably accurate and penetrating analysis of *Troilus*. Here again it resembles Henryson's other poems: both the *Fables* and *Orpheus and Eurydice* are attempts to bring out the most profound meaning of the pre-existing narratives. But as well as being both an occasionally ironic tribute to Chaucer and a commentary on his poem, it is also a serious moral poem parallel to *Troilus*. Henryson takes Chaucer's characters and situation, and uses them to explore the same problems that Chaucer deals with—the meaning of earthly "wele and wo," for instance—though he does not always arrive at the same answers. The resemblance with Henryson's other poems still holds, for both the *Fables* and *Orpheus* are, in the end, serious poems about morality.

Denton Fox
Introd., in Robert Henryson, *Testament of Cresseid*,
ed. Denton Fox (London: Thomas Nelson, 1968), pp. 20–22

The one comprehensive examination of *Orpheus and Eurydice* which has yet been published is John MacQueen's, in his *Robert Henryson: A Study of the Major Narrative Poems*. My own more limited investigation began with two questions: what are the sources of Henryson's account of the Muses, and what is its relationship to the rest of his poem? In answering the first question I have indirectly contradicted MacQueen's assertion that the passage is based on Boccaccio's *De Genealogia Deorum*; in answering the second I hope to show that this seemingly trivial factual correction can lead to a contradiction or at least to a questioning of MacQueen's central assumptions. MacQueen holds that our reading of *Orpheus and Eurydice* must be governed by the *moralitas*—a versification of part of [Nicholas] Trivet's commentary on *De Consolatione Philosophiae*—which follows the narrative in all three sixteenth-century texts. He interprets the function of the Muses in accordance both with this belief and with their Fulgentian and Macrobian significances: for him they represent the pure intellect from which Orpheus (who in Trivet represents the *pars intellectiva* of the soul) is descended, and the harmony of the spheres whose discipline it is Orpheus' duty to imitate in the moral world of man. Nowhere in the narrative or the *moralitas* is such an interpretation made explicit, but we might confidently suppose that it was implicit if Henryson had indeed used *De Genealogia Deorum*, or any other full and coherent presentation of Fulgentius' and Macrobius' allegories. Such, however, is not the case. His true source, the *Graecismus*, offers a medley of Fulgentian and non-Fulgentian interpretations, which its author seems to regard as he regards his other scraps of etymological or mythological information—as interesting but unrelated facts which every schoolboy ought to know. Of allegory in the proper sense—a system of interpretation, not an arbitrary collection of interpretations—it contains no trace. Admittedly Henryson could still have tried to impose an allegorical purpose on his refractory material, had he so wished. Of such a wish, however, I can find no evidence; on the contrary, as we have seen, his adaptation is rather more eclectic and unsystematic than its original. His treatment confirms what the nature of his source suggests: that he expected his audience to appreciate the passage as a display of cyclopaedic erudition for its own sake—as it was appreciated by Gavin Douglas. . . .

At one point at least, therefore, an allegorical reading of *Orpheus and Eurydice* must break down. Two inferences are possible: either Henryson has wavered uneasily between an allegorical and a non-allegorical method, or (as I prefer to believe) he intended the *moralitas* to provide an optional and added level of meaning, not the obligatory key to the entire poem.

Dorena Allen Wright
Medium Aevum, Vol. 40 (1971), pp. 46–47

The Testament of Cresseid is from start to finish a poem built upon courtly love premises. This is to say nothing about Henryson's personal beliefs as a Christian. For the purposes of his poem he has created a make-believe love cosmos which contains several elements adapted from medieval thought—*adapted* from medieval thought, not symbolic of Christian spiritual realities. Sydney Harth is right in saying that "Henryson was a conscious artist whose aim in *The Testament of Cresseid* was to tell an old story anew." Harth is wrong, however, in his belief that Henryson is being ironic in describing his poem as a "tragedie" or that this is not "a particularly moving poem, or one which is unusually disturbing or profound." *The Testament of Cresseid* is a moving poem because Henryson has endowed his fictional world with much of the complexity which makes real life moving and profound.

Part of this complexity has been explored by Duncan Aswell and John MacQueen, whose analyses of the planet-gods as symbolic of the forces of growth and decay I consider not incompatible with my view of the poem. The progressive deepening of Cresseid's character, the reader's growing awareness of the instability of human life, the narrator's fine sense of balance whereby he portrays Cresseid both as a victim of circumstance and as a woman responsible for her own downfall—all contribute (and I agree in this respect with [E. M. W.] Tillyard) to make the *Testament* a poem which "through being truly tragic . . . takes itself right out of its medieval setting and allies itself to the tragic writings of all ages."

Dolores L. Noll
SSL (July, 1971), pp. 24–25

The gods of Cresseid's theology are vindicated because . . . their punishment is just and does lead to her moral regeneration. Cresseid and, by implication, the narrator learn to accept divine justice even when they cannot fully understand it. The narrator's understanding is somewhat greater than hers, however, because he is a Christian who sees the value of "Cheritie." Yet there remains a disquieting sense that the problem has not been completely resolved. We see that Cresseid's theology, from a Christian perspective, is severely limited; yet when we turn to the narrator, we fail to learn much more about the workings of God's justice. What does happen to Cresseid after death? Dante, Langland and the author of *St. Erkenwald* ventured to admit righteous pagans to paradise who had received special gifts of sanctifying grace from God. Chaucer was somewhat more cautious, dispatching Archite and Troilus to pagan "heavens." Henryson is more cautious still. While never confirming it, the poem also never denies the possibility that Cresseid may be saved. Such ambiguity is characteristic of much late medieval theology, which claimed that God could use his absolute power to suspend the ordinary law and accept a sinner from the Church. Henryson thus leaves God's options open, implying an unconditional acceptance of divine justice.

Readers who remain dissatisfied with this conclusion should not fault Henryson for failing to resolve all the questions his poem raises. Such readers should take their quarrel beyond the poem to the theological tradition it implies. The poem itself suggests simply that (1) divine justice has been vindicated in the actions of the pagan gods, (2) the Christian God whom they represent must, by implication, also be just, and (3) whatever God may choose as the ultimate resting place for Cresseid's soul will therefore be just. But since this justice, though itself reasonable, transcends human reason, it must be accepted on faith.

John McNamara
SSL (July–October, 1973), pp. 106–7

In choosing as his theme the definition of Christian experience by contrasting it to pagan, Henryson is following the example of his master Chaucer. *Troilus and Criseyde* explores the dilemma of a religious (if not specifically

Christian) personality like Troilus who, finding himself in a pagan universe, establishes as his point of stability a distressingly wayward human being. Henryson's imitation of Chaucer is both profound and—somewhat surprisingly for a so-called minor poet—innovative. For Henryson adds to the expression of the theme a presumably fifteenth-century narrator who is an unabashed if markedly unsuccessful pagan. Like Cresseid, the narrator is a votary of Venus. He tells us that he is "ane man of age" who "traistit that Venus, lufis quene,/. . . My faidit hart of lufe scho wald mak grene" (23–25). At the opening of the poem we find him demonstrating his loyalty to the goddess by braving the bitter cold "to pray hir hie magnificence" within "myne oratur." But the "northin wind" forces him to "remufe aganis my will," and he withdraws to a warm fire and a strong drink. Again like Cresseid, the narrator's initial withdrawal is a retreat, an act of self-protection. It is also a retreat in self-understanding. He has trusted in Venus and yet he spends the evening reviving his faded heart not with blood "flowing in ane rage" but with a "fyre outward" and the "phisike" of a drink, cozy but alone. Obviously Venus is untrustworthy, a lesson so obvious as to verge on tautology. But the narrator refuses to draw this conclusion. Nor does he draw the secondary conclusion, that "ane man of age" should not be concerned with reviving a faded heart in the first place. He prefers instead to nurture a hothouse alternative to genuine revival, to retreat from reality into the fantasy of love stories.

The final and clinching analogy to Cresseid is that his withdrawal, originally an evasion, leads him precisely to the lesson he wished to avoid. The lesson is found, of course, in the very love stories that are his only "sport," *Troilus and Criseyde* and its brilliant companion, the "vther quair." Does the narrator, like Cresseid, learn the lesson? At the end of his poem he tells "worthie wemen" that "this ballet schort/[Was] Maid for *ȝour* worschip and instructioun" (610–11), a deflection of the lesson away from himself that bears a dismaying resemblance to Cresseid's strategy in her complaint. But in the last analysis Henryson declines to give us enough information to answer the question. With true Chaucerian reticence, he refuses to say.

Lee W. Patterson
PQ (October, 1973), pp. 713–14

In his book *Chaucer and the English Tradition* (1972), Ian Robinson speaks of Henryson's *Fables* as "those very lively and charming poems which one yet sometimes feels like calling *only* charming and lively." He goes on to refer to the author as a "comfortable old schoolmaster." There is a good deal of the schoolmaster in the "Preaching of the Swallow," as we have seen; but this *Fable*, at least, should never be called "*only* charming and lively." It is hardly charming at all, and its lively sketches of nature and country life serve a larger purpose. I have tried to show how the encyclopaedic, didactic and narrative parts of the poem all contribute to the treatment of a single, named, moral topic. The poem displays various aspects of Prudence, as that virtue was understood in Henryson's day, by means of formal exposition and narrative example. Thus Prudence plays the same part in this poem as Patience does in the *Gawain*-poet's *Patience*, or Justice in the Fifth Book of Spenser's *Faerie Queene*. Generally speaking, whatever the other attractions of the poems concerned, this type of ethical construct has found little favour with modern readers. They think it wrong that a poet should be content merely to expound and illustrate a familiar moral idea such as prudence, justice or patience. It seems too servile or too scholastic an exercise. The obvious answer to this objection is that much can be done, by a skilled and imaginative poet, with a familiar moral topic, as the "Preaching" itself shows. But the case of Henryson's poem prompts a more fundamental reflection.

Many traditional moral ideas still regarded as familiar, even commonplace, survive in modern times only in drastically simplified and weakened versions. "Prudence" is an extreme case of this simplification and weakening, since the term in modern English (where it is rarely used) denotes little more than the not-always-lovable quality which saves people from overspending or going out without a raincoat. The connection between such common caution and the noble capacity to hold in view past and future, as well as present, has been broken off, with the result that we would not want to call God (or Blake's Bard) "prudent." Prudence is, in fact, a shadow of its former self, like at least two of the other three cardinal virtues—justice, temperance, and fortitude. In her last book, Rosamond Tuve showed how the theory of the cardinal virtues, originating in classical antiquity, was integrated into Christian thought, producing the rich and complex ethical tradition drawn upon by Spenser. Henryson belongs to the same line. "The Preaching of the Swallow," like the Second and Fifth Books of the *Faerie Queene*, provides an opportunity to rediscover, as Tuve did, what a cardinal virtue was like in its heyday. Much that must have been familiar teaching to an audience around 1500 is there in the poem for us to learn, brought to life—as it must have been also for a contemporary—by the power of Henryson's imagination.

J. A. Burrow
EIC (January, 1975), pp. 35–36

THOMAS HOCCLEVE (or OCCLEVE)

ca. 1370–1450

Hoccleve's syntax has never received thorough study. The most noticeable characteristic to a modern reader is the endless number of lines containing inverted word order, as in these typical examples selected at random from the *Tale of Jereslaus' Wife*: "And vndir thee/my brothir heer shal be" (v. 31), "Haaste I me wole/fro thennes away" (v. 42), "That thow me kneew/thow blisse shalt the tyde" (v. 532), and "That he vn-to yow/nat entende may" (v. 602). Of course Hoccleve has not done anything unprecedented. Inverted word order is traditional in Middle English verse; it can be found in Chaucer, Lydgate, and all the tail-rhyme romances. The influence of French word order is one explanation for it, poetic license another, and the demands of meter and rhyme a third. Some examples of inverted word order in Middle English are possibly vestiges of the earlier state of the language.

In one respect Hoccleve's syntax differs from Lydgate's. Almost everyone who has written about Lydgate has called attention to his loose syntax. "Drawled-out and incompact," [J.] Schick remarks, "are the first epithets which one would most readily apply to the style of the monk's productions. His sentences run on aimlessly, without definite stop, and it is often difficult to say where a particular idea begins or ends. One certainly has the impression that the monk never knew himself, when he began a sentence, how the end of it would turn." A good way to appreciate the difficulty of Lydgate's syntax is to read the recent edition of the *Life of Our Lady*, which has been given no editorial punctuation. But even the most carefully punctuated texts of his works are often ambiguous in syntax. One cannot say for certain whether the ambiguity is a result of his ignorance in grammar, or his misfortune in having his works copied by careless scribes, or his belief that loose syntax and rambling sentences, along with aureate diction, would help produce an elevated style. Whatever the case may be, the point of this discussion is simply that loose syntax is a fault of which Thomas Hoccleve cannot be accused. In all his verse there is hardly a single instance of syntactical ambiguity.

Jerome Mitchell
Thomas Hoccleve (Urbana: Univ. Illinois Pr., 1973), pp. 73–74

WILLIAM LANGLAND

fl. 1370–1400

George Kane and E. T. Donaldson, eds., *Piers Plowman: The B Version* (1975)

[*Piers Plowman*] was a book much read until new modes of literature swept in with the Renaissance. Then for three centuries it was almost undisturbed, and when a revival of sorts occurred in the nineteenth century the re-discoverers of the poem were not the common folk who had helped fill William Langland's audience. They were, out of linguistic necessity, philologists for whom, both as teachers and writers, the poem was to become valuable material. They and their successors have approached it as sermon and as allegory, as epitome of literary lore and as theological tome, as rhetorical sampler and specimen of Late Middle English. . . .

To speak of him is to speak of a poet who is first a missionary, then a contemplative, then a sociologist—and who is also a writer because he will reach the largest possible number of the weak and wandering. The majority of his critics commend him greatly but regret his failures as an artist. They speak of the lack of unity and poetic sensibility, and they wish that in his labors he had brought the C version nearer to structural perfection. When he is commended, it is for his passion of conviction, the strength of which must have given him a compulsion to study the mysteries that trouble us all. And he must have studied in solitude for the greater part of his life, for he attained a level of scholarship rare even among our great poets. He seems to me to be more impressive in this regard than, for example, Chaucer, Shakespeare, Pope, Whitman, and Frost. . . .

Langland is praised for the uniquely masterful synthesis of classical, patristic, and medieval lore which constitutes *Piers Plowman* and for the breadth of his vision. Excepting the mystics, who have not his stories to tell nor his complaints to shout, he is alone and centuries ahead of his time as one whose writings are directly autobiographical. The power of the man could not be throttled by mere convention; in point after point we see him shrugging or wrenching off the shackles of the Middle Ages and producing a work that, as an anatomy, is Renaissance but, as autobiography, strictly modern.

His editors and the analysts of his allegory and language have, I think, been fair to him as far as they have gone. But he has received few words of thanks from the thousands to whom he has provided *entertainment*, and in their silence on this sole aspect of his poem is to be found the most serious oversight in his critical reception. All the other writers of his rank have from their beginnings been applauded as public performers, *pleasers* of the crowd, good company for the hours of leisure. And undoubtedly in his own beginnings and for a while after, Will Langland was most kindly and warmly thought of—most gratefully remembered for the lives he had enriched, for the bite and balm of his stirring lines. He had sung better to the commoners, in some ways, than their balladmakers had sung: he had voiced their woes and their worries as no one had done before; with a work of great substance and beauty he had done honor to the poorest; and we think today that large numbers of his countrymen read his lines and heard them. If they did, Langland must have held a high place in their minds as a supplier of entertainment.

William M. Ryan
William Langland (New York: Twayne, 1968), pp. 123–24

In brief, [Langland] used the tradition, as he used everything else that came to hand, to call men back to the great truths of religion. Langland was anything but the "blind traditionalist" who defends unquestioningly the *status quo*; in fact he was always doing battle against religious practices which, he considered, had become traditional for the wrong reasons. Comfortably pious persons get short shrift from him, for he doubts that they can save their souls by fasting and churchgoing if they do not have charity for the poor. The popular ways of gaining indulgences he condemns almost entirely. The traditional pilgrim with staff and scrip is, for him, a figure for satire. And the miracles that fill medieval story are rather surprisingly absent from his book of visions. The dreamer finds himself in odd places, but he is not carried there by rudderless boats.

The miracles described in *Piers* are the great miracles of Scripture. Scripture (understood literally and figuratively) is the standard by which all else is measured. The basis of Langland's attack on the corrupt practice of indulgences is that it bypasses the law. On Judgment Day, he thunders, a man will be safe with the Ten Commandments, not with bought pardons. The professional pilgrim is condemned because he does not seek first the Truth taught by the Scriptures; Langland's pilgrims must follow Abraham, Moses, and Jesus. And the Jews are condemned because they reject the Messias taught by their own Scriptures. Whatever else Langland questions, he accepts with his whole mind and heart the authority of Scripture and its continuing relevance to both the affairs of men and the doctrines of the Church.

Actually, Langland does not separate doctrine from practical affairs as most men do. He had no patience with the philosophers and dialecticians who tended, then as now, to make theology a subject in the university curriculum, and he rebuked those priests who preached over the heads of the congregation in the language of the schools. His Trinity is no philosophical abstraction but the God of Israel, whose justice and mercy can be understood only insofar as they are practiced.

Ruth M. Ames
The Fulfillment of the Scriptures: Abraham, Moses, and Piers
(Evanston, Ill.: Northwestern Univ. Pr., 1970), p. 10

Piers's virtue is instinctive and simplistic. It is derivative from an established pattern of life in which he has always existed; that is why the pastoral image of a plowman as an ethical norm is so useful to the poet.

This is not a reflection on Piers, but he is as unable to provide the prerequisites for that way as Envy or Sloth or Robert the Robber; and the whole force of the poem's analysis has been directed not to human behavior as such but to its basis, not to corruption and virtue as such but to the problem of turning the one into the other. Piers's virtue is *pietas* rather than *caritas*. What the action of the half acre brings home to the reader more than anything else is the growing anger and puzzlement, even resentment, of Piers as the whole gamut of means available to the well-intentioned for the amelioration of society are inexorably revealed, one by one, to be useless for anything but temporary palliation. What Piers represents is simply not the answer to the tragic character of the human situation.

The satiric function of the figure of Piers as a foil for the folk is obvious; what is less immediately obvious, though no less important, is that Piers is still more fundamentally the complement to the Dreamer, to whom he is related in a way which the modern reader cannot help associating with Yeats's self and antiself and which the poem's use of personifications would have made natural in its own time. The two seem like complementary poles in a cumulative portrayal of Everyman. Piers is all purity, practicality, authority, confidence. He is disciplined, extraverted, productive. He sees life in terms of its manageable elements; he is totally unprepared for a world which does not respond to recognized treatment. He has a contractual conception of the relationship between God and man, an "Old Testament" conception, quite innocent of the consciousness Paul saw as its corollary, in which the very awareness of law brings a self-knowledge which is a kind of death: "I had not known sin but by the law. . . . The commandment which was ordained to life I found to be unto death." Piers's account of the way to Truth does not confine itself to the Ten Commandments. Its emphasis on "loue & louȝnesse," the role of grace and mercy, and references to the pope, the sacrament of penance, and so on, make it clear that no identification between Piers and a pre-Christian ethic in the historical sense is intended. But his emphasis is on the fulfillment, point by point, of an established code, and above all on the confidence that a man who fulfills this code can count on an equally established and predictable response from God: Truth is "þe presteste payere þat pore men knowen," and Piers can say, "þeiz I sey it myself, I serue hym to paye" (A 6. 36). In Piers's view, in contrast to Conscience's in the Meed debate, God gives not "reward" but justice. In short, although the content of Piers's religion is not "Old Testament," the contractual psychology of it is.

But in our recognition of what Piers exemplifies in the religious sense, we must not forget that he is also one kind of emblem of man as artist, *homo faber*, mind and will shaping the elements of his world as form shapes matter; he is, as the fourteenth century called the poet, a "maker," not with words but with the elements of his environment.

Elizabeth D. Kirk
The Dream Thought of "Piers Plowman" (New Haven, Conn.: Yale Univ. Pr., 1972), pp. 76–77

Piers is in many ways the cognitive key to the poem. The revelation of his nature is an ongoing process within it, parallel to the ongoing revelation of Christ's nature during his lifetime, which Conscience describes at the beginning of Passus XIX. In Passus V, he is an enigmatic figure, prone to error and to the partial understanding which is in keeping with his figural nature at that point in the poem. When he first enters the *Visio*, he is an evident leader, but of an ambiguous sort. Indeed, it is not at all clear whether he is anything more than a simple fourteenth-century plowman, susceptible to all the blunders of a limited human nature. But in Passus VII he is revealed, though obscurely, as a genuinely figural character, whose being has a dimension beyond the literally human. During the course of the *Vita*, Piers becomes more and more figural, and in this process his outline becomes clearer. He is identified with Peter, with Christ, with right will, with the teaching of the three Do's, with true charity. Piers is the revealer of charity and of history in Passus XVI; his is the fruit which grows on the Tree; his are the arms in which Jesus jousts, his is the pardon, and it is to him that the Holy Spirit is sent in Passus XIX. When Will first beholds the redemptive figure who enters at the beginning of Passus XIX, he sees not Christ but "Pieres the Plowman . . . paynted al blody" (XIX. 6).

It is extremely difficult to put all these manifestations together into a conceptually coherent character. Piers, like Dowel, seems to be an "infinite," but if one regards them as the stages in a progressive revelation, figurally conceived, they become less mysterious. By Passus XIX, Piers Plowman, too, is a redeemed and redemptive word; consequently, one must put together the various aspects under which he appears at different points in the poem in exactly the mutually significant way in which Conscience draws together the various themes of the poem in his discourse on the names of Christ. Piers can only be understood as a *figura*, the sign (actually a series of different manifestations) which reveals partially but truthfully the divine pattern of charity acting within human time and history. To ask "who is Piers Plowman" and expect a completely articulable answer is to be as naïve and misled as Will is when he first asks "what is Dowel"—and for very much the same reasons. The question misconceives the real nature of its object, for it assumes that it has a limited, knowable nature. But Piers is the *figura* within time, "the changing aspect of the permanent" progressively revealed until the end of time, the vehicle through which the ineffable is articulated within the limitations of human experience.

The old sort of word, the language of virtue and of vice, the established language of the Church itself, has proved inadequate finally to express truth, done in by its own complex verbalness, which makes it an easy prey for the sophistry of Antichrist. But Piers, the ineffable *figura*, the "infinite" sign of truth, who cannot be expressed fully in terms of any human concepts, seems to promise the new language and new understanding which Conscience seeks after the collapse of the old.

Mary Carruthers
The Search for St. Truth: A Study of Meaning in "Piers Plowman"
(Evanston, Ill.: Northwestern Univ. Pr., 1973), pp. 169–71

Langland's poem is an exceptional fulfillment of possibilities inherent in the dream tradition; it is the most complex, most sophisticated instance in pre-Spenserian English of the interiorizing and the more profoundly distinctive personalizing of allegory that derives from this tradition. His poem represents—clearly, impressively, and poetically—a way of organizing and conceiving experience, and a way of exploring the self while searching for Love and Truth, which are implicit in this tradition and without which *The Faerie Queene* would not be the inner, echoing poem, the imagined and remembered experience it is. J. V. Cunningham has observed that "What a writer finds in real life is to a large extent what his literary tradition enables him to see and to handle." He adds that the one term is tradition, "not unalterable but never abandoned" as "the other term is always experience." I should extend these observations; in the hands of great poets, sources are likely to become analogues; and in the realm of ideas, every true analogue is potentially a source.

Besides belonging to England's poetic past, *Piers Plowman* belongs to the history of thought and belief. It centers on the character Will and reflects some of the more radical statements formulated in the Middle Ages to affirm the freedom and responsibility of the will, yet it also proves to be progressively reconcilable with *The Faerie Queene*, a poem informed deeply by Protestantism, indeed by a faith showing Calvin's influence. Taken together, these poems readjust a number of our presuppositions, simplified by catch-words like *free will, predestination, justification, Catholic* and *Protestant*, *medieval* and *Renaissance*, which have got in the way of understanding. Many years and many differences in taste and outlook separate these two poetic *summas*; but to the extent that *Piers Plowman* seems an unlikely match for *The Faerie Queene*, it is because Langland's poem is the grandfather of Spenser's and not because his poem is a different species. The theological differences between the poems are in significant ways more superficial than their likenesses, as is actually the case with the systems of thought—even Scotus's and Calvin's—behind them.

Judith K. Anderson
The Growth of a Personal Voice (New Haven, Conn.: Yale Univ. Pr., 1976), p. 3

The sense throughout the three texts [of *Piers Plowman*] is one of continuous intellectual and spiritual growth, openness and receptivity, just as within each text there is a dynamic principle at work by which more and more is revealed to the dreamer as he grows in capacity to understand. The truths of the faith are expounded forcefully enough by Holy Church in Passus I, but the dreamer (and Langland) must learn them anew out of the need from within, and the poem therefore dedicates itself to giving a life more pressing and more dramatic to those truths, "rendering imaginable what before was only intelligible." As a dramatic poem, a process of continuous but halting discovery, its procedures are ruminative rather than dialectic, and Langland has no grand design, no scholastic principle of organisation. He was not a professional scholar and tough and complex passages of exposition (such as the Tree of Charity, B. XVI) rub shoulders with the simplest kind of homilectic commonplace, but as a theologian he had tremendous intellectual energy, which often enables him to leap great divides that his scholastic contemporaries hesitated over, and an intellectual open-mindedness which enables him to entertain if not to endorse the most advanced speculation—one reason why he could be so radically misread by revolutionaries like John Ball in the fourteenth century and by Protestants in the sixteenth.

Derek Pearsall
Old English and Middle English Poetry, Vol. I of *The Routledge History of English Poetry*, ed. R. A. Foakes (London: Routledge & Kegan Paul, 1977), p. 179

JOHN LYDGATE

ca. 1370–1450

Derek Pearsall, *John Lydgate* (1970)

It is not wise to make extravagant claims for Lydgate as a poet—and I hope that an enthusiasm for neglected causes will not have led me into folly. Indeed, in most of the senses in which we ordinarily understand the word, Lydgate is not a poet at all, for he can never, even at his best, rivet us with the uniqueness of his language, or enrich our awareness of words. But this in itself would only argue for a broader definition of what we mean by poetry, to include the practice of "crafty" rhetoric, for it is essentially as a professional craftsman and rhetorician that we should see Lydgate. Here is the value that he has for us; for, by the very bulk of his work and the massive centralness of his position, he forces us to re-examine our notions of medieval poetry, or poetry itself, and to modify easy assumptions about its nature. Sometimes the quality of his writing does not make this a very valuable exercise in itself, and, having established the nature of a tradition, one has to admit that Lydgate does not represent it at its best. This is why it is useful to regard him as a type of the Middle Ages, an introduction to medieval literature, presenting its themes and methods in their basic form, without the complications of experiment, ambiguity, or even, sometimes, of individual thought.

The very mechnical nature of his processes is thus often invaluable for understanding those like Chaucer who used them more freely and independently, and every reader of medieval literature should therefore be able to *use* Lydgate in this way. It follows from this that we do great wrong to regard Lydgate as anything but typical of his age. His roots are deep in the medieval tradition, he is impregnably medieval, and there is in his work no sign of movement toward the Renaissance, except in so far as he responds fitfully to the prompting of his sources. With all this said, none of it very exciting for those who think that understanding is not enough, it should be added that at his best—and it is a rare best only in the context of his enormous output—in parts of the *Troy Book*, the *Fall of Princes*, the *Life of Our Lady*, and in some of the shorter courtly and religious pieces, his eloquence can transcend its own journeyman professionalism and, rising to its theme, can speak to us with sense and sonority across the chasm that the passage of years has opened up.

Derek Pearsall
John Lydgate (London: Routledge & Kegan Paul, 1970), pp. 298–99

What Lydgate does [in "Horse, Goose, and Sheep"] according to his own admission, is to use the contrivance of "Poetis of old fablis" in order to chastise the "oppressiouns & malis" of each estate so that they might be moved "Bi exanplis of resoun." The usage of a parliamentary fiction is particularly appropriate since it was this body which was specifically charged with service to the "common profit." The usage of animal debaters allows Lydgate to show how each animal-estate is failing to fulfill its social obligations. Their own speeches suggest the reasons for this failure—greed and pride have replaced necessary "social affection" and concern for neighbors. Though none of the animal-estates admits its failure, the evidence and argument that each makes for supremacy and the final verdict rendered by royal authority make these failings both dramatically and explicitly clear. Indeed, the final verdict of the lion and eagle would seem to be Lydgate's reminder to Henry VI of the role that he should take in matters of the state. Certainly in the exchange of the poem—in the blindly proud pleadings and *ad hominem* rebuttals—it is only the *Vicar dei*, the *Rex Christus*, who can restore any kind of order, who can impose any kind of harmony on the estates which stand at odds.

Lydgate's originality—and I almost hesitate to use that term without some qualification—is not in the estates philosophy expressed in the poem, nor in the *debat* pattern or beast-fable parliament fiction that he uses. Rather, it would seem to be in the combination of all these commonplace patterns and with the rhetorically skillful double argument he gives each debater. This may be a modest originality by modern standards, but in terms of medieval poetics which glorified in the re-statement and embellishment of accepted truths, it was certainly enough to satisfy many medieval readers and perhaps even a few modern medievalists who can laugh *with* rather than *at* the prolific monk of Bury.

David Lampe
AnM, Vol. 15 (1974), pp. 157–58

SIR THOMAS MALORY

ca. 1410–1471

Unlike Thackeray, Malory does not claim to be omniscient in the world of his book. The most subtle and pervasive type of omniscience is that of irony from a superior level of consciousness. This is most effective when it reveals a mind which is not only better informed but also more sophisticated and more introspective than the minds of the characters. This it does in Thackeray, who knows more of the way of the world than his characters, knows more particular facts, and especially knows himself and his readers.

In contrast, Malory seems to be very much on the same level as his characters, in knowledge as he is in power. The irony which comes from an author's superior knowledge of the world was of course as available to a medieval author as to a modern one, and perhaps more conspicuously so if the author visualised himself reading aloud to a circle of patrons. It may have been in such readings that Chaucer discovered the effectiveness of assuming the (intermittently transparent) *persona* of a henpecked onlooker, which he uses so successfully in the *House of Fame* and the General Prologue to the *Canterbury Tales*. The reader shares or seems to share the secret thoughts and feelings of the narrator in a way the characters in the story do not. This intimacy makes the narrator very important, even if the characters are clearly in some way better than he is, even if the narrator only knows his own weaknesses. . . .

Malory's commentary on his characters rarely goes beyond what could be provided in a few words by any observer without special insight. As with every other generalisation about Malory, there are a few minor exceptions to this. The most important of these few is the narrator's observations on the attempt by Gareth and Lyonesse to anticipate their wedding:

> This counceyle was nat so prevyly kepte but hit was undirstonde, for they were but yonge bothe and tendir of ayge and had nat used suche craufftis toforne. [V 333–35]

For once, the narrator is coming close to that omniscience which puts him on one level and the characters below him on another. Even a little of that would destroy the impression of objective fact which the *Morte Darthur* achieves. And the example of commentary above, sympathetic and endearing though it is, suggests that we should certainly lose by the exchange. It is trivial enough when compared with the unexpressed intuitions latent in the dialogue. It seems certain that Malory was able to show things he could not have explained, and which he would have spoilt by attempting to explain.

P. J. C. Field
Romance and Chivalry (Bloomington: Indiana Univ. Pr., 1971),
pp. 147–49

It is a measure of Malory's tragic sense and evidence of his political concerns that Arthur's tragedy is directly attributable to his weaknesses as a king. At the point in the French text where the king calls up the vicissitudes of fortune to explain his fall, Malory's Arthur simply declares all "erthely joy ys gone" (863). Here, as in the scene with Bedwer, the king understands that his loss of charisma is responsible for the fragmentation of his fellowship. The famous dream which occurs the night before the battle with Mordred is drastically reduced in Malory's account. The effect of this reduction is to change the interpretation of the entire tragedy implicit in the French account of the dream. The wheel of fortune in the *Mort Artu* is used as an explanation of the events leading up to Arthur's death, and Arthur's dream functions as a commentary on human frailty and the inevitability of the king's decline. Malory's abbreviated and cryptic version does not mention the wheel by name, and seems to work more as a description of Arthur's emotional state than as an explanation of its causes. Here as elsewhere Malory prefers to read the story as a tragedy with well defined political causes than as a generalized tragedy in which the specific human event is dwarfed by fortune and mortality. . . .

The seams of the Arthurian world are exposed in Malory's version as in no other. But paradoxically the tragedy is if anything more compelling for what we know about its origins. Were the story simply a fictional vehicle for rules of government, Arthur's passing would carry no greater emotional force than the final catastrophe of *Gorboduc*. But instead of reducing the moral complexity of the story's themes, Malory's political rendering of the legend enriches the story by allowing its paradoxes to emerge from the shroud of myth. The political idealism and political morality of the first four books show us why the Arthurian ideal deserves its reputation for true magnificence. And as the paradoxes of the story are then allowed full play we see that the order, civility, and ritual of this society of peers is only one half of a Janus-faced creature which also contains anarchy, fratricide, and the will to potential self-destruction. The politics of the story are only incidentally instructions for good government; primarily they are used to account for all aspects of the "mysterious" collapse of a perfect society. The tragic sense of Arthur's passing is preserved and even sharpened because politics for Malory is a very large category; it subsumes the history, the morality, and to a large degree, the religion of the story. Not only do we know that Arthur's passing is an irrevocable event, but we have learned that even the re-creation of Arthurian society as a cultural model or historical ideal must be at best an illusory and dangerous comfort.

Elizabeth A. Pochoda
Arthurian Propaganda (Chapel Hill: Univ. North Carolina Pr., 1971), pp. 138–40

The last paragraphs of the *Morte Darthur* epitomize Malory's method of dealing with the problems raised by his inherited history. He retains the historical facts and the consequent tragic pattern they suggest, just as he retains the fact that Bors takes religious vows. Then he modifies their effects by additions such as Bors's leaving the hermitage to carry on the chivalric life. The result is not a coherent pattern of tragedy but rather what Stephen Miko calls a "tragic emulsion," in which the elements of tragedy are held in suspension, never quite coming together to produce a tragic effect. They are held apart by the thematic, essentially comic elements that prevent the historical pattern from coalescing. Consequently, the end is neither completely tragic nor purely comic. As Edmund Reiss writes, we are left in doubt whether to be "wholly delighted or thoroughly disenhearted by what has happened." That doubt can never be completely resolved, for it is this mixture of joy and sorrow that lends the conclusion of the *Morte Darthur* its peculiar force and beauty. Perhaps, after all, Caxton was right; he best characterized this complex book when he humbly beseeched the noble lords and ladies of his audience "That they take the honest actes in their remembraunce, and to folowe the same; wherein they shall fynde many joyous and playsaunt hystoryes and noble and renomned actes of humanyté, gentylnesse, and chyvalryes. For herein may be seen noble chyvalrye, curtoyse, humanyté, frendlynesse, hardynesse, love, frendshyp, cowardyse, murdre, hate, vertue, and synne. Doo after the good and leve the evyl, and it shal bringe you to good fame and renommee."

Larry D. Benson
Malory's "Morte Darthur" (Cambridge, Mass.: Harvard Univ. Pr., 1976), pp. 247–48

SIR THOMAS MORE

1478–1535

Since . . . the bulk of More's polemical work was written in great haste under tremendous pressure, and since most of his nonpolemical works were written at greater leisure, one obvious difference is that the latter, as a group, tend to be more polished. Obviously, also, More would make greater efforts to achieve literary polish in the nonpolemical category, since the exhibition of literary elegance would be one of the main objects of the work. Good examples are his *Richard the Thirde*, his epigrams, and his *A Dialoge of Comfort*, written during his imprisonment in the Tower. The one polemical work to which More had time to give some finish is his *Dialogue Concernynge Heresyes,* the careful construction of which has already been discussed. It stands in sharp contrast to the piecemeal and formless character of all his other polemics, including the *Supplicacion of Soules*, the first book of which contains the central dramatic device of the "souls" but lacks total structure.

More's noncontroversial works also tend to be somewhat less repetitious than the polemical, again chiefly for the reason that when the former were written, More had time to edit what he wrote. *Richard the Thirde* and *Utopia* are not at all repetitious, and it should be remembered that the prolix More of the later polemics was at one time master of the concise epigram. The *Dialogue Concernynge Heresyes* is repetitious, but here the repetition is still controlled and, as was pointed out, should be regarded as part of More's polemical technique. It is in the *Supplicacion of Soules* that he begins to lose control and weary his readers with unnecessary repetition. Evidently the habit carried over later to the noncontroversial *Comfort* which, of course, More wrote under a different kind of pressure.

Understandably, the tone of the polemics is sharp—except the work against [John] Frith—while that of the nonpolemical works is not. Yet in the area of tone the two categories tend to blend, for some of the wonderful satire of *Richard*, the *Utopia*, and the epigrams is essentially the same as the kind of satire More used against his opponents. There is the same masterful characterization and dramatization, as well as the same keen eye for the ridiculous—such as in the Anemolian ambassadors section of the *Utopia* and the picture of Barnes or the David-Bathsheba section in the

Confutacyon, where More ridicules [William] Tyndale's distinction between sinning and not sinning.

Rainer Pineas
Thomas More and Tudor Polemics (Bloomington: Indiana Univ. Pr., 1968), pp. 218–19

The Fathers were to [More] giants in the earth, the greatest men besides the Apostles who had ever lived. Their moral example radiates throughout all his works. Even in the *Utopia* there may be some reflection of his feelings towards them in the Utopian conviction that the spirits of the dead hover ever about on earth to encourage the living. All these men were resolutely committed to the Catholic Church. But if the Reformers were correct, all of them had been in error. For More the error was not some mere peccadillo, something which could be glossed over in the name of something called the "Gospel." The error was fundamental to their whole understanding of themselves, of the universe, and of God. In More's mind saintly men could not have been *so* wrong. "I laye you also that if it had bene otherwise and that they had therin damnably bene deceiued, then liuyng & dying in damnable error they could not haue bene saintes." I do not believe we exaggerate if we say that ultimately More's defence of the Catholic Church, built as he conceived it on the foundation of the Fathers, was a defence of the cosmic value of goodness.

In large measure too More's defence of the Catholic Church was a defence of the idea that God was constantly active in creation. This was the more profound theological principle behind More's incessant emphasis upon the importance of the miraculous. God moved in the world in ways that were unmistakable. The Fathers possessed holiness of life and a plenitude of grace, and God had "opened theyr eyen and suffered and caused them to see the trouth." He had confirmed their teaching "by many a thousand myracle both in their liues & after their deathes." But if the Reformers were correct, the Fathers had fallen into catastrophic error and God had remained silent for centuries until the advent of Luther. In phraseology this thought usually was embedded in the argument that if Tyndale and Luther were correct, "then hath Chryste broken all hys promyses by whyche he promysed to be wyth his chyrche all days to the worldes ende." This is a rhetorical expression of an attitude which could not understand how God as Christians conceived Him could remain quiescent while so much error was abroad among people who lived saintly lives and believed they knew God's will. The implication was that if Luther's protest were allowed, the conception men had of God would be so changed as to become unrecognizable.

R. C. Marius
Traditio, Vol. 24 (1968), pp. 404–5

More's concern with the Erasmus-[Martin van] Dorp controversy and his composition of *Utopia* were continuous if not indeed coeval. But this increases the difficulty of thinking of *Utopia* as a work predominantly scholastic rather than humanist in character. It requires us to suppose that while one part of More's mind was most intensely focused on the sort of thing that most concerned Christian humanists in his letter to Dorp, the other part of his mind dealing with *Utopia* fell or had just fallen into a pattern of thinking which at that very time he was holding up to ridicule and contempt. For in his letter to Dorp one of the strategems by which More defended Christian humanism was a devastating and unqualified attack on school philosophy from Peter Lombard on. The intellectual profit to be derived from the supposition above stated is hardly adequate to compensate for the excessive and unnecessary stress to which it subjects our credulity.

The same observation applies to a second way of thinking about *Utopia* and its author which emphasizes their medieval orientation and dissociates them from Erasmus. The Utopian commonwealth, the argument goes, was patently a heathen, not a Christian, state. To anyone reared as More had been in Catholic orthodoxy there was an obvious distinction between the four pagan virtues, which were accessible to heathen reason, and the three Christian values, which were not. By basing his *Utopia* on the distinction between Temperance, Courage, Wisdom, and Justice on the one hand and Faith, Hope, and Charity on the other, More both follows the medieval tradition and gives point to his satire on contemporary abuses in Christian Europe.

J. H. Hexter
The Vision of Politics on the Eve of the Reformation: More, Machiavelli, and Seyssel (New York: Basic Books, 1972), pp. 67–68

For the Augustinian there is a great gulf between the ideal of natural law and the specific circumstances of experience, so that ultimately the category of natural law gives way before a strict juristic machinery and a Pauline endorsement of "the powers that be." In the structure of paradox of Book 2 of *Utopia*, those details of Utopian life and conduct that encourage a *naturrechtlich* perspective compete with others that assume that no appeal is possible from positive to natural law. Thus, Utopians do not make international treaties because a positive form of an international understanding would be redundant (197/18–23), but in domestic matters Utopians are warned to observe private contracts with care (165/23–25).

More got from Augustine no particular social or political doctrine, such as that of the just offensive war, but rather a feeling for the inevitable mingling of good and bad in any social or legal order. It may be objected that he did not need to read any books to find out that politics was irrational. *The City of God,* though, may have helped him to give form to his own distaste for "politic" solutions. The "dimension métaphysique" that enabled More to gain perspective on Plato's myth of the rational state is essentially Augustinian.

Readers from [Guillaume] Budé . . . to [R. W.] Chambers and [J. H.] Hexter have characterized Utopia as *Hagnopolis*, holy community. I have been concerned with More's criticism from an Augustinian point of view of the Stoic-Christian or rational version of *Hagnopolis* or the Christian state. But *Hagnopolis* may take the form not only of the Stoic-Christian community but also of the theocratic state; there is, that is to say, a fideistic as well as a rationalistic formulation of the ideal of a Christian politics. It may be well, then, to consider More's work in relation to theocracy for a moment.

The problem with a fideistic formulation of a Christian politics is no different from that with the rational one. For theocracy turns out to be only a disguised version of the rational state. To move in the direction of theocracy is, in the Augustinian perspective, to make larger claims for the state than are justified by the basic assumption that the state is an accidental legal order existing only to secure earthly peace. We have seen that Augustine was at pains to define the state in this manner in Book 19 of *The City of God*.

Augustine himself confronted this problem in connection with the Donatist controversy. As a propagandist for the Catholic Church he was necessarily concerned with bringing heretics into the fold. But it was inconsistent with his own skeptical view of *politike* to justify *on religious grounds* political compulsion to join the visible Church. His final position on this question was in fact to move in the direction of theocracy, that is, to justify coercion of Donatists and others to join the Church (as any religious would) on religious grounds. But in view of the fundamental Augustinian assumption that the state exists only to secure "the peace of Babylon," a theocracy such as Calvin's Geneva could be only an exact parody of the *civitas dei*: any attempt to realize the Word in time, in society, disfigures the essential teaching of *The City of God*. . . .

Martin N. Raitiere
Studies in the Renaissance. Vol. 20 (1973), pp. 164–65

In explaining why he thinks *Cynicus, Menippus,* and *Philopseudes* are worth reading, More is at pains to disarm critics who may object to Lucian's paganism. He insists on the propriety of disregarding the paganism of ancient authors in favor of the benefits they confer. Though brief, the conviction and clarity of this letter [to Thomas Ruthall] make it a notable example of Christian humanism, if by that term we signify the reaction of Christian scholars, *both* as Christians and as scholars, to classical civilization. Too often a vague or superfluous phrase, "Christian humanism" is in this instance appropriate, even if defined so broadly, because More is commenting on Lucian both as an appreciative reader and as a discriminating Christian. To approach every classical text in the same way he treats Lucian would be as tedious or pedantic as the passion for allegorizing in mediaeval exegetes, but the letter to Ruthall is justified by More's purpose and—we suspect—by the character of the person to whom the letter is addressed.

Clever, witty, and entertaining though Lucian is, More does not suggest that pleasure should be the main reason for reading him. Pleasure is mentioned only in the opening lines, where he alludes to the Horatian maxim about the twofold aim of poetry. Lucian's dialogues are defended chiefly because of their moral worth. If read correctly, their effect will be salutary, despite the writer's paganism. Ignore the paganism but enjoy, and take to heart, his exposure of fraud and hypocrisy. This discrimination by More is important, but we must repeat that his letter dwells on the *utile* rather than the *dulci* of Horace's phrase. In both respects it is characteristic of the more impressive apologies for literature, including pagan literature, that we meet in the sixteenth century. To teach delightfully is the highest aim, and the best justification, of literature: this is the doctrine we meet in Erasmus, in Sidney, in Spenser. "Artistic means to ethical ends" sums up the method, value, and pleasure of literary art, in the judgment of the humanists. They were better informed about ancient literatures than their mediaeval predecessors and correspondingly more sophisticated and more critical about language and style, but in their presuppositions about the purposes and utility of literature they had more in common with their mediaeval predecessors than with us. Where More seems a truer humanist, perhaps, is in his admonitions on testing a text for genuine and spurious contents and judging it from different standpoints. He is too sensitive and too scholarly to be patient with the palpable fictions so common in saints' lives. Truth is not served by pious frauds or faked miracles.

Craig G. Thompson
Introd., in *The Complete Works of St. Thomas More*, Vol. III,
Part 1, ed. Craig G. Thompson (New Haven, Conn.:
Yale Univ. Pr., 1974), pp. xliii–xliv

Continuous critical arguments about More's ideas in the *Utopia* prove that through the satiric devices of irony, inversion, juxtaposition, and indirection, he succeeded in detaching himself from the work. Some would say, in fact, that he succeeded too well. Perennial controversy centers around two questions which result from his aesthetic distancing: who is the satiric spokesman, and what is More's attitude toward communism? As I have suggested, Hythloday usually seems to represent More's views; in the debate in Book 1, however, the conservative, accommodating argument of *More* and the liberal, philosophical views of Hythloday seem to reflect More's own indecision about court service. The second question is more difficult. Although it is impossible to determine how More actually felt about communism, the speculation most valuable in interpreting this work is that based on the Christian humanism fundamental to More's own Weltanschauung, as revealed in his life and in his writings. His traditional attack on folly in the *Utopia* is effective largely because of the aesthetic distance or double satiric removal that he achieves through the ironic handling of *More* and Hythloday, paradoxical names, juxtaposition of values, and especially indirection, techniques which, since the work's publication, have amused readers and confounded biographically oriented critics.

Irma Ned Stevens
Moreana (November, 1974), p. 24

Thomas More has generally been paired with Erasmus as one of the leading representatives of Renaissance humanism, and his *Utopia* has been widely read as a provocative expression of humanist ideals. With the works of fifteenth-century humanist educators like Vittorino da Feltre and Aeneas Silvius and of contemporaries like Erasmus, the book shares certain fundamental doctrines: a faith in man's educability; a conviction of his potential goodness, rationality, and willingness to cooperate with his fellows; and a belief in social planning and the transformation of social institutions as the best means both to improve society as a whole and to raise the individual to the heights of human possibility. However, while More's *Utopia* reveals a clear relationship to Renaissance humanism through its sharing of such basic doctrines and assumptions, it also possesses a deeper relationship to the tradition than the existence of doctrinal similarities alone might suggest.

Going beneath the level of doctrine, More is linked to the humanist tradition at the fundamental level of language. His *Utopia* is organized about a few key images which not only generate his conception of human nature but also inform his vision of the natural order, dictate the construction of Utopia's social institutions, and even determine the distinctive features of the island's topography. . . . More shares with his humanist predecessors and contemporaries these images and the sets of terms they generate in the course of being elaborated, and if he differs from them in any way, it is in the degree to which the images dominate his thought and receive concrete embodiment in his vision of Utopia. Where the humanists thought of education as a kind of agriculture and longed for a world transformed at least metaphorically into a garden of innocence, More's artistic imagination treats those metaphors literally, making the Utopians into a race of farmers and the Utopian state into an immense walled garden. . . .

Filled with a cautious faith in man's potential for goodness and rationality, but fearing his ever-present inclination to vice, More follows in the footsteps of the humanists and designs a rigidly controlled environment where freedom of movement, religious dissension, and sexual association are carefully restricted. Not trusting men to amuse themselves honestly, he has their leisure-time activities supervised so that only constructive games, work like gardening, and self-improvement through continuing education are really tolerated. Finally, More takes the constant monitoring the humanists desired to the point where no one in Utopia can ever escape public scrutiny. No wonder Erasmus and [Peter] Giles, [Joseph de] Busleiden and Budé wrote admiringly of More's work—the enclosed garden of Utopia is a colossal version of the educational environment they all desired for their children and dreamed of as a model for a brave new world.

Wayne A. Rebhorn
ELR (Summer, 1976), pp. 141–42, 155

JOHN SKELTON

ca. 1460–1529

Skelton's verse . . . is permeated with musical statement and metaphor drawn from various divisions of music known to the medieval scholar: musical theory and practice, sacred and secular music, and musical ideas. In finding musical imagery especially apt for characterization, punning, and witticism of many kinds, Skelton is remarkably like Rabelais a generation later; indeed, some of their allusions are practically identical. Far more than Rabelais, however, Skelton shows himself everywhere in touch with practical musical matters—with musical services in the church and the chanting of the liturgy for various occasions, with the training for that type of service, and with secular musical practices both instrumental and poetic. There is little evidence that Skelton ever "read music" in depth at any university; and there is no evidence at all that he knew the *Musica* of Boethius, the standard text in music in university lecture halls for centuries. But his practical knowledge of music is everywhere paramount.

It seems more than reasonable to conclude, then, that Skelton received his secondary education as a scholar in a choir school somewhere in England. And as a student in the university, he would have studied music as well as the other disciplines of the quadrivium (arithmetic, astronomy, and geometry) before proceeding to the bachelor of arts. Later, as tutor to the future King, Skelton may have had an important part in shaping the musical studies of this young boy destined to become famous for his musical abilities and compositions. It is not unlikely, moreover, that the laureate himself was a lutenist.

Nan Cooke Carpenter
John Skelton (New York: Twayne, 1968), p. 120

Speke, Parrot is a typically mediaeval work of art in that the system of ideas on which it is based is external to it. It is not, in the language of Coleridgean criticism, an organic whole; on the contrary, it is manifestly incomplete without the co-operation of an audience of informed readers. It is designed for a community of Christian readers, and like most mediaeval art, it cannot be wholly alive apart from such a community. This may or may not seem a drawback to a modern reader; but the poem's dependence on its readers offered Skelton an artistic opportunity of which he took full advantage. Had he spelled out his equation of Wolsey with Antichrist, the result would have been merely denunciatory, even platitudinous; but by basing the poem on an allusive use of materials traditionally understood as revealing the doctrine of Antichrist, he was able to invite his reader into a conspiratorial rediscovery of the old doctrine in a new guise. As it is, Antichrist is writ large all over the poem. Yet no matter how commonplace the idea, the reader who discovers it for himself, alone with the poem, cannot but feel that he is being initiated into secret and dangerous matters. This would be so, even if five thousand others were simultaneously undergoing the same initiation. The meaning of the poem is an open secret, and intentionally so. Open, it is commonplace; secret, it is dangerous.

F. W. Brownlow
SP (April, 1968), p. 137

Skelton's satire, in fact, is nothing else but the aggressive expression of his orthodoxy in moral and political matters. In accordance with an approved medieval formula, he made satire a branch of didactic literature. He was the author both of dogmatic treatises such as *The Book How We Should Flee Sin* and of satires intended in his own words, "uyce to reuyle/And synne to exyle" (*Colyn Cloute* v. 11–12).

He spent time lashing his contemporaries whenever their malice or their back-sliding seemed to imperil the community, "the commune weal." He was guided, then, less by an ideal of individual moral perfection than by a vigilant anxiety for the public welfare. Considering the position he occupied in relation to his sovereign, it is not difficult to understand the importance he attached to the part he was called upon to play. Skelton wrote satire with the outlook of a scholastic theologian. Behind every one of his satires it is possible to discern an armature of logical and somewhat harsh reasoning, according to which, since the prevailing orthodoxy was founded upon the great medieval synthesis of Aristotelian Thomism—the alliance of reason and faith—the enemies of England's king, of the Universal Church and of the poet-laureate Skelton must inevitably, by definition, be either fools or heretics.

Such in essence is Skeltonian satire: personal, topical, corrective, it denounces one by one the enemies of Skelton, of the English monarchy and of the established religion. It is akin to ecclesiastical censures and to the chastisement administered in school. It is quick to wield the birch and to fulminate anathema. When it is inspired by the lofty sentiment of duty, it can be bold to the point of rashness: at such times it subordinates every other consideration of rank or person to the general interest. But it can also be quarrelsome, captious, and about as polite as a gamekeeper to a poacher, with something cruel and gloating in its denunciation which reminds one of the procedures of medieval justice. It delights to pillory the enemies of the public welfare, leading the chorus of jeers and gibes.

Maurice Pollet
John Skelton: Poet of Tudor England (London: J. M. Dent, 1971), pp. 186–87

[Spenser's] *Shepheardes Calender*, of course, has much greater depth, complexity, subtlety, and sophistication than *Colyn Cloute*, but lacks the directness, vitality, and immediacy of Skelton's poem. Above all, the *Calender* has E. K., who, through his emphases, queries, and helpful details can be a guide to the allegory—or throw up a protective cloud of mystification if the allegory becomes too plain. As E. K. tells us, he composed his glosses because otherwise he "knew many excellent and proper devises both in wordes and matter would pass in the speedy course of reading, either as unknown, or as not marked." E. K. also complicates matters by making references to, and attacking things, in terms of the anti-Catholic propaganda elicited by the Alençon marriage controversy of late 1579, and thereby puzzles later readers in regard to the ecclesiastical eclogues. (The latter, probably written a year or two before the glosses, reflect a somewhat different climate of religious opinion.) Furthermore, the dramatic form of the *Calender* enables Spenser to return again and again to his central issues of concern in the separate eclogues. And the *Calender*'s anagrams can tease us into thought about the drift of the poem.

In much the same way Skelton reflects the problems of his age in the looser structure of *Colyn Cloute*. Colin, Skelton's spokesman, in his outbursts of rage or in his reports on the ecclesiastical views of various lay critics, can either cudgel the authors of these views or evaluate, qualify, or partially discount the views themselves.

Whatever the obvious differences in the two poems, it should be thoroughly evident by now that both Skelton and Spenser were committed to the established Church of their time—Skelton as a conservative Catholic, and Spenser as a conservative Anglican—and wished to see reform come from within this Church by improvement in clerical morals and education, not from without by changes in doctrine. But both were a little pessimistic. To Skelton, Christ and Thomas à Becket and two or three unnamed contemporary prelates were foils to the many worldly, indifferent, or corrupt pastors. Spenser, too, held up a handful of contemporary bishops as models of, or spokesmen for, the clerical ideal, but found his most telling contrast in the pre-Reformation or the biblical past—where shepherds were the direct opposites of their modern counterparts.

It should be realized, finally, that Skelton's *Colyn Cloute* was an important influence on Spenser in the composition of the *Shepheardes Calender*. Spenser found many of his central themes, devices, and procedures in Skelton's poem and, in general, like Skelton, wished to hold a poetic mirror up to the political and ecclesiastical problems of his own time, to stress similar political and religious ideals, and to attack those forces that were disturbing the proper balance between classes that should exist in the nation and the church.

Paul E. McLane
SP (April, 1973), pp. 158–59

JOHN WYCLIF

ca. 1330–1384

As a thinker Wyclif was an extremist. In his earlier, metaphysical, phase he pressed his conclusions beyond the limits of reason; later, when he turned to theology and ecclesiology, he went beyond the bounds of faith. Yet, like most medieval dissidents, his premisses belonged to Christian tradition; and to Wyclif his outlook embodied it. To make the cause of his divergence exclusively intellectual would be as mistaken as to see it solely in terms of his personal fortunes. That Wyclif's progression to heresy was not simply an autonomous development of his ideas without reference to experience can be seen in his changed tone after 1378 and more especially in the conclusions he drew from the Eucharist—conclusions which had been open to him philosophically for fifteen or more years. Equally, it shows that his ideas were not independent of his experience in the world of affairs. Indeed, more than with most scholastics, it would be artificial to separate in Wyclif the thinker from the man and to attribute his heresy to one rather than the other. At most, events accentuated a fundamentally constant orientation. This was largely determined by his metaphysics and temperament; they gave a unity to much of his theology and ecclesiology, which was both his strength and his weakness. It enabled him to set his protest against the Church within a comprehensive theoretical framework and to conduct it on a variety of fronts. He brought to it considerable dialectical skill and sometimes eloquence. This made him a formidable opponent even when, as so often, he was defending the indefensible. His conviction and undoubted sincerity gave him certainty at a time when the dominant intellectual climate was doubt. These attributes combined to establish his supremacy at Oxford: it took official action after his departure to destroy it.

On the other hand, being wiser after the event, we can perhaps more easily recognize Wyclif's flaws: he was unsubtle and repetitive; the system, for all its elaboration in work after work, turns out on closer inspection to be little more than a few guiding threads cocooned in endless words; the arguments, rigorous in themselves, lack structure; the exposition consists in reiteration rather than development; the dialectical agility hides mental rigidity; the certainty was more often an inflexible resolve to force square pegs into round holes. But if these are shortcomings in a thinker, they can be a source of strength in an advocate. In the latter role Wyclif was supreme. He left an imprint upon history which cannot be effaced. For this reason, however much we may dismiss his ideas on a purely intellectual plane, we cannot ignore them.

Gordon Leff
Proceedings of the British Academy, Vol. 52 (1966), pp. 147–48

Modern opinion, although divided about the authorship of the two translations called Lollard unanimously disclaims anything but an editorial and inspirational function for Wyclif himself. There is excellent evidence for [Nicholas] Hereford's participation in the early translation of the Old Testament, and fairly firm reason for believing [John] Purvey to have overseen the production of the later version. [Eric] Fristedt postulated a third attempt, a revision of the early version, edited by Wyclif himself, but if it ever existed, it is now lost. There are several modern writers who suggest John Trevisa as the author of the later version, but the only testimony comes from Caxton, and some interesting, but inconclusive circumstantial evidence. The later version was almost certainly completed twelve or so years after Wyclif's death, but he may have supervised or encouraged its undertaking, and Purvey would have been the likeliest person to have been entrusted with his friend's project.

Wyclif's belief in the sufficiency of the Bible and his wish to reproduce the New Testament Church in the fourteenth century necessitated an English Bible. He saw that while theology in his day still rested on scriptural authority, "the enforcement of the Church's jurisdiction rested on canon law."[1] Designing, in a way typical of him, to attack the source of the abuses he saw around him, Wyclif conceived the very large objective of replacing canon law with a vernacular Bible. In addition to a reformation of the organization of the Church, the demand for a return to New Testament Christianity required that an understandable text of the whole Bible be made available to the people. Why these two aims could not be met in a single translation lies in an explanation of the principles of the translation of scripture in mediaeval times.

For the purposes of scholarly debate, and for the bases of Church organization, there was only one method for Bible translation uniformly found acceptable before the sixteenth century. W. Schwartz writes that "the method of word-for-word translation was considered to be the surest safeguard against any alteration of the original thought. It was considered to render the contents of the Bible in its entirety without any mistakes, and to protect the translator from a change of God's word and from heresy." Such an approach to translation was called "construe" and was advocated, according to Miss [Margaret] Deanesly, by "the strictest school of translators." Only such a method, then, would suffice for Wyclif's plan to reform Church organization. Rather than mere ineptitude in the English idiom, as was formerly believed, the literalness of the early version may have been part of a careful plan to meet the most rigid specifications for an English Bible.

Peggy Ann Knapp
Sp (October, 1971), p. 714

ELIZABETHAN AND JACOBEAN LITERATURE

Kenneth Friedenreich, editor

ROGER ASCHAM

1515–1568

Quattrocento Humanism in its early stage seemed to represent a shift toward a "cleaner," less shadowy, more precise, more delimited conception of discourse. But by the end of the century a neo-allegorism was established within Humanist exegesis (e.g., Landino's *Disputationes Camalduenses*) and a suppler conception of symbolism was flourishing in both north and south, from the philosophy of Pico della Mirandola to the comic art of Rabelais, whose ninth and tenth chapters in the *Gargantua* constitute a kind of manifesto of the modern practice. . . .

[Ascham's] approach to language was nothing if not "clean," and in this regard he bears a superficial resemblance to such great Italian schoolmasters of the early Humanist phase as Guarino [da Verona] and Vittorino da Feltre. In contrast to the Spenserian dark conceit, Ascham's characteristic trope was the simile, wherein his lively ingenuity was never allowed to blur the strictest logic and the sunniest translucency. The contrast operates in fact not only forward but backward with a predecessor like Sir Thomas Elyot. Ascham had no affinity for the kind of ritualistic relation Elyot drew between dancing and virtue. The elaborate articulation of Elyot's symbolism reveals a consciousness attuned to metaphysical correspondences, about which Ascham was far less curious. He represents a kind of interruption in the continuous line from Elyot to Spenser and Sidney, an interruption whose divergence can be measured by the distance between dancing and archery.

It would be easy and perhaps expected of a latter-day critic to deplore this interruption. But it could be argued that in fact the English language at mid-century required precisely the clarity and control which the Cambridge

Humanists strove for. It could be argued that the remarkable evolution of English prose during the hundred years that followed was promoted by the erudite simplifications of Ascham and his generation. Such arguments are not subject to proof. But there is much that is certain for which we can be grateful. For it can be said with assurance that Ascham brought a kind of distinction to that option, that cultural style which remains in most respects so distant from our own. In his firm literary sense, his respect for lucid precision, his lively advancement of English prose style, his hostility to the divorce of tongue and heart, his faith in human craft, his capacity for delight and his passion for order, his melding of quiet beauty and decorous action into the luminous ideal of comeliness—in all these respects he enriched the cause of Humanist enlightenment. A generation later his sturdy traditionalism and his somewhat narrow pieties would already doubtless have appeared quaint. But at the particular stage of his country's cultural evolution during which he wrote, as an inchoate movement groped toward self-consciousness, Ascham made to his culture a precious contribution. With a few other men, and more effectively than most, he gave it a feeling for the beauty of discipline and the discipline of beauty, the lovely accuracy of seemly action and proper speech. Almost everything he wrote concerns the way human art achieves what he called "the perfect end of shooting." His love of art, conceived so broadly and finely, seals him as a true son of that Renaissance he partly distrusted and nonetheless served with felicity.

Donald M. Greene
ELH (Winter, 1969), pp. 623–25

Ascham [in *The Schoolmaster*] is clearly making use of the *Odyssey* to solve a contemporary problem, that of whether or not the young gentleman should make what came to be known later as the Grand Tour. Just before he begins his interpretation of Homer he explains that "Sir Richard Sackville, that worthy gentleman of worthy memory . . . was most earnest with me to have me say my mind also what I thought concerning the fancy that many young gentlemen of England have to travel abroad, and namely to lead a long life in Italy." The passage supplies an alternative to the modern critical attempt to get at the author's intention by means of the work. Ascham certainly disregards Homer's intention in the *Odyssey* altogether, but what he substitutes gives an interesting insight into sixteenth-century criticism.

Ascham finds himself in a particular situation: he is asked to speak to the question of the Grand Tour. He at first says the youth should not go, but then adds, in the beginning of the interpretation above, "Yet if a man will needs travel into Italy. . . ." Ascham's problem is to prepare this traveller, and he does this by making the *Odyssey* applicable to this situation: Ulysses is the model to be followed in wisdom and caution by the English youth who do go to Italy. It is almost as if the *Odyssey* is an indeterminate object on which Ascham thrusts the burden of his own problem of preparing the tender pilgrims for what they will meet in Italy. This is a temporary use of the work to resolve a problem about a cultural habit; when there is no longer a problem there is no longer any need for the interpretation. There is, in other words, nothing permanent in this view of the work. As Ascham might well say, this use of Homer "works" for the moment; it aids in resolving the problem (for sixteenth-century readers, we assume) and hence it does what Ascham intends it to. . . .

Historical consideration of sixteenth-century criticism is inadequate because it has failed to approach such writers as Sidney, Ascham, and Elyot in terms of the basic assumptions developed explicitly or implicitly by these critics. It has failed to accept these men as systematic thinkers, but has insisted on breaking down their works into isolated interpretations and statements that appear ridiculous when removed from a theoretical substructure that renders them valid. Ascham, the primary subject here, provides one of the most extensive sources of humanistic thought and criticism of the period, and yet *The Schoolmaster* has been relegated to the dustbin of educational historians. Even beyond this necessary historical re-examination the similarity between Ascham and [Cleanth] Brooks suggests that sixteenth-century works may be valuable to modern criticism: the critic who understands the assumptions underlying his own works will be most likely not to mislead his readers (the New Critics should have been clearer about the moral or social orientation of their criticism, for example). Such a critic will be able to see the influence of his own particular experience and to control it or make it clear; he will then be able to place his own comment in relation to that of others and perhaps see the critical predilections of the age in which he lives. The study of sixteenth-century criticism, both related to and distant from modern criticism, is useful in promoting this kind of awareness.

Robert M. Strozier
EIC (Winter, 1972), pp. 400, 406–7

SIR FRANCIS BACON

1561–1626

We are now in a position to consider precisely the relationship between Bacon's method (in the *Novum Organum* and the *Essays*) and the tradition of Platonic-Augustinian dialectic. There are many points of contact (some of which will have already occurred to my readers), but they find a single source in a shared distrust of the human mind. Like Plato, Bacon deplores the tendency of the mind to equate its immediate horizons with the horizons of reality, and, again like Plato, he devises a mode of proceeding that prevents the mind from resting too easily in the satisfaction of closed and artificial systems. They are alike, too, in what they oppose. Where Plato turns away from rhetoric (at least in its sophistic guise), Bacon turns away from the syllogism, and for the same reasons. The conclusions processed by a syllogism are true only with the circle of its own order ("The syllogism commands assent to the proposition, but does not take hold of the thing—xii"); in the larger context that circle excludes they are neither authoritative nor (necessarily) helpful. The deliberations of a syllogism are defensive rather than exploratory; it is committed from the beginning to something that is assumed to be true (as the rhetorician is committed to popular belief) and will admit evidence only in support of it. Rather than challenging received notions, a syllogism builds on them (syllogisms do not permit examination of their basic premises) and therefore confirms the mind in the opinions it already holds. In short, the syllogism is a conservative form which (like rhetoric) induces complacency rather than encouraging change.

It is change, of course, that is promoted both by dialectic and by the method of induction, change not only in the discernment of what is true and real, but in the mind that is to be the instrument of the discerning. Dialectic and the method of induction are refining processes and what they refine (in their early stages) is the understandings of their users; they clear away debris, remove film, expose error, prevent sloppiness, encourage rigor, sharpen perception. In the words of Milton, they "purge with sovrain eye-salve that intellectual ray which *God* hath planted in us," making it more "fit and proportionable to Truth the object, and end of it."

But it is precisely here, where the two operations are most similar, that they must be sharply distinguished. The truth to which the understanding will be made "fit and proportionable" is for Plato, Augustine, and Donne a truth above the phenomenal world, while for Bacon it is a truth about the phenomenal world. In the light of this one difference (which makes all the difference) the points of similarity become points of opposition. . . .

In short, while the dialogues of Plato and the sermons of Donne are self-consuming, Bacon's *Essays* are merely self-regulating; his words may be, as he terms them, seeds, living not so much in their references as in their effects, but they will flower in other words rather than in a vision, and in words which do have the referential adequacy that is presently unavailable.

Stanley E. Fish
Self-Consuming Artifacts: The Experience of Seventeenth-Century Literature (Berkeley: Univ. California Pr., 1972), pp. 151–54

The fate of the *New Atlantis*, though it was influential for some years and though it names some scientific goals that still prevail, has upheld Bacon's belief that the acroamatic method is a very dangerous one to employ. Like most of his other works of fable-making, it has contributed to his reputation as a tradition-bound Renaissance man. Even [Thomas] Sprat, author of the *History of the Royal Society*, fails to see that Bacon is demythologizing natural studies by employing myth itself, or that he is following his own method of inquiry by comparing in the *New Atlantis* things which do not exist with things which do. Less learned readers will see the work as a light on antiquity perhaps, but the "sons of science" will read it for the light it throws on nature. The ancient and revered art of mythologizing will yield its powers to the new maker of myths, and the emphasis for study will henceforth be on the uncharted side of the similitude (the things which are or can be). Thus both the writer and the reader will be protected in this initial stage of the development of the new learning.

Bacon understands his role in intellectual history and plays it well: though the path to true knowledge through fables has been "narrowed," there is nothing to prevent science's spokesman from using his wit to create new myths from old ones to serve as vehicles to carry men along to greater things. Because the devices of poetry make content "appear" sacred and venerable, Bacon will use his considerable talent in that direction to provide the new mythology. He will do so, "not for the value of the thing," but in the interests of the advancement of learning and the relief of man's estate. Thus he accomplishes as a stylist what his mentors in ancient Rome and on the Continent fail to accomplish. Instead of thrusting his new ideas at readers with no consideration for their imagination or passions, he employs myth and metaphor to enchant every faculty of his readers' minds. Certainly this is a dangerous risk to take, as subsequent events have demonstrated, yet Bacon remains in favor with both groups to whom the *New Atlantis* is addressed, though, in our own age, those audiences' roles have been reversed. Those who still participate in the romance of science and technology continue to cite Bacon as one of the fathers of the age of reason. Those who regret the losses and compromises entailed by a commitment to naturalism are turning increasingly to a study of Bacon as a poet and fabulist. He was among the last to enjoy the best of both worlds.

James Stephens
Francis Bacon and the Style of Science (Chicago: Univ. Chicago Pr., 1975), pp. 170–71

FRANCIS BEAUMONT
1584–1616

and

JOHN FLETCHER
1597–1625

F. T. Bowers, ed., *The Dramatic Works in the Beaumont and Fletcher Canon* (1966–), in progress, 3 vols. to date

The masque has recently received new critical attention. Books on the subject have appeared, important masques have been reprinted, and the 1968 volume of *Renaissance Drama* dealt exclusively with this form. The relation of the masque to the Jacobean drama still needs reexamination, however, with emphasis not merely on mechanical connections—who borrowed an antimasque from whom—but on the stylistic influence of the masque on the new tone of drama in the Jacobean period. From this viewpoint the contribution of Beaumont and Fletcher is central, particularly since they developed and popularized the other characteristic Jacobean form, tragicomedy . . . .

The simultaneous emergence of these two extravagant forms was not accidental. Both are romantic, even antirealistic. Laurels go to the poet who manipulates the situation most spectacularly, not, as in realistic drama, to the one who best conceals his controlling hand. Furthermore, the leading authors of Jacobean masques and tragicomedies knew each other's work. . . .

The abbreviation of the masque impelled by theatrical circumstances might suggest that isolated masque elements could occasionally be as effective as "full" masques. [Ashley] Thorndike, who did not differentiate masques from masque elements, counted "distinct masque elements occurring in eighteen of their plays." These masque elements, isolated bits of the masque requiring less preparation than a full masque, help fashion the abrupt changes of mood and meaning in a Beaumont and Fletcher tragicomedy. They may appear alone or together with a full masque; in either case, such elements permit a particularly continuous and flexible penetration of the masque into the drama. Repeated shifts to the more formal style serve as reminders of the artifice of the play, constantly pulling the audience back from the brink of serious involvement. In this way masques and masque elements can resolve a critical difficulty of tragicomedy, and Beaumont and Fletcher exploit them with increasing frequency throughout their careers.

The masques in Beaumont and Fletcher's plays helped overcome another difficulty of tragicomedy: destroying conventional comic and tragic expectations. The concealed denouement is often considered the central and distinguishing characteristic of Beaumont and Fletcher's tragicomedy. The audience should have no idea how or whether the dilemma will be solved. Normally a play creates a set of tragic or comic expectations, but in tragicomedy both must be kept in uneasy balance. Beaumont and Fletcher abjured any helpful reference to the way things really happen, while their technique of surprise inhibited them from furnishing the audience decisive information unknown to the characters (as in *Measure for Measure*). They found another way to destroy comic or tragic expectations by shifting the entire play into a mode formal enough to be free of conventional logic. Their dramas are organized formally, as [Arthur] Mizener has illustrated, and within this formal organization constant shifts from the familiar to the fantastic disorient the audience.

Masques throughout the Beaumont and Fletcher canon create these shifts from real to unreal, remind us of the factitious nature of the performance, and destroy conventional comic or tragic expectations. A full masque was not essential for achieving these results, and in practice masques introduced into plays had to be abbreviated. A masque in a drama could not lead to one or two hours of reveling with the ladies, and its author could not hope for elaborate scenery or complex machinery. What remained, then, was a short, spectacular entertainment, normally including some music, dancing, and the entry of fabulous or exotic characters.

Suzanne Gossett
MP (February, 1972), pp. 199, 201–2

ROBERT BURTON

1577–1640

The *Anatomy of Melancholy*, a massive treatise of scientific and humane learning, ends with the quiet, anti-climactic advice that its readers "be not solitary, be not idle"—an almost vapid remark to make to close out a book of these dimensions. Burton's eloquence concerning man's need to love his fellow man by loving God, the appeal to place human despair in the context of divine mercy, these end with a sort of tinkling inconsequence in a plea to "be not idle." Tinkling and inconsequential after the clarion call to charity, except that reverberating through the *Anatomy* to its very last word is the essential humanizing, civilizing force of industry that reforms the essentially inhumane, barbarous natural state of man which is idleness, *id est*, melancholy. The Preface's climactic movement, this section of the argument *a partibus ad totum*, describes man as he is by nature in contrast to what he might be by art and industry. . . .

The *Anatomy*'s form is not limited to one expression, as the structural analyses of the Partitions have shown. Digression and equivocation, like Burton's constant "yet nevertheless" that allows him to shape and order the seemingly shapeless "facts" of knowledge, speak the truth that this book is no mere finished Pharaoh's tomb which destroys its form by being finished. For the *Anatomy* is never finally finished, its form is always open to new views, yet it is always made, an artifact complete and whole but never unused, never useless. So, I would argue, Burton's book does not cancel itself out by representing melancholy with all that disease's chaotic symptoms. Instead it cures melancholy constantly by being what it is, the useful structure of the scholar's cure, the apparent idleness that is never really idle but is always working to cure its author and its readers through their very busyness with it.

The *Anatomy* is so constantly and so consistently a thing in production that it can reappear "corrected and augmented by the author" eleven years after that author has given up time for eternity. Scholars have the effective means of civilization as the very tools of their trade: method and composition. So Democritus Junior indicates how method and composition can work if the means themselves are the end. His curious transition from the general view of the world to the views of institutional man ends, we have seen, in his reasonable but illogical move "*a partibus ad totum*, or from the whole to the parts." . . .

To restate roving as a progression "*a partibus ad totum*, or from the whole to the parts"—even if the world appears so chaotic that the order is artificially imposed—is to reform the chaos and so to prove that the things of the world are disordered but its structure is not permanently impaired; paradise can be regained.

Ruth A. Fox
The Tangled Chain: The Structure of Disorder in "The Anatomy of Melancholy" (Berkeley: Univ. California Pr., 1976), pp. 248–49, 258–59

THOMAS CAMPION

1567–1620

While it is important in the study of song to stress the independence of poetry and music, the influence of the arts upon each other is clearly a matter of great interest. In strophic songs, for example, the choice of words and images in successive stanzas must match the recurrence of the same musical phrases. Such a discipline, in addition to that required for the production of good rhyming verse, might be expected to limit the variety and vitality of word music. A more obvious influence is that of the events, images and emotions expressed in the poems on the musical form created for them. No body of work is more instructive about such influences than the song books of Campion in which (to quote him) "I have chiefely aymed to couple my words and notes lovingly together."

It is significant that Campion used the lute song rather then the madrigal for setting his poems. Both forms were at the peak of their fashion and development during Campion's creative life; but while the madrigal was a predominantly polyphonic form in which several voices carried the words through an often complex web of imitation, the lute song was predominantly homophonic, a melody with accompaniment. The words fitted to the melody were at the focus of attention and could be clearly understood, in contrast with the overlapping and repetitious phrases that commonly appeared in the madrigal. "To sing to the lute," said Castiglione in *The Courtier*, "is much better [than counterpoint], because all the sweetness consisteth in one alone, and a man is more heedfull and understandeth the feate manner, the aire or vaine of it, when the eares are not busied in hearing any more than one voice?" Although the composers of polyphony often took great pains to represent every nuance of emotion or action described in the text with appropriate illustrative music, they reflected the subject matter rather than the actual phrases of the poem. It is therefore not surprising that there is a larger proportion of good poetry in the song books than in the madrigal collections.

Edward Lowbury, Timothy Salter, and Alison Young
Thomas Campion: Poet, Composer, Physician (London: Chatto and Windus, 1970), pp. 38–39

THOMAS CAREW

1594?–1640

Carew's demonstrated knowledge and mastery of both Donne's and Jonson's poetry surpasses, I think, that of any other poet up to 1640. And Carew often surpasses Donne in the evocation of sensuous and sensual (rather than dramatic) immediacy. . . . And Carew sometimes surpasses Jonson in courtly elegance and decorative compliment. How much he owes those achievements to his own temperament and how much to French and Italian poetry (particulary to [Giambattista] Marino, a number of whose poems Carew translated and whom he may have known in Paris) is impossible to determine. One can, however, see not only his mastery of some effects of Donne and Jonson but also his departures from their practice almost everywhere in the lyrics. . . .

The grandest public occasion to demand Carew's talents was answered by his masque, *Coelum Britannicum*, designed and produced by Inigo

Jones and presented before the King at Whitehall on Shrove Tuesday, 1634. Sir Henry Herbert, George Herbert's younger brother, Master of the Revels since 1623, called it "the noblest masque of my time to this day, the best poetry, best scenes, and the best habits," and the Queen remarked (in French) that she had never seen such fine costumes. . . .

The passage in Carew's masque which I find most impressive and most touching (and which Carew did not get from [Giordano] Bruno) is Mercury's neo-Spenserian rejection of Hedone, or Pleasure, after her claims of sovereignty . . . and her masque of the five senses. It suggests, I think, that Carew, like some later poets, had come to know by experience that a simple sensuous hedonism may be one of the most painful of all creeds, particularly for a man past thirty-five, but that it was about all he had.

Joseph H. Summers
The Heirs of Donne and Jonson (New York: Oxford Univ. Pr., (1970), pp. 68–69, 74–75

GEORGE CHAPMAN

ca. 1559–1634

A. Holaday et al., eds., *The Plays of George Chapman: The Comedies*, Vol. I (1970)

Chapman usually draws his myths, whether directly or indirectly, from *The Metamorphoses*; in fact, all the major poems from the 1590s are stimulated by Chapman's dislike for the changing taste in Ovidian poetry, from the mythological to the erotic. . . . Donne was a force in the newer vogue for Ovidian eroticism. . . . Chapman's kind of poetry is old-fashioned in comparison to Donne's; but, like many late practitioners of an art, he gains greatly in sophistication because of that. The strategems which the winds of change moved Chapman to deploy result in complexities, tensions, and density that make his best work extremely interesting technically, as well as remarkable poetry. One recurring example of such sophistication would be his skill at typological adaptation of myths. As he explains in the [*Free and Offenseless*] *Justification*, poets "have enlarged, or altred the Allegory, with inventions and dispositions of their owne, to extend it to their present doctrinall and illustrious purposes" (*Poems*, p. 327). Understanding Chapman's handling of myth never is merely a matter of having read the same books, although admittedly that helps. Rather, it is necessary to appreciate the flexible systemization of myths that had evolved by Chapman's time, enabling the commentators, emblematists, and poets to adapt freely among typological equivalents, a procedure at which Chapman was a master. . . .

If, as I argue, Chapman brings to his skirmish with the erotic Ovidians the heavy artillery of Plato's condemnation of dramatic poetry, what are we to make of sonnet 10 in *The Coronet*, which praises the greatness of classical drama and urges its revival while condemning the contemporary theatrical abuses? First, there is nothing new about the probability that Chapman, like any other humanist, used his classical proof-texts selectively, either not noticing inconvenient and contradictory materials or simply ignoring them for tactical purposes. Which is to say, he found it convenient to apply the weight of Plato's censure to erotic poetry of the mixed mode; he intended to extend it no further. Certainly he would have disavowed the attack on Homer. Second, Plato talks about the *abuse* of the dramatic mode, permitting the inference that it could be employed unobjectionably. Chapman believed that the great classical dramatists achieved this, and that he could emulate their achievement.

In *Ovids Banquet of Sence* Chapman imitates "the fretful part" of man in dramatic narrative, writing with the full expectation that many of his readers will misapprehend the imitation. Although he firmly locates the poem in an interpretative context—by the abuse of vision both in action and intellectual hierarchy, by Ovid's abuse of relational and mental hierarchy, by the perspective metaphor, by the bent-stick emblem, and by his entire manipulation of point of view—he expects that many will lack the "meanes to sound the philosophical conceits." To a modern audience this readiness to permit the deception of the unwary for illustrative purposes, making them unwitting exempla of the poem's thesis about sensory deception, perhaps will smack of coterie verse, written only to gratify an attitude of superiority assumed by the poet and his friends. Such a response would be mistaken, for the only admission requirements to this inner circle are learning and reason. Chapman's poem implies a definition of poetry that evolves from the humanist tradition of *ut pictura poesis* and that is still consonant with the general vision of Horace's *Ars poetica* from which the catch phrase is lifted. The "*Enargia*, or cleerenes of representation," required in "absolute" poems and paintings alike is a matter of viewing experience with mind and body together, intelligently and with a moral responsibility—to paraphrase Arnold, of seeing life steadily and seeing it whole. By projecting such a definition and upholding it as a standard, Chapman lays fair claim to having written an "absolute" poem.

Raymond B. Waddington
The Mind's Empire: Myth and Form in George Chapman's Narrative Poems (Baltimore: Johns Hopkins Univ. Pr., 1974), pp. 17, 150–51

JOHN CLEVELAND

1613–1658

The witty hecatomb ["On His Mistress"] is instructive on several counts. Not only does it give us some insight (perhaps unnecessary, of course) into the practice of invention on the part of those poets Cleveland dislikes, but it also gives us an indication of the degree to which invention is consciously practiced by Cleveland himself. As moderns, we sometimes tend to think of analysis by invention as something which is *post facto*, an operation of the critic in his efforts to describe a poem; but Cleveland shows us unambiguously that such is not the case. Invention is, as its name implies, not a function of the critic but of the creator, of the poet.

Therefore, the term "Clevelandism," applied invidiously or not, is a term which finally aims at describing the kinds of invention Cleveland found of particular use. It aims, too, at emphasizing the characteristic ways in which wit functions in Cleveland's poems, just as it aims at describing the lengths Cleveland sometimes goes to achieve a witty situation. The term, in other words, is not necessarily limited to the abuse of a word or a phrase; it can be applied to the peculiarities of structure which identify many of [his] poems. . . .

The range, then, of his primarily nonsatirical political poems is quite remarkable. Cleveland in his own time was more famous for his satirical poems, and he is still justly more famed for his exercises in satire; but he should not be overlooked as a poet capable of direct political statement. His muse was sometimes justly rage and sometimes merely bewilderment, but he always seemed aware of the meaning of events and of the portent of change. . . .

Regarding Cleveland as a master of rhetoric and admitting the prejudices of successive ages against rhetoric mixed with poetry should help us understand why it is difficult to appreciate some of his work. Reviving Cleveland is probably a job similar to that of reviving the Mannerist painters, whose incompetence has been taken for granted until our own century. Recent art historians began to see that their work was not technically deficient but basically rhetorical in nature: it was designed to affect a viewer in a way he might not like but could not ignore.

The purposes of Cleveland's energy, inventiveness, audacity, and simple shock are clearly of this order. He does not lose control of his poems, as careful examination of the prosody shows. Criticism which asserts Cleveland had no control of his materials seems unwarranted by careful reading of the poems and prose. Cleveland knew what he was doing, and we cannot help but admire his brilliance. He remains one of the most inventive lyricists of his time—and of the style which virtually ended with him. And perhaps more important for the post-Romantic reader, Cleveland must be considered an absolute master of what we have come to call the English satire. His genius as a satirist in his own day had no peer. In terms of the history of English literature, Cleveland must be considered original, brilliant, and among the first rank of satirists in the language.

Lee A. Jacobus
John Cleveland (Boston: Twayne, 1975), pp. 48, 79, 152–53

SAMUEL DANIEL

1562–1619

It is important that we allow ourselves to see Renaissance poetry as poetic representation rather than simply oratorical persuasion. Many of Daniel's rhetorical figures become meaningful only in context of the larger gestures of the poem. For example, his reiterative word-play stresses ironic contrasts of attitude, but also a certain continuity of concern in the poem, the concern embodied in a tone of voice and a presence which apply themselves gravely to the "topics" of life as they arise. That is, word-play may support certain ironic contrasts in local passages, but it also represents the continuing process of thought and commentary which is the major subject of the poem and which sets its "pitch" and tone. Such word-play is not merely ironic, interruptive and fragmenting, but indicates the continuing concern of the speaker for his subject, his continuing struggle to be present to life. It gathers together and harmonizes the individual addresses of thought, the transitions, extensions and reservations of attitude which extend the length of Daniel's poems. . . .

At the level of technique Daniel seems bent upon selecting and adapting rhetorical strategies so as to turn them from their normally emphatic clarifying role toward the non-public, personal and "directly expressive." Once again the sensitive reader may feel in Daniel a deep conflict—a respect for the presence of inward thoughtfulness crossed by the desire to imitate that thoughtfulness, and so publicize it, as carefully as his knowledge of literary devices permitted. His speakers are more deeply concerned with literary composition than with poetic effectiveness, the former being the more personal, the latter the more satisfying. We are hesitant to determine where the speaking voice is issuing *from*, and so we say it is the man himself. We must be getting the "poet himself." Or are we getting only his concern with the question of being present to himself and to the "questions" of living in the world? This latter concern would militate against a vivid sense of location, for all thinking is undeniably "here"—and elsewhere.

Rhetorically considered, the formation of this style depends on an eclectic mingling of figures, being as they are common tools, but always, hopefully, with that Sidneian "inward touch," that inspection of the relation of honest feeling to its artistic expression which so absorbed the attention of Astrophil. Such a style cannot be considered in Daniel's case a mingling of poetic figures with prosaic matter. Much of the rhetoric is directed to specific representations of the speaker's stance, balance, and manner of discourse, rather than to isolated vivid turns and "effective" argumentation.

Anthony La Branche
in *The Rhetoric of Renaissance Poetry*, ed. Thomas O. Sloan
and Raymond B. Waddington (Berkeley: Univ. California Pr.,
1974), pp. 136–39

THOMAS DEKKER

1572–1632?

The action of *The Shoemakers' Holiday* moves back and forth, in the fashion of many Elizabethan plays, between two contrasting sets of attitudes: integrity, spontaneity, and good cheer on the one hand—duplicity, pretense, and rigidity on the other. Obviously, the first set is extolled and the second condemned. The main plot—which follows the rise of Simon Eyre from humble cobbler, to Sheriff, and finally to Lord Mayor of London—is rooted in folklore and was a very well-known legend in its time. Its being so well-known may account for its subordination to the antiphonal movement between the contrasting sets of attitudes. (None of Simon's elevations is actually shown on stage, only the domestic excitement preceding those appointments.) The sub-plots—first Rowland Lacy's courtship of Rose and second "dead" Rafe's return from the wars to his unfortunate Jane—are also absorbed into this pattern of alternating attitudes. There is narrative interest in the old legends which constitute the three plots, but the impact of Dekker's interpretation and treatment of those legends derives from the play's antiphonal movement. . . .

The pattern of the play is maintained through four acts by an antiphony between the robust and the puerile, between sincerity and duplicity, between industry (shop-style) and indolence. The play's center, both in arrangement and in meaning, is the scene . . . in which Simon condemns "the courtier" for his "torne inner linings" while "Hans" leads his fellow-journeymen in a morris. The plots come together in Act V, scene 2, the episode in which Rafe and his merry men rescue Jane from Hammon at church door at the same time that the Earl and Sir Roger are tricked by Firk into forestalling the wrong wedding. . . .

The play's underlying theme is . . . appropriately punctuated even if the King is not specifically identified. But the King . . . is identified—implicitly—and the identity is significant. He is Henry V, the former madcap prince, the most renowned of folk-heroes, the hero-King of the middle class. He may, I think, be viewed as the embodiment of the theme of *The Shoemaker's Holiday*, a blend of the best of two worlds: the courtier's world of honor and the commoner's pragmatic world. He is the lord who is at home in the tavern, as Lacy is at home in the shop. He, too, has hated the "painted Images" and has been contemptuous of those whose "inner linings are torne." . . .

In summary, *The Shoemakers' Holiday* is constructed about the ironic implications of Simon's conventional attack on courtiers in Act III, scene 3. The attributes of Simon's courtier are embodied in a pretentious citizen and those of the good citizen in a disguised courtier. A man's "inner linings" are more important than birth or rank. The play presents its contrast between those attitudes it is celebrating and those it is condemning in the antiphonal manner common in Elizabethan drama. First we see falsity and arrogance, next warmth and candor—and so on until the concluding scenes culminate with the image of a hero-King pronouncing victory for the forces of humility and good will over those of false pride and blind adherence to the past.

Michael Manheim
SEL (Summer, 1970), pp. 316, 321–23

JOHN DONNE

1572–1631

Helen Gardner, ed., *The Divine Poems*, 2nd ed. (1978)
Wesley Milgate, ed., *Satires, Epigrams, and Verse Letters* (1967)
———, ed., *The Anniversaries, Epithalamions, and Epicedes* (1978)

Logical structure is, of course, no novelty in Donne's poetry; but the exhaustiveness of the argumentation in "The Extasie" is unusual. The mind is not darting about in agile hyperactivity, but steadily accumulating analogies and data bearing on a single point; and when that first brief is complete, the same patient accumulation begins upon a second. It's probably this palpable intention to make a final statement, a summation, that is responsible more than anything else for the belief that "The Extasie" is one of Donne's great poems. The exhaustiveness, combined with the logical perspicuity, ought to be impressive.

If we start with this overt structure, it all seems plain sailing: (1) Thesis: the ecstatic union of souls, its commodities and discommodities; (2) Antithesis: the claims of the body for satisfaction, giving rise to (3) Synthesis: the true relation between soul and body defined, followed by (4) a slow dissolve as "we'are to bodies gone." But immediately scruples arise. Isn't this altogether too suspiciously lucid? It's a commonplace of human psychology that wonders of clarification can be wrought by schematising, into sequence and series, mental happenings which are in fact simultaneous and indistinguishable. If the body did, in fact, lie mute while the soul reasoned itself into a *cul-de-sac*; and if the soul next, recognising its predicament, implored the body to develop *its* position; and if the mind then stepped tactfully between the disputants and proposed a mutually acceptable formula; then Donne's synthesis might be a matter of great human import. But as it is, one cannot be at all sure how authentic it is. . . .

The pity of it is that the poem which classically creates a meaning for wholeness should revert dismally to its own dichotomies. If the knot is subtle, Donnie is subtler, and he proceeds to its unravelling. What had been insight is converted into rationale. Analytic intelligence sets about re-applying its discoveries in the old dualistic terms, justifying what, given "That subtile knot, which makes us man," needed no justification. "To'our bodies turne we then." It is desperately bathetic, and possible only because, even at the heart of the synthesis, there had been a poison of contradiction: "So must pure lovers soules descend."

In its context that ought to mean, "There is as deep a fittingness in the soul's descending as there was in the blood's aspiring: 'As . . . So . . .' And the soul demonstrates its true purity by accepting that fittingness." But in the light of the poem's ending, it seems also to mean, "Bodily life being what it so sordidly is, the soul must compromise its purity by this descent, and its best resource, having done so, is to brazen it out with a stout pretence that nothing has really changed in the process": "Let him still marke us, he shall see/Small change, when we'are to bodies gone." The affectation of undergoing this shameful metamorphosis self-sacrificially, for the benefit of "Weake men," serves as well as another to conceal the degradation, the *mésalliance* of the soul with the inferior body.

The poem ends, as quoted, on a note of urbane defiance—defiance for which the synthetic union of soul and body has never been anything more than an expedient fiction.

The problem of the proper relation between soul and body, it hardly needs saying, remains as obscure as ever. Donne gropes his way out of the room he has plunged into darkness. Soul is, in a superficial sense, triumphant. Impotent itself, and overweening in its impotence as only conscious purity can be, it has nevertheless forced the body to act out its avid theoretical lusts, preserving its purity by a proxy debauch. Perhaps it's this perverse and barren triumph that makes the dulcet tones of the last quatrain faintly repellent: lilies that fester smell far worse than weeds.

Wilbur Sanders
John Donne's Poetry (Cambridge: Cambridge Univ. Pr., 1971), pp. 98–99, 103–4

There is a poetic type to which, I think, Donne's verse aspires, though it does not conform to that type's conventions. That is the hymn, named in the "Progresse." "These Hymnes," he says, "may work on future wits"; "These Hymnes" shall be the lady's issue, until the Day of Judgment cut them off. Several sorts of hymn were known to Renaissance theorists, the hymns of the gentiles praising their gods and the hymns of the Christian in praise of his single Deity. The psalms of David were the major models for the Christian hymn, which therefore tended to be a subspecies of the poetry of praise; Spenser's *Fowre Hymnes* manages to recapitulate, with a Christian cast given the vocabulary, the high philosophical aims attributed by Renaissance critics to ancient hymnodists. In speaking of the Christian hymn, Scaliger says that by its means the soul is led from the prison of its body to the wide fields of contemplation, to which region the hymn's reader is also translated. Chiefly, the hymn should make clear the great gulf between God and man, and man made aware of his "imbecillitas." Certainly this definition of the hymn is congruent with what Donne does, and "imbecillitas" has its peculiar application in his poems. But all the same, though this might be its theme when handled by Christians, the hymn proper, with its supposed classical models, was quite different, and dealt rather with the descent of the soul to earth than with the (Christian) ascent of the soul to heaven. Donne borrows devices from the literary kind, indeed, as usual fused with other literary implications, such as the soul's flight and passage through the spheres; but Donne's poems, for all their arrival in heaven, begin on earth and take their measurements from human experience. Furthermore, the classical hymn derives from philosophical convictions, and his poems manage to undermine precisely these.

What can these [anniversary] poems be called? They are, in each case, what the poet called them—the first an anatomy, the second a progress, *ad hoc* forms pointing rather to theme than to structure, indeed named to suggest their formal independence and creativity. The first poem is an examination of the world dismembered into "peeces" and into smaller "worlds" of cosmology, intellection, and experience. Since the "Anatomie" is by definition future-oriented, looking to a later cure, it is no wonder that the poet fitted his material to that scheme, to lead toward the progressions of the second year, the *Second Anniversary*, far less unhappy than the first. The same sort of justification may be made for "Progresse," the name given to a sovereign's formal removal from one seat to another. Practically speaking, the term consolidates the recurrent imagery of statecraft and ruling ("When that Queene ended here her progresse time"); thematically, it stresses the movement forward from despair to hope, from decay to renewed health, from intellectual confusion to spiritual revelation. The lady's soul makes that progress, on its way fusing with the poet's soul, to carry him along, the first of her imitators, on a meditative passage to heaven. The medical "Extasie," the "Lethargie," from which the world and poet suffer in the first poem turns into the environmental ecstasy offered by heavenly experience; the condition of ecstasy is, then, normalized in the course of the poem.

Rosalie L. Colie
in *Just So Much Honor: Essays Commemorating the Four-Hundredth Anniversary of the Birth of John Donne*,
ed. Peter Amadeus Fiore (University Park: Pennsylvania State Univ. Pr., 1972), pp. 212–13

Donne's poetry of certain love has [an] inclusiveness. "Sweetest Love," "The Good-Morrow," "Lecture upon the Shadow," "The Computation" and "The Relique," amongst other poems, all have [a] capacity for concentration and breadth. "The Relique's" most gravely delighted tribute can include the "cynical" parenthesis about womankind being "to more then one a Bed"; the theme of that extraordinary poem, "Negative Love," is in a way demonstrated in Donne's positive declarations, which show an awareness of the difficulty and danger of love in the larger world. At the same time, these positive love-poems particularise intimacy with changing passion and sensuousness. The sensuousness is various, to be sure, and at times resides less in local life of a detail than in a diffuse musicality, as in "The Paradox," an almost abstract piece of witty argument where physicality is that of ordered sound, not that of invoked experience.

Physicality, of one kind or another, is the rule in Donne. It belongs, however, not only to the positive love-poetry but also to what we may like to describe, albeit crudely and temporarily, as Donne's poetry of destructive and rejecting passion. "Loves Diet" is a destructive poem, both in theme and passion, but has a purchase on wholeness. If "Loves Growth" conveys the knowing, marginal sense of pain, winter, and dishonesty, "Loves Die" hurls its scorn so as to reveal scorn's loving origins. The way the poem moves (in both senses of that word) is through wit, ironic and derogatory, and repulsive sensations. Wit and sensation work together in the images of obesity—"combersome unwieldinesse," "burdenous corpulence"—in the idea of sucking sweat instead of tears. Such images are presented as unattractive, visually and tactilely, and are also contemptuously argued: "made it feed upon/That which love worst endures, *discretion*," or "I let him see/'Twas neither very sound, nor meant to mee." Sometimes the stroke of wit depends entirely on the strong sensations, as in the last stanza, where love can be called "my buzard love," without argument, fitting in immediately with the imagery of flight, recall, and sport, but taking its contempt and its offensiveness in its culminating definition of the food of love as carrion. The poem is a most serious act of rejection, and also in a sense about itself. It works through great control and economy, forcing resentment out in these physical and cerebral ways, until the release of the last stanza. At the end the imagery of the diet is dropped once the "buzard" makes its logic felt. The feeling is one of release, the poem now exhibiting the ease and heartless play it has been attempting in the diet. . . .

The state of not caring, of cutting love down to size, of "lowering" it, has only been achieved slowly, through the whole poem, and the marked disappearance of contempt and irony in the sense of freedom makes it very clear that the "odi" is part of the "amo." In contrast and change it has created for us the sense that value has existed, and must be destroyed. The hostile feeling, and the devaluation of love shows the process of cynical feeling, and creates an apology for it. Better a buzzard than this kind of falcon?

Donne's so-called cynical poems seem to reveal cynicism, to show it as something created. I am not trying to argue it out of existence in order to claim a life-affirming creativity, but rather to suggest that destructiveness is shown as the other side of love, in the poetic process.

Barbara Hardy
in *John Donne: Essays in Celebration*, ed. A. J. Smith (London: Methuen, 1972), pp. 79–80

The intense awareness of a need for others, expressed in its personal, dependent way in the first miserable anxiety about [Donne's] infectiousness, comes to its stronger and more impersonal expression in the passage "No man is an *Iland* . . ." of Meditation 17. But even in the early statement of the theme he expresses it in the ultimate Christian form of horror and distress at the possibility of separation from God:

> *O my God*, it is the *Leper*, that thou hast condemned to *live alone*; Have I such a *Leprosie* in my *Soule*, that I must die alone; alone without thee? Shall this come to such a *leprosie* in my *body*, that I must die alone? Alone without them that should assist, that shold comfort me? (Expostulation 5)

Separation from God is closely linked for him with separation from man, and even in Prayer 5, in terms that again recall "A Hymne to God the Father," he associates the opinion of others with his own faith when he prays God to

> preserve this *soule* in the faculties therof, from all such distempers, as might shake the assurance which myselfe and others have had, that because thou hast loved me, thou wouldst love me to my *end*, and at my *end*.

In Donne's hands the Christian idiom is shot through with the realities of a sensitive and intelligent man's experience, and the whole plan of the *Devotions* gives the religious concepts a firm anchorage in human events and emotions. Readers who can enter into the sombreness that marked his outlook—in spite of the robust vigour of his mind—will probably have no difficulty, however far they are from accepting his doctrines, in following him in his self accusations and regrets. It may seem altogether more difficult, if not out of the question, for the non-believer to find any parallel to the affirmations, centrally his faith in the redemption, through which Donne achieves his reassurance. For it is a reassurance, something far more positive than mere resignation in the face of death, that he achieves.

We have to see that what his faith does for Donne in his sickness, for Donne in this world, is to convince him that his self-condemnation need not and must not be total and final. And non-Christians too, suffering from a deep sense of worthlessness, do in favourable circumstances, or with the right kind of help, come to terms with it, not by condoning what they have cause to deplore but by coming to believe that in spite of everything they can accept themselves, that there remains some worth in being the person they now are. Reconciliation to himself, though not to his past failures, is what in terms of human experience Donne achieves through his faith.

D. W. Harding
in *John Donne: Essays in Celebration*, ed. A. J. Smith (London: Methuen, 1972), pp. 400–401

Donne's *Anniversaries* resemble in several respects the contemporary poetry of compliment. First, they clearly assume that the chief function of praise is didactic, proposing Elizabeth Drury as in some sense a model for us. Second, the speaker of the *Anniversaries* expresses both public griefs and fears and his own sorrow, resembling most closely perhaps those speakers in the Prince Henry elegies who bewail the general sinfulness held to be responsible for the Prince's death but also associate themselves with it. Third, the *Anniversary* poems employ the full range of available topics, including those chiefly used of princes; but they reflect the trend (evident when we compare the elegies for Prince Henry with those for Elizabeth) toward the Christianization of the poetry of praise by deriving its topics from the Christian order. Finally, these poems are in the vanguard of a trend in the poetry of compliment toward greater unity and analytic rigor, often achieved by extended exploration of a particular issue or topic. . . .

The method of the *Anatomy* is analytic rather than progressive; it gains its force by reiterating [Elizabeth Drury's] loss and tracing its effects upon the bodies of all the "worlds" which constitute the order of nature. The organization of the topics is strictly logical, beginning with man whose Fall was the root of all the evils described, and then taking up the ever-widening ramifications of that Fall throughout the world and the universe. The first section displays the loss of man's heart, and the consequent rottenness and decay of man's whole substance, who is himself a microcosm and the "heart" of the macrocosm. The second section analyzes the corruption and decline of the whole world's frame and substance due to the rottenness of its heart, man. Part three shows the extension of this decay to the exterior and immaterial parts which constitute the beauty of both microcosm and macrocosm. And part four shows the further expansion of these effects throughout the entire body of the universe, as interaction between the realms of earth and heaven, nature and grace, are almost wholly disrupted.

The significance of Elizabeth Drury as manifestation of our primal innocence is similarly extended. In the first section, her recapitulation of that primal perfection is seen to intensify the almost total corruption of man's substance and faculties now, demonstrating thereby that man's only hope lies in transcending the natural order by religion. In regard to the macrocosm, the world's susbstance and beauty, her manifestation of primal innocence serves not only to emphasize the world's loss but for a time seemed to offer some hope for its restoration, a hope blasted by her death. In regard to the failure of correspondence, her life demonstrated the limited effect which even the manifestation of primal innocence restored by grace could have in stimulating natural virtue, and her death removed all hope for any amelioration of nature by higher influences. This brings us directly to the focus of *The Second Anniversary*, the order of grace, which, though it does not restore nature as such, does regenerate man.

Barbara Kiefer Lewalski
Donne's "Anniversaries" and the Poetry of Praise: The Creation of a Symbolic Mode (Princeton, N.J.: Princeton Univ. Pr., 1973), pp. 39, 259–60

Holy Sonnet XIV provides a particularly apt illustration of [Donne's] mannerist assault upon the normal patterns of logic or belief. It is obvious enough that the violence of the opening lines performs the same function as "Spit in my face . . . ," plunging the reader into the self-flagellative mood of the meditator:

> Batter my heart, three person'd God; for, you
> As yet but knocke, breathe, shine, and seeke to mend;

But it succeeds also (and almost unnoticed) in impatiently brushing aside the conventional conception of prayer as a plea to God for an alleviation of suffering and for a merciful mitigation of the punishments incurred by sin. Here the longing is not for a remission but for an intensification of torture in the knowledge that suffering must precede forgiveness and frailties be purged painfully away before the hard-won faith can be attained. Once again, the path Donne chooses is tortuous and steep, bypassing any easy roads to penitence and forgiveness. That is why the sonnet invokes the Trinity here—a phenomenon rare in the writings of Donne who, in the Jesuit tradition, tends to address himself almost exclusively to Christ. For the invocation introduces into a position of prominence God the Father, as the symbol of vengeance or retribution, the prerequisite for atonement. In the triplet sequences which correspond to the respective members of the Trinity—"knocke, breathe, shine" and "breake, blowe, burn"—first place is assigned to the crushing of the human spirit as the necessary prelude for the inspiration of the Holy Ghost and the warming or cleansing benevolence of the Son (here, as elsewhere, identified with the life-giving sun). The vehemence of the opening has served, therefore, not only to subvert the conventional view of prayer but also to presage the violent, searing torture which the speaker demands in place of the shedding of guilt traditionally conferred by the Church upon its prodigal sons. . . .

In a magnificent peroration, the imprisoned soul pleads for divine rescue from this subservience to worldy lusts, conjuring up an image in which the spiritual meaning dwarfs the physical anomaly, again by inverting normal logical perspective:

> Divorce mee, untie, or brake that knot againe,
> Take me to you, imprison mee, for I
> Except you enthrall mee, never shall be free,
> Nor ever chast, except you ravish mee.

The subtlety here—that serious word-play in Donne's religious writing—is the double meaning of "enthrall," which compresses within itself the polarized elements of the image. On the surface level, the soul absurdly asks to be "enslaved" in order to be freed. But "enthrall" means also to "fascinate"; a man entranced becomes oblivious of the factual world about him, withdrawn and totally absorbed in his inner experience or meditation. So here, the agonized soul recognizes that, since reason has failed, it can achieve its release from the tyranny of the flesh only by means of a willing submission to the divine ecstasy which, on breaking the "knot," raises the soul from the body. In that sense it must be enthralled in order to be free. And the image reaches its climax in the concluding line

> Nor ever chast, except you ravish mee.

Murray Roston
The Soul of Wit: A Study of John Donne (Oxford: Clarendon, 1974), pp. 172–74

MICHAEL DRAYTON

1563–1631

For all his antiquated ways—and from the standpoint of fashion they had a faint mustiness almost from the beginning—Drayton's sentiments place him among the increasingly vocal faction of his day known as "the Country," which one historian has aptly described as "that large, indeterminate, unpolitical, but highly sensitive miscellany of men," who would rebel "not against the monarchy (they had long clung to monarchist beliefs) nor against economic archaism (it was they who were the archaists), but against the vast, oppressive, ever-extending apparatus of parasitic bureaucracy which had grown up around the throne and above the economy of England." Drayton is one of the few articulate literary spokesmen for the Country at a time when virtually all the worthwhile English poetry belongs to the ambience of Court and City. Poets of this milieu, with its sophisticated liberality and ease, are seldom moved to protest against laxity in government or against desecration of nature and tradition.

Drayton's poetry must have had a large audience, given the frequency with which his works were reprinted in the earlier seventeenth century, but what kind of readers were they? I have given some account of the friends and associates who form the core of this audience, many of whom, like Drayton, had roots in the English midlands, with its viable tradition of nonconformism and independence. They do not seem to have shared the tastes, let alone the values, of those who enjoyed Donne, Carew, Herrick, or the Cavaliers. Nor was Drayton's readership like that of Ben Jonson, which consisted of "small circles in which aristocratic and cultivated people knew each other intimately." On the contrary, it is fairly certain that Drayton was attempting to write for a national audience, as is hinted in his dedicating the 1627 volume to "the noblest gentlemen of these renowned Kingdoms of Great Britain." . . .

Drayton also shares the Neo-Classical sense of the public man, a concern so dominant in his poetry that characters and lyric personae are often intolerably flat and two dimensional. This is explained in that, taken as a whole, his poetry chronicles the moment in English history when the society became aware of itself as a nation. Drayton carries on the epideicticism of medieval and Renaissance poetry, with origins that reach into remote human antiquity, but there is a difference; for whereas the earlier poets grounded their praise and blame in the deeds of single men or factions, Drayton's subject is finally his whole nation. The Britannia on the title page of *Poly-Olbion* is a mythic depiction of the national self, as venerable as Arthur, Alexander, or any of the old "worthies." Drayton's work thus belongs to an era in the history of European poetry that begins with Camoens and Tasso and continues through Tolstoy. This transition from individual to national epideicticism corresponds to the change that takes place in the chivalric hero. On the surface, the world of Drayton's narratives resembles that of Malory's romances—a world of courtly amours, tournaments, single combats, and the like; but the fortunes of Mortimer, Robert of Normandy, the Black Prince, and others in Drayton's pantheon are inextricably grafted to those of the whole nation. In *The Battle of Agincourt* the old quest for fame and personal virtue becomes a search for national fulfillment, just as, in Tudor society, the old chivalric knight yielded precedence to the statesman and field general. Drayton's heroes belong ostensibly to the chivalric tradition, but they derive their real significance from their roles in government—or, as in the cases of Gaveston or Queen Margaret, in the undoing of government.

Richard F. Hardin
Michael Drayton and the Passing of Elizabethan England
(Lawrence: Regents Press of Kansas, 1973), pp. 132–35

Michael Drayton's *Poly-Olbion* is usually approached as a curiosity, the longest topological poem in English, curious in its antiquarian learning and still more curious in its apparent design to chart with a cartographer's accuracy every tract, river, mountain, forest, dell in Great Britain. Scholarly studies of *Poly-Olbion*—Gerhard Buchloh's *Michael Drayton, Barde und Historiker, Politiker und Prophet* and Alice d'Haussy's *Poly-Olbion; ou, L'Angleterre vue par un Élizabéthain*—have for the most part attempted to evaluate the poem in terms of its use of antiquarian materials. Yet, though we must be aware how Drayton's work is rooted in the historical traditions of Elizabethan England, we must not forget its poetical design. Drayton divided *Poly-Olbion* not into chapters or books, but into songs, and consistently he subordinates whatever history he is recounting to the lyrical mode of these songs. In his preface, moreover, he promises readers pleasures of a poetical order. For our delight Drayton will create a perfect world of nature in which we may hear "harmless Shepheards . . . some exercising their pipes, some singing roundelaies, to their grazing flocks" and may see "dainty Nymphes in their simple naked bewties, bathing them in Crystalline streams." . . .

Drayton in writing topological pastoral is dealing with a very special kind of poetry. The nymphs and shepherds to whom he alludes in his preface are, of course, the actual features of the landscape anthropomorphized. Thus forest nymphs are not merely nymphs who inhabit forests, but the forests themselves; hill shepherds, not the conventional complainers upon hillsides, but the hills. This genre of pastoral, which is of venerable ancestry, had newly been given voice in Drayton's time by Spenser in *Colin Clouts Come Home Again* and in Book IV, canto 11 of *The Faerie Queene*, the "marriage" of the Thames and the Medway. But Drayton's purposes in using topological pastoral are not those of his master Spenser. Whereas Spenser had used it as embellishment to complement the main action of the poem and had relegated it to set pieces, Drayton uses it as his principal device. Topological characters are the main characters in Drayton, topological "action" the only action of his poem. However these ladies and gentlemen of the landscape may resemble real or fictional heroines and heroes, they do not exist in Drayton's pastoral to call these to mind. Humanity has been excluded from *Poly-Olbion* except as topological characters themselves look at human beings and the world of men.

Thus, Drayton's kind of pastoral requires some adjustment on the part of the reader. Held together as it is by a series of dramatic incidents in which the persons of the landscape are described as and act like human beings, *Poly-Olbion* consistently tempts the reader to view it as a pastoral masque in which "hills" and "rivers" are merely human beings in fancy dress. . . .

Drayton has created this little drama perhaps for the sheer fancy of it, perhaps to glance wryly at the absurdities of romance that it mimics. What is most important, however, is that in telling his story of rivalry and rejected love, he has taken care to "ground" it in topological truth. We see the landscape better, not worse, for Drayton's story. Consistently Drayton aims to transcend nature, to heighten it, to render it—as Sidney said the artist must—yet more golden, but never to deny it.

Stella P. Revard
SEL (Spring, 1977), pp. 105–7

JOHN FORD

1568–after 1638

'Tis Pity She's a Whore is rare among Caroline tragedies in its use of multiple plots. In the foreground action, a bourgeois youth makes love to his sister; the background draws in various stories concerning their acquaintances in Parman society—and a greedy, lustful, jealous, vengeful, murderous, and hypocritical group they are. How one interprets the interaction between main and subplots is important, because on this relationship rests the overall structural design of the play. . . .

What really defines the interaction between main and subplots is a sliding scale of social acceptability. The incestuous and the non-incestuous are all driven by identical feelings and desires, by rabid egotism, power lust, jealousy, and vengefulness. Who will stand and who will fall is determined by the degree of overt sexuality manifested: the more passion there is in a person's jealousy, the more his cruelty springs from lust, the more certain he is to face social isolation and a violent death. Only the cold and chaste

—whatever their egotism—rank among the normal, the rational, the safe. . . .

The complexity of *'Tis Pity*'s overall design lies in the interaction of the various subplots with the main plot and with one another. We are not being asked to condone incest because Parma is full of people at least as wicked as the lovers. We are being asked to see the underlying relationships which join socially unacceptable kinds of behavior to behavior which, although equally egotistic and destructive, avoids passion and claims to work through justice. The moral world of *'Tis Pity* is all of a piece. Honor (men's self-image, their drive towards power) governs everywhere; fantasies of sovereignty over fate abound. Each man lives in a private kingdom, and is king. Simultaneously, everyone lives in society, and some expressions of the secret will are more acceptable than others. Those free of sex and wed to "reason" are most acceptable of all. So, while every individual occupies a private place and views every other as part of *his* universe, all men together occupy an objective universe where their atomistic desires are in constant turbulence, constant tension. The pattern of reverberation and interaction, of clashing wills bound to universally similar drives, constitutes the pattern through which we in the audience must discern justice. The picture which emerges is a heavily ironic one.

Some critics have assumed that Ford is so obsessed with abnormal psychology and the hothouse world of personal relationships that he finds the only true reality in private vows. Moralistic interpreters go so far the other way that they sometimes reduce the play to the level of *exemplum* and deny the characters any inner life at all. Actually, Ford's achievement is an integration of private and public which produces an analysis of human behavior shot through with the lurid illumination of an uncompromising irony. The overall design cannot be "reduced" at all.

A. P. Hogan
SEL (Summer, 1977), pp. 303–4, 316

GEORGE GASCOIGNE

ca. 1535–1577

When we scan the whole body of Gascoigne's lyric poetry to determine what is and what is not valuable, the first quality that strikes us is the intensely personal character of the poetry. The poems are the subjective record of emotions, of feelings, and of reactions to the surrounding world. For the most part, Gascoigne makes himself the subject of his poems, and we see him in a variety of attitudes—examining his relations with ladies of the court, his loss of youth and subsequent loss of attractiveness, his failures, his fear of dying, and so forth. At other times, he writes of his reaction to the changing society around him. In either instance, the poet is recognizable behind the poem; he is not obscured by it, partly because he seldom relies on artificial conventions. His lyric poetry is an extension of himself, of all parts of his personality, and is not bland or impersonal as is so much of the contemporary poetry.

A second quality of Gascoignes's poetry is its variety. In its subject matter, its mood, its verse form, and its technique, it achieves great breadth of applicability and effect. The subject matter includes many aspects of love; it includes social criticism and self-analysis. Its approach is philosophic, religious, mock-serious, and didactic. His poetry enters nearly all fields and experiments with nearly all kinds of verse form. His mood varies from tenderness to harsh cynicism, but the emphasis is on pessimism.

Finally, the question of whether all this poetry is or is not good boils down to poetic technique; and we have found that, when Gascoigne borrows the technique of the Petrarchan imitators, his poetry is usually poor. But most of the poems which do not imitate are successful; some, excellent. Gascoigne usually writes to discover or establish a truth in poetry. That truth may vary from showing the validity of an old Latin proverb to precisely delineating the position of a certain lover in his quest for satisfaction. To establish truth, he uses proverbs, examples, similes, metaphors, analogies—in short, the usual poetical or rhetorical figures. Upon occasion he uses a symbol. When the truth is established, or proven, the success of the poem usually depends on the depth or sophistication of the particular truth. But, when the truth is reinforced by the mood of the poem, however created, either through diction as in "Lullabye" or through poetical figures as in "Gascoignes Wodmanship," so that the content and the mood interact and cause tension or irony to result, the poem can approach brilliance, as these two poems do.

Thus, to answer satisfactorily the question of Gascoigne's ability as a poet, we can say at least that the following qualities of his verse are valuable: the variety of his verse form and content; the accuracy of his social and psychological perception; the control of tone he exhibits in his lighter poems such as "Gascoignes Recantation" and "Gascoignes Araignement"; and his departure from the tradition of Petrarch.

Ronald C. Johnson
George Gascoigne (Boston: Twayne, 1972), pp. 72–73

Gascoigne has, by his use of the lullaby metaphor [in "Lullabie"] found a profound link between what before were perceived as mere opposites; this link presupposes a specific way of seeing experience and how it might be represented in poetry. And this way is far different from that underlying the enumerative method. Topics here are not simply abstract conceptions by which to judge experience as if it could be isolated into atomic units of significant substance. Thus, the possibility is opened for a different kind of poem, a true alternative to the still prevalent literary modes of the fifteenth-century lyric: the cataloguing encomium or complaint. Such poems might provide the wherewithal to examine relationships not as if they were fixed and static, but rather as the result of a process that paralleled the relational character of actual experience. Many of Wyatt's poems are precisely the kind that make relationship itself the center of interest, often the relation between the old way of composing and perceiving the experience of love set against something new and painfully difficult to apprehend, which he calls by many names, among them newfangledness or change. Newfangledness, as a topic, was long familiar to the medieval poets, but never treated by them as fit for analysis in complex relation to other topics. Like Wyatt, Gascoigne sees complex relationship itself as a vital subject for poetry. More particularly, he sees that through available poetic structure, he can connect apparently antithetical aspects of experience. The poet's task for him, then, is to invent a controlling figure of sufficient richness and appropriateness to give the poet tonal scope to do justice to the complexity of the experienced relation. And that "Lullabie" is not a mere accident is attested to by another of Gascoigne's poems, "Woodsmanship," which links youth and age (or at least middle age) in a yet richer and more serious way. . . .

The principle of composition Gascoigne employs, however he came upon it, gave him an instrument of considerable range in dealing with common human experience. Moreover, each of these principles assumes a way of perceiving reality. The mannered and schematic tonality in [Thomas] Vaux's poem ["The Aged Lover Renounceth Love"] is the direct result of a categorical way of seeing reality, while Gascoigne's more open, subtle (though no less formal) voice is the direct consequence of a more fluid and relational way of seeing things. Indeed, it might be said that the topic of poems that come from this mode of seeing is always relationship itself. And it is this latter kind of poem that seems to me to appear in the Renaissance for the first time in numbers that suggest it is as characteristic of the time as it is uncharacteristic of fifteenth-century poetry. I have already mentioned its presence in Wyatt and have noted that Gascoigne's most impressive poem, "Woodsmanship," partakes of the mode, as does also Ralegh's "Even Such as Time," Sidney's "With How Sad Steps," and Jonson's "On My First Son." It might be argued that the structure of Shakespeare's great tragedies is akin to that of these poems, leading the auditor to a perception not of categories but of relationships.

Leonard Nathan
in *The Rhetoric of Renaissance Poetry*, ed. Thomas O. Sloan and Raymond B. Waddington (Berkeley: Univ. California Pr., 1974), pp. 69–71

ROBERT GREENE

1558–1592

James IV, probably Greene's last play, does not deserve one critic's epithet of "moral tragedy"; it does, however, bring coherence to its jumble of literary bits and pieces and provides a complex view of human passion and its social effects. In response to the potential intricacies of his subject, Greene elaborately complicates two features of the play: its treatment of dramatic illusion and its handling of romantic, pastoral, and comic conventions. Finally, the play makes no claim to a satisfactory comic resolution of the moral and social crises it presents. . . .

Greene ordinarily links the two chief plots of his play by the simplest and most common method: a single character (Ida) appears in both the story of James's attempted adultery and in the contrasting story of pure young love, purely achieved (Ida and Eustace). . . .

Greene evidently had the skill necessary to organize this sort of multiple parallel among diverse activities and tropes. In common with some of his fellow playwrights, he also probes—sometimes skillfully, sometimes confusingly—the relation between dramatic illusion and the dual realities represented by the theater audience and the stage audience. The frame story of Bohan and Oberon—within which the play of James IV, his wife, and his love nominally serves as an exemplary anecdote—does raise the question of illusion. More importantly, the combination of frame story and internal play enlarges Greene's technical resources in achieving his overall effect. . . . Greene has encircled the conventions of the internal play with another illusion having conventions of its own and dramatic aims necessarily different from those implicit in the internal play. Indeed, he has underlined the greater reality of Bohan and Oberon; after all, "even" they agree that they witness a theatrical event. I would argue that this complex structure has two effects: it forms part of Greene's challenge to many conventions of Renaissance drama and romance, and it signals his attempt to penetrate beyond the standard situations and responses. . . .

Although Greene has rather mechanically separated the representatives of opposed attitudes toward love between the frame plot and its interior play, the interior romance itself frequently abandons convention or introduces new possibilities in order to diversify its portrayal of love. To achieve its full effect, the play must end with a contradiction between its courtly interior and misanthropic circumference. . . . By exaggerating the play's literariness, by turning conventional situations upside-down, by erecting a complicated set of theatrical illusions, Greene argues that complex human emotion cannot be simplified through dramatic and romantic commonplaces.

First trials in any new form often depend upon an analytic power which in turn creates structural images and oppositions such as the frame-interior play division in *James IV*. Only the greatest of Elizabethan dramatists could achieve synthetic resolution hard upon this sort of analytic discovery, and it is no grave charge that Greene made only an original step rather than an entire journey. *James IV* deserves to be read as more than a strong hint of Shakespeare's future and rival successes in romantic comedy. With all its flaws of haste, incomplete development, and unsatisfactory amalgamation of literary forms, the play anticipates the darkness of *Measure for Measure* as well as the light of *As You Like It*.

A. R. Braunmuller
ELR (Fall, 1973), pp. 337–39, 350

FULKE GREVILLE

1554–1628

How can the compressed abstractions of Greville's best lyrics secure the same imaginative assent that generations of cultivated readers have granted to the much broader epic narrations of Dante or of Milton? One way that they can do so, as I have been concerned to point out, is by being examined largely in terms of their emotional consequences, by being employed to judge experience that is universally accessible. Another way is simply that which has been universally acknowledged, even by those critics who do not much like it: by the "sheer power of mind" which distinguishes their presentation. . . .

Greville's lyrics can offer us the pleasures of cogency in a direct and highly pressurized form. To appreciate them we have only to allow poetry a resource possible to any use of language, and to see this resource not as frozen rigidity but as potential liberation, as one of the few and fallible means we have to explore the inner spaces of our nature. For what these pleasures finally imply involves yet another principle of Renaissance orthodoxy and modern heresy: they imply that we delight in learning and that poetry can teach. . . .

What, therefore, the poet communicates, and what we perceive with aesthetic pleasure, is nothing more nor less than an understanding of experience and of ourselves. There are to be sure many ways of understanding, just as there are many kinds of poetry, many kinds of order that can be imposed. Greville's is one kind; indeed, it is the most obvious kind, and for this reason possibly the most efficient. For to express emotions as they emerge from a chain of reasoning is not only to discipline and comprehend those that we may share, but also to enable us to become aware of those that we may not. Our own feelings are often sufficiently baffling; those of others which do not coincide with our own, which are elicited by different objects and formed by different experiences, are wholly so, unless their motives are communicated to us by some mental process which is mutually known or knowable. And to obtain pleasure in the process as it unfolds in a poem is one way by which we may be led to an awareness of what is beyond the narrow limits of our actual experience, or indeed of what is within it had we only noticed. The effect of such poetry is to get us out of ourselves, to enlarge our perception of the world by providing through the understanding not only an understanding but a full, sympathetic, and disinterested contact with other human beings. In whatever guise it presents itself, this is a precious gift: it is the gift of civilization, and we cannot afford to refuse it.

Richard Waswo
The Fatal Mirror: Themes and Techniques in the Poetry of Fulke Greville (Charlottesville: Univ. Pr. Virginia, 1972), pp. 165–67

GEORGE HERBERT

1593–1633

In all, the direction of will defines man's spiritual condition, and Herbert in nothing represents Reformation interests and attitudes more clearly than in putting such weight on will. The urgings of the self, according to his constant message, are opposition to God and the means of our destruction. To bend our will in childlike submission to God's is the way of holiness and the condition of grace. . . .

What speaks most strongly in the poem ["Holy Baptisme, II"] is the sense of man's entire helplessness and emptiness until helped and filled by God. No spiritual effort is possible for him, no escape from his wretchedness as the useless anomaly in a creation dedicated to function. He is nothing until grace is given and only emerges into significant being as the factor which defines his individuality, his will and self-purpose, is lost in God. Faced logically the situation is a hopeless conundrum, as the mock-logic of "The Holdfast" makes clear. . . .

The great chain concept is explicitly rejected for man in Herbert's poem; humans are omitted from the ordered associations of the creation. Will has made a breach which only the destruction of the will can close again, and while Herbert and Protestantism are free to contemplate the order and plenitude of the creation in general, their vision of continuity finds a gap at man. This is of course a staggering exception, and it means that when the metaphysical imagination of the seventeenth-century Protestant attends to its primary subject, the relations of man with God and the problems of salvation, it occupies itself with a wholly different framework of ideas and metaphors, those of discontinuity, opposition and conflict—dualism so decided as to have suggested the term "Manichean" to the critics cited earlier [I. A. Richards and Murray Krieger].

But the dualism, as we have seen, can be conquered by the action of God's grace and the grace-motivated subjugation of the will. It is a condition in which hope outweighs despair and which, I have argued, leads in poetry to excitements of opposition and reconciliation. In Herbert, it leads to certain other poetic qualities. . . .

Despite his virtuoso mastery of his art and his manifest pleasure in artifice, Herbert will be plain. Plainness may, of course, have been legislated by other considerations than simply the need to put down will. Ruth Wallerstein and others would put us in mind that Augustine had rhetorical as well as theological importance to seventeenth-century poets and that a long tradition descending from Augustine prescribed a low style in preaching. But Herbert seems to give his reasons fully in the second "Jordan" poem where, in a series of brilliant and striking images, he deplores fancy effects in religious verse as contaminations of self. . . . The plain style, on the other hand, works the self out, and that overthrow and submission—with no concessions to the idea of progress or improvement—was, of course, a basic Reformation project.

William H. Halewood
The Poetry of Grace: Reformation Themes and Structures
(New Haven, Conn.: Yale Univ. Pr., 1970), pp. 106–7, 110–11

In order to make [the] reunion of Christ and nature possible in [*The Temple*], Herbert must rehabilitate not only such modes as the song and sonnet but also pastoral. Rather than merely repeating conventional purling streams and the artifices of Arcadian courtship, he must draw them into the precincts of the temple's symbolism and make them an aspect of the incarnation, a habitation of the Word. In the temple it is possible to recreate such an emblematic universe of symbols that look backward toward Eden and forward to paradise restored. By reconstituting these in the poetic enclosure of *The Temple*, Herbert seeks to find God again making "one place ev'ry where." The heart, the temple, and the poem, the symbolic objects, views, "window-songs," and ritual patterns that the priest and the poet arrange for the reader may then become an epitome of a greater creation, a single organic and harmonic order. . . .

Within *The Temple* proper, the purgative functions of verse accomplish more than the moral redirection of the youthful reader. As an imitation of Christ, a poem offers an image of original beauty; as personal expression and confession, it clears the way for the poet's own union with God; as rhetoric, it negotiates between the poet and God and between the poet and his audience; as narrative, it recapitulates history and discovers in the temporal progression of the Old and New Testaments an anagogic reality that continually prefigures paradise; and as description, it discovers recurrent signs of paradise in the seasons and in nature's potentially emblematic objects. The structure of *The Temple* through the first sequence of poems (to "Easter-wings") is a complex overlaying of these functions of poetry and of several modes of progression: the poet's and the reader's initial entry into the "temple"; the historical events of Christ's life that set the pattern for the church's liturgical offices, sacrifice, death and rebirth, and all symbolic passages from the old to the new dispensation ("The Sacrifice," "Good Friday," "Redemption," "Sepulchre," "Easter"); the poet's search for an appropriate medium ("The Altar," "The Thanksgiving," "Good Friday," "Easter," "Easter-wings"); and the sinner's handling of the barriers that sin erects against the mystical repast ("The Reprisal," "The Agonie," "The Sinner," "Redemption"). These modes of progress are recapitulated in "Easter-wings," which sorts them out and clarifies them, in a preliminary way, before they become the substance of subsequent detailed explorations of the three "temples"—heart, poem, church—and their epitomizing of patterns dispersed in nature and in scriptural chronicles.

Harold Toliver
Pastoral Forms and Attitudes (Berkeley: Univ. California Pr., 1971), pp. 118–21

One of the particular virtues of Herbert's poetry is its provisional quality. His poems are ready at any moment to change direction or to modify attitudes. Even between the title and the first line, Herbert may rethink his position. There are lines in which the nominal experiences or subjects have suffered a sea-change, so that the poem we think we are reading turns into something quite other. The more extreme cases occur in Herbert's "surprise endings," in what Valentina Poggi calls his "final twist," in which Herbert "dismisses the structure, issues, and method" of the entire poem, "rejecting the established terms" on which the poem has been constructed. A case in point is "Clasping of Hands," which ends, after playing for nineteen lines on the notions of "thine" and "mine," with the exclamation, "Or rather make no Thine and Mine!" In cases less abrupt, Herbert's fluid music lulls our questions: we scarcely see his oddities, or if we see them, they cease to seem odd, robed in the seamless garment of his cadence. . . .

The inveterate human tendency to misrepresent what has happened is nowhere more strongly criticized than in Herbert. Under his repetitive and unsparing review, the whole truth finally becomes clear. Herbert knows that to appear pious is not to be pious; to pay formal tribute is not to love; servilely to acknowledge power is not to wonder; to utter grievances is not to pray. His readers, often mistaking the language of piety for the thing itself, are hampered by dealing with an unfamiliar discourse. We have a rich sense of social deception in human society and can detect a note of social falseness in a novel almost before it appears; but it sometimes does not occur to us that the same equivocations, falseness, self-justifications, evasions, and defensive reactions can occur in a poet's colloquies with his God. We recognize defiance when it is overt, as in "The Collar" or "Affliction" (I), but other poems where the presentation is more subtle elicit assenting readings and token nods to Herbert's sweetness or humility. Herbert spoke of himself in "Affliction" (IV) as "a wonder tortur'd," and his own estimate of himself can be a guide in reading his poems. . . .

It makes little difference to Herbert where he finds his *donnée*—in the images of courtly poetry, in the Bible, in his personal experience. The artless borrowed beginning soon becomes the scrutinized personal statement. The anxiety that must have made Herbert want to begin with the safe, the bland, the familiar, and the taken-for-granted coexists permanently with the aggression that impelled him almost immediately to criticize the received idea. He seems to have existed in a permanent reversible equilibrium between the two extremes of tradition and originality, diffidence and protest, the filial and the egotistic. His poems do not "resolve" these extremes into one attitude; rather, they permit successive and often mutually contradictory expressions of the self as it explores the truth of feeling. At any moment, a poem by Herbert can repudiate itself, correct itself, rephrase itself, rethink its experience, reinvent its topic. In this free play of ideas lies at least part of Herbert's true originality.

Helen Vendler
The Poetry of George Herbert (Cambridge, Mass.: Harvard Univ. Pr., 1975), pp. 25, 54, 56

ROBERT HERRICK

1591–1674

However much he owes to Jonson, Herrick is more than an imitation or smaller Jonson. I make the point aggressively because it has been fashionable for some years to patronize or even denigrate Herrick's achievement. One can easily see what might support that fashion. Even at their best, the 2500 or so epigrams and lyrics of *Hesperides* and *Noble Numbers* are like bonbons in at least one respect: tasting too many at a sitting can result in severe discomfort. And even read in moderate numbers, Herrick's poems often seem too facile, and some of them are silly as well as repetitious. Herrick is often afflicted with archness. . . .

Herrick tends to be at his best when he is celebrating festivals, English or Latin or natural (Jonson may have suggested the direction; "Ceremonies for Christmas" and "Ceremonies for Candlemas Eve" are examples), and when he is writing of evanescence. The word "superficial" may be justly applied to much of Herrick's poetry, but it is one of Herrick's strengths rather than weaknesses that this is so. Herrick is continually concerned both with the surfaces of natural and human beauty and with the linguistic surfaces of his poems. And he is concerned often in a special way with the intricacies of appearances, the subtleties of surfaces and what they suggest: lawn, silk, crystal, cream, water, skin as they partially or momentarily reveal a lady's body, a lily, strawberries, pebbles, blood, and bone. A man who so loves the surface beauties of this world almost inevitably comes to feel the poignant brevity of such beauty and of this life. That is the subject of "To Daffodils," one of Herrick's loveliest poems. . . .

Joseph H. Summers
The Heirs of Donne and Jonson (New York: Oxford Univ. Pr., 1970), pp. 56–57

In a sense Herrick often redeemed his Celtic paganism by lightly classicizing it, and his classicism by lightly Christianizing it. Similarly, he redeemed love-making by having it lead directly to marriage. One of Herrick's longer poems, "The Hock-cart, or Harvest Home" (55 lines) seeks to create the quality of country life by presenting it in terms of a rural festival. The element of ceremony will be found in the repetition of certain words (e.g., "Come . . ." or "Some . . ."), and a certain "Devotion" appears in the blessing of crops and in drinking. Anyone with a decent edition will know that Herrick draws on Tibullus, *Odes*, II. i and can see by comparison how the classical, pagan spirit has been acclimatized. Herrick's debt is real, but his poem is very English. Dedicated "To the Right Honourable Mildmay, Earle of Westmorland," it addresses the "Sons of Summer, by whose toile,/ We are the Lords of Wine and Oile" (1–2). The message simply says, Drink today, because tomorrow you must work:

> And that this pleasure is like raine,
> Not sent ye for to drowne your paine,
> But for to make it spring againe. (53–55)

I can see many virtues and interests in this. How interesting that the *carpe diem* urging should enter the social realm. How much we can prize an accurate and unvarnished explanation. But the rigid stratification of society and the unblinking affirmation of "paine" for the hinds and "Oile" for the gentleman is too much for me. (How much more generous Jonson's "To Penshurst" is.) My distaste does not extend to Corinna; the rituals employed by Herrick in his vain effort to win her are to me the timeless ceremonies and decencies of the heart.

The best religious poetry of the Cavaliers seldom rates being called their best poetry, but it does emphasize the importance of ceremony. Herrick's "Ceremonies for Christmasse" is to be sure in the *Hesperides*, and it is no more Christian than Jonson's *Christmas his Masque*. Not that I think with Bunyan that it is sinful to enjoy oneself. "Ceremonies for Candlemasse Eve" (the feast celebrating the Virgin's presentation of Christ in the Temple) concludes with ceremonies suggesting very well the way in which observation of rites is a way of dealing with the times.

> Green Rushes then, and sweetest Bents,
> With cooler Oken boughs;
> Come in for comely ornaments,
> To re-adorn the house.
> Thus times do shift; each thing his turne do's hold;
> *New things succeed, as former things grow old.*
> (17–22)

There is much to commend in ceremonies growing from the natural cycle of the seasons or the cycles of marriage, birth, and death, because recognition of such fundamental cycles provides a ritual that affirms facts of life that our powers of abstraction often conceal.

Earl Miner
The Cavalier Mode from Jonson to Cotton (Princeton, N.J.: Princeton Univ. Pr., 1971), pp. 192–93

It has been said that Herrick's poems show clear affinities to the masque genre. Nowhere is this relationship more suggestive than in the verses of the courtly persona. His is a stylized, highly ordered, and, in some ways, simplified world. Events are important because they actualize the little ritualistic codes which make up the courtly existence. Each lyric in this vein is essentially the working out of one small part of the court experience, presenting little real anxiety, little worry or human difficulty, but rather the surface brilliance of an ultimately successful masque. Taken together, the whole body of courtly lyrics makes up a masque of this form of life. Each poem presents one more aspect of the particular urban sensibility and to enjoy the poem is to participate, perhaps even cultivate, that sensibility. The reader's participation is similar in this respect to the final dance of audience and actors in the court masque—it unites him in the celebratory rite of the courtly world. . . .

Like his pastoral counterpart, [the strictly courtly] persona is more concerned with the presentation of a *poetic* ceremony than with anything else. That is, he is not concerned to present a verse-compliment, to display his wit, or to glorify a particular person; he is concerned with the presentation and the artistic amplification of a given moment of poetic celebration. Whatever the ostensible subject of the poem, the voice of this persona directs the reader's attention to the strictly literary act which the poem involves. . . .

It is not necessary to regard every poem in the *Hesperides* as ceremonial to see that celebration is the governing intention behind most of them and that the poetic ceremonial is the shaping principle through which that intent is most often actualized. By transforming literal and private actions into significant, public rituals, Herrick's poems continually isolate and re-present, in heightened and ordered form, key moments of human experience. By freeing these moments from temporal control, the poet leads us to an understanding of what each involves. Surely one measure of his success in demonstrating how meaningful these ritual moments are is the freedom and the ease with which we, as readers, can commit ourselves to the constructed rites.

To a large extent, however, the true success of the *Hesperides* lies not with individual poems. There are, certainly, some poems here as fine in their way as any of the century—"Corinna," "Delight in Disorder," "The Night-piece, to Julia," "The Argument," the "Sack" poems, and so on—but it is a feeling of joy and festivity, even of a kind of free abandonment to the vitality of communal impulses, which is evoked by a reading of the volume as a whole. The artistic stasis which Herrick achieves within the limits of his poetical garden does in fact go far beyond the mutability concerns giving rise to the book. In this way Herrick raises larger questions about the act of creative writing itself and the function of poetry within the framework of human experience.

To pursue this line of thought but one step further, it is possible perhaps to see the *Hesperides* as a kind of poetical dialectic. By using different personae, Herrick is able to pit one ceremonial approach to existence against another, to show that each is significant on its own terms and within its own limits, and to demonstrate that the *poetic* ceremonial, the rite of artistic or imaginative creation, is one means of actualizing all these approaches simultaneously.

A. Leigh Deneef
"This Poetick Liturgie": Robert Herrick's Ceremonial Mode
(Durham, N.C.: Duke Univ. Pr., 1974), pp. 106–7, 192

RICHARD HOOKER

1554–1600

If he is read today at all, Richard Hooker is read as the author of a single work, the massive treatise *Of the Laws of Ecclesiastical Polity*. Yet his other writings, if one includes Chapters iv–vi of Book VI, the "tract of confession" over which the dispute arose at Hooker's death, amount to one-quarter of his extant work. Largely unexplored, they reveal the essentially inward bias of his mind, and they set forth, independently of the disciplinarian context of the *Laws*, the doctrinal assumptions that underlie its defense of established polity. From the perspective of these non-*Polity* writings, the *Laws*, for all its length, its wealth of illustrative detail, and meticulous argumentation, is simply an application *in extenso* of more general principles that Hooker enunciates elsewhere. Predestination and free will, grace and assurance may seem to have little bearing on the question of the authority of bishops as opposed to that of lay elders, or the ecclesiastical supremacy of the Queen. But to see these doctrinal issues as Hooker himself saw them is to see the arguments of the *Laws* in a perspective nearer to Hooker's own, one less colored by the pervasively controversial bias of his lay collaborators, George Cranmer and Edwin Sandys, the later partisanship of his biographer, Izaak Walton, and the ecclesiastical authority of his superior and patron, Archbishop Whitgift.

There is evidence that his contemporaries too saw Hooker as a theologian, and not primarily as a political theorist. Among his friends, Lancelot Andrewes feared more for the safety of the sermons and early tracts at Hooker's death than for the "three last books" on church polity. The plans of Hooker's literary executors to publish those books were frustrated by Andrewes' insistence that a "tract of confession," evidently written in the 1580's, be inserted into Book VI. Among his foes, his early antagonist, Walter Travers, attacked Hooker publicly for doctrinal error. . . . Similarly, the authors of *A Christian Letter*, the only published answer to the *Laws* in Hooker's lifetime, accuse Hooker of sacrificing the faith of the Church to an expedient defense of its established polity. . . .

His lifework was conceived as an attempt to cleanse of every ambiguity and to ground in all possible certainty this fundamental truth of human experience. Thus, the theme of truth in its inward and subjective dimension, as assurance, certainty of belief, solidity and resolution of conscience, became the central concern of his thought. It is first articulated in the *Tractates*; later, it is exemplified in the *Laws* and applied to the defense of his own Church. To the question, where was a man to find faith—that sense of personal vindication before an all-seeing and all-powerful God within a subjective world where absolute value was deemed fundamental to man's nature as a human creature—Hooker's answer combined a compelling and humane exposition of the central tenet of Reformation theology, justification by faith, with a massive restatement of the central tradition of reason in Western European thought.

W. Speed Hill
ELR (Summer, 1972), pp. 173–74, 193

BEN JONSON

1572–1637

Jonson's finest achievement probably lies in his ability to arouse in us a total conviction of his moral integrity, of the good man searching himself and others, of the good life being glimpsed and sought for with strenuous effort. And it does not exclude other qualities. When he addressed various of his contemporaries, his skill with epigram frequently produced wonderful *obiter dicta*. . . .

Jonson's conception of the good man is precisely that, a conception, an artistic creation and a view of life. How far we may go toward identifying the values in what is created with those in the life is always a question. Physicians often neglect their health or mistreat themselves, and the moralists often find it easier to lead than to follow. We have the evidence of the extraordinary number of poems celebrating him after his death to understand that although his contemporaries knew Jonson's considerable faults ("Hee's not a man hath none"), they accepted them and the man because of his far greater virtues. And although some may question whether poetic evidence can be accepted for biographical fact, this much is certain: Jonson had the ability as a poet (and *I* think the fortitude as a man) to meet disaster. The epigrams on his son and daughter are too well known to quote. A less familiar poem ["An Execration upon Vulcan"], and one of Jonson's most charming, humorously remonstrates with the god of fire for burning his house in November, 1623.

Earl Miner
The Cavalier Mode from Jonson to Cotton (Princeton, N.J.: Princeton Univ. Pr., 1971), pp. 66–67

Jonson's perception of the price that men are willing to pay in order to preserve their illusions governs the structure of *Volpone*, just as it governs the structure of *The Alchemist*. In both plays there is a point at which it seems that the action must come to an abrupt end. In *Volpone* this point is reached at the end of Act III, when Bonario prevents the rape of Celia. In *The Alchemist* it is postponed until IV.vi, the scene in which Surly reveals himself to Subtle and Face, making it clear to them that he now knows exactly what has been going on. Again it looks as though the truth must come out, and again it fails to. Guided and manipulated by Face, the gulls unite to get rid of Surly because he is a threat to their hopes. And, once more, Jonson hammers home the part that self-deception has played in the comedy. . . .

While *The Alchemist* confirms that self-delusion and self-deception are, indeed, the things that Jonson "isolates for sardonic inspection," it also tells us even more than *Volpone* does about the way in which illusions can be stimulated until they bloom into gigantic fantasies. The processes used by the alchemists, together with their technical jargon, are part of the play's essential texture. . . .

Jonson, I suggest, shared Swift's distrust of the imagination. It is surely significant that he does not, so far as I can recall, use the word at all in that final section of the *Discoveries* which he devotes to the subject of poetry, though it is there, if anywhere, that one might expect to find it; and it can scarcely be an accident that it is precisely the more romantic plays of Shakespeare that elicit his scorn: "*Tales, Tempests*, and such like *Drolleries*" (*Bartholomew Fair*, Induction, 130) and "some mouldy tale,/Like *Pericles*' ("Ode to Himself," ll. 21–22). It was not, quite obviously, that he was without imagination. The plays he wrote are ample proof of the contrary. But, in so far as Jonson the dramatist is concerned, that imagination only seems to have worked at white heat when he was dealing with the follies, the vices, and the crimes of which man is capable. Whenever he seeks to give a positive representation in a play of the ethical values by which he set such store, something seems to go wrong. Cicero, in *Catiline*, is clearly meant to embody these values. Orator, moral philosopher, and statesman, he has Jonson's unqualified approval. It is his undoing. He is allowed to commit dramatic suicide by talking himself, the play, and the audience to death. Similarly, when Jonson tries to show sensual attraction between a man and a woman developing—admittedly, with much encouragement from the man's friend—into deep and disinterested friendship, as he does in *The Devil Is an Ass*, he cannot make it convincing.

G. R. Hibbard
in *A Celebration of Ben Jonson*, ed. William Blissett,
Julian Patrick, and R. W. van Fossen (Toronto:
Univ. Toronto Pr., 1972), pp. 73, 77–78

It has become increasingly clear in recent years . . . that *The Alchemist* no longer produces . . . laughter in everyone, for a number of new readings of the play have been appearing which make it sound very grim indeed. Although they are not yet in the majority, there are enough of them to constitute a significant trend—one, moreover, that seems to be growing and involves many other comedies of the period as well, so that it should be worth examining in some detail. . . .

It is much easier to identify this trend than to explain it, or even to determine what kind of explanation should be sought. Some would say that the trouble with these critics is their lack of a sense of humor, but there is no reason to believe their psychology is basically different from ours simply because they do not laugh at everything we find laughable (although this is usually all that the accusation means). Others would see it as the result of their reading drama in the study rather than watching it in the theater, but that does not get us very far either. . . .

It seems to me, however, that most if not all of these readings do have something in common—they are "thematic," in the broadest sense of that term, since they assume the particular characters and actions of each play are not really significant in themselves but only as examples or symbols or allegories of some general idea about the human condition, which is the real subject of the play. And these general ideas, by their very nature, do not define any specific emotional response: just as the concept of "chair" can tell us nothing about the color of any given chair, so the popular themes, such as "appearance vs. reality" or "art vs. nature," say nothing about the tonality or feeling of each play from which they have been abstracted. Indeed the same "central theme" can be abstracted from comedies of very different emotional textures and even from tragedies—thus one of the critics quoted earlier finds "the issues and implications are much the same" in *Sejanus, Volpone*, and *The Alchemist*, while another claims that "every play Jonson ever wrote revolves around" the same "principal themes" or "central issues" (which brings us back to the homogenization of Jonson, where we began, and points to a relationship between it and thematic analysis and these over-solemn readings of comedies that otherwise would not conform to the hypothesized Jonsonian ideal). It is therefore easy for a thematic reading to pass over or actually alter the comic quality of a play, and since most of these themes, again by their very nature, have an aura of profundity about them, one can see why they have proved so helpful in the process of decomicalization; even the simplest farce of identical twins, for example, can be upgraded by this means into a serious "demonstration" or better yet "exploration" of the "problem of personality identity" or of "Entfremdung." . . .

It should be evident that this kind of perspective will destroy almost any comedy it encounters—not only satiric comedies or comedies of intrigue, but also much more romantic comedies, since they too usually include activity that would qualify, from such a viewpoint, as a sin or at least a crime. . . . If this trend continues long enough, we may eventually witness the death of comedy, not (as in [George] Steiner's treatment of tragedy) on the public stage but in our scholarly press.

Richard Levin
SLitI (Spring, 1973), pp. 85, 92–94

THOMAS KYD

1558–1594

Arthur Freeman, *Thomas Kyd: Facts and Problems* (1967)

In *The Spanish Tragedy,* Kyd provides England with her first major tragedy, as well as with one of the first defenses of the play as an art form. However, the play undertakes its defense more along distinctly Aristotelian than broadly Horatian lines, for in acknowledging the profit which man receives from art, its concern is more specifically with art as an experience which helps man come to terms with the conditions of his world than with art as an instrument for morality. Rather than focusing on the teaching of what it is to be or not to be a good man in a flawed world, the play explores what kinds of responses can make it possible for man to endure the pain and suffering which such a world has in store. The focal point of this exploration is Hieronimo. Once he recognizes that gods and institutions do not exert an absolute control over man's destiny, his search for a meaningful response leads him to art, which, by mirroring his experiences, also helps him to learn their universal quality, a lesson which gives him some relief from his torment. Throughout Hieronimo's struggle to select the best form in which to cast his perceptions, Kyd seems to be using the Renaissance notion of poetry as a speaking picture for the touchstone against which to judge Hieronimo's success. As Hieronimo moves from the oratory of the soliloquies, to painting (in the Painter addition), to metaphor and song in the Bazulto scene, and finally to the playlet of the last scene, the conclusion inevitably emerges that drama is the form most capable of expressing the human experience because it is both *poesis* and *pictura*, and has, as well, real sound and action. . . .

In the frame episode, Andrea, who, I suggest, will change during the course of the play, searches in a thoroughly casual and unworried manner for a resting place in the underworld. Because he has no opinion at this point about what his future either will be or should be, his narrative carries no indication that revenge might be in order. When the three judges of the dead are unable to agree on his resting place, Minos sends him to Pluto. With smiling ease and a playful spirit, Prosperine gains from Pluto the chance to name Andrea's future. Her decision to give him to Revenge is not prescriptive, but descriptive. She names what the future will be because she knows how men turn circumstances into chaos. We might compare the function of Kyd's frame to that of the gods that frame some Greek tragedies; in both cases the frames are universalizing agents which indicate that the main action of the play depicts general truths about man and life. . . .

The ending scene of Andrea and Revenge reminds us that Hieronimo's play is contained within this frame and that the frame itself is part of an even larger construct. Andrea's inappropriate and unseeing response to the catastrophe of the play's end interrupts the audience's involvement with Hieronimo, and gives the audience an opportunity to gain a perspective on the impact of the work as a whole. Because *The Spanish Tragedy* contains both Andrea and Hieronimo, its matter stretches beyond what either one alone or both characters together can embody.

Donna B. Hamilton
ELR (Summer, 1974), pp. 204–5, 217

Three of the most troublesome incidents in Thomas Kyd's *The Spanish Tragedy* are the varient descriptions of Don Andrea's death, the play-within-a-play, and Hieronimo's biting out his tongue. Perhaps none of these events can be fully defended—save to an Elizabethan audience fond of battles and spectacles—but all can be understood if considered as concomitant to one of the play's major themes: deception through words. . . .

We find in Kyd's world of unexplained whispers, false messages, suspected letters, and lunatic ravings a marked emphasis on the deceptiveness of words. The characters themselves call our attention to words and their import with such phrases as "honey'd speech" (I, i, 30), "good news" (I, ii, 85), "ill news" (I, iii, 53), "envious, forged tale" (I, iii, 93), "fair answer" (I, iv, 94), "trifling words" (II, i, 44), "fair words" (II, i, 52), "pleasing words" (II, i, 124), "flattering words" (III, ii, 75), "kind and courteous words" (III, xiv, 82), and "the vulgar, liberal of their tongues" (III, xiv, 74). In fact, "word," "words," "speech," "speak," and "tell" appear in the play's dialogue more than eighty times, while the words "revenge" and "vengeance" appear less than thirty times. Of course, statistics alone reveal little about a work of art, but when they are this one-sided, we should begin to wonder whether critical emphasis on the play's theme of revenge has not resulted in neglect of another important theme.

Kyd makes it clear early in the play that we can trust the words of no one on the stage. This disquieting fact is initially established through the several descriptions in Act I of Don Andrea's death at the Battle of Alcantara. . . .

The play's three most troublesome incidents referred to earlier—the five versions of Don Andrea's death, the play-within-a-play, and Hieronimo's biting out his tongue—are complementary parts of one of *The Spanish Tragedy*'s major themes: deception through words. Rather than brushing aside these incidents as signs of carelessness or textual corruption or sensation-mongering, we should recognize them for their dramatically effective function in *The Spanish Tragedy*. Primarily through them Kyd makes a strong statement about what happens to man and society when honest and open communication is not the essential aim of anyone. In the world of *The Spanish Tragedy*, where no one's words can be trusted, where unexplained letters abound, where whispers and screams can decide a man's fate, where vows are violated, and where messages are either lost, blank, or distorted, men move further and further apart through the very medium which should unite them: speech. Perhaps, indeed, "harmless silence" is the only alternative, for as one Portuguese nobleman observes, "now I see that words have several works,/And there's no credit in the countenance" (III, i, 17–18).

Carol McGinnis Kay
SP (Spring, 1977), pp. 20–21, 37–38

JOHN LYLY

1554–1606

In legend, Endymion was a young and handsome shepherd who slept under enchantment upon the heights of Mount Latmus. His beauty so moved the cold heart of the moon goddess—called Selene in Greek mythology and Diana or Cynthia in Roman—that she descended from the heavens to kiss him and lie at his side. When Endymion awoke, she had disappeared, but his spirit had been so moved by his dreams of her that he prayed for Zeus to grant him immortality to sleep forever on the heights of Latmus. The tale is another version of the stories of Diana and her sacrificed lovers.

Lyly's interpretation of this story [*Endymion*] was first performed before the Queen on Candlemas Day at night. Candlemas, celebrated in the church calendar on February 2, honors the presentation of the infant Jesus in the temple and commemorates the purification of the Virgin Mary. At the festival, candles for the altar and other sacred uses are blessed. Candlemas is a day in which the burning light is sanctified as Mary's chastity and purity are celebrated. Chastity to Lyly meant participation in the timeless world of the spirit; it was not directly opposed either to marriage or to sexuality. Chastity was an ideal—a virtue not so much of the body, as of the soul. The dogmatic insistence on the chastity of the body grew out of man's need to emerge out of his mortality into the immortal world of the spirit; finally, in religion, it was the spirit alone that mattered. But, for Lyly, the spirit must be in the body.

The day is, therefore, a festival for the promise of a new world emerging out of the old—a new world signaled in the church year by the appearance and consecration of light in Mary and later in Christ's presentation in the temple. In Lyly's play, Cynthia is the chaste moon; she is, thereby, analogous to the Virgin. Endymion's rapture is for the moon whose light constantly represents in its wavering the continuing promise that light will shine in the darkness. The moon's literary association with chastity in the classical stories of Diana unites its physical presence with ethical value.

The moon, thus, embodies light and purity within the physical structure of the universe. But Diana, in classical stories, is frequently a harsh and unrelenting goddess, similar to the Diana Lyly draws in the earlier portions of *Gallathea*. Lyly's virgin, on the other hand, is the virgin whose purity allows her to suffer for the world by bearing its twin burdens of time and history.

The problem for Lyly then becomes how to show his word is real; how to demonstrate that the world of his word is one with the world of his flesh; how clearly to manifest his sense that the world within is one with the world without. His solution secularizes the meaning of John's Gospel. When John wrote, "And the Word was made flesh, and dwelt among us," he meant Christ born into Jesus. Lyly would mean Cynthia born into Elizabeth. For "Cynthia" is Elizabeth made into the Word, and Elizabeth is Cynthia's Word made flesh to dwell among us. Elizabeth's rule by divine right and Elizabeth's authority over the spirit in the world bring together in her royal self the spiritual world and the earthly city. She is the source of earthly order and the incarnation of divine will.

Because Cynthia is finally both word and flesh, both image and body, within the play *Endymion*, Endymion himself is able to be transformed. Because Elizabeth's presence is the actual, or implied, incarnational link between mundane reality and transcendence, the world itself and those who live in it can be changed. We see in Lyly the sense of the real as the potentially ideal *and* the sense of the ideal as the potentially real.

Peter Weltner
ELR (Spring, 1973), pp. 27–29

Like all Elizabethan drama and like all allegory, *Endimion* is anachronistic: it combines past, present, and promise into one fable. As a "pagan" story, it occurs in ostensibly pre-Christian time, in the era of Athenian Pythagoras and his companion seer, Gyptes. These "historical" characters are introduced in order to transcend time, so that Lyly can quietly emphasize the typological resonances of Endimion's renewal and turn them to a contemporary application. Gyptes and Pythagoras fare rather badly in this story: they lose a dispute to Cynthia, having to surrender unspecified "ridiculous opinions," and they have no luck in freeing Endimion. Yet once Cynthia has learned and showed her power, they "fall from vaine follies of Phylosophers to such vertues as are here practised" and "chuse rather to liue by the sight of *Cynthia*, then by the possessing of all Egipt" (5. 3. 286–92). Here is a clear reflection of the scriptural progression from nature to grace. Pythagoras is probably a namesake for the most famous representative of pagan naturalism; Gyptes, whose herbs fail, is probably Zatchlas Aegyptius from the second book of Apuleius, the herbalist who temporarily brings back from hell the soul of a poisoned man so that his body can testify against an adulterous wife. Such a literary antitype must yield to a better shadow of that power which undoes both snake and venomous herb: both Pythagoras and Gyptes give way to Cynthia as the corrupt enlightenment of gentile philosophy gave way to the lord of love.

This is not flattery of Elizabeth, that "vain" monarch of modern notoriety. It is a challenge to her capacity for grace, to her ability to see beyond her own veil of mortality. For implicated in the mystic resonance and pagan time of *Endimion* are allusions both mundane and contemporary. Whether Lyly is asking favor for himself, for the earl of Oxford, or for some unknown other, hardly matters: none of these is a hidden equation for Endimion. What counts is Cynthia's mercy, which the allegory makes general for all of Elizabeth's right-minded subjects, all of them potential particulars in this vastly more universal case. This is why Lyly can honestly discourage the "application" of pastimes while still pointedly decrying the attempts of envious persons to inspire his queen's displeasure: "Dread Soueraigne, the malicious that seeke to ouerthrowe vs with threats, do but stiffen our thoughts, and make them sturdier in stormes: but if your Highnes vouchsafe with your fauorable beames to glaunce vpon vs, we shall not onlie stoope, but with all humilitie, lay both our handes and heartes at your Maiesties feete" (Epilogue). This is not special pleading for just one subject, but the application of a fable in which Elizabeth is encouraged to be her full majestic self. *Endimion* is a program for bringing the heavenly kingdom to earth; it is a mirror in which ruler and subjects alike should seek their better selves.

Robert S. Knapp
MP (May, 1976), p. 366

CHRISTOPHER MARLOWE

1564–1593

When the Epilogue [in *Doctor Faustus*], equivocal as all else, enjoins the wise from practicing "more than heavenly power permits," it does not condemn "wonder at unlawful things," though Faustus begins his tragic career precisely by wondering. In some interpretations, as we have seen, the play itself can become an "unlawful thing" both in the study and upon the stage. But there are more things in heaven and in hell than are dreamt of in dogma of any kind. If Marlowe's play is not homiletic but dramatic, not doctrinaire but dialectical, not dogmatic but tragic, the spectacle may evoke but not answer Faustus' question, "What doctrine call you this?" If with Faustus we attempt an answer, the spectacle shows only that he has been torn to pieces by unresolved and unresolvable terms, each term a hell, nor are we out of it until we leave the theater to realize that the play is only a play at last, perhaps something more than "nothing but to delight the mind" but also limning for us what we had forgotten we had always known, that "these are but shadows, not substantial" (xii.55) and that fundamental ontological oxymora are not for dramatic spectacle to resolve but to show, not to mean but to be. The Epilogue permits wonder before such a spectacle, the Scholar, woe. Woe and wonder, then, for the passionate suffering of Faustus, hero of the spectacle, who asks, "What means this show?"

Max Bluestone
in *Reinterpretations of Elizabethan Drama*, ed. Norman Rabkin
(New York: Columbia Univ. Pr., 1969), pp. 82–83

Marlowe's translations of and frequent borrowings from classical literature and his fascination with the individual's potentialities mark him as a humanist. Yet he is generally pessimistic about man's endeavors, and he sees the tragic implications inherent in the humanistic tendencies of his time. In particular, he views with profound irony the replacement of the traditional Christian view of man as a sinful, limited creature, obliged to accept humbly the limitations of his life, with the new view of man as a fully self-sufficient and worthy being, able to master his world and make desired changes in his life. Because it turns away from a theocentric approach to life, humanism does more than challenge man to create a new, secular order: it threatens him with intellectual and moral chaos if he does not. And man—laboring to find a more liberating approach to art, politics, personal relationships, and natural science—finds himself at the end of his tether when he recognizes the incredible paucity of his abilities to accomplish these goals. With no God to help him, the product of radical humanism ironically tries to fashion a flawless destiny by disregarding the accumulated wisdom of his traditions. But his efforts are constantly menaced by futility, for the limitations he has hoped to leave in the past he now discovers within himself. And so the long-desired freedom from history and necessity does not arrive, for he is, after all, only man, trapped in time and subject to the decay of flesh. Moreover, perceiving himself to be alone in the universe and fully responsible for his own fate, he bears a terrible burden of guilt for having failed to achieve the perfection he has imagined for himself.

The acute sense of loss suffered by Marlowe's protagonists, their self-obsession, their estrangement from other men and God—these are the characteristics of the most widespread psychological malaise of men in the past century and a half, a malaise which often goes under the name of alienation. Better yet, perhaps, it is humanism with a vengeance, for it originates in an overestimation of human potentialities. The growing sense of limitation and despair in his plays thus makes Marlowe the first modern English dramatist, and his heroes share this predicament with individuals in the present age: they either have no viable traditions to guide their actions, as is the case with Tamburlaine, or they seek to ignore them, as Edward, Barabas, and Faustus do. They choose to act in ways unsanctioned by the wisdom of the ages, try to enjoy themselves in prohibited ways, or try to create unnatural contexts for self-expression. His protagonists reject their conventional identities, as defined by their medieval and Renaissance cultural heritage, and reach for an ideal, improvised, but illusory self. . . . These are moral and intellectual voyagers who have cast off from the psychic boundaries of the Old World, and only after it is too late do they recognize that they are lost.

Charles G. Masinton
Christopher Marlowe's Tragic Vision: A Study in Damnation
(Athens: Ohio Univ. Pr., 1972), pp. 10–12

Critics tend to ignore the close parallel between the means taken by Mortimer to effect Edward's death and Isabella's means. Mortimer employs the lightborn featherbed and red-hot spit which, as we have suggested, are as much indicative of his own vicariously satisfied "desires" as symbolically making Edward die the way Mortimer has promulgated how Edward lived. Isabella employs the dead-sea technique, Mortimer himself, and she is far more careful than he that she shall not be discovered.

Mortimer's fall, like Niobe's which Marlowe makes him imitate in his boast that he is too great for fortune to harm, is inevitable; he draws too much attention to himself; his hand is written too plainly for it to be unidentified despite his half-hearted attempts at equivocation and concealment. There is remarkable poetic justice in the way he is made to describe himself entirely in terms of fortune's wheel. He had reached the summit and there was no movement possible but tumbling headlong down. That Marlowe should have the new King give instructions to have his father's hearse fetched so that Edward may have Mortimer's "head" offered to it, is a remarkable ironic twist to the Mortimer-Edward relationship exhibited throughout the play.

But perhaps the play's greatest subtlety is that Isabella should be sent only to the Tower on "suspicion," and although a searching trial is promised, the young King's expression that he could not "thinke her so vnnaturall," and his refusal to let her speak because her words force him to tears and he will pity her if she speak again, cast all in doubt. The young King shedding tears of grief over his father's death is yet inclined to think well of his mother. Both Edward *and* Isabella triumph and are defeated in this. All the Gavestons, Spencers, and Mortimers of this world have been exploited in vain for an impasse which will ever remain an impasse even in death, judged from the new King's stance, but judged from the whole play the focus has to be different.

The voice of Edward screaming in his long day's journey into his marriage's loneliness is in some senses more dramatically powerful than Faustus'. Faustus' empty threat to burn his books, and his fear of being torn in pieces, are quite inconsequential compared with Edward's plea for warmth, understanding, and love, and his being physically torn apart, and dismembered.

The one jewel Edward had left with which he attempted to dissuade Lightborne from the dreadful deed was really the jewel of his soul. His mind was more steadfast on his God as his body became too weak to resist, but his own eternal jewel was commended into the hands of his God, and there was no heinous sin written on it of "vilde and loathsome filfthinesse" (*Faustus*), as far as *his* conscience was concerned.

In his ending Edward successfully pointed out where the real stench emanated that corrupted the inward soul with such heinous sins as no commiseration may expel, not even the son's pity for his mother. Nothing can wash away the guilt of Isabella and Mortimer. The play's final symbolism of young King Edward III distilling tears from his eyes as he offers up Mortimer's head to the hearse of his father's murdered ghost in the presence of his mother asking to be allowed to "moorne for my beloued lord,/And with the rest accompanie him to his graue" and yet arraigned on "suspicion" is perfect. The grouping in this symbolic way is the nucleus of the play. Gaveston and the Spencers, and all the rebellious nobles, were but incidental to all Edward's reign, which was but as a scene acting out that argument.

John P. Cutts
The Left Hand of God: A Critical Interpretation of the Plays of Christopher Marlowe (Haddonfield, N.J.: Haddonfield House, 1973), pp. 237–38

If young Elizabethan writers were initially inspired to reinvestigate Ovid through a partly subversive delight in witty eroticism, what they eventually discovered was a much deeper and more disturbing range of expression. Perhaps the most important conclusion to draw from the examination of Ovid's poetry with which this chapter began is that the alternative to an orthodox "Elizabethan Ovid," an Ovid made safe for the Christian reader, is not necessarily a frivolous, indulgently decorative, decadently "Italianate Ovid." Even in Marlowe's translation of the *Amores* one can see, along with the obvious interest in Ovid's urbane sexual comedy, a sensitivity to the violent pathos and psychic torment which disrupt and complicate both the wit and the lyricism of these remarkable poems. The epyllia of the 1590s represent a further exploration of that characteristic Ovidian ambivalence which Marlowe and some of his contemporaries were beginning to probe in the 1580s. A close, uncondescending look at these explorations may reveal for the modern reader, as perhaps it would have for the late Elizabethan reader, a rather surprising awareness of the contradictions as well as the comedy and excitement inherent in human sexual experience. . . .

In making the case for *Hero and Leander* as a seriously perceptive as well as an entertaining poem about erotic experience, I have had to give less emphasis than I would have wished to certain more generally recognized features of Marlowe's writing, particularly to the sheer fun of his extraordinary verbal wit. In an effort to redress the balance somewhat, let us see how Marlowe's more extravagant conceits might be accommodated within the view of the poem I have been arguing for. One critic [Paul Cubeta] has found Marlowe's conceits so extravagant that he urges us not to take them seriously: Marlowe conceives of his narrator, he says, as a "hack poet . . . with an over-active awareness of his literary heritage and almost no ability to master it poetically." While this view seems to me entirely misdirected, it does point to the way in which the carefully distanced narrative persona allows Marlowe to indulge in flights of stylistic fancy which otherwise would have been impossible. . . .

I have dealt with Marlowe's *Hero and Leander* as a self-sufficient poem throughout this chapter because I am convinced that it can and should be read in this way. Marlowe narrates only a "fragment" (proportionately a very large "fragment") of the entire story, but he treats this "fragment" with a remarkable unity of conception and execution. It is impossible to know exactly what Marlowe thought of the state of his poem when he died. It is hard to imagine how he would have made good on his muted but unmistakable forebodings of tragedy had he wanted to and had he lived to be able to. The irony with which he explores both the comic and the serious imperfections in the love of Hero and Leander would have made the tragedy of their deaths very difficult to realize artistically, if not emotionally and intellectually.

William Keach
Elizabethan Erotic Narratives: Irony and Pathos in the Ovidian Poetry of Shakespeare, Marlowe, and Their Contemporaries
(New Brunswick, N.J.: Rutgers Univ. Pr., 1977), pp. 35, 114–16

Criticism of *The Jew of Malta* has persistently sought a satisfactory explanation for the apparent change in Marlowe's conception of his hero, Barabas, who seems cast in the first two acts in the familiar mold of a Marlovian superman, but who is somehow transformed in the last three acts into a comical revenger. Until recently, there was widespread belief among the play's critics that its text was corrupt, and that the radical transformation of Barabas after act 2 was the work of a redactor, probably Thomas Heywood, and not Marlowe.

The corrupt-text thesis is probably best known as given by Tucker Brooke: "It is beyond question that the vigorous flow of tragic interest and character portrayal with which the play opens wastes away amid what, for the modern reader, is a wilderness of melodrama and farce. The change is so marked as to suggest grave doubt whether the tragedy as we have it can represent the conception of a single man." This opinion was transmitted to generations of Marlowe students, for whom the Tucker Brooke edition was a standard for many years. Although Tucker Brooke judiciously added his belief that Marlowe was no doubt responsible for the outline of the final acts, subsequent critics have frequently cited only his unqualified assertion that the text of *The Jew of Malta* is corrupt.

T. S. Eliot argued against this opinion as long ago as 1919, suggesting instead that *The Jew of Malta* was actually a farce, and that we had all along misunderstood the humor which accompanies Barabas's metamorphosis. Through the first half of this century, Eliot's view of the play met with little favor, primarily because it went against a prevailing conception of Marlowe himself as a profoundly serious artist, a conception whose origins lie in nineteenth-century criticism of the dramatist.

However, once the corrupt-text thesis was called into question by such critics as Leo Kirschbaum and J. C. Maxwell, many more commentators came to see the drama as written wholly by Marlowe and, consequently, became more sympathetic to Eliot's view of the play, seeing the farce in *The Jew of Malta* as evidence of Marlowe's larger ironic vision of the world. While ironic readings of the play have proliferated in the last dozen years, an inevitable reaction against the ironists has set in, characterized by a desire to explain the immense stage success of *The Jew of Malta* through a study of Marlowe's dramaturgy—his arrangement of scenes, his depiction of minor characters, and his manipulation of audience sympathies. . . .

In a review of the stage history of *The Jew of Malta* (1968), James L. Smith reasserted that in spite of its supposed defects—a corrupt text, an outrageous villain-hero, ambiguities in character portrayal, meaning, and dramatist's intent, Marlowe's play has enjoyed considerable success on the stage, far more in fact than it has in the libraries of critics. Smith argues that the play must be first interpreted as sensational theater, a view expressed variously by A. L. Rowse, Brooke, [Alfred] Harbage, and [T. W.] Craik. As Smith's paper shows, the recent production of the play provides a vindication for Eliot's view of *The Jew of Malta* as farce. . . .

The play, admittedly, raises certain insoluble problems for the majority of people who, alas, only know it through reading. The play will defy attempts to unify it or make it consistently conform to any particular theory of tragedy or farce. Therefore, it is in terms of the experience of *The Jew of Malta* in the theatre that the criticism of the play will surely be most productive, because in such a way the play's genuine problems can be distinguished from those specious ones imagined by over-zealous critics.

Kenneth Friedenreich
PLL (Summer, 1977), pp. 318–19, 334–35

JOHN MARSTON

1576–1634

H. H. Wood, ed., *The Plays of John Marston* (1934–38), 3 vols.

Antonio's Revenge has generally been accepted as the rather unsuccessful product of Marston's attempt to write a serious Kydian revenge tragedy. The similarity between its plot and those of *The Spanish Tragedy*, *Titus Andronicus*, and *Hamlet* have been pointed to repeatedly and, understandably, most scholars see Marston as "at first a little clumsy in handling the technique of tragedy." Because the ending apparently takes no account of the wanton brutality Antonio has effected, they sense a gross failure in the conception of the "poor orphan" revenger deserving of the audience's sympathy to the end. The final vow the revengers make to become "constant votaries" does not attest Marston's awareness of the tarnished nature of his heroes, for he makes it clear that their retreat does not involve penance. The morality of the revenge seemingly goes unquestioned, yet it is far more difficult to sanction Antonio than Hieronimo or Hamlet. . . .

Marston wrote his play largely in response to what he saw as the amorality of Kyd's treatment of the revenging hero. Fredson Bowers follows Lily B. Campbell in emphasizing orthodox Elizabethan thought on private revenge, and claims that Hieronimo's final actions would have lost him the audience's sympathy. There are dangers in this sort of legalistic approach. Obviously Kyd is vitally concerned with moral issues, but their dramatic treatment need not reflect codes of behavior that apply outside the theater. . . .

It is a matter of fact that the major revenge tragedies after Marston's—[Henry Chettle's] *Hoffman*, [Tourneur's] *The Revenger's Tragedy*, [Chapman's] *The Revenge of Bussy D'Ambois*, and [Tourneur's] *The Atheist's Tragedy*—reject the heroic revenger. . . . *Antonio's Revenge* should be seen as the first in a group of plays that, largely on moral grounds, reject Kyd's concept of the revenger. There is no reason to assume that Marston put aside his accepted role of moral teacher for this play, and Jonson did imply that Marston's plays were commonly regarded as the kind a clergyman might have written.

Philip J. Ayers
SEL (Summer, 1972), pp. 359, 361, 374

Marston's admirers have always had to contend with the possibility that he is an incompetent, whose "literary sins were committed in invincible ignorance, and often with high seriousness" (R. Ornstein, *The Moral Vision of Jacobean Tragedy*, 1960, p. 152). The solution which recent enthusiasts have adopted is not to minimise the author's alleged vices, but to produce a formula which converts them into virtues. By treating Marston as a parodist, his plays' notorious defects have been converted into illustrations of his sardonic humour. If parody on this scale is to work, author and audience must know where they are. It is essential that the dramatist should not be mistaken for an exponent of what he ridicules. This requires both settled design, and a dramatic technique of sufficient clarity to convey it unambiguously. Defenders of the two *Antonio* plays proceed from the latter to the former, deducing from the presence of stylistic parody Marston's intention to ridicule courtly intrigue and the conventions of revenge. In fact, these are plays in which his habitual irresponsibility is most pronounced, and their stylistic opportunism simply demonstrates his incapacity to handle plot and agent in any integrated design. . . .

The enduring fascination of the revenge motif lies in its vicarious release of grievance, by criminal act in just cause. No other dramatist of the period indulged these pleasures as fully and as sadistically as Marston in [*Antonio's Revenge*]. The scenes of violence are not the most prolonged, nor the bloodiest, yet they succeed in being the most brutal by imitating so skilfully the electric excitement, the abruptness of actual violence. To make the idiotic courtier Balurdo one of Piero's murderers is not a mistake; it perfects the scene's horrific glee. In the murder of Julio we find the same mounting hysteria, from the "punches" with which Antonio obscenely rehearses his stabs, to the mangling of the body. This is what Marston does best. Yet, incredibly, Marston still represents the murder of Piero as a work of purification. Images of purgation replace the images of putrescence which have filled the play. Piero becomes the solitary scapegoat of evil, so that, after his removal, the band of grave senators (especially invented for the purpose) can congratulate his killers on "ridding huge pollution from our state" (V.iii.130). Antonio exclaims, "First let's cleanse our hands,/ Purge hearts of hatred, and entomb my love" (ll. 154–5, Mellida having died in Act IV of a broken heart). The naïve cathartic assumptions of these lines betray an ethic of revenge as involuntarily sanctimonious as it is collusively brutal. To find the detachment of parody in this play is to substitute for it the play we wish Marston had written, and to perceive less clearly than his own astuter contemporaries where his true force lay. Where Marston ignorantly led, others knowingly followed, and to recognise his survival in their work may be the best quarcentenary tribute we can pay him.

T. F. Wharton
EIC (Fall, 1975), pp. 357, 367–68

ANDREW MARVELL

1621–1678

Pierre Legouis and E. E. Duncan-Jones, eds., *The Works of Andrew Marvell*, rev. ed., Vol. I, *Poems*, Vol. II, *Letters* (1971) (based on Margoliouth's ed.)

D. I. B. Smith, ed., *Andrew Marvell: The Rehearsal and The Rehearsal Transpos'd* (1971)

The allegorical imagination is essential not only to the metaphysical conception of the soul's temporal life, but also to the description of certain problems of a social and political nature. The reason is that when social and political questions are entertained as variants of religious and philosophical questions, the language of metaphor is indispensable; for Marvell, the metaphysical and the political, the religious and the philosophical are mutually defining categories of understanding. Whatever is of philosophical interest to him has inevitably a religious dimension and all political conceptions have for him, as for his time, profound metaphysical implications. To paraphrase Marvell's description of the civil war, whichever was at the top of his poetry—history or philosophy—the other was at the bottom. And religion is everywhere the axletree of that polarity. The meaning of history, the definition of nature and of love, and the revelation of grace are all expressed by means which the allegorical imagination makes available to consecutive discourse. The mythic image and the visionary narrative are poetic forms by which the philosophical conception of the soul's temporal life can be set forth in terms of the dramatic confrontation of the Resolved Soul—as lover, as hero, philosopher, shepherd, the poet himself—and his fate. Man's life is the soul's journey, the soul's battle, the soul's tranquility: the temporal life of the soul is a life in nature. But it is, as well, a life in history. And precisely because the allegorical imagination can give form to the notion of permanence, it is well-fitted to describe the nature of change, the course of history. Entertaining a double perspective, the poet thus enjoys the opportunity for an "ironic" judgment of history, for the celebration of the hero as well as the acclamation of Providence. Because the allegorical imagination offers the means of conceiving of the opposition of two realms of being, it can express complex notions of causality. By identifying logical and temporal priorities, Marvell can create emblems and symbolic narratives through which to speak feelingly of such paradoxes as the love born of despair and impossibility, of the conjunction contingent upon opposition, of the annihilation which is creation, of the ruin which is birth.

In short, the allegorical imagination, deploying mythic ambiguity, is a mode of conception especially congenial to the ironic temper; however, so much has been written of Marvell's detachment, his "ironic vision," his remarkable capacity to remain aloof, that it might be useful to stress the conviction that underlies the disinterest, for it is only an unquestioned fundamental assumption that can be the fertile ground of irony. Marvell's recognition of the inescapable ironies attendant upon the fact of matter's limiting spirit is the spur not only of humor but of definition and judgment. His critical spirit invigorates because it is confident, because it springs not from hatred but from despair, the only ground of action; not from resignation but from resolution. *Resolution* is the generative power as much of Marvell's acceptance of Cromwell as it is of the lover's recognition of the "rough strife" which is passion; or of the poet's definition of the love of his soul as the child of despair and impossibility; or of the Shepherd's discovery that grace is not to be reduced to "meer Morality." Love, heroic action, and contemplation are all modes of the mediating heart and mind, acts of the Resolved Soul confronting his fate, which is time. If separation is the condition, resolution is the predicate: the wedges that separate are the wedges that join. Marvell throughout his poetry confronts with resolute imagination the absolute contingency of freedom and necessity, transforming that philosophical conception into the drama, the "story," of the Resolved Soul.

Ann E. Berthoff
"The Resolved Soul": A Study of Marvell's Major Poems
(Princeton, N.J.: Princeton Univ. Pr., 1970), pp. 31–33

Marvell was capable of transforming real landscapes into imaginary disciplines, as when, in "Upon the Hil and Grove at Bill-borow," the "Groves of Pikes" are assimilated to the natural copse on Bilbrough Hill; he presents us his most inelastic natural scene in the Fairfax gardens at Appleton House, evidently in fact already planted in military design. The severe contrast between the notion of strict military discipline and the notion of a garden (delicate plants, lovely colors, sweet smells, diaphanous insects) is deliberately forced, to demonstrate at its extreme point the interpenetration of the retired by the involved, the fragile by the solid, the evanescent by the concrete.

If one may draw a moral from Marvell's practice in these poems, it is that the pastoral cannot provide a satisfactory working-model for lives as men and women must live them, complicated beyond help from the pastoral paradigm. Just because the pastoral is so "useless" in interpreting human life, it is important for its recreative, dreaming beauty all the same. In the "Mower against Gardens," the competition is between nature and artifice, between *otium* and *negotium*, between a reduced pastoral and an adumbrated georgic style of life. The poet, one feels, knows the values of both meadows and gardens, and rejects the competition to embrace a world in which all sorts of flowers and plants may grow.

Rosalie L. Colie
"My Echoing Song": Andrew Marvell's Poetry of Criticism
(Princeton, N.J.: Princeton Univ. Pr., 1970), pp. 40–41

Judging after the fact, we can see that Marvell's most comprehensive idea of the poem's imitation of paradise required a compromise between static emblems that close out the world (while admitting the divine image) and reformative agents that seek to change a faulty reality. We see him seeking that compromise not in the Elizabethan way, in images of royalty or in the militant church of a Red Cross Knight but in those historical reforms of his time that press for spiritual renewal—in what we might call Puritan-Platonist "actional emblems." They offer a progressive revelation of the sphere above in yearly accomplishments and regard time as the stages of renewal. The pilgrims of "Bermudas," to take an instructive example, leave prelate-torn England and travel to an eternal spring where nature is "enamelled," where rocks bespeak gospel, and where the grassy scene itself is a divine "stage." Their work in rowing the boat across the "watry maze" keeps them from sinking in time's circles; it is accompanied by their own art, a kind of work song, which is an important part of their "doing": "What should we do but sing his Praise/That led us through the watry Maze." The reformed church-boat, returning to an earthly version of paradise, is thus, like Cromwell, an active instrument of historical transformation in which all pull together for change. Like their cousins the Arcadian shepherds, the pilgrims are free of masters, but unlike Arcadians they are no longer tied to purely natural seasons: their paradise transcends time even though it can be realized only in time.

The paradisal island and the Protestant craft are obviously a quite different locality and "conveyance" than Herbert's temple, from which the poet invokes God to descend into institutional and sacramental embodiments. But despite this difference, the poem itself in both Herbert and Marvell seeks to provide a sacramental image of paradise, to model the divine pattern and render the praise due it; and the tension between temporalized images and eschatological reality is basically unresolvable. For Marvell in the later satires, the pastoral element shrinks in proportion before a multitude of follies and England's general failure to attain the goals of the Reformation. The bond between the greater and lesser heavens is broken, and poems are no longer effigies of paradise. Whereas for Herbert the temple as purified heart, sacramental poem, and church is not vulnerable to so general a failure and the poet can find security in its epitomizing enclosure, for the later Marvell the poet is forced to conceive of poetry as a rhetorical weapon in the chastisement of follies and the implanting of moral standards.

Historical incarnations of divine harmony are the subject also of much of Milton's pastoralism, especially in the early poems. . . . Thus both in Marvell's gradual abandonment of visionary politics for practical politics and in Milton's view of paradise regained, we see an acute stage of the dissociation of those levels of pastoral that Marvell in "Upon Appleton House," Milton in "Arcades," and Herbert in *The Temple* labor to join. That dissociation, which includes the divorce of social and transcendental pastoral, will be reconsidered in Pope, Thompson, the romantics, and eventually Frost and Stevens. Each of these in his own way questions anew the possible reunion of the sacred and the natural in the *locus amoenus*—and what such a reunion might portend for the poem and visitants to its mirrored landscape.

Harold E. Toliver
Pastoral Forms and Attitudes (Berkeley: Univ. California Pr., 1971), pp. 148–50

The situation rendered in the "Dialogue [between the Soul and the Body]" exhibits, along with aspects of the debate, those of a personal altercation. Each participant looks upon himself as the injured party, detailing the miseries of his own experience and acrimoniously inculpating the other. A quarrelsome pair, they come across somewhat as a mismated man and wife and indeed are even more indissolubly joined "until death do them part." Like Adam and Eve in *Paradise Lost* when fallen and bickering, "they in mutual accusation" spend their time, "but neither self-condemning." The narrator adds, "of their vain contest appeared no end." This verse, that ends Book 9, will do as a motto for some critical misapprehensions of Marvell's poem. Harold Toliver considers it "a dramatic contest between antagonists who need each other," and either might have the "final word, which by the nature of their fusion cannot be final." J. B. Leishman, going still farther, holds that the work is "almost certainly incomplete," and must originally have "continued through several more ten-line stanzas." If a mere altercation it might indeed have proceeded on or stopped inconclusively, but the contention has another facet, that of the debate, which is the delimiting factor and key to the arrangement.

As an undergraduate at Cambridge, Marvell would have assisted at and participated in the academic disputations embedded in the curriculum, and the imprint they left on his mind is apparent in this composition. He by no means reproduces a disputation in its elaborate totality, but he includes sufficient particulars to suggest a performance of the type, particulars such as: the set speeches; their equal length, as if time limits had been fixed, except that the last runs slightly longer; their being addressed, except again for the last, not to the opponent, though exerting a determinant effect on his subsequent discourse, but to some third party, either directly to the reader or else to some other judge or a moderator supposed present at the occasion; the orderly presentation of the arguments; and the impressive command of formal devices of logic and rhetoric in the argumentation. . . . However these roles are assigned, the interest very much lies in the skill of argumentation on both sides of the question.

The debaters of the thesis are personifications of two of the terms. They postulate kinds and degrees of offenses. Body offends with physical. Soul with psychological and moral evil. The latter kind is, in the values of the poem, the gravest, far more grievous than any bodily affliction, and the word "Sin" has religious implications, presently to be examined, that extend beyond moral evil. Soul affirms these values by having no comeback when charged with sin, he tacitly acknowledges defeat. Body's second speech, its significance hinted at by the special features earlier remarked, proves, by virtue of this charge, conclusive, and for him a disputatious triumph. Critics approach the poem with so fixed an expectation of a triumph by Soul that they are unable to respond to the reversal of that expectation. The reversal can have been calculated by Marvell as the crowning touch of wit in a performance witty throughout.

Joseph Pequigney
in *Tercentenary Essays in Honor of Andrew Marvell*,
ed. Kenneth Friedenreich (Hamden, Conn.: Archon, 1977),
pp. 90–91

THOMAS MIDDLETON

1580–1627

The basic pattern of *A Chaste Maid in Cheapside* can be viewed as an expansion of the triple hierarchy, since it includes four distinct plots arranged in an order of descending importance. As in the case of many of the three-level dramas, this is also the order of their inception. The action opens with the main plot, which centers on the efforts of Touchwood Junior to win Moll Yellowhammer (the "chaste maid" of the title) despite the violent opposition of her parents, who want her to marry Sir Walter Whorehound. The second plot, beginning in the second scene, deals with the Allwit household, where Sir Walter has for years been carrying on an affair with the wife and supporting the complaisant husband. The third scene initiates the third action, the story of the barren couple, Sir Oliver and Lady Kix, who finally acquire a child through the ministrations of Touchwood Senior. And in the fourth plot, which does not get under way until Act IV (and so is the briefest and least developed), Tim Yellowhammer courts and weds a supposed Welsh heiress only to discover she is Whorehound's former mistress. . . .

The formal integration of [the] structure, which is still more elaborate, is articulated through the analogical interrelationship of these four lines of action. Each of them is based on a sexual triangle involving two men and a woman; and in their treatment of this triangle the first and fourth plots make up a comparable pair, as do the second and third. Both plots of the first pair are stories of young couples who eventually marry, conceived in such a way that one seems the exact opposite of the other. . . .

In this structure the sex-money equation plays a very important role, although here, unlike *A Mad World, My Masters* and *Michaelmas Term*, it is not divided between separate plots but lies at the heart of all four . . . and so serves to unify them in terms of a common rather than an analogous subject matter. . . .

Because it epitomizes this conception of the sex-money equation, the Allwit plot can be called the satirical center of the play; but that does not mean we should follow some of the critics in writing off the main-plot romance as a mere "neutral frame" on which to "hang the more interesting comedy of fleshly passions and follies," for the story of Moll and Touchwood, although not as intriguing as plots two or three, is at the structural center, modifying and being modified by these subordinate actions, not only in the causal connections between them (which were all seen to work through the main action), but also in the emotions they arouse. The very audacity of the Allwit plot and of its comic replica in the Kix plot is emphasized, and at the same time kept within appropriate bounds, because it is framed by the conventional main action and the equally conventional inversion of that action in plot four. And conversely these unconventional plots create the general environment that gives the love story its special significance, perhaps most impressively in the much admired "realistic" episodes of the promoters and the christening. They are included partly for their independent satiric import, but they also help to define with marvelous vividness the identity of "Cheapside," the home of the Yellowhammers and Allwits and the center of the middle-class world whose sordid carnality and commercialism, shown in these scenes corrupting the "religious wholesome laws" of Lent and the sacrament of baptism, constitute the real enemy of Moll and Touchwood, and the background against which the triumph of their love is made to stand out as something uniquely attractive—as the comic miracle expressed in the title of *A Chaste Maid in Cheapside.*

Richard Levin
The Multiple Plot in English Renaissance Drama (Chicago: Univ. of Chicago Pr., 1972), pp. 194–95, 200–202

Women Beware Women is an experiment which partly fails, especially in the last Act; yet the play as a whole is some indication of what Middleton intended to do with serious drama. His use in tragedy of a plot activated by one character playing upon the frailty of another, tentatively suggested in the main plot of *A Fair Quarrel*, was an instinctive step in his development. For it provided opportunity for the realism in dialogue and background which makes the reading and acting of this play a continually fresh experience. The total effect upon an audience is of an intimacy with the characters which makes their contrarieties acceptable.

Middleton's obvious innovation is of a new type of tragic hero in the figure of Leantio, with his capacity for depth of feeling and his aspirations balanced against his limitations and innate vulgarity. To make such a character credible and to keep him in his proper place within the pattern of the play was no mean achievement. And the women characters are made up of similarly disparate elements. The post-Restoration qualities often noted in Middleton can be seen, surprisingly, here. The Bianca of the middle Acts, her aspirations to "fashion"—how often is the word on her lips!—the hard sparkling wit of her replies at the banquet, the coldness of her taunts to Leantio, would not be out of place in Congreve. Yet the same character is brought to the limits of mortality before the play closes, and this without violence to that hard consistency of character which anticipates later seventeenth-century comedy.

In all this the influence of Webster, whose own modifications to the pattern of Revenge Tragedy in his two greatest plays made such an impact on the theatre, should not be ruled out. It is possible that Webster's tragicomedy *The Devil's Law Case,* with its social implications, its substitution of the merchant for the prince as hero, was in Middleton's mind. . . .

For tragic intensity Middleton substitutes tensions within the characters which, though often generated by circumstances, are moral in the long run. Like the majority of mankind they are people of good intention, with motives rather confused than mixed. It is the character of comic stature brought up against an acute psychological or moral challenge—the challenge faced by Beatrice [in *The Changeling*] on her wedding night or by Bianca as she sees her bridegroom die at her own hands—that gives to Middleton's tragedy its characteristic edge. One is driven to the conclusion that the violence of the closing scenes of the two tragedies is largely a concession to a mode. With Middleton there are no heights or depths in the passions of the flesh, only a retardation of the spirit which it takes the reversals of life, not an encounter with the universal mysteries in death, to cure. Thus at the catastrophe there is nothing to regret, nothing to condemn or admire, only a good deal to understand.

Dorothy M. Farr
Thomas Middleton and the Drama of Realism: A Study of Some Representative Plays (Edinburgh: Oliver and Boyd, 1973), pp. 94–96

Thomas Middleton, like Cyril Tourneur and Ben Jonson, pioneers in the development of a situation which, never resolved on stage, requires the spectators to utilize their personal values as the measure of judgment on every character in the play. The world of *Women Beware Women*, more specifically, is characterized by a general abandonment to passion. Involving both aristocratic and mercantile classes in its web of intrigue, it is one of the most extensively decadent societies in the entire range of Jacobean-Caroline tragedy. The focus, similar to that of [Tourneur's] *The Revenger's Tragedy*, is exclusively upon sexual depravity, concerning both the lechery and lust which seek physical gratification at whatever cost to another and the avarice which barters flesh for position and wealth. No fewer than five sexual relationships form the basis for the action, only one of which—and that one only for a period of days—is morally sound. . . .

If the stage world of *Women Beware Women* has seemed lacking in moral force and direction, the end results are almost rigidly conventional. The reward of sin is death, and, although no positive force has been visibly active throughout the play, the guilty destroy themselves with precise effectiveness. With the spectators in a position to place all of the pieces together, they alone can receive the full impact of the tragedy. And, as in the work of Jonson, Tourneur, and Ford, for them alone is catharsis possible. Without question they will face society beyond the theatrical doors with a renewed conviction of teleological design. They will face their Jacobean realities with the additional reminder that tragedy is rarely a matter of isolated private decision, that more frequently it will be the consequence of human interaction. Hell has come to earth and its name is humanity disposed to using others merely as means of achieving its own satisfaction. While this stage world lacks characters of full tragic stature, the greatest degree of sympathy—albeit mixed with disdain and condemnation—is reserved for Brancha, Isabella, and Leantio—figures whose descents into corruption and villainy are not entirely self-motivated and who most clearly reflect the complex societal forces culminating in the tragedy of the individual. Perhaps most importantly, by dramatically increasing the number of individuals who communicate privately with the spectators, Middleton has captured amidst his broad scene of societal corruption and tragedy the sheer loneliness and isolation of its victims. In a world in which human depravity sets its own rules of conduct, the individual is ultimately a stranger and genuine love and friendship are virtual impossibilities.

Larry S. Champion
ES (August, 1976), pp. 411–12, 424–25

THOMAS NASHE

1567–1601

Rather than Shakespeare . . . I would suggest Dickens, if some other writer is to be invoked in order to help define Nashe's quality. It is Dickens who comes most constantly to mind as one recognizes the vividness and wit of Nashe's thumbnail character-sketches. In *Pierce Penniless*, for instance. . . .

The sheer energy of the writing is also Dickensian. There is often the resourcefulness of a musician devising variations on a theme. In the opening of *Have with You to Saffron Walden*, for example, his theme is the fact that Doctor Harvey has published some more pamphlets, and the aspect that he takes up for comical exploitation is the great bulk or weight of them. . . .

One is never so aware of this skill, of Nashe's essential character, and hence of his limitations, as in his last published writing, called *Nashe's Lenten Stuff*; and in this the comparison is not with Shakespeare or Dickens as much as with James Joyce. People who knew Joyce well sometimes say that in his last years the only passion he had was for words themselves. Granted, one does not quite feel this to be so with *Lenten Stuff* (the birch-branch-swinging prose-style takes him heavenwards, but he comes back, feet firmly on the ground, to say, for instance, that "that which especially nourished the most prime pleasure" in him was the sight next morning in Yarmouth harbour of ships driven in by storm overnight, their sails now spread out against the sky). . . . But words *qua* words are certainly a main delight in the author's mind here: he indulges his own kind of scribblede-hobble as the nonce words come thick and fast . . . and the full vigour of the English language matches up with the zestful humour. . . .

And yet Nashe does represent something more than a collection of laughs and images, vivid lines and well-rounded sentences. What he enunciates is little to what he knows; what is explicit doctrine is little to what is expressed and communicated. *Summer's Last Will* is a branch which has grown, out of roots that have clutched: an age-old condition of life is presented, where the seasons are no mere backdrop, and where the medieval *ubi sunt* theme is given a modern realisation through the imminence and urgency of the plague. . . . There is also the energy which is eternal delight, and which finds expression in the writer's love for words. . . .

Nashe is an entertainer, an artist conscious of his craft, proud of success, apprehensive of failure. But "no man ever wrote so well," Chesterton said of Stevenson, ". . . who cared only about writing." Nashe wrote of the human scene without reverence but with savour. We can at least do the same for him.

J. B. Steane
Introd., in Thomas Nashe, *The Unfortunate Traveller, and Other Works*, ed. J. B. Steane (Baltimore: Penguin, 1972), pp. 38–40, 43–44

Many commentators regard the Nashe-[Gabriel] Harvey quarrel essentially as an important event in literary history, one that helped to set the course of English prose in the seventeenth century: it arose Phoenix-like from the smoldering ashes of the Martin Marprelate controversy; it anticipated the bold and succinct prose of Bacon because in their extravagantly written pamphlets, both Nashe and Harvey helped to undermine the fortress of ornate Ciceronian prose which was then the dominant style. In the broad context of literary history, this assessment of the Nashe-Harvey quarrel is surely tenable. However, even while Nashe's critical reputation rests largely on his talents as a professional man of letters, and although his flyting with Harvey has been recounted many times, surprisingly little has been said about the substance of particulars in the quarrel itself. Of course, Nashe and Harvey debated in earnest no single issue throughout the long duration of their quarrel; its free-wheeling and inordinate manner could not engender or sustain weighty arguments. Nonetheless, there appear to have been genuine differences of opinion between the antagonists that went beyond personal animosities and that contributed to the protraction of their pamphlet-war.

A palpable issue that Nashe and Harvey argued about was the rise of the professional writer at about the time their quarrel ignited. In *Foure Letters and Certaine Sonnets* Harvey expressed his contempt for this new class of writers, who were paid to pander to the public's appetite for the bizarre and the sensational. Nashe responded with *Strange Newes, of the Intercepting Certaine Letters*. Here, the posture of a professional writer, characterized by a fierce sense of indignation, informs the mode of Nashe's response—as a news pamphlet—and provides him with potent ammunition to engage Harvey. At the heart of *Strange Newes* lies its author's esprit for the writer's craft. But to see why Nashe considered the mode of newswriting as a most appropriate way to confute Harvey we must examine, in addition to the contents of *Foure Letters*, the state of the news industry at the close of the sixteenth century, for it provided much of the work for the enterprising ranks of professional writers. . . .

In *Foure Letters*, and to a greater degree in *Strange Newes*, there is an energy which, I believe, must arise from the power of fiercely contested opinions. There is little question that the antagonists held disparate views of the function of literature and literary enterprise. For Harvey, literature serves to preface and enhance great public actions; for Nashe, literature is a vehicle by which one displays virtuosity, entertains and excites readers, and most important, by which one earns a living. Nashe's opinions are embodied by the very public format of *Strange Newes* as Harvey's are by private epistles "made public." Only a man whose career was both as unfortunate and insular as Harvey's could quixotically take on a London literary establishment of growing importance; only a man such as Nashe with a vested interest in the advance of this London publishing trade could achieve remarkable success in celebrating a mode of writing then in its infancy. Nashe sustains the aura of excitement and sensationalism throughout *Strange Newes* while he ingeniously dispels the assertions of his opponent with élan. Although, as the quarrel intensified, issues were obfuscated in favor of more personal and strident invective, the impression remains that at the outset of the exchange, at least, one issue did incite Nashe and Harvey. Nearly four hundred years later, we are able to apprehend the urgency and eagerness coloring Nashe's defense of the literary professionals. Amid current interest in "the new journalism," it might be wise to remember that Nashe made discoveries about writing in the news mode long before Tom Wolfe or Norman Mailer.

Kenneth Friedenreich
SP (October, 1974), pp. 451–52, 471–72

To most of Nashe's readers, artistic coherence in *The Unfortunate Traveller* is . . . chiefly notable for its non-existence. . . . It seems worth suggesting that, in our anxiety not to force a bogus unity on the book, we may have overlooked some interesting cases where one point *does* connect with another, where arrangement seems purposeful, and where there is some consistency in the ideas beyond the basic purposes of entertainment and stylistic display. That is all I want to claim; but if the claim seems reasonable it may suggest a slight re-adjustment in our judgment of Nashe's achievement.

To begin with a simple point: one cannot help noticing that, in the rich variety of the book, one kind of atmosphere seems increasingly predominant. There is, especially towards the end, a sense of oppressive heat and physical corruption. Sweating, tortured flesh becomes an obsession. The motif is introduced fairly early, in the description of the sweating sickness. . . .

Against this violent and corrupt world, Nashe sets the pleasure garden of the summer house in Rome. This is not, I think, simply a piece of "fine writing" indulged in for its own sake. It provides a vision of life that is diametrically opposed to the chaos outside the garden, and correspondingly extreme. It is in itself a model of the world, "a heauen and earth comprehended both vnder one roofe." But it is a model of the world before the Fall, a world of harmony, order, and innocence: the music of the spheres is heard; the wolf and the lamb lie down together. As Nashe's description continues, the past tense begins to take on special force, and this model of Eden seems to fuse with the real, "historical" Eden in the writer's mind. . . .

The last extended episode of the book, the execution of Cutwolfe, takes up some earlier strands of action, and weaves a similar, though simpler, pattern of revenge. Cutwolfe is being executed for murdering Esdras of Granada, the robber who raped Heraclide and stole Diamante, and for whose crimes Jack was very nearly executed. Jack was rescued as a result of the dying confession of Bartol, one of Esdras' confederates, whom Esdras killed in a quarrel. Cutwolfe was Bartol's brother, and his murder of Esdras was an act of revenge. But it is also connected with the rape of Heraclide, a connection made plain in Cutwolfe's narration. . . . The detailed description of Cutwolfe's execution makes a logical culmination for *The Unfortunate Traveller*: it takes up, for the last time, the motif of tortured flesh that runs through the book; and it provides one last spin of the wheel of violence and revenge that controls the action in Italy. After this, Jack's return to the English camp provides a sharp and genuine sense of relief.

But, as I have indicated, no great claims can be made for tight organization or consistent purpose in the first two-thirds of the book. We must return to the earlier statement that *The Unfortunate Traveller* is not a fully coherent work of art. It survives chiefly as a grand, grotesque entertainment, alive with comedy and horror, with the flamboyance of Hieronymus Bosch but without his concentration of purpose. It is worth noticing, however, that what coherence can be detected in the book points forward to later developments in the English novel. Nashe pulls some sections of his work together through devices which the novelists who followed him were to use more purposefully—interrelated strands of action, a coherent pattern of images (centered here on the frailty of the flesh), and a development in the central figure which, though rudimentary, anticipates the now-familiar theme of the education of the hero.

Alexander Leggatt
SEL (Spring, 1974), pp. 31–32, 46

SIR WALTER RALEGH

1552?–1618

Deep pessimism, linked with the dramatic sense of life, is central to *The History of the World* and to much of Ralegh's poetry as well. The play metaphor was a conventional vehicle for such pessimism. It had been used for centuries to suggest the limitations of man's life on earth, its transience, its unreality, its lack of freedom, the instability of its greatness. Yet, paradoxically, the actual effects of the dramatic sense in Ralegh's life seem bound up with an intense optimism about the possibilities of human achievement and a belief in man's power to control his destiny. In the final scenes of his life, for example, Ralegh's role-playing (when it was not simply, like the feigned illness, a device to gain time) was an assertion of human dignity. At a moment when circumstances conspired to reduce him to total impotence, his theatrical self-possession acted out the integrity and even the freedom of the individual. And, of course, this is only the extreme example. At those other moments of his life when we most sense the histrionic sensibility, as in the assault on Cadiz, the 1603 treason trial, and the two voyages to Guiana, Ralegh's theatrical heroism similarly affirmed the power of the human will over fortune. . . .

In Ralegh's life and art . . . one finds not the realization of a single tradition but a struggle between opposing forces. On the one hand, the play metaphor as an image of life's limitations reaches back to medieval theologians like John of Salisbury, to Fathers of the Church like St. John Chrysostom and St. Augustine, and to a diverse array of classical authors. Behind all of these is most probably the Book of Job with its dark picture of human fortunes manipulated and marked by God. Ralegh's self-assertive theatricality, on the other hand, has its intellectual origins in those Renaissance writers who saw in man's mimetic ability a token of his power to transform nature and fashion his own identity. . . .

The artificial world which had this supreme actress [Queen Elizabeth] at its center was Ralegh's world during his years of happiness, fortune, and influence. The self-dramatizing that was the essence of the court deeply influenced his life, coloring not only his relations with the queen but his entire personality. His theatricalism in the crucial scenes of his life, his sense of himself as an actor in a living theater, his capacity truly to believe in the role he played though it was in many of its elements an evident fabrication, his self-manifestation in poetry and prose are all profoundly related to the example and effect of the remarkable woman on the throne of England.

Stephen J. Greenblatt
Sir Walter Ralegh: The Renaissance Man and His Roles
(New Haven, Conn.: Yale Univ. Pr., 1973), pp. 30–31, 55

SIR PHILIP SIDNEY

1554–1586

Jean Robertson, ed., *Sidney: The Countess of Pembroke's Arcadia* (1971)
Katherine Duncan-Jones and Jan van Doorsten, eds., *Miscellaneous Poems of Sir Philip Sidney* (1973)

In Sidney's idea of fiction [in *Apology for Poetry*] there is one essential precondition: the proposition that each man's "erected wit" or "inward light" permits him to know perfect truth and goodness. Eternal truth thus can be "conceived" and in that sense imitated by the human mind. If need be, the mind can then use this general design, pattern, or "foreconceit" to fashion or "feign" a material manifestation of that truth (or some portion of it). By impressing such true patterns upon the raw stuff of nature, including that of his own body or his various bodies politic, man can convert the brazen natural world into a golden one. Sidney evidently found nothing precious or mysterious in this belief. Because it is the mark of man that he can "discern beauty," he can impose the idea of a temple upon a cave and that of a constitution upon the anarchic state. In doing so, he may parallel the creativity of nature by working with the things of nature, but he will never merely "follow" her. It is more likely that he will imitate God, the original designer and maker.

In his original state, Sidney's man is thus a knower and maker—that is to say, a poet. His powers of conception and creation define his humanity.

However, it seemed to Sidney that modern man had increasingly fallen away from his high origins. Erected wit, which "maketh us know what perfection is," had given way to "infected will." In the *Arcadias,* that slide is graphically demonstrated when princes turn idle seducers and a nation degenerates into a mob. It is not that reason (the "erected wit") has withered away, but that passion (the "infected will") has usurped its governing power. When that happens, man becomes less a knower and creator than a blind user and consumer. He is increasingly the slave to things in nature and to fortune and fate within history. Knowledge dwindles into cold philosophy, and action into history's "old mouse-eaten records." If the errant human will is to be converted and the erected wit to be restored, a force as strong as passion must homeopathically oppose passion; men must be brought to love, not merely to "know," truth and goodness.

At this point, Sidney turns to the mediatorial poet. Unlike most other modern men, the poet cannot have severed his intuitive contact with eternal reality; to be a conceiving "maker" at all, he must know and love truth. If he were concerned with himself alone, his only "poem" might be the unwritten (*a-graphos*) conception that results. All about him, however, are men in whom knowledge has declined and love has turned to passion.

Partly for their needs, but partly also for the sake of the idea that he loves, the poet will utilize his own communion with eternal truth as the "fore-conceit" or meaning which guides him as he fashions a seemingly living manifestation of that truth. This "lively" image of truth will be so admirable that other men may love it and emulate it. . . .

Sidney always assumes the quality of liveliness (*energia*) in a poem, but by itself it might be dismissed as a trick of style. More essential is his belief that knowledge (*gnosis*) must be realized in action (*praxis*), of some kind. Three partially obscured principles of movement are inherent in that doctrine. . . .

A principle of movement "outside" the fiction proper will produce at least a limited narrative and dramatic movement within it—a practice or "action," in the purely literary sense considered by Aristotle. Although "speaking" debates in the *Old Arcadia* and "picturing" narratives in the *New* may seem static, the movement of inter-involving characters among those arguments and pictures nevertheless comprises a significant general action. The characters even come to major reversals and recognitions, as if gradually proving general knowledge within their particular action.

Jon S. Lawry
Sidney's Two Arcadias: Pattern and Proceeding (Ithaca, N.Y.: Cornell Univ. Pr., 1972), pp. 2–3, 10–11

I cannot think it useful to number and categorize the roles Sidney plays. In a rhetorical structure such as he has created, *any* role could fit. And if we cannot find an artistic pattern in the roles, we cannot find a master *persona*, a standard to judge affectation in terms of the poem itself. Instead, we see Sidney casting about, using for his compulsive purpose whatever comes to hand. Great critics have disputed whether *Astrophil and Stella* tells a story, and if so what kind. This is a non-problem. The work chronicles a series of attempts to persuade. This is narrative of a sort, but of a peculiarly rhetorical sort. It stands halfway between life and literature and draws indiscriminately from both. Its protagonist is first fictional, then the real and historical Sir Philip Sidney. Both "story" ("real life") and consistent artistic metamorphosis of this ("*persona,*" "pure poetry") enter in only as they serve a predominantly rhetorical purpose. *Astrophil and Stella*'s mixture of fact and fancy makes perfect sense in its own terms. Only under the wrong formal expectations does it seem inconsistent.

Perhaps this is the moment to confront another famous and irrelevant problem—Sidney's sincerity. Sidney sincerely wants to persuade. His desire is sincerity itself. This he is obliged to tell us and, in the first four lines of 1, he does. All that comes after serves this purpose. He makes poetry out of his effort to find a "voice," to be sincere, but he makes poetry out of a good many other occasions and feelings and problems, too. We can quarrel with the end in view. Seduction, however fancy the language, may be wrong. But this has nothing to do with Sidney's "sincerity" in trying to bring it about. We can say that real love is sincere love and neither has anything to do with sex. Sidney would simply disagree, and we should have to kiss both Astrophil and Stella good-bye. We can say that, granted the end and the conception of love, Sidney was not justified in pretending to feelings he did not possess. He would reply that the force of desire to change—and fabricate—one's feelings was part of the story he was telling. *Astrophil and Stella* was about "sincerity." The only argument about the sincerity of *Astrophil and Stella* that might avail would be that he had not warned us about his rhetorical purpose. But he not only does this in the first four lines, he does it again and again. The force of desire is continually before our eyes. None of the charges will stand. Sincerity, except as a theme, is irrelevant to *Astrophil and Stella*, one of the non-problems that have plagued the poem. . . .

Sidney's thinking about language is a tool (the double-edged sword of rhetoric), like his thinking about everything else, to be *used* not pondered.

So too it is with the proverbial popular wisdom. Sidney confronts it. He sees that it will not do. It is manifestly inadequate to cope with experience, as anyone can see when he simply juxtaposes the two, as in 5. But we cannot say that he transcends it. He confronts desire, he confronts the ambivalent, lying heart of language, but he goes beyond neither. Nor does he coherently relate them one to another. These are fantastic objections, of course. Look what he does do. He makes of his own desire the great poetic representation of Desire in English. But because his purpose remains rhetorical throughout, he can neither anatomize desire, as Shakespeare does in sonnet 129, nor follow it through consummation into middle age, as Shakespeare does in 138. He cannot yoke desire and the censor in a brilliant philosophical pun, as Shakespeare's dazzling 135 does. Nor, of course, does Sidney attempt any of these Shakespearean purposes. Neither meditative nor philosophic, *Astrophil and Stella* begins and ends in the begging mode.

Richard A. Lanham
ELR (Spring, 1972), pp. 110, 115

Considering the wide range of sources from which Sidney drew his material, it is not surprising that the *Old Arcadia* does not readily fall into any one category. Although the Eclogues contain pastoral poems with short prose links in the manner of Sannazaro's *Arcadia*, and the main story is a prose narrative with interspersed lyrics in the manner of the *Diana* of Montemayor and Gil Polo, the *Old Arcadia* is not really a pastoral romance concerned with the celebration and examination of love in an ideal world to which the heroes have retired from the world of chivalry. Arcadia is very far from being such an ideal country; it contains no magic healing centre such as the cave in Sannazaro or the temple of Diana in Montemayor. The lady Felicia, who resides in this temple, and to whom the lovers take their problems for resolution, and from whom they receive mysterious predictions of happiness to come, is a development of the benevolent oracle of the Greek romances, which, instead of threatening disaster, has "assumed an almost contrary character and become a symbol of the second chance" [Mary Lascelles]; whereas the oracle which has caused Basilius foolishly to dwell among shepherds, and to make the boorish Dametas guardian of his daughter Pamela, is an oracle of menace on the older pattern of the terrible Greek myths, and it is Basilius's attempts ("menaced by fortune") to evade the fate predicted that bring him and his to near disaster. No reproaches whatever are levelled at those who consult the oracle in the Greek prose romances, or directed to the unhappy lovers who resort to the lady Felicia in the *Diana*, but Sidney makes his disapproval of Basilius's idle curiosity ("in vain to desire to know that of which in vain thou shalt be sorry after thou hast known it") abundantly clear, both in his own voice, and in the unavailing sage counsel of Philanax.

Sidney, then, has availed himself of a pastoral setting for a story of a very different kind from the *Diana*. Even pastoral, the lowest of the eight kinds of poetry Sidney lists in the *Defence of Poesy*, is defended, not by reference to the ideal world portrayed in such works as the *Diana*, but for its ability to comment on moral and political questions. This emphasis was determined by Sidney's desire to prove that even the humble pastoral is superior to history and philosophy in its power to teach. . . .

Firmness of structure was Sidney's most individual contribution to prose fiction, and had the *Old Arcadia* rather than the *New Arcadia* been printed in 1590, we might have been spared some of the long-winded imitations of the seventeenth century, and the criticisms of the *Arcadia* voiced in the eighteenth century.

Jean Robertson
Introd., in Sir Philip Sidney, *The Countess of Pembroke's Arcadia (The Old Arcadia)* (Oxford: Clarendon, 1973), pp. xxxiv–xxxv, xxxvii

The biographical intrusion [in *Astrophil and Stella*] works by hints and sometimes guesses; but its recurrence makes it strangely, even mystifyingly, insistent. It adds an extra depth, and also an enigmatic quality, to any poem in which it occurs. When, for instance, Astrophil warns Stella's sparrow against too much boldness with her, he is probably warning Philip Sidney also, as well as himself (the last syllable of his name is the same as the first syllable of the sparrow's):

> Good brother *Philip*, I have borne you long . . .
> Leave that sir *Phip*, least off your necke be wroong.

What exactly Sidney might be warned to stop doing we can only guess. It may be something to do with Penelope in so far as she is sometimes identified with Stella, and perhaps he is being warned against making this very identification; but we cannot be sure. There are similar mysteries any time there is biographical intrusion. What we need is some way of describing the general effects which this always has, for I think it is done for deliberate and important artistic effects which are quite precise, even though in particular instances there are other subtleties too.

In *Astrophil and Stella* it is Sidney who is glimpsed at moments behind Astrophil, and not the other way about. In other words, the biographical intrusion is not meant as a form of personal confession, but rather as a way of adding another character to the drama. Similarly, Penelope Rich is glimpsed at moments behind Stella; and the way that the main "Rich" sonnet opens on the world of historical fact is dramatic: the fact becomes an element of the fiction, and gives a sort of solidity to the drama. The sudden references to reality have the effect of making us more aware of the fiction, more conscious that the sequence is mainly fiction. Awareness of the author, and of his guiding hand in the affair, increases our appreciation of the sequence as a made thing, an artefact, something that did not merely happen, and consequently increases our delight in the skill the poems reveal. . . . The chief reason for the biographical intrusions into the dramatic fiction which is *Astrophil and Stella* [is] to make us more aware of the poetry as art, and consequently more aware that art is related to things outside itself. I believe the effect is deliberately calculated by Sidney. He was as aware as anyone can be of the paradoxical nature of art. Artistry is needed when we wish to appear natural, since poetry is always made by a human being,

> The only creature ever made who fakes,
> With no more nature in his loving smile
> Than in his theories of the natural style . . .

There is also the paradox that subject-matter which is painful in itself becomes pleasant in art:

> Oft cruell fights well pictured forth do please.

This is reminiscent of the *Apology*:

> That imitation whereof Poetry is, hath the most conveniency to Nature of all other, insomuch that, as Aristotle saith, those things

> which in themselves are horrible, as cruel battles, unnatural monsters, are made in poetical imitation delightful.

His *Apology* shows too how seriously he took fiction, and how aware he was that fiction, by its very difference from some kinds of fact, bears a closer relation to others.

J. G. Nichols
The Poetry of Sir Philip Sidney: An Interpretation in the Context of his Life and Times (Liverpool: Liverpool Univ. Pr., 1974), pp. 87–89

EDMUND SPENSER

1552–1599

The fact that [*The Faerie Queene*] was described by him as a "continued Allegory or darke conceit" is Spenser's way of defining the kind of reading it required. To read on is to absorb at once the story and the allegory; they are not separable and in both there is the common factor of movement. *The Faerie Queene* is one of those works of art which depend for their quality upon cumulative effects. Each event in the scene slides into the next, and ultimately needs the context of the whole poem to give it its full force. For those critics of classical inclinations who admire "form" of the kind supplied by order, proportion, and outline, this is a distressing method of procedure; perhaps it is to every critic, whatever he admires, since it drives him to vagueness, half-truths, and tedious modifications of every statement he would like to make precise. But it is the only type of structure which Spenser found he could use satisfactorily if he were to say all that he wanted to say in *The Faerie Queene*. The generous pattern of *The Shepheardes Calender* offered him a similar variety but when he attempted in other works more limited, stricter kinds of design he was defeated by the requirements of their plan. What he needed was a multiple form which he could shape to any purpose as it arose. Consequently the only kind of consistency we can look for is consistency of formulation to meaning, never consistency of formulation here with formulation there.

Allegory for Spenser has become a means of submitting an unsystematic habit of thinking to an imaginative type of expression. It enabled him to regulate the quantity, the quality, and the kind of significance he desired at any given stage in the poem. The last thing it was designed to be was a system in itself. This might imply a state of considerable confusion, but for Spenser multiple allegory was positive and constructive in its outlook. It offered a medium where many different kinds of material could find their place. It became for him a dimension, a mode of perception, never a fixed scheme to which all poetic thought had to be subordinated. . . .

It is one of the inherent virtues of the framework he had adopted that so many different levels of meaning can be introduced easily without labour or repetition. He does not have repeatedly to point his morals in the fashion of the emblem book, but can trust the conception to run by itself once it is established. It is, therefore, a means of economy. Once set in this context in each Book, all become part of a changing story. Spenser had not left his form at the stage where a single isolated example stands alone. The assumption of a moral idea formulated in terms of narrative was for him only a beginning: the narrative will vary as the idea grows and will develop more branches; each Book will be different; there will be different relations between the literal and allegorical meanings; there will be different ways of indicating the relationship, from the most explicit (as in the Abessa and Mammon episodes) to the merest suggestion by context, analogy and contrast (as with Malengin); but always the allegory is there. *The Faerie Queene* is written in its shadow and belongs to its world.

Rosemary Freeman
"The Faerie Queene": A Companion for Readers (Berkeley: Univ. of California Pr., 1971), pp. 69–71

The Faerie Queene is a splendid ceremony about the necessity for ritual, pattern, and ceremony in life, so as to contain and control the demonic forces within and around us all. The poem is about continuity and anarchy and how each reasserts its potency in the path of the other's power. As an image of continuity, Arthur appears often, as we know, but remarkably he reappears in canto viii of every book save Book III and thus initiates the redemptive movement of each book. In III,viii, we do not meet Arthur. Instead, here near the center of the poem, the anarchic forces are most concentrated. Here we first meet that embodiment of illusion and travesty of substance, the False Florimell, and the very principle of deceptive flux, Proteus. Throughout, Arthur seeks the ennobling visionary core of experience; near the core of the poem, vanity and mutable illusion are manifest. The dialectic—or what we called the dual impulse—goes on forever at the heart of epic.

The reader ought to be aware of the grand patterns, the alternations of day and night, dark and light; of the metaphors of health and disease, government and strife, art and nature, time and eternity. He should be alert to the alternating rhythms of birth and decay, garden and city, and to the occurrences of those two crucial words, "ruin" and "moniment." Finally, one must watch for the technique of relevant digression, where a small story or episode or myth, seemingly intruded for no purpose, in fact catches and crystallizes the poem's larger concerns.

Some of the most interesting patterns in the poem result from the repetition of similar episodes or images, with the further result that the poem (and reader) acquire ever expanding perspective, increasingly dense versions of experience. For instance, the monster Error (I,i,14) is repeated in Duessa's "many headed beast" (I,viii,6;16) and again in the great Dragon (I,xi), each version of monstrosity summing up and enriching the previous one. So also the boar imprisoned by Venus in a cave (III,vi,48) in its way foreshadows the snake beneath Venus' feet (IV,x,40), the crocodile subdued in Britomart's dream at Isis Church (V,vii,6), or the lion under Mercilla's throne (V,ix,33). Again, the beast that feeds on women, released by the Witch from a cave (III,vii,22f) prefigures the Blatant Beast whose bite is slander (V,xii,37f), while the Beast's assault on Serena (VI,iii,24) is an image completed and expanded by the tiger's attack on Pastorella (VI,x,34–35). . . .

The poem draws constantly on itself as a reservoir of past history and human experience, always impressing on us—as the poem seems to start over and over—how different substances are from surfaces, and how we must learn to discern the true from the false. In this vast world of *déjà vu*, of repetitive phenomena, of recommencements, only wariness and cumulative experiences will guide us to the single and abiding visionary core. . . .

The vision of Romance is always restoration of lovers and of lands, the reestablishment of edenic sentiments and landscapes. And in Romance, whether narrative poem or drama, the symbol for the harmony of sentiment and place, and for the wholesome continuity of human and physical nature, is the deeply satisfying reunion of the generations.

A. Bartlett Giamatti
Play of Double Senses: Spenser's "Faerie Queene"
(Englewood Cliffs, N.J.: Prentice-Hall, 1975), pp. 68–69, 75

It is true that upon first reading *The Faerie Queene* we are apt to proceed discursively—that is, a new reader probably starts with the first line and intends to read through to the end. This is the procedure for reading a novel. And it is likewise true that we, modern readers, will perceive the poem phenomenalistically—that is, we will attempt to know the poem by its phenomena, by the events it describes; and we will assume that the poem has no other existence. Perhaps as heirs of the New Criticism, we will assume that the poem has no existence except the words of the text, which we should respond to as phenomena, and we may forget that there are other constituents in a poem's meaning besides our own affective response to these stimuli. To concede the worst, we might admit that a modern reader may experience *The Faerie Queene* like Joseph Spence's mother—that is, as "a collection of pictures." He will read it discursively and phenomenalistically, reflecting the assumptions about time and ultimate reality which prevail in our own day. He will work inductively, piecing the poem together from fragmentary data like a scientist arriving at a hypothesis based on empirical observation.

That, however, is only half a reading of *The Faerie Queene*. . . .

To understand *The Faerie Queene* as it was intended, we should strive to reorient our thinking to accord with assumptions that prevailed in Spenser's day. We should read it in the context of an ontology which placed ultimate reality on some suprasensible level, and in the context of an epistemology which made truth dependent upon perception of that ultimate reality through exercise of the intellect rather than the human sensory apparatus. *The Faerie Queene* projects a world view different from our own, and a sympathetic approach is prerequisite to making any headway in it. We must take at face value Spenser's announcement of a foreconceit in the title, and we must accept literally the confidences about method he reveals in the letter to Raleigh. We must strive to reconstruct the foreconceits of glory and magnificence which he bodies forth in Gloriana and Arthur, and which he unfolds even further to our view in the multitude of knights and ladies (both good and bad) that inhabit the microcosm of Fairyland. We must learn to relate each episode not only to adjacent episodes in the durational narrative of its own book, but even more cogently to the encompassing pattern of Arthur's quest and to the enduring ideal inherent in Gloriana's court. Then we will perceive the endless variety of the world around us; and because the episodes of *The Faerie Queene* conform with our own experience, we will accept the events as true. Moreover, because in their totality they lead to a greater whole, to a vision of life not only in its completeness but also abstracted to essential beauty, we will have an aesthetic experience by reading Spenser, an experience wherein we will recognize the relationship between art and nature and reality that aspires to. We have reached the limit of words, even the limit of poetry.

S. K. Heninger, Jr.
in *Contemporary Thought on Edmund Spenser*,
ed. Richard C. Frushell (Carbondale: Southern Illinois Univ. Pr.,
1975), pp. 96–98

The nature of Spenser's allegory in the final cantos of Book I [of *The Faerie Queene*], and the sense in which he can be said to provide a context for subsequent unfoldings, may be illuminated by looking at the corresponding episodes at the climax of Book II. This comparison has become a hackneyed examination question; since [A. S. P.] Woodhouse's classic article, it has been rehearsed, in one version or another, by almost every critic of the poem. Whether grace and nature, faith and reason, *mens* and *ratio*, or some other sets of terms provides the conceptual matrix, descriptions of these twin events tend to sound much like each other. But those who want to emphasize a distinction between the episodes usually make things more difficult for themselves by failing to note the chief difference: that the dragon-battle and the Bower of Bliss are unlike as metaphors. [Robert] Kellogg and [Oliver] Steele are on the right track when they observe that Guyon's adventures are "set forth in poetic images made philosophically significant by generations of medieval and Renaissance mythographers, but essentially independent of a mystical Christian significance."

It is not really possible, of course, to argue that any images in *The Faerie Queene* are "independent of" Christian significance. They are all subsumed by a theory that saw pagan myths as versions of the one truth; and circumscribed, in the poem, by a system of cosmic references that ultimately converge in a single source. Within the poem, however, Spenser makes a distinction between Guyon and the Red Cross Knight as a Faery knight and an English one, respectively; and this is reinforced in the canto of the chronicles where the same distinction is drawn between Guyon and Arthur. . . .

Book VI of *The Faerie Queene* has received its due from critics only since the renaissance of Spenserian studies over the past quarter-century. This is not surprising, for in his last completed book Spenser achieved the most original and unexpected of his imaginings, and one that is congenial to our modern taste for self-contemplation. Consequently, we are probably better equipped to understand what the poet is doing in this book than any previous generation of readers has been. The readings of Book VI by recent critics have made clear that the final book is a parable of the power and limitations of the imagination. . . .

The poet who steers his course through the poem does not reach a haven, and not merely because he was prevented from finishing his work. Spenser's actual death occurred less than three years after he published the six completed books of *The Faerie Queene*, but a different sort of death overtook the poem before that happened. The final canto of Book VI terminates in the moment of writing, and life invades art as Calidore spoiled Colin's vision, as the Brigants ravaged the homestead of Melibee. The Blatant Beast is a monster whose presence blurs the boundaries of fiction. England of the 1590's becomes an extension of the allegorical landscape as the Beast "raungeth through the world againe" (xii.40); the indecorum of its behavior, rending "without regard of person or of time," causes the leaching away of the poet's strength. He can no longer maintain the power of his fiction to resist simplistic reading and the malice of the envious. For one who traffics in words, this failure of his words to defend their own integrity is a kind of death, and Spenser reinforces this notion in his final descriptions of the Beast. "As the poem ends we are left in no doubt whatsoever that Spenser regards the Blatant Beast as the particular enemy of poetry and of himself as a poet." And the enemies of poetry work through the poet's medium, by attacking and finally silencing his words. That silence is death, and so the Beast is appropriately a sibling of the first and last enemy in *The Faerie Queene*. It "realizes completely the Dragon figure of earlier books," in particular the Dragon of Book I whose mouth opens into Hell. . . . Like Serena in the woods, the poet awakens from his nightmare and finds it truth.

Isabel G. MacCaffrey
Spenser's Allegory: The Anatomy of Imagination (Princeton, N.J.: Princeton Univ. Pr., 1976), pp. 343, 400–402

The legend of chastity is organized symmetrically. At the center of [Book II of *The Faerie Queene*] Spenser places the cool and shady Garden of Adonis, which represents the chaste heroine's potential for self-realization, as the presence of the Genius might indicate. The periphery of the book is hedged by the nocturnal life of the loci of Malecasta and Busirane, which represent an overheated erotic desire. Britomart passes through the last two loci chastened but unhindered; she does not visit the locus of recognition, however, because the realization of her love is deferred to another legend. Amoret, on the contrary, is nurtured in the Garden, and Britomart's identification with her interests emerges at the juncture of the two books. Thus the legend as a whole has the entrance-exit pattern of its own locus of recognition.

Britomart achieves the quest meant for Scudamour, and in the sequel, Scudamour visits the locus of recognition perhaps in some sense meant for Britomart. It is Britomart who requests Scudamour's account of the Temple of Venus. The two eductions of Amoret, then, must be another instance of the structure of recurrence. Just as Britomart enterprises the field version of this education (at the House of Busirane), she also experiences a field version of the scene of recognition, when she is acknowledged as a Venus figure by Artegall. As the poem stands, this acknowledgment signals the effective accomplishment of her quest: the enamoring of her future spouse. Their meeting is placed at the center of Book IV; that is, halfway between the lovers' respective legends, and also halfway between the symbols of Venus and Adonis, and Isis and Osiris. . . .

The end of Spenser's legend is the uniting of the faithful and the true. Truth, if she is going to prevail, needs a champion. And the champion, if he is going to prevail, needs to know what he is doing. Spenser's theme, though, is the establishment of faith, and to be a legend of faith the story must not end in marriage, but in trothplight, or betrothal: that is, in a renewed pledging of faith. Near the end of the Apocalypse, John says that his words are "faithful and true." This serves to identify his "moste wonderful Propheticall or Poetical Vision," as Harvey called it, with the messianic horseman whose ride to victory the vision has announced and whose name—Faithful and True—the vision has revealed. Such an alignment of word and person makes the point that the New Testament in Christ's blood is not only a sacrifice, but also a sign, a disclosure of "the word of truth," which requires faith. At the House of Holiness, Fidelia carries not only a cup, but also a book. Spenser's first legend, we have endeavored to show, has as many analogies with Fidelia's book as with her cup. Indeed, the pages of such a book, "with bloud ywrit," must manifest the sacramental color pattern in yet one more place. The legend of the Redcrosse knight, in its loving elaboration of this pattern, has many of the qualities of the Church's principal ceremony, but it is no idol. As the reformers said of the cup, its efficacy derives from the Word annexed to it. . . .

We may now summarize the place of the two sixth cantos. Midway between the Bower of Bliss and the House of Busirane Spenser describes the Garden of Adonis, his vision of fruitful chastity, as opposed to either the sterile promiscuity of the Bower, or the traumatized virginity of the House. The meeting of Britomart and Artegall is similarly placed. It belongs to the pattern of reconciling conflicts in this legend—here a conflict in which Britomart appeases the jealous Scudamour and tames the savage Artegall. It is therefore placed midway between the legends of chastity and justice. Friendship exists chiefly among the virtuous. Thus this canto forms a principal link in that golden chain of concord that is also the Arthurian chain of the virtues.

James Nohrnberg
The Analogy of "The Faerie Queene" (Princeton, N.J.: Princeton Univ. Pr., 1976), pp. 281–82, 628–29, 635

SIR JOHN SUCKLING

1609–1642

Thomas Clayton and L. A. Beaurline, eds., *The Works of Sir John Suckling* (1971), 2 vols.

Among the group of poets conveniently labeled "Cavalier," John Suckling has in particular been stereotyped. Largely because of the set anthology pieces and the limited critical studies, "Natural, easy Suckling" is commonly seen as an unabashed rakehell and a dilettante writer whose amateur love poetry is synonymous with libertine cynicism. This characterization, like the more inclusive designation "Cavalier," neatly places Suckling's poetry in a literary and a philosophical tradition; but the depiction is misleading. While some of his more famous poems apparently endorse a cynical vision of love, the entire canon reveals this is only one response in a complex and even sensitive search for the wisdom in love forbidden to the "fond lover."

The short lyric "Out upon It," often cited as a typical Suckling poem, epitomizes both the traditional manner and the essential crux of his love poetry. Unlike John Donne's intensely personal immediacy, the dramatic opening stanzas establish a public, somewhat detached mode. The speaker, highly conscious of more traditional poetic attitudes, casually affects a deliberate pose. . . .

When he can distance himself, as in "A Ballad upon a Wedding," the need to conceal his own ambiguous attitude is less immediate; as a result the tonal complexity is more effective. With the persona of the rustic, Suckling creates a speaker completely outside his own identity; and the fictional context, the most complete development of the conscious posture, ensures a completely controlled freedom. Through the speaker, who with wide-eyed wonder narrates "things without compare," Suckling presents his own version of the epithalamium; paradoxically his ironic acceptance of this venerable poetic form produces unique emotional immediacy. . . .

The poem juxtaposes the physical description and these sexual witticisms partly to avoid any possibility of cloying and insincere sentimentalism; but beauty and sexuality are also in accord with the spirit of the epithalamium. After the marriage is celebrated and as the consummation approaches, the sexuality implied in the first part of the poem becomes more overt. Activity now replaces the more static description in the poem's first half, and the tempo begins to gather momentum with the progressive accounts of the feasting, drinking, and dancing. The activity of the carousing people accentuates the wedding couple's desire to be finally alone, and their frustrated anticipation is vicariously experienced by all who help them celebrate. With masterful timing Suckling builds and prolongs this yearning; then he suddenly collapses the urgency in his final stanza. . . .

The best gloss . . . of Suckling's love poetry is a statement by C. S. Lewis in *The Allegory of Love*: "cynicism and idealism about women are twin fruits on the same branch—are the positive and negative poles of a single thing."

Raymond A. Anselment
TSLL (Winter–Spring, 1972–73), pp. 17–18, 30, 32

CYRIL TOURNEUR

1575–1626?

In Cyril Tourneur's *The Atheist's Tragedy; or, The Honest Man's Revenge* we find again the three levels of the [low comedy] formula—the first portraying the conflict between the "atheist," Baron D'Amville, and his antagonists, Charlemont, the "honest man," and his beloved Castabella; the second, the adulterous affair of Levidulcia and Sebastian; and the third, Languebeau Snuffe's attempted seduction of Soquette. And again we find that the critical commentary, which has grown considerably over the past thirty years, deals almost exclusively with the first level. This is quite understandable, for the most striking feature of the play (as the double title suggests) is its development of general theses opposing atheism and private vengeance through the careers of D'Amville and Charlemont, respectively. Yet even in these didactic terms it can be shown that the second action and, to a lesser degree, the third contribute to the formulation of the "doctrine" of the main plot, as a necessary consequence of their integration into the hierarchic structure of the work as a whole. And this structure will turn out to be the most elaborate yet encountered, since it in itself necessarily reflects the highly self-conscious and systematic program entailed in the play's ethical commitment.

The first two levels are related through their common form; they are both villain-hero or retribution plots, focusing on the criminality of D'Amville and Levidulcia and their deserved punishments (indeed, D'Amville's atheistic Machiavellianism makes him a much more typical protagonist of this genre than those discussed earlier). But while this is an essential aspect of the analogy between these levels, the detailed dramatic and conceptual scheme in which that analogy is worked out takes as its basic components not the plots themselves but their major characters —D'Amville, Charlemont and Castabella (who, it will be seen, are treated as a single unit), Levidulcia, and Sebastian—and the moral positions represented by them. . . .

The hierarchic arrangement serves the general purpose of the formula by providing a context that "places" the three components and our responses to them, but it also takes on a more specific function within the particular ethical orientation of this play. The intermediate characters of the second level and their burlesque counterparts of the third fill in the continuum between the extremes of the main action, which seems to force these extremes still further apart and thereby sharpens and clarifies the personal and ideological contest enacted there. At the same time, they enhance the sense of "coverage" (implicit in the formula itself) by exhausting all of the possibilities defined by the moral scheme, and so tend to universalize the villain-hero "retribution" plot that reappears in all three actions (for the Snuffe episode is a comic version of this plot, terminating in his comic discomfiture). The repetition of that plot pattern constitutes the formal parallel relating these separate levels, while the differentiations among them insure that the gravity of the crime and punishment at each level is commensurate with its place in the emotional hierarchy. Therefore the combination of the positive and negative aspects of the fundamental analogy suggests a comprehensive demonstration of the "wages of sin" and of the omnipresence of a punitive providence throughout all the various manifestations of human depravity and frailty. (A similar effect was noted in [Thomas Lodge's] *A Looking Glass for London and England,* which is even more openly didactic.) And it also has the complementary result of isolating and emphasizing by contrast the virtue of Charlemont and Castabella and the beneficent power of this same providence that protects and rewards them.

Richard Levin
The Multiple Plot in English Renaissance Drama (Chicago: Univ. Chicago Pr., 1972), pp. 74–75, 84–85

Within the metaphor and metaphysics of *The Revenger's Tragedy* time has little place, and the revenger and his victims appear tied to the same stake. Nothing is problematical, all is ordained, conforming with monotonous regularity to the coinage of Vindice's brain. If the undoing of the Duke is, as Inga-Stina Ekeblad would call it, an "exemplum horrendum," it figures in a strangely unorthodox homiletics. . . . The schema is self-determining—as perfect as it is inflexible.

A vision or fiction of conduct as mechanically contrived and of human nature as reduced to a few spastic gestures may be made to work very well for farce or satire, but it is hard to imagine it as working well for tragedy. This is especially so when the contrivances are as ironic and intricately interlocked as those which—to use again one of Tourneur's own most insistent words—swell his world. . . .

My quarrel, however, is not with Tourneur's right to his theme of "Why this is hell!" nor with any seriocomic decorum per se. A good Calvinist, viewing all sin as a fall out of freedom into necessity, might well find such a decorum ideal; and the joke of the slave of passion who dreams himself an architect of fortune can certainly bear repeating. I wish merely to stress both the aesthetically and the ethically disturbing consequences of Tourneur's having channeled the power of his intelligence and imagination into a reiterated definition of that convulsive moment when the time-ridden destroy themselves; to argue that this obsessive patterning is ultimately *undramatic* if drama is taken to imply conflicts and their resolution in time; and to insist, lastly, that it represents a very harrowing rigidification of consciousness. . . .

He is a Dante *très manqué,* whose responsiveness to his experience, while sporadically moving and brilliant, is ultimately self-entangling and self-nullifying. In what other play of its period, one may wonder, is subject installed so patently at the expense of object? The Duke, Lussurioso, Spurio, and the Duchess cross the stage in abstract silence, visible only that they may be absorbed into Vindice's poetry (half diatribe, half dithyramb) of "this present minute," no more real than fat folks or the usurer's son, and decidedly less real than the presiding skull. The Depraved, the Skull, the Revenger, and the versification itself, hectically contracting and expanding, all are of a piece—"Savage, extreme, rude, cruel, not to trust"—bearing witness to that sinewy thread their maker's brain lets fall through every part. What Gide called the "state of dialogue" is not to be found in the play. The skull is the agent in a realm where no effective counteragent exists; and while Vindice addresses his beloved volubly, the very soul and secret of her responding eloquence is, inevitably, her grinning silence.

B. J. Layman
MLQ (Spring, 1973), pp. 29–31

THOMAS TRAHERNE

1637?–1674

Traherne . . . was part of that latitudinarian movement in theology which centered on the Cambridge Platonists. Like them he was concerned with finding the foundations of Christian belief on which all men could agree. Like the Cambridge Platonists he was also attracted to the philosophic tradition of liberal Christian theology, and like so many other liberal theologians of the times from Erasmus to Le Clerc, he had an enthusiastic interest in a revival of pre-Nicene theology. In Traherne's case, as in that of Servetus (who does, incidentally, closely resemble Traherne in his doctrine of Man), the figure of Irenaeus was conspicuous.

It is necessary to establish this background because in Traherne's most interesting writings, the *Centuries* and *Poems*, he provides little acknowledgment of his sources. Besides, his own rare vision has often the effect of transmuting the quality of what he derives from elsewhere. It is for this reason that the Pelagian argument has been formulated by critics. It is a hypothesis which might seem to fit the facts when the author himself leaves his theoretical precedents so undefined. But it would seem clear from the background we have described that we might well expect to find Traherne's theological sources among the pre-Nicene Fathers of the Church, and I suggest the hypothesis of St. Irenaeus, rather than either Pelagius or Augustine, is one which will fit the facts in a most satisfactory manner. . . .

We may . . . conclude, as we began, by suggesting that it is confusing to discuss Traherne, as critics have consistently done, in terms of an orthodoxy which is Augustinian. The Pelagian heresy and scholastic discussion of "states" of human nature are foreign to the vision of Irenaeus, and are not helpful for explicating the position of Traherne who assumes an Irenaen type of theology. A discussion of the theological background of the seventeenth century makes it clear that Traherne was more than likely to indulge an enthusiasm for such a teacher as Irenaeus, and we can see from *Roman Forgeries* that Traherne had indeed a special interest in this early father. However, as with any discussion of Traherne's sources, we should add that he, more than any other devotional poet of the period, possessed a vision which was unique, and he stamped all he borrowed with the impress of his own peculiar mystical sensibility. Moreover, he was less interested than most writers of prose in the period with acknowledgment and demonstration of scholarly sources. However, Traherne found not only a comparably unique mentor in Irenaeus, but a fellow spirit as well. It may be concluded of Traherne's individualism no less than that of Irenaeus himself. . . .

Patrick Grant
ELH (Spring, 1971), pp. 44–45, 61

HENRY VAUGHAN

1621–1695

French Fogle, ed., *The Complete Poetry of Henry Vaughan* (1964)

The private and personal qualities of Vaughan's sensibility do not . . . obscure the fact that he drew deeply on the Augustinian conceptions which the age made available and gave them full play in the structural dynamics of his poetry. The first poem of *Silex Scintillans* is "Regeneration," which employs a title already hallowed by Herbert's use and treats what we have seen to be the essential and dominant theme of Augustinian-Protestant spirituality. . . . The poem can be seen as a somewhat rambling and uncompressed variation on the theme of Herbert's "The Collar," which it echoes closely in its first lines (almost matching its second line word for word), and Herbert's speaker, of course, protests at his bondage to God, not to the world. . . .

Vaughan perhaps shows a similar indifference in the arrangement of episodes in the last half of the poem. There seems no clear reason, for example, why the "new spring" announced in line 38 and described and expanded in the following stanza could not suffice as an adequate symbol of regeneration. Line 40, "The unthrift Sunne shot vitall gold," seems to say almost all that logic requires (Grace is given unthriftily, indeed with infinite generosity; it comes suddenly and without warning—"shot"; and what it gives is the gift of true and transformed life—"vitall gold"), and the remaining lines of the stanza, at once profuse and delicate, beautifully satisfying each bodily sense, would seem to render the new spring with the necessary imaginative particularity. The allegory goes on, however, shifting away somewhat from an account of the speaker's own spiritual condition, but not departing from the themes of Reformation Augustinism. . . .

The poem seems to suffer from an allegorical overplus, a purpose expansive in the manner of Bunyan, but expressed in a form not suited to such expansions. In fact, however, there is less wasted motion than may appear. The last four stanzas depict not merely a series of emblems of grace, but (with no less interest from the standpoint of Augustinian theology) the soul's perplexity among them. The mind and senses tire with the effort to understand, but persist with anxious questions, wondering, desiring, musing, listening, turning, seeking. . . .

One can maintain then that Vaughan's "Regeneration" is a theological poem, without casting doubt on the ultimate authenticity for the poet of the experience it reports: Vaughan need not have gone through "conversion" himself (although it is likely that he did) to know the Protestant drama of the soul in vivid detail and assent to it feelingly.

William H. Halewood
The Poetry of Grace: Reformation Themes and Structures in English Seventeenth-Century Poetry (New Haven, Conn.: Yale Univ. Pr., 1970), pp. 127–28, 130–31, 133

It is difficult to speculate further about the motives which prompted Vaughan's powerful interest in imagery drawn from the Book of the Creatures. It may have been partly a reaction against dualistic and Manichean elements in Puritan polemics. Their attacks on the materialism or fleshliness of Anglo-Catholic ritual, iconography, and liturgical symbolism tended to emphasize the incompatibility of spirit and matter and thus to magnify and render crucial a philosophical problem which had always been dormant in Christian theology. Their attitude tended to minimize the possibility that matter was sanctified by pious uses and ultimately to weaken belief in God's love for the Creation. Among the potential consequences of these attempts to purify spirit from the contaminations of matter were the cancellation of man's responsibility for evil, the liberation of temporal affairs from the rule of God's law, and the undermining of faith in the temporal manifestation of God's goodness. . . .

Vaughan's preference for a poetic language with a maximum potential of intelligibility can be seen . . . in the fact that his natural metaphors are usually organized in terms of the broadest, most salient concepts of popular science rather than in terms of the more abstruse and technical concepts which gave Donne a reputation for pedantry in his own day and for toughmindedness in ours. The central principle by which most men organized their conception of the cosmos was still, as it had been in ancient and medieval times, the figure of the Chain of Being or Ladder of Creation—a figure made up by the coalescence of various aspects of ancient philosophy and mythology, Biblical exegesis, Ptolemaic cosmology, astrology, and popular scientific lore. The broad outlines of this conception of the cosmos as a unified, hierarchical system, a *discordia concors* which encompasses and disposes various plenitude with order and regularity, make up the "metaphysical" features of Vaughan's natural imagery: the concentric spheres, the immutability of the heavens, the flux of the elements, the supremacy of reason, man's primacy in the natural world, stellar influence, the decay and renewal of the cosmos, the correspondences between different orders of being. These ideas were basic components in the intellectual world-view of the time.

James D. Simmonds
Masques of God: Form and Theme in the Poetry of Henry Vaughan (Pittsburgh: Univ. of Pittsburgh Pr., 1972), pp. 43, 147

One of the most influential Anglican interpretations of The Song [of Songs] in the seventeenth century is Bishop Joseph Hall's *An Open and Plaine Paraphrase, upon The Song of Songs* (1609). Hall's interpretation of the verses most pertinent to "Regeneration" helps illuminate Vaughan's position. Hall assigns to Christ the verses immediately preceding the one Vaughan uses as an epigraph: "A garden inclosed in my sister, my spouse; a spring shut up, a fountain sealed. Thy plants are an orchard of pomegranates, with pleasant fruits; camphire, with spikenard. Spikenard and saffron; calamus and cinnamon, with all three of frankincense; myrrh and aloes, with all the chief spices: A fountain of gardens, a well of living waters, and streams from Lebanon." Hall explains that the garden is enclosed so that it will not be "carelessly open, either to the loue of strangers, or to the rage of enemies. . . ." Vaughan's temple in nature, the "garden inclosed," is, then, unlike the organized church, safe from the "rage of enemies." . . . Significantly, Hall interprets the plants of the garden as faithful children who grow up in the Church, and the fragrances as symbols of their holy obedience. In Vaughan's description of the grove, he emphasizes those sensuous aspects of the Anglican worship to which the Puritans particularly objected, the stained glass and the incense. In light of Hall's interpretation, Vaughan's description ironically redounds against the defilers of the Anglican ritual who were—in Vaughan's view—anything but obedient. . . .

Vaughan's "Regeneration" . . . is an account of the poet's own personal pilgrimage from a false spring of worldly pursuits to a genuine springtime of the soul. Brilliantly developed by means of rich and pregnant allusions, the poem charts a quest for spiritual rebirth. Central to this journey is the pilgrim's discovery of the House of God in nature, where he learns lessons of the mysterious working of Grace and of faith in times of adversity. It is in the enclosed garden that he hears the rushing wind whisper "Where I please" (I. 80). Vaughan describes the temple of nature in terms that remind the reader of Anglican architecture and ritual, the earthly church denied to Vaughan by the Parliamentary triumph. As a result of that triumph, Vaughan apprehends in nature the enduring Church, the Spouse of God, which is safe from the vicissitudes of the religiopolitical strife of his immediate experience. In this sense, "Regeneration" is a public poem as well as a personal one.

Vaughan's discovery of a temple in nature has implications for the continuing evaluation of him as a nature poet. In the best of the many studies emphasizing Vaughan's relationship to nature, James D. Simmonds speculates that among the motives that prompted the poet's interest in nature imagery "may have been partly a reaction against dualistic and Manichean elements in Puritan polemics. . . . Their attitude tended to minimize the possibility that matter was sanctified by pious uses and ultimately to weaken belief in God's love for the Creation. . . . The violent contemporary attacks on the traditional liturgy may have contributed to the intensity of [Vaughan's] interest in the traditional view of the relation of Nature to God on which the liturgy was based." One can go beyond this to the view that Vaughan, driven from his church, found the immanence of God in nature, as Herbert found it in the liturgy of Anglicanism and Jacob in the vision at Beth-el.

Claude J. Summers and Ted-Larry Pebworth
JEGP (Fall, 1975), pp. 358–60

JOHN WEBSTER

ca. 1580–1634

The White Devil isn't a play of the order of [Kyd's] *The Spanish Tragedy* or [Tourneur's] *The Revenger's Tragedy*, where the moral alignment follows the obligation of revenge and allows one to talk of heroes, Machiavellian villains, avenging justice, and the like. Nor has it anything in common with a work like *Hamlet*, whose action develops some settled concern into a dialectic to which every speech dynamically contributes. The counterpointing of scenes in *Troilus and Cressida* may be the nearest thing Shakespeare affords to the relativism of *The White Devil*, but Webster's play has little in common with a movement which allows as much scope to the heart's drastic gestures as to the world that keeps giving them the lie. Webster's far more limited sense of human possibility allows no such insights as Troilus or Hector or old Shallow incarnate, and consequently no such effective moral scourge as Thersites.

A closer comparison might be John Donne. *The Progress of the Soul*, written in the same decade as this play, is an exuberant attempt to carry through a thoroughgoing sceptical relativism in an account of the economy of fallen nature. But its vision of the civic jungle has—and assumes—an assured purposefulness that's quite missing from Webster's play, and one simply can't take the action of *The White Devil* as predicating man's predatoriness, or the relatively of our judgements in respect of absolute truth. Donne's is a menacing world but we knew just where we stand in it. Webster's is desperate because that's just what no one who inhabits it can know.

The decisive matter is what the characters make of their world, and perhaps what they don't or can't make of it. For all the furniture of counter-reforming zeal, inquisitions of morals included, there's really no metaphysical dimension in the play at all. Effectively the characters don't admit in their lives anything beyond the here and now, which death simply negates. . . . What then do they live by? Nothing in the play warrants our speaking of "a world of evil," or even of anything so revolved as Machiavellism. Only the successful working of Francisco's plot suggests that people's actions aren't all blind self-will and momentary expediency, mocked by ironic circumstance. Even Francisco's devious control is pointedly casual, and limited, so that however Webster meant it we see him not as a Machiavellian but simply as the least vulnerable performer in a game of pride, a self-justifying avenger whose justice is itself wholly in question. The absence of a central moral focus makes it meaningless to place him in relation to Brachiano or Vittoria or Flamineo, for all their impulses present themselves as arbitrary attitudes and choices. If we look for settled motives or principles we find only local values—wifely loyalty, motherly love, family solicitude, the motions of the victim in the world of this play. But the submissive virtues themselves aren't so much coldly exploited as simply over-vulnerable in a world where men are seeking to impose their wills at random, moving dimly round each other like self-enclosed atoms whose reaction is the only check upon action. . . .

In a world where people respect each other so little our pity is not much in place. The characters hardly claim as much as our respect. For most of its course the play seems arranged to resist our sympathies, opposing intolerance and deviousness on the one hand to effrontery and headstrong self-will on the other—striking enough qualities but none of them especially admirable. If we feel that it does nonetheless allow people a kind of grandeur in the end it can only be the final episode which sublimates their scattered powers and at last offers us something in human nature to esteem. All the play allows us for our unreserved respect is the way the three meet their deaths when they see that they have to; and they invite our approval because it's only then that they acknowledge each other, and each other's defiant pride.

A. J. Smith
in *John Webster*, ed. Brian Morris (London: Ernest Benn, 1970), pp. 86–88

John Webster has been called decadent or obsessed with death because his plays do frequently resemble a charnel-house of the imagination in which the audience cannot escape the knowledge of their own death and therefore react, on occasion, with the disgust and disbelief that are naturally aroused by this uncomfortable thought. Webster forces his audience to regard this unpalatable fact because it is only once it has been accepted that the full value of the other elements of his composition can be appreciated. The intricate spider's web of intrigue, "policy," and death which surrounds the Duchess [in *The Duchess of Malfi*] creates a darkness both in the language and the lighting of the stage which concentrates attention upon her own perspective of the world. . . .

There is a distinct danger that the calmness with which the Duchess accepts her death may leave the audience unmoved by its terror. The fear and agony of Cariola, biting and scratching as the cord goes round her neck and struggling to avoid the inevitable by a vain succession of increasingly improbable pleas for a stay of execution, remind them that death is, at the last, still terrible. For Cariola life itself is still a thing of value and she properly fights in its defence. If the Duchess does not struggle it is because only her love for Antonio has made her life of value to her and the acceptance of death has now become the only available expression of that love. It is the only expression left because her marriage with Antonio cannot observe the "degree, priority and place" of a world ordered by Ferdinand and the Cardinal. The Duchess appeals beyond the customs of her society to the natural world where the birds in the fields are free to choose their own mates. Her family is an expression of that natural order and her courage in its defence provides a hint of the power which might translate it into a new political reality. The Renaissance court now seems a devious labyrinth which obstructs the very human nature it had once liberated. It can still crush the Duchess but it cannot control indefinitely the power which she represents. Webster's observation of the troubles which afflicted his society is both accurate and prophetic. . . .

The play is a carefully constructed dramatic equation whose "solution" depends upon the value that we are ourselves prepared to assign to some of its unknown quantities. The structure and the imagery both seem to suggest that within the framework of the poisoned fountain or standing pool of the opening and the deep pit of darkness which is its end, John Webster has succeeded in presenting one woman's psychology which is misinterpreted, religiously, socially, and psychologically in terms of the masculine ideology of her brothers. The problem is not one that requires an answer since what is being dramatised is the unresolved clash between vital and competing human instincts and the imperfect control exercised by man's turbulent intelligence. Webster does not offer us a solution but a report in which the growing darkness of the "sensible hell" perceived by Bosola is lit for a moment by the flash of "I am Duchess of Malfi still."

Nigel Alexander
in *John Webster*, ed. Brian Morris (London: Ernest Benn, 1970), pp. 104, 110–12

SIR THOMAS WYATT

1503–1542

Joost Daalder, ed., *Sir Thomas Wyatt: Collected Poems* (1975)

It is not. . . . by accident that Wyatt's poetry at its best is pervaded by feelings of nostalgia at the sacrifice of old conventions and the securities of sophisticated communal feeling these represented; nor, consequently, is it accidental that such a sacrifice should give to the lover in Wyatt's poems such a dramatic insecurity. Wyatt's search for assurance is significantly an appeal against conventional feeling to that which is "within," to the real state of the affections. It is this characteristic of his best work that has led to the claim that he introduced the introspective note into English poetry. The decay of the habitual modes of life left the individual adrift in an ethically chaotic world and, critical of what was taking place about him, he was forced to search within himself for the materials out of which to construct some sound discipline of life.

It was this moment of social collapse, so well recorded by More, [Thomas] Starkey and Wyatt in their different ways, that made Protestantism appear spiritually significant and made it conceivable that a reformation of life could take place around the inner convictions of the enlightened individual. In a society still possessing a strong code of opinion and conduct such a conception would have seemed merely eccentric. . . .

The bulk of Wyatt's poems, and those of the new company of courtly makers to which he belonged, still appraise the affections in the language of feudalism. This is not to say, of course, that other kinds of appraisal were not being made; a man would seek to procure his lady's favour by service, but he would also put her in remembrance of him by presenting her with some costly trinket. . . .

In general, pre-Elizabethan poetry bears witness to the fact that the heart's affections were conventionally accepted to be as natural and as unchanging as feudal bondage. Although Wyatt's poetry expresses a sense of the inadequacies of this presumption, it is still largely constrained by it. "Who so list to hount," for example, alludes to the untouchability of Caesar's wife in a line—"Noli me tangere for Cesars I ame"—which relies for its irony upon Christ's use of the phrase *Noli me tangere* ("Touch me not for I am not yet ascended unto the Father," John XX:17), and his command that we should render unto Caesar the things that are Caesar's and unto God the things that are God's (Matthew XXII:21). By conflating these two commands the line surreptitiously convicts the lady (thought by some to have been Anne Boleyn) of rendering unto Caesar the things that are God's. Thus, whilst recognizing the royal prerogative, Wyatt creates an awareness of a higher allegiance and so feeds into his poem a sense of the inadequacy of an affectional tie sanctioned by degree alone. Nevertheless, this sense of inadequacy is only stealthily at work behind an overt acquiescence to the claims of degree.

Raymond Southall
EIC (Winter, 1972), pp. 364–65, 368–69

Wyatt's poems often deal with courtly love in a very literal sense; but courtly love was closely tied up with courtly politics (as in Anne Boleyn's case), and Wyatt's reactions in both spheres show consistency. The death of Thomas Cromwell, for instance, is described in much the same language in poem CLX as Wyatt uses elsewhere in his love poems. The editor of Tottel's *Songes and Sonettes* actually thought that the poem was about "the death of his loue." Clearly Wyatt thought of Cromwell as offering the security which at other times he expected from women. This time, his grief is on record outside the poem; and we find Wyatt writing that his *only trust* is in Cromwell and the King. Much of his verse is about the loss of, or betrayal of, trust. It is often impossible to decide whether he is referring to a treacherous mistress or to a deceitful enemy at Court. Certainly his courtly experiences account for his fear and hatred of slander, the more dangerous because it is concealed. We need only think of the malicious Bonner, a persistent enemy, to whom Wyatt owed his imprisonment in 1541. Poems that refer to a sudden, unhinging shift in the favours of Fortune can be seen as related to this confinement, or for example to Wyatt's spell in the Tower in 1536, when he witnessed the fall of others besides. This event is specifically alluded to in poems CXLIII and CXLIX.

It is true that on the whole Wyatt's life was not unsuccessful, given the circumstances of Henry's regime, but he suffered enough misfortune to explain the melancholy tone in much of his work, and his condemnation of the vices which he saw around him or was the victim of. He encountered a good deal of frustration in his diplomatic work, and he witnessed the duplicity of Charles V, on which he comments in his letters, and perhaps in poem CV. In his first letter to his son, he speaks as though he has gone through "a thousand dangers and hazards, enmities, hatreds, prisonments, despites and indignations." He blames his own "folly and unthriftiness" for this, as he does more than once in his verse; but it is significant, and fully consistent with what we find in the poems, that already in 1537 he saw his life as made up of these depressing experiences. It is only natural that in several poems we see Wyatt turn away from the courtly life (outwardly alluring, but perilous and nauseating underneath), and express a preference for a quiet, humble, and anonymous life.

This may sound as though he tended to indulge in easy escapism, but such is not the case. He remained involved in the courtly life until his sudden death, but tried to steel his nerves by enduring suffering patiently. He instructed his son to read Seneca, the Roman Stoic philosopher, who left his stamp on some of Wyatt's verse, and he was influenced, too, by Boethius and by Plutarch's *Quyete of Mynde* (Wyatt's title), which he translated. Quiet of mind is indeed what Wyatt in several poems professes to be his aim.

Joost Daalder
Introd., in *Sir Thomas Wyatt: Collected Poems*, ed. Joost Daalder
(London: Oxford Univ. Pr., 1975), pp. xvii–xviii

SHAKESPEARE

Harold Kollmeier, editor

WILLIAM SHAKESPEARE

1564–1616

Personal

Some voyagers [into Shakespeare biography] have preferred to take journeys of discovery. We tend to regard Caroline F. E. Spurgeon as an heroic, although not unfeminine, figure from an already somewhat remote past: a principal architect (with G. Wilson Knight and Wolfgang Clemen) of that profound shift in emphasis away from historicism and the study of the play as an action or an assemblage of characters or the embodiment of a philosophy, and towards a conception of the play as dramatic poem conveying meaning primarily through word-pictures. To think of Miss Spurgeon is to think of her classifications of figures, and of the brightly colored charts at the back of *Shakespeare's Imagery and What It Tells Us* (1935). . . .

What manner of being emerges from the application to biography of [a] revolutionary method which unlocks the "storehouse of the unconscious memory"? Shakespeare (we learn) had a healthy mind as well as body, and was cleanly in his habits, with a fastidious disdain for dirt and foul odors. A quiet chap, annoyed by noise, but practical rather than a dreamer: he made creative use of his silences, for he was busily absorbing impressions, registering them like a sensitive photographic plate. The countryside and fresh air appealed to him more than urban pleasures. Shakespeare enjoyed reading; horses he loved, as he did most animals, except spaniels and house dogs (probably because of the filthy practice of feeding them at table in those days). Bowls he played with zest, and he was an expert archer. "He was, indeed, good at all kinds of athletic sport and exercise, walking, running, dancing, jumping, leaping, and swimming." A homey and domestical sort too, neat and handy when it came to household chores, especially if they involved carpentry. He preferred, however, to steer clear of such indoor nuisances as smoky chimneys, stopped ovens, and guttering candles. The attributes of the inner man Miss Spurgeon sums up in five words: courage, sensitiveness, balance, humor, and wholesomeness. (The acute sensitivity, she grants, coexists oddly with the courage.) Of all the virtues, he most prized unselfish love; fear, rather than money, he regarded as the root of evil. If Shakespeare can be described in a word, it is *Christ-like* (perhaps that helps to explain his carpentering hobby). Thus do new critical methods furnish a modern variation on age-old bardolatry.

Samuel Schoenbaum
Shakespeare's Lives (Oxford: Clarendon, 1970), pp. 747–49

General

The much debated question of act division in Shakespeare has been a scholarly red herring, diverting attention from the real issues and seriously impeding our understanding of the plays' organization. The question whether Shakespeare knew and followed the Horatian five-act rule has probably seemed to many critics an arid subject, which they could afford to ignore. Possibly the issue has even discouraged some from embarking upon serious, inductive studies of structure. The subject *is* arid precisely because, as recent scholarship has demonstrated, act division plays no part at all in Shakespearean structure. . . .

Especially since Granville-Barker, we have come to understand that Shakespeare's usual practice in relating scene to scene is to select and dispose his material so that each scene comments upon the one preceding. A play is in effect a series of pictures held up for comparison in pairs, first scenes 1 and 2, then 2 and 3, and so forth. In most cases, scenes are presented in roughly chronological order, but the progression of time is by no means regular and steady: Shakespeare will leap over days, months, or even years if necessary to find the next significant moment to hold up before us. These two freedoms, complete freedom of choice in the episodes to be dramatized and almost complete freedom in temporal sequence, allow him to make nearly every scene count.

To a mind accustomed either to a predominantly psychological literary form, like the modern novel, or to a classical style of regular and logical narrative development, the sequence of scenes in a play by Shakespeare is likely to appear capricious and arbitrary. Like the relations between the various episodes within an individual scene, the relations between scenes are often determined by other than narrative concerns, and we will have no difficulty following the logic of a Shakespearean play if we keep this in mind. The temptation scene in *Othello*, for instance, is preceded by the brief and apparently irrelevant scene which shows the Moor on his way to inspect the fortifications of Cyprus (II,ii). An Elizabethan sensibility, accustomed to thinking analogically, would have no difficulty relating this episode to the temptation scene, which reveals how inadequate Othello's personal fortifications are against Iago's siege.

Mark Rose
Shakespearean Design (Cambridge, Mass.: Harvard Univ. Pr., 1972), pp. 20–21, 74–75

Shakespeare's plays are presented in ever new productions, each one of which will emphasize one particular interpretation and display the talents of its director and actors. The devoted Shakespearean will seek out many different productions and slowly build up a complex memory-system which will provide him with a multiple response for each favourite play; but by this time he may well be devoted to the pursuit and not to the quarry.

In such a well-informed and various world, the survival of individual, open, imaginative and creative response poses yet another major problem. How can we avoid the secondary response, see the goods and not the package, maintain a crucial ignorance, but not a *naïveté*? We have a virtually free access to books of learning and have been encouraged since youth to pass examinations, so that it now seems natural to have an informed opinion on any subject worth the study. Yet we know that deepest experiences are not examinable, and that verbalization stops short of accounting for those moments when we have recognized truth and moved outwards towards the encompassing of its new experience. Somehow we must defend our own creative response and strengthen it. This will not mean burning our books or trying to reconstruct primitive conditions. Rather we must examine the processing which art receives today, and our own consumption of it. We must use new skills responsibly, without expecting too much from them. . . .

Our response to Shakespeare poses these difficulties in extreme form. He inherited beliefs and expertise we no longer possess. He responded to social and political realities that can only be reconstructed painstakingly by analysis and description. He wrote plays for a kind of theatre that no longer exists and cannot be reconstructed. He wrote texts for actors to explore and recreate rather than for the solitary reader, and he was aware of an audience that shared its pleasures. He has left no direct testimony of his intentions and we know only a little more than nothing about his private life. Obviously we can use many aids to understanding and consequently the books written about his plays and the productions of them in theatres throughout the world are unequalled in quantity and growing frequency. While there is no doubt that Shakespeare has survived through all the changes of time, that only increases the danger that his plays will be processed more completely. By making him our own, we may have lost what he can, uniquely, offer.

John Russell Brown
Free Shakespeare (London: Heinemann Educational Books, 1974), pp. 1–2

The physical theater and its arrangements of space are always a part of any play performed within that theater. We have almost lost sight of this basic theatrical fact because the theater of modern realism—like the movie theater which developed from it—with its elaborate scenery and its darkened auditorium has created an illusion of reality, causing audience and theater magically to vanish. But the play space of the Renaissance London theater with its "heaven" and "hell," its outside framing structure and internal galleries, its pit and its platform stage, was starkly present during all performances in the public playhouses. Nor did the playwrights try to ignore this theater.

Among Renaissance English dramatists such open acceptance of the theater is commonplace, but Shakespeare was particularly insistent on "detaching" his audience from any illusion about the reality of the scenes and characters before them and calling attention to the fact that the full scene includes the theater and the audience sitting inside it watching a play. The most obvious device used for this purpose was, of course, the placement on stage of an audience watching a play-within-the-play, as in the production of "Pyramus and Thisbe" in *A Midsummer Night's Dream*. This stock device forces the actual audience to remember that they are in turn simply another group of players in a larger play, and that the physical theater in which they sit is not final reality but simply another stage on which a longer play is being enacted before an unseen audience.

Because of its involvement in the plays presented in it, the structure of the physical theater becomes most important to Elizabethan and Jacobean drama, and it would be most helpful to know with certainty the answer to such questions as exactly how large was the stage? or did all public theaters have upper or inner stages, or "stations"? But how much real need is there finally for the endless pursuit of exactly accurate answers to such questions as these? In some ways it might be enough to accept a general "type" of theater and then spend our effort on trying to recover its symbolic values. . . .

Perhaps the most interesting thing about the Elizabethan public theater is that it was obviously a model in plaster and wood of the conservative world view of the late Middle Ages and the Renaissance. It was a *mappa mundi*, which constantly, though silently, said that the soaring poetry and brave sound of the human voice which dominated the stage and claimed the theater were ultimately contained by an enduring reality, a fixed cosmos of earth and heaven and hell, which were not made by the players and which existed before and after the brief moments in which the stage was filled with movement and activity.

But within this larger theater, which seems to have stood for limit and "reality," there were numerous smaller "internal theaters," or a more or less constant "theatrical situation," which provide the surest and best information we have to answer our most crucial questions about the fundamental nature of this theater. To know what the theater truly was, we need to understand not so much the dimensions of the physical theater as the way in which all the elements which composed the total "theater," including the stone and timber, worked together to create a characteristic "stance" or condition of being and striving. This stance is enacted for us by a great many characters within the plays, characters who are their authors' doubles, even in some ways their competitors who achieve what their creators strove for unsuccessfully.

Alvin B. Kernan
SQ (Winter, 1974), pp. 1–2

The History Plays

If I lay too much stress on what is original and individual in the History Plays, it is because recent scholarship has so often declared them conventional in form and substance and traditionally staid in their political and moral attitudes. We are asked to believe that the Shakespeare who blazed the path in tragedy for Chapman, Tourneur, Webster, Beaumont and Fletcher, Middleton, and Ford was content to follow the lead of the plodding didacticists who supposedly created the genre of the History Play, and like them dedicate his art to moralistic and propagandistic purposes. The pity of this scholarly insistence on the conventionality of the History Plays is that it threatens to turn living works of theater into dramatic fossils or repositories of quaint and dusty ideas. Instead of bridging the gulf of the centuries, the historical approach to the History Plays seems to widen it by identifying Shakespeare's mind and art with a past that viewed through the lens of scholarship appears more remote than ever before. . . .

No doubt the History Plays were more topical in their concerns than Shakespeare's other drama. They were also uniquely "public" plays in that they dealt with the political anxieties and patriotic enthusiasms, the shared memories and aspirations which make a people conscious of their oneness and destiny as a nation. Necessarily, therefore, Shakespeare was constrained in these plays by Chronicle "fact" and by accepted opinion. He could no more think of making Richard III a Yorkist Hamlet than he could deny Henry V his praise as a conquering hero. But if one does not expect Shakespeare to be emancipated in his political attitudes or recklessly heterodox in his interpretations of history—an Elizabethan revisionist or debunker of eminent Plantagenets—neither does one expect him to step forward in the History Plays as the laureate of Tudor royalism. One could imagine him in a time of national peril dedicating one or two plays to what he thought were necessary patriotic purposes. Can we believe, however, that he dedicated nine plays—the weightier part of all the drama he wrote before *Hamlet*—to the claims of orthodoxy? And can we imagine that a dramatic form as prescribed and conventional as the History Play is made to seem allowed scope for the artistic development which made him capable of plays like *Hamlet* and *King Lear*? . . .

What we need is not a less historical approach to the History Plays but a more rigorous methodology for that approach. . . .

Hardly cynical in his portrayal of human behavior, Shakespeare nevertheless records in the History Plays the ease with which men turn their coats and alter their allegiances and yet remain men of conscience. He allows us to savor the irony of ingenious political rationalizations, but he is not quick to brand equivocations of loyalty hypocrisy. He knows that politics is the art of accommodation and survival, and he knows too that because political theoreticians invoke metaphysical absolutes it is difficult for them to adjust to changing circumstances without seeming to abandon their principles.

Robert Ornstein
A Kingdom for a Stage: The Achievement of Shakespeare's History Plays (Cambridge, Mass.: Harvard Univ. Pr., 1972), pp. 2–4, 27

The Comedies

Whereas classical and Italian comedies pictured the life of a city, Shakespeare very nearly pictured the life of a whole nation. In the two parts of *Henry IV*, he conjured up an image of the varied ranks and regions of Britain, such as no one had seriously attempted since Chaucer. . . . Nevertheless, there are some striking omissions from his comedies. Although he refers repeatedly to the countryside, he shows little or nothing on the stage of the life of yeomen or farm-workers, which he must have known well. He shows none of the interest in the condition of the peasants as a subject for drama that appears in the writings of Ruzzante or Lope de Vega; he is a national playwright, but he looks towards London. And even in his urban scenes, he shows little or nothing of the working life of the craftsman or apprentice or the ordinary shopkeeper in staple trades, by comparison with a contemporary like Dekker; he shows bourgeois householders and tradesmen, but his merchants deal in luxury goods like the goldsmith in *The*

Comedy of Errors, or they are the moneylender and the patrician venturer of Venice. His stage world gravitates towards the great house or the court. He depicts the gentry from outside, but they stand at the centre.

Secondly, his comic vision remains very largely a vision of the stage. To quote Bernard Shaw . . . he shows us ourselves, but not our problems; or rather, he has none of the ambition that actuated writers of Shaw's time to represent people struggling to solve their problems rationally, under lifelike conditions. On the contrary, even in his most serious comedies, he reverts to the ancient conventions of Fortune and trickery; even the earnest and privileged Duke of Vienna [in *Measure for Measure*] corrects the vices of his government by subterfuges more devious than those of a slave in Plautus. In part, Shakespeare's reliance on the ancient conventions of comedy sprang from realistic if not unavoidable assumptions, however; he could expect much less than men like Shaw from rationality in human affairs because his society was much more fragile than theirs, living closer to the starvation-line, much more exposed to the pressures of Nature. And in part, Shakespeare's attitude seems to reflect a conscious bias or choice. His people live through their emotional problems in comedy precisely by being transformed or disguised, by coming into contact with the special conditions of the stage. Shakespeare does not, as a rule, invite his audience to escape from normal psychological conditions by forgetting what they are like, but he invites them to contemplate special conditions, which are not presented as typical of life in general, but are contra-distinguished from everyday life outside the theatre by devices carried over from the comic tradition. The theme of the place of comedy itself in social life is usually latent in Shakespeare's plays and often comes near the surface.

Shakespeare's preoccupation with the real influence of the monarch, even in comedy, and, at the other extreme, his preoccupation with the idea of play-acting, set him apart from all but his immediate predecessors. They reflect his historically novel situation, as a professional playwright in a mainly commercial theatre, writing for, and even in a sense creating, a national public, but depending first and last on aristocratic and royal favour. At one pole of his comic world is the actor-poet, at the other, his ultimate patron, the prince.

Leo Salingar
Shakespeare and the Traditions of Comedy (Cambridge: Cambridge Univ. Pr., 1974), pp. 255–56

The Tragedies

What meaning can there be in the term "Christian tragedy," in particular as applied to Shakespeare? There would be no controversy, I assume, if this term were generally reserved for tragedies which have Bible story as their subject matter, such as Peele's *David and Bethsabe* or Milton's *Samson*; for then it could be taken for granted that "Christian" carried a denotation like that of the adjective "science" in our term "science fiction." But most users of the term "Christian tragedy" have in mind not story classification, but a Christian quality in the *Weltanschauung* of the author. . . . Although admittedly the term "Christian tragedy" can be used in diverse senses, the most meaningful usage would seem to be in connection with some distinctively Christian understanding of man implicit in the art work, as evidenced by a mimesis of human experience in accord with principles of discrimination traditionally Christian.

It is in this sense that I consider the word "Christian" a valid way of characterizing Shakespearean tragedy. It runs the risk, however, of being associated with the loose and half-informed notions of Christianity which many moderns have. That is, it can be misused as an umbrella under which to attribute to Shakespeare sentimental meanings, or impressionistically didactic ones, which his plays do not really imply but which the critic develops and denominates as Christian. . . .

The hero's utterances must not be confused with the playwright's feelings. And further, we ought not to suppose that if the tragedy as a work of art is to be called Christian its hero must have or develop a Christian ethic. Rather, what may be said to qualify a tragedy as Christian is the author's unstated Christian world view, by the light of which he understands and orders what happens to and within a hero whose attitude and choices are morally defective. . . .

"Souls in their very sins," says St. Augustine, "seek but a sort of likeness to God, in a proud and perverted, and so to say, slavish freedom." A playwright who knows this fact, it seems to me, has a basic clue for the structuring of Christian tragedy. He will recognize that tragedy can be a dark analogue of Christian redemption, a blind version of Atonement. Recall, for example, besides Hamlet's priestlike behavior, Macbeth's taking of a cup at the striking of a bell and celebrating pale Hecate's rites; or the elaborate language of sacrificial offering with which both Brutus and Othello envelop their crimes; or Romeo's drinking the cup at "Saint" Juliet's tomb-altar; or Richard II's imagined humiliation as a Christ betrayed by Judases. In each case, the tragic hero has taken as his god some imagination of his own heart, to which he then offers his life in an unintended mimicking of divine action.

The Shakespearean hero's defective action shadows Christian paradigm, in the same sense that falsehood inevitably depends upon truth, or the corruption of anything depends upon the good it corrupts. By ineradicable implication, a perverse nobility implies nobility, a defiled humanity implies something great that can be defiled. . . . Thus tragedy, paradoxically, points us to the high calling man might have achieved, by showing us the empty shadow of it which he has chosen as his fate.

Roy Battenhouse
Shakespearean Tragedy: Its Art and Its Christian Premises
(Bloomington: Indiana Univ. Pr., 1969), pp. 134–35, 264–65

THE ROMANCES

It has been pointed out that the chief obstacle to the movement of the comedies toward their festive conclusions often takes the form of a rigid or unreasonable law—the laws governing the disposition of marriageable daughters in *A Midsummer Night's Dream* and *The Taming of the Shrew*, the law which upholds Shylock's bond, the law of primogeniture in *As You Like It*, the King of Navarre's silly edict, and so forth. In several of the plays the obstacle is a blocking or "killjoy" figure who is repressive, anti-social, and generally unmusical—the heavy father of *A Midsummer Night's Dream*, Shylock, Malvolio, and so forth. Although the wishes of the lovers, their sense of identity, and finally the social vision of the plays themselves gain in value and integrity as a result of their being tested by these counter-romantic laws and figures, the threat they pose to the romantic vision of the play is not very grave. . . .

There is a sense then in which the romances would not have been possible without the preceding tragedies—I do not mean psychologically impossible, but *structurally* impossible. For like *Paradise Lost* and *Samson Agonistes*, Shakespeare's final romances subsume tragedy in the process of transcending it—not only *The Winter's Tale*, where the first three acts form a tragedy unto themselves, but the other romances as well. The adversity (if that term is not altogether too bookish to describe what a character like Leontes undergoes) presented in these plays does not resemble that of the comedies so much as that of the tragedies. There is nothing in the comedies to compare with the loss and isolation of Pericles, though there is much in *Lear*; nothing to match the rage and desperation of Leontes except in *Othello*; no counterpart to the humiliation of Hermione and Imogen other than that of Desdemona and Cordelia. Side by side with the magical speech-music of each of the last plays exist the harshest cacophanies of the tortured soul familiar from the great tragedies. If it is true that many of his tragic heroes try in vain to romanticize or redeem themselves to the bitter end . . . and that this effort is an essential part of their tragedy, the suffering principals of the romances—Pericles, Posthumus, Leontes, Alonso—are stripped of all hope or illusion of redeeming themselves, are rendered "absolute for death" (in a way that Claudio, to whom these words are addressed in *Measure for Measure*, never really is), and this is essential to their redemption. The tragic heroes, and we along with them, persist in expecting romance and get tragedy; the romantic protagonists are disabused of all romantic expectations and get romance. . . .

Because their protagonists expect the worst, the endings of the romances come to them, and I venture to say to us as well, as nothing less than a "miracle" in a way that the endings of the comedies do not.

Howard Felperin
Shakespearean Romance (Princeton, N.J.: Princeton Univ. Pr., 1972), pp. 60–64

The Comedy of Errors

It is my contention that this early Shakespearian comedy needs to be studied for the way it employs the structural pattern of separation and union—a pattern that is central to almost every comedy written, but one that informs the language, characterization, and action of *The Comedy of Errors* in a way that has not been explored in the past. This basic structural pattern, moreover, underlies a complex of thematic statements and restatements of ideas either closely or loosely related to separation and union. In *The Comedy of Errors* separation is represented by references to, and acts of, severing, untying, releasing, divorcing, freeing, and losing; these are balanced by different representations of union: binding, tying, fastening, uniting, confining, and finding. What is more, the implications of separation and union are profusely widespread. Separation, for example, becomes associated in the play with categories such as illogicality, chaos, and domestic dissolution; whereas union is linked with logic, order, and domestic stability. . . .

Before looking at the separation-union idea itself we should understand that another aspect of structure in *The Comedy of Errors* is the play's solid base made up of four interlocking levels of reality: family, commerce, state, and cosmos. The last of these does not have as prominent a role as do the first three; nevertheless, it *is* present; and, as we shall see, it does receive clear expression before the close of the play's third scene. In turn, the social situation (commerce and state) is not central to the play's meaning as is the domestic. Although the ties of family in the play are temporarily severed, causing, of course, separation, we see that those ties are actually extremely strong ones: brother seeks to be united with brother; son with mother; and father with son. The principal search is for the natural bonds that hold a family together as well as a search for individual members of that family. In a more general way all four levels are marked by a drive toward overcoming estrangement or division; and helping to underscore the importance of domestic, social, and cosmic ties (or the lack of them) is the separation-union antithesis, which helps to create ironies and ambiguities that make this play throb with dramatic and comic vigour. When in the denouement the ironies and ambiguities subside (meaning, of course, that the comic absurdities are at an end), a society and, more importantly, a family, are re-united. Happiness ultimately prevails in the world of the play. Just how Shakespeare effects this outcome with conviction is appreciated if we look at the separation-union pattern and its connexion with the four levels I have outlined.

Vincent F. Petronella
MLR (July, 1974), pp. 481–82

Love's Labour's Lost

The final songs contain everything in the play. Though they are presented almost as an afterthought, *Love's Labour's Lost* is incomplete, and unimaginable, without them. They receive almost unanimous praise, even (or especially) from critics who dislike the rest of the play. The songs represent a magic moment in *Love's Labour's Lost,* a moment which seems of a different quality and order from what has come before it.

And yet the songs explicate what has preceded them and are themselves best explicated by it. The first chapter showed that in the range of stylistic parodies encountered in the play there seemed no obvious rhetorical center, no voice to be relied upon. But that voice is heard, triumphantly, in the final songs. . . . The songs are touchstones . . . an exemplum and model for the right use of language.

The songs are not simple or "natural," in the usual sense, but are perhaps the most carefully crafted things in the entire play. They represent not the rejection of Art for Nature, but the rejection of bad art for good art, for sophisticated stylistic devices are used with assurance in the songs: rhyming, inverted word order, frequent alliteration, punning ("To-it" and "towit"), low to middle diction, and an insistent if uncomplicated syntax ("when" = "then," with a free use of "and" connectors that carry us along effortlessly). The meter is a carefully regulated ground-tone of iambic tetrameter, and the planned irregularities—the spondee of "mocks married men" and the anapestic surprise of "When icicles hang by the wall"—are strikingly effective. Holofernes would be astonished.

The point, as in the first chapter, is that, to say anything, we have to use a common body of rhetorical constructs and devices, although some schemes, such as periphrasis, are suspect from the start. *Love's Labour's Lost* in effect has debated the use of such devices, and if the parody and exaggeration in the play show us how not to use them, the last songs show what can be done with them. The rhetorical devices are essentially the same in both cases; what makes the difference is the imagination employing them.

That the songs seem a moment out of or beyond the play constitutes their triumph. They *are* still in the play, in the realm of the imagination, without seeming to be. The play proper, we think, ended some moments ago and this is simply being tacked on. But it isn't. Where the three earlier theatrical sections were self-consciously emphasized, the songs are introduced on a more casual note. It is crucial that they follow immediately upon Berowne's comment, "That's too long for a play," for as the play begins to turn back to artifice, away from the harshness of Marcade's outer world, the songs are offered as the perfect fusion of Art and Nature, inner and outer. And, as Shakespeare announces that his materials are too long for the traditional dramatic model, he concludes his play with one of the most traditional of all dramatic models, the medieval *conflictus*.

William C. Carroll
The Great Feast of Language (Princeton, N.J.: Princeton Univ. Pr., 1976), pp. 206–7

Henry VI, Part I

A literary artifact . . . is a museum-piece; what life it might truly have had has perished with the necessarily narrow set of emotional and cultural conditions to which it answered; to pretend that those conditions are available when the piece is reintroduced later is to make it its own parody. Now in *1 Henry VI* everything is only too obviously "artifact" in this sense—not just its admirable design, but its portrayal of history as monuments, its personages, its dramatic conventions, and its language. Everything is, as it were, deliberately turned to stone. Yet, do we not recognize as somehow essentially "Shakespearean" the dramatic consciousness that seems always aware of what it ostensibly excludes; that provides for its own vulnerability by containing its own criticism?

Such a drama embodies its own potential negation, and is truly willing to abandon its hold on the old in order to create the truly new. Thus Shakespeare's work characteristically cooperates in its own continuous exhaustion and demise. And so it is, though inchoately, with his earliest play. My argument is that *1 Henry VI* does *not* in fact rest contentedly with its stiff spectacular dramatic accomplishment, its too-easy manipulation of history, its Senecan postures and Heroick Song. The curious sense of original life beneath all the brassy opacity is the play's dis-ease by which it pre-empts and embodies our live discomfort. Thus the imperatives of drama, history, and speech, that proclaim themselves in stone only to melt at once into chimera, are not only exhaustible, but surpassable. And thus the play's counter-consciousness not only affords an ironic perspective upon the language and the characters who mouth it, but commences a potent exploration into the *true* relationship of "history" and "play." But that is possible only when the theater has become metatheater—self-aware and self-fulfilling. . . .

As a "fantasia" *1 Henry VI* plays upon the very notion of historical reality, the ontology of the past. In testing out ways in which the past claims to signify in the present, Shakespeare must have marvelled to discover how easily that supposedly intractable material dissolved, how easily he could manipulate it and produce solid "effects" such as, for instance, Nashe wondered at in beholding "brave Talbot . . . after he had lyne two hundred yeares in his Tombe . . . fresh bleeding" on the stage. For thus does "art and baleful sorcery" win over Charles, Talbot, Burgundy, Henry, Nashe, and us. Too easily, in fact, and in our case at least, not lastingly. Something was wrong with a concept of the past, solemnly chronicled in the texts or monumentalized in conventions of dramatic speech and form, that so readily turned to self-parody under the scornful dramatist's pen. That readiness, indeed, saved the play itself from petrifaction, but it also meant that, in the ease of its contempt for the petrified past which it affected to present "fresh bleeding," *1 Henry VI* had missed the real issue between the artist and his matter.

John W. Blanpied
SEL (Spring, 1975), pp. 215, 226–27

Richard III

Traditionally, *Richard III* is regarded by "orthodox" critics as part of a grand design celebrating a providential concept of history and political order, derived chiefly from Edward Hall, a design that is worked out in the eight plays from *Richard II* to *Richard III* and merges them into an epic narrative of England. Other critics have emphasized the play's resemblance to Senecan tragedy, to the morality play, and to Marlowe. But historical doctrines and literary traditions do not explain what makes Richard run. . . .

In *Richard III* the protagonist acts always for two audiences, his dupes in the play, who never learn the truth about him until too late, and the auditors in the theater, who are never misled because he takes us into his confidence in his soliloquies, making us his accomplices. He speaks five soliloquies in this play, four of them purposefully concentrated in the first three scenes, so as to make us as soon as possible his confidants in crime. Although we may feel uneasy about it, our virtuous superego is lulled, and the naked id awakes to vicarious enjoyment of Richard's virtuosity in villainy. He uses as both agents and dupes people who, for the most part, willingly play the parts he assigns them, and who therefore deserve the consequences. This may account, in part, for the powerful hold of the play from Shakespeare's day to our own. The stripping of our defenses to lay bare our unofficial selves, the same selves strongly appealed to by Falstaff, becomes an important key to Shakespeare's technique. We are caught off guard as we are drawn into Richard's plots. We know his game because he has told us about it. The play puts us in the position of being able to say "I could have told you so" to the simple gulls as we smugly watch their misfortunes unfold. . . .

We are in it with Richard before we know it, for his existence "depends on a kind of conspiratorial collaboration with the audience" [Wilbur Sanders], and the line separating spectator from player is stretched so thin that the demarcation becomes precarious as Richard seduces us along with his other victims, although we remain comfortably immune. . . .

We know Richard's self-declared unfitness for love because of his deformity, a defect repeatedly thrown in his face in *2* and *3 Henry VI*. Except for its visual presence, it is displaced now by more serious defects of character expressed in his resemblance to various venomous and ferocious animals, an insistent imagery that becomes dominant. He is called hedgehog, poisonous bunch-backed toad, bottled spider, dog, bloody boar (this nine times, a telling epithet because a boar was Richard's heraldic emblem) and its variants rooting hog and foul swine, wolf, cockatrice, hellhound, and carnal cur. Quite a menagerie. These comparisons to malignant animals, twenty-nine of them in all, are distributed among most of the important characters and persist throughout.

Waldo F. McNeir
SEL (Spring, 1971), pp. 171, 173–75

Titus Andronicus

When T. S. Eliot so flamboyantly denounced *Titus Andronicus* as "one of the stupidest and most uninspired plays ever written," he naturally invited rebuttal. But while an apology for *Titus* can certainly be erected, the fact is that the imputed stupidities of the tragedy attract far more interest than any of its mediocre achievements. Indeed, if we would only persist in the study of those very "stupidities" that many critics would rather forget, we would discover that the ways in which the figurative language imitates the literal events of plot makes *The Tragedy of Titus Andronicus* a significant dramatic experiment. In the play's spectacularly self-conscious images that keep pointing at the inventive horrors in the plotting, in its wittily-obsessive allusions to dismembered hands and heads, and in the prophetic literalness of its metaphors, *Titus* reveals its peculiar literary importance.

The peculiar language of *Titus Andronicus* is particularly apparent in the literalness of its central metaphors. In a play preeminently concerned with the mutilation of the human body, *Titus* makes nearly sixty references, figurative as well as literal, to the word "hands" and eighteen more to the word "head," or to one of its derivative forms. Far from being divorced from the action as many critics claim, the figurative language points continually toward the lurid events that govern the tragedy. The figurative language, in fact, imitates the gruesome circumstances of the plot, thus revealing that Shakespeare subordinates everything in *Titus*, including metaphor, to that single task of conveying forcefully the Senecan and Ovidian horrors that he has committed himself to portraying.

Such a relationship between language and event is really quite strange. Ordinarily metaphor is endowed with the capacity of extending almost infinitely the imaginative compass of a play. Through its embedded metaphors especially, a play usually translates its immediate events in images that reach far beyond the poor limitations of the stage. In *Titus Andronicus*, however, metaphor, for the most part, draws its images directly from the narrower events of plot. It becomes literalized. This is a very daring and even dangerous enterprise to undertake. Deliberately relinquishing its natural prerogatives, metaphor strives instead to unite language and action in an endeavour to render the events of the tragedy more real and painful. . . .

This unrelieved and, in truth, witty exploration of the relationship between language and event marks a notably disinterested, even detached, involvement in the values of language with respect to dramatic events. This cool distance between the playwright and his materials helps to explain one of the distinguishing features of *Titus Andronicus*—the odd way that this tragedy leaps with an inextinguishable wittiness toward the multiple perceptions that ordinarily belong to the world of intellectual comedy. . . .

Whatever our final aesthetic judgment concerning the merits of *Titus Andronicus*, we must understand that we are dealing, not with a paucity of imagination, but with an excess of dramatic witness, with a talent untamed. However flawed the tragedy may be in other respects, we must grant that the playwright has exploited the language of the stage with inventive brilliance and has taxed the resources of drama in making death and mutilation vivid to us.

Albert Tricomi
SS, Vol. 27 (1974), pp. 11–12, 14, 19

The Taming of the Shrew

There is an abundance of evidence in Shakespeare and other Elizabethans to show that jigs were not the only dances that could be interpreted as miming the sexual impulses of animals. In fact, this was one of the charges in the Puritan crusade against all dancing. The pavane took its name from the peacock, and the mating dance of that bird was proverbial. . . . The galliard, as Sir John Davies informs us in *Orchestra*, was "a gallant daunce, that lively doth bewray/A spirit and a vertue masculine," qualities reflected in the etymology of its name, which combines connotations of bravery with gaiety and high spirits. . . .

If Petruchio's conquest of Kate is a kind of mating dance with appropriate strutting and biceps-flexing, she in turn is a healthy female animal who wants a male strong enough to protect her, deflower her, and sire vigorous offspring. Petruchio's elemental force differentiates him from the numerous old pantaloons who people the comic world of the play, especially the Bianca plot. . . .

The animal imagery in which the play abounds is a prime reason for its disfavor with the critics, who find such terms degrading to Kate and to the concept of matrimony. True, Petruchio undertakes to "woo this wildcat" (I.ii.196) and punningly vows "to tame you, Kate,/And bring you from a wild Kate to a Kate/Comformable as other household Kates" (II.i.278–80). Likewise, there is the nodal metaphor of hawk taming, and at the end he wagers on her obedience as on his horse or his hound. But these images are less the mark of the master than his tribute to the animal spirits that they both share. He is perfectly willing to style himself "a combless cock, so Kate will be my hen" (II.i.229). If she can be compared to the jennet in *Venus and Adonis*, inwardly eager but coyly standoffish, Petruchio's behavior recalls the stallion's in that poem: "Anon he rears upright, curvets, and leaps,/As who should say, 'Lo, thus my strength is tried,/And this I do to captivate the eye/Of the fair breeder that is standing by' " (279–82). Shakespeare's easy acceptance of the facts learned in Warwickshire barnyards, his evident sympathy for all animal life, should forestall any critical squeamishness on our part.

Michael West
in *Shakespeare Studies VII*, ed. J. Leeds Barroll (Columbia: Univ. South Carolina Pr., 1974), pp. 68–70

The Two Gentlemen of Verona

Clearly this very early play is in many ways a piece of apprenticeship (so that one natural reason for anyone's "disgust" with it is that it is not as good as the rest of Shakespeare) and a seed-bed for themes, characters and situations which are to be developed in later plays. But it can be unhelpful to pre-judge the play according to notions of development: to assume that the reason why *The Two Gentlemen of Verona* troubles us is that Julia is not as "rounded" as Viola, that the Proteus-Valentine relationship is not as fully realized as the friendship of Bassanio and Antonio, or that the outlaw scenes do not have the thematic importance of their counterparts in *As You Like It*. What is more helpful, if we want to see what impulses produce the particular inconsistencies of *The Two Gentlemen of Verona*, is to relate the play to the sonnets. Whatever the exact chronology of either play or sonnets, a kinship between them has long been a recognized fact. It consists both of verbal echoes—similar, often Petrarchan, topics and conceits being developed through similar vocabulary—and of a kind of plot similarity. Whatever the true story behind either play or sonnets, in both cases Shakespeare is creating a fiction to explore the joys and agonies, the betrayals and fulfilments, of interconnecting love relationships. Proteus, the betrayer of both love and friendship, is most like the Youth of the sonnets, with an element of the Dark Lady; Valentine and the two girls all share features of the sonnets' "I": adoration of the beloved, faithfulness, constancy; and Valentine in the end takes up the all-forgiving and renouncing position of, for example, Sonnet 40. Obviously I am not concerned here with "plot" similarities as indicating any autobiographical truths behind these works: the "truth" of the sonnets lies in Shakespeare's dramatic ability—unique among Elizabethan sonneteers—to create a sense of "what it feels like" in a given human situation. . . .

When love poetry is transferred to the stage, when the inner drama of a sonnet's "I" and "thou" has to be translated into the flesh-and-blood interaction of two lovers and probably also their conflicts with several other "I"s and "thou"s, then the problem is further confounded. In *Romeo and Juliet* Shakespeare partly solved it by contrasting the empty attitudinizing of Romeo's love for Rosaline with the beauty of the formality which surrounds and expresses his love for Juliet, from their first meeting on a shared sonnet. . . .

The lovers in *The Two Gentlemen of Verona* can liken each other to the sun, or the moon, or the stars, can be blinded by love or weep floods of tears, or generally draw on the stock-in-trade of Petrarchan love poetry. But, as in the sonnets, Shakespeare in this play also shows an awareness that conventionalized language, like conventionalized behaviour, may be false. In this self-consciousness about conventional language and situations lie many of the play's inconsistencies, but also much of its sense of life.

Inga-Stina Ewbank
in *Stratford-upon-Avon Studies 14*, ed. D. J. Palmer and Malcolm Bradbury (New York: Crane, Russak, 1972), pp. 34–37

Romeo and Juliet

Shakespeare . . . methodically constructs and maintains a sympathetic portrayal of Romeo and Juliet. The spectator is by no means blind to the excesses of passionate love, and on brief occasions both principals anticipate the worst possible consequences; but, with no internal struggle and with other figures manipulated to reflect the admirable characteristics of the young lovers, the structure of the play literally does not permit the audience to develop a critical posture. Instead, the greater antipathy is directed against what at one moment is branded as destiny and at another is depicted as a deadly feud. In the final analysis the two are synonymous;

the destructive force that converges on them is no malevolent or sadistic deity but an all-too-human hatred and envy which divides society into two armed camps admitting no commerce of affection.

More specifically, the terms "star-crossed lovers," "death-marked love," and "misadventured piteous overthrows" in the Prologue must be seen in the context that defines them. Numerous surrounding references clearly describe the fate which limits human freedom in this society as the rivalry of two rich families: "two households," "alike in dignity," "ancient grudge," "new mutiny," "civil blood," "civil hands," "fatal loins of these two foes," "parents' strife," "parents' rage." And the feud is the subject of the first 118 lines of Act I as the struggle involves, in turn, the servants, the youth, the aged, and the prince in a mounting crescendo of senseless terror. The servants fight from sheer habit, not from cause, asserting that this quarrel between their masters and the servants is "all one" to them. They know nothing of motive and are not concerned to know, questioning only whether the law is "of our side" in provoking an altercation. Nor is young Tybalt capable of greater reflection; to him it is sufficient that swords are drawn and that he hates all Montagues. Cruel humor is added as old Montague and old Capulet, each restrained by his wife, hobble on stage determined to leap into the fray. The prince denounces the lot of them as "rebellious subjects, enemies to peace" (i, 79), "beasts" (81) whose "pernicious rage" (82) and "cank'red hate" (193) has bred "civil brawls" from an "airy word" (87).

Verona's fate, in brief, is the human condition. To be sure, references to destiny in the play suggest a strong confluence of malignant coincidences and no effort of human logic can minimize the sense of an ominous design that seems to control the lives of the young protagonists. At the same time, each incident is clearly seen as the fruit not of the stars but of human hatred.

Larry S. Champion
Shakespeare's Tragic Perspective (Athens: Univ. Georgia Pr., 1976), pp. 83–84

Richard II

There is an artistic pleasure in the evocation of a medieval ethos in *Richard II*, not a political nostalgia for an earlier time. There is no intimation that England under Richard was a prelapsarian paradise, a world of order and harmony that was to be destroyed by a primal sin of disobedience. The opening scenes introduce us to a world which already knows violent contention and mortal enmity, in which men have shed the blood of their nearest kin and fear their father's brother's son. . . .

To find in the great speeches of *Richard II* an "Elizabethan World

Picture" and in its plot a depiction of the brute realities of power politics is to distort Shakespeare's sense of the complex relationship between political ideals and political realities. As a matter of fact, the poetry of *Richard II* does not declare the universality of cosmic harmony; it speaks instead of the universality of contention and change. It suggests that if hierarchy is natural, sovereign place is neither fixed nor immutable. Stars fall and consume themselves; rivers overflow their banks, and clouds dim the radiance of the sun. . . . Such conceits do not project Shakespeare's belief in analogical order; they express in dramatic verse his awareness of man's will to discover pattern and stability in a universe of disorder and flux. There would be no need for metaphysical conceptions of hierarchy if every king, baron, and commoner were as he should be.

So responsible seems Richard for the calamity that befalls him, and so inevitable seems his tragic fall, that one cannot believe Shakespeare wanted to persuade his audience that Richard should have been allowed to continue the rash blaze of riot which threatened to destroy England. According to [E. M. W.] Tillyard, the doctrine of *Richard II* is "entirely orthodox. Shakespeare knows that Richard's crimes never amounted to tyranny and hence that outright rebellion against him was a crime." Yet in fact Richard was guilty of the lawlessness which medieval and Renaissance theorists defined as tyranny. Accused of tyranny by his contemporaries, he is called a "wanton Tirant" in *Woodstock*, whose author makes much of the corruption of the law by Richard's rapacious favorites. Shakespeare grasps the more important issue of Richard's political lawlessness and leaves no doubt that at his worst he was, as *The Mirror for Magistrates* declares, a monarch who "ruled all by lust."

When a king recklessly endangers the foundations of law and plunders his country, what is an honorable subject to do? . . .

Instead of providing an ideological solution to the problem of political loyalty in *Richard II*, Shakespeare makes us aware of its enormous difficulty. We realize that men bow to circumstances in bowing to kings. Since there is no alternative to the rule of Henry, it is "right" for Aumerle to kneel before him; and if Henry is not the rightful heir to the throne, he is nevertheless the true king. Like Aumerle, Henry must bow to necessity.

Robert Ornstein
A Kingdom for a Stage: The Achievement of Shakespeare's History Plays (Cambridge, Mass.: Harvard Univ. Pr.),
pp. 103, 105, 113–14, 123–24

A Midsummer Night's Dream

The "dream" of Midsummer night is a vision, the moment of "sacred" time in which those capable of visionary perception can see the whole, the full harmony that grows out of endless reconciliation, or the real concord of what, under the aspect of ordinary time, seem to be opposites: winter and summer, male and female, life and death, reality and fantasy. I cannot agree with [C. L.] Barber when he says, "The actual title emphasizes a skeptical attitude by calling the comedy a dream." Such a vision is not extra-terrestrial; it is not, as [Paul A.] Olson suggests, the Platonic Abstract available to reason alone. Quite the contrary, reason, the analytical, distinguishing faculty, interferes with the perception of this kind of truth. The vision of endless reconciliation is a "midsummer night's dream"; it is effected through the medium of imagination which ignores or blurs the distinguishing limits and dimensions of things. The lunatic, lover and poet are especially qualified for visionary perception because they are "of imagination all compact." In their eyes the lines of demarcation between subject and object, or reality and fantasy, are erased.

Emblematic of the play's dream, or vision, is Bottom's dream. Bottom is not, as he is accused [by Olson] of being, the natural who "will not see God's secret at the bottom of things." He is, rather, a visionary, whose very synesthesia suggests a wholeness of perception that denies the partiality of any one sense: "The eye of man hath not heard, the eare of man hath not seen, man's hand is not able to taste, his tongue to conceive, nor his hearte to report what my dreame was" [IV.i.214–217]. He is aware, moreover, of the futility of trying to define the indefinable, of trying to report in ordinary language a moment that transcends ordinary experience. He knows that what he has perceived can only be expressed in the imitative synthesis of poetry: "I shall get Peter Quince to write a ballet of this dreame, it shall be called Bottome's Dreame, because it hath no bottome" [IV.i.229–235]. The dream is "Bottome's dreame" because it gives shape to that recurrent pattern that underlies the movement of ordinary life; yet it is bottomless because in every recurrence the pattern renacts the archetypal sacred moment.

Rose A. Zimbardo
in *Shakespeare Studies VI*, ed. J. Leeds Barroll (Columbia: Univ. South Carolina Pr., 1970), p. 36

The Merchant of Venice

The structure of Shakespearian comedy reflects a principle of Elizabethan aesthetics that "oftentimes a dischorde in Musick maketh a comely concordance " [from the Epistle Dedicatory to Spenser's *The Shepheardes Calender*]. "How shall we find the concord of this discord?" asks Duke Theseus in *A Midsummer Night's Dream*, and the answer lies not only in the characteristic action of the comedies, leading through confusion and conflict to clarification and reconciliation, but also in their blending of contrasting tones and moods. Shakespeare's development in comedy could be traced in terms of the increasing subtlety with which disparate elements of tone are brought into concordance with each other, from *The Comedy of Errors* with its fusion of romantic and Plautine motifs, to the complex and precarious harmonies of *Twelfth Night*.

The Merchant of Venice occupies a special place in this progression, as a play in which the discords are so powerful that it almost becomes a tragedy. In *Love's Labour's Lost*, the fragile and artificial comedy is shattered at the end by the sombre entry of Mercade, bringing news of death; *The Merchant of Venice*, on the other hand, establishes a keynote in its opening lines which suppresses the comic spirit of mirth and merriment. There is little playful laughter and not much wit, until they break out in the conclusion. Instead the prevailing tone is serious, and this current of feeling is modulated from Antonio's sadness, through the grim conflict between Shylock and his enemies, and the solemnity of the casket scenes, to the gravity which attends even the lovers in their ecstasy: they are never merry when they hear sweet music.

The seriousness of comedy is itself a paradox, a *discors concordia*. Yet the comic seriousness of *The Merchant of Venice* lies deeper than its potential for tragedy or its moral themes; the play operates at the fundamental level of feeling, as its action stresses the primacy of the affections, and after the tragic and moral conflicts are over, the serious spirit is transmuted into the effect of music at Belmont. "Nothing is good, I see, without respect," says Portia sententiously as she hears this music:

> How many things by season season'd are
> To their right praise and true perfection!
> Peace. . . . (V.i. 107–8)

The harmony is sweeter in the silence of the night, and also after the discords of the preceding action; this comic resolution reduces the passions to a serene contentment which is still serious in tone, but from which the play can come to rest in a relaxed good humour. Among the happy lovers as they leave the stage, Antonio is the odd man out, the discord that "maketh a comely concordaunce," for his part remains "a sad one."

D. J. Palmer
in *Stratford-upon-Avon Studies 14*, ed. D. J. Palmer and Malcolm Bradbury (New York: Crane, Russak, 1972), pp. 119–20

Henry IV, Parts I and II

Falstaff is complexly monstrous in the variety of his animality, but he is more intricately and at the same time more essentially monstrous in what he is as man and animal in one figure. The joining of the two in him has relationship to that figuration of doubleness in the mermaid which Montaigne takes to have an essentially grotesque quality, or to the figuration of doubleness in the centaur, equally favoured in the grotesque tradition of the Middle Ages and the Renaissance. But in Falstaff the beast and the non-beast are not joined with so violent an opposition to each other or so sharp a line of demarcation between them as to make a centaur form of the kind that Shakespeare brings the mad Lear to find in women. . . .

A figure of doubleness that may well be taken to exhibit an aspect of Falstaff is one put forward by his own wit but not for application to himself. He calls the Hostess an otter and, when the Prince succumbs to curiosity and demands his reason, says: "Why, she's neither fish nor flesh; a man knows not where to have her" (*I Henry IV*, III. iii. 144–45). The Hostess inevitably falls into the trap and protests that any man knows where to have her. Falstaff is a human being as much as the otter is a land creature and he is a brutish being as much as the otter is a water creature. The joining of man and beast in him, like the joining of creatures in the otter, is so much by way of interpenetration that it is not always easy to know where to have him. And of course he does not protest that he can be had.

For instance, Falstaff has all the animal desire that Lear attributes to centaur womanhood, but in him the beast is not by any means all beneath the girdle. It penetrates so far into what is above the girdle that it helps to make him the sensual man, the natural man *par excellence*, and yet it leaves generous space within him for a something more than natural. This other something affords him a lively understanding of his own grotesqueness as man and beast together, and of its relation to a general human grotesqueness with reaches of high and low even greater than his own.

Willard Farnham
The Shakespearean Grotesque (Oxford:
Clarendon, 1971), pp. 54–55

Julius Caesar

The political struggle in *Julius Caesar* is between members of a common weal, whose duty to it is never in question. It is a body composed of members unequal yet mutually dependent and responsible collectively for the general good. It is in health when each member executes his proper and vital function; it is disabled or diseased when any member fails in his public duties or encroaches on the functions of others. In this context, the most conspicious cause of Brutus's failure is not his politics but his lack of political skill. His amputation of the head for the patriotic purpose of benefiting the commonwealth actually deals it a mortal blow, and his failure to anticipate, let alone control, the subsequent paroxysm invites the operation of less scrupulous surgeons. At the conclusion, he has earned a name as the noblest Roman, but in terms of the common weal, nobility is not enough.

There is a special irony too, that in spite of his devotion to a social ideal, Brutus plays a lonely and tragic role, not less lonely because it is self-imposed. At the opening of the action, he has convinced himself that the commonwealth is threatened by the imperial designs of Caesar, and that it will be enslaved if he is crowned. At whatever expense to friendship, he feels an enormous sense of public duty to set it straight. . . .

Such idealism proceeds with the greater effect from a patrician with a proud republican ancestry; and it is sharpened quite as much by Antony, whose suave and ruthless political dexterity mocks the common good, as by Cassius, who as a practical politician recognizes the political potential of Brutus, but is no more capable of understanding Brutus's insusceptibility to political persuasion than he is of the idealism which prompts it. "What you would work me to I have some aim" (1.2.162) is not, as Antony publicly announces, the murder of a friend for personal gain, nor yet, as Cassius would like to have it, Brutus's consent to substitute his own image for Caesar's, but a reluctant admission, since he does not envy Caesar, that Caesar's crescent power has become a jeopardy to commonwealth, and that he must be the necessary instrument to preserve it. When Cassius holds the mirror up to Brutus, he is asking him to see what is not there to see. For an image of a very different character is most certainly taking shape in Brutus's mind as Cassius speaks. In the present disposition of affairs, he begins to see himself, not as a rival to Caesar, but as a "conservator of the common weal" . . . acting in his ancestral role as defender of the liberties of Rome against a potential tyrant. As patriot-idealist, he must implement his ideals with action—not an easy decision to make since he must weigh the too obvious personal cost (the death of his friend) against the gain to the common cause. "Poor Brutus, with himself at war," must choose between public and private loyalties, and the choice must be his alone.

W. G. Zeeveld
The Temper of Shakespeare's Thought (New Haven, Conn.: Yale Univ. Pr., 1974), pp. 84–86

As You Like It

The tendency of *As You Like It* to keep before us the artificial basis of the pastoral design is closely linked to its stress on the relativity and subjectivity of the experience of sojourn. The forest is constant in its imaginary character and changeable in each contact with a separate imagination. The essential subjectivity of pastoral thus emerges with considerable force; and since each character's encounter with Arden differs, the play offers a growing awareness of the fundamental relativity of human experience. This is much more so in *As You Like It* than in, say, Montemayor, Sidney, or Lodge. But it nonetheless springs from the idea of pastoral, and is a logical extension of the tendency in the eclogues to show nature reflecting human moods, and the themes of self-discovery and self-knowledge in the pastoral romances. It is again a case of Shakespeare seeing the full possibilities of a subject and exploiting them with uncommon skill. . . .

Everywhere this world gives back to its inhabitants and visitors the images of their own selves and preoccupations. Adam and Orlando find it hostile because they are lost and hungry; when they have had a square meal its savage character vanishes, to return for as long as it takes Orlando to forgive Oliver and dispatch the lioness. Corin sees in his flock the image of his own peace and contentment, while Touchstone, exercising his fascination with sexuality, turns it all into "the copulation of cattle," with Corin as presiding pimp. Touchstone comes closest to acknowledging the subjectivity of pastoral experience. "Ay, now am I in Arden," he remarks on arrival, "the more fool I" (2.4.15). And he goes on to demonstrate this intensification of selfhood, proving a much apter and funnier clown in the forest than he ever was at court. . . .

The typical plot of the pastoral romance—upon which most writers intent on adapting pastoral to the stage might be expected to concentrate their attention—held little genuine interest for Shakespeare in this play. He was content to rely on Lodge for the main events, and his treatment of the story line, as a number of critics have noted, was more than a little perfunctory. The plot of *As You Like It*, its complications and outcome, clearly exists as a means to something else that occupies most of the playwright's interest.

It is this fact, I suspect, that has led so many critics to suppose that Shakespeare had little interest in pastoral when he wrote *As You Like It*, and that it was mostly a convenience upon which his comic achievement could be reared. But a closer look suggests that his interest in pastoral was very great indeed, and that he brushed past its external trappings only in order to get at its essential themes and discover its rationale, recognizing that the appeal of pastoral lay not in shepherds, shepherdesses, or pretty songs, but in its imaginative vision of life, a vision that partook of both mythical and intellectual elements.

David P. Young
The Heart's Forest (New Haven, Conn.: Yale Univ. Pr., 1972), pp. 50–51, 69–70

Twelfth Night

Many of the conflicts of *Twelfth Night* seem to be concerned with the contest between human will and suprahuman control; yet, the latter manifests itself in various ways and is called different names by the characters themselves. As each contest between the human will and another designer works itself out, the involved characters recognize that their will is fulfilled, but not according to their planning. The individual's will is finally secondary to a design that benevolently, but unpredictably, accords with what he truly desires. For example, when Olivia, at the end of Act I, implores Fate to accord with her will in allowing her love for Cesario to flourish, she has no idea that her will must be circumvented for her own happiness. Yet the substitution of Sebastian for Cesario in her love fulfills her wishes more appropriately than her own design could have done. . . .

The playwright, like the comic providence in the play, has understood "what we will" and has led us to a pleasurable fulfillment of our desires, but in ways which we could not have foreseen or controlled. The substitution of the final line, "And we'll strive to please you every day," for the refrain, "For the rain it raineth every day," is a crucial change. Like the incremental repetition in the folk ballad, this pessimistic refrain has built a dynamic tension which is released in the recognition that the play is an actual experience in the lives of the audience, even though it is enacted in an imagined world. The players, and the playwright who arranges them, are engaged in an ongoing effort to please the audience. The providential design remains incomplete within the play's action and only promises a "golden time"; similarly, the playwright promises further delightful experiences for his audience. The subplot's action, on the other hand, is limited within the framework of revenge; the revenge of the subplot characters elicits Malvolio's cry for revenge.

Malvolio is the only one who refuses to see himself in a subservient position to a larger design. And possibly because that design is too small, we cannot feel that his abuse and final exclusion from the happy community of lovers and friends allows the golden time to be fulfilled within the play. Feste's manipulation of Malvolio resembles the playwright's manipulation of his audience's will, but in such a reduced way that we cannot avoid seeing the difference between merely human revenge and the larger benevolence that controls the play's design.

Joan Hartwig
ELH (Winter, 1973), pp. 501–2, 513

Hamlet

The play persists in taking its audience to the brink of intellectual terror. The mind of the audience is rarely far from the intellectual desperation of Claudius in the prayer scene when the systems in which he values his crown and queen collide with those in which he values his soul and peace of mind. For the duration of *Hamlet* the mind of the audience is as it might be if it could take on, or dared to try to take on, its experience whole, if it dared drop the humanly necessary intellectual crutches of compartmentalization, point of view, definition, and the idea of relevance, if it dared admit any subject for evaluation into any and all the systems of value to which at different times one human mind subscribes. The constant occupation of a sane mind is to choose, establish, and maintain frames of reference for the things of its experience; as the high value placed on artistic unity attests, one of the attractions of art is that if offers a degree of holiday from that occupation. As the creation of a human mind, art comes to its audience ready-fitted to the human mind; it has physical limits or limits of duration; its details are subordinated to one another in a hierarchy of importance. A play guarantees us that we will not have to select a direction for our attention; it offers us isolation from matter and considerations irrelevant to a particular focus or a particular subject. *Hamlet* is more nearly an exception to those rules than other satisfying and bearable works of art. That, perhaps, is the reason so much effort has gone into interpretations that presume that *Hamlet*, as it is, is not and was not satisfying and bearable. The subject of literature is often conflict, often conflict of values; but, though the agonies of decision, knowing, and valuing are often the objects of an audience's concern, an audience rarely undergoes or even approaches such agonies itself. That it should enjoy doing so seems unlikely, but in *Hamlet* the problems the audience thinks about and the intellectual action of thinking about them are very similar. *Hamlet* is the tragedy of an audience that cannot make up its mind. . . .

When Hamlet seems suddenly mad, the audience is likely for a minute to think that it is mad or that the play is mad. That happens several times in the course of the play; and the play helps audiences toward the decision that the trouble is in themselves. Each time the play seems insane, it also is obviously ordered, orderly, all of a piece.

Stephen Booth
in *Reinterpretations of Elizabethan Drama*, ed. Norman Rabkin
(Cambridge: Cambridge Univ. Pr., 1969), pp. 151–52, 159

How much of a fool is Polonius? This question lies behind most of the discussions of the character by actors as well as by other critics. It goes back, of course, to Samuel Johnson's famous statement that in Polonius Skakespeare depicts, not folly, but "dotage encroaching upon wisdom." This pronouncement flatly contradicted stage tradition, for not only had the role been played by a low comedian ever since the Restoration but the advice to Laertes (which gives Polonius his chief claim to wisdom) had long been omitted in performance. . . .

Looking back over the actors' descriptions of Polonius, we get the impression of several different kinds of personality: one Polonius is bustling, another suave; one is kindly and well-intentioned, another self-seeking and hypocritical. But when we compare the answers to the basic question "Is he a fool?" we find, I think, that the differences are mainly a matter of definition and emphasis (and sometimes of sympathy). Particularly if we were able to compare stage performances that deliberately attempted to convey these various interpretations, I suspect that in some passages at least all of them would seem comic. Those actor-critics who have argued most strongly for a wise and capable Polonius—Elizabeth Griffith, [Joseph Shepherd] Munden, [J. H.] Barnes, and [Arthur] Byron—have nevertheless mentioned characteristics that would probably elicit laughter from the audience, no matter how they were explained by the performer himself. . . . Munden and Barnes probably did hit upon an interpretation that could be projected in the theatre: laughter would be aroused, but it would not necessarily be aimed at Polonius' folly. This would be true, at least, in the scenes with Hamlet—though even here some members of the audience might well laugh, sadly or sardonically, at the ultimate folly involved in attaining political and social goals at the expense of personal identity and self-respect. But what of "Your noble son is mad?" And what of the scene with Reynaldo? (In some cases the latter question would not arise, for the scene has frequently been omitted.) Byron's description of a serious and worthy Polonius gives an interesting insight into his own purpose and manner in acting the part, but it does not really explain away the laughable element in the character. Tediousness and self-assurance (traits which Byron admits in Polonius) may build patience or provoke disgust in real-life associates, but if well acted, this combination normally produces laughter in a theatre.

It is equally true that none of the actor-critics, even those who call Polonius a "fool" or "clown," consider him completely simple-minded. To speak in stock company terms, their conceptions would, in general, call for a character actor rather than either the Low Comedian or the First Old Man. The dramatic rationale for such a Polonius is well explained by George Skillan: The character "cannot be a straight part" or "he would be flat and purposeless." Since the other major roles are "strong and intense," a "singularly different" type is needed for relief. But, although eccentricity is appropriate to Polonius, buffoonery is not. Comedy is his "*mould*," but "*tragedy comes out of his mistakes. This means that the element of his foolishness must not become absurd.*"

Carol Jones Carlisle
Shakespeare from the Greenroom (Chapel Hill: Univ. North Carolina Pr., 1969), pp. 129–30, 135–36

The Merry Wives of Windsor

To search for thematic imagery in *The Merry Wives* would be folly: the play has neither the intellectual nor the emotional intensity for that. There are, however, some interesting groups of imagery that influence one's attitude to story and characters, and certainly there are some that help to establish atmosphere.

The main group, not surprisingly, could be described as that arising from the typical domestic life of a family in a country town. "Choked with a piece of toasted cheese" (and other cheese references), "one that makes fritters of English," "half stewed in grease like a Dutch dish," "have my brains ta'en out and buttered," "rain potatoes," "bowl'd to death with turnips," "as blue as bilberry," "as crest-fallen as a dried pear," "laid my brain in the sun and dried it," "knit a knot in his fortunes with the finger of my substance," "Welsh flannel," "a cockscomb of frieze," "cannot creep into a half-penny purse, nor into a pepper box," "cooled, glowing hot, . . . like a horse-shoe," "to the forge with it, then; shape it: I would not have things cool," "like a barrow of butcher's offal," "like a glover's paring knife" are representative; and, not to forget the out-of-doors, there are the delightful "these lisping hawthorn-buds" and "he smells April and May." While not strictly an image, perhaps, "plucked geese, played truant, and whipped top" gains the same effect. Amusingly some of the oaths and terms of abuse have this country flavour too: "You Banbury cheese," for example, or "mechanical salt-butter rogue." . . .

The legal and financial group is not so easily explicable: that love and marriage are so often seen as arrangements to be made formally is only a partial explanation. "Lay to pawn," "fee-simple, with fine and recovery," "the register" (of follies), "fee'd every slight occasion," "exhibit a bill in the parliament," references to (legal) "suits" and inheriting, and, particularly, "like a fair house built on another man's ground, so that I have lost my edifice by mistaking the place where I erected it" and "build upon a . . . promise" may even have an autobiographical rather than a dramatic significance (although "I will be cheaters to them both, and they shall be exchequers to me" is clear enough). Military images help to reinforce the idea that some see woman's purity as an object to be attacked and defended (e.g. "lay an amiable siege to the honesty of this Ford's wife," "the ward of her purity," and "her defenses which now are too too strongly embattled against me").

Some of the most vivid images have to do with ships and places and exploration. A few of these link with the previous group (e.g. "this voyage toward my wife," "board," "above deck," and "under my hatches") and those used by Falstaff reinforce the notion of his exploring for treasure ("sail like my pinnace to these golden shores," "they shall be my East and

West Indies," and "she is a region in Guiana," for instance). The Host's, however, are far more exotic, and build up the impression of his ebullience —such as "my Ethiopian," "Castalian-king-Urinal," "Anthropophaginian," and "Bohemian-Tartar." Falstaff's "Pickt-hatch," "like Bucklersbury in simple time," and "the Countergate"—together with "red-lattice phrases" —are distinctly English and from his own background.

H. J. Oliver
Introd., in William Shakespeare, *The Merry Wives of Windsor*, ed. H. J. Oliver (London: Methuen, 1971), pp. lxxvii–lxxix

Troilus and Cressida

Troilus exhibits a time element that produces persons and situations not elsewhere found in the plays. It has often been pointed out how frequently it invokes time and its powers. Time is of course one of the most frequent topics of the commonplace not only in Shakespeare but in all Elizabethan literature; the most notorious and by its very familiarity the most reassuring of *topoi*. It is merciless, devouring, all-conquering. Or it can conquer everything except love, everything except art. Or it is both judge and redeemer, serving "to unmask falsehood and bring truth to life." We are lulled by these commonplaces, which seem not only familiar to us but doubly familiar from their frequent and regular recurrence in the miniatures of lyric and in the discursive poetry of high sentence. Moreover, as Kenneth Muir for one has pointed out, there are actually even more references to time in *Macbeth* than there are in *Troilus*. It is evidently not the emphasis on time that counts here but the dramatic use made of it. In all Shakespeare's other plays we feel that the present time as enacted on the stage, not only depends upon the past but is in the service of the future. Lear has made his plans: the action will reveal their consequences; the unseen future will underwrite a return to normality of a kind, be guarantor, as Edgar says, of "we that are young." But in the formal impact of *Troilus* there is neither past nor future: everything takes place in and ends in, the present. . . .

Let us consider the first scene of Act III, in which Pandarus, Paris and Helen chatter together and sing a song about love. It is like a glimpse in a nightclub, but whereas in real life the spectator might be sufficiently intrigued—enough of a novelist as it were—to wonder about their relationship and about the rest of their lives, Shakespeare inhibits even so small an attempt at coherence, by depriving the characters of the slightest historical and personal significance. The scene makes us feel as confused and unresponsive as if we ourselves were in the same state as the other guests in that nightclub, immersed in the same experience of the contingent and the banal. No novelist can do this, because in drawing our attention to the contingent and the banal he puts us on the outside of it, and manipulates it so that it is fully under our control. This difference is crucial. In novel time the absurdity of the contingent becomes a positive pleasure to be entertained by; but in *Troilus* we are too be-nightmared by the world of the moment to contemplate it with this enjoyment. Like the actors themselves, we are borne passively on the moment by moment tide of the drama, and we find when it is over that we still cannot get it into shape.

John Bayley
EIC (January, 1975), pp. 57, 59

All's Well That Ends Well

An early Morality Play such as *Mankind* is built on the assumption that ends are governed by means. If the Morality figure wishes to reach ultimate "good," he must achieve that end by means of the "good" life. Good deeds always yield good ends. Or we may find the opposite case presented. In *Cambises*, a late development of the Morality-cum-tragedy, the eponymous villain destroys himself through his evil actions. . . . Evil can never lead to good. For the Morality playwright, this kind of moral causation was fundamental to his artistic universe. In contrast, the title *All's Well That Ends Well* points to a completely unorthodox ethical position; for, on the literal level, it indicates that ends do justify means. Helena's contention, "All's well that ends well yet,/Though time seem so adverse and means unfit" (V.i.25–26), affirms her acceptance of this unconventional moral belief. For her, "unfit" actions may be used to attain desirable ends; the means are irrelevant if the conclusion is personally satisfactory. . . .

Shakespeare in *All's Well* was taking a new approach to the Morality, attempting to give the form a new sophistication. Here Shakespeare holds his mirror not up to nature but to the Morality Tradition. . . . Ostensibly the play is a refutation of the Morality ethic, since Helena gains her desired end through questionable means. But this interpretation depends largely on how one looks at the action of the final scene, and it will be one of the purposes of this essay to suggest that the play does not truly end "well" for either Helena or Bertram. From this stance, the play may be seen as an ironic or even comic confirmation of Morality ethics, where we are shown what happens when bad means achieve their proper ends *without metaphysical intervention.* The effect is similar to what the twentieth century calls "black humor" (an effect not at all alien to the Renaissance sensibility as readers of Sidney's *Arcadia* attest), where the audience laughs at an essentially serious situation when it is presented in a comic light. . . .

As a practitioner of deceit, Helena obtains a deceptive man for her mate; like has drawn to like; and the Nature which Helena elects to follow in the first scene has closed the gap in their fortunes. The end of the play thus returns to the Morality pattern. The means have governed the end, no matter how earnestly Helena declares otherwise. The King's skeptical statement, "All yet *seems* well" (1.329, italics mine), points to the reality underneath the final reconciliation. Deceptive means have led to the union of two deceivers; we feel that they heartily deserve each other, and we are invited to surmise what the outcome of their union will be. The cycle has not ended. Diana, who helped to deceive Bertram, receives her reward from the King: "Choose thou thy husband, and I'll pay the dower" (1.324). At the end of a traditional Morality Play, vital lessons have been learned; good and evil have been defined. Here, the King, like the other characters, retains a moral obtuseness which will lead by moral causality to recurring cycles of deception. For the sophisticated audience, the effect is darkly humorous—a comic Morality Play.

W. L. Godshalk
SQ (Winter, 1974), pp. 62, 70

Othello

The meaning of the play . . . is closely linked with opinions widely held about Africans in Shakespeare's day. . . . There were Africans then living in London . . . but the portraits of the Africans, or Moors, in English Renaissance drama were made up from qualities ascribed to them in classical and contemporary travel books. Prominent among supposed Moorish qualities were marked sexual capacity and promiscuity, a savagely jealous regard by male Africans for chastity in their wives, and an astonishing credulity, often accompanied by a belief in magic. Moors were said to have ungovernable tempers and to be pitilessly cruel. Africans were also then, in point of fact, usually either Mohammedans or pagans, so that playwrights found African characters useful for ready association with conduct that was both uncivilised and un-Christian. Dramatists tended to classify Moors by degrees of blackness, and by the time *Othello* appeared two broad types, distinguished by make-up, had been established. Invariably the black Moor, or negro, was a bad character, amply endowed with evil Moorish qualities; but the other type, of lighter complexion and called a "white" or "tawny" Moor, was normally noble in bearing and character, though he might have some of the "barbarous" qualities presumed of all Africans. . . . It would, though, be very difficult to produce a fully sympathetic Moorish portrait, and particularly so in a context involving the murder by a Moor of his European wife.

These facts help to suggest, at its simplest level, the probable response to *Othello* by Shakespeare's audience. Although it has been denied that Othello is a negro, this is to ignore clear textual evidence, and also events before Othello's entrance seem intended to establish first a conventional, if extreme, reaction to a black Moor. . . . Shakespeare obviously faced large technical problems in seeking to present Othello as an honourable murderer, who could retain or, rather, gain sympathy. . . . Qualities specifiably Moorish in their eyes must not take sole possession of the portrait, however useful they might be for some purposes, or the effect would be far from tragic. . . .

The dramatist's only solution was to persuade his audience to transcend the old familiar stock responses to Moors, unite with Othello in a common humanity, and so attain that degree of identification with the play's hero without which tragic effects are impossible. Accordingly, the source of the tragic feelings which the play sought to inspire is to be found in Othello's own development, belated and never complete, beyond simple attitudes associated with his background towards a broader view of human relations, one at once more realistic and more elevated then that with which he begins. Although Othello acts often in conformity with Elizabethan ideas about Moors, he acquires added dimensions from this attempt to overcome his limitations, and in the total portrait the preoccupations of a type blend with qualities common to all men. . . .

So, race is never the sole determinant of Othello's behaviour . . . and a capacity for self-dramatisation, an unpleasant taste for self-pity and other quite ordinary human failings are often prominent in him. At the same time, however, the artistic opportunities afforded by the very special quality in Othello's response towards general human problems are not sacrificed, as is particularly evident, in terms of the play's ideas, from the struggle that takes place between the two Moorish types, between the upper and lower elements in human nature, in his character. The play gets its meaning, in fact, from the course and outcome of this struggle, from the process of self-development in Othello.

K. W. Evans
in *Shakespeare Studies V*, ed. J. Leeds Barroll (Columbia: Univ. South Carolina Pr. 1969), pp. 124–25, 131–32

Measure for Measure

The Duke . . . has but one concern: that people see and accept the constraints of the law as necessary for their own happiness. In effect, the Duke says to Juliet and to Claudio: your failure to delay sexual satisfaction pending the arrangement of the dowry is a self-injury—the result of which will be a certain unhappiness in your lives; what came too quickly and too easily—without the tensions and delay caused by social barriers—will more quickly exhaust itself than if it had remained subject to those barriers. The essential damage, in other words, will be to your capacity for happiness. . . . Angelo and Isabella present something different. They both set the highest value upon external restraints—but neither seems personally to require them or able to profit from them. In both, the path to sexual gratification is quite fully blocked from within. If Lucio, Pompey, and the street life, as well as Claudio and Juliet, represent the unhappiness that results from the lack of external restrictions upon the sexual impulses, Angelo and Isabella represent the unhappiness that results from excessive reenforcement of the original internal restraints. That is, societal anxiety about this very matter—the necessity for external barriers—has, in both of them (through parents and educators), effected an exaggeration of the internal barriers so strong as to prohibit any possibility of satisfaction. The asceticism of both is the manifestation of an exaggerated fear of the reminder of the original incestuous desires and of those coprophilic and sadistic impulses which "have proved incompatible with our aesthetic ideas." Angelo has led an exaggeratedly "clean" life—it is his virtue—and he cannot be tempted by the "strumpet,/With all her double vigour" (II, ii, 184–185). But, the appearance of Isabella, who is announced to him as "a very virtuous maid,/And to be shortly of a sisterhood,/If not already," (II, ii, 20–22) tempts him beyond his control. The *inaccessible* woman, because she is "safe," and because she is the essential reminder of his past desires, arouses him. But, even as she does so, the old defensive pattern makes itself even more strongly to see sexuality as foul and degrading. In this scene, at line 16, Angelo refers to Juliet: "Dispose of her/To some more fitter place, and that with speed." A scant six lines later, *after* the Provost announces Isabella, Angelo (superfluously) repeats the order: "See you the fornicatress be remov'd./Let her have needful but not lavish means;/There shall be order for't." The temptation dimly stirring in Angelo at the announcement of an interview with a "very virtuous maid" arouses his anxiety, and automatically the "her" of the initial order becomes the "fornicatress" of the latter, with the additional stringency of "needful but not lavish means." That it is Isabella who causes his anxiety is demonstrated in the next line to the Provost who has turned to leave: "Stay a little while." He does not wish to be left alone with her. . . .

The very idea of sexuality—"There is a vice that most I do abhor/And most desire should meet the blow of justice;" (II, i, 29–30)—is painful to Isabella because it associates itself too easily with her old incestuous wishes, and must therefore be denied. It is understandable that she wishes to enter a nunnery, and that she finds the restraints of the sisterhood not strict enough. Clearly, Shakespeare finds the extremes of both Angelo and Isabella as unfortunate as those of Lucio and Pompey.

Stephen A. Reid
The Psychoanalytic Review, Vol. 57, No. 2 (1970), pp. 276–79

King Lear

The play uses pastoral structure to get at pastoral ideas—to arrive at basic man and a purified order of human values that encompasses public justice and private compassion—but once having arrived at the theme of human feeling, Shakespeare goes on to treat his material according to the tragic mode. The Aristotelian formula of pity and terror (underlying the Donatan woe and wonder) reinforced the propriety of the theme for tragedy, and the combined affective and didactic bias of Renaissance poetic theory channelled it into an attempt to stir up an analogous emotion on the part of the audience.

The pastoral-romance structure, like the reconciliation scene that is also from romance, is finally ironic, in the sense that both contribute to the meaningful pattern of life without ultimately having the power to define it. *King Lear* is tragedy, and neither pastoral nor romance, for all the use it makes of those modes. The last glimpse back to pastoral in the play (and it is fittingly to pastoral elegy) is a measure of the difference. One of the standard conventions of pastoral elegy is the comparison between the protagonist's death and the rebirth cycle of vegetative nature, a comparison which points to man's alienation from a nature that he is otherwise harmoniously part of and which formulates the anguish and tension that the final consolation of the elegy then overcomes. Another form this questioning frequently takes is "Why this person and not someone less worthy?" There is an analogous moment in *King Lear* when Lear emerges with the body of Cordelia in his arms. The reduction motifs that culminated in the pitiable figure of unaccommodated man with whom Lear identified himself make the question of worthiness impossible for Lear to ask. And there is no lush nature in our experience of the play to give the vegetative comparison resonance. Instead, Lear's despairing cry is formed in terms of animals such as those which all along have been vehicles in the negative comparison that sought to define justice or humanity:

> Why should a dog, a horse, a rat, have life,
> And thou no breath at all? (5.3.306–7)

The riddle, the incomprehensibility, the anguish are what we are left with. For King Lear there can be no final consolation.

Nancy R. Lindheim
in *Some Facets of "King Lear"*, ed. Rosalie Colie
(Toronto: Univ. Toronto Pr., 1974), pp. 181–82

Macbeth

If *Macbeth* can be said to figure forth an image of the horror of hell, labor without rest or meaning should perhaps be considered part of the punishment called pain of sense. It involves bodily pain and it results from the inordinate pursuit, as Aquinas defined it, of a mutable good. If so, it leads logically to the punishment . . . which torments specifically the senses. . . . In *Macbeth* . . . we . . . find, more than in any other of Shakespeare's plays, a concentrated torment of the tragic hero's senses and so great a torment that it has brought the play a unique reputation, usually ascribed to other causes, for its sensory imagery. Much of the poetic quality of the play, and much of the vividly perceived imagery, results, I suspect, not so much from Macbeth's poetic nature as from the fact that his senses, and the imagination that afflicts them, are singularly excited by a specific kind of punishment.

Not all of Macbeth's senses, or those of his Lady, are equally affected. The protagonists are tormented almost entirely through the eye and through the ear. There are, to be sure, occasional references to the suffering of other senses. Macbeth does, after all, bend up "*each* corporal agent" to his terrible feat. The poisoned chalice will, figuratively, be commended to Macbeth's own lips, and he later refers not simply to having felt fear but to having *tasted* it (V.v.9). He has "*supp'd* full with horrors" (V.v.13). He feels, according to Angus, his "secret murders *sticking* on his hands" (V.ii.17). Lady Macbeth is especially obsessed by the sticking; and one of Shakespeare's finest touches is her feminine displeasure with "the *smell* of the blood still." Taste, touch, and smell can become a part only of the dialogue—and at best the imagery—of a stage play, whereas sight and sound can be a part of the action. But in a play notable for the way in which sensation is made meaningful, it is tempting to look for a more organic explanation. Shakespeare's poetry can both mean and be. . . .

The eye and the ear are the principal members whereby Macbeth and Lady Macbeth are tempted and offend, and so the two protagonists are appropriately punished through them. They also, especially Macbeth, offend through the imagination, and the imagination affects the body primarily through vision and hearing.

Paul Jorgensen
Our Naked Frailties: Sensational Art and Meaning in "Macbeth" (Berkeley: Univ. California Pr., 1971), pp. 157–58

That all the deceit and falsity in Macbeth's Scotland is to be apprehended as semantic disorder might be inferred from Lady Macbeth's comment on her husband's face: it is, she tells him, a book where men may read the strange matters that are forming in his heart; and she advises him to make it in that sense illegible (I v 59–60). It is not true then that "there's no art/To find the mind's construction in the face" but rather that people like Lady Macbeth and the first and second thane of Cawdor have all but destroyed that art. Duncan himself, one must suppose, is a perfect refutation of his own maxim. "The order of God's creatures in themselves is not only admirable and glorious, but eloquent," and Scotland's anointed king is an active part of that eloquent order. Cast in the right role, and playing it with perfect grace, he will suit the word to the action and modulate his voice and countenance in such a way that his kindly and gracious heart will be manifest to all men. His whole manner will be like a garment that cleaves to its mould by the aid of use: it will fit.

But Macbeth and his wife, being committed to a permanent "faith-breach" (V ii 18), are compelled to make their faces "vizards" to their hearts, disguising what they are (III ii 34–35). Macbeth himself has to "put on" the semblance of manly readiness because his "naked frailties suffer in exposure" (II iii 125–126, 132) or because he cannot endure his wife's taunts that she would "shame to wear a heart so white" as his (II ii 64). He has to "mask" his "bare-fac'd" savagery from "the common eye," wailing at the fall of the men he himself strikes down (III i 118–24). And among his guests, he must try hard to "sleek o'er" his "rugged looks," since "the rugged Russian bear" and the shag-haired villain or demi-wolf that he is beginning to resemble does not become the royal banquet table (III ii 27; III iv 100). The sleeking of Macbeth's rugged looks is perhaps the most potent of all the dress-disguise images. By the lightest of associative means, it calls up the terrible spiritual transformation which has taken place in him and at the same time defines the conflict between civility and barbarity which is implicit in the banquet scene. The likening of Macbeth's uneasy looks to bristling or shaggy hair puts him in the catalogue with the "rough, rug-headed [Irish] kerns,/Which live like venom where no venom else" (*Richard II*, II i 156–57); with the mad rebel Cade who seemed "like a wild Morisco" or "a shag-hair'd craft kern" (*II Henry VI*, III ii 356–57); with "the rugged Pyrrhus" and "Hyrcanian beast" (*Hamlet*, II ii 444); in short, with the hirsute, cave-keeping creature which man becomes once again when he defies humane statutes that purged the gentle weal.

T. McAlindon
Shakespeare and Decorum
(London: Macmillan, 1973), pp. 159–60

Antony and Cleopatra

Language must act to indicate quality and character, but here it does more: by reaching to the heart of the moral problems faced by Antony and Cleopatra, the language of their play makes us realize anew the ingrained connection between speech and style of life. The "square" of Roman speech and Roman life has its values, which we recognize the more easily as we see those values betrayed by Romans; the "foison" of Egypt, both its fertility and its corruption, find expression in the *agon*. If one felt that the play were only an essay in style as life-style, then one might draw back from it as superficial and trivial; but *Antony and Cleopatra* seems to be more than a presentation-play of theatrical and unpersoned types, more also than the *psychomachia* to which it is occasionally reduced. . . .

In a sense quite different from that of the morality-play, *Antony and Cleopatra* is about morality, about *mores* and ways of life—not by any means just about sexual morality, although problems of sexuality are not ignored—but about lives lived in moral terms. "Style" is—especially in the Attic-Asiatic polarity—a moral indicator, but here displayed as deeply thrust into the psychological and cultural roots of those ways of life. In this play, a given style is never merely an alternative way of expressing something: rather, styles arise from cultural sources beyond a character's choice or control.

At the beginning of the play, this does not seem to be the case: Antony doffs and dons Egyptian and Roman styles, of speech and of life, apparently at will and at need. By the play's end, he has settled for a manner of speech and behavior proved by his decisive final actions to be the signature of his inmost nature. That is to say, his style can be seen not only to express his deepest sense of self, but also to relate to the consequences of his life-choices. . . .

Far from ideal lovers, Antony and Cleopatra demand a language for their love which rejects conventional hyperbole and invents and creates new overstatements, new forms of overstatement. In the language itself, we can read the insatiability of their love, as the language seems to make hungry, too, where most it satisfies. Nothing is enough for these two, not even the most extravagant figures of speech.

The language Antony and Cleopatra use, the language others use about them, is stretched at its upper and lower limits, to express their high and low gestures as bigger than lifesize. It is interesting that Antony and Cleopatra do not bewitch others' imaginations only by their charismatic presence; their great qualities are praised, described, referred to, and criticized mostly in their absence. These two are watched by a world fascinated even when disapproving; they are staged in a play of their own making, with the world as their willing audience. But they do not really play for that audience: their imaginative acting is all for each other, and in their mutual absorption they do not care who happens to look on at the spectacle. Of course the Romans cannot keep their eyes off them; beneath the language of official disapproval, one can see Roman fascination with this un-Roman style of life, with this abundant, prodigal, excessive manner of doing things. Their bounty knows no winter but is, in Antony's word, always "foison."

Rosalie Colie
Shakespeare's Living Art (Princeton, N.J.: Princeton Univ. Pr., 1974), pp. 178–79, 198–99

Timon of Athens

In several important respects . . . the play lacks coherence and consequently fails to achieve either the power or the significance of Shakespeare's earlier works. Timon's character is too rigidly drawn, both in prodigality and misanthropy, the result of Shakespeare's determination to prevent the spectators' close emotional identification with the character. The protagonist's final moments, unrelieved by even the slightest suggestions of insight into the human condition, are increasingly aberrational; as his attitude grows progressively more extreme and illogical, the spectators' dislocation becomes complete. At the same time the subplot fails to function convincingly in the establishment of a secondary character whose illumination or compassion could provide the rationale for tragedy. Then too, many of the characters surrounding Timon are strangely impersonal, labeled only by profession or occupation.

Nevertheless, the structure of the piece—albeit applied to the action like a straitjacket—provides a signpost for charting the perspective of Shakespeare's final tragedies. Concerned with a vision of evil and its operation different from that of the middle tragedies, he utilizes the very devices by which heretofore he has depicted the private, inner struggle with passion and thus has provoked close emotional rapport between the spectators and the protagonist. Now, however, he demonstrably blocks such a relationship, at least in part, in order to place a greater emphasis on the forces of evil that operate on the protagonist from without. The soliloquies spoken by this principal, instead of depicting a moment of crucial decision, emphasize a particular state of mind. Or, spoken by a minor character, they signal the veracity of some observation about the protagonist and the situation he confronts. Instead of one or two such characters who rivet attention on the central figure. Shakespeare utilizes multiple pointers to direct the spectators' attention to the public dimensions of evil. Moreover, by developing a second figure to whom is transferred at least a part of the emotional impact of the tragic illumination arising from the protagonist's experience, he not only avoids the total emotional commitment to the protagonist that would block the spectators' realization that the judgment against evil must fall equally upon the individual and upon those around him; he also stresses a similar fact about the wisdom, heroism, compassion, or sacrifice which the protagonist achieves—that such a quality, in touching and influencing the life of another, also has its public dimension.

The assertion of Shakespeare's final plays, to reiterate, is that no tragedy occurs only in the isolation of the protagonist's soul, in terms of either the destructive forces that produce it or the fundamental insights achieved concomitantly with devastation and death. To a degree, such is obviously the case in all Shakespearean tragedy, but the emphasis in the earlier plays is on the individual and the anguish of his internal struggle. In the last plays, Shakespeare broadens the perspective in order to emphasize both the personal and societal nature of such tragedy. While *Timon*, then, is not among Shakespeare's great tragedies, the structural complexities, which here fall short of the mark, do provide the groundwork for more powerful and more successful efforts in both *Coriolanus* and *Antony and Cleopatra*.

Larry S. Champion
Shakespeare's Tragic Perspective (Athens: Univ. Georgia Pr., 1976), pp. 217–18

Coriolanus

The sexual images, references, and hints in this play seem to have several functions. First, they provide a plain (and to my mind unequivocal) statement that war is a quasi-sexual activity, or that sex and aggression are profoundly linked. I regard the servants' dialogue in IV.v as a virtually "unfiltered" statement of a theme that the imagery has repeatedly suggested. Next, they throw light on the characters of several of the dramatis personae, and especially supply an important part of the puzzle of Coriolanus's mind. The imagery suggests that for him too war is a manifestation of sex, and that both together must be considered as related to his problem of identity. . . . Finally, the sexual images, in revealing the bent of Volumnia's disposition, suggest through her a further general statement on sex. For Volumnia sex is part of the mechanism of power; her boy exists to fulfill her needs. She is the one triumphant figure that survives the play, the savior of Rome. There is an astringent irony in the juxtaposition of the two final scenes—the feted mother, the butchered son. The honors that she had once preferred even to the "embracements of his Bed" are hers. "Welcome Ladies, welcome" (V.v.9). The ironic effect of this tiny scene would be infinitely greater if it were staged *after* the death of her son: but are Shakespeare's intentions any less clear for making her triumph the penultimate scene? . . .

The main public issue is a mindless war; in no other play does Shakespeare spend such little time on the formal motivations of the war. In the histories he spends much time, if sceptically, on the claims that can be advanced for the justice of this or that war. But in *Coriolanus*, the Romans fight because they are attacked ("the Volscies are in Armes," I.i.242) and the Volsces fight because they fight (I,ii.); not even a token justification is written in. The play becomes then an extended analysis of Coriolanus's reaction to the news—"I am glad on't" (I.i.243); and to establish this analysis, we must turn to the dominant formative influence in his life. From Volumnia, we derive a strong impression of the interlinked impulses of sex and power. Her son, "my good *Martius*," resorts to war as a means of compensating for sexual uncertainty. Both he and Aufidius find the key issue of war to be an imposition of their will upon their major rival. In all this, the images of heterosexual activity hold in general metaphoric status. (The main exceptions are the servants' dialogue, and Cominius's blunt picture of the aftermath of defeat.) They pose, therefore, a familiar question: is the metaphor a means of illuminating the central activity of the play, war and politics, or is the metaphor the true focus of Shakespeare's gaze? The question is unanswerable; and we can no more resolve the sex power-drive distinction today than could Shakespeare. We must, then, fall back upon the position that the play's main emphasis is upon the foreground, the unending struggle of human beings to dominate one another.

Ralph Berry
SEL (Spring, 1973), pp. 314–16

Pericles

The significance of *Pericles* for our study of the final romances, for our understanding of Shakespeare's work as a whole, is not that it reveals Shakespeare undergoing (like one of his own romantic characters) a religious conversion or that it reflects the senility or serenity of his old age. Nor is it to be sought, as I for one believe, on the level of technical experimentation justified only by its fruits in *The Winter's Tale* and *The Tempest*. Anticipations of the romances to come are numerous and tantalizing—one thinks of the double recognition scene to be reenacted in *The Winter's Tale*; of Pericles' decision to forego the less rare action of vengeance on Cleon as prefiguring Prospero's; of Marina as a Proserpine figure snatched away by the pirate Valdes to the underworld of Mytilene, where she becomes its queen and brings renewal, like Perdita after her. Such features no doubt reveal a good deal about the romance poetics and mythic substructure common to all the last plays. Perhaps more importantly, however, *Pericles* reveals Shakespeare reassessing the premises on which his art had always been based, wholeheartedly returning to that kind of drama which to a great extent had helped shape his own, and attempting to recover the inclusiveness of old tales like those which, in Sidney's words, "holdeth children from play, and old men from the chimney corner."

For like Marina's own art as described by Gower, the art Shakespeare employs in *Pericles* exerts its appeal on the naïve and sophisticated alike and is itself naïve and sophisticated at once. . . .

The peculiar power and universality of *Pericles* and the subsequent romances, it seems to me, has less to do with their "conventional" or "mythic" or "archetypal" dimension than with their medieval dimension. Or perhaps the two are finally inseparable and the same, to the extent that the apparent crudeness and naïveté of such plays is the condition of their power and universality. Because virtually everything in such plays is subordinated to a didactic purpose: they begin not in the middle of an action but at the beginning and proceed linearly to the end; they frankly announce and reiterate their designs on the audience; and their characters are simplified types rather than complex personalities. They may strike us as technically crude, yet there is an important sense in which they hold the mirror up to nature as faithfully as the most sophisticated of plays, which we mistakenly equate with naturalistic.

If there is any truth in these contentions, they may help to explain why *Pericles* should have been among the most popular of Shakespeare's plays in its early years and among the least popular of them thereafter, as well as why it has very recently begun to regain a place for itself in contemporary repertories.

Howard Felperin
Shakespearean Romance (Princeton, N.J.: Princeton Univ. Pr., 1972), pp. 172–74

Cymbeline

The masque-like quality of *Cymbeline* has long been recognised but it has not been realised that the approach through masque and pageantry in the early years of the seventeenth century can tell us more about the meaning of *Cymbeline* than can the purely literary approach. We have seen that the Stuart inheritance of the Tudor myth was the theme of the performances at court in 1610 and 1611 in honour of Prince Henry. To James, the Stuart king, were now applied the legends of the British History. As a new Arthur, ruling over a new Great Britain, James presided over the shows in which his son and heir, Prince Henry, was being brought to the fore as the reviver of chivalry. . . .

I suggest that *Cymbeline* was written about 1611 when the masques were building up the British History in relation to James and his children, and that it was revised in 1612 to make it fit the rejoicings over Princess Elizabeth's engagement but *before the death of Prince Henry*. In this form it would have been a play fitted to reflect both the valorous personality of the living Prince Henry and the marriage of his sister to the Elector Palatine. When, at the end of *Cymbeline*, King Cymbeline-James presides over a family consisting of two sons, a daughter, and a son-in-law, the play would reflect a moment in the history of James's family before the death of Henry but after it became certain that Elizabeth would marry the Elector Palatine, that is a moment late in 1612, when poets, playwrights, masque-writers, were busy preparing their works in celebration of Princess Elizabeth's coming marriage.

A revealing comparison which can be made between *Cymbeline* and another contemporary work is the comparison with the masque which Thomas Campion wrote for the wedding, with production by Inigo Jones. In this, the poetry combined with elaborate scenic effects to express the harmony of the spheres blending with the harmony of the royal wedding. . . .

The performance is close to the atmosphere of *Cymbeline* with its dreams and visions. Philarmonus, the soothsayer in *Cymbeline*, interprets the mysterious prophecy in terms of universal harmony; he is something like the presenter of a nuptial masque, a masque similar in atmosphere to others presented in honour of Princess Elizabeth's wedding. In *Cymbeline*, Shakespeare has combined his reflections of the Prince Henry type of masque, with chivalrous youths issuing from caves, with themes which might verge on a nuptial masque for his sister. The combination of masque-like presentation of Prince Henry and his brother with masque-like effects for their sister does not, perhaps, fuse quite satisfactorily. The boys in the cave are too young; the eldest boy does not quite represent the adult Prince Henry as he was at the time of his sister's engagement. Shakespeare did not have time to rewrite the whole play; he had to use the 1611 version, adding to its British imperial visions suggestions of the further destiny of the British Imogen through her marriage to a representative of the Holy Roman Empire.

Frances Yates
Shakespeare's Last Plays: A New Approach (London: Routledge & Kegan Paul, 1975), pp. 47, 52–53

The Winter's Tale

What do we expect as we approach the final scenes? Remember that we still have no inkling that Hermione is alive. Coming to the end of the play knowing that Hermione is alive dulls our response to Shakespeare's artistry here, just as coming to the beginning knowing that she is innocent dulls our response to the skill with which he builds his grounds for Leontes' jealousy. We expect nevertheless a number of reunions at the end of the play: Leontes with Perdita—this should be the main one—but also Leontes with Polixenes, Polixenes with Florizel, and Camillo with Leontes. We expect not only reunions, but forgiveness, and young love overcoming the objections of Polixenes, since the shepherdess is, after all, a princess. This is the ending we expect. It is the usual ending for comedy. Shakespeare, of course, has his surprise up his sleeve and, in addition to all that we expect, he will give us also the reunions of Leontes, Perdita, and, indeed, Polixenes with Herminone. Of all the reunions, that of Leontes with Hermione is his climax—it is the forgiveness beyond all deserving and hope which is the point of this play. . . .

The statue, like the bear, reminds us immediately of the dramatic medium. We no sooner see the statue than we recognize the actress—or in Elizabethan times the actor—in the costume of Hermione. But note that this very recognition of the dramatic pretence prevents our being certain how we should respond. Hermione is still dead—or is she? If the wild bear has been played by a tame bear, or a man in a bear suit, how else would we stage a statue but to have it represented by the actor who played the character the statue itself represents? The presence of Hermione on stage, then, does *not* immediately tell us that Hermione is alive. Even if we catch the statue breathing, we have no clue—for we know the actor has to breathe. Shakespeare plays upon our uncertainty. . . .

I could not pick the exact point at which an audience should decide that Hermione is, after all, alive. But Shakespeare does his utmost to hold it off as long as possible. Just as he has insisted originally that Hermione is dead, so he insists that the statue is a statue, carved by "that rare Italian master, Julio Romano, who, had he himself eternity and could put breath into his work, would beguile nature of her custom, so perfectly is he her ape" (V, ii, 93–95). Critics argue over the origin of the name Julio Romano. That seems to me less important than why it has been brought in at all. Surely it is here as part of the general insistence that we not suspect the statue of being anything more than a statue. And then, when we see it, hope after hope is raised, to be explained away or withheld from proof. The statue is wrinkled, unlike the Hermione of sixteen years ago. . . .

We must resolve *our* doubts. Once again, notice how closely Shakespeare has involved us, the audience, in the ongoing dramatic process. We suspected Hermione before Leontes became jealous; similarly here, we are not simply watching to see how Leontes will take the living Hermione—we are forced through the process of ourselves coming to recognize that Hermione is alive. It is not something we knew all the time; it is not even a miracle which is reported to us or staged for us: it is a miracle in the full effect of which we participate.

William H. Matchett
SS, Vol. 22 (1969), pp. 102–3

The Tempest

The Winter's Tale celebrates the triumph of art; *The Tempest* is concerned with its limitations. The central theme is discipline, restraint, the hard labor through which one earns freedom. The two inhuman characters, Caliban and Ariel, conceived in a mode not quite allegorical but close to it, define the theme's opposite poles. So long as he is intractable, ineducable, the earthly monster Caliban will remain a slave. Ariel, too, is a slave, but of a different quality, and overarching *The Tempest* rainbowlike is the story of Ariel laboring hard for the freedom that Prospero grants him in the play's final line. Prospero's own story relates to the same theme. In Milan he indulged himself in his magical studies to the exclusion of his princely responsibilities, with the result that he lost his dukedom and found himself exiled to the enchanted island. On the island he has learned to govern a new little commonwealth, restraining Caliban and employing Ariel usefully. Equally important, he has learned to use his magic, his art, not merely for his own delight but for a purpose, to help mend the natures of his former enemies—or, in the language of this play, to help them find themselves—and in the process to earn his own freedom. Throughout the play, even as he demands discipline from others, Prospero shows the strictest self-control, in particular restraining his impulse to revenge, choosing the rarer action instead. The ultimate mark of his self-control, and self-knowledge, is his lenten renunciation of the art that has both imprisoned and freed him, his vow to break his staff and drown his book.

Curiously enough, *The Tempest* has sometimes been seen as one of Shakespeare's more self-indulgent plays. We recall [A. C.] Bradley's remark about Prospero's long expository speech to Miranda in the second scene, that "Shakespeare grew at last rather negligent of technique." Actually, this episode is an emblematic statement of the play's theme. Prospero is educating his daughter, teaching her what she is, and the reason the episode seemed awkward to Bradley is that Shakespeare has contrived it to emphasize the effort self-knowledge requires, for Prospero is continually interrupting himself to demand that his pupil pay attention. So far from being sloppy in technique, *The Tempest* is one of the most disciplined, most severely controlled plays in the canon.

Mark Rose
Shakespearean Design (Cambridge, Mass.:
Harvard Univ. Pr., 1972), pp. 172–73

SONNETS

The perfectly appropriate word "riddle" has followed the sonnets through most of their critical history. The only problems one labels "riddles" are ones that have solutions: riddles sound as if they had solutions; they usually contain the clues necessary to their solution. Shakespeare's sonnets do not present a reader with a constantly dominant organizing principle, but . . . provide an abundance of evidence of organization. At the point where readers finish the sequence and try to think about it whole, the professionals among them have traditionally wanted either to rearrange the sonnets to suit the terms of one of the systems in which the poems cohere or to demonstrate that one such system governs the sequence as it stands. A riddle tests its audience's intelligence. If a reader cannot see the answer to the riddle, if he cannot see the organizing principle for a collection so obviously and insistently coherent, he may feel like a dunce, and he may be panicked into what an early rearranger called "a pertinacious adherence to a principle of continuity," biographical, thematic, or stylistic. . . .

Although the multitudinous potential frames of reference and systems of interrelation for the sonnets can panic the mind of a reader into arbitrarily maintained distortions, the same qualities can be a source of great solace to the same reader while he is reading, before he demands a definitive statement from himself. A reader has a sense always as he reads through the sonnets that each poem, each line that he reads, is in a specific relationship to what has gone before and that he can know what that specific relationship is. He is always on familiar ground, but he never knows just what that ground is. For example, the great number of different kinds of phonetic and substantial connections made among the sonnets by repetition of the various ideas that can be expressed by *bear* and *bare*, and by repetition of all the various forms and senses of the words themselves, gives the whole sequence an illogically powerful aura of coherence.

Perhaps the happiest moment the human mind ever knows is the moment when it senses the presence of order and coherence—and before it realizes the particular nature (and so the particular limits) of the perception. At the moment of unparticularized perception the mind is unlimited. It seems capable of grasping and about to grasp a coherence beyond its capacity. As he reads through the 1609 sequence, a reader's mind is constantly poised on just such a threshold to comprehension. The source of that pleasurable sense of increased mental range is the same multitude of frames of reference that frustrate him when he looks for a single label or formula by which his mind may take personal possession of the sonnets.

Stephen Booth
An Essay on Shakespeare's Sonnets (New Haven, Conn.: Yale Univ. Pr., 1969), pp. 12, 14

MILTON, AND NEOCLASSICAL LITERATURE

John T. Shawcross, editor

JAMES BOSWELL

1740–1795

Marshall Waingrow, ed., *The Correspondence and Other Papers of James Boswell Relating to the Making of "The Life of Johnson"* (1969)

Charles N. Fifer, ed., *The Correspondence of James Boswell with Certain Members of the Club* (1976)

Boswell's stock has gradually risen since persistent searching in our century and the necessary capital brought to light an unprecedented mass of hidden material. The Boswell papers have provided the evidence that was needed to reexamine Boswell's biographical art and to understand better the creative process that produced the great *Life*. They also brought to the fore his preeminence in the area of autobiographical writing; and, through the gradual publication of the Journals and other personal documents in accessible trade editions, he has recently come to be popularly known as a journal writer of great merit. . . .

Boswell was not the kind of biographer that can be successfully imitated. Yet, as he sought to adhere to the truth—even if he never intended to present all of it—and as he refused either to eulogize or to defame, he established the standard for excellent biography. It was not chiefly in his regard for truth, however, that he influenced biography in the nineteenth century; instead, it was in the nineteenth-century view of the *Life of Samuel Johnson* as a specimen of that form of expression which was a major feature of romanticism. According to this view, Boswell's experience and his knowledge of Johnson were dominated by his inner self; in other words, he knew Johnson by knowing himself in Johnson. . . .

He had a deep-rooted respect for authority, and he often gave oral and written expression to his approval of the ancients as critics and as arbiters of taste. In his verse, which seldom achieved a fair competence and never rose above it, he was often guilty of the worst excesses of poetic diction; but in his prose he emulated with some success Addison's ease and lucidity. His ideas concerning inspiration and enthusiasm betrayed the faults which the neoclassicists sought to correct, but the restraint which the tastes of the time demanded curbed his impulses when the occasion required decorum, and it influenced his prose style. . . .

The uniqueness of this contribution is the deliberate fusing of Boswell's own life story, his own experiences, with Johnson's story. The coalescence of ordinary experience with artistic achievement seems in his case to have been exceptional. Elements in and outside Britain to which he was exposed and which attracted his attention permeated his mind and art and nourished his peculiar genius. At no stage in his adult life did he ever seem to be unconscious of this fact. Ever aware of the enrichment which his wide experiences and interests would inevitably bestow upon his biographical work, he seems to have sought out experiences and to have cultivated interests for the sake of the monumental *Life of Samuel Johnson* to which he had committed himself. He can thus be said to have planned much of his life deliberately out of considerations primarily artistic.

A. Russell Brooks
James Boswell (New York: Twayne, 1971), pp. 151–52, 155

There are two major ideas about Johnson and his temper that Boswell sets out specifically to combat in the *Life*. The first is that he is naturally and habitually rude (Mrs. Thrale's "natural roughness of manner"). The other and more serious view is that he was indiscriminate in his violence and would readily attack even his best friends with all the venom with which he might have attacked an "American." The first view of Johnson's roughness Boswell most commonly negates by showing (as in the anecdote in which he corrected Mrs. Thrale above) that if Johnson is sometimes impatient it is always and only when he has been provoked by ignorance pretending to knowledge, vanity, etc. This is the way in which he dramatizes all the incidents of this kind of the *Life*. . . .

Boswell uses two methods for countering the view of Johnson as sometimes cruel and brutal even to his friends. One is to explain again and again the understandability of Johnson's occasional attacks in light of the great physical and psychological burdens he fought against so heroically all in his life. The outbursts are made symptoms of that struggle and not evidence of an essential malice or ill will. The final and most compelling statement of this idea of the "understandability" of Johnson's outbursts is made appropriately in the concluding sketch. . . .

But the artist in Boswell must have realized that theoretical explanations of what might have been considered a serious flaw in Johnson's character were doubled-edged at best. It was apologizing for Johnson. His most effective way of dealing with such incidents is to dramatize or report them in such a way as to show that the common (stereotypic) view of this aspect of Johnson's behavior does not do justice to him—does not tell the whole story. He confronts the best known instances of Johnson's attacks on his friends directly, to show that when viewed in the proper context, when the whole story is known, Johnson's essential goodness, his fundamental kindness and honesty with himself, make these outbursts merely foils for the greatness of heart and the breadth of compassion that lie beneath these outward manifestations of his brooding and troubled spirit.

William R. Siebenschuh
Form and Purpose in Boswell's Biographical Works
(Berkeley: Univ. California Pr., 1972), pp. 65–67

ROBERT BURNS

1759–1796

Robert T. Fitzhugh, *Robert Burns, the Man and the Poet: A Round, Unvarnished Account* (1970)

SAMUEL BUTLER

1612–1680

Charles W. Daves, ed., *Characters* (1970)

THOMAS CHATTERTON

1752–1770

Donald S. Taylor, ed., in association with Benjamin B. Hoover, *The Complete Works of Thomas Chatterton: A Bicentenary Edition* (1971), 2 vols.

Murray Warren, *A Bibliography of Thomas Chatterton* (1976)

WILLIAM CONGREVE

1670–1729

Herbert Davis, ed., *The Complete Plays of William Congreve* (1967)

In this prologue [to *The Way of the World*] Congreve stated that his play would contain "some new Thought," but this newness is hardly apparent unless the title is to be taken seriously. The world is very much at issue in this play; in fact, it might have been called "The World Well *Found*" as a response to the subtitle of Dryden's *All for Love: or, The World Well Lost.* Congreve sets out to create two lovers who are as ideal as Anthony and Cleopatra, and he then has them come to terms with their world and succeed in it. Witwoud even refers to Millamant as "handsome as Cleopatra"; and, like Anthony, Mirabell confesses that he is in love in spite of a rational awareness of his folly. She is so beautiful that she is always accompanied by a convoy of beaus; he, so handsome that every woman in the play is in love with him. Unlike Anthony, Mirabell has learned the ways of the world and is able to outwit his Octavius, Fainall, at every turn.

The world in which they succeed is that newly sophisticated eighteenth-century London that Congreve loved. The city produces its Witwouds and Petulants, parasites of the coffee and chocolate houses, men who are symptomatic of the ego deflation that comes with impersonal crowds; for they seek some kind of notoriety to draw attention to themselves to compensate. Witwoud enters asking whether any messages have come for him, and Petulant is so desirous of being thought important that he hires people to call on him or calls upon himself in disguise. . . .

In spite of Congreve's refusal to acknowledge the relationship between his plays and the real world, they are very much about a world—one which is here and now. If Christian ideals were inescapable because so deeply imbedded in his age, Congreve does his best, nevertheless, to avoid mentioning them. In this respect, Congreve was little different from most contemporary writers of comedy; but the world of Congreve's comedies is so complete and convincing that [Jeremy] Collier's sense of a deliberate exclusion of serious Christian content is understandable. Mirabell operates on the assumption that, within his world, the most important point is love, marriage, and the way he and Millamant can manage to live together as individuals and as a family. She is concerned about her liberty and her tea table, about how they will appear in public and about how she may avoid associating with fools just because they happen to be her husband's relatives. Swift left his sermons, Addison his prayers, Steele his *Christian Hero*; but, in spite of Congreve's devout education, there is little in his life or writings to indicate a leaning toward religion. And Congreve's art is not only secular in its avoidance of religion. *The Way of the World* establishes a concept of art and civilization, of manners and morals, which finds its fullest expression in the wit, intelligence, and moral values of Congreve's hero and heroine.

Maximilian E. Novak
William Congreve (New York:
Twayne, 1971), pp. 156–57

Millamant's plight reflects Congreve's dramatic concern with the problems of experiencing genuine emotion and still behaving with due decorum within a world of artificiality. *The Way of the World* thus brings us full circle from [Etherege's] *The Man of Mode*, which was concerned with various methods of suppressing emotion in order to behave with brilliant artificiality. Still, neither Millamant nor Mirabell throws good sense or good manners to the winds for the sake of sheer, unmitigated passion. Mirabell sees to it that the financial situation is well in hand, and Millamant sees to it that she can maintain as much autonomy and glamour as possible even after marriage. This measure of control, this degree of calculation, seems inevitably necessary in any world where some degree of artifice and a large degree of economic and social realism are necessary in order to survive (but where the expression of emotion beyond artifice is equally necessary in order to live richly and fully instead of merely managing to exist by duly observing the proper forms). Congreve's hero and heroine are thus experts in the art of social survival; they both manage to control the society around them. . . .

So the unique beauty of *The Way of the World* may be in part the result of the passion bestowed upon and portrayed within it. And the fact that the passion survives without any illusions is the best possible evidence that it is genuine. There just do not seem to be any illusions at all in *The Way of the World*, and that is why it is never sentimental or false. Clearly the world portrayed (like its heroine) has plenty of faults of its own. It is full of artifice, vanity, conniving, and arrogance, and it poses very real dangers for its inhabitants. But somehow Congreve makes it possible for us both to understand his social world and to like it. He shows us how to accept and enjoy it with all its faults, and ultimately he even allows us to like it for its faults when we relish the lascivious Lady Wishfort and the malicious Fainall, even as we sympathize with Mrs. Fainall and triumph with Mirabell.

Harriet Hawkins
Likenesses of Truth in Elizabethan and Restoration Drama
(Oxford: Clarendon, 1972), pp. 136–38

ABRAHAM COWLEY

1618–1667

Historically, it is not difficult to place Cowley's contribution. His *Davideis* is the first "Christian" epic, his Preface the first open argument for converting previously "pagan" poetry to biblical subjects. Milton's great poems—*Samson Agonistes*, *Paradise Lost*, *Paradise Regained*—are in the tradition of Cowley's Old Testament epic. To Cowley's popularization of the irregular English "Pindarics" one can trace the odes of Gray, Collins, Wordsworth, Shelley, and others. Addison, Johnson, Lamb, and Hazlitt owe a debt to the essays in verse and prose.

The great theme in all his works, as Robert Hinman's excellent *Abraham Cowley's World of Order* demonstrates, concerns "experimental philosophy" [science]: the poems and prose reveal a significant occupation with the concept of order and with the role of poetry in achieving it. In an age of political and social instability, when the institutions of men were at best expedient and transitory, Cowley looked for order and permanence through art; enduring values were to be established in poetry, the human manifestation of the divine harmony. . . . The concept of order in art owes something to Ben Jonson, whose influence on Cowley has not been sufficiently noted.

It is not strange that Cowley has always been seen as the follower of Donne, but one ought to realize that many of Cowley's major ideas about poetry reflect Jonsonian concepts as well. Cowley and Jonson were both interested in what poetry could teach about life and its conduct. Cowley has no set of critical observations in prose such as Jonson's *Timber*, but he too is interested in how poetry mirrors that symmetry and that plan in the universe which are not always apparent to men. . . .

The mixed strains of Jonson and Donne are obvious in Cowley's work, and he felt their influence so strongly that one finds it difficult to determine what a characteristically Cowleyan idiom is. Not content to sing only with the past, Cowley faced a world whose foundations were changing so rapidly that a new poetic idiom was not sufficiently developed for what he intended to do. "Truth" to Cowley and to Jonson were really very different, for they were found in different places. Jonson looked to the traditions of the past; Cowley, to natural phenomena and to the science of the future. By the time of the *Davideis*, Cowley, caught up in that future world, was attempting to see his hero in terms of contemporary truth. And, as Donne tells one as early as 1611–12, the old truths were crumbling away and there was as yet nothing to replace them. Cowley's very contemporaneity—his desire to speak in the language of the new truths—makes him an exciting figure.

James G. Taaffe
Abraham Cowley (New York:
Twayne, 1972), pp. 122–24

WILLIAM COWPER

1731–1800

The Task came into existence because Lady Austen, in answer to Cowper's complaint that he had no fit subject for a blank-verse poem, told him to write about a sofa. The jest and the subject matter demanded as a reply a poem in the mock-heroic tradition, and Cowper began with a burlesque of *The Aeneid*. . . . In choosing mock heroic as his vehicle, Cowper assumed a double perspective on reality, mocking both past and present, but at the same time seeing the shortcomings of one as the strengths of the other. His elevation of a mean object seems unnatural, and the fact that he began with a parody of Virgil implies that an age which can praise only furniture has fallen from the greatness of Augustan Rome.

But Cowper's design is more complex than this attitude implies. If the history of man is to be organized according to the genesis of the devices on which he has sat, the past, which can boast only three-legged stools and crude chairs, must defer to the present. And, although the very fact that Cowper can conceive of history in this way comments on the luxury and triviality of the present, the past, which could not afford the luxury of being trivial, must also admit its limitations. Civilization does not always progress downhill.

Cowper soon realized that mock heroic did not suit his deepest feelings. Unnatural elevation of syntax and diction has to be accompanied by a real concern for the heroic potential in man and his falling away from it; instead, Cowper was more interested in the way improvements in furniture reflected the rise from barbarism to modest refinement and then to luxury. That he made aldermen and priests, two of his favorite subjects of attack, contribute to the growth of instruments of leisure suggests his basically religious motivation. He was more interested in the excesses to which luxury had carried man than in the falling away from a primitive ideal of heroism. . . .

The structure which replaced mock heroic has a strong personal or subjective bias. In contrast to mock heroic, in which the poet does not intrude, but allows tradition to dictate order, *The Task*, as it evolves, is informed by the "I" who offers his experience of life as an alternative to the images of corruption which cluster around the central figure of the sofa. Hence the long-held truism that *The Task* cannot be enjoyed unless we have a good understanding of Cowper's life has its foundation in the very techniques which the poet chooses. If we are to find a unifying principle in the work, we must explore the mind that produced it. The order is not that of an epic or pastoral or essay, but is organic to the poet's imagination. Psychic tensions, preoccupations, and aspirations become the organizing principle.

William N. Free
William Cowper (New York: Twayne, 1970), pp. 101–3

DANIEL DEFOE

1660?–1731

Certainly the most persistent attribute of Defoe's longer narratives is their profusion of circumstantial detail, and . . . the author has been criticised for failing to be sufficiently selective, for burdening his fiction with all the details his invention produced, regardless of their inherent interest or germaneness to the central story. But if at times he permitted the circumstantial method to get out of hand, it seems quite clear that it was nevertheless a *method*, a specific device for obtaining verisimilitude. The detailed style is not, as some scholars would have it, a reflection of Defoe's tape-recorder mind, interest in good book-keeping, or deficient sense of proportion, let alone his inveterate mendacity. What argues most strongly against such views is evidence that the proliferation of circumstantial detail in the fiction often rises proportionately in ratio with the unfamiliarity or incredibility of his subject matter. . . .

Defoe's judicious application of circumstantial detail . . . makes the unfamiliar not only credible but exciting. . . . [His work] testifies to the author's careful manipulation of invented facts so as to secure verisimilitude and the reader's interest. To argue that the realism of . . . countless . . . effective passages is the product of something other than artistry, and that the circumstantial style is not a premeditated device, is simply to depart from the critical line of least resistance.

Again and again we find in Defoe's works accounts which, however fantastic or unfamiliar, achieve the ring of truth solely because the author has his fictitious narrators display such sedulous accuracy, such attention to factual minutiae, in recounting them.

E. Anthony James
Daniel Defoe's Many Voices: A Rhetorical Study of Prose Style and Literary Method (Amsterdam: Rodopi, 1972), pp. 125–26

Among Defoe's longer narratives, *A Journal of the Plague Year* is *sui generis*. His other narrators are autobiographers who place themselves at once in the middle of events, shaping and altering their surroundings from act to act. Their task is to present themselves at the expense, finally, of the world, to extract freedom from various kinds of necessity. In place of these expansive conquests, the *Journal* offers a detailed and carefully compelling picture of necessity in the ultimate human forms of disease and death. The semi-anonymous H. F. lives at the contemplative edge of that necessity, mysteriously immune to the plague so that he can record the inscrutability of natural process. Defoe's other narrators appropriate their environments, converting them from historical and geographical entities into emanations of the infinitely resourceful self. The saddler's account is rooted in and limited by the historical moment of the plague, and it is surrounded as well by the verifiable documents and maps of an actual London.

These differences are hardly surprising. The *Journal* is pseudo-history in the service of expert political propaganda, and the saddler is necessarily an adjunct to these purposes, a witness to events whose reactions support rather than convert their reality. . . . . The source of our concern and what we participate in as readers is the process of ordering an unprecedented intrusion of natural chaos called the plague, and what the saddler leads us to fear is the dominance of disorder. In short, the saddler is not a lesser Crusoe; he is an intensified and almost abstract version of the ordering self that we have seen in Defoe's other narratives.

The plague is an extended moment of total uncertainty, an exaggerated, nearly metaphysical version provided by history of the random destructiveness of an environment. Perfectly, one can add, that environment is both natural and social. The plague is a natural disaster attendant upon commerce and urban crowding, perpetuated and complicated by the conditions of social life.

John J. Richetti
Defoe's Narratives: Situations and Structures
(Oxford: Clarendon, 1975), pp. 233–34

JOHN DRYDEN

1631–1700

John A. Zamonski, *An Annotated Bibliography of John Dryden: Texts and Studies, 1949–1973* (1975)

David J. Latt and Samuel H. Monk, *John Dryden: A Survey and Bibliography of Critical Studies, 1875–1974* (rev. ed., 1976)

It is one of the ironies coloring shifting politics in the century that the anti-royalist, anti-Catholic writers of England should borrow arguments from the monarchomach writers, many of them Jesuits, who provided the philosophical grounds for rebellion against a king sympathetic to the Protestant cause in France. Dryden was not the last person to observe irony and ambiguous metaphors. For the purposes of his new poem [*Absalom and Achitophel*], a biblical parallel would obviously enable him to steer a surer course through events variously interpreted in his day.

His choice of a "parallel" from sacred history was unquestionably his major poetic decision. It gave his Tory treatment of contemporary events a seemingly divine sanction unavailable to other analogies, and enabled him to suggest an outcome to matters still very much undecided. The choice was one of a metaphor controlling far more explicitly than those of *Mac-Flecknoe* the actions, characters, and meaning of his poem. The nature of that control depended upon a further decision, whether the metaphor should be cast in the imagery and allusions typical of *Annus Mirabilis*, in the reciprocally functioning metaphors of *MacFlecknoe*, or in terms of some new principle. He chose novelty. He chose to describe contemporary experience as if it were unvaryingly biblical. As a result there is very little indeed in the poem that cannot be read as an expansion of 2 Samuel. One could do worse than read *Absalom and Achitophel* as a biblical poem, and one would find it difficult to prove, on the evidence of the poem *in vacuo*, that it concerns anything other than the biblical story. The metaphorical vehicle of biblical history has swallowed up the metaphorical tenor of Restoration history. Like nature, however, readers abhor vacuums, and we know from the epistle "To the Reader" and the evidence of history that a contemporary tenor is conveyed by the biblical vehicle.

If we could read the poem as it was read on that mid-November day of 1681 when it first appeared, we would approach it with the tense excitement that men feel when the threat of civil war is in the air. Words and names that might mean several things on other occasions would now mean but one. But we cannot read as if we were Dryden's contemporaries, and at our distance in time we are less involved in the events themselves than in their poetic expression, especially in the workings of the metaphor, difficult as they are to describe. It is not easy to designate the metaphor, whether as parallel, analogy, allegory, or what. For the fact is that to Dryden and his age, and to the workings of the poem, the vehicle has a greater truth than the tenor. Even today we accept the biblical analogy as something less partisan than Dryden's picture by it of Restoration history. Believing as he did that monarchy was divinely ordained, the imperfect demonstration of that truth by his account of the happenings he witnessed very nearly makes Restoration history a metaphor or type of the biblical.

As in *MacFlecknoe*, so in this poem, there is an exchange of metaphorical roles, except that now the exchange is between the explicit and sustained pole of metaphorical vehicle and an implicit but sustained pole of metaphorical tenor.

Earl Miner
Dryden's Poetry (Bloomington:
Indiana Univ. Pr., 1967), pp. 109–10

By the beginning of 1682, the year in which Dryden wrote *Religio Laici*, the conditions which warranted his answers to both deism and Catholicism in that poem already existed. The long-standing controversy between Protestants and Catholics in England had increased and sharpened during the years following the Restoration, reaching an unprecedented intensity during the crisis over the Exclusion Bill beginning in 1679. To this well-entrenched topic for the polemicists had been added, more recently, the challenge of deism, swelling gradually until it had become "so common a *Theme* among the *Scepticks* of this *Age*" that it too required the attention of Anglican apologists.

Hardly any such apologists had yet appeared in the field against the deists, however. . . . [Edward] Stillingfleet's *Letter to a Deist*, almost the only effort of this kind, could offer Dryden little help. Stillingfleet's procedure in his book had been to engage in a minute examination of details in order to answer his opponent's objections to the Scriptures. The Anglican churchman's concern with specific passages of the Bible is excusable in a treatise; it would be insufferable in a poem. Dryden's arguments are of a more general order, and more commonplace.

For convenience sake, I shall outline Dryden's arguments in the first half of *Religio Laici*, up to the point where the "*Digression to the Translatour*" signals the beginning of the second half:

I. Necessity of Revelation (ll. 1–125)
   A. Inadequacy of natural religion (ll. 1–92)
   B. Our dependence on revelation for the means of atonement (ll. 93–125)
II. Proofs That This Revelation Is Contained in the Bible (ll. 126–67)
   A. Superiority of its teachings to those of other religions in answering the ends of human life (ll. 126–33)
   B. Antiquity of its laws (ll. 134–37)
   C. Character and circumstances of its authors (ll. 138–45)
   D. Confirmation of its doctrines by miracles (ll. 146–51)
   E. Its remarkable reception in spite of so many hindrances, internal and external (ll. 152–67)
III. Answer to the Objection of the Deist (ll. 168–223)

No one has previously taken the trouble, I believe, to outline Dryden's arguments, and it is sometimes assumed that he has arranged them in haphazard fashion which defies the common requirements of logical structure. This outline, therefore, is worth some attention, for it reveals that Dryden's arguments form a coherent sequence of ideas in which each principal stage of the discourse depends on the one which immediately precedes it. Thus, his demonstration of the necessity of revelation leads to the question of where this revelation is to be found, and his affirmation that it is contained in the Bible leads to a consideration of the objection to this theory.

Phillip Harth
Contexts of Dryden's Thought (Chicago:
Univ. Chicago Pr., 1968), pp. 95–96

When Milton in *Samson Agonistes* invented a language very different from his epic manner, he used it to express antithetical attitudes. Although the work is modelled in its outlines and in many conventional details on Greek tragedy, it seems purposely to alter the function of that form—originally evolved for performance before vast public audiences as part of a national and religious festival—in order to appeal to the solitary reader's feelings, to evoke his most private and inward responses in so far as possible abstracted from or lifted out of his identity in the social world. The style seems designed, then, not to accumulate the wealth of associations conserved in literary and social language, but to lay bare some irreducible core of meaning. It insists upon the truth of a vision which finally escapes articulation. . . .

The view of the morality of language expressed in *Samson Agonistes* goes beyond distrust of human speech to renunciation of it as the chief threat to the soul's proper, silent communion with God. The limits of language are not bounds appropriate to man's creaturely nature . . . but violations of his essential identity, his wordless, inward self. The poet's function, then, is not . . . to learn a purified language suited for conversing with God, but to invent a style . . . which surmounts the limits to language to recreate perfect silence.

Dryden never fully explored the implications of this view, but the parallels . . . with *Samson Agonistes* in *All for Love* show that he strongly felt their attraction. In that play he creates a situation and characters virtually abstracted from the particularities of setting so richly exploited in his Shakespearean model, portrayed in a language largely stripped of the social accents so precise in his own satirical style, as if to examine human society in its fundamental patterns, human feelings reduced to their essential elements. The image which he then lays bare in the play, for all its inconsistencies, is of a world in which relationships are meaningless and feelings inexpressible because finally dependent on language which is both arbitrary and threatening. This world, the main emphasis in the play underlines, it is the Hero's achievement to renounce for a state of wordless and unconscious oblivion: Antony escapes, like Samson, into inertness and silence. But his release is more passive than Samson's fierce negation of experience, and the play ends in large confusions which prevent any clear assertion that his death represents an heroic triumph over the limitations of society and all things human. *All for Love* celebrates the world of words well lost, but not the heroic image regained of immutability and silence. It shows Dryden to have been sympathetic with certain attitudes at the heart of Milton's dramatic poem, and the superiority of *All for Love* to all his other plays suggests that his sympathy was deeply felt. Yet the confusions and contradictions in the play also reveal that Dryden never fully apprehended Milton's vision in its magnificent and ferocious clarity.

Anne Davidson Ferry
Milton and the Miltonic Dryden (Cambridge, Mass.: Harvard Univ. Pr., 1968), pp. 178–80

Dryden's chief norm for drama is exactitude and wholeness of design. He is not fascinated by imagination merely as an instrument of discovery; undisciplined originality would not have gained much credit with him. Nor does he pay much tribute to style, insisting that words, like the coloring of a painting, are mere surface and of no value if the design is badly wrought. What he does lavish praise upon and what he himself excels in is disposition, the interrelation of parts within a whole. He often censures ancient as well as modern French dramatists for "narrowness" of plot and "fewness of persons." An abundance of distinct characters and a large, historically significant action would be, for Dryden, major ingredients in a good play.

Because the architectural merit of a play, its draftsmanship, is more important to Dryden than the novelty of its content or the language in which it is executed, he makes continual use of an architectural metaphor to designate the various parts of a play. Ben Jonson once compared the fable of a play to the place where a building is to be erected, and Davenant called *Gondibert* "this new Building" with such distinct parts as "the outward frame, the large rooms within, the lesser conveyances, and now the furniture." Dryden makes more elaborate use of the metaphor. He employs it first of all to distinguish the work of fancy from that of judgment in the making of a play. In the preface to *Secret Love* (1668), Dryden calls judgment the "master-builder" which restrains fancy and is its proper "surveyor," and contrasts judgment to self-love, which would let fancy run astray. Judgment is in charge of the "fabric and contrivance" of the play and may determine "without deception" whether the finished piece is faithful to the model or "pattern." Fancy, on the other hand, gave judgment the "perfect idea" of the pattern which the master builder now follows. In *An Essay of Dramatic Poesy* (1668), Neander also calls judgment the "master-workman" in charge of raising a building. In the construction of a play, this builder needs "many subordinate hands, many tools to his assistance," including "history, geography, or moral philosophy." The master builder even needs verse, for this is a "rule and line by which he keeps his building compact and even."

Also by means of the architectural metaphor, Dryden distinguishes the plot, characters, manners, and thoughts in a play. He consistently compares the plot or fable with the underground parts of a building, or the foundation; this part should be sturdy, for on its solidity rests the entire building.

Anne T. Barbeau
The Intellectual Design of Dryden's Heroic Plays
(New Haven, Conn.: Yale Univ. Pr., 1970), pp. 149–51

The essential differences between *Religio Laici* and *The Hind and the Panther* are not so much matters of doctrine as differences in attitude toward metaphors and images which correlate with, and perhaps even determine, differences in epistemology and belief. For Dryden, Anglicanism and Roman Catholicism came to represent distinct orders of imagination, both of which, at their best, could succeed in imaging spiritual truth. The Anglicanism espoused by *Religio Laici* succeeds by virtue of its ability to mold intellectual abstractions into a dynamic outline of divine reality. The Roman Catholicism of *The Hind and the Panther* takes a different route: it avoids metaphor and false images by surrogating a dazzling monstrance of mystery. Like Daniel's visions, *The Hind and the Panther* had to remain "closed up and sealed." Dryden believed that satire in general should proceed "figuratively, and occultly"; and in *The Hind and the Panther*, particularly, the occult is of crucial importance. . . .

The Hind and the Panther makes a program of the mysterious. In it Dryden decided to "launch"—"In the same vessel which our Saviour bore/Himself the Pilot" (I, 130–32)—into the "abyss of light" (I, 66): he committed himself to the darkling revelations of divine truth which emerge from God's secret mercy to man's reason and from the occult symbol of tragedy and triumph which the poet's reason was allowed to create from the mysteries of Daniel and primitive English Christianity. In the "abyss of light" Dryden attained the final stage in the surrogation of light images for the divine essence. The metaphor of a "throne [of] darkness in th' abyss of light" indicates a realm beyond metaphor; it creates an image beyond imagination, a conceit which defies concrete conceptualization. With this image—and in *The Hind and the Panther* as a whole—Dryden showed us that allusions need not be merely descriptive or definitive, that at their most striking they are powerfully invocative and infinitive. In *The Hind and the Panther*, Dryden attempted to approximate the shape of the divine by creating immeasurable correspondences and resonances. He recognized that one of the things poetry and religion have most in common is a sense of intellectual infinitude.

Each of Dryden's religious poems is an act of faith; each renders a central imaginative process of its belief (as Dryden understood it) and each relies, for its own wholeness, on God's gracious aid. From a formalist point of view, we might say that it is the planned leap or gap itself—the architectonic void supported between proposition and conclusion—which gives these works much of their power. In *The Hind and the Panther*, indeed, Dryden found a way to import *infinite* spaciousness. But there is a cultural or spiritual dimension to both poems for which no formalism can account. In both, the poet's imaginative reason remains inadequate without revelation or illumination from without. In both, a vision of truth is impossible without first entering the chaos and trusting to a higher power.

Sanford Budick
Dryden and the Abyss of Light: A Study of "Religio Laici" and "The Hind and the Panther" (New Haven, Conn.: Yale Univ. Pr., 1970), pp. 234–36

The critical standards that Dryden uses are ultimately empirical, resting on the particulars of style, "thought," and characterization which experience has proved effective. Yet he does not, like Johnson, appeal to the taste of audience or readers as the final critical standard. Although he consistently maintains that the business of an author is to please his age, he grows increasingly distrustful of audience taste. Dryden's final critical appeal is to that fuzziest of notions, the "imitation of nature," a concept which he uses in a confusing variety of ways. He does not, like [Thomas] Rymer, ask for a literal but decorous representation of the probable. Nor does he, like Johnson, treat art as a judiciously generalized slice of life. Rather, what Dryden most frequently seems to want in art is "nature wrought up to a higher pitch" . . . made more stimulating and hence more effective. Inevitably then, Dryden tends to see the "imitations" as a demonstration of the creative powers of the artist. . . .

Dryden hedges his claims for individual creativity by insisting that its products must be checked by judgment, but in essay after essay he finds imagination (or fancy) the vital creative power. Dryden never has much use for "natural imitation" . . . even in comedy. Consequently, he attaches great importance to the free imaging-power of the mind, and it is impossible for him to reduce art to life, as Johnson does. Dryden's attention is mostly fixed on the skill with which the work is wrought, since his dislike of the abstract keeps him from speculating about the author's motives. . . .

In sum, Dryden is a transitional figure in whose works the traits of both legislative and descriptive criticism are clearly discernible. We find in his criticism change (increasing emphasis on the powers of individual artists) and some distinct modes—speculative, prescriptive, and explanatory, as I call them. In critical theory as in literary practice Dryden is a syncretist, trying to reconcile and use what he finds best in the English, French, and Classical traditions.

Robert D. Hume
Dryden's Criticism (Ithaca, N.Y.: Cornell Univ. Pr., 1970), pp. 27–29

Threnodia Augustalis and *Britannia Rediviva* complete Dryden's attempt to record the sacred history of the English nation. A comparison of *Threnodia Augustalis* and *Britannia Rediviva* with the Restoration panegyrics reveals in Dryden's last official poems considerably more emphasis on the divinity of the king and a marked reluctance to involve the English nation in the process of redemptive history. In neither *Threnodia Augustalis* nor *Britannia Rediviva* are the English people able to participate in the renewal and restoration that Dryden had prophesied so often in the past. The diminution of the metaphor is noticeable both in Dryden's isolating the divinely sanctified monarch from the life of the nation and in his substituting abstractions like "Faction," "Domestick Treachery," "th'ungrateful Rout," and "Godless men" for the English people's earlier identity as a blessed if recalcitrant nation. Both characteristics suggest a growing rigidity in Dryden's handling of political issues—a loss of the ability so supplely and powerfully demonstrated in *Absalom and Achitophel* to see nation and king unified in terms of sacred metaphor.

Threnodia Augustalis begins not in the Edenic state nor in the past of Jewish history but with a reminiscence of the classical golden age. . . . The choice of the golden age as an expression of political security and harmony does not in itself signal a change in Dryden's handling of the relationship of English history to the past. . . . What does mark a change and what points to a retreat from the tensions of contemporary affairs is the fact that the image of the golden age is simply posited at the beginning of the poem and is not involved in the expression of either the immediate past of English political life or of an ideal toward which the nation should strive. . . .

Yet for all its typological detail, *Threnodia Augustalis* fails to make a case for the king as an expression of divine monarchy in the political life of the English nation. Like David and Christ, Charles and James are redemptive kings, but in the design of the poem Dryden fails to allow for redemptive action. Although the poem concludes with a prophecy, it is drawn exclusively from classical literature and not, as in the past, from sacred history or classical literature combined with biblical apocalypse. . . . The poem closes as Dryden enumerates the signs of a prosperous reign for James. But Dryden's belief in the possibility of political redemption is faltering. . . . [There] are subjunctive petitions bordering on a despair of realizing such a wish. And, indeed, the emphasis on faith and belief seems to be another signal that Dryden is turning away from English political life as an area that can respond to the promise that God recorded in Israelite history. Furthermore, Dryden's shift from prayer to vision is unconvincing (ll. 503–4), for there has been nothing in the poem to suggest that "They do" believe. Dryden's vision seems to be no vision at all, but a weary repetition of the props of a political fortune in which he seems no longer to believe.

Steven N. Zwicker
Dryden's Political Poetry: The Typology of King and Nation
(Providence, R.I.: Brown Univ. Pr., 1972), pp. 109–10, 113–14

At the center of Dryden's theory of literature is doubleness. What I mean by doubleness is perhaps best explained by illustrations of what I do not mean. Doubleness does not mean the presence of antinomies, antitheses, paradoxes, polarities. All of these suggest such tension between two values or sets of values as precludes sustained coexistence. Both the Manichean heresy and Hegelian dialectic are examples of such structures in that they organize two different forces or ideas or values in ways that embody this kind of tension. In the Manichean heresy conflicting values compete for supremacy, for that state or stasis, however temporary or partial, when one has conquered the other. In Hegelian dialectic there is a similar conflict between mighty opposites, with the difference that thesis and antithesis merge into a new synthesis which becomes immediately a new thesis predicating a new antithesis in a continuing dialectic. Both of these examples describe a situation which is unstable as a result of the competition between equal or nearly equal forces, and which consequently must progress to a new situation. A third example of what I do not mean by Dryden's doubleness is in the relation between good and evil according to traditional Christian doctrine. The situation in this example is much more stable because evil is understood as merely a perversion of good; sin is love misdirected. The stability results from good's subsuming of evil; because good is of a higher order than evil, there can be no ultimate competition between them. . . .

If we picture Dryden's criticism as a dramatic struggle between mutually exclusive values, we are projecting onto his sensibility a psychomachia which, interesting as it might be in itself, is not typical of his mind. He perceives literary qualities in terms of complementaries—both/and; a statement of preference in an exclusive sense, either/or, tends to be the last kind of statement that Dryden wishes to make. There are values in French drama and there are values in English drama, and any responsible theory of literature ought to respond to both sets. The French can learn from English elevation to enlarge the scope of their drama, and the English can learn from French justness to manage their variety better. Dryden's well-known definition of a play in the *Essay of Dramatic Poesy* emphasizes precisely this doubleness: *a just and lively image of human nature.*

His articulation, then, is conjunction rather than disjunction. But if it is conjunction, it is not synthesis. The terms held together by *both* and *and* are never transcended. Fancy and judgment, Dryden tells us, both perform essential functions in the creation of art, but they never merge into any third term. When on rare occasion they are incorporated into a new concept and given a new name, such as imagination or wit, they are not subsumed into a new product, nor do they ever lose their existence as individual concepts referring to distinguishable processes. When Dryden uses wit in an inclusive sense, it is meant to contain the fancy and the judgment in the way that a bag contains apples.

Edward Pechter
Dryden's Classical Theory of Literature (Cambridge: Cambridge Univ. Pr., 1975), pp. 11–13

GEORGE ETHEREGE

1634?–1691?

Frederick Bracher, ed., *Letters of Sir George Etherege* (1974)

HENRY FIELDING

1707–1754

All three of Fielding's novels, but most clearly *Tom Jones*, were written to be read ideally in the way we have been reading the so-called art novel since the time of Conrad and James. Each book is an intricate reflexive system that cannot be fully grasped with only one reading. Even in the relatively simple instance of Sophia's bird, not only does the episode affect our reading of all that follows, but our retrospective awareness of what follows influences our understanding of what actually happened in the early episode. No incident or action can be discussed in isolation from its context in the novel as a whole without at least partly distorting its meaning.

It is not really surprising that modern critics accustomed to reading novels in just this fashion should so often misread Fielding. Slapdash comic playwright, Grub Street journalist, genial old eighteenth-century essayist and humanist, by tradition he is hopelessly entangled with all those qualities that in our popular mental image typify the literature of his age and divide it from ours. The entanglement goes back in one respect to Fielding's own contemporaries, some of whom imagined *Tom Jones* and *Roderick Random* to be the work of the same writer. Such a mistake could only have been made by failing to see the overwhelming difference between Smollett's practice of writing novels as freehand narrative improvisations and Fielding's conception of the novel as a work of art. The notion of Fielding as a kind of Smollett with fancier style and more fastidious nose has vaguely persisted. For some of the reasons I have tried to trace above, many critics of our age have had little inclination to test the validity of this tradition by giving Fielding a really fresh reading.

It would be foolish to argue for the intrinsic superiority of Fielding's kind of novel to others. Fielding is different from Richardson, not necessarily better or worse. With all his artistic sophistication, there are clearly realms of experience that his kind of writing and his kind of sensibility cannot reach. But what should be avoided by intelligent criticism is to canonize one particular variety of the novel.

Robert Alter
Fielding and the Nature of the Novel (Cambridge, Mass.: Harvard Univ. Pr., 1968), pp. 24–25

Though its presence and importance in *Tom Jones* are evident . . . literary portraiture in Fielding's novels is richest and most varied in *Joseph Andrews.* At the same time, however, the nature of Fielding's characterization has changed. His figures are still tied to his ethical system, but the ideals of that system, as they are embodied in the characters, seem no longer as absolute and cerebral.

In general, Fielding moves away from ethical types in *Tom Jones*, creating, instead, a large number and wide range of social and psychological studies. This change is evident in such people as Di Western, Lady Bellaston, Squire Western, and Mrs. Waters. Very few people in this novel have predominantly ethical functions. And unlike the situation in *Jonathan Wild* and *Joseph Andrews*, these central ethical figures are not major characters, like Adams and Wild, but minor ones, like Thwackum, Square, and Allworthy. Tom, for example, is a paragon only in a limited and somewhat sentimental sense. Significant names are the best index to this development: in *Tom Jones* the use of such names—great reduced from *Joseph Andrews*—is restricted to a small number of minor personages.

This change in the nature and techniques of Fielding's characterization is accompanied by a decline in the use of his major forms of direct literary portraiture. Only limited use is made of elaborate descriptive conventions in his 1749 novel. There is no emblematic portraiture, and only one really full-length idealized delineation. Except for Captain Blifil's epitaph, it does not employ the biographical character sketch in its full form, and it makes only limited use of the direct character sketch. Fewer figures are described by this device in *Tom Jones* than in *Joseph Andrews* and *Jonathan Wild.* The form and uses of the direct sketch also change: psychological characterization is not presented in unified, full, set-piece delineations of personality but in numerous two- and three-sentence passages that are dispersed throughout the novel.

Sean Shesgreen
Literary Portraits in the Novels of Henry Fielding (DeKalb: Northern Illinois Univ. Pr., 1972), pp. 150–51

Despite his conviviality and good humor, Fielding is not the easiest of novelists to get to know. For someone who talks so openly to us, so directly about the nature and aims of his art, he offers us surprisingly little sense of himself and few insights into the recesses of his mind. In spite of the restless energy of his plots and his freewheeling commentary on all kinds of literary and actual experience, he is not really open and frank; he seems permissive, but he moves quickly from tone to tone and posture to posture so that his own personality is seldom directly visible and his privacy is never at stake. Very quickly we become acquainted with the social qualities that make his prose and his postures so engaging: he is genial and pleasantly garrulous; he sees the humor in everything including himself; he loves life and savors its every moment; he is tolerant of others without compromising his own strong beliefs; he is uncommonly decent and fair, unwilling to settle for the easy trusts and distrusts of majority taste.

But even after long acquaintance, we may have no firm knowledge of his private self, of who he is when the pen is put away or the company has gone home. Fielding's readers have always had difficulty imagining him in his private chamber, for like the greatest of his heroes, Tom Jones, he seems to belong at the Mermaid Tavern or on some pleasant path or in a verdant bed in pursuit of or in company with a very human other, not alone meditating upon his self. Yet Fielding is a contemplative man, too, and behind his smile is both facetiousness and benevolence, a complex temperament and a calculating mind. Any telling portrait of him must finally reconcile his discriminating eye with the facetious gestures and farcical postures that first strike us, for the worlds of his imagination—playful stages, wayward journeys, tuneful verbal rhapsodies, essays in becoming—are ordered by fine distinctions among human pleasures. Whatever his song, he always moralizes it and not just with an ordering dance in the last act or a graceful turn at the end of the journey. . . .

Fielding's career was shaped by historical forces just as surely as by psychological ones, and in its interaction of external and internal pressures it indexes the clash between medieval and modern that Fielding's contemporaries lived with every day. Time took away his inherited expectations and diluted the allusive power of the past, instead thrusting upon Fielding occasions and audiences that hardly seemed promising for one whose intellectual and personal ancestry was humanistic and aristocratic. But his responses to shifting tides of taste creatively transformed difficulty into opportunity, and he is a poignant example of the trapped artist who rejects the role of victim and instead carves out a place for himself in literary history. Fielding was no Vergil, and he provided no continuing paradigm for literary careers, but he did work out viable compromises between tradition and the burdens of the present, and his career is significant because it both articulates a recurring historical problem and suggests how literary forms and rhetorical strategies develop from occasions transformed.

J. Paul Hunter
Occasional Form: Henry Fielding and the Chains of Circumstance (Baltimore: Johns Hopkins Univ. Pr., 1975), pp. 3–4

JOHN GAY

1685–1732

Julie T. Klein, *John Gay: An Annotated Checklist of Criticism* (1973)

The Beggar's Opera, wrote Pope, was "a piece of Satire which hit all tastes and degrees of men, from those of the highest Quality to the very Rabble." All classes and all men come within the arc of its satire; no one is left unscathed. Yet it is the method of Gay's irony to keep maintaining the illusion that this is not so at all; that although things are in a bad way in this society there must surely be exceptions somewhere to the general rule; someone must be kind, someone must be honest, someone must be heroic. Throughout the play Gay keeps suggesting possible exceptions to the general rule of bourgeois possessiveness and self-interest, possible avenues of romantic freedom and escape, possible evidence of a primitive honesty; only regretfully, ironically, to dismiss such possibilities, to shut off the avenues and to reject the evidence as we approach more nearly. . . .

Two distinct views of man as a "sociable animal" were . . . current at the time at which Gay wrote *The Beggar's Opera*: the sceptical Hobbesian view, and the more optimistic view of Shaftesbury, which argued that sociability, like the other human passions, was both instinctive and conducive to the common good; that self-interest and social interest might be the same. There is little doubt, I think, that the Hobbesian view pervades *The Beggar's Opera*; but Gay's achievement is to throw up as an ironical alternative the sentimental Shaftesburian view of things, appearing, as it were, to weigh the two social theories judiciously in the balance, hinting that there *might* be exceptions to the general Hobbesian rule.

Ian Donaldson
The World Upside-Down: Comedy from Jonson to Fielding (Oxford: Clarendon, 1970), pp. 165–66, 177–78

OLIVER GOLDSMITH

1730–1774

A. Lytton Sells, *Oliver Goldsmith: His Life and Works* (1974)

No longer should it be necessary to puzzle over Goldsmith's self-conscious antisentimentalism toward weeping comedy and trite romances and his seeming contradiction in writing a sentimental novel. No longer should it be necessary to view Goldsmith as turning soft—as one of the first pre-Romantics. If *The Traveller* and *The Deserted Village* are no longer read as autobiographical you-can't-go-home-again poems and are recognized as deliberately rhetorical, then the view of Goldsmith as becoming a man of sensibility is untenable. It is here, however, that one may take issue with those who have made as strong a case as it is possible to make for these two poems. Given the two prime modes of writing as Goldsmith saw them —the craft of persuasion and the craft of satire—one can little doubt that Goldsmith's craft of satire is what still speaks to us directly today. Despite the very able analyses of *The Traveller* and *The Deserted Village* made in the last decade or so, I do not think that we can suspend our taste and maintain the greatness of Goldsmith's verse and then use another set of poetic values to read contemporary verse. . . .

Rather than labeling Goldsmith an "amuser," we may instead interpret him as an amiable satirist. Goldsmith himself, as we have seen, would not think of this label as a contradiction in terms. For some, no doubt, satire must be corrosive—must be the lashing mode of Juvenal or Swift—but this is to limit its range too narrowly. Satire should be conceived as a spectrum in which the color is determined by the technique and by the ends for which a particular work is designed. In the past critics have called Goldsmith a comic writer, forgetting that comedy is a criticism of life and ignoring exactly what it is Goldsmith is criticizing. Goldsmith-as-amiable-satirist demands that his moral motives as they are expressed in the structures of the works themselves be defined as well as his means; indeed, aesthetic understanding is impossible without an understanding of function. If Swift is placed at one pole of eighteenth-century English satire and Goldsmith at the other, we will have a much better grasp of the mode's surprising range, refinement, and versatility. We will no longer think of Goldsmith as merely an amuser but second only to Chaucer as a master of the art of amiable satire.

Robert H. Hopkins
The True Genius of Oliver Goldsmith (Baltimore: Johns Hopkins Univ. Pr., 1964), pp. 234–36

If the narrative technique used by Goldsmith in *The Vicar* [*of Wakefield*] is viewed in the perspective of those major earlier novels of the same basic type—i.e. first-person fictitious memoirs—with which he can be assumed to have been familiar, it is possible to make the following main points.

First of all, there is no earlier major first-person novel in which a narrator-agent of Dr. Primrose's kind—a middle-aged parent of the amiable-humorist type, who has troubles in marrying off his daughters—is used. As a rule, in novels dealing with "amours," the narrator-agent is more directly involved, for instance in the way that Marianne is in Marivaux's *La vie de Marianne*, or Jacob in the same writer's *Le paysan parvenu*. On the whole, the narrators of first-person fictitious memoirs tend to be either *picaros* (genuine, as in *Lazarillo de Tormes*, or modified in some way, as in *Gil Blas* or *Roderick Random*), travellers (as Gulliver or Robinson Crusoe), or young lovers. The focus of narrative interest usually lies in a comparatively early period of their lives, when they either had to struggle hard for their existence, or travelled widely, or were involved in more or less complicated and extended love affairs. Though he simplifies (and excludes the many female protagonists), Goldsmith himself was not wide of the mark when, in 1759, he claimed that the heroes of modern "romances" were usually "young men of spirit, who go through a variety of adventures, and at last conclude a life of dissipation, folly, and extravagance in riches and matrimony."

Seen in this perspective, *The Vicar* is also exceptional in that the action is exclusively concentrated within a very brief but crucial period in the life of the narrator-agent and his family, with no reference at all made to his birth and earlier life. It is hard to find a first-person fictitious memoir before 1760 that does not follow the autobiographical pattern and start off leisurely, with a more or less extended account of the protagonist's birth and ancestry, only very gradually arriving at the action proper. . . .

By avoiding calling attention to the double point of view—that of the experiencing I and that of the narrating I—which a narrative of this kind may involve, Goldsmith escaped a trap into which many an allegedly didactic writer of first-person narratives before him had fallen. . . . Goldsmith lets his narrator comment ironically on the failings of other characters in his surroundings, but his own shortcomings are mainly left to be judged by the reader and the implied author in tacit understanding behind the narrator's back. . . .

In composing his novel, Goldsmith only had to go a few steps further in the same direction in order to create an ironic, yet fallible, narrator-agent of a more plausible and less exotic kind than the one that existed in embryo in his *Chinese Letters*. By making the protagonist of his novel a full-blooded amiable humorist with a naïveté more marked than Lien Chi's, and yet retaining some of the latter's ironic distance to his fellow-beings, by restricting the scope of the satire considerably, and by making him the central figure and narrator of a more complex and less romantic action than the thin frame-story of the *Chinese Letters,* he could add a new and original dimension to the art of first-person narrative in the tradition of the English eighteenth-century novel.

Sven Bäckman
This Singular Tale: A Study of "The Vicar of Wakefield" and Its Literary Background (Lund, Sweden: C. W. K. 'Gleerup, 1971), pp. 111–13

THOMAS HOBBES

1588–1679

Hobbes writes on morals as a moralist. His primary aim is to demonstrate what men ought, and what they ought not, to do. In pursuing this aim he introduces, and explains, certain moral concepts, of which the most important are *right of nature, law of nature, obligation,* and *justice.* But his interest is in using these concepts in moral conclusions, not in explicating them.

When the contemporary moral philosopher turns to Hobbes, however, his concern is with the concepts themselves, rather than the conclusions in which they appear. He wants to analyze moral terms, not draw moral conclusions. This shift of interest is entirely legitimate, but it is not always sufficiently noticed. . . .

There are two opposed lines of argument which have been pursued by Hobbes's scholars, and which are equally mistaken. The first is to claim, correctly, that Hobbes's *conclusions* have a prudential basis, and to infer, incorrectly, that Hobbes's *concepts* are prudential. The second is to claim, correctly, that Hobbes's concepts are not prudential, and to infer, incorrectly, that Hobbes's conclusions do not have a prudential basis.

The plausibility of these mistakes has been increased by two factors. The first is the supposition, usually tacit, that if Hobbes's concepts are not prudential, and not merely legal, then they must be moral in a sense of "moral" correlative but opposed to that of "prudential." This is wrong; as we shall show, Hobbes's concepts are *practical,* moral in so far as "moral" means "practical," "concerning what to do," but not in so far as "moral" means "opposed or superior to prudential."

The second is the supposition that Hobbes's concept of obligation must be defined in terms of his concept of the law of nature. This we shall show to be mistaken—and badly mistaken, in that it rests on a misunderstanding of our ordinary concept of obligation.

David P. Gauthier
The Logic of Leviathan: The Moral and Political Theory of Thomas Hobbes (Oxford: Clarendon, 1969), pp. 27–29

Hobbes's state of nature . . . is a picture of civil society as Hobbes sees it, with all the civil bonds dissolved by a process of abstraction. The human animal which inhabits Hobbes's mythical state of nature is not the Aristotelian animal who exists in tension between his origin and his fulfillment, nor is he simply "instinctive" man antecedent to all society (a creature that would be pure fiction); but he is rather the typical seventeenth-century man as Hobbes sees him, released from the network of institutions and obligations which constitute society. . . .

The method for discovering what is "natural" about anything, including men and political society, then, is for Hobbes this process of analytical dissolution which he calls "resolution." As Rousseau acutely was to observe in the next century, he actually failed to complete his appointed analytical task. What he depicted as man in the state of nature was still a political animal, one who was released from the bonds of obligation and authority but who was still clearly a social product. Nevertheless, whatever failings Hobbes had in carrying out his analysis, the nature of the intellectual project he had in mind is quite clear: to reach the "real" components of any "complex whole" such as political society, one must intellectually "resolve" it into its constituent elements. . . .

Hobbes goes even further. Nature is not only characterized by a lack of human or political order; it is even a force working against order in some ways. "Nature dissociates," he says, "and renders men apt to invade and destroy one another." The "natural lusts of men," he says elsewhere, "do daily threaten each other." The political task which faces men, therefore, is not to attain that order which nature has provided for them, but rather to escape the intrinsically ill condition of meer nature.

The disorder of meer nature, standing as it does in such stark contrast to the orderliness of Aristotelian nature, helps to explain the radically creative force which Hobbes attributes to the word of the sovereign. Given the anarchy of meer nature, the voice of the sovereign must serve as the *logos* —the origin of order. For nature herself is now bereft of its *logos*; it has been stripped altogether of its ordering force. Man must therefore create and invest such a force on his own as a work of artifice. He must build "an Artificiall Man . . . of greater stature and strength than the Naturall for whose protection and defense it was intended," namely, "that great Leviathan." Only through such a creation can man save himself from the suicidal consequences of remaining in a state of nature.

Thomas A. Spragens, Jr.
The Politics of Motion: The World of Thomas Hobbes
(Lexington: Univ. Pr. Kentucky, 1973), pp. 106–8

SAMUEL JOHNSON

1709–1784

James L. Clifford and Donald J. Greene, *Samuel Johnson: A Survey and Bibliography of Critical Studies* (1970)

Johnson's tremendous sensitivity to language places him in the small handful of literary critics of the very highest rank in the English language—some, like Yvor Winters, have not hesitated to place him, alone, at the top. His preparation as a critic was unequalled—some nine years spent in minutely examining the texts of masterpieces of English from the sixteenth to early eighteenth centuries, noting the subtle semantic differences of English words and phrases, finally assembling the results of his labors into the first modern dictionary of the language: a dictionary, as he put it, "for the use of such as aspire to exactness of criticism or elegance of style," a dictionary whose method formed the basis of all later scientific and historical study of the language. And the first application he made of that knowledge, to the explication of the difficult and often corrupt text of the greatest of English writers, Shakespeare, laid a monumental foundation for all future explication of it.

Nowhere is Johnson more modern than in his criticism of poetry. Students now identify the close scrutiny of poetic text with "the new critics" of the twentieth century, and applaud as "modern" Mallarmé's dictum that poetry is made up of words, not ideas, and Eliot's footnote to it, that in criticism "The spirit killeth, but the letter giveth life." They have only rediscovered what Johnson, long before, preached and practiced, in his rejection of archaism of vocabulary and distortion of syntax—of writers like Gray who "thought his language more poetical as it was more remote from common use" and Collins who "affected the obsolete when it was not worthy of revival, and . . . puts his words out of the common order, seeming to think, with some later candidates for fame, that not to write prose is certainly to write poetry." With Wordsworth and Pound and Eliot, Johnson believed that the language of serious poetry, addressed to the contemporary reader, must be essentially contemporary. We think of a concern with imagery in poetry as a characteristic of modern criticism: but no critic has been more intent than Johnson on fully realizing the imagery of the poetry he studied—the words "image," "imagery," and "imagination" (the image-creating faculty) occur many dozens of times in *The Lives of the Poets*, and Johnson has no greater praise for a poem than to say that its imagery is novel and effective, and no greater censure than that its imagery is inept or trite.

Donald Greene
Samuel Johnson (New York: Twayne, 1970), pp. 218–19

It is because Johnson is skilled in shifting from voice to voice that comments about his "style" can be so misleading. The nineteenth-century recoil from his writings largely took the form of attacks, like Macaulay's, on what was thought of as his "style." It was assumed that he wrote always in his own sincere person and that therefore he had one style; and that this style was unremittingly polysyllabic, fraudulently—that is, merely mechanically—antithetical, and hence uniformly pompous. William Hazlitt's objection to a fancied uniformity is typical: "The fault of Dr. Johnson's style is that it reduces all things to the same artificial and unmeaning level." But such a view will not survive close application to the writings in all their variety.

The charge of ostentatious polysyllabism is easiest answered. Often the polysyllables complained of are not Johnson's at all: they belong to his ridiculous characters, and on such occasions Johnson flourishes big words with a cunning satiric consciousness of their absurdity and its effect on the reader. . . .

When in a piece of writing Johnson does establish an elevated stylistic norm, giving us much antithesis and balance and offering an abnormal number of Latinate polysyllables, he frequently does so to provide himself with a grid against which the blunt and the monosyllabic will show with special energy. In this he behaves like a poet who establishes a regular texture of meter and rhyme and line-length so that significant variations from these things can take place and the spectrum of expression be widened. . . .

His styles are those appropriate to a number of occasions, or genres. Even various kinds of conversations are genres, and in them as well as in written occasions he senses the necessity of literary conventions. Indeed, in conversation "stated and prescriptive" actions and reactions constitute the essential dynamics. He often chided Mrs. [Hester Piozzi] Thrale for her practice of gross flattery, and it is true that much of his criticism of her usages was moral in intent: envy is so powerful a human passion that to praise anyone highly in company is immediately to rouse against him as many secret enemies as there are persons present. But in addition, much of his criticism of Mrs. Thrale's flattery is more purely literary: flattery that deviates from the conventional is like bad writing—it produces the opposite rhetorical effect from the one designed by its practitioner.

Paul Fussell
Samuel Johnson and the Life of Writing (New York: Harcourt Brace Jovanovich, 1971), pp. 76–77, 80

Johnson looked back on his play [*Irene*] with the humility of a proud man who is not too proud to learn from his mistakes. . . . Johnson did not succeed and he knew it. But surprisingly . . . he totally failed to perceive why this was so. What he must originally have conceived was a drama of ideas, but instead of designing an action in which ratiocinative dialogue could be appropriate, and instead of providing characters who could plausibly speak it, he followed the example of [Addison's] *Cato* in forcing his moral ideas into a plot that emphasizes suspense and intrigue. We have seen how carefully he developed these elements, but the suspense he tried to attain was of a mechanical kind (will the characters succeed in their scheme or be betrayed?) when the moral suspense of Irene's conversion ought to have been at the center. The love-plot adds further distraction, and in such a framework Johnson's moral ideas inevitably seem extraneous. His characters must desist from the action demanded by the structure of the play, and must disregard the passions which are supposed to be driving them, in order to expound doctrines which, to make matters worse, are dull.

Need Johnson have failed? I do not say that he could have achieved a true *drama* of ideas like Schiller's *Wallenstein*, where moral and philosophical issues rise out of a human (and dramatic) predicament. But another kind of model was available. Instead of irrelevantly condemning [Milton's] *Comus* for its lack of sprightly dialogue, he might have perceived that it would have been a far better guide than *Cato*. And when he objects to *Cato* in almost the same terms, it is clear that he has not really reflected on the difference between the two. . . . The truth is that *Irene* is undramatic not because the characters talk too much, or because more should have been done with the expedients of suspension and the stratagems of surprise, but rather because the drama itself is misplaced, and centers on a not very fascinating action instead of on the intellectual and moral issues that really matter to the author.

Leopold Damrosch, Jr.
Samuel Johnson and the Tragic Sense (Princeton, N.J.:
Princeton Univ. Pr., 1972), pp. 137–38

Johnson's participation, however brief and didactic [in *Rasselas*] in an imitation of *Don Quixote* entitles us to generalize about his relation to traditions of the novel. All misadventures of a bookish hero in an incurably practical world are imitations of *Don Quixote*, if we are willing to use the phrase in a very general way. The number and variety of narratives which conform to this model, precisely, crudely, or by derivation, is astonishing; it includes most of the better-known seventeenth-century prose burlesques, much of the new realism in eighteenth-century England. The experience of disenchantment and disillusion, which *Don Quixote* both pursues and evades, evolves easily into Bildungsroman, itself an archetype for the conventional novel. The Cervantic paradigm may be modified in the other direction also, away from personality and back to concept, away from realism toward satirical fictions organized around the disparity between ideal and actual, theory and practice, art and nature—*Gulliver's Travels*, for example, or *Candide*. In its own abbreviated and idiogrammatic way, Johnson's fiction touches all these bases; his protagonists are always mocked or educated or disillusioned, and sometimes all three at once.

Johnson as narrator is hardly more than a dilettante in realism, Cervantic or otherwise, but the aspect of *Don Quixote* which is less an imitation of life than a parable on the relation between literature and life—for humanists, a perennial concern—attracted him strongly. . . .

In many respects, then, Johnson's tastes coincide with those of early masters of English fiction. Not only does he share their aversion to heroic romance and their interest in psychological complexity of character; he was also, as everyone knows, bored by "histories of the downfal of kingdoms, and revolutions of empire," and strongly drawn to domestic fictions and to intimate biography. . . .

But even in the eighteenth century, and even within Johnson's frame of reference, realism could mean many things. It could mean a rough-and-tumble picaresque comedy of discomfiture, for which Johnson showed no special enthusiasm: he virtually ignores Quixote's broken bones. Yet the applauder of Falstaff and Sir Andrew Aguecheek can have no insuperable aversion to "low" tavern scenes, to the realism of cakes and ale. Johnson's appetite for Shakespearean realism is somewhat diminished by neoclassical assumptions about language and decorum: he is happy that Shakespeare's senators are sometimes buffoons, but cannot bear that a true hero use the language of the stable; a scene which aspires to tragic dignity is spoiled for him by the admixture of undignified words, even if they are realistic. There is more than a residue of Renaissance doctrines of the separation of styles in Johnson. He respects narratives which "exhibit life in its true state" because they are true, not because they are beautiful; and realism is for Johnson rather a mode of expression, appropriate to lower genres, than a way of looking at life itself—he sees *Roderick Random* and *Tom Jones* as versions of comedy, not as the distant ancestors of *Ulysses*.

Carey McIntosh
The Choice of Life: Samuel Johnson and the World of Fiction
(New Haven, Conn.: Yale Univ. Pr., 1973), pp. 23–24, 28–29

JOHN MILTON

1608–1674

A Variorum Commentary on the Poems of John Milton. Vol. 1 (1970), *The Latin and Greek Poems*, ed. Douglas Bush, and *The Italian Poems*, ed. J. E. Shaw and A. Bartlett Giammati; Vol. 2 (1972), in three parts, *The Minor English Poems*, ed. A. S. P. Woodhouse and Douglas Bush; Vol. 4 (1975), *Paradise Regained*, ed. Walter MacKellar

Don M. Wolfe, gen. ed., *Complete Prose Works of John Milton* (1953–), 7 vols. in 9 parts to date

William Riley Parker, *Milton: A Biography* (1968), 2 vols.

POETRY

There is involved in "Lycidas" an assault upon the poem's own assumptions, which the poem, in the act of making itself, recognizes and progressively strengthens. This attack is exemplified, both in the kind of microcosmic enactment of language . . . and in the larger tactical manoeuvre of the pastoral spectacle, thrice set up to be undermined. The total attack, both formal and linguistic, can be thought of as the stylistic correlative to the deeper assault of experience upon the sense of order; and the restoration of equilibrium in convention and language corresponds to, validates and intensifies the deeper restoration of a sense of design in reality. It is because of this inclusive and highly sophisticated strategy that the poem, to quote Douglas Bush, "is at once an agonized personal cry and a formal exercise, a search for order and a made object, an affirmation of faith in Providence and an exploitation of pastoral and archetypal myth." One more paradox can be added to the description of this unprecedented poem in which everything has a precedent. It is both a powerfully allusive essay in a convention and a highly controlled denial of that convention. . . .

"Lycidas," as one comes to realize progressively, is full of significant symmetries arranged as affirmations of its three part structure. The three forms of irresponsibility have already been noted and it is well-known that the outburst of questioning in each part is stilled on each occasion by a form of divine reassurance. . . . Perhaps it is best to say that each part discloses a different face of God or, more precisely, a different form of man's recognition of God's nature. The God who calms the first wave of doubt is the god of justice and emphasis is laid on his impartiality, his "perfect witness," and on the "all-judging" power that weighs all things fully and impartially in its balance. The god of the second part is the apocalyptic god of retribution whose single blow is sufficient to crush the armies of the godless. To make understanding doubly clear Milton defines the specific quality of each reassurance, immediately after the reassurance has been offered. Significantly, these definitions occur in those two crucial passages that admit the violation of the pastoral decorum. We return to normality from the "higher mood" of justice; we return again to it from the "dread voice" of retribution.

The third recognition of God is the one recognition that can truly answer man's agony. It is the consciousness not of justice but of the power beyond justice, not the might of him who wields the two-handed engine but instead the "dear might of him that walk'd the waves." . . . The third resolution transcends the law and so reminds us that there are energies in this poem which even the law cannot silence. If peace is to be won it can be won only through the higher satisfaction of redemptive love. . . .

As the dolphins waft Lycidas to Byzantium, they surely guide us also to the recognition that salvation lies not with the god of hosts, nor with the exact dispenser of Olympian justice, but in "the blest Kingdoms meek of joy and love" which establish both our dignity and dependence.

Balachandra Rajan
The Lofty Rhyme: A Study of Milton's Major Poetry
(Coral Gables, Fla.: Univ. Miami Pr., 1970), pp. 49, 53–54

"Epitaphium Damonis" breaks through to a new level of poetic technique. Again, the problem is the death of a friend, a very close friend now. But the poem moves both within and beyond the pastoral tradition, and its resolution depends in part on its self-consciousness of its form, its awareness of moving dynamically beyond the poetic conventions within which it began, and the dynamism arising from the poetic conventions it surmounts.

Samson Agonistes brings the traditions of Greek tragedy to bear on the recurring question of the justice of God's ways. Whether it is Milton's last poem, the next-to-last, or earlier than that seems unanswerable on a basis of external evidence. Its conservatism in its use of the Greek tragic tradition, however, argues against its being a very late work. While it uses its Greek models skillfully and not slavishly, it tends to remain content within its tradition (unlike "Epitaphium Damonis," *Paradise Lost*, and *Paradise Regained*); it tends to use the Greek tragedies as general models, not as instruments for creating a new pattern adapted uniquely to this poem. Where "Epitaphium Damonis," *Paradise Lost*, and *Paradise Regained* repeatedly create functional dissonances between themselves and their respective traditions and then use these dissonances as instruments to arrive at extra-poetic resolutions, *Samson Agonistes* tends simply to use the tragic form as a vehicle for the Biblical story; and the tragic tradition in the play is more a generalized mode or vehicle than it is an implement whose function is to create the patterns of clashes and harmonies with the poem itself in order to arrive at a culminating insight.

But *Paradise Lost*, like "Epitaphium Damonis," refuses to rest within its tradition. It establishes itself again and again as an epic poem, yet at the same time it drives itself, somewhat like "Epitaphium Damonis," from more conventional epic positions early in the poem to concepts of higher virtue at the end, and to the explicit exaltation of the Christian virtues of patience and humility over the conventional epic virtues of physical courage and martial skill. Like "Epitaphium Damonis," *Samson Agonistes*, and many of the early poems, *Paradise Lost* is ultimately a dialectic poem; it seeks for the justification of God's ways. Like "Lycidas," "Epitaphium Damonis," and *Samson Agonistes*, it ultimately finds this justification, this answer to its extra-poetic problems, by poetic means: by its epic hero who learns to suffer for Truth's sake, and who journeys forth to seek the Paradise within.

Paradise Regained in many ways takes some of the unrealized implications of *Paradise Lost* to their logical conclusion and uses the epic tradition with even greater subtlety and sophistication than *Paradise Lost*. . . .

The structure of the poem is as much anti-epic—a renunciation of the epic and a transcendence of the epic—as it is epic; but just as "Epitaphium Damonis" both uses and transcends pastoralism to achieve its poetic vision, so *Paradise Regained* uses both its acceptance and its rejection of the epic tradition to arrive at its ultimate extra-poetic resolution—the discovery of the self through the struggles of the spirit.

Ralph Waterbury Condee
Structure in Milton's Poetry from the Foundation to the Pinnacles
(University Park: Pennsylvania State Univ. Pr., 1974),
pp. 177–78

In 1671 Milton grouped together two poems under the title *Paradise Regained. A Poem. In IV Books. To which is added Samson Agonistes.* He did so with good reason: the two works were companion-pieces, comprising the poet's final words on Christian heroism, and providing a Christian definition of the two great poetic modes, the heroic and the tragic. Although *Paradise Regained* is a brief epic, *Samson* a tragedy, both are brief heroic poems with the common subject of a hero coming to knowledge of his identity through temptation: Christ in the darkness of the wilderness, and Samson in the darkness of his own blindness, struggle against the sins to which the old Adam had succumbed, raising finally an inner Eden from a "waste Wilderness" (*PR*, I.7).

Milton's readers would, I believe, have recognized at once that in addition to a similarity in subject the two works shared a similarity in structure as well; for the structure of both works emerges largely from the structure, based on Adam's temptation in Eden and Christ's in the wilderness, established by Spenser in the Legend of Holiness and imitated by Giles Fletcher in "Christ's Victory on Earth." In *Samson*, Milton's borrowing from his Spenserian heritage is confined primarily to the poem's "middle" and Samson's confrontation with Manoa, Dalila, and Harapha, or the Flesh, the World, and the Devil. In *Paradise Regained*, however, the borrowing is much more comprehensive; it extends to virtually every major structural aspect of the work. Following Spenser and Fletcher, Milton employs a linear triadic sequence in which the first day is linked to the Flesh, the second to the World, the third to the Devil. Also like Spenser and Fletcher, Milton makes the World-temptation a composite one, but he goes beyond Spenser to make the World include not only one but two temptations to the

Flesh, the World, and the Devil, the first occurring in the banquet-wealth-glory sequence, the second in the Parthia-Rome-Athens sequence.

Underlying *Paradise Regained* is Milton's desire to outdo his great English master and his triadic structural triumph in the Legend of Holiness. As a result, Milton goes beyond Spenser not only in the amplification of the World-temptation but also in the addition of two structural features: first, a fusion of the Flesh-World-Devil sequence of the three days with another triad, Christ's mediatorial roles as Prophet, King, and Priest; second, the imposition of a tetradic book structure. Milton's additions, however, are exactly that, additions; they do not supplant but supplement the structure he inherited from Spenser and Fletcher. The result is a work of a vigorously mature and seasoned artistry, a brilliant structural tour de force with everything in perfect measure and proportion.

Patrick Cullen
Infernal Triad: The Flesh, the World, and the Devil in Spenser and Milton (Princeton, N.J.: Princeton Univ. Pr., 1974), pp. 125–29

Paradise Lost

I would like to suggest something about *Paradise Lost* that is not new except for the literalness with which the point will be made: (1) the poem's centre of reference is its reader who is also its subject; (2) Milton's purpose is to educate the reader to an awareness of his position and responsibilities as a fallen man, and to a sense of the distance which separates him from the innocence once his; (3) Milton's method is to re-create in the mind of the reader (which is, finally, the poem's scene) the drama of the Fall, to make him fall again exactly as Adam did and with Adam's troubled clarity, that is to say, "not deceived." In a limited sense few would deny the truth of my first two statements; Milton's concern with the ethical imperatives of political and social behaviour would hardly allow him to write an epic which did not attempt to give his audience a basis for moral action; but I do not think the third has been accepted in the way that I intend it. . . .

The wariness these encounters with demonic attraction make us feel is part of a larger pattern in which we are taught the hardest of all lessons, distrust of our own abilities and perceptions. This distrust extends to all the conventional ways of knowing that might enable a reader to locate himself in the world of any poem. The questions we ask of our reading experience are in large part the questions we ask of our day-to-day experience. Where are we, what are the physical components of our surroundings, what time is it? And while the hard and clear outline of *Paradise Lost* suggests that the answers to these questions are readily available to us, immediate contexts repeatedly tell us that they are not. . . .

Satan's initial attractiveness owes as much to a traditional idea of what is heroic as it does to our weakness before the rhetorical lure. He exemplifies a form of heroism most of us find easy to admire because it is visible and flamboyant (the epic voice also admires: the "though in pain" of "So spake th' Apostate Angel, though in pain" is a recognition of the steadfastness that can belong even to perversity; the devil is always given his due). Because his courage is never denied (instead Milton insists on it) while his virtue and goodness are (in the "allegations" of the epic voice), the reader is led to revise his idea of what a true hero is. If this poem does anything to its readers, it forces them to make finer and finer discriminations. Perhaps the most important aspect of the process I have been describing—the creation of a reader who is fit because he knows and understands his limitations—begins here at I. 125 when Milton's authorial corrective casts the first stone at the ideal of martial valour and points us towards the meaningful acceptance of something better.

Stanley E. Fish
Surprised by Sin: The Reader in "Paradise Lost" (London: Macmillan, 1967), pp. 1, 22–23, 48–49

There is . . . in *Paradise Lost*, not only a respect for the great cultural traditions of the past, but also a kind of witty devaluation of them, or inversion of them. It is not enough to say that Milton is writing under the influence of Greek, Latin, and Renaissance poetry; still less, that he is "showing off" his erudition. What Milton is "showing off" is usually his poetical virtuosity, challenging the severest comparisons. . . .

I think that there is demonstrably in *Paradise Lost*, what there demonstrably always was in Milton, throughout all his writings: a sardonic wit, a sense of the absurd, an amused contemplation of scale and perspective, a growling sense of the comic, which finds expression often in a quiet or surreptitious deflationary technique, very often about the poetry itself, about the kind of poem *Paradise Lost* is expected to be. Perhaps the qualities I have been indicating in *Paradise Lost* are a little more perceptible if it is compared with an epic poem which was quite definitely not a joke against the Epic: a religious heroic poem on the ancient model which we know that Milton read and—at least in his youth—admired: I mean the *Christiados* of Girolamo Vida. . . . In comparison with the *Christiados, Paradise Lost* scintillates with wit and dazzles us with subtlety and variety. . . .

The interesting achievement of twentieth-century criticism of Milton is to make us perceptive of . . . variations of style and sensibility in the poem. From the older critics of Milton one supposes that they found him grand but somewhat monotonous. What they admired they described eloquently.

But they did not admire Milton nearly enough. We may flatter ourselves that we can take a good deal of *Paradise Lost* in a double and richer sense. We have learnt to feel that Satan is a comic figure as well as a tragic figure; that Adam and Eve are domestic characters as well as archetypal figures; that Milton responds to and understands—as surely a poet must—both rebellion and obedience; that the poem is about Providence as well as Damnation; and that it is a poem about love both human and divine; that the poem means *us*. Extreme views have been expressed about Milton. But I can think of no poet whose critics have, in the last generation, so educated and sensitised his readers.

And now by a lucky chance we are perhaps in a peculiarly happy condition for becoming close to *Paradise Lost*. Contemporary critical theory and practice have accustomed us to the notion of the "anti-novel" and the "anti-hero." It is now at last obvious what *Paradise Lost* is. It is the anti-epic. Wherever we turn we find the traditional epic values inverted. It closed the history of this poetic genre in England—the epic form as understood by Petrarch, Ronsard, Vida, or (for that matter) Boileau and Dryden. It closed the history of the epic (for you will not expect me to comment on the unspeakable labours of [Richard] Blakemore, [Richard] Glover, and [William] Wilkie).

Never was the death of an art form celebrated with such a magnanimous ceremony, splendid in ashes and pompous in the grave. The death of tragedy was a mere decline into a whine and a whisper. But the death of epic was, in Milton's hands, a glorious and perfectly staged suicide.

T. J. B. Spencer
in *Approaches to "Paradise Lost,"* ed. C. A. Patrides (London: Edward Arnold, 1968), pp. 89–90, 97–98

The role of the Son finds its counterpart in the role of Satan, and we cannot begin to understand the function of one without a complete awareness of how the other functions. In another instance, God's act of creation operates most significantly when viewed in the light of its opposite, the defeat of Satan in Heaven. Carrying the idea still further, we can see how the Son's entrance into Chaos and return to glory in Book VII is contrasted with Satan's entrance into Chaos in Book II and return to ignominy in Book X. Or, to cite a critical commonplace, the contrast between the holy Trinity of God, Son, and Spirit and the unholy Trinity of Satan, Sin, and Death allows us to see how the divine world is parodied by the degenerate. As obvious as these contrasts might appear, they serve to indicate the importance of dialectical reasoning to *Paradise Lost*. Indeed, Milton's reference in *Areopagitica* to the necessity of learning by what is "contrary" should determine the very way in which we approach Milton's epic. For to understand the polemical nature of *Paradise Lost* is to come to terms with the essential oppositions that manifest themselves on all levels.

With the dialectical approach as the basis of my study, then, I propose to discover a common referent by which the oppositions of the poem find expression. That referent, as I shall argue, has to do with the idea of creation in all its aspects: conception, pregnancy, birth, and offspring (both sublime and degenerate). I shall suggest that Milton as a poet speaks in a language of birth in order to dramatize such events as the warring of good and evil, the fall of angels and men, the redemption of man through grace, God's creation of the universe, and the poet's creation of the poem.

Michael Lieb
The Dialectics of Creation: Patterns of Birth & Regeneration in "Paradise Lost" (Amherst: Univ. Massachusetts Pr., 1970), p. 7

The reason why *Paradise Lost* as a whole "does not profoundly trouble, profoundly satisfy us, in the manner of great tragedy" [A. J. A. Waldock], is that it is *not* a tragedy. It is an epic which *contains*, among other things, a tragedy, that of Satan. When the narrator of *Paradise Lost* proclaims, "I now must change/These Notes to Tragic" (IX, 5–6) he has to be referring to those "Notes" with which he will describe the Fall of Man, but not necessarily to all the remaining notes of the poem. . . . The term *tragic* does apply to the *catastrophe* of Satan's drama and to the *crisis* of what will be classified as the tragicomedy of Adam and Eve, but it does not apply to all that transpires in Books IX–XII. For these books embody the resolution of the plot of a kind of history play—that of the Son of God. This drama contains, integrates, and unifies Satan's tragedy and Adam and Eve's tragicomedy, but is itself contained within the outer framework of the epic form. This structure of interlocking dramatic units can be crudely diagrammed as follows:

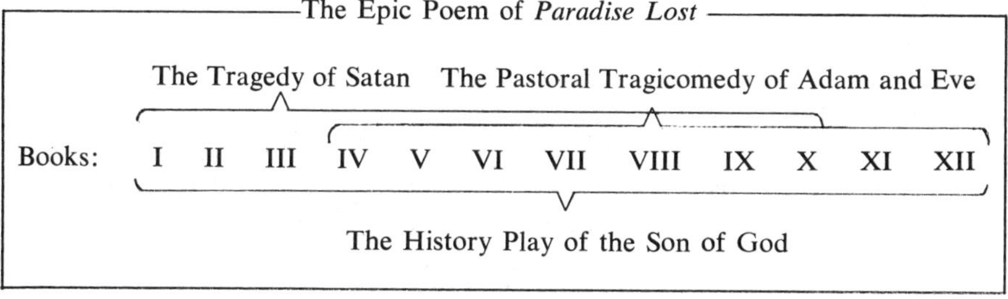

One need not be a purist to be disconcerted by the use of terms like tragedy, tragicomedy, and history play in connection with an epic poem, but as Lily B. Campbell has noted, in the seventeenth century such terms "were applied to nondramatic as well as dramatic writing." Furthermore, since the time of Aristotle students of the drama have had difficulty in agreeing upon their terminology.

Roger B. Rollin
in *Milton Studies*, Vol. V, ed. James D. Simmonds (Pittsburgh: Univ. Pittsburgh Pr., 1973), p. 5

Paradise Regained

Milton's *Paradise Regained* is obviously indebted to the biblical "brief epic" tradition in regard to conception, structure, epic devices, and even verbal echoes. Clearly it is also indebted to the "epic" exegetical and literary tradition of the Book of Job for some aspects of the hero and the structure. When, however, we examine Milton's use of these generic traditions we get a measure of the distance between noble intention and distinguished achievement, and we see how tremendous are the transformations wrought by the true artist.

It is now evident that Milton's statement about the brief epic does refer to traditions important for the understanding of *Paradise Regained.* His distinction between the "diffuse" and the "brief" epic does point to two separate categories of biblical epic, and we have seen that until the mid-seventeenth century the brief epic category contained a preponderance of the biblical poems. It seems likely also that Milton's four-book format derives from the precedent supplied by many of the best-known and most influential brief epics. . . .

Moreover, it is clear that Milton's reference to Job as the model of a brief epic has its sanction in the fact that the Book of Job itself was often described as an epic, that the Jobean theme was often given "epic" literary treatment, and that the structure of the Book of Job had already been imitated in other biblical and Christian epics, most notably in [Robert] Aylett's *Joseph*, and [Joseph] Beaumont's *Psyche*. . . .

The style of *Paradise Regained* . . . no less than its relationship to generic traditions and its vast all-inclusive theme, supports the poem's claim to the status of brief epic. Coleridge's encomium on the work as "in its kind . . . the most perfect poem extant" is perhaps the appropriate final tribute to Milton's consummate art in conceiving his brief epic according to the demands of the higher moral and spiritual heroism and in executing it without sacrificing either epic dimension or the decorum appropriate to this very special subject. The perfection is not merely formal, for the poem in large measure succeeds in its attempt to incorporate, evaluate, and order the whole complex of Classical-Judaeo-Christian values which constitute the intellectual heritage of Western man. The particular ordering vision, like all human things, is partial. But the poem's dramatic situation—

Christ's search in the wilderness to comprehend his nature and discover his mission, his subsumption of the past but rejection of its dead literalisms, his abjuration of the many evil or ignoble or imperfect or less perfect modes of action which would preclude attainment of the highest concept of personal excellence and mission—presents a myth of human process, of human striving toward ideals of comprehension and order, of wisdom and noble action which must remain relevant and powerful as long as such ideals hold any meaning for us.

Barbara Kiefer Lewalski
Milton's Brief Epic: The Genre, Meaning, and Art of "Paradise Regained" (Providence, R.I.: Brown Univ. Pr., 1966), pp. 102–3, 355–56

In the usual reading *Paradise Regained* concerns what we now call an identity-crisis; in the reading I wish to propose it centrally concerns the choice of a life-style. The two, I hazard, are not the same, and Milton would not have confused them. The one is exclusive, asking as the all-important question "Who am I?" The other is inclusive, asking "How is man to live?"

Since the meaning of *Paradise Regained* depends on how we read its action, and its action depends on how we read its crisis, our understanding of what Milton has to say about the regaining of Paradise necessarily turns on how we conceive of a brief passage near the end of Book IV. Unlike *Paradise Lost, Paradise Regained* has been allowed—even by twentieth-century commentators—to have an unmistakable crisis. No one, to my knowledge, has ever suggested shifting it from the two crucial lines where Satan, having set Jesus on the pinnacle of the temple, taunts him to hurl himself down, relying on the angels to rescue him, and Jesus answers (IV, 560–61). . . .

Tempt not the Lord thy God, he said, and stood.
But Satan, smitten with amazement, fell.

Commentators have further been able to agree that the protagonist's standing is the victory foretold by the angelic choirs in Book I and now celebrated by them in their prophetic rejoicing over the ultimate defeat of the enemy. But that apparently is as far as commentators will go in agreement. . . .

Few critics have regarded Milton as an advocate of "negative capability" or even of a "wise passiveness"; yet on such matters of ultimate mystery this was his constant doctrine: Let us be wisely ignorant. What then would he have said to readings of *Paradise Regained* that make its meaning turn on sudden secret mysterious revelations from on high to the protagonist, not one of which is narrated in the gospels—his main source—and not one of which is so much as indicated by a single word in his poem? . . .

To misquote the clear meaning of Luke—and thereby make Jesus misquote the clear meaning of Deuteronomy—would have been anathema to Milton. And would he have reversed his principle for the sake of his poem? But to make the sentence mean what? That Jesus is announcing his divinity to *Satan*, telling Satan not to tempt him—as though only then aware of what his interlocutor had been up to for three days—and in thus announcing and telling, declaring himself Satan's God. Who would want to be Satan's God? Not the supremely rational hero of *Paradise Regained*. . . .

To take *Paradise Regained* as centrally concerned with establishing the identity of its hero—whether for the adversary or for the hero himself—is thus to lose Milton's purpose in writing. No discovery that the protagonist is the God-man who may henceforth go about his business in full confidence of who he is could give the impulse that named this poem the regaining of Paradise and filled it with arguments and counter-arguments on possible ways of life. To read it as a "Who am I?" poem is to limit it to a mimesis of the particular, a matter for the historian-chronicler-biographer-theologian; to read it as a "How am I to live?" poem is to see its availability as the mimesis of a universal action, a program for every man. The mystery of the God-man is framework, accepted by the poet from the gospel story, believed, and thought of as not to be added to, complicated, or amended; the centre of the poem is the dialogue Milton invented for his two main agents.

Irene Samuel
in *The Prison and the Pinnacle*, ed. Balachandra Rajan (Toronto: Univ. Toronto Pr., 1973), pp. 111–12, 118–20

Samson Agonistes

Catharsis . . . emerges as a principle of structure in the drama. Each of the three central episodes in *Samson* treats one of the tragic passions. Manoa seeks to comfort Samson but in fact increases his grief. Dalila, appealing to sexual passion masked as compassion, asks his pity. Finally Harapha and the Philistine Officer try to excite his fear. But in Samson all these passions are reduced to just measure. . . . The resolution of the temptation by fear is especially instructive. Samson defies the threats of the Philistine Officer because what he now dreads most is the loss of "Favour renew'd" by "venturing to displease/God for the fear of Man" (1357, 1373–74). Purgation does not eliminate passion but reduces it to "just measure": the brave man, says Aristotle, fears what ought to be feared. So Samson fears God. And by this fear, which is the beginning of wisdom, he is delivered from the fear of men or anything that they can do to him. But the homeopathic formula of like against like does not always work this neatly. A more general idea of passion is at work in this strange therapy.

For the Renaissance, as we all know, the moral life turns on the control of passion by reason. And it is significant that all Samson's temptations—even the sensual lure proffered by Dalila—take the form of debates. This is equally true of *Comus*, *Paradise Lost*, and *Paradise Regained*: a temptation that does not threaten to seduce reason did not seem to Milton fit subject for a tragedy, an epic, or even a masque. Samson's victory over temptation is shown in the fact that he wins all his arguments. What he replies to his tempters is, if not truth, certainly closer to truth than what they say to him. Yet compared to the unmoved hero of *Paradise Regained*—and surely this comparison is intended—Samson does not strike us as a very reasonable man. . . .

The imagery of purgation relates Samson to Adam; the imagery of lustration relates him to Christ. To understand his catharsis is thus to understand the triadic pattern of *Paradise Lost, Paradise Regained*, and *Samson Agonistes*. This pattern was first observed by F. M. Krouse in his brilliant book on *Samson* and the Christian tradition. I believe that the parallelism can be extended to the triple temptation in all three poems; however that may be, the essential outline is clear. In *Paradise Lost* we see man fallen; in *Paradise Regained*, we see man restored; in *Samson* we watch the agony of man between. The action of the drama repeats the pattern we have traced through history in the last two books of *Paradise Lost*, as Samson moves from the likeness of Adam to the likeness of Christ. Milton's tragedy is a mimesis of the redemptive process at work in the life of the individual and the race, an action not of men but of man. . . .

He is one of the great heroes of faith, those patriarchs and martyrs who, having finished the course, are become examples to all who follow them and who, compassed about with so great a cloud of witnesses, must run with patience the same race. Samson prefigures us: the poet, the reader, all who in darkness and bondage share the *agon* that leads from paradise lost to paradise regained.

Sherman H. Hawkins
in *Milton Studies*, Vol. II, ed. James D. Simmonds (Pittsburgh: Univ. Pittsburgh Pr., 1970), pp. 223–24, 227

The preface [to *Samson Agonistes*] does indeed throw some light on [Milton's] concept of tragedy, but it is light of one wavelength; it does not include the entire spectrum. This work obviously omits certain highly important aspects of poetic imitation and purgation that receive expression in his other writings. . . . The preface to *Samson Agonistes* is, as he himself declares, an apologia or defense. Even in his verse and prose epistles his remarks on his literary tastes or his literary plans appear to be partly conditioned by his awareness of the personality and interests of the men he is addressing.

His statement on "passions well imitated" obviously does not exhaust his opinions on the objects of tragic imitation. His remarks are selective, and the selection has been made primarily for rhetorical purposes. In defending tragedy on the ground of its utility (as the "moralest" and "most profitable" of all poetic genres), he had the best possible reasons for stressing the passions (rather than action or character or thought) as the object of poetic imitation. Expressed in this form, his argument anticipated, and refuted in advance, one of the most common ethical objections raised against tragedy—that it imitates the passions and corrupts character. . . .

It was common rhetorical practice . . . to anticipate an opponent's arguments and thus forestall him by refuting them in advance. Several of Milton's arguments in defense of tragedy could serve, accordingly, as replies to the objections a hostile reader might raise under the shadow of Plato's authority. In particular, his remark on "passions well imitated" could forestall an appeal to Plato's strictures against dramatic imitation of the passions. His medical image, moreover, enabled him to answer Plato with Plato, pitting the poet-physician simile of the *Laws* against the statements in *The Republic*. His allusion to the poet's ability to "temper" and moderate the passions might likewise rebut Plato with one of his own arguments. For in *The Republic* the philosopher had asserted that "a good man, who has the misfortune to lose his son" will indeed feel sorrow; but "though he can not help sorrowing, he will moderate his sorrow." Similarly, Milton's long catalogue of rulers who had composed tragedies might constitute a reply to Plato's contention that tragedy would corrupt the future guardians of the state.

John M. Steadman
in *Calm of Mind*, ed. Joseph A. Wittreich (Cleveland: Case Western Reserve Univ. Pr., 1971), pp. 200–201

Samson Agonistes follows a common tragic pattern: the hero, looked on as something monstrous or unacceptable, is killed or exiled, or as in Samson's case is forced by his character, by religious or moral necessity, or by circumstances, into a position where death is inevitable. This pattern is also Christian. It is related to Milton's often-repeated ideal of Christian heroism, of plain heroic magnitude of mind, of the single just man rejected by his fellows, or of the suffering of the saints. With unadorned heroism, Samson defeats worldly greatness: physically, with no other weapons than his bare hands, spiritually, with nothing but the divinely-inspired strength of his will. He sets his plainness and determination against human strength and glory. The Chorus, when it describes the kind of man God chooses to deliver his people, describes Samson. . . .

Although Samson is pitiable and fearful, a man who is degraded, dirty, and outcast, nevertheless he remains great, noble, and heroic. He is both abject and splendid at the same time. The negative elements, far from detracting from his greatness or merely contrasting with it, actually add to it. We think no less of Oedipus, Job, or Lear because they are set apart from common values and the ordinary preoccupations of life. . . .

Manoa, when he speaks the eulogy for Samson, can think of no greater or more appropriate praise than this:

> *Samson* hath quit himself
> Like *Samson*. . . . (1709–10)

As a man, he is something greater than a king, a knight, a leader, or a judge. *He has become himself.* The idea that Milton's Samson is foolish, ignoble, stronger in muscle than in mind or spirit, has long been discredited, though presumably a few critics will never be lacking to raise the point once more. As Arnold Stein among others has shown, Samson's intellectual capabilities are discriminating and powerful. Yet Milton has retained or even added to many of the barbaric attributes of the biblical Samson. They make his hero not less but more heroic. By a more vital principle of decorum than Samuel Johnson was willing to allow, things normally not thought heroic deepen and humanize, even elevate, Samson's character. If he had been drawn as a straightforwardly civilized and refined hero, a Renaissance gentleman, as a few critics assume, he would have verged on the priggish, or become an empty abstraction like Addison's Cato. Milton plainly has successfully avoided this danger. His Samson has gained in intellect, but he has not lost his physical presence. He has not only human weaknesses, but human strengths. He combines intellectual vitality and nobility of spirit with the starkness of a biblical prophet. But his heroism cannot be reduced to any one class or tradition. His analogues, with like qualities of essential greatness, are the heroes of three traditions: Job, Oedipus, and Lear.

Anthony Low
The Blaze of Noon: A Reading of "Samson Agonistes"
(New York: Columbia Univ. Pr., 1974), pp. 59–61

PROSE

The very nature of [tract-writing] demands a popular, ephemeral, immediate, localized style. Tract-writing in fact demands the nationalistic ad-hominem zeal that Milton was very well able to employ. It does not demand this larger, more unwieldy resonance of big words and intricate periods, full of forecasts out of time. It is no wonder that Milton was not the most effective of pamphleteers. But his many-levelled Miltonic music is immensely interesting as the creation of a mind both Puritanical and literary, and especially as the autobiography of this great poet. . . .

There are of course many reasons why this highly literary prose, created by and creating an "I" whose whole life is based on literature, could never be mistaken for the literary Anglican style. This "I" has devoted himself to a worldly goal, and his tracts are his weaponry. His autobiography, literary though it is, is delivered straightforwardly, though defensively, and involves considerable temporal and factual detail. Most importantly, it is the same kind of spiritual autobiography that other Puritans wrote, except that it is translated into literary terms. He documents the ways in which it was recognized that he had a gift for poetry, just as others documented the incidents that brought them to be receptive of God's grace. His discussions of himself are always a combination of lamentation with rejoicing. In the early prose, he knows he has the gift, but complains of his unripeness; in the poetry, he worries that he has come to write too late. The same kind of nervous assertiveness is observable in other Puritans: This is who I am—but will I make it? In Milton, as in others, the certainty overrides the doubts.

And it does that, finally, because of his acceptance of himself as God's instrument. However we read him, as polemicist, autobiographer, prophet, or literary critic, that is clear. He may lament, like Jeremy (whose words he cites), that God has made him a prophet in an ill time, but he accepts his role. The tracts sometimes seem disconnected because he sees himself called in so many different ways, and they succeed to the extent to which he himself succeeded in making his several vocations into one, in seeing that present rage must prepare for future song, or in seeing how nevertheless to manage raging and song and criticism all at once.

Joan Webber
The Eloquent "I": Style and Self in Seventeenth-Century Prose
(Madison: Univ. Wisconsin Pr., 1968), pp. 216–17

General

In *The Lives of the Poets*, where he is describing *Paradise Lost*, Dr. Johnson writes that . . . Milton . . . would characteristically choose "a subject on which too much could not be said, on which he might tire his fancy without the censure of extravagance." Such choices, and the aesthetic they imply, may be ascribed to a preference for "transcendental forms." Such forms seem to arise in literary history when authors have apparently exhausted all the natural resources of their art and seem also to arise, with less reason, when a cultural group believes it has entered a period of definitive decadence or even final apocalypse.

Initially we may define a transcendental form as any poetic structure that by design includes more than its traditionally accepted generic limits—the classical limits of its genre—would allow it to include. As containing form this structure will apparently be held together by an immanent order. As symbolic matrix, however, this closed and immanent order will display a countering activity of all its details, exploding out from the containing frame, transcending limits formally accepted. . . .

While the critical theory of Kenneth Burke has often been devoted to the problem of the transcendental symbol, his definition of the transcendentalism of Emerson will serve to remind the reader that all such symbolism is a kind of "pontification," "the building of a *terministic bridge* whereby one realm is *transcended* by being viewed *in terms of* a realm 'beyond' it." Burke argues for Emerson's *Nature* and more widely for other similar works that insofar as things of this world, "things here and now," are treated in the terms of a realm *beyond*, "they thereby become infused or inspirited by the addition of a *new or further* dimension." . . . From such statements the historian of philosophy can trace a long line of thought back to the Platonic theory of ideas, the source for all such theories of mediation. To the extent that poetic fictions attempt such crossing from one realm to another or attempt a vision of the material in terms of the ideal, they too have a root in the Platonic tradition, and during the Renaissance this inheritance is strong. Neoplatonic thought is radically transcendental, and the major literary forms in a period of influential Neoplatonism will show transcendence. Yet it is one thing to speak of "transcendence" within a work, and another of the "transcendental form" of a work. The former is textual—the parts are set forth to yield an image of one world "in terms of" another world beyond it. Yet the modular nature of all symbolic textures provides that certain overall forms will follow from those textures. Thus, to give a homely analogy, it is possible to make much better curvilinear architectural forms with poured concrete than with wood or cinder blocks. The modular unit influences the containing shape. Infinitely delicate details articulate the whole universe. There lies our main problem with the masque [*Comus*], for even though the texture can be shown to be predominantly magical, as we have seen, there remains the question of containing form.

Angus Fletcher
The Transcendental Masque: An Essay on Milton's "Comus"
(Ithaca, N.Y.: Cornell Univ. Pr., 1971), pp. 116–18

Milton's entire literary career was devoted to his design of eclipsing the classical orators and poets and then forging a new literary tradition just as Christ had eclipsed his types and superseded their teachings with his own. Throughout Milton's prose works he invokes the classical orators and theorists but only to distinguish himself from them. Milton, in other words, obtains to the ideal that Cicero and Quintilian articulated by mastering style and form, but he also supersedes Cicero and Quintilian by deriving a new standard of eloquence from the models of Christ and St. Paul. When Milton invokes the tradition of Isocrates, Demosthenes, and Cicero it is to make differentiations; when he invokes Christ and St. Paul it is to establish "the knit of identity." Milton and Milton's Christ may cast a dubious eye on specious rhetoric but not without also embracing the "loudest Oratorie" of which Milton was the Renaissance's greatest master.

In his prose works Milton was intent upon establishing a sharp opposition between the true and false orator. This is what he does in the Defenses, opposing himself to Salmasius, More, and company; it is also what he does in *Paradise Lost* by contrasting Satan and the epic narrator. . . .

Milton asks his audience (a total culture) to reorient the reigning values and when necessary, to discard them, so as to bring them in line with his own moral vision. Herein lies the difference between the figure of the epic poet in *Paradise Lost* and in *Paradise Regained* and the figure of him in previous epics, and from this difference emerges Milton's complicated relationship with his audience.

Milton not only draws his moral character from the orator; he derives from him his epic stance as well. Epic, more than any other literary mode, is bound to cultural history and class divisions. The oral epic belonged to the "people" and was sung to them. The Renaissance literary epic, however, recognized class divisions and was addressed to an aristocracy defined along economic lines. The poet, therefore, addresses an aristocracy; and though he assumes, like Ariosto, an artistic superiority, he proceeds to draw his values from those whom he addresses and from the culture he celebrates. In Milton, there remains a strong sense of elitism—and a continuing interest in audience. This is true from the First Prolusion, where Milton chastises his audience for its ignorance, to *Paradise Regained*, where through Christ he says that his audience should bring to books "A spirit and judgment equal or superior" to those qualities possessed by their authors (IV.324). In *Paradise Lost* Milton hopes "fit audience [to] find, though few" (VII.31). What distinguishes Milton from his epic predecessors is the fact that his "fit" audience is finally a moral rather than a social category of readers. Moreover, though Milton knows that the full comprehension of his art is restricted to this "elite" he also knows that the moral vision he articulates must be made accessible to all.

Joseph A. Wittreich, Jr.
in *Achievements of the Left Hand: Essays on the Prose of John Milton*, ed. Michael Lieb and John T. Shawcross (Amherst: Univ. Massachusetts Pr., 1974), pp. 45–47

SAMUEL PEPYS

1633–1703

Robert Latham and William Matthews, eds. *The Diary of Samuel Pepys* (1970–76), 9 vols.

The *Diary* brings us into intimate contact with one of the most remarkable men who ever lived and, yet, a truly average man with typical faults as well as virtues. To use a good, if overworked, phrase, Mr. Pepys was the "divine average"; for, in many ways, he was the best of men. When death lurked and danger threatened, he did not run and hide; he stood his ground —in plague and fire and war, and he watched in open-mouthed wonder. He did, though, what average man has done since time began: he took part in things. There were crises in Pepys's day as in ours. Average men today, and always, will face fire and flood, pestilence and deprivation with quiet determination as did Pepys.

The paradox of the *Diary* is that average days to average men are not ordinary at all, for they assume a vast importance to each man. There is no evidence anywhere in the *Diary* that Pepys thought of himself as special or as remarkable in any way. Vain and self-conscious he was, indeed, and lovably and delightfully so; but the sin of pride—of vainglory—was not a sin of Samuel Pepys. The average man who reads the *Diary* may be pleased to recognize himself in Mr. Pepys. When Mr. Pepys viewed the Coronation, he stationed a comely woman next to Mrs. Pepys so that from a distance he could watch her decently; when pestilence came, he rubbed himself with plug tobacco as any man might do to ward off evil by reaching into the dark, backward abyss of time to invoke a charm or to practice a forgotten rite; but Pepys stayed among the comfortless and dying; when fire broke out, Pepys ran to see it but stayed to put it out. These great events happened on average days, for any day is an average day; but Mr. Pepys threaded the events together by taking part in them. The secret of the power of Mr. Pepys and his *Diary* is that Mr. Pepys shows an average man that, while doing average things, if he take his part in the daily round, his days, too, are filled with meaning and living wonder.

The literary quality of the *Diary* depends, to a large extent, on its simplicity of style and on the personal grace revealed in Mr. Pepys's way with words. He wrote down what he witnessed and shared of the life about him while the incidents were fresh in his mind. . . . It is, in fact, a spontaneous record of things as they happened from day to day. Mr. Pepys's friend and contemporary, John Evelyn, wrote a wonderful diary, too, and always it invites comparison with Pepys's; neither suffers from the comparison.

Evelyn's diary represents the edited and thrice-pondered account; Pepys's represents things as they happened, on the spot.

Ivan E. Taylor
Samuel Pepys (New York: Twayne, 1967), pp. 150–51

After all is said, the origins of so deeply personal a document [as a diary] must themselves be personal. One origin is certainly the vanity which is so clearly marked a feature of Pepys's character. Another, equally certainly, is his love of life. The diary is a by-product of his energetic pursuit of happiness. The process of recording had the effect, as he soon found out, of heightening and extending his enjoyment. It enabled him to relish every experience more than once—not only at the moment of its happening but also in its recollection. But possibly the most important part of the explanation may have been his concern for neatness, which showed itself throughout his life in many forms—in his carefully arranged library of books marshalled by size, or in his taste for formal gardens and English Renaissance architecture. His handwriting was small, shapely, controlled. The very inditing of the quick slim symbols of shorthand probably gave him a palpable satisfaction. Similarly, it is likely that the diary itself, fully and regularly kept, tidy and neat, had the effect of making life itself seem neat and tidy—the quotidian chaos reduced to order, each day's events packaged and tied up in a rounded summary.

He was by nature a man of system, and one to whom the keeping of records was necessary to the art of living. The diary was one of a series of records, which by the 1660s included petty-cash books, account books, letter-books, memorandum books and also more idiosyncratic records such as his "book of tales" and his list of private vows. All were means to a disciplined life, methods of canalising the stream of experience—the diary best of all, because it was the most comprehensive and the most intimate.

Robert Latham and William Matthews
Introd., in *The Diary of Samuel Pepys: A New and Complete Transcription*, Vol. I (London: G. Bell, 1970), p. xxviii

ALEXANDER POPE

1688–1744

Pope's different couplet styles in the eight poems of this study depend upon the complex and subtle handling of just two basic features of the couplet—balance and closure. If this seems like an oversimplification, let us remember that balance implies nonbalance, and closure implies the opposite, the open or suspended couplet that is incomplete in meaning. Closure is more frequently a characteristic of the couplet than of the line, since the couplet is more often complete in meaning than the line. Balance is a characteristic either of the line or the couplet; and while Pope frequently balances or parallels one line of the couplet against the other, he more frequently balances one-half of the line against the other half. The handling of balance and parallelism is a correlative of the handling of sentence structure; and it seems a fruitless task to try to determine which comes first, the line and the couplet or the sentence, or which determines the form of the other. They are a *Gestalt* and occur together, just as in the greatest works of art form and content are felt to be the same. But one can make, at least, a slight generalization about Pope's handling of the relation between the couplet and the sentence: in his early poems he shows a tendency to compose in terms of line structure, in the later poems in terms of the sentence. This does not make a late poem a better poem, necessarily, than an early one; it makes it a poem with a different kind of couplet style. . . .

The balanced line is the basic feature of the couplet upon which Pope based his stylistic developments. Generally he used less balance in the later poems and depended less on zeugma and chiasmus. With less antithetic balance, he used fewer inversions; and if one grants Pope the same liberty of inversion as is usually given other poets, his inversions were not frequent in poems later than the *Essay on Man*. As a result, the continuity from couplet to couplet grew simpler, less patterned, and more proselike.

John A. Jones
Pope's Couplet Art (Athens: Ohio Univ. Pr., 1969), pp. 199–200

Pope's poetry, like the book he was accustomed to call Scripture, begins with a garden and ends with a city. To be sure, the city in Revelation is a holy city, whereas the city in the *Dunciad* of 1743 is a version of Augustan London. Yet both are in an important sense visionary, and beyond the *Dunciad*'s city looms another that is more abiding: the eternal City of man's recurring dream of the civilized community, only one of those names is Rome.

As for the garden, so far as we have evidence today, Pope's quasi-Horatian *Ode on Solitude*, celebrating the quiet life of the gentleman-gardener-farmer, was "the first fruit . . . of his poetical genius" [Owen Ruffhead]. Nor is anyone today ignorant of the poet's early and lasting association with settings horticultural and rural. First Binfield, then Chiswick, then the villa at Twickenham, and throughout his life, at home and on summer rambles, the landscaping and planting carried on by himself and his aristocratic friends. It is curious that this side of his personality and work should have gone almost unnoticed by nineteenth-century critics, who, following [Joseph] Warton, usually consigned him to the outer darkness of artificial and urban poets. Considering that he was a lifelong gardener of some renown; considering that he chatters repeatedly in his letters about broccoli and pineapples, about prospects and wilderness; considering that he left behind him a substantial body of verse having to do with the natural scene, and was among the leaders of a landscaping movement which so modified the character of rural England, the oversight of Romantic critics seems at first glance extraordinary. . . .

[Pope] *is* a city poet, not simply in the obvious ways [the Romantic critics] saw, but in deeper ways they failed to see. His poetry has apocalyptic mutterings in it from his earliest years; it shapes itself again and again in patterns that exhibit loss converting into triumph or, for satiric ends . . . triumph that in fact is loss. And always in Pope the thing that is being lost, or lost and recovered, or lost and recovered and lost again, is a vision of the civilized community, the City. . . .

To be a great satirist, a man must have, literally and figuratively, a place to stand, an angle of vision. For Pope . . . the garden and the grotto supplied this. They supplied a rallying point for his personal values and a focus for his conception of himself—as master of a poet's "kingdom," a counter-order to a court and ministry that set no store by poets, a community bound by ties quite other than those uniting the "pensioners" of St. Stephen, as he sardonically calls the members of Walpole's parliament. In a sense, they supplied him too with the materials of a *Selbstentwurf*, nourishing his feelings and imagination in the way that at a later time the tower and the swan would do for Yeats. Through them his retreat at Twickenham became, not only in his own eyes but in those of a number of his contemporaries, a true country of the mind.

Maynard Mack
The Garden and the City: Retirement and Politics in the Later Poetry of Pope, 1731–1743 (Toronto: Univ. Toronto Pr., 1969), pp. 3–5

The poem itself [*An Essay on Man*] suggests that the reader should know more than one side of most of its arguments. *An Essay on Man* is not a gratuitous piece of system-making but a refutation of specific points of view, specific ideas. Pope included to some extent both the ideas that he rejected and those he submitted in their place. His own comment on his purpose suggests, even further, that he was purposely placing himself within a range of ideas, since he asserts that he was "steering betwixt extremes of doctrine seemingly opposite." If he was consciously steering between extremes, he was referring to a range of ideas rather than to a single refutable position. The range would presumably have limits of relevance; that is, every author's ideas on a subject would not be relevant. Some assertions might be too wild in direction or too radical in implication; but even those authors who worked within the bounds of a similar frame of reference and an acknowledged awareness of supposed orthodoxy (even without agreement on its contents) used many important ideas with a variety of intention that sets up an observable spectrum of implications and interpretations.

If the ideas Pope steered between are *seemingly* opposite, then he evidently felt that they were not necessarily opposite but that some mistake in either the statement of the doctrines or some false conclusion stemming from them made them appear to conflict. When the implications of an idea are the source of heterodoxy or orthodoxy, then the spectrum of thought formed by a variety of implications becomes important. . . .

One of Pope's concerns in the writing of the *Essay* was to state his case but to extricate himself from certain difficulties perceived by his contemporaries to be attached to the position he favored. He did not choose merely to assert but also to deal with contemporary reaction to the supposed direction of his assertions. One part of my intention in the present study is to discover how well Pope understood the direction of his own argument as it would have been understood by his well-informed contemporaries. I do not, however, intend to decide whether he escaped satisfactorily according to the armed vision of the twentieth century, or even according to the individual conclusions of his contemporaries. Nor would one be justified in asking whether he arrived at the one acceptable adjustment of ideas, for it is perfectly apparent that there neither was nor is any such thing. Some progress can be made, however, toward ascertaining the status and direction of the solutions he employed, which in turn will show us some of the ways in which his mind worked—and, it must be repeated, show this against a contemporary spectrum of opinion rather than against a single set of beliefs, whether of Pope's day or our own.

Douglas H. White
Pope and the Context of Controversy: The Manipulation of Ideas in "An Essay on Man" (Chicago: Univ. Chicago Pr., 1970), pp. 3–4, 8

The divine creative power of the word is, as Aubrey Williams has brilliantly demonstrated, a central concern of *The Dunciad*. Between the *Essay on Man* and the final version of *The Dunciad*, Pope wrote most of his greatest satiric verse. His apparent assumptions shifted: the implicit metaphysics of *The Dunciad* is closer to Donne than to the *Essay on Man*. Having experimented with wit and with perception as focuses of aesthetic control, the satirist committed himself at last to the crucial importance of judgment, the manifestation of that reasoning ability which makes man not merely *animal rationis capax*, but *animal rationale*, and which, at its best, makes him little lower than the angels. Again in this final long poem his aesthetic principles reflect the moral concerns that are his explicit subject. His verse demonstrates the devastating energy of the judgmental faculty, which the poet, almost alone, retains in a world dominated by forces of antireason. It shows that judgment can be a powerful poetic resource, organizing the brilliances of wit and commenting on the meanings of perception. . . .

The Dunciad depicts a state of affairs in which the observation of nature has become itself a form of perversion, leading men away from instead of toward God. Observation of society is unrelieved horror. Moreover, the possibility of false perception is more vivid than in the earlier poem, where the asserted blindness of men is readily counteracted by the poet's clear vision. The poet's vision provides the clarities of *The Dunciad*, too, but as in T. S. Eliot's *The Waste Land*, a poem significantly resembling Pope's, clarity reveals confusion. By the end of the poem, the poet can see nothing: there is no longer anything to see. The muse obeys the power of Dulness, the great anarch who lets the curtain fall, and universal darkness eliminates the possibility of perception. . . .

The Dunciad, with its elaborate structure of physical images for moral conditions, translates [George] Berkeley's insights into another realm. . . . Despite the existence of received ideas about morality, every man must finally see for himself where good and evil lies. Men are likely to see wrong, but even more likely to judge wrong. Like the moon-watcher, Pope's dunces misinterpret their own perceptions. And their mistakes are more sinister than his because in the moral world, Pope suggests—going one step farther than Berkeley—perception alters reality. Those who see men as things help convert them to things; men who understand words as restrictive forces make them so; concentrators on insects become what they see. The relation between imagery and "reality" in *The Dunciad* is complicated by the fact that the prevalence of dunces alters the nature of reality. The extravagant imagery that condemns the disciples of dullness reflects not only the satirist's disgust but the victims' true nature and their self-perceptions. The proportions of each component are difficult to determine.

Patricia Meyer Spacks
An Argument of Images: The Poetry of Alexander Pope
(Cambridge, Mass.: Harvard Univ. Pr., 1971), pp. 84–86

SAMUEL RICHARDSON

1689–1761

T. C. Duncan Eaves and Ben D. Kimpel, *Samuel Richardson: A Biography* (1971)

A considerable part of Richardson's achievement in character portrayal . . . is dependent upon his scenic achievement. Attitudes, movements, spatial relationships, qualities of voice are so specified that the reader envisions the entire scene exactly as it would have occurred in real life. It was Richardson who developed the dramatic, realistic, vivid, dimensional, and temporal scene and based much of his novels upon it. Hence, it was possible for him in *Pamela* and *Clarissa* to present the relatively limited but unified plots of the drama in novel form, for this narrative technique allowed him to concentrate on fewer episodes and emphasize character rather than action. Even though *Pamela II* and *Sir Charles Grandison* have little plot, they are far more unified and harmonious than most earlier novels because of the new emphasis upon the dramatic scene. But as well as dramatizing the individual scene, the novelist dramatizes the point of view through which the scene is observed. He develops the characterization of each narrator at great length, depicts in detail his or her present state of mind and previous emotional involvement in the recreated scenes, and thus brings to life all levels of action in the world of the novel. . . .

A performed drama is immediately real to our senses; it creates life before our eyes. We see the people and events, hear the voices and clamor of life. These same dramatic qualities are suggested by the playbook: dialogue and stage action are transcribed in words which suggest a pattern of images that create in our minds the entire scene. It was this dimension that fiction required in order to create the illusion of a more normal world and treat life more seriously. Until 1740 the novel was a vehicle for improbable tales, semirealistic love affairs, and unusual personal histories. With its rudimentary narrative techniques the genre could relate no more. Its basic method of summarizing episodes and quickly narrating a multitude of adventures made its success dependent largely upon the excitement of events. Its techniques could not create real people; thus, it could hardly portray realistic situations and concern itself with important moral and social matters. What was required was a dramatic dimension that could create the inner lives and outward existences of human beings.

Richardson achieved this dimension by writing his novels to some extent as he would have written plays. . . . To understand Richardson's dramatic methods as a novelist, the three general techniques with which his characters write their letters must first be established. Frequently more than one of these techniques appear in the same letter, but each is used for different purposes.

In the Preface to *Clarissa* Richardson discusses the letters of that novel: "All the Letters are written while the hearts of the writers must be supposed to be wholly engaged in their subjects." . . .

Richardson's second technique of epistolary writing dramatizes the correspondent rather than action. . . . Richardson's third technique is in direct contrast to his self-revealing manner of writing, though it too furthers the reality and fullness of his characters. . . . Richardson's novels present many fully described scenes that are obviously a result of his knowledge of the theater.

Ira Konigsberg
Samuel Richardson & the Dramatic Novel (Lexington: Univ. Pr. Kentucky, 1968), pp. 102–4, 107, 110

The difference between the morality of *Clarissa* and the morality of *Sir Charles Grandison* is the same as the difference between the "realism" of the two novels. The realism of *Sir Charles* depends on accurately observed manners; its morality is based on maxims about what human conduct should be, approved by Richardson's class and by his own conscious mind. These maxims are grouped together and given the name of Grandison, and various actions are devised to illustrate them and are then reported with due attention to plausibility. The actions are "true to life," but one can never be allowed to imagine the feelings of the man who performs them. The maxims do not depend on feelings but on rules, and these rules demand that the embodiment of the maxims even *feel* correctly—that is not feel in any way which another human mind can recognize. The realism must remain on the surface or the morality will become ambiguous. In *Clarissa* the morality *is* the feelings, and the surface realism is subordinated to the imagined characters. If the reader tries to identify with Sir Charles, realism and morality both evaporate; if he does not identify with Clarissa, the impression of reality is impoverished and the moral effect is reduced to a series of platitudes.

It is, of course, possible to read Richardson's novels as allegories or myths. Like all the major realistic novels, they embody an outlook on life, a set of values, which can be stated in abstract, general terms. We might even suggest a "mythos" for *Clarissa*, the perennial conflict of the demands of the ego—its desire to assert itself at the expense of others against its desire to remain independent of others. The Lovelace part of our minds can fulfil itself only by dominating our fellows and lowering them in order to put us on at least a relative height; the Clarissa part can learn to be independent of the invidious comparison and to assert its independence even when violated and humiliated. Such a conflict lends itself very well to the "determining emotional pattern" which, according to Maud Bodkin, "corresponds to the form of tragedy." If the tragic archetype is "an ambivalent attitude toward the self" arising from the contrast between "a personal self" and "a self that is free to range imaginatively through all human achievement," then this archetype is built into *Clarissa* both in the conflict between the two main characters and in the development of the heroine. Lovelace throughout, and Clarissa to a lesser degree at first, can be taken as embodying "the self of imaginative aspiration," "the power-craving"; Clarissa's final mood is an ideal example of the other pole of tragedy which "satisfies the counter movement of feeling toward the surrender of personal claims and the merging of the ego within a greater power." The story itself thus gives us that "organization of the tendencies of self-assertion and toleration" which according to Miss Bodkin creates the tension which gives rise to "the distinctive tragic attitude."

T. C. Duncan Eaves and Ben D. Kimpel
Samuel Richardson: A Biography (Oxford: Clarendon, 1971), pp. 616–17

In a general sense [Sir Charles Grandison] is the embodiment of complete personal virtue, the image of a nearly perfect human being; in addition he also serves the more limited function of demonstrating the behavior of a man who engages in all of his specifically masculine social roles without fault. To a certain extent, the characterization of Grandison is an answer to some of the unresolved problems of the earlier works; and if Richardson consciously addressed the portrait of his hero to Fielding as a rebuke for the rowdiness and vulgarity of Tom Jones, Sir Charles' perfectly prudent conduct provides an equally appropriate response to the weakness of farmer Andrews, the failures of Clarissa's father, the milksop Mr. B., and the corrosive evil of Lovelace. Not one of these had been a complete and satisfactory man; the virtuous among them had been weak or absent, while the villains had been all too personably effective in their wickedness. Now at last in Grandison man would assume his rightful role within both the family and society at large. His rule would be just because it would be directed to the benefit of all who relied on him; and his authority over the dependent members of society, the women and children, would be warranted by his power to protect them and to effect good for them. . . .

Only when we understand the vital importance of Sir Charles' taking an active part in reestablishing order can we understand why Richardson causes him to behave in a manner which may seem arbitrary and officious. Grandison bustles into his uncle's home to relieve him of a plaguey mistress and present him with a dutiful wife. Such actions scarcely befit the relationship: nephews do not arrange marriages for their uncles, and men in their twenties seldom presume to dictate to men twice their age. Those are the offices which might more suitably be performed by a father for his son, and they seem appropriate to Sir Charles only when we recognize his role as an agent for establishing social coherence. It is in this role—perhaps the central role he is called upon to play—that Grandison most fully exhibits the busy-ness, the incessant (and often unrequested) activity that becomes faintly offensive to a modern reader.

Richardson is drawing on the notion of the Saint here; and several traits essential to that Puritan ideal contribute to this picture of the moral man as one who is active in the world around him. . . .

Sir Charles' meddlesome nature has several sources or justifications: he must reestablish the order of family government by offering firm, moral, masculine leadership; and he lives in a society which views socially useful works as a sign of virtue and in which activity itself is deemed commendable.

Cynthia Griffin Wolff
Samuel Richardson and the Eighteenth-Century Puritan Character
(Hamden, Conn.: Archon, 1972), pp. 190–93

The idea of writing fiction in letters was not new, nor did Richardson ever claim to have invented it. What he did invent was the idea of using letters, along with other techniques, to achieve the equivalent in the novel of the experience of drama. His "new Manner of Writing—to the Moment" was essentially the creation of a fiction which could seem to be happening "now" rather than recollected in tranquillity; and to be shaping itself from moment to moment, rather than to a pattern perceived and articulated with hindsight and by an author. As in drama one must seem to experience directly for oneself rather than through an authorial filter. . . .

Richardson's "letters" are in many ways unlike letters that people actually write, and unlike other epistolary fictions also, to the extent that they are to the moment dramatic narratives, attempts to catch living voices in a dramatic present. . . . His letter-writers write letters, not dramatic narratives and dialogues, they write at moderate length and with a formality of style that acceptably imitates contemporary correspondence, and the experienced "tense" of the action is always past, although only recently. . . .

Richardson is an "epistolary novelist" certainly; but to lay the emphasis there is to mistake a technical means, however central, for the formal end itself: the novel as drama. Richardson not only wishes to produce an experience that is "like" drama; he creates by the imaginative process that is characteristic of the true dramatist, whether it be in verse monologues, stage plays, epistolary novels, or any other convention.

The forming vision, the "shaping spirit of imagination," is the process of dramatic projection, where the author formally banishes himself, and creates by becoming each of his characters. He tries to see through their eyes, and use their distinctive voices. He cannot be identified with any of them, and is not formally responsible for anything they may say. It can be a matter of some difficulty to establish what he himself "thinks"; and this can only be done in the light of the complex creation as a whole. For, "how can it be said I and not Charlotte dressed Aunt Nell? —Here I sit down to form characters . . . I am all the while absorbed in the character. It is not fair to say—I, identically I, am any-where, while I keep within the character." Richardson is the pioneer of "point of view" fiction. In reading him . . . we have to enter the points of view of *all* his characters, to form an overall comprehension that is greater than any possesses; and we have no obvious authorial presence to help us. By formal definition, no single point of view is "reliable." Where there is only one narrator for a given action, we may have to accept the narrative of speech, gesture and action, but it is always dangerous to accept the interpretation the narrator puts on these, and always necessary to read between the lines of the other characters, to discover their points of view.

Mark Kinkead-Weekes
Samuel Richardson: Dramatic Novelist (Ithaca, N.Y.:
Cornell Univ. Pr., 1973), pp. 395–98

How faithfully . . . does *Pamela* reflect Richardson's expressed theories about fiction? Following his precepts, Richardson makes the reader's involvement with Pamela, his exemplary character, the key to the novel. Pamela's letters written "to the moment" in Richardson's preferred manner create a sense of vivid immediacy that heightens the emotional tension and allows the reader to share with Pamela the uncertainty of "events undecided." In accordance with his tenets Richardson gives Pamela some flaws of character so that she emerges, through the candid self-revelation of her letters, as a believable young girl consistent in her actions and development.

Pamela is marred by some flaws of structure and technique. Attempting to establish the verisimilitude which he thought was important to secure the interest of the reader, Richardson sometimes succeeds only in calling attention to the inherent improbability of Pamela's letter-writing proclivities. Richardson's choice of a one-sided structure in *Pamela*, the chief reason for his problems in verisimilitude, also forced him to use a single point of view, Pamela's herself, and this damages the presentation of the other characters in the novel, notably Mr. B. Although Richardson strives to indicate the latent good qualities in Mr. B. that Pamela's virtuous conduct brings to life, the reader's knowledge of Mr. B.'s mind and emotions is too slight, and he is not entirely successful.

The inadequacy of Mr. B.'s characterization tends to call into doubt Pamela's status as an exemplar when she marries him. Anticipating these objections, Richardson very carefully not only establishes good credentials for Mr. B. but stresses that Pamela's resistance is based upon moral principle and a sense of her own integrity, and that, in fact, her greatest struggle is with her own attraction to him. Internal conflict is Richardson's fundamental subject—"in the minutiae lie . . . the unfoldings . . . of the heart," as he wrote to Lady Bradshaigh—and in this struggle lies the chief example that Richardson wished to give his readers.

Richardson's purpose in writing—to give moral instruction through exemplary characters—required him to show those characters being forced to make fundamental moral choices, and this interior drama creates the emotional tension characteristic of Richardon's best work. Although the latter half of the original *Pamela* establishes Pamela's role as a complete exemplar, it is much less interesting primarily because this inner tension is lacking. The decisions that Pamela and Mr. B. have to make in this portion of the novel are not really questions of morality but of social propriety. They must decide how to cope with the hostility of Mr. B.'s relatives and friends, how best to care for Pamela's parents, how to rear Mr. B.'s illegitimate daughter, and how to establish Pamela in her proper dignity without undue ostentation. All of these problems require delicacy rather than moral purpose. The final portion thus becomes a conduct book in the sense that Emily Post is a conduct book; it instructs in the social graces. The first part, on the other hand, has been like *Pilgrim's Progress*: it shows moral choices.

Elizabeth Bergen Brophy
Samuel Richardson: The Triumph of Craft (Knoxville: Univ. Tennessee Pr., 1974), pp. 70–71

The most noticeable and direct influence of Richardson on major English literature was to come through [*Sir Charles*] *Grandison* rather than his earlier novels. The narration by letters became associated with the courtship tale as Richardson had developed it: *Evelina* (1778) is a most successful example. But young ladies could be shown entering society, observing manners, and falling in love, without sustaining themselves by constant sessions of letter-writing, and the novelist could tell their story without recourse to epistles. Jane Austen, who owes much, both directly and indirectly, to Richardson's novels, and especially to *Grandison*, flirted with the epistolary novel only in her juvenile stories. Material and perceptions deriving from *Grandison* went into a kind of novel for which the letter mode seemed but a cumbersome device. The real importance of what had been achieved by Richardson, especially in *Clarissa*, went unnoticed, and, before Richardson's own popularity had waned, the epistolary form was considered *passé*. . . .

Richardson's novels are great images of consciousness. They express, in their divers ways, the fact that no one is merely passive and static, that in the inmost recesses of being the consciousness is always alive and growing. Every person, even the humblest servant-girl, is a consciousness involved in creating its own nature and destiny at every moment. To refuse this great work is impossible. To wish to refuse it, to desire not to be, as do Belton and Mrs. Sinclair, is the sin against the Holy Ghost which cannot in the nature of things be forgiven. Unconsciously to attempt to evade the arduous and exciting task, as Clementina does, is an invitation to disaster. The possibility of error is ever-present—very well, that too must be accepted. "It is good for me that I was afflicted," says Clarissa, who in her ultimate maturing accepts both responsibility and mistake. Men and women must face and explore the ironic connection and apparent incompatibility of the rapacious desire of love and the knowledge of identity, which is the acknowledgement of the nature of freedom, both of oneself and of others, of the beloved object too, who is also subject.

We find in Richardson an expression of the spirit making itself and its world, understanding both its nature and its passion through that nature and passion. The strenuous drama of inner event, the intensity and complexity of the experience of living are reflected in the form of each novel as well as in the matter of the tale itself. Richardson's novels will always be of interest as long as we are concerned with the search for the reconciliation of love and freedom, and with how much may be endured in our quest for fulfilment.

Margaret Anne Doddy
A Natural Passion: A Study of the Novels of Samuel Richardson
(Oxford: Clarendon, 1974), pp. 372–73, 382–83

JOHN WILMOT, EARL OF ROCHESTER

1647–1680

David M. Vieth, ed., *The Complete Poems of John Wilmot, Earl of Rochester* (1968)

Rochester's distinctive technique as a poet involves the simultaneous manipulation of several conflicting levels or planes of experience. The point at which two or more such planes intersect is the poem, and the name of the resulting effect is irony. To be sure, something resembling "Rochesterian irony," as it may be called, can be found in other Restoration poets and might even be considered an essential element in all good poetry. . . .

Even after Rochester's poems have been placed historically and biographically, they retain a uniqueness that probably accounts for their perennial appeal to readers who care nothing about the seventeenth century and know little about their author. In the best of the poems, an open-ended, Pirandello-like quality makes them seem forever contemporary, especially in the modernized format adopted for this edition. This quality is nowhere more apparent than in Rochester's masterpiece, "A Letter from Artemisia in the Town to Chloe in the Country," whose structure resembles a room full of mirrors endlessly reflecting one another.

Which of the poem's many characters represents the truth? It may be the booby squire who dies in serene possession of "the perfect joy of being well deceived." Or it may be the whore Corinna who skillfully dupes him and finally poisons him, or the penetrating "men of wit" such as the one who initially ruined Corinna. Or it may be the "fine lady" who argues so plausibly in favor of fools as lovers—although, as Artemisia observes, she knows "everyone's fault and merit, but her own." Artemisia speaks self-righteously of the traditional spirituality of love, but she proves to be little more than a gossip-monger, powerless against those who reduce love to a mechanical operation of the spirit and who conform so completely to fashion "that with theirs ears they see." These, in turn, as the violently synesthetic image implies, have foregone the immediacy of experience. Perhaps the norm is suggested by Chloe, Artemisia's correspondent, who may stand for the reader but whose presence is entirely a creation of Artemisia's words. Being analytical rather than synthetic, in the manner of the best Restoration comedy, the poem offers no clear synthesis.

In a sense, the structure of "Artemisia to Chloe" simply illustrates the multiplicity of assumed identities or personae used by Rochester as speakers in his poems, thereby raising the philosophical question of identity which has been such an insistent concern in the twentieth century. Logically, in a literary construct based on intersecting planes of experience, with immediacy of experience a desideratum, there must at the point of intersection be a perceiving or participating consciousness, the "I" of the poem. This inherently unstable identity is defined largely by its relationship to the intersecting planes. Enriching the situation further, Rochester's poems, to the extent that they are a coherent body of expression, acquire a corporate unity as projections of what we imagine to have been his real-life personality. To a greater or lesser degree the "I" of each poem is always Rochester, even when the speaker is a woman.

David M. Vieth
Introd., in *The Complete Poems of John Wilmot, Earl of Rochester*, ed. David M. Vieth (New Haven, Conn.: Yale Univ. Pr., 1968), pp. xxxv, xl–xli

It is largely the poems of crude obscenity not by Rochester, read in old editions or heard about, which foster the impression, still current, that Rochester was only a debauched sensualist and sensationalist.

Although such a view of Rochester is no longer seriously argued, other views, equally inadequate in their exaggeration or simplification, are still offered. Rochester has recently been described as a "spiritual explorer," yearning for transcendence of mere sense, a destructive and unintelligent nihilist, and a traditional "Augustan," sharing a complex of Christian-classical values with Dryden and Pope. My own position is that little is gained by affirming or denying that Rochester is an "Augustan" or an "explorer," terms that have been applied with little critical precision and about which there has been (and, I suspect, can be) little agreement.

My view is that Rochester, very much a product of the Restoration, socially, intellectually, literarily, is best understood in such contexts. By no means a mindless sensationalist, a merely sadistic rake, nor a would-be Christian pilgrim lost in doubt's boundless sea, he is a perplexed rather than a dogmatic doubter, delighting in the parody of heroic convention and tradition (as found in Cowley and Waller, for example), attracted to heterodox and paradoxical notions, yet a poet and a man in search of certainties—in love, court life, friendship—which continually elude him. He is shifting, uncertain, undisciplined, able to combine within a single poem widely differing views and tones. His poems are sometimes anxious, sometimes cool and controlled, sometimes "talky," sometimes lyrical, and at the same time savage and gay. They are more memorable and valuable for their intensity and "energy" (a quality contemporaries admired), for their vigorous flow, than for their thought or formal perfection.

Dustin H. Griffin
Satires against Man: The Poems of Rochester (Berkeley: Univ. California Pr., 1973), pp. 4–6

RICHARD SHERIDAN

1751–1816

Cecil Price, ed., *The Dramatic Works of Richard Brinsley Sheridan* (1973), 2 vols.

Madeleine Bingham, *Sheridan: The Track of a Comet* (1972)

As criticism, *The Critic* attacks failings among audiences, critics, and playwrights; but it also points out correspondences between bad art and bad humanity. In criticizing audiences, it indicts the popular taste for sentimental drama and for foreign entertainments—taste that allows bad playwrights to flourish. In criticizing critics, it indicts excessive permissiveness on the one hand (through Dangle) and excessive censoriousness on the other (through Sneer). It also exposes the vanity prompting critics to arbitrate taste for the public, and it condemns the hypocrisy they practice in supporting their pretensions. The discourse on puffing in Act I elaborately damns irresponsible newspaper criticism of the sort that deliberately misleads the public, preying upon its mental and moral weaknesses.

And actually Mr. Puff's tragedy, the work of a critic-turned-playwright, criticizes critics in suggesting that they often misunderstand the art they criticize. Criticism of playwrights in *The Critic* attacks personal vanity, which promotes testiness and hostility to all criticism, however sound; and, of course, it attacks incompetence of the sort illustrated by Puff's play. Each of Puff's "rules" . . . emphasizes a presiding flaw in contemporary tragedy. And the text of his play illustrates yet other flaws: improbable motivation, erratic characterization, fragmented dialogue, contrived argument, shallow pathos, inexact entrance and exit cues, eddying action, flabby verse.

The recurring patriotic appeals made by *The Critic* clearly indicate that the play does not limit its interests to theatrical matters. At the very outset, Mr. Puff's preoccupation with bad art corresponds to his flawed patriotism and in turn to his ineffective humanity. And Puff's chicanery infects the world of politics and commerce as well as the world of art. Through Puff, as a matter of fact, Sheridan makes his most penetrating observations upon art and life. As a professional puffer, Puff reduces deception to rule. Through intricate falsehoods, he offers to exploit human vanity; and he succeeds. As a playwright, he attempts similar stratagems: he reduces art to rule, applying to it the same dishonest principles he applies to life; and he fails. The point is, of course, that art resists deceit more successfully than life does; that, while art may flourish for a time in the hands of practical deceivers, it will eventually betray the deceivers in their deceit. First and last, art is an instrument of truth. It draws upon many forms and conventions—some of them spectacular and artificial, others scrupulously realistic—but always it supports and reveals truth.

As though to ratify these affirmations about art and truth, Sheridan seizes control of Puff's play at the close. He implies that masques have little legitimate place as appendages to tragedy; but he demonstrates that they serve important artistic ends when they function in their own right and celebrate honest human experiences. Throughout the play, Sheridan has emphasized the correlation between bad art and bad humanity, especially as expressed through flawed patriotism. At the close, in a splendid patriotic masque, he celebrates art's proper function as an instrument of honor and truth.

Jack D. Durant
Richard Brinsley Sheridan (Boston: Twayne, 1975), pp. 120–21

TOBIAS SMOLLETT

1721–1771

Smollett's importance as a mid-eighteenth-century novelist stands secure. As a young man, he had to challenge the established reputations of Richardson and Fielding, which he successfuly did by grasping a large portion of the public interest with *Roderick Random*. At the end of his career, Smollett had to confront the popularity of Sterne, whose appeal to readers suggested a turn in literary taste, a demand to feed an appetite for sentiment that would balance the customary harsh diet of satire. Smollett responded with *Humphry Clinker,* a novel that could not detract from Sterne's substantial hold upon the public's enthusiasm; but, nevertheless, it managed to make a highly respectable place for itself within the new climate of opinion. To discuss the eighteenth-century novel without considering Smollett's contribution to the genre would, therefore, be as impossible as discussing the poetry of the age without giving full attention to the work of Pope.

But what *was* Smollett's contribution to the novel of his own time? To be sure, his methods of characterization offered none of the fine psychological probing of Richardson's, and his plots had none of the dramatic sense that Fielding brought from his plays to the novel. Smollett lacked the wild imaginativeness of Sterne that even two hundred years later makes *Tristram Shandy* still seem a daring fictional experiment. And yet Smollett gave much to the new genre, helped to shape it for his own period, and directed it in ways that continue to have significance today.

For his own time Smollett, together with Fielding, demonstrated that the novel was an appropriate means for carrying on the Augustan tradition of satire. Pope had made poetry an effective instrument for satirizing society; Swift had accomplished the same purpose with a variety of prose parodies. By introducing the Continental picaresque form into the eighteenth-century English novel, Smollett provided another method for attacking the social vices and abuses that had aroused the wrath of his Augustan predecessors. Like Pope and Swift, he turned to a traditional genre instead of initiating a new one; but, also like them, he adapted and altered what he took so that it became something quite different from what it originally had been.

In a variety of other ways, Smollett gave added breadth to the eighteenth-century novel. His nautical characters in *Roderick Random* and *Peregrine Pickle* introduced a new type into English fiction. In his Gothic scenes in *Ferdinand Count Fathom,* Smollett first brought the materials of romantic Jacobean and Elizabethan drama into the novel; and he did so a dozen years before the publication of Horace Walpole's *Castle of Otronto.* Although not the first example of novel serialization, *Launcelot Greaves* was indeed the first by a major novelist. Finally, with *Humphry Clinker* Smollett demonstrated how the epistolary form could gain effectiveness from presenting the same materials from a multiple point of view.

Robert Donald Spector
Tobias George Smollett (New York: Twayne, 1968), pp. 146–47

From our point of view in the twentieth century, Smollett appears to link the end of one tradition, the great tradition of classic picaresque, with the beginning of another tradition of related and derivative works . . . and the common element of both groups, the one that leads up to Smollett and the one that leads away from him, is the interaction between a hero who is bright, quick, often naïve, and clever, and a society which is both powerful and cloddish, that interaction being a series of what we can loosely call games. Those interactions are at once endlessly various, inventive, surprising *and* limited, constricted, and predictable. . . . Smollett's pivotal position, at the end of the classic picaresque tradition, as translator of [Alain René] Le Sage and assimilator of a wide range of earlier works, and as a precursor of the abrasive absurdities of the neo-picaresque that follows him, guarantees his ability to provide us with patterns of game not only peculiar to himself but suggestive of the nature of the genre. . . .

It would be a mistake, I think, to systematize the restraints that act upon the play of Smollett's picaros. Their guilt or embarrassment or remorse is always momentary, always highly specific; they improvise their moral response to experience. Smollett's narrative judgments of them are likely to be problematic, embedded in his rhetoric, every bit as *ad hoc* as their views of themselves, and just as unsystematic. The texture of Smollett's rhetoric, for example, is filled with man-beast images, which serve, among other things, to remind us of the sub-human possibilities that are always open to his human character, open, certainly, to his exuberantly mimetic picaros who are always in danger (to choose one of Smollett's own favorite beast metaphors) of becoming baboons. And the action of the novels is filled with reminders that the picaros, being skilled mimes, could lie, cheat, steal, and gamble so as to lay waste around them if they wished; but their play most often succeeds against the vain and the arrogant and they never become the vicious and indiscriminate confidence men which they have every native skill to become. In short, Smollett so constructed the characters of the picaros as to keep them in a perpetually unbalanced tension between their lust for game on the one hand and their moral constraint on the other.

Philip Stevick
in *Tobias Smollett: Bicentennial Essays Presented to Lewis M. Knapp*, ed. G. S. Rosseau and P.-G. Boucé (New York: Oxford Univ. Pr., 1971), pp. 112–13, 129

Arriving in London for the first time, Roderick Random and the faithful Strap [in *Roderick Random*] attempt to dress in a manner befitting the capital. Strap's attire, in keeping with his friend-servant status, is less elegant than Roderick's but he does sport a "short crop-eared wig that very much resembled Scrub's in the play." This allusion to the eighteenth-century costuming of the servant in Farquhar's *Beaux Stratagem* is merely one of numerous dramatic allusions running through Smollett's novels. The high incidence of such allusions recalls Smollett's own efforts as a playwright and indicates a lifelong fascination with dramaturgy and actual stage practice that makes him, as George M. Kahrl claims, "a rare example of the influence of the stage upon the novel." Such influence appears most obviously, perhaps, in the frequent tableaux-scenes that occur in the novels. This static arrangement or grouping of characters derives immediately from stage blocking and ultimately from the group composition of painting. . . .

Smollett's use of the "stage passions" undoubtedly undervalues the individual's internal emotional state. This undervaluation does not mean that Smollett denies the reality of such a state, but rather that to him, its inner workings are less accessible and, ultimately, less relevant to the total human condition than the individual's life in society. Smollett's "realism" is a realism of characters acting in context. . . . Smollett, through the "stage passions," sought to sound in his characters not the music of the unique but the music of humanity.

Thomas R. Preston
SP (January, 1974), pp. 107, 124–25

SIR RICHARD STEELE

1672–1729

Shirley Strum Kenny, ed., *The Plays of Richard Steele* (1971)
Calhoun Winton, *Sir Richard Steele, M. P.: The Later Career* (1970)

LAURENCE STERNE

1713–1768

David Thomson, *Wild Excursions: The Life and Fiction of Laurence Sterne* (1972)
Arthur H. Cash, *Laurence Sterne: The Early and Middle Years* (1975)

The question of Sterne's comic art emerged briefly in our consideration of his typography, which we saw, in the light of Bergson's theory, as a gestural revelation of the absurd assumptions behind printed language. To spatialize the flux of experience, to impose the mechanical upon the living, is to falsify life and—although custom may obscure the fact—to act comically. It is hard to see the end of the ramifications of Bergson's theory; when overlaid upon Marshall McLuhan's *Gutenberg Galaxy*, it suggests that man's history since the written alphabet has been one unrecognized comic error. And when viewed in connection with the problem of personal identity, it suggests that a similar error lies in our own sense of our selves. At this point, we are tempted to say that the theory explains too much; but it is perhaps more accurate to say that, despite problems readily identified by other theorists of the comic, Bergson nonetheless describes certain aspects of the comic and penetrates to a level of human behavior in which the comic—and other aspects of man's nature, as well—may be grounded. Just where and how the comic differentiates itself then becomes the problem for the theorist of the comic. Here I would again retreat from matters beyond my competence and suggest merely that although *Tristram Shandy* and Bergson's theory mutually explicate one another at several levels, the richness and complexity of Sterne's work challenges the adequacy of Bergson's formulation.

If typography is one level, another obviously is that of posture, gesture, and expression; for certain of the elaborate images of Sterne's characters can be considered not merely as parodic extensions of a mimetic technique but also as formally comic in themselves, disrupting the normal imaginative continuity of the fictive action to reveal as comic in fact what is comic by right, that is, the necessary imposition of rigid form on the flux of life. . . .

Character as permanent, or fixed, identity exists in close connection with the comic perspective. Bergson would argue that a character is one who has failed to adapt to the ever-changing flow of life. Yet we can begin to sense an inadequacy in Bergson's account of the comic, which is purely pejorative and negative, when we consider how triumphantly adaptable the great comic characters are in maintaining their fixations. Their fixity accommodates challenge and change; their stasis is dynamic. . . . All experience reveals the further reaches of their essential sameness. And it may be that the real root of the comic mode lies in the time-transcending nature of personal identity, which assimilates all sequential experience to the immediate unity of the self. If this is so, the really interesting connection is that between the comic character and the reader in whose mind he becomes comic: the essential sameness through time of the one in fiction can be seen as a figure of the sense of identity of the other in life. Bergson accounts for the comic *forms*, but not for the source of our interest in these forms; and in the view I am working toward, the comic finds its ground in a fundamental feeling of livingness, of confidence, of permanence in the face of change.

William V. Holtz
Image and Immortality: A Study of "Tristram Shandy"
(Providence, R.I.: Brown Univ. Pr., 1970), pp. 138–39, 141

There are occasions when Sterne [in *Tristram Shandy*] literally dramatizes the processes of reading; he writes dialogue for the reader; at least, he writes words for some of the parts the reader has to play. And in this way he very effectively symbolizes the reader's essential relationship to what he reads: he is in effect defining the reader as a kind of actor.

It is not just that he asks the reader to take *these* parts and speak *these* words. But in doing so he draws attention to the characteristic situation of a reader. For these imagined readers, the lady and the critic, by no means eclipse the reader; they stand for him, but they do not usurp him. They are, as we have seen, embedded in the fiction; but the reader is not. He is still outside it, and they are what he is reading about. Any attempt to write the reader into the story will have this result, for the reader has to be the person for whom all the rest is written. He cannot be shown in the work, for it is to him that everything must be shown. Yet reading does seem like entering a new world, the world of the novel, and Sterne's imaginary readers help to show how this can happen. They are an invitation to the reader to act out different versions of himself; they allow him to assume various identities within the fiction. This is not to say that he identifies himself with these characters. At least, if he does so, it is without losing his own identity. Sterne is proposing a controlled and deliberate commitment to the fictional roles. He wants the reader to be able to "play" another character and yet remain himself. . . .

John Preston
The Created Self: The Reader's Role in Eighteenth-Century Fiction (London: Heinemann, 1970), pp. 205–6

Tristram makes his game from this classical method of narrative. Two changes signal a shift to the game sphere. He juggles two or three of these narrative-speech progressions at the same time. He digresses for pleasure, not from narrative need. If we were to try, impossibly, to disentangle the narrative threads of *Tristram Shandy*, we might find a narrative-speech-narrative-speech pattern for Walter Shandy, one for Toby, perhaps one for Yorick. Tristram's game, or part of it, is to juggle them, to let them fall finally into a meaningful superposition, one atop the other. Yorick must dive for a chestnut when we expect Walter to dive for the mysteries of name-giving; Tristram must kiss the critic's hand when the context leads us to expect him to kiss another part of the body; Toby, amidst the birth pangs that produce Tristram headfirst, must discourse on not hurting a hair on a fly's head. This alternation creates a Thucydidean pattern raised to the third power. Tristram controls the interweaving. He is no jocular Joyce, however, only pretending to trust God for the second sentence. Behind the pretense of chaos may lie careful chronology, but not always a master intelligence.

Process literature this novel is, vaguely realizing itself toward a termination coincident with the author's conscious intention. Sterne's preconscious voice, Tristram, confesses throughout the novel both that he really is helter-skelter and that he only seems so, that the digressions interrupt the main story, are the main story. Confessions aside, he does not proceed at random. But his consistent principle in digression and juggled narrative hardly satisfies critical expectation. Tristram does as he pleases. Yet if, as is generally recognized, his game is the novel itself, should it surprise that his playing seeks play's characteristic reward? He is not a Shandy for nothing.

Richard A. Lanham
"Tristram Shandy": The Games of Pleasure (Berkeley: Univ. California Pr., 1973), pp. 95–96

For Sterne all knowledge—rational, emotional, and imaginative—is subjective. Each man makes his world conform to his own pleasure and predisposition. The result is a simplification and distortion of reality. All experience is essentially ironic in nature. That which is most explicitly or obviously presented as truth is usually an inversion of another truth, a more basic truth, which is hidden but implied. But, because there is never an absolute truth (only a number of possible points of view which must be balanced against one another) statements, people, appearances are not simply the opposites of what they seem. They are themselves *and* their opposites. The problem which the reader faces in approaching *Tristram Shandy* is identical to the problem he faces day by day, mystery inside ambiguity, in the maze of his own life. Sterne calls upon him to relate to the novel as he must relate to any part of his own experience. For the novel, like the jester's riddle, is as complex, ambiguous, paradoxical—as humorous and absurd—as life itself. Upon the mind purged by confusion and cleansed by laughter Sterne impresses a new vision of reality which contains within itself a simplifying truth about the nature of man, who aspires despite his limitations, who persists despite his defeats, who, though locked in isolation, is still capable of loving.

The overriding irony of the work derives from the relation of the apparent confusion of form and theme to the actual structural and conceptual order. The close parallel between Sterne's theory of art and his philosophical view of reality must again be mentioned. The experienced world is made up of random impressions which are given meaning by the perceiving eye. Similarly, a man's life, Sterne tells us through his characterizations, appears to the observer to be little more than eccentricity and choas. But the appearance cloaks a principle of organization bestowed by the coherence of the individual's personality. The most bizarre fantasies, the most illogical associations, reveal their internal logic to anyone who can project himself into the wonderland of another's mind. Instead of abnormality there is only a variety of different perspectives.

All of life, Sterne seems to say, is an irony; each man who lives it is an ironist—his functioning largely unconscious—for he composes the mysteries of those appearances which are extensions of himself. But each man is therefore his own enemy, victim of the ironist within, alienated as he attempts to unravel the secret of his own identity as well as the identities of others. To write as Sterne does is to consciously imitate life while standing apart from it. It is to become the ironist as jester, not wholly part of society, not completely human. Sterne creates Tristram, who stands between the ironist and the victim, the writer and the reader, the creator and the interpreter. In him, on a human and fallible level, both partial selves come together, and living and writing are joined in the same mysterious function.

Tristram Shandy is, then, an astonishing reflection of reality, of its discontinuity as well as its coherence. It is an elaborately formed complex of interrelated ironic patterns which belong to the fundamental ironic concept.

Helene Moglen
The Philosophical Irony of Laurence Sterne (Gainesville: University Presses of Florida, 1975), pp. 5–6

JONATHAN SWIFT

1667–1745

Irvin Ehrenpreis, *Swift: The Man, His Works, and the Age*, Vol. II (1967)

It is irrelevant . . . to talk of Gulliver's character; he has no character, he is a cipher. Perspective is pertinent to our reception of Gulliver because the first law of his composition is that every relevant fact is available to the eye. To understand Gulliver it is only necessary to look at him, to see what he does; the fact that he is delivered so completely to one of five senses is the gist of the comedy. The eye is selective, a specialist. If, on the basis of what we see in Gulliver, we choose to guess what we do not see, that is our privilege. We cannot be prevented; but we can be discouraged. Beyond what is delivered to the eye, there is, in fact, nothing at all. Gulliver has a lively role, but its comic force consists in its limitation. He is what he does, what we see him doing, there is nothing beyond what we see. More to the point, there is nothing beneath what we see, no underground man to be sensed beneath the detail of his imprisonment. We are bewildered, then scandalised, by *Gulliver's Travels* because we expect depth and we are held to surface. Swift laughs at our sentimentality and frustrates it. Gulliver is a fraction, not a whole number. If the reader tries to gratify himself by completing Gulliver, tries to add intimations of character, soul, feeling, depth, then he convicts himself; he is a sentimentalist, Swift's favourite butt. It is Gulliver's condition to be a fraction; that is, the human average. The book challenges us to deny the equation. . . .

Gulliver's Travels achieves by mockery what [John Gay's] *The Beg-*

gar's Opera achieved by good humour, the feeling that we are all human together. Gay wanted to comfort people with this reflexion: Swift had a different purpose. But it was one effect of the *Travels* to bring people together, if only in a sense of their folly. The perspective imposed by the work implies that at some level our militant differences are trivial and we should be ashamed to pursue them. . . .

Denis Donoghue
Jonathan Swift: A Critical Introduction (Cambridge: Cambridge Univ. Pr., 1969), pp. 162–63, 186–87

Knavery and foolishness, the discordant terms of the *Tale* [*of a Tub*]'s conflict, are separate; and yet they meet together in the persona of the *Tale*. The combining of the two aspects in the modern persona is like the discordant harmony that ironically conjoins knavish Peter and foolish Jack, the two religious leaders who had sought above all else to be unlike. . . .

This marriage in the *Tale of a Tub* of fool and knave ultimately renders, the reader must feel, a piece of poetic justice. Seen in the light of tradition, their integration is nicely appropriate. For just as Peter and Jack deserve to be associated because of their machinations, their gullibility, and their vanity, so the fool and the knave of a long tradition had been identified. In Solomon's Proverbs, fool and knave are indistinguishable, folly and vice together accommodated by the single term "fool." Fool and knave alike in biblical tradition are proud, aggressive, and boastful; both are prattlers and talebearers; both are self-reliant "single" men, who trouble their own houses; both are considered deceitful to others, while they themselves love to be deceived. Fool and knave in Proverbs are curious *and* credulous. Swift, in the *Tale of a Tub*, suggestively recurs to this older tradition and in doing so mounts the finest comic irony upon the boards of his dramatic house: knave and fool in the *Tale*, for all their insistent conflict, appear at the last, like Donne's famous pair of compasses, men whose sphere and whose circularity are the same.

This *mixtus*, this wavering, this ground swell of backward and forward jostling and confusion that pattern the *Tale of a Tub*'s conflict among the parts of its singular organization reflect exactly the subjective impasse in the modern persona himself, between knave and fool, with fool turning knave and knave metamorphosing into fool—all before our eyes. With a vengeance is "Imagination at Cuffs with the Senses" . . . for this is the central and continual conflict that we discover in the *Tale*.

John T. Clark
Form and Frenzy in Swift's "Tale of a Tub" (Ithaca, N.Y.: Cornell Univ. Pr., 1970), pp. 76–78

JAMES THOMSON

1700–1748

Thomson's great achievement is to have fashioned a conception which, by bringing nature to the forefront of his poem [*The Seasons*], became a new poetic way of defining human experience. Thomson was not the first nature poet to write in English, but he was the first to provide an effective idiom in which science, religion, natural description and classical allusion blended to describe the glory, baseness and uncertainty of man's earthly environment, holding forth the hope of heavenly love and wisdom.

Thomson did not deny the actuality of wickedness, the hunter-killers, the wealthy aristocrats disregarding human need and squandering their wealth, the religious exploiters and the brutal executors of injustice. Nor did he deny that aspects of nature seemed, at times, jealous and vindictive, destroying good men and sparing the wicked. But these aspects existed simultaneously with others, with the comic, exhilarating, joyful transformations. This double view he accepted, but he did not accept any simple moral arithmetic in nature and he did not believe that virtue or benevolence was directly rewarded on earth. . . .

The seasons provided Thomson with a naturalistic basis for change which, by its cyclical pattern, permitted limited progression in any one season while relating the whole to God's power. But the cycle of the seasons is not the circle of perfection, and in the poem the cyclical repetition, like the confrontation of opposites, does not lead to a whole. It leads to a temporary completion that introduces a new beginning. Scientifically, change was explained by the traditional assumptions of the transformability of the four elements, but Thomson mixes this view with a description of observed natural changes. The speaker absorbs the scientific explanation by mixing natural description with personification, by using the same term in a literal and metaphoric sense. A knowledge of science can assist man in understanding nature, but such knowledge cannot provide answers to ultimate questions. . . .

Thomson's defects are of two kinds: he is limited in his knowledge of man and in the range of his understanding of human behavior; and, within the range to which he confines himself, he sometimes uses techniques formalistically to conceal his inadequate grasp of a situation or to cajole the reader by flattery or sentimentality. The poem can become overly scientific and excessively formal or overly sentimental, the types of dangers that Thomson risks by using the mixed form and scientific or abstract terms. There is always the risk, too, that repetition will rub off the rough individual edges of a general term and make it vague and indefinite. Thomson tries to avoid succumbing to such faults by employing a fragmentary structure which prevents any readily accepted generalization, and in this he is overwhelmingly successful, even when he introduces scientific explanations and terminology.

Ralph Cohen
The Unfolding of "The Seasons" (Baltimore: Johns Hopkins Univ. Pr., 1970), pp. 324–25, 329–30

A degree of vagueness still persists when we attempt to isolate and describe those qualities that characterize Thomson's view of external nature. That view is implicit in his pictorialism. Clearly his models are heroic and ideal, not naturalistic. Thomson can no longer be considered a precursor to Wordsworth, an anachronism partially redeeming the barrenness and aridity of Augustan poetry. But he is still associated far too frequently with the picturesque movement of the later eighteenth century. . . . Thomson is "picturesque" only in the sense that he composes his scenes of nature "like a picture." The narrower meanings of the term are of later derivation and cannot be applied retrospectively to the poet of *The Seasons*.

The Seasons is Thomson's major work, a poem whose evolution spanned almost his entire career. It reflects his preoccupations both intellectual and aesthetic over a twenty-year period. So various are its scenes of rural life that it is possible to find and extract from its context a particular passage to illustrate almost any style. Looked at more generally, however, *The Seasons* reveals itself as typical of the age that produced it. Its originality cannot be denied, but its inspiration and pictorial sources are largely unchanged from those of Thomson's contemporary, Alexander Pope. The decorative rococo and baroque styles assume a greater importance in Pope's work because his landscapes tend to be representative of more traditional poetic subgenres—the pastoral, the estate poem. Thomson's *Seasons* was not such a recognized type, so of necessity he became more of an innovator, but only in his methods, not in his sources.

Evidence suggests that these sources are largely pre-Claudian [Claude Lorrain]. Thomson, while first writing *The Seasons*, was learning to reconcile his northern heritage and his love of rugged natural terrain with the new landscape architecture coming into vogue and with the traditional artistic pantheon he learned to appreciate during the time of his pictorialist apprenticeship in London. He was not yet ready to assimilate the fully realized Claudian ideal, or to trade his own varied poetic canvases for the notably less diverse pastoral vistas portrayed by Claude. . . . Thomson appears to have solved certain problems in depicting landscape (the prospect view, diffused lighting) and used certain techniques (aerial perspective, chiaroscuro effects) in ways strikingly similar to the methods used by [Adam] Elsheimer and [Paul] Brill. Finally his ability to elevate the landscape of fact into the heroic mode resembles that of the two

Northern painters and such Italians as [Jacopo da] Bassano, a circumstance that helps to explain his appeal to later poets who found his landscapes more natural and less artificial than those of Pope.

Thomson's unique but limited talents were stimulated to best advantage by the time and place in which he was fortunate enough to exercise them. His work gave an added impetus to the landscape movement in both the verbal and the visual arts until his educative influence on his successors came to be out of all proportion to his own stature as a poet.

Jeffry B. Spencer
Heroic Nature: Ideal Landscape in English Poetry from Marvell to Thomson (Evanston, Ill.: Northwestern Univ. Pr., 1973), pp. 294–95

HORACE WALPOLE

1717–1797

W. S. Lewis, gen. ed., *The Yale Edition of Horace Walpole's Correspondence* (1937–1965), 34 vols.

The *Anecdotes* is basically an archeological compendium, not a critical history of art. It contains very many "brief or trifling articles" on artists. As Walpole himself admits, "This work is but an essay towards the history of our arts; all kinds of notices are inserted, to lead to further discoveries." He intended the work "as an impartial register of, not as a panegyric on, our English artists." Yet this does not mean that he does not employ his critical faculty "in commending and blaming" (III, 316–17, 432). His essay on a contemporary, William Hogarth (including the comprehensive catalogue of Hogarth's prints), may be cited as an excellent illustration of his art criticism, judicious yet balanced by sympathetic warmth and appreciative understanding of Hogarth's artistic and moral aims. Walpole, always sensitive to the ability of the best artists to portray and evoke emotion, seizes on just this quality in Hogarth's "delicate and superior" comic satire—"familiarized by strokes of nature and heightened by wit, and the whole animated by proper and just expressions of the passions." But Walpole also believed that "as a painter he had but slender merit," thinking that that was not the real bent of Hogarth's genius. Nor was he impressed by Hogarth's so-called discovery of the principle of grace—the serpentine line of beauty. There are, then, in the *Ancedotes* enough evidences to show Walpole in the capacity of serious art critic as well as art historian. From this point of view, his critical opinions are most interesting for our study and may contribute to an understanding not only of his taste but also of his personality.

Among his best essays are those dealing with architecture, and his remarks help explain the alterations at Strawberry Hill. He writes with verve when he focuses on architecture, especially his favored Gothic style. His prose becomes animated, often crackling and sparkling with irony and epigrammatic wit, and he exhibits the confidence of an expert. . . .

In general, Walpole is an exciting critic, praised for his taste and competence by all who have written on the subject. He often writes with vigorous pungency—as of Piranesi who "has a sublime savageness in his engravings like Salvator Rosa." He takes his stand on fashions: William Chambers' *Treatise on Oriental Gardening* is "a work that tended to bring back all manner of bad and whimsical taste." He writes zestfully and yet judiciously, with shrewdness and sensibility in his penetrating critiques of Hogarth as well as Reynolds. Praising and blaming these artists in detail, he demonstrates his shrewd insight and sensitive intelligence. The essay on Hogarth is still considered a standard one on the subject. He errs only when he is concerned with the works of his close friends and social equals.

Martin Kallich
Horace Walpole (New York: Twayne, 1971), pp. 83, 86

WILLIAM WYCHERLEY

1641–1716

[A major] area of meaning comprehended in the term *generosity* as it was used in Restoration comedy is the complex of ideas surrounding the word *plain-dealing*, a term often used in the plays and always with favorable connotations. That Plain-dealing was indeed a part of the content of *generosity* may be supposed from the fact that several comic heroes specifically labeled *generous* are notable for the plainness of their dealings as well. For example, Congreve's "generous Valentine" poses as "Truth" in his mad scene; Wycherley's "generous Captain" Manly is the title character of *The Plain Dealer*; Farquhar's "generous creature," Silvia, is "too plain" in speech. Plain-dealing may be the form that the classical virtue of Wisdom or Truth takes in Restoration comedy. . . .

Restoration comedy is not artificial. The view here espoused that these plays recommend Plain-dealing is irreconcilable with any view which assumes that protagonistic characters are affected or artificial in their behavior. It would exclude the classic "comedy of manners" approach generated by Charles Lamb and passed on to Kathleen Lynch by John Palmer: "In the comedy of manners [says Palmer, quoted in Lynch] men and women are seen holding the reality of life away or letting it appear only as an unruffled thing of attitudes. Life is here made up of exquisite demeanour." The "manners" approach to *The Plain Dealer* therefore requires that honest Manly be an object of satire, not of admiration.

Ben Ross Schneider, Jr.
The Ethos of Restoration Comedy (Urbana: Univ. Illinois Pr., 1971), pp. 96, 98–99

Probably, inspired by [Molière's] *Le misanthrope*, Wycherley [in *The Plain-Dealer*] had originally planned to show the baseness of society by letting an extremist measure it against absolute moral standards and, at the same time, to show the folly of flinging oneself against socially necessary compromises and deceptions. He had used a similar plan in *The Country-Wife*, in which Margery's absolute naturalness brings out the artificiality of everyone else, while simultaneously demonstrating the inadequacy of naturalness in a social setting. Such a scheme would require Wycherley to treat all his characters with detached amusement. Even when he exposed depravity, as in the Widow Blackacre's scene with her hired false witnesses, he would retain his sense of humor. The reader can laugh at the paradox that the Widow is honest since she pays people for perjuring themselves, for he is not emotionally involved with these characters and no direct appeal is made to his moral judgment. In order to satirize the two extremes of oversocialized and antisocial man, Wycherley would have to accept as his standard the best moral level that his society offered: Freeman's decent expediency would be the norm, and the expectation of anything higher than this norm would be folly.

Yet the conclusion seems inescapable that Wycherley was not satisfied with the norm. Into a world which recognized only Elizas and Olivias, Alitheas and Lady Fidgets, he introduced Fidelia, who obviously does not belong.

Katharine M. Rogers
William Wycherley (New York: Twayne, 1972), p. 86

EDWARD YOUNG

1683–1765

Henry Pettit, ed., *The Correspondence of Edward Young, 1683–1765* (1971)

Conjectures on Original Composition in a Letter to the Author of "Sir Charles Grandison," published in May, 1759, is an astonishing production for a man of seventy-six. Its exuberant, forward-looking attitude, its repudiation of dependence on the past, its stress on originality and individual self-confidence, its indignation at pettiness and servility to rules, its ranking

Shakespeare with the greatest of the Greek dramatists, its hope for future writers equalling or surpassing the great writers of the past—all suggest a youthful vigor of mind and imagination unusual at his age. It would be an incredible production if it indicated entirely new convictions on his part. While it shows the final development of his views, it does not contradict his past writings. It was no impromptu production, but the result of long deliberation and careful revision. . . .

Young . . . turns to the main theme and, in a metaphor of gardens, plants, and growing things, which is a dominant metaphor throughout, he introduces his major terms: "The mind of a man of genius is a fertile and pleasant field . . . it enjoys a perpetual spring. Of that spring, *Originals* are the fairest flowers: *Imitations* are quicker growth, but fainter bloom." He indicates that he will use the term "Originals" for those who imitate nature, and "Imitations" for those who imitate authors. The first is always superior to the second: "An *Original* may be said to be of a vegetable nature; it rises spontaneously from the root of genius; it *grows*, it is not made." Since thoughts, as well as words, get worn with use, writers should think for themselves: "We may as well grow good by another virtue, or fat by another's food, as famous by another's thought."

Why is it, he asks, that there are so few originals? It is largely because the writings of the past overawe writers of the present: "They *engross* our attention, . . .; they *prejudice* our judgment in favour of their abilities . . . and they *intimidate* us with the splendor of their renown." Although writers of the past are of great importance to those of the present, they should be admired, not copied. This distinction between copying and imitating other writers leads him to a differentiation between the relative value of genius and learning. Learning is "a great lover of rules"; genius, with less interest in rules, "has ever been supposed to partake of something divine," and surpasses learning, great though its worth is.

Isabel St. John Bliss
Edward Young (New York: Twayne, 1969), pp. 143–45

ROMANTIC LITERATURE

Betty T. Bennett, editor

JANE AUSTEN

1775–1817

Given the number of Jane Austen studies that have appeared in the last decade, some justification for this book is called for. It offers perhaps two original proposals: first, it makes the unusual assumption that *Mansfield Park* is fundamental to Jane Austen's thought—not the counter-truth it has traditionally been considered—and second, working from a detailed and positive reading of this controversial work, it proposes a thematic unity to her fiction. As my title implies, such a unity resides in Jane Austen's conception of the "estate" and in her idea of "improvement." For Jane Austen, in *Mansfield Park*, the estate as an ordered physical structure is a metonym for other inherited structures—society as a whole, a code of morality, a body of manners, a system of language—and "improvements," or the manner in which individuals relate to their cultural inheritance, are a means of distinguishing responsible from irresponsible action and of defining a proper attitude toward social change. . . .

Against the regulated hatred, the detached irony, and the subversive morality that much recent criticism has stressed, it is necessary to take more seriously a Jane Austen "thoroughly religious and devout" [Henry Austen, 1818], who has the additonal "merit . . . of being evidently a Christian writer" [Archbishop Whately, 1821]. In this connection it is appropriate to mention one important response to deprivation that is dramatized in Jane Austen's novels which seldom finds its way into critical commentary. At times of greatest distress the "reduced" self in Jane Austen's fiction is apt to fall back on its "resources," an idea which suggests a Christian stoicism, an inner resilience in the face of adversity. Elinor Dashwood, Fanny Price, and Anne Elliot all at times approach a kind of Christian heroism which recognizes that, whatever the distresses of the moment, this world is not after all the place of ultimate reward. . . .

If her fiction looks forward to modern themes and responses (as in *Persuasion* and *Sanditon* I believe it does), it also grows out of an eighteenth century novelistic concern with the predicament of the dislocated individual. It is in the eighteenth century novel that the recurring pattern of Jane Austen's plots—the movement from a condition of initial security to a period of isolation and then to a final reinstatement in society—finds its origins. It is there, too, that individualism, often viewed in religious contexts, has interesting implications for a consideration of Jane Austen's fiction.

Alistair M. Duckworth
The Improvement of the Estate: A Study of Jane Austen's Novels
(Baltimore: Johns Hopkins Univ. Pr., 1971), pp. ix, 8, 10

I have pointed out how Jane Austen's simple, lucid, even formally "correct" language can overlie a deeper complexity of meaning contained within it. I have tried to make clear that the existence of both surface and depth are essential to the aesthetic significance of *Emma*, which, among other things, teaches us that trivialities of ordinary life are important because the "simple" facts of commonplace existence are in reality complex. The nature and function of Austen's language, even in its smallest details, reflect the form of her novel as an aesthetic whole. . . .

Her community is the genteel novel-reading public of her day. The range and significance of her literary references are restricted. Her satire is seldom generalized and is always kept within the traditional scope of lighthearted novelistic comment. She never appeals to her readers except as novel-readers. Even the pervasiveness of her irony may be a sign of her awareness of the limitations of her audience, in that irony tends to disguise complexities of meaning. Moreover, it is plain that a great deal of what Jane Austen must have actually experienced never appears in her fiction. Hers may have been a sheltered and uneventful life, but much of it she chose to exclude from her novels. . . . *Persuasion*, like many of Wordsworth's poems, is concerned primarily with recurrence, with the processes of emotions as defined by experiential repetitions. Like Wordsworth, Austen becomes interested in the relation of feeling *now* to feeling *then*, of the novel to the familiar. The comparison to Wordsworth is not arbitrary. It helps to explain why, in moving away from logical, ironic representation, Jane Austen did not move farther in the direction of the pictorial and metaphoric. Probing more deeply into the sources, persistence, and significance of personal emotion, she sought not that which separates the private from the rest of the world but different, more fundamental, bonds between the individual and his surroundings. Even more important than "romantic" description in *Persuasion* is Austen's delineation of the qualities of her heroine's sensibility which make her so appropriate a character both to respond to the immediacy of sensory impressions and to dramatize constancy of affection.

Karl Kroeber
Styles in Fictional Structure: The Art of Jane Austen, Charlotte Brontë, George Eliot (Princeton, N.J.: Princeton Univ. Pr., 1971), pp. 25–26, 46, 83

That tight and demarcated little world, which may seem to us so restricted in its scope and in its assumptions about reality, becomes enormously exhilarating and liberating; it offers to those who are capable of exerting themselves to discover its meaning the control of the essential qualities of their lives; it challenges our own narrowness, our assumption of powerlessness or rebellion. The restrictions in the world of Jane Austen's heroines do not make their choices less significant. As boundaries become clear and close and alternatives are few and final, choice becomes more heroic. The more valuable way to approach her novels is not through the list of all the mighty matters and all the odd corners that she omits, as though her primary concern were to reject or withdraw from what she could not or did not want to touch in art. It is not helpful to say, with one critic of many, that she "feels compelled to tidy up life's customary messiness," because to say that is to make an assumption about life that is not hers. She knows, and she shows us in her novels, messy lives, and most people are leading them, even when the surface of life seems proper; but custom is not the first fact of life. Life is not a disorder to be ordered, a given mess on which those of tidy compulsions impose a tidiness. It is not a meaningless heap from which meaning is extracted by reduction and exclusion. Meaning is the first fact. It is obscured by inexperience, by miseducation, by deception, above all by internal blindness, but it is there and it is clear to the opened eye. . . .

Jane Austen's world is full, it has all the parts it needs and all of them are fully given to us as far as they are needed. All parts become luminous in a defining vision. Each part is located, each part can be explained, as far as it must be for purposeful word and action. Strong feelings rise in her characters, rightly and necessarily at moments of crisis, with pleasures and pains beyond what they have ever felt: the characteristic accompaniment of this increase of feeling is an increase in articulateness; they must often struggle for it but their stature is in proportion to their willingness to try for it and their eventual success in achieving the brightness of command.

That definition, clarity of atmosphere, fullness of articulation, with which she gives us the actions of men and women in common life, give her stories such original simplicity that it is understandable why even sophisticated critics have thought of her as a primitive.

Stuart M. Tave
Some Words of Jane Austen (Chicago: Univ. Chicago Pr., 1973), pp. 33–34

What makes this issue of communication in Jane Austen's fiction so noteworthy is the degree to which her writing is pervaded by the conscious formulation of style and structure as parts of the moral or psychological process, and by her ability to integrate completely any one mode of communication, any single "bit of ivory," within the total framework of each novel. Hence, to analyze her patterns of style and narrative form is to investigate some of the most crucial aspects of her meaning. . . .

I seek to establish specific links between individual Jane Austen techniques and her eighteenth-century predecessors as part of my general interest in style, or technique, as meaning. Hence Jane Austen's moral philosophy can be illuminated if we compare, say, her ironic diction, not only with similar structures in eighteenth-century satire and novels, but also with the moral philosophy which consciously explores attitudes towards word usages in the eighteenth century: the multiple nuances of "pride" and "prejudice" in her fiction are more accessible if we can compare such ironic usages with the implications of the terms as used by a predecessor like David Hume. Similarly, the thematic significance and the structure of other narrative techniques acquire more meaning if they can be compared with explicit eighteenth-century commentary on imagery, conversation, or letter writing. In short, Jane Austen's style is not only integrated with her meaning, but also with the philosophical traditions which she inherits from the eighteenth century. This is appropriate enough: Jane Austen's style and meaning suggest, on the whole, that the very notion of tradition is central to her moral insights and her narrative techniques as an ironist. I am not referring here to the Janeites' narrowly self-serving notion of tradition, but to Jane Austen's capacity to perceive social traditions in dual terms: on the one hand, the traditions of behavioral reality, and, on the other, the revered traditions of moral idealism.

Lloyd Brown
Bits of Ivory: Narrative Techniques in Jane Austen's Fiction
(Baton Rouge: Louisiana State Univ. Pr., 1975), pp. 9, 13

Jane Austen's attitude to social distinctions in the upper reaches of society has been called that of a "Tory radical": which is accurate provided we recognize that over all in the novels her Toryism carries more weight than her radicalism. For a novelist during the revolutionary era, form and manner are decisive indices to partisanship, and an analysis of Jane Austen's characteristics in the light of contemporary practice reveals, unarguably, the lineaments of the committed conservative.

Study of the novel of the 1790s shows how the two types of partisan differ in placing the hero in his environment. One test of allegiance is the degree of sympathy with which a novelist views the feelings of his hero. Another, whether the plot, broadly, suggests a victim suffering at the hands of society, or a misguided individual rebelling against it. The first issue arouses real differences of interpretation among readers of Jane Austen, and is best left to an examination of the individual novels. But on the second, the question of her plot—or, for the two are hardly separable, her form—some preliminary generalization is possible.

Jane Austen moves turn and turn about between two plots, which can be crudely characterized as built about the Heroine who is Right and the Heroine who is Wrong. The first type, the Heroine who is Right, acts as spokesman for conservative orthodoxy. Elinor, Fanny, and Anne advocate principle, duty, and the sacrifice of private inclination to the service of others. The Heroines who are Wrong arrive at this state of true understanding only late in the day: they begin in intellectual error, brought about in Catherine by immaturity and false lights, but in Elizabeth and Emma by the more spiritual-looking errors of pride and presumption. In these three novels the dénouement follows the heroine's discovery of her mistake, and Elizabeth's exclamation is representative. "I have courted prepossession and ignorance, and driven reason away . . . Till this moment, I never knew myself." The moment of self-discovery and self-abasement, followed by the resolve in future to follow reason, is the climactic moment of the majority of anti-jacobin novels.

Marilyn Butler
Jane Austen and the War of Ideas (Oxford: Clarendon, 1975),
pp. 165–66

Not many people now think of Jane Austen as the gentle, secluded spinster who gives us a picture of quiet, "ordinary" uneventful life in a humdrum rural society, preaching the tired clichés of a conventional and superficial morality. Yet G. K. Chesterton's "paradoxical" over-reaction to this kind of thing—"[Her] inspiration was the inspiration of Gargantua and of Pickwick; it was the gigantic inspiration of laughter. . . . She was the very reverse of a starched or a starved spinster; she could have been a buffoon like the Wife of Bath if she chose"—though a salutary corrective to the older view, hardly tells the whole truth either. It is interesting that what startled Chesterton into writing this was the recently recovered juvenilia, in particular *Love and Friendship*, written when Jane Austen was fourteen. Since R. F. Brissenden's brilliant analysis of this satire and other juvenile pieces, in which he audaciously links her with her contemporary Sade as a deflater of the sentimental "image of man as a social, sympathetic, generous, benevolent, and good-natured being," picturing him rather as "an isolated, anarchic, selfish, cruel, violent, and aggressive being," we have become uneasily aware that there are depths of the knowledge of evil—as well as of good—in Jane Austen's writings for which perhaps none of Chesterton's illustrations provides a very exact parallel. . . .

Jane Austen is no mean psychopathologist. One needs to remember that she grew up in the great age of English caricature, when Hogarth's engravings were on every wall, and Gillray, Rowlandson and the Cruikshanks were producing their twisted, grotesque distortions of the human frame. "Hogarth's moralizing, Gillray's irony, Rowlandson's comedy, Newton's burlesque," Mrs. George, the greatest scholar of the genre, characterizes some of them. All those terms could be applied to Jane Austen's vast zoo of monstrosities—as could such more recent ones as "surrealism," "black humor," and "the absurd."

Donald Greene
in *Jane Austen: Bicentenary Essays*, ed. John Halperin
(Cambridge: Cambridge Univ. Pr., 1975), pp. 262–63, 276

The actual experience we have in reading *Persuasion* is possible primarily because Jane Austen's art conveys to us at least something of a peculiarly modern terror: that our only recourse amid the accelerations of history is to commit our deepest energies to an intense personal relationship, but that an intense personal relationship is inevitably subject to its own kind of terrible precariousness. . . .

The self that we encounter in the consciousness of Anne Elliot is clearly and profoundly imperiled by the dead weight of an outmoded past. (Surely the brilliant opening of the novel, with Anne's absurd father finding his fullest sense of reality in the contemplating of "his own history" in the Baronetage, supports such a reading.) Hence, the emphasis in the early chapters on Anne's awareness of the passage of time—of the eight empty years that have gone by since she might have had Frederick Wentworth for her own. And hence, too, our sense at the close of *Persuasion* that we have just been participants in the recapturing of the past, but of a past (unlike Wordsworth's, say, or Proust's) capable of a vital *re-creation* into newfound harmony with the actualities of Anne Elliot's present world.

William A. Walling
The Wordsworth Circle (Autumn, 1976), p. 336

WILLIAM BLAKE

1757–1827

In both the [Book of Job] itself and in Blake a strong emphasis is thrown on the destroyed and reintegrated *community* of Job. This is essential for that aspect of the symbolism in which Job represents not simply *a* man but mankind as a whole. And yet Job has to be an individual too, for Satan's assault on him is part of a struggle between alienation and identity in which the former carries its conquests up to the very last stronghold of the latter, which is the individual consciousness. Everything Job has, as distinct from what he is, disappears into the illusory satanic world of time. He is alienated from his own body by his boils, and from society by the accusing or "Elect" friends, leaving Job himself in the isolated position of the "Reprobate" prophet, the scapegoat driven like Elijah into the wilderness, with only his wife to represent the "Redeemed." Finally Elihu, pointing to the stars so far above him, alienates him from his earlier view of God, who is now wholly replaced by the accuser. With the turning point of Plate 13 the community starts rebuilding again, extending to a risen God in Plate 16, the friends in Plate 18, and a still larger community in Plate 19. . . .

Blake's Vision of the Book of Job was certainly a work of the creative imagination, but what made it possible was a powerful critical analysis of the book. This criticism performed what we are slowly beginning to realize is the essential critical act: it put the Book of Job into its literary context. That context, the Christian Bible as a whole, lay of course ready to hand. Yet to comprehend the story of Job as a microcosm or epitome of the whole Bible, and to comprehend it as intensely as Blake did, and as the quotations on the engravings show that he did, took a critical mind of first-rate quality.

Northrop Frye
in *William Blake: Essays for S. Foster Damon*, ed.
Alvin S. Rosenfeld (Providence, R.I.: Brown Univ. Pr., 1968),
pp. 230, 234

Blake, however often he may have stretched out of easily recognizable shape the forms he inherited, did in fact remain profoundly indebted to the pictorialist masters of his youth. But in viewing the largest revelant context for Blake's union of the arts, we must understand that literary pictorialism is by no means confined to scene-painting of the kind that Lessing attacked or to the visual personifications of the anti-Pope school. The tradition we are concerned with in defining the verbal-visual in Blake goes far beyond Collins, Thomson, or the Wartons in time and quality. It includes the sacramental icon as well as the natural image, prophetic vision as well as empirical imitation. It is a complex and ageless tradition that has been variously embodied at different moments of cultural history. Blake, as he always did with the influences that played upon him, adapted this broad and diverse tradition to his own special purposes. But reject it or ignore it or treat it as irrelevant—that he seems not to have done. To Blake and his picture-poem inheritance may be applied what Christ said of Jewish law and prophecy: that he came not to "destroy but to fulfill" it (Matthew 5:17).

Jean H. Hagstrum
in *Blake's Visionary Forms Dramatic*, ed. David V. Erdman and John E. Grant (Princeton, N.J.: Princeton Univ. Pr., 1970), pp. 82–83

The central image of Blake, from whenever he first formulated his mythology, is Ezekiel's; the *Merkabah*, Divine Chariot or form of God in motion. The Living Creatures or Four Zoas are Ezekiel's and not initially Blake's, a priority of invention that Blake's critics, in their search for more esoteric sources, sometimes evade. Ezekiel, in regard to Blake's *Jerusalem*, is like Homer in regard to the *Aeneid*: the inventor, the precursor, the shaper of the later work's continuities. From Ezekiel in particular Blake learned the true meaning of prophet, visionary orator, honest man who speaks into the heart of a situation to warn: if you go on so, the result is so; or as Blake said, a seer and not an arbitrary dictator.

I have indicated elsewhere the similarities in arrangement of the two books, and the parallel emphases upon individual responsibility and self-purgation. Here I want to bring the poets closer, into the painful area of the anxiety of influence, the terrible melancholy for the later prophet of sustained comparison with the precursor, who died still in the realm of loss, but in absolute assurance of his prophetic call, an assurance Blake suffered to approximate, in an isolation that even Ezekiel might not have borne. For Ezekiel is sent to the house of Israel, stiffened in heart and rebellious against their God, yet still a house accustomed to prophecy. God made Ezekiel as hard as adamant, the *shamir* or diamond-point of the engraver, and that was scarcely hard enough; Blake knew he had to be even harder, as he wielded his engraver's tool.

Harold Bloom
The Ringers in the Tower: Studies in Romantic Tradition (Chicago: Univ. Chicago Pr., 1971), p. 66

With "The Progress of Poesy" . . . Blake seemed to feel that Gray had assumed the dishonorable role of Virgil to a corrupt Augustus, so that while, as before, certain of Gray's poetic insights emerge as true and richly suggestive, the argument of the poem taken as a whole is degrading to the poet and destructive of his muse-seeing "infant eyes." That those eyes were not permanently blurred or destroyed "The Bard" stands as powerful evidence, for there poetic prophecy addresses itself fearlessly to kingship. Yet the "Ode for Music" and, for other reasons, the "Epitaph on Mrs. Clarke" and the "Elegy Written in a Country Churchyard" betrayed (to Blake) how fallible Gray could be in his role as poet of vision.

In his illustrations to "The Bard" Blake allowed certain of his own developing mythological elements to entangle themselves with Gray's, drawing together sometimes contradictory lines of association: chief of these are the glimpses of the dead bards as ancient Britons (later described by Blake as "naked civilized men, learned, studious . . . wiser than after-ages") and at the same time as a trio of vindictive and punishing furies.

There are, to be sure, suggestions of both prophecy and vengeance in Gray's portrayal of the bards, and in another mood Blake might have found it important to separate the two in the name of eternal salvation. But I suspect that Blake's mood was influenced in part by the conditions of the time, and that he was willing to let such contradictions pass—and indeed to build on them in his designs—in his greater eagerness to display the necessity and potential power of bardic denunciation of a government founded on war and the persecution of poets. It has always been true, he maintained, that "Art Degraded, Imagination Denied, War Governed the Nations," and while Gray doubtless intended no radicalism, still his poem does present a vision of poetic power in the face of bloody suppression, of the final victory of art and imagination over a government that degraded and denied them, and ruled by war.

Irene Tayler
Blake's Illustrations to the Poems of Gray (Princeton, N. J.: Princeton Univ. Pr., 1971), p. 157

Our understanding of Blake, especially in his late work, is still so encrusted with defining analogies to the impulses and traditions of mysticism that it is necessary to emphasize that for him imagination is a matter of perceptions and representations. Indeed, he suggests that forms of mental process descend in validity as they forsake material particularity for the opposite pole of mystery. The sensed phenomenon and its abstraction are equally landscapes in which we live and act, and to try to work apart from the images, like the mortification of the body, is a retreat into the darkness of the cavern.

It follows that Blake is not interested in any God, paradise, or fulfillment which is unavailable to the immediate experience of the body. The withdrawal from direct perception as a trusted mode of cognition—the path carved out for us by Plato, Paul, and Descartes—produces a fatal gap between the real and the perceived, as does the empirical subordination of sensory detail to mental pattern; and when what we take to be ultimate reality is removed from the world of appearances, so too is paradise, which is the state of our complete involvement in that reality. In *The Marriage of Heaven and Hell*, Blake describes the retreat of the gods to the sky, the disappearance of the sense of divine humanity from the things around us, and our subsequent style of worshipping realities that transcend our present experience (11, E37). His suggestion is, further, that the distance between paradise and our senses is simultaneous with that between involuntary impression and conscious recognition. The cognition spoken of in the following marginal comment to Berkeley's *Siris* is a kind that, when it comes, bursts apart the world of our customary experience. . . . The feeling in Blake, as in Wordsworth, Coleridge, Shelley, and Keats after him, is that our present experience can be made whole only by putting an end to the compartmentalization of our awareness into unrelated, and often conflicting, modes of knowing; and, like the later poets, Blake finds that for such wholeness, a visionary knowledge and experience—one in which the distance between the subject and the object disappears—must be sought through the body and the senses. Eden will come about, Blake tells us, through "an improvement of sensual enjoyment" (M.H.H.: 14, E38).

Thomas R. Frosch
The Awakening of Albion: The Renovation of the Body in the Poetry of William Blake (Ithaca, N.Y.: Cornell Univ. Pr., 1973), pp. 26–28

One might have expected that the publication of G. E. Bentley, Jr.,'s monumental Clarendon edition of *Vala; or, The Four Zoas* in 1963 would stimulate a tradition of commentary on the drawings. In fact, however, with the partial exception of one design . . . nothing like this has developed.

Bentley's data-filled chapter on the drawings raises a number of interesting questions and makes some valid interpretational points; but there are a number of errors in the data, and some major premises of his argument are too confidently and uncritically employed, at times after having been introduced in a tentative way. An example of this is the assumption that the emphasis in Blake's pictorial art generally changed from illustration, in which pictures correspond to a text, to illumination, in which no such correspondence is evident. Something like this development has been claimed by other critics as well, but in fact it is not clear that the percentage of such correspondence is much less in the case of the late *Jerusalem* than the early *Marriage of Heaven and Hell*. Even if in general Blake's art actually progressed in the direction alleged, this would not provide a valid basis for making inferences applicable to any particular page in the *Vala* manuscript. In the first place, at any point in his career Blake was capable of aligning text and pictures on either nearby or considerably separated pages. Moreover, the fact that a picture in *Vala* has been altered tells nothing of when the alteration was done. Blake might in the space of a day or two have tried out several versions of a picture; thus the amount of ascertainable connection between any text—any *surviving* text, we must constantly recall, in this much-altered manuscript—and any version of the picture is much more likely to have an intellectual or aesthetic cause than to be the result of a Blakean stylistic or organizational predilection.

John E. Grant
in *Blake's Sublime Allegory: Essays on "The Four Zoas," "Milton," "Jerusalem"*, ed. Stuart Curran and Joseph Anthony Wittreich, Jr. (Madison: Univ. Wisconsin Pr., 1973), pp. 141–42

Let me say bluntly that I am not grateful to Yeats for inaugurating the kind of Blake research of which Miss Kathleen Raine is the recognized high-priestess in our time. Blind to Blake's genius, it generates blindness, and perpetuates a cult that, whatever it serves, doesn't serve Blake or humanity. The notion that by a devout study of Blake's symbolism a key can be found that will open to us a supreme esoteric wisdom is absurd; and to emphasize in that spirit the part played in his life's work by Swedenborg, Boehme, Paracelsus, Orphic tradition, Gnosticism, and a "perennial philosophy" is to deny what makes him important. . . .

It was in this combined clarity and intensity of conviction that the sense of human responsibility he so signally represents was manifested. There is no paradox here—or in what follows: it is a question of giving the due force to the phrase "human responsibility." The conviction was a creative drive, and it led him, in his most ambitious attempts, the major prophecies, into difficulties that defeated his art. He takes up in them a challenge so formidably presented in the totality of *Songs of Innocence and of Experience*. He commits himself to what it is customary to describe, with a good deal of reason, as epic treatment, although Shakespeare counts for essentially more in it than Milton does: it is not merely the verse that is positively un-Miltonic. . . .

Blake's reaction against Newton and Locke represents the really momentous new development associated with the complex spiritual and cultural eruption that we call the Romantic Revolution—eruption of ideas, impulsions, and intransigently conscious human needs. His compellingly presented conception of an ultimate human responsibility that, while the reverse of hubristic, manifests itself in human self-reliance—bold, yet deferential towards the life whose source is not to be possessed (though we may cut ourselves off from it and perish)—recommends itself peculiarly to our needs at this crisis of human history.

F. R. Leavis
in *William Blake: Essays in Honour of Sir Geoffrey Keynes*, ed. Morton D. Paley and Michael Phillips (Oxford: Clarendon, 1973), pp. 80–81, 83

Newton's increasing appearance by name in Blake's epics is . . . perhaps the least significant evidence of Blake's concern with Newton's system as a vital threat to the Human Imagination. The development of Blake's thought from his concept of "Urizen" as an adequate projection of the Newtonian world-view through his displacement of Newtonian features throughout his mythic universe—in the several Spectres, the Sons and Daughters of Albion, the Shadowy Female, and the consolidated form of Satan (the Newtonian "Reactor")—is symptomatic of his continual attempt to solve, among others, the particular complex of problems which center in the imaginative appeal of Newton's system. Many central components of Blake's poetry reveal his struggle to exorcise the consolidating forms of anti-imaginative forces from his own imagination. . . .

In the intricate labyrinths of Blake's developing myth we continually find many striking parallels to complex tensions embedded in Newton's own system. As we have seen, significant crises in Blake's poetic struggle, such as the development of his doctrines of Limits, States, pulsational time, variable ratios, measurement, expanded sense perception and the Vortex, the problem of the mathematical usurpation of time, as well as the peculiar "hermaphroditic" unions and divisions that take place in Blake's poetry, bear much more than terminological, imagistic, or conceptual connections to Newton's own system. What I have been arguing throughout is that *structural* parallels between crisis of vision in both Newton and Blake penetrate quite deeply to their similar motives as intellectual problem-solvers. Further, I feel it is no more than fair to insist not only that these parallels are illuminating and instructive of tensions in Blake's and Newton's intellectual constructions but also that from his own point of view Blake would not be surprised to find such parallels obtaining. In fact, Blake came to recognize the structure of Newton's system as so central to his own power as a poet to reveal Satan in his secret identity, "in his System," that in his final vision he construes the intellectual structure of Newton's system as a consolidation of the elements of normal perception which attempt to substitute for and fulfill the true drives of the imagination.

Donald D. Ault
Visionary Physics: Blake's Responses to Newton (Chicago: Univ. Chicago Pr., 1974), pp. 161–63

To the question often raised, whether Blake considered his poems or his designs the more important, the best answer is drawn from his comment to Dawson Turner (who wanted the pictures "without the Writing") that printing the pictures alone meant "the Loss of some of the best things," that the pictures "when Printed perfect accompany Poetical Personifications & Acts, without which Poems they never could have been Executed" (Blake to Turner, June 9, 1818). And certainly the poems can stand alone, while many of the pictures cannot. Yet the poet's work is not perfectly "done" until that moment when the reader, travelling the line of text, becomes a spectator, seeing at one pulse beat the "single visualizable picture" (these words are Northrop Frye's) and then, between that and the next pulsation, leaving these mortal things, text and picture, to enter into Noah's rainbow, into "the eternal world that ever groweth" (these are the words of the Fairy who dictated *Europe*): "then he would be happy." . . .

It has become customary among students of Blake's pictures to suppose that very many of them do not directly concern the text, since we have never possessed an even rudimentary reading of them all—a lack which it is one purpose of this book to remedy. The larger pictures, it is true, have become increasingly familiar, at least on the simple story level of the postures and interaction of the Zoas. Yet the mulitudinous but minute, even microscopic, animals and vegetations, or banners, scrolls, tendrils, even delete signs and snails and spiders, have been so overshadowed by the large pictures—or so difficult to associate with the text in any concreteness even when made out—that they have seemed even to our finest scholars little more at times than "irritating forms of punctuation." . . . We may be sure that Blake used an engraver's magnifying glass when drawing some of his minutiae—consider the tininess of the bird in its nest in *Jerusalem* 3. Spectators are well advised to use one for the marginal pictures in *Milton*, the interlinear population of *America*, and the marginal wraiths illuminating "The Keys to the Gates." . . .

David V. Erdman
The Illuminated Blake: All of William Blake's Illuminated Works with a Plate-by-Plate Commentary (Garden City, N.Y.: Doubleday, 1974), pp. 10, 13

What we should talk about . . . is how Blake expanded upon the whole tradition of Milton illustration, how, even when his designs abandon established iconography, they continue to have important conceptual ties with the tradition of which they are a part. This premise involves the rejection of a more common one, which would have us believe that Blake knew very little, that he created *ex nihilo*. The more popular thesis may have the weight of critical tradition on its side, but there is evidence to the contrary provided by Blake's art, which shows that he possessed an impressive knowledge of the arts—of painting, illustration, and engraving—and subdued their traditions to his own purposes. . . .

The version of Blake's idea of Milton that Harold Bloom asks us to accept is different from the one presented here. Originally under Milton's sway, Blake wrote *The Four Zoas* "in the formal shadow of *Paradise Lost*, and *Milton* less darkly in the shadow of Job and *Paradise Regained*"; but in *Jerusalem*, Blake bursts beyond the tyrannies with which Milton afflicted him, going "at last for prophetic structure to a prophet, to the priestly orator, Ezekiel, whose situation and sorrow most closely resembled his own." Blake "followed Milton, to the line of prophecy," Bloom allows; but he finally casts off the counterfeit Milton for the authentic Ezekiel, crossing over, in the process, "from the theatre of mind to the orator's theatre of action." It is not possible to find a formulation that more boldly defies the delineation of Blake's Milton advanced in this book; but Bloom's formulation also defies the fundamental attitudes toward Milton that can be gleaned from Blake's portrayals of Milton and illustrations for his poetry, not to mention Blake's own writings.

Joseph Anthony Wittreich, Jr.
Angel of Apocalypse: Blake's Idea of Milton (Madison: Univ. Wisconsin Pr., 1975), pp. 4–5, 247–48

A critical tradition of some length and dignity has treated Blake as a symbolist, first with the proviso that he had to invent his own symbols, later with the argument that his symbols were archetypal, whether of Jungian or fundamentally literary shape. Along with this appellation, Yeats's phrase describing Blake as a "too literal realist of the imagination" has tended to stick. But Yeats's phrase has such variable meaning that unless carefully applied it obfuscates or misleads. Though he may be regarded at some very high level of abstraction as belonging to the same tradition as Baudelaire's, Blake is not a symbolist at all in the obvious sense implied by the famous sonnet "Correspondances," and his techniques have little in common with Mallarmé's or with those of any of the poets discussed by Arthur Symons in one of the first studies of the symbolists. Yet Blake may be treated as a more complete symbolist than those who have gone under the "symboliste" banner, if one means by symbolist a poet who regards literature as a "symbolic form" of experience, in the sense that has become common since [Ernst] Cassirer. The view of Blake's work as more complete in its implications for critical theory than that of any poet generally regarded as symbolist has not been asserted, though implied in Northrop Frye's pioneering *Fearful Symmetry* and exploited in Frye's own subsequent theoretical work. . . . He has had a germinal influence on the theories of numerous modern writers and made the most complete utterance of a philosophy of literary symbolism in his time. I shall see Blake as providing a transition from purely neoclassical English views of language to those developing in the later nineteenth and earlier twentieth centuries. . . .

Blake's view suggests that we create symbolic worlds, and that these are for all practical purposes the only worlds we have. What we have made them makes us what we are. We can only make a world with a language, indeed *in* a language. There is nothing imaginable independent of a medium to imagine *in*. Our languages constantly die into use and must be reborn. Further, each language has its own limits and requires its opposite. Blake's vision of language was that myth precedes science and reason, that the latter feeds on the former. But he also believed that in his time the devourer's language had so dominated reality in the form of "Single vision & Newton's sleep" that civilization itself was in danger unless the contrary mythic language of poetry and art rose to the challenge of spiritual warfare.

Hazard Adams
Blake Studies, 7, 2 (1975), pp. 143–44, 168

GEORGE NOEL GORDON, LORD BYRON

1788–1824

Bryon's "coherence," as a whole, becomes realized in the definition of his various, metahistorical character; the coherence of his individual works, on the other hand, depends upon *poiesis*, the symbolic organization of immediate and dramatic materials. A work like *Childe Harold's Pilgrimage* illustrates both of these facts about Byron's poetry, for on the one hand it contains the story (or at least *a* story) of his metahistory, and on the other it presents that metahistory in a dramatic and symbolic form. Byron-the-narrator tells his own story and in the process not only discovers what his life means, but finds that its meaning proliferates and develops as the story continues. The poem is a journal that eventuates in an autobiography, for the overall coherence that the latter form pretends to and that the former (at least by intention) does not, becomes realized in the total work within the narrator's own act of self-discovery. *Our* experience of the work involves the perception of this self-dramatization and self-discovery in the narrating poet, whose purpose in writing is "to create" himself—"and in creating live/A being more intense." . . .

In *Childe Harold's Pilgrimage* it is through Harold that we come to know Byron's crooked man, and it is by fostering the Harold elements in himself that the narrating poet exposes the twistedness that marks all life. In Mother Goose the story concludes:

> And they all lived together
> In a little crooked house.

Which is approximately the moral of *Childe Harold's Pilgrimage*. If the crookedness at the root of life cannot be removed, it can be made straight in the attitude of the artist's imagination. *Childe Harold's Pilgrimage* takes its evil a good deal more seriously than does the Mother Goose poem, however, and this difference is well defined in a passage from Auden's eulogy for W. B. Yeats. The lines might as well have been applied to Byron, another of Auden's favorite poets.

> Sing of human unsuccess
> In a rapture of distress;
> In the deserts of the heart
> Let the healing fountain start.

Perhaps Auden was thinking as much of Byron as he was of Yeats anyway, for the last two lines distinctly echo a famous verse in Byron's "Stanzas to Augusta": "In the Desert a fountain is springing."

Jerome J. McGann
Fiery Dust: Byron's Poetic Development (Chicago: Univ. Chicago Pr., 1968), pp. 66, 93

To study the apparent confusions of imagery and structure in [Byron's] work, and the apparent rootlessness of his attitudes toward characters, actions, and ideas is to see them as strategies, as means to a comprehensive end which, paradoxically perhaps, exchanges the hieratic finality of "I affirm" for the profane unpredictability of "I would affirm." Hence what one may call the imagery of contradiction in *Don Juan*, "Mazeppa," and *Childe Harold* III–IV. . . .

Byron's skepticism has its limits too, and not merely in terms of his being "awed by his own audacity" and refusing to face directly the full implications of his thought ([Edward Everett] Bostetter). Something more affirmative appears in his work at least as early as *Lara* (II.X); and, occurring later in the very heart of his idio-satirical and heroic works, contrasts with and potentially redefines their dominant temper. This is a third, viable option in Byron's thought, the peculiar form of humanism and stoicism that may be called counter-heroic. It rebukes the desperate activity of the heroic no less than the desperate passivity of the idio-satirical, by virtue of its austere sense of responsibility to be principled and humane in action, to acknowledge without collapse the normal perplexities and corruptions of existence, to profit and be honored by the opportunity of confronting the self and the universe through suffering. Significantly it does not arise to meet ordinary threats to the perennial values of society, threats such as mercenariness, hypocrisy, folly, cruelty, and ambitious envy. These failings, identified as such and referred to confessed standards of conduct and belief, become objects of ridicule and scorn. But what are the confessed standards of the idio-satirical or of heroicism? Counter-heroic humanism opposes a state of emotion or passion which has been unnaturally enlarged and which therefore attains power, a virtual authority, usurping or redefining the area of value. It veritably recreates, and does not in the manner of conventional satire restore (as a painting) the terms of value. Its typical bête noire, then, would be Glory, or war, or any form of political egotism. And a typical though not necessary instrument for it would be satire.

Michael G. Cooke
The Blind Man Traces the Circle: On the Patterns and Philosophy of Byron's Poetry (Princeton, N.J.: Princeton Univ. Pr., 1969), pp. 100, 181–82

More than one literary historian has wondered how Byron planned to clean away the corruption of public taste and reform the excesses of the contemporary theatre by writing plays that he declared were never designed for performance and that could be truly appreciated only by remote posterity. In the Preface to [*Marino*] *Faliero* Byron stated, "I have had no view to the stage; in its present state it is, perhaps, not a very exalted object of ambition." This he affirmed emphatically in the Preface to his next volume of three plays: "In publishing the following Tragedies, I have only to repeat, that they were not composed with the most remote view to the stage." In his correspondence he repeatedly insisted that his plays were for a "mental theatre," and that the kind of drama he was trying to write was as opposite to the English theatrical tradition "as one thing can be to another." "They might as well act the Prometheus of Aeschylus" as perform *Faliero*. . . .

Just as popular taste and current fashion had challenged Byron to make a dramatic innovation and to defend and describe it, so his susceptibility to public opinion chilled his enthusiasm for playwriting and caused him to abandon it as a serious enterprise. Byron's reaction to his public had always been a mixture of concern and indifference. He would declare that he never coveted fame, that, except for the tales, none of his work was in a popular style, that he would have his say in spite of public disfavor, and that posterity would appreciate the merit of his plays. On the other hand, while he was writing the third act of *The Two Foscari* he wanted to know what the response to *Marino Faliero* had been. . . . When he read the cold reviews of *Faliero*, he was discouraged and felt even more depressed about the hostile reception of the later volume of three plays. Thereafter he ceased to wage a theoretical campaign in his letters.

Truman Guy Steffan
Lord Byron's "Cain": Twelve Essays and a Text with Variants and Annotations (Austin: Univ. Texas Pr., 1969), pp. 23–25

Shelley and Byron lived by extremely different moral and intellectual principles, but Shelley could appreciate within the antiromanticism of *Don Juan* a humanitarianism which gives positive direction to the burlesque assault upon sentiment and solemnity and cruelty. What he approved of as "wholly new" was what we should call a new kind of romanticism, freed of anticlassical excesses, returning from the mountains and lakes to the "stove of society" and reducing all the rituals of civilization and the postures of individuals to risible absurdity, and yet quietly asserting an immense hope for individuals and nations. The modern criticism which reads *Don Juan* as completely reductive, as "spoiling" everything with its facetiousness, is the expression of a much later and more thoroughgoing cynicism, not romantic but existential.

In these comic cantos Byron has outgrown the Byronic hero; instead of looking at his faces in a mirror he looks out upon the contemporary world which is yet the world of his origin, the world that cannot and yet still does survive, in order to observe how one does, in reality, live in such a world; the "need of fatality" turns into a recognition of (improbable) necessity. What Byron intended to do with the nominal hero, the youthful Juan, was something of a joke, but a true historical one. After a rake's progress through the Mediterranean, continental, and English centers of the prerevolutionary world of Byron's infancy Juan was to make his gesture of allegiance to the new world in revolutionary Paris, only to end at the guillotine. It would be a comic variant of the destiny of every one of Byron's radical aristocrats. Freedom ne'er should want an heir—but was notoriously profligate of her sons.

An art thus based on historical reality suited a poet who valued "actions" above rhymes and considered poetry only a "next best" occupation for times when "we cannot contribute to make mankind more free and wise" by participation in "more serious affairs." From 1818 to the end of his life he kept *Don Juan* going for entertainment, for his comment on freedom and wisdom and all the magnanimous humor of his conversation and correspondence. More earnestly he could still write a "Prophecy of Dante" (1819) defining poetry in Promethean terms. But he kept a bid in for participation in more serious affairs as they might develop in Italy, in England and in Greece.

David V. Erdman
in *Shelley and His Circle*, Vol. III, ed. Kenneth Neill Cameron
(Cambridge, Mass.: Harvard Univ. Pr., 1970), pp. 317–18

"How the devil should I write about *Jerusalem*, never having yet been there?" quipped Byron in 1816. He found no irony in his having written about Jerusalem only the year before in the Hebrew Melodies. Childe Harold had not journeyed to the Temple; nor had Byron embraced the religion of the Jews. The Hebrew Melodies are not a collection of hymns or psalms brimming with the faith of the Old Testament. They are merely thirty poems Byron wrote at various times during 1814 and 1815 and then gave to Isaac Nathan (or intended to do so), who in turn set them to music. But it is just this fact that binds the poems together, for they share in the essential unity of Byron's lyric corpus. In their own peculiar way, they almost seem to be a later edition of Byron's *Hours of Idleness*, his best-known collection of lyrics. The seemingly biblical poems are *Byronic*. We can best perceive their unity by comparing the poems with the entire body of lyric poetry Byron wrote before 1816.

The themes and postures of the Hebrew Melodies at first seem nothing more than varying restatements of thoughts expressed in many of Byron's earlier lyrics (and in the first two cantos of *Childe Harold*). But the comparison reveals differences as well. The Hebrew Melodies share to some extent a community of biblical subject; they have been influenced by the conventions of the national-melodies genre; and they are in the main dramatic lyrics. As we shall see, because of these differences, in the Hebrew Melodies, more so than in the earlier lyrics, we are made to experience and to understand the romantic myth of sympathy that the Byron of 1815 wished to articulate. With this in mind, we can say that generally the Hebrew Melodies differ in kind, because they differ in degree. Their variety is the variety of Byron's early collections and of the lyrics published with his longer poems. Anyone attempting to classify the poems must recognize these facts. Joseph Slater finds that "nine of the poems are Biblical in subject but Byronic in treatment; two are love songs; five are reflective lyrics, neither Jewish nor Christian; and five are expressions of what might be called proto-Zionism" (nine are unaccounted for). We should not be surprised, for Byron's *Poems on Various Occasions* were not much different.

Thomas L. Ashton
Byron's Hebrew Melodies (Austin: Univ. Texas Pr., 1972),
pp. 65–66

"I am not a cautious letter-writer and generally say what comes uppermost at the moment," Byron wrote on November 14, 1822, in an unpublished letter probably addressed to Mary Shelley. That in part is why his letters are such a clear mirror of his personality, of its weaknesses as well as its strengths, and why they reflect more accurately than any of the records left by his contemporaries the brilliance and charm and wit of his conversation, universally acknowledged to be extraordinary by those who knew him. Medwin's and Lady Blessington's accounts of his conversation, revealing as they are of the substance of his attitudes and prejudices, fall short of giving the true flavour and piquancy of his frankest letters. And Iris Origo says aptly of Teresa Guiccioli's recollections of his spoken words: ". . . she has no ear for any style but her own. It is possible that Byron's meaning is what she conveys; it is hardly possible that that is how he expressed it!" In the end he must be his own Boswell, and in large measure he succeeds better than Boswell himself (the Boswell of the journals) in exposing the many facets of an engaging egoist, a romantic with a balance of common sense which always brings him back to earth and to an honest recognition of his own frailties and limitations.

It is true that one side of Byron—and an important one—is seen in only occasional glimpses in the letters. There is little of Childe Harold or Manfred. That tortured spirit found expression in his poetry, always the safety valve of his deepest feelings. The letters do run the gamut of his emotions and moods, but always with a lighter touch. If one compares some of the letters he was writing from Italy at the same time that he was composing the last act of *Manfred* and the fourth canto of *Childe Harold*, one will see how successfully Byron could shut off one side of his divided self from the other. In the end we need both the poetry and the letters to see the whole Byron.

Leslie A. Marchand
Introd., in *Byron's Letters and Journals*, Vol. I (Cambridge, Mass.: Harvard Univ. Pr., 1973), p. 1

Don Juan . . . when taken with *Beppo* and *The Vision of Judgment* (which could be absorbed into the scheme of the main effort), stands as a remarkable achievement: (1) it creates one of the few new directions in English poetry since the Renaissance, not for its stanza form but for its use of the character of the *persona* and tone rather than narrative or theme as unifying principle in a major literary work; (2) *Don Juan*, though sometimes called an anti-epic, is a true epic in a new mode, markedly unlike even its Italian predecessors in its choice of hero and in its emphasis on love, humanity, tolerance, and honesty, rather than traditional moral virtues of obedience to abstractions like heroism and patriotism or to the wills of capricious gods. . . . Now, with the perspective of a century and a half, we can see that *Don Juan* fulfills Shelley's descriptions of the epic in *A Defence of Poetry*. . . .

Byron's poetry drew upon the fundamental values of the Judeo-Christian tradition, blended with them a skeptical tolerance for diversity that derives from the highest ideals of Classical civilization, and concentrated his study on the behavior of men both alone and in society. *Don Juan* incorporates all the central themes of later Western literature, and it does so more pertinently than does any other work written by one author under a single title. Goethe's *Faust* is at once too intellectual and too aristocratic in its perspective; Byron, though beginning with *hidalgos* and treating aristocrats of all nations, deals primarily with elemental human emotions and attitudes. His hero is modern Everyman, whose quest takes him not to an ideal Helena through supernatural agency, but to a foreign social context by a series of accidents. Tolstoy's *War and Peace* says nothing about human life that is not clearly stated in *Don Juan*. Browning's multiplicity of possible viewpoints, Eliot's vision of a spiritual *Waste Land*, Stevens's identification of the human imagination as the author of the Supreme Fiction, Henry James's exploitation of manners as signs of morals, and even Kierkegaard's outcry against smug conventionality in religious observance are all woven integrally into the texture of Byron's poem. Only the exclusive visions of extreme beatitude (like *Epipsychidion* or *Four Quartets*) or unremitting horror (dozens of twentieth-century works) lie outside its boundaries. For *Don Juan* is both a social and a positive poem, as it must be to bridge the stream of time between the Enlightenment and the modern world.

Donald H. Reiman
in *Byron on the Continent: A Memorial Exhibition, 1824–1974*
(New York: Carl H. Pforzheimer Library and New York Public Library, 1974), pp. 48–50

Byron is, with Wordsworth, one of our two great topical poets—in the sense of "regional," sinking roots into a *topos*. Wordsworth's topos is a narrow one, the Lake District, and this limits his appeal to the European reader. Byron's is a very broad one, the whole of Europe and the Mediterranean world, and this makes him strange to the English reader. Mosques, temples, bazaars, dervishes, pashas, deserts, wadis, don't go down very easily to a palate accustomed to clergymen, farmers, public-houses, markets, churches and cottages. So that Byron has never seemed quite real to an English audience, though his work was very real to himself and to his Mediterranean readers. As we come closer to Europe in what remains of this century we shall probably come closer to Byron. . . .

We shall never understand Byron's "Nature poetry" if we attempt to approach it through the fixities and definites of the Wordsworthian schema, or via Coleridge's symbolic universe of God speaking to man through a physical cryptogram. Byron's Nature is endlessly fluid . . . a theatre of exchange among a variety of planes. The snowflake is an ethereal visitant, a heavenly star or flower descending on the barren but heroic surface of the rock. It would appear to have little contact with "the fury and the mire of human veins." But it is the point of Byron's inclusive vision, here in a nuclear and later in a wealth of expanded forms, to link up the human and the natural-divine not in a metaphysical synthesis, like Wordsworth's, but in a working family relationship. . . . In Blake's phrase, "For the human family we live," and the human includes the natural and the divine. This is Byron's major theme of reciprocity, of self-giving, of sacrificial death and resurrection. It suffuses *Childe Harold*: with its opposite, assertion of the selfhood against the communal good, it forms the dramatic agon of the Turkish Tales. Nor, even in these projections of human passion, is the snowflake, now in the form of the wild flower springing from the barren rock, forgotten. . . .

Bernard Blackstone
Byron: A Survey (London: Longman, 1975), pp. xi, 18–19

Byron's sense of wonder is for the extent of the world's variety, which represents an "Order" beyond our desire or imaginings. In *Don Juan*, Byron makes a great virtue of not comprehending the world in a unified, integrative, or closed system. By giving in completely to the surprises of his life, by emphasizing that, even in retrospect, one appreciates and can respond to more than the achieved order of events, Byron in fact opens his mind not merely to further experiences as such, but to further, possibly altogether different, experiences of order. Byron's world is not a system; it is a network of systems and orders, some of which may overlap in some ways, some of which do not. . . .

Coleridge postulates exactly what *Don Juan* refuses to postulate. According to Coleridge, the purpose of a narrative is to convert a series into a whole. But Byron meant to sail directly into that wind, and to say, as it were: the purpose of this narrative is to convert the whole (i.e., the human world) into a series. Everything that is the case is taken for granted, not in the order of form, but in the form of experience. . . .

The notorious lack of form in *Don Juan*, then, is in one respect a repeated attempt to draw distinctions. Byron wants to show what things are by placing them in contexts where differences are brought out by making the parts stand free and clear of each other. Meanings and observations are literally particularized; separations act to clarify the reality of context, of things standing in relation to other things. Finally, as items are moved along a narrative line, the complex but determining importance of context for understanding any thing, or act, or person, is raised to a critical perspective. The consequence of this procedure—this refusal to allow free particulars to fall back into some conceptual or idealized unity—is not only to train the eye, and mind, into careful perspicuity of particulars and their particular significance but to impress upon the mind the precise nature of context: that it is a functional reality, always present and comprehending particulars, that it is a real Idea, actual Form.

Jerome J. McGann
"Don Juan" in Context (Chicago: Univ. Chicago Pr., 1976),
pp. 103, 109, 114

However valuable these mutual allusions and borrowings may be in demonstrating the influences Byron and Shelley provided for the "form" of each other's poetry, their antagonistic philosophies and the record of this antagonism in their poetry written from 1816 through 1823 provide the more important evidence for a study of the interaction of their "two spirits." Shelley's *Julian and Maddalo* (1818–19) may be the only major poem that explicitly juxtaposes the melioristic Shelleyan and the fatalistic Byronic spirits, but after 1816 the two poets frequently used their major works to debate their philosophical differences. Their opposition may be traced not only in their lyrical poetry, in which each poet imaginatively objectified his personal hopes and fears, but also in their narrative and dramatic works, in which the "fictionalized" heroes directly reflect each poet's self-consciousness or his artistic struggle "to idealize and to unify" his imaginative prehension of the human condition. This does not mean that Byron is in every respect Manfred or that Shelley is Prometheus, but it does mean that as imaginatively constructed perceptions of the real world that does or should exist, *Manfred* and *Prometheus Unbound* distinguish Byron's and Shelley's philosophies. If, as John Buxton regrets, we can never listen to Byron and Shelley "talking," we can at least experience the two poets' dialogue in their poetry.

Charles E. Robinson
Shelley and Byron: The Snake and the Eagle Wreathed in Fight
(Baltimore: Johns Hopkins Univ Pr., 1976), p. 5

JOHN CLARE

1793–1864

John Clare, born July 13 in Helpston, was a farm laborer and a poet. His first volume of poetry, *Poems Descriptive of Rural Life and Scenery* (1820), was received enthusiastically, resulting in three editions in its first year. Although Clare brought out subsequent volumes of poetry, including *The Village Minstrel* (1821), *The Shepherd's Calendar* (1827), and *The Rural Muse* (1835), his fame rather quickly subsided. Afflicted by spells of insanity, beginning in 1823, Clare was confined from 1837 until the end of his life to asylums. There, during periods of lucidity, he continued to write poetry. He died on May 20, 1864.

J. W. Tibble, ed., *Poems of John Clare* (1935)

J. W. and A. Tibble, eds., *Prose Works* (1951)

J. W. and A. Tibble, *Clare: His Life and Poetry* (1956)

It is true, as [John] Middleton Murry says it is, that Clare's vision does not ever "pass beyond itself," or at least it never did so successfully until the asylum-poems; it is true, too (and very well said), that we feel that this vision can leave "no margin for other faculties." At the same time we should be wary of the assumptions behind criticism of this kind; and particularly the assumption that for a descriptive poem to have content, it must pass beyond itself, into meditation or whatever. The poems of Wordsworth and of Keats, against whom Clare is here being measured, do obviously pass beyond themselves in this way; and although we are right to admire the "organic unity" in their poems, the way in which image and idea coalesce, it is nevertheless true that there is always some part of their content which is separable from the images that have given rise to it. . . . But if the description does not lead us to the more abstract content of the poem, then for Murry, and for Keats and no doubt for all of Clare's contemporaries, the description was either superfluous, or the poem somehow *purely* descriptive in a way that precluded its having *real* content.

But Clare's purely descriptive poems do have content, I want to suggest, which, although it is hardly at all separable from the description in which it inheres, is nevertheless perhaps evidence that Clare "thought about" what he saw—if it is thus that content arises. The content of "Winter Fields" is precisely the accuracy of the description, the richness and the completeness of it, understood in this particular way, that it is a body of knowledge, a set of details, that Clare has arrived at in this particular place, and not elsewhere. The content of the poem thus becomes the sense of place that the imagery and the language (and I shall argue later the syntax) together express, though they can none of them fully express it without the others. The sense of place that the poem expresses is that "*this* is how it is *here*"; and the poem thus contributes to the content that the larger part of Clare's poetry seeks to express, the particular individuality of Helpston.

John Barrell
The Idea of Landscape and the Sense of Place 1730–1840: An Approach to the Poetry of John Clare (Cambridge: Cambridge Univ. Pr., 1972), pp. 130–31

We can profitably turn to Clare's *Shepherd's Calendar*, and see the revolution he is beginning, perhaps unconsciously, to effect. Gone are the echoes of style caught from Thomson and Cowper; gone are the moralistic episodes, the illustrations of Divine Immanence. Even poverty is not held up as a thing to be looked at and pitied from a distance. The truth to nature that so many of his predecessors talked vaguely about, is here seen, not only in clarity and variety of detail, but in the economy of the style, the energy and movement that had been denied to them. Clare does not preach; nor, on the other hand, does he simply regurgitate the vignettes and genre-sketches that abound elsewhere. Clare achieves here, for the first time in a long poem, a plangent tone of regret untinged by sentimentality, a poem on country life that is neither didactic nor moralistic. For many, it was precisely the tone of moral reflection that appealed to them in his early work. In the context of the literary tradition it is remarkable that Clare could write a poem on country life so free from the trammels of current expectations. . . .

It is Clare's directness of language which most immediately and noticeably marks him off from his predecessors. It would be true to say that no other poet of the eighteenth or nineteenth centuries wrote as Clare did: absorbing the influence of such writers as Thomson and Milton, Pope and Cowper, Keats and Collins, the numerous Elizabethan writers he admired, he evolved a style that was completely individual, true to his own needs and intentions. If we can appreciate the merits of this style, in its broadest sense, we shall be able to see what it is that makes Clare of particular interest, in what way he is distinguished from other writers in this apparently limited genre. We shall see also, perhaps, that the genre is less limited than it appeared.

Mark Storey
The Poetry of John Clare: A Critical Introduction (New York: St. Martin's, 1974), pp. 84–85

SAMUEL TAYLOR COLERIDGE

1772–1834

Kathleen Coburn and Bart Winer, eds. *The Collected Works of Samuel Taylor Coleridge* (1969ff.)

However distressing his years from thirty to forty-three, Coleridge emerges from them and from the next three years at Highgate as at least one of the half-dozen greatest critical interpreters in the history of literature. Reservations based on the incompleteness of his work or his use of the insights of other men have had no serious effect. If he is vulnerable in ways that most critics are not, he transcends them in other, more important respects; and if he exposes himself more, it is partly because he attempts more.

His resources—intellectual, imaginative, emotional—were enormous. What makes him almost unique is the active union of qualities usually found only separately or in smaller combination. To begin with, in philosophic profundity he excels every other English critic. For anything really comparable we are forced to turn almost exclusively to the seminal reinterpretation of literature and art begun in late eighteenth-century Germany, to which, like Coleridge, we ourselves owe so much but to which—again like Coleridge—we are forgetful or cavalier about acknowledging our debts. At the same time Coleridge possesses what is so rare in the general theorist of art: the close practical grasp of form and style, the direct perception of the thing as it appears in the concrete, for which English empirical criticism, whatever its theoretical weaknesses, is unrivalled. He is one of the foremost in the long line of English poet-critics for which no other literature offers a counterpart, and which extends from Sir Philip Sidney through Ben Jonson, Dryden, Addison, Johnson, Wordsworth, Shelley, and Arnold, to Eliot. And the point to be stressed is that these two ordinarily diverse interests or gifts not only reinforce and extend each other but together form something greater than the mere sum of the parts—something different (to use one of Coleridge's favorite distinctions) in "kind" as well as "degree". . . .

Walter Jackson Bate
Coleridge (New York: Macmillan, 1968), pp. 143–44

There is [a] tension . . . that will be seen to run like a kind of leitmotiv through much of Coleridge's religious writing. It is the conflict between his "dynamic philosophy" and his Christian faith. On the one hand there is his conception of reality as organic process, prompted by his reading of Spinoza and deepened by his reading of Kant and later of Schelling. It is the spirit of, for example, the "conversation poems" with their sense of "the one life within us and abroad." For all its lurking possibilities of pantheism (which he shunned all his life), this philosophy attracted him strongly both emotionally and intellectually. On the other hand there is, very simply, his commitment to the Christian faith.

In a sense, much of Coleridge's religious thought is an attempt to reconcile the dynamic philosophy and the Christian faith. His speculations about the Trinity, for example, are to some extent a function of this struggle: for Coleridge, the Trinity offered the only viable alternative to pantheism; in this way alone can God be conceived of as at once "the same and other," and in this way alone can dynamic process be compatible with the Immutable. His conception of the Logos, too, is part of this tension: the Logos is the eternal pattern of Creation, but this pattern is still to be worked out toward its perfection in the "divine humanity." Coleridge's notion of symbol, too, and of "consubstantiality," as an attempt to confront the dynamic problem of the One and the Many, will be seen to be of crucial importance for his idea of faith, Redemption, and the Sacraments.

In these instances—as in so many others—we will find that, although the problem is not resolved and a final synthesis constructed, usually a balance is achieved. And this is probably how it should be, after all, when one is dealing with what he admits to be, as Coleridge does, ultimately mystery. This is why Coleridge's religious writings must be seen as—to use Walter Jackson Bate's words—"brilliant, searching, conservative, boldly speculative, and (increasingly) humble—humble before the mystery of the unknown, and the mystery, in particular, of Christianity."

J. Robert Barth, S.J.
Coleridge and Christian Doctrine (Cambridge, Mass.: Harvard Univ. Pr., 1969), p. 13

Firstly, Coleridge's borrowings are not only real, but so honeycomb his work as to form virtually a mode of composition. Secondly, he was, on the evidence, a deeply neurotic man. Thirdly, he expected much of himself and his friends expected much of him, but his blocks and frustrations compressed his powers in a humiliating and often impotent bondage—his dejection was indeed caused by his loss of the shaping spirit of imagination. Fourthly, his cultural situation was isolated, and, compared with the philosophical activities of Germany, provincial. "Great indeed," said Coleridge, "are the obstacles which an English metaphysician has to encounter." Then against these facts we have to take account of his huge erudition, his meditative habits, his flashing insight—even Carlyle concedes him "a subtle, lynx-eyed intellect" and speaks of "his pious, ever-labouring, subtle mind." Thus we can see, perhaps, the elements that might fuse into his unorthodox and disingenuous mode of composition: on the one hand, the sense of understanding and insight into problems that baffled lesser minds (and did not even exist for many), and on the other, the humiliation before his neurotic incapacity to perform the mere busy work necessary to body forth his insight. We may then be able to see in, say, the translations of the *Biographia*—a book, as [Sir Leslie] Stephen notes, "put together with a pitchfork"—a kind of intellectual promissory note. We may be willing to concede that the psychological background of such borrowings was not a dearth of ideas, but a profusion of ideas along with a dearth of energy. Why, otherwise, "plagiarize"? If one intends to steal the tiara, rather than merely borrow it, surely one does not keep it intact but rather dismantles it and resets its gems. Why lay oneself open to reproach? Why copy verbatim? . . .

For our present purposes it is enough to say that the imagination, either as posited in the thirteenth chapter of the *Biographia* or as elsewhere formulated, is conceived by Coleridge as functioning in a way that does not grow out of his Schellingian paraphrases, in a way that in fact frees him from dependence on such borrowings. For Coleridge the function of the imagination was to emancipate the poetic concern from any Spinozistic implications, or, to put it another way, to establish the harmony of the moral concern with poetry. Coleridge's formulations were not borrowed or fabricated in response to any temporary fashion or problem; they were gradually evolved as reflections of the deepest and most permanent needs of his intellectual awareness.

Thomas McFarland
Coleridge and the Pantheist Tradition (Oxford: Clarendon, 1969), pp. 28–29, 157

If we use the episode of *The Watchman* as a gauge of the firmness with which Coleridge propounded his true beliefs, we find, in general, frankness rather than evasion, and restraint rather than timidity. It is true that he withheld much of his fire on such specific issues as the iniquities of the Two Acts; but so did the whole reform-party. He was not too prudent to speak out on what he called "first principles," nor to challenge received opinion in every issue of *The Watchman*. He charged the Church of England with teaching hatred in the name of the God of love (p.11) and ridiculed the miracles of the New Testament (p. 52); he called the Two Acts breaches of the Constitution (p. 13); he declared that the possessions of the rich rightfully belonged to the poor (p. 64); he predicted that by providential means kings and potentates would shortly be overthrown, and a good thing, too (pp. 65–66); he quoted with approval a declaration in favour of the rights of man (p. 372) and that nations other than France and the United States, which had been "too long the dupes of perfidious kings, nobles, and priests, will eventually recover their rights" (p. 373); he urged the enlargement of the right of suffrage in England (p. 209); he asserted that in the purer and more radical days of the French Revolution "the victories of Frenchmen" were "the victories of Human Nature" (p. 270); and he likened [William] Pitt to Judas Iscariot and hoped that he would be struck by a thunderbolt (p. 167). But if these extracts, chosen as instances of candour, give an impression of rashness or bombast, as well they might, the impression is false. The tone of *The Watchman* was prevailingly temperate—kept so, I think, because Coleridge believed that the knowledge of truth was best disseminated in a climate of thoughtfulness and in "cool and guarded" language.

Lewis Patton
Introd., in *The Watchman* in *The Collected Works of Samuel Taylor Coleridge*, ed. Kathleen Coburn and Bart Winer (Princeton, N.J.: Princeton Univ. Pr., 1970), p. lviii

Critics, historians of thought, even philosophers, giving Coleridge the highest sorts of praise, lament his lack of a system. But for that lack, they say, he might have been the greatest thinker, philosopher, teacher, moralist, etc., that England ever produced. Yet, suppose he had hewn or hammered himself into a firm, sound, complete structure, would he not have become his own contradiction? He did not even believe in a closed system. He believed in growth, the "free life," with a deep antipathy to "the confining form"; he had what he called a "rooted aversion to the *Arbitrary*"; systems and system-making do tend to become at some point arbitrary. He preferred "method" to system, and it will be protested by some that he did not achieve method either. But that depends on what you mean by it. He said somewhere that the shortest path gives one the knowledge best, but the longer way round makes one more knowing. The fragments he left us in such quantities certainly necessitate the longer way round. They tantalize us into wishing to understand him, and then, willy-nilly, into facing the questions he raised. The trick he plays on us is the educator's trick, who says, "What do *you* think?", i.e., "Do it yourself." Inquire of yourself—setting out from the grimmest realities of the Self, and Self-consciousness, so as not to end there.

Kathleen Coburn
The Self-Conscious Imagination: A Study of the Coleridge Notebooks (London: Oxford Univ. Pr., 1974), pp. 76–77

Coleridge's quest, which begins in "Effusion XXXV," can be called a search for a substantial, unified self. "All our Thoughts," he wrote in a notebook in 1807, "all that we abstract from our consciousness & so form the Phaenomenon Self is a Shadow, its whole Substance is the dim yet powerful sense that it is but a Shadow, & ought to belong to a Substance." His meditations on the goal of the quest were most frequent after the publication of his greatest poetry and when he was severely depressed by his failure to reach the goal. The definition of the goal became clearer when he was farthest from it, but the basic problem confronting him was explicit in "Effusion XXXV." The goal of a properly individuated self, he came to learn, could be attained only with the realization of its two aspects: first, the assurance that the self is grounded in a reality outside the self, a reality that can be embodied in objective symbols in nature and, more importantly, in other persons; and second, an active will that unifies the conscious and unconscious, the past and the present, and individuates the self from the undifferentiated oneness of either the One Life or the unconscious.

The first part of his goal is most clearly conveyed in his meditations upon love relationships. Kathleen Coburn has noted that he often attempted "to describe his own consciousness of his need to feel himself as real, and to be reassured of his own identity by means of objects, including love-objects and symbols." The picture of Coleridge as a transcendentalist who delighted in carrying his speculations on the nature of the self into the realm of Platonic ideas obscures his deep need for a ballast in the empirical world. Whenever he penetrates beyond the bounds of the sensory, whenever he crosses the line between immediate sensation and the world in which there are no anchors in sense, he often retreats, frequently in fear, because his imagination represents the ideal world as insubstantial.

Paul A. Magnuson
Coleridge's Nightmare Poetry (Charlottesville: Univ. Pr. Virginia, 1974), pp. 4–5

It will, I hope, become apparent that an essentially coherent idea of human relationship did exist for Coleridge. Its most important manifestations may tentatively be summarized as:

the recognition of personality, rather than conduct, as the starting-point of morality;

the essentiality of love, which is part of the striving of the individual towards the "one Life";

the origin of self-consciousness, morality and Reason itself in the individual's sense of "otherness";

and the vital function of religion and the developing social state in breaking through the individual's insular subjectivity and incorporating him into the stream of history.

To all of this the poetry of the great early creative period forms a strange but indispensable commentary, suggesting, through its recurring image of the fountain, that the real sources of love and joy are still mysteries not susceptible of explanation. . . .

Coleridge's attempt to see men as they really are, and not as their conduct represents them, was, in part, a reaction against the heavy emphasis that had been placed on conduct by some eighteenth-century moral philosophers, and the attempt of Jeremy Bentham to become the Newton of the moral world and "introduce a mathematical calculation on subjects of morality." Yet it was difficult for Coleridge to step entirely out of this dialectic, much as he longed for freedom from the eighteenth-century modes; he could not quite assert with Blake's confidence that man has no body distinct from his soul. Kant's subjective-objective distinction provided him with a possible answer, and in *The Friend* he used it to separate jurisprudence, and the punishments inflicted by the State for its own preservation, from morality, which he conceived to be entirely subjective, in the sense that it is the motive that justifies or condemns, and only God can know a man's true motives.

John Anthony Harding
Coleridge and the Idea of Love: Aspects of Relationship in Coleridge's Thought and Writing (Cambridge: Cambridge Univ. Pr., 1975), pp. 5, 41–42

Coleridge's meditative poems are too often read as mirrors of his distressed psyche, his postures of abasement and passivity seen as indicative of life-long emotional dependencies. To be sure, it is hard to find anywhere in his poems the manly strength he admired and envied in Wordsworth, and such clusters—to return to Kenneth Burke's term—as the recurrent images of the upraised-eye invite us to dwell on their "personal" overtones. But inherent in such psychoanalytic criticism is the risk of a self-blinding tendentiousness that neglects in the poems the possibility of a subtler art than psychoanalysis prepares us to imagine. The danger in reading the art so much in terms of the life is that we may settle for too easy a version of the life and then let the outlines of that version shape our expectations of the art.

I have tried in this book to balance the natural inclination to confessional readings by presenting evidence for interpretations of the poems that emphasize in Coleridge the capacity to shape the materials of distress into an unobtrusive but highly wrought poetic art. The point is that Coleridge's craft and subtlety as a meditative poet have been underestimated. Readers are entitled to find in his poems evidence of the self-pity and weakness that undoubtedly were major aspects of his personality, but the success or failure of his art ought not to be judged exclusively or even primarily on such a basis. Implicit in the readings offered here is my sense that the elaborate analogies informing the poems are a source of significant aesthetic pleasure. The remarkable play of his analogical imagination, drawing as it frequently does on a rich literary context, generates in the reader those combinations of expectation, gratification, and further surprise that are essential elements in the success of any art. There can be no doubt that Coleridge sought in his poems to transcend the merely personal and "idiosyncratic" or "accidental": the evidence indicates, I think, that in such poems as "This Lime-Tree Bower My Prison," "Frost at Midnight," "Hymn Before Sun-rise in the Vale of Chamouni," "Dejection: An Ode," and "To William Wordsworth" the elements of distress and anxiety are presented in a vision of theodicy achieved by the exertion of will and the play of imagination.

Reeve Parker
Coleridge's Meditative Art (Ithaca, N.Y.: Cornell Univ. Pr., 1975), pp. 242–43

THOMAS DE QUINCEY

1785–1859

In a N.B. postscript to the original magazine publication of "On the Knocking," [De Quincey] called that piece "psychological criticism." He was a psychological critic and what he valued was a criticism which started with an effect and gave reasons. It was not enough for a critic to feel, or to know what he liked—he must be able to generalize, universalize the psychology of the effect. Thus De Quincey was willing "to set aside any judgement that may be given until something more is consulted than individual taste," and he argued that criticism should be "governed by canons less arbitrary than the feelings, or perhaps the transient caprices, of individuals." . . .

For his part, he espouses two principles: "First, I shall not assume that all, which reconciles itself to my own feelings, is therefore sound. I shall not take it for granted, as is usually done, that the feelings (which speak a determined language) justify themselves," and "Secondly, which is a point of more uniform importance, I shall not make the Poetry ministerial to the purpose of displaying myself . . . but shall make myself ministerial to the Poetry." Addison's criticism, he objected, "rested not upon principles, but upon mere fineness of tact." Taste, tact was not satisfactory: criticism should be based upon "just principles of art."

It is partly this emphasis on principles which has made some commentators call De Quincey a preceptist. In fact, [George] Saintsbury claims De Quincey may be said to have been almost the "instaurator of . . . preceptist criticism." Similarly, [Horace A.] Eaton puts him "with the dogmatists of the eighteenth century" and [W. A.] Dunn speaks of his "categorical style of criticism." [René] Wellek has placed him more precisely, pointing out that De Quincey belongs "to the empirical psychologist tradition of the British, and to the emotionalist trend, descending from [John] Dennis through [David] Hartley to Wordsworth."

John E. Jordan
Introd., in *De Quincey as Critic*, ed. John E. Jordan (London: Routledge & Kegan Paul, 1973), pp. 35–36

MARIA EDGEWORTH

1767–1849

For Irish society in the last quarter of the eighteenth century the novels of Maria Edgeworth provide a truly excellent source of information and intelligent comment. In *Ennui* the role of the ideal estate-manager is thoroughly explored; in *Ormond* the churches and education are discussed at considerable length with great sympathy and understanding; in *Rosanna* elections get their due notice; and in *Vivian* again politics and the people is an important theme. To some extent the views expressed are relevant and more than relevant to the themes of this book. And in the disapproval she feels for Thady Quirk's son, Jason, in *Castle Rackrent* there is an excellent example of how the principles of the later years were foreshadowed at an early stage.

Nevertheless what was written, albeit generally under the Union, about a period before it and what is not directly geared to situations as they actually came upon her are in many ways less valuable as evidence about the Ireland of the first half of the nineteenth century than letters and memoranda composed spontaneously from day to day. In these and these alone one can see best the Canute-like quality of so many of her thoughts and actions; the curiously Louisa M. Alcott quality transferred into some place reminiscent of the western frontier; the dilemma of the liberal "White" in a quasi-colonial situation and the quest for integration of the deserving "native" into "White" society along lines still trodden by bodies such as the South African Progressive Party. So too one can make out the bold design of the Repealers in an age groping towards democracy for the United Kingdom. With the Repealers in this game were the Chartists, the Anti-Corn Law League and even the much neglected yet fascinating Anti-League of the protectionist tenant-farmers. Among a bunch of failures the Repealers came off best. Just why, shouts from the pages of Maria's correspondence.

By 1849 the world of the novel *Patronage* was over and done with as surely as that of its fellow *The Absentee*. Often in the 1790s Maria claimed politics were "above" her "capacity and information." Experience made it impossible for her to say that and ring true about the "now" of the 1820s and on, whatever had been the case during the "then" of the Grattan régime. Working as a "Friend of the People," above and alongside, but not merged in with it, she recorded her "As it Happened." This should belong to posterity.

Michael Hurst
Maria Edgeworth and the Public Scene: Intellect, Fine Feeling, and Landlordism in the Age of Reform (Coral Gables, Fla.: Univ. Miami Pr., 1969), pp. 27–28

It would be a perverse biographer who sat down to compose a portrait from which [Maria Edgeworth's] charm and humour in old age are deliberately omitted. On the other hand a different picture of Maria Edgeworth emerges from a perspective that is not personal but literary. Just what did Scott (or for that matter Turgenev) read into her novels that was so well worth copying? Scott himself now seems to be receiving his long-overdue reassessment; but even during the twilight of his reputation earlier this century, no one denied that in his day Scott had as wide an influence on European literature as any English writer has ever had. A formative influence on him, if Maria really was that, ought to arouse some interest; especially when she also attracted the notice of Stendhal and Turgenev, the pioneers of the two greatest European traditions in the novel. The fact is that Maria's most important stories, together with the personal and intellectual influence that went into them, reveal a great deal about the roots of early-nineteenth-century realism. To understand why she succeeded is to have a clearer insight into the conditions that brought the major Victorian novels into existence. . . .

The reason for Maria Edgeworth's literary importance lies in her development of the techniques of documentation, and in her intelligent understanding of the social scene. The social novel became the dominant form of the first half of the nineteenth century, both in England and Europe, not because of individual writers but because it studied middle-class life and reflected middle-class attitudes. Its explicit reference to real life and fascination with detail was the literary counterpart of the empiricism of the industrial innovators, and so it naturally appealed to the educated but not aesthetic prosperous classes, and to the rapidly expanding proletarian readership. Not only for Maria Edgeworth and Scott, but for Dickens, Thackeray, Mrs. Gaskell, and George Eliot, society itself often becomes the central character. . . . Maria Edgeworth's genre, so often nowadays called in a derogatory way "the provincial novel," does not exist as a separate entity, as the study of its first critics has shown. Her successors may have had a different (and often much more critical) attitude to society, but their concern was, like hers, a detailed and accurate re-creation of the organism as a whole, and not of individuals extrapolated from it. There is the same unbroken line of development as between Defoe and the great novelists of the 1740s.

Marilyn Butler
Maria Edgeworth: A Literary Biography (Oxford: Clarendon, 1972), pp. 8–9, 485–86

WILLIAM HAZLITT

1778–1830

The aim of the present study is to indicate some of the principal ways in which Hazlitt vindicated the self-authenticating nature of the poetic principle against both a hostile empirical epistemology and what he conceived to be the misguided attempts of contemporary poets and critics to construct a non-scientific and extra-poetic alternative. He viewed the age in which he lived as one of abstraction. His conviction of the harm arising from the contemporary emphasis upon generality is the key to his entire critical outlook, theoretical as well as practical. To this conviction can be traced his dislike of systems, doctrines, theories, dogmas, parties and sects. The general role assigned to him in the following pages is similar in many respects to that occupied by Matthew Arnold later in the century. Hazlitt is unique in one respect, however. The theory of abstract ideas which is the principal theoretical justification for his criticism of all forms of abstraction is entirely original. Its implications, whether as a philosophical theory or as a psychology of artistic perception, are revolutionary, and it constitutes the most important single factor in an understanding of his literary criticism. It is essentially the theory of a painter trained originally as a philosopher, and emphasizes the important role played by painting and philosophy in the formation of the mature literary critic.

Roy Park
Hazlitt and the Spirit of the Age: Abstraction and Critical Theory
(Oxford: Clarendon, 1971), p. 2

The souring of [Hazlitt's] temper had begun [early in life]. His frequent moves as a child—from Maidstone to Bandon to Philadelphia to Boston to Wem—had given him no opportunity to form lasting friendships; his only close ties had been with his parents and his older brother and sister. He had learned to echo their grown-up talk, to court their approval, to accept their narrow standards. Yet rebellion was in his blood, and once his reading had exposed him to the world beyond his father's parsonage, he rebelled—rebelled at home and even more at the New College at Hackney. Unfortunately he could not do so without offending his parents—wounding them—and wounding himself even more. Then came his frustrating attempts to prove himself, first as a philosopher, later as a painter—and the humiliation that followed his foolish conduct with the girl at Keswick.

Again he tried to perfect his art and to finish his metaphysical essay. He married Sarah Stoddart probably less for love than for a meager security while he strove to develop his talents. But his paintings were still rejected, and his essay, when finally published, was ignored. As a writer for the magazines he enjoyed some success. Soon, though, he was refusing, like his father before him, to exercise discretion—stubbornly flaying those who disagreed with him and, inevitably, exposing himself to painful reprisals. As he wrote in 1829, he had at first been "treated as a cipher," later "set upon as a wild beast." But it had been his "misfortune (perhaps) to be bred up among Dissenters, who look with too jaundiced an eye on others, and set too high a value on their own peculiar pretensions." And his defense was to "take refuge in a sort of misanthropy and cynical contempt for mankind."

Ralph M. Wardle
Hazlitt (Lincoln: Univ. Nebraska Pr., 1971), p. 494

THOMAS HOOD

1799–1845

Few would contest that during the last decade of his life (the years from 1835 to 1845) Hood wrote many of the poems that have established his surest claim to remembrance, and a reinterpretation of this period is desirable from both a biographical and a critical point of view. First, a sizable amount of new material—unpublished letters and doctoral dissertations—is now available, material ignored or unused by previous biographers; easily four-fifths of the unpublished letters date from the last ten years. Moreover, no previous study has adequately taken into account the importance of the personal crisis in Hood's life that took place during the winter of 1834–1835: it clearly determined the course the remainder of his life would take. From his own despair Hood looked upon the injustice prevalent within English society with newly opened eyes.

Second, the writings of the last decade of Hood's life have not received adequate critical interpretation. Deeply troubled by the widening rift between the "two Englands," Hood sought through his humanitarian poems to bring about some kind of reconciliation "between Rich and Poor," between "Hate on the one side and Fear on the other." This study examines in detail his interest in social and humanitarian causes and shows that it did not arise suddenly late in 1843 with the publication in *Punch* of "The Song of the Shirt," but was, on the contrary, an interest of many years standing. It also traces later developments in Hood's rich vein of grotesque poetry, known for its abrupt undercutting of the dramatic illusion, and explores the all-important influence of German romanticism—an influence hitherto ignored—upon these poems. Nor has anyone recognized the extent to which many of Hood's poems, to borrow Johnson's phrase, "point a moral." "One use of Victorian laughter . . . ," observes a recent critic, "was to ridicule in order to correct, or at least to unsettle, things and ideas which those who laugh take very seriously." This was Hood's intent in what I call his "poems of moral humor." The detailed interpretations of all three of these themes—the humanitarian, the grotesque, the moral—are, I believe, basically new.

John Clubbe
Victorian Forerunner: The Late Career of Thomas Hood
(Durham, N.C.: Duke Univ. Pr., 1968), pp. vii–viii

LEIGH HUNT

1784–1859

The power of the living theatre probably represents the strongest personal force in Hunt's opera reviews. He was drawn to theatrical criticism initially by a curiosity about the "strange superiority of the mimetic" attributes of the stage; the particular appeal of the performers and their art continued to play a vital role in his opera criticism. But his penetrating analyses went far beyond the superficial accomplishments or deficiencies of the singers. His energies were absorbed by *revealed* drama—to such an extent at times, it would seem, that he could not "tell the dancer from the dance." He strove to capture the performance in the very process of its dramatic realization. This aspect of his criticism tended to supplant discussion of opera vehicles themselves. For he focused on the dramatic substance itself—the episodes and situations that breathed life into the theatrical experience. In this respect his criticism often goes to the heart of opera, revealing that special quality of the art form wherein vocal nuances blend with melodic expressiveness, capturing and projecting the essence of dramatic characterization.

Two complementary forces at work in Hunt's character—his self-assurance and his self-doubt—find expression in his opera criticism. The former quality underlies the confidence and assertiveness, curiosity and challenge, that distinguish his reviews. Under stress, however, Hunt becomes overconfident, tending to make provocative attacks, rash assumptions, mistaken generalizations. The quality of self-doubt is evident in his questioning attitude, his need to reexamine, his openness of mind and freedom from dogmatism. At times, a distrust of his own opinions leads to a certain hesitance, ambivalence, and inconclusiveness in his reviews.

The shifts noted in Hunt's attitudes on opera owe much to an interplay between these forces, the one quality serving as a corrective to the other. Thus he gained the capacity to seek new experiences and to learn from them. For the overall trend of these shifts is toward a greater catholicity of taste and toward sounder, more realistic judgments.

Theodore Fenner
Leigh Hunt and Opera Criticism: The "Examiner" Years, 1808–1821 (Lawrence: Univ. Pr. Kansas, 1972), pp. 234–35

The central conception of "Angling" is . . . a humanitarian appeal that Charles Lamb would have found surprising but that Shelley and Byron would heartily approve. Leigh Hunt was something of a *bon vivant*, but though he undoubtedly took as much delight in eating roast suckling pig as Lamb did, he could not have described the process of roasting with equal delight. Hunt would have tried to ignore the prior history of his tasty meal. He disliked facing the hard realities from which the newly urbanized civilization of nineteenth-century London conveniently shielded him. (Note the revulsion he feels for mud, weeds, and stones.) Lamb and Shelley both looked squarely at the origins of "animal food" and came to some opposite conclusions about what their personal behavior ought to be. Shelley tried to maintain a vegetarian diet in the most carnivorous society in Europe; Hunt continued to enjoy his meal, while averting his eyes from the kitchen and the butcher shop.

Hunt's criticism of anglers—particularly of Izaak Walton—also lacks some sense of history. When Walton and other sportsmen of the seventeenth century spoke of the harmlessness of their pastime, they were not comparing it with riding, walking, skating, playing at cricket or rackets, dancing, or listening to music (lines 39–41). Walton specifically compares angling with hunting with hounds and with falcons, and in the speech in which Piscator speaks of anglers as harmless, he says that "most Anglers are, quiet men, and followers of peace; men that were so simply-wise, as not to sell their consciences to buy riches," contrasting angling with the quest for military glory, commercial wealth, or political or ecclesiastical power. . . .

For his own time or ours, Hunt's message to fishermen has greater merit. In an age that recognizes greater kinship among all sentient creatures than did the seventeenth century and that has evolved as one of its higher ideals a reverence for life, there is certainly no harm in reminding men that the fisherman's pleasure is the fish's agony. Leigh Hunt and journalists of his type have probably aided popular awareness of some of the profounder problems of modern ethics by oversimplifying them.

Donald H. Reiman
in *Shelley and His Circle*, Vol. VI, ed. Donald H. Reiman
(Cambridge, Mass.: Harvard Univ. Pr., 1973), pp. 1078–80

JOHN KEATS

1795–1821

Jack Stillinger, ed., *The Poems of John Keats* (1978)

I have often wondered whether we could find any more comprehensive way of taking up the whole of English poetry during the last three centuries—or for that matter the modern history of the arts in general—than by exploring the effects of . . . accumulating anxiety and the question it so directly presents to the poet or artist: *What is there left to do?* . . .

So with the English Romantics. Keats, who certainly faced enough personal difficulties, would become really despondent only (except after his fatal illness began) when, as he told his friend Richard Woodhouse, he felt that "there was nothing original to be written in poetry; that its riches were already exhausted—and all its beauties forestalled." . . .

For one thing, there is what we can only call a profound opening up for literary treatment of the "inner" life of the individual. In exploiting this the

Romantics relied on at least a hundred years of British empirical psychology. The theme was not taken up without some reluctance. As Wordsworth says at the start of *The Prelude*, he would have preferred to write an epic, romance, or long philosophical poem, and he refused to publish *The Prelude* until he could also show a long work of a more traditional kind. The critical remarks of Keats in his letters, where we see him casting about for his own direction, express the same uneasiness: this poetry of the inner life could forefeit objectivity and range. But at the same time, there was a sense of both its originality and its profound importance. For this poetry, as it "martyrs itself," in Keats's phrase, "to the human heart," not only comes closer to some modes of "truth." It also conveys a new sense of the adventure and possible joy of living. The feeling of this was so strong that Wordsworth, in the Prospectus to *The Excursion*, proclaims that the "Mind of Man" is "My haunt, and the main region of my song," and goes on to voice his "high argument," how the mind can through its own creativity and love make a paradise of common things. The appeal of the subjective theme was powerful enough to deflect Keats from his admiration of the great "objective" genres of the past, making him wonder whether Wordsworth was not "deeper than Milton . . . [Milton] did not think into the human heart, as Wordsworth has done." And in the first of the great odes, "To Psyche," he commits himself to building a temple to this "latest-born" promise for art—the "untrodden region of the mind."

Walter Jackson Bate
The Burden of the Past and the English Poet (Cambridge, Mass.: Harvard Univ. Pr., 1970), pp. 3, 5, 123–24

The true schism in Romantic poetry is not between the real and the ideal but between self-consciousness and vision, between nakedness (in Yeats' sense) and myth, between existential anguish and imaginative self-transcendence. The true poetry of actuality for the Romantics is not a poetry of naturalism and "process" but a poetry of personal quest or crisis, a poetry of self-confrontation. What makes the "Ode to a Nightingale" so central, not only for Keats but for all of Romantic literature, is the way it dramatizes these contrary strains, the way it charts a circuitous but definitive course through visionary and naturalistic aspiration to tragic self-definition and self-knowledge. . . .

Keats himself, I am convinced, can now rejoin the other Romantics, can now be rescued from our need for his supposed health and sanity as he was once rescued from an earlier need for aestheticism and decadence. He need no longer be our refuge from the negative emotions of modern literature, from its violence and desperation and apocalyptic longings. Keats too had within him an intransigent and threatening negativity, what Baudelaire calls "the sensation of an abyss"—a "violence of . . . temperament continually smothered down," as he once said. To say this is not to impress Keats into the service of modernism or nihilism but only to insist that he achieved health and selfhood through intense inner conflict, and that this conflict has much to teach us.

There is a positive side to the Romantic experience of crisis: a creative autonomy of self, a conquest of new territory for the spirit. "That which is creative must create itself," Keats wrote. "By our own spirits are we deified," said Wordsworth in "Resolution and Independence." "I see, and sing, by my own eyes inspir'd," Keats proclaimed to Psyche. But both poets knew of the contingency and peril, the deep inner stress, that attended such godlike freedom and presumption. . . . Romantic self-consciousness is always a double consciousness: innocence and experience, joy and terror, creativity and madness. Romantic poetry improves the quality of our own self-knowledge by recalling us to this double vision.

Morris Dickstein
Keats and His Poetry: A Study in Development (Chicago: Univ. Chicago Pr., 1971), pp. xiv–xvi

One can . . . describe what Keats's poems are about, and in the description at least partially account for his peculiar excellence. He wrote on most of the standard subjects: nature, poetry, art, love, fame, and death. But in the over-all view, his significant poems center on a single basic problem, the mutability inherent in nature and human life, and openly or in disguise they debate the pros and cons of a single hypothetical solution, transcendence of earthly limitations by means of the visionary imagination. If one were to summarize the career in a sentence, it would be something like this: Keats came to learn that this kind of imagination was a false lure, inadequate to the needs of the problem, and in the end he traded it for the naturalized imagination, embracing experience and process as his own and man's chief good. His honesty in treating the problem and his final opting for the natural world, where all the concrete images of poetry come from and where melodies impinge on "the sensual ear" or not at all, are what, more than anything else, guarantee his place "among the English Poets." . . .

Characteristically, the speaker in a Romantic lyric begins in the real world (A), takes off in mental flight to visit the ideal (B), and then—for a variety of reasons, but most often because he finds something wanting in the imagined ideal or because, being a native of the real world, he discovers that he does not or cannot belong permanently in the ideal—returns home to the real (A′). But he has not simply arrived back where he began (hence "A′" rather than "A" at the descent), for he has acquired something—a better understanding of a situation, a change in attitude toward it—from the experience of the flight, and he is never again quite the same person who spoke at the beginning of the poem. . . .

It is not really necessary to place Keats historically—in any sense in which he is "romantic" we are still today in the same "romantic movement" —but it happens that the structure embraces two dominant tendencies in the literature of his time, the desire to transcend the world of flux and the desire to merge with that world, and it helps explain the way in which both of these contradictory tendencies may exist, as they so often do, in the same work.

Jack Stillinger
The Hoodwinking of Madeline, and Other Essays on Keats's Poems (Urbana: Univ. Illinois Pr., 1971), pp. 100–103

During the winter of 1817–1818, Keats proceeded to develop his favorite chemical analogy through a number of related metaphors as a means of exploring the mystery of poetic creation. The formulation was of invaluable service as a way of articulating the kinds of reaction from which poetry sprang and which it in turn occasioned. Nevertheless it raised as many questions as it solved. The scientific operations he found most useful by way of comparison were suggestive in a variety of ways; the very terms they employed were subject to a number of different implications once one sought to adapt or extend them. While science, particularly chemistry, provided a method for understanding the changes and reactions taking place within the world of physical energy and matter, there was no simple or exact means for applying such principles in order to explain imagery, sensation, emotion, thought, and the various combinations and relationships between them. The larger context, one which kept shifting in his mind, was fundamentally poetical and would have to be worked out in terms of his verse itself. It was just here that the problem, far from depressing him, was proving so stimulating. For it was one, as he realized, that could be resolved not merely in terms of the metaphors and speculations that preoccupied him in his letters but through the new inferences and values these were continually assuming in his poetry. The problem, that is to say, could be settled only through the coherence and discipline (the outgrowth of self-discovery) sustained composition demanded—through the act of creation itself. Indeed the shifts and conflicts in his own attitude toward certain major aspects of the question had already begun to provide that kind of dramatic tension from which great poetry often springs. . . .

Stewart M. Sperry
Keats the Poet (Princeton, N.J.: Princeton Univ. Pr., 1973), pp. 70–71

Let me set down three propositions. First, that embarrassment is very important in life. Second, that one of the things for which we value art is that it helps us to deal with embarrassment, not by abolishing or ignoring it, but by recognizing, refining, and putting it to good human purposes; art, in its unique combination of the private and the public, offers us a unique kind of human relationship freed from the possibility, which is incident to other human relationships, of an embarrassment that clogs, paralyses, or coarsens. Third, that Keats as a man and a poet was especially sensitive to, and morally intelligent about, embarrassment; that the particular direction of his insight and human concern here is to insist upon raising the matter of embarrassability (whereas some other writings and people furnish a different kind of principled relief for us, by means of the cool tactful pretence that the possibility of embarrassment does not arise when we are in their company). I should stress that the attempt is not in any way to search out Keats's psyche, but to get closer to a sense of his special goodness as a man and as a poet; to see the shape of his imagination, and the truth of it. I am aware that this constitutes no kind of biography (but then there have recently been three invaluable biographies, by Walter Jackson Bate, Aileen Ward, and Robert Gittings), and that there are many essential kinds of literary criticism not at all attempted here. But without at all lessening the achievement of Keats's poetry there is a good deal in T. S. Eliot's bringing together Keats, Goethe, and Baudelaire as "men who are important first because they are human prototypes of new experience, and only second because they are poets."

Christopher Ricks
Keats and Embarrassment (Oxford: Clarendon, 1974), p. 1

Keats's texts can to an extent be repaired simply by correction of the most obvious mistakes in the current standard editions. I have not very often, in Section IV.2, concerned myself with errors in [H. W.] Garrod's headnotes and apparatus (of which there are a great many, perhaps a thousand or fifteen hundred in the recording of variants in the fine print of the apparatus) or with mistakes in [Miriam] Allott's textual notes (which too frequently are based on Garrod's misinformation). My focus has been the texts themselves, and these can be rid of at least most of the errors and inconsistencies in new issues of Garrod's and Allott's editions, revised according to the lists given at the beginning of this section. I would not trust my collations, and the details of the histories in Section IV.2, as a basis for a fresh editing of the poems, but they should serve in the interim as a basis for correction.

I think, however, that a fresh editing is in order. Texts aside, Garrod's arrangement of the poems makes no sense, his introduction and headnotes are considerably out of date, and his cumbersome and error-filled apparatus does as much harm as good. Allott's chronological arrangement is much to be preferred, and her critical annotations, which would amount to some four hundred pages in small type if they were printed all together, are excellent; but she modernizes spelling, punctuation, and the like inconsistently, and she provides too little textual information to serve the requirements of serious scholars and critics. "What is needed now," wrote [Stuart M.] Sperry in 1967, "is a full-scale re-editing of the poetry in the light of all available evidence bearing on text, dating, and allusion . . . a modern edition—something akin to the so-called variorum—that accurately provides for any given poem all known readings of any textual authority together with all available facts bearing on dating, allusion, and contemporary criticism." For some of these latter matters—the historical background and critical annotations—Allott's edition answers the need quite nicely. But the textual work still needs to be done.

Jack Stillinger
The Texts of Keats's Poems (Cambridge, Mass.:
Harvard Univ. Pr., 1974), pp. 282–83

In what follows I suggest, daringly, that "To Autumn" has something to say: that it is an ideological poem whose very form expresses a national idea and a new stage in consciousness, or what Keats himself once called the "gregarious advance" and "grand march of intellect." . . .

My argument runs that "To Autumn," an ode that is hardly an ode, is best defined as an English or Hesperian model which overcomes not only the traditional type of sublime poem but the "Eastern" or epiphanic consciousness essential to it. The traditional type was transmitted by both Greek and Hebrew religious poetry, and throughout the late Renaissance and eighteenth century, by debased versions of the Pindaric or cult hymn. Only one thing about epiphanic structure need be said now: it evokes the presence of a god, or vacillates sharply between imagined presence and absence. Its rhetoric is therefore a crisis-rhetoric, with priest or votary, vastation or rapture, precarious nearness or hieratic distance ("Ah Fear! Ah frantic Fear! I see, I see thee near!"). As these verses by William Collins suggest, epiphanic structure proceeds by dramatic turns of mood and its language is ejaculative (Lo, Behold, O come, O see). Keats's "Hesperianism" triumphs, in "To Autumn," over this archaic style with its ingrained, superstitious attitude toward power—power seen as external and epochal. The new sublimity domesticates with the heart; the poet's imagination is neither imp nor incubus. Though recognizably sublime, "To Autumn" is a poem of *our* climate. . . .

Autumn's "conspiring" function is comparable to that of the guardian genius, the *natale comes qui temperat astrum.* An idea of poetic or personal destiny enters, in however veiled a form. The poet who writes this ode stands under the pressure of an omen. As summer passes into autumn (season of the year or human season), his dreaming deepens into foresight.

. . . In fear of early death, and sensing riches his pen might never glean, Keats evokes a figure of genial harvests. Three times he renews his surmise of fruitfulness, three times he grasps the shadow without self-defeating empathy. Even fruitfulness is not a burden in "To Autumn." This, at last, is true impersonality.

Geoffrey Hartman
The Fate of Reading, and Other Essays (Chicago: Univ. Chicago Pr., 1975), pp. 124–25, 126–27, 146

Yeats, following Nietzsche, uses the term "antithetical" for the anti-natural imagination, which is intellectual, and opposes this to the primary self, which is emotional. Where Milton largely removes ambivalence from the antithetical (or seemed to have for those who followed), poets since him have had to acknowledge that the antithetical other whom they address as "Thou" (in its various forms) has a degree of power over them, in part because they have idealized it. The wish for "poetic character" is a wish for identity, and to see it in another (as seems inevitable) is to grant that other not only power but a measure of self-love. If this sounds suspiciously like Freud's formula for the ego confronting the super-ego as it is projected onto an external object, it is, for this is the first term of the oxymoron. To open oneself out to that power, as Keats does with Moneta in *The Fall of Hyperion,* is the second term and brings the poet *past* the renewed narcissism of Freud to a state of vision, the unfolding of the rose. Here primary meets antithetical, and the poet seems to transcend subjectivity, settling for neither a compensating emotion nor the antithetical sublime but a fusion, however brief, in which emotion and intellect are united. During this moment the poet achieves the paradoxical state that Yeats thinks of as being "self-possessed in self-surrender," a recognition that, ironically, self is only whole when it surrenders to other. . . .

Keats, as the extraordinary poet he was, seeks the meeting place of self and other, the scene in which the power of presence may be made accessible to the poet's feelingful perception. The poet here must concede priority to otherness, but indirectly he proves that without his own presence the sublime other would have no priority. In other words, he needs the heightening that the sublime provides, but he completes or defines that sublimity as he engages it. This, broadly, is the relationship portrayed in *The Fall of Hyperion,* one of the most magnificent poems Keats wrote (even if in some need of revision, and if fragmentary), and one of the most moving in the language.

Stuart A. Ende
Keats and the Sublime (New Haven, Conn.: Yale Univ. Pr., 1976), pp. 29–30, 145

Insufficient attention to Keats's place in the tradition of natural religion has led several . . . scholars into difficulty when they attempted to deal with the poet's religious thought. Apparently unaware of the historical roots of Keats's theological ideas, John Middleton Murry regarded him as an original religious thinker, almost as a prophet bringing a special revelation from God. Clarence Thorpe likewise believed that Keats devised a special religion for himself, involving a kind of Platonic quest for and worship of absolute Beauty. An opposite tendency in criticism has disregarded the evidence of Keats's serious involvement with religious concerns, speaking of him as though he were an early exponent of modern secular humanism. This approach often necessitates interpreting Keats's religious language in non-religious terms, as is done in a recent study [by Stuart M. Sperry] when an obvious reference to the Deity ("the great Power") is understood as signifying "an endless potential for creation, an ideal of beauty latent amid the elements of human perception." The fact is that Keats was neither an evangelist nor an agnostic. He was an earnest seeker after truth who believed in the existence of a Supreme Being and who felt a need to investigate the consequences and ramifications of that belief. . . .

The relationship that Keats posits between human intelligences and the Divine Intelligence is not unlike the relationship [Coleridge] understood to exist between the individual human reason and Divine Reason: the first was seen as a mental analogue or counterpart of the second. Moreover, Coleridge was willing to speculate that human creatures might enjoy some type of existence in God before their earthly conception, but insisted that these preexistent entities could not be considered fully human since they would lack the kind of individual identity that comes only during life on earth.

Whenever or wherever he found them, Keats was interested in these doctrines primarily because they provided a foundation and gave a kind of theological legitimacy to the system that he was offering as an alternative to Christianity.

Robert M. Ryan
Keats: The Religious Sense (Princeton, N.J.: Princeton Univ. Pr., 1976), pp. 4–5, 202

WALTER SAVAGE LANDOR

1775–1864

Walter Savage Landor symbolized for Yeats the complete man of action who "topped us all in calm nobility when the pen was in his hand, as in the daily violence of his passion when he laid it down." . . .

Yeats's image is drawn from Landor's unquiet personal history, but it also reflects the peculiarly Roman qualities in his writings, their eloquence and strength. These find their greatest scope in the English prose works of his later years, notably the *Imaginary Conversations*. But earlier on in his career many ambitious experiments were made in Latin. . . .

Landor's sensitivity to tradition, great though it was, did not prevent him from developing a highly individual style. For Landor, as Connop Thirlwall pointed out, resembled no other author, ancient or modern. His style "is the style of Landor and it is marked with the stamp not only of his intellect but of his personal idiosyncrasy." Thirlwall continues: "No doubt the author's poetical faculty is more largely developed in the longer compositions; but the shorter are more deeply impressed with the signature of the man; not always indeed in the most winning aspect. . . . Now and then harmlessly playful, but much oftener instinct with the bitterest sarcasm." These shorter poems have never been edited or annotated, and being of an occasional nature, they can be difficult to follow, especially when Landor chooses to be stylistically obscure. In the case of Landor's political and satiric verse, several poems were sent to newspapers and journals of the day, and their topicality is lost on the modern reader. Leicester Bradner has commented: "He is a poet who is impressive in anthologies and disappointing in the bulk. . . . A judicious selection of the idylls and epigrams would do much to raise Landor's reputation as a Latin poet."

A judicious selection is certainly needed, but one that represents the man in all his moods and undertakings, not simply the bereaved lover or the stoic philosopher of the English anthologies. Landor imparted an engaging, sometimes an alarming directness of address to even his most commonplace verses and he touched on contemporary issues with a lively and discerning mind. An important aspect of his writings is their sheer bulk; this immense productivity lies behind each small poem and is sustained over a lifetime. Something of the man and the daily violence of his passion is lost, if selection is too rigorous. It would be a pity to cage such characteristic expansiveness within too rarefied an anthology, even in the interests of calm nobility.

Andrea Kelly
in *The Latin Poetry of English Poets*, ed. J. W. Binns (London: Routledge & Kegan Paul, 1974), pp. 150–51, 158–59

THOMAS MOORE

1779–1852

Hoover H. Jordan, *Bolt Upright: The Life of Thomas Moore* (1975)

By a bitter irony Moore's name has acquired a reputation for obsequiousness when in fact he was throughout life so bold in utterance as to make many contemporaries wonder why he did not spend the greater part of his days in jail. At this juncture, seeing [his] letters "seasoned with plenty of the then favourite condiment, treason," as Moore characterized them, his mother requested that he never take so hazardous a step again, and "as any wish of hers was to me a law," he promised not to write further articles. Even [Robert] Emmet [leader of an Irish uprising against British rule] remonstrated with him in the course of their walks together in the countryside. . . .

In 1808, as the first two numbers of the *Irish Melodies* were appearing, Moore readied two satires for publication, issued anonymously by [James] Carpenter in 1808, and written in what he called a "stately, Juvenalian style." Neither proved very popular: "Intolerance" had only one edition, "Corruption" only two. They did, however, permit him to assume a role which he found especially attractive—that of political moralist—in which he could admonish England for its conduct toward his home land. Anticipating possible mob violence in Ireland from the first stirring of the populace by [Daniel] O'Connell as a result of the defeat of the Catholic Emancipation Bill which the Whigs introduced in 1806, and subsequent violence against English repression in general, Moore declared of his satirical intention that he wished to awaken England to the necessity for reform before revolution became imperative. . . .

Taking matters familiar to the modern cultural anthropologist, physicist, or chemist as a basis for attacking bigotry, Moore did not endear himself to fundamentalists in religion; if their assertion be true that he was more responsible for changing the tone and morality of the first half of the century than anyone except perhaps Byron, it was not possibly so much from the effect of the Little poems as from Moore's often-stated ecumenical beliefs and internationalist view of mankind, which were hostile to restrictive ideas.

Hoover H. Jordan
Bolt Upright: The Life of Thomas Moore, Vol. I (Salzburg, Austria: Universität Salzburg, Institut für Englische Sprache und Literatur, 1975), pp. 26, 166, 169

THOMAS LOVE PEACOCK

1785–1866

To re-open the case of Peacock, like any other, calls for fresh evidence. Many previously unpublished letters by Peacock, Shelley and [Thomas Jefferson] Hogg, and new biographical research, have appeared since the last books on Peacock and the last complete edition, and largely modify those previous verdicts. Yet the most recent book on Peacock is a reprint, without any alteration, of the one [J. B.] Priestley wrote in 1927 before even the later Halliford [Edition] volumes had appeared.

But I shall also attempt a fresh and more scrupulous weighing of previous evidence. For instance, "The Four Ages of Poetry" will be balanced against the usually ignored "Essay on Fashionable Literature." *Melincourt* will be given much more attention, and the representation of Coleridge in *Nightmare Abbey* entertained more seriously, than is usual. Fuller credit will be given to the "Memoirs of Shelley," and to the music reviews and articles. The latter particularly deserve extended treatment because literary critics give them only a passing mention, and because they appear not to be known by music historians—who, however, when introduced to them are impressed by Peacock's intelligence and knowledge.

The established idea of Peacock will be taken for granted as the background of this study, and so Priestley, [Carl] Van Doren and [A. M.] Freeman rarely cited—or reiterated. Above all this study, unlike theirs, will present the complexity of Peacock in preference to fixing a clear-cut judgement.

Howard Mills
Peacock: His Circle and His Age (Cambridge: Cambridge Univ. Pr., 1969), pp. 5–6

Peacock came to face what Wordsworth, Coleridge, Keats, Shelley, Byron, all struggled with: the question of whom to write for. Peacock was to recognize that the initial reaction to "Kubla Khan" and "Christabel" among the reviews and "reading public" was childish and wrong. His first essay, an unfinished piece on "Fashionable Literature," denounces both readers and reviewers and laments the plight of the imaginative poet. Not always kind to Coleridge, Peacock was clearly aware of what he had to face. His response to his own readers is fascinating to watch. At about the time of his first novel (written in 1815) he sensed that there actually was no public to write for. He did not conceive, as Wordsworth had, of trying to create a responsive audience. He felt that such an audience as could listen to poetry was no more—had passed with the previous century when readers and reviews were more receptive. His decision was to stop writing for a particular audience, and the result was a series of iconoclastic novels and essays and, paradoxically, his best long poem—*Rhododaphne*. No longer bound by the idea of reviews, he was no longer tied to what he had thought the requisite sentiments and language for serious poetry. . . .

But this is not to say that Peacock's seven novels, or the five "novels of talk" are mere *romans à clefs*, as it were exhausted when the various portraits are deciphered. After one has identified Mr. Mystic of *Melincourt* with Coleridge, Scythrop of *Nightmare Abbey* with the young Shelley, relatively little has been accomplished. For Peacock's characters are at once more and less than the individuals they suggest or on whom they may be based. They and the books wherein they live become increasingly independent of the world they seem so unmistakeably to burlesque.

Peacock may have conceived of his satiric portraits as a way to quit himself for his exclusion at Bracknell; if so, his method tends to work against him, or at least to reveal his more complex response. A remarkable change occurs in his novels, for though they begin by satirizing intellectual fads, they move away from satire into the realm of comedy. The process here is generic as much as biographical. By an almost imperceptible process, light, intellectual irony usurps the initial militancy. Works that begin as mock utopias, as showcases for a collection of harmless lunatics, gradually turn into play utopias, of which the narrator approves and about which his laughter is gentle.

Carl Dawson
His Fine Wit: A Study of Thomas Love Peacock (London: Routledge & Kegan Paul, 1970), pp. 6–7, 160–61

ANN WARD RADCLIFFE

1764–1823

Two of the most celebrated mysteries in [*The Mysteries of*] *Udolpho* elicit a book full of suspense from the reader before they dwindle into the aftermaths of the novel's two most questionable *expliqués* or revelations: the mystery of the letters which Emily must burn without reading, and the mystery of the black veil behind which Emily does indeed look—but does not speak of. Both mysteries are intensified because Emily sees and reveals just enough for us to imagine abominations which are worse than the reality, though perhaps not much worse. Although our confidence in our moral discrimination and our rational powers is shaken, Mrs. Radcliffe's technical virtuosity is called into question in both instances, along with her artistic integrity. Why, after all, did she fail to tell us what Emily saw in the letters and behind the veil? . . .

What Mrs. Radcliffe may be trying to give us is a kind of wordless metaphor for the defensive vacuum her heroine's mind sustains itself in (and with) in a state of shock. Emily's silence is therefore a legitimate rhetorical gesture illustrating a state of mind so delicately balanced in its own confusion that the words which would truly clarify for it what the lady thought she saw would bring it tumbling down. . . .

Mrs. Radcliffe's *expliqués* are usually manifest afterthoughts. But if we do care to take it seriously, it does in itself supply sufficient motive for Emily's unwillingness to admit in words or image to herself the horrible implications of such a crime, which would thereby serve as a precedent for the murder of her aunt and herself. More likely, we may assume that there is one Mrs. Radcliffe at work in the midst of Emily's confrontation with the unimaginable horror behind the veil and another at work during the process of rationalizing it away. The real—or at any rate the esthetically interesting—Mrs. Radcliffe is the first one, the one who knows and writes that "human reason cannot establish her laws on subjects lost in the obscurity of the imagination, any more than the eye can ascertain the form of objects that only glimmer through the dimness of night." The second Mrs. Radcliffe is the prim moralist about her official business of tidying up and airing out her chamber of horrors by letting in the dry light of reason and common day.

Eugene B. Murray
Ann Radcliffe (New York: Twayne, 1972), pp. 128–29, 131–32

SIR WALTER SCOTT

1771–1832

Scott was a Tory, but his Toryism was neither reactionary nor subservient. It did not prevent him from opposing a Tory government of his own friends and patrons when they proposed to make what he considered injudicious changes in the banking laws of Scotland. In the three slashing Malachi Malagrowther pamphlets he defeated the Government singlehanded. Nor did his unfaltering Protestantism debar him from publicly espousing the cause of Catholic emancipation. . . .

Far from being founded on a blind attachment to the past and an uncritical fear of change, Scott's Toryism represented a balanced awareness of the degree to which the individual and society are shaped by the historical past and the forces that have created social institutions. He distrusted sweeping panaceas and felt suspicious of radical reforms that might subvert the habits of order and endanger society's equilibrium. For Britain, with its long-established government, he believed in a monarchical and aristocratic organization, but he did justice to the republican Swiss. . . .

Scott's very rationalism was thus rooted in an awareness of the power of tradition over men's minds and hearts. "He understood," one critic [in *TLS*] puts it, "every type of enthusiast," but "could clothe himself in no enthusiasm, whether exalted or extravagant." He saw that unchecked enthusiasm led to fanaticism, and fanaticism, no matter how noble appeared the cause, J. A. Bramley summarizes, "robbed men of their balance, destroyed their judgment, perverted their sense of truth, and finally ended by destroying their sanity, charity, human compassion." Scott's massive sanity perceived these dangers and preserved him from all extremism.

It was this fusion of judgment and control that shaped the man he became. His character was an achievement, not a gift of nature. On the foundations of a crippled body and a passionate heart he built, by a discipline of the reasoned will, the figure the world saw. Beneath the frank and open brow there were hidden veins of reserve. Beneath the bright cheerfulness lay depths of skepticism, even of disillusion. "Life could not be endured," he wrote somberly, "were it seen in reality." . . .

What Scott does—and for the first time in either fiction *or* history—is to dramatize the basic processes of history. He created a revolution, [George Macaulay] Trevelyan notes, by being the first to show that "thoughts and morals vary according to the period, the province, the class, the man." And since his time all history has learned from him. It learned, as G. M. Young observes, that what men *thought* was happening was as important as what was really happening, and their feelings as significant as fact. It learned to listen to what the people were saying. It learned that history embraces the common man as well as kings and statesmen.

Edgar Johnson
Sir Walter Scott: The Great Unknown, Vol. II (New York: Macmillan, 1970), pp. 1253–54, 1260

Scott . . . was very much on the side of the Establishment in these troubles. Like other gentlemen of the time, and to a greater degree than many, he was throughout his life liable to intermittent panic at the thought of popular insurrections and of mobs in action. . . .

All this may make Scott appear a mindless reactionary of the most extreme kind. But in fact his political and social views, which remained very much the same throughout his adult life, were well considered and in some respects perceptive. He feared and hated what the Industrial Revolution was making of workers, and his analysis of the process would have been accepted by Marx. It had destroyed the organic society, in which he profoundly believed. He was a paternalist; he believed in the rights and responsibilities of property; he believed in the dignity of the individual. Two quotations from letters written by Scott in 1820 will make clear his position once and for all. He is arguing in favour of arming the poor where they can be trusted, for the great thing is to prevent a class war, "that most dreadful of evils, a *servile* or Jack Cade sort of war." . . .

"Natural superiors" may make us wince, and it is true that though in his novels Scott could introduce stupid and ridiculous landed proprietors and contrast them with intelligent and dignified peasants, he did in his conscious political thinking believe in a natural order which put the landowner (ideally, benevolent, educated and responsible) at the head of local social groupings. But Scott's diagnosis of how things got the way they were sounds more modern. . . .

This diagnosis puts Scott in line with the Victorian "prophets" Carlyle,

Ruskin and William Morris. It is worth remembering that the Industrial Revolution began in Scotland (on Clydeside) in Scott's youth. In deploring its social and moral effects while welcoming all possible technological aid for what Francis Bacon had called "the relief of man's estate" Scott showed that he was caught up in a contradiction in which most of the great English writers of the nineteenth century were to be involved. It should be added, before this aspect of Scott is left, that he was personally a humane and generous man, kind and thoughtful to his own tenants at Abbotsford, with a great gift for commanding loyalty and affection from those who depended on him.

David Daiches
Sir Walter Scott and His World (New York: Viking, 1971),
pp. 60–62

If it is to the nineteenth-century intellectual tradition known as "historicism" that the modern imagination owes its sense of the unique character of past epochs, no historian helped spread the notion more effectively than Walter Scott. Yet, by a curious paradox, Scott has lost much of his impact in his own realm, fiction, in part because of a critical tendency to judge him in modern terms, without attention to the historically special qualities that make him the novelist he is. When Scott is placed within his proper intellectual milieu, his work is seen to be alive with historical concerns which, while they are not, indeed, precisely our own, are expressed in esthetic forms that can stand as an example to the fiction of any time. To begin by placing Scott within the history of ideas, then, is not to assign him a narrow and outmoded interest; instead, we may come to see his achievement as offering a challenge to the art of our own day. . . .

Historical tradition is the subject but not the norm of Scott's fiction. The temporal dimension of his novels is necessary to trace the historic course of certain values, e.g., those of chivalric heroism, but it is not an absolute guarantor of any one set of values. This argument cuts two ways: it not only excludes the Burkian interpretation but also the Marxist progressivism found in Lukács's reading. Scott's fiction can stand in justification neither of a traditionalist *status quo* nor of a revolutionary historical trend—which Lukács holds up as the inner meaning of these works. The only affirmation Scott makes is of the historical process—of the workings of history itself, which make it certain that no political or social group can make an unqualified claim to credence, though they may conditionally stand for social progress. Thus the appropriate context for Scott is neither Marx nor Burke but Scottish intellectual life—including the speculative historians, who were more concerned to define the form of historical progress than to insist upon a set of ends already achieved or to come. Scott's vision of history is open-ended and free, neither a validation of the past nor an invocation of a necessary outcome on the horizon. Scott was not an ideologist but a dramatist of ideas, and his historical thinking is closer to being an esthetic contemplation of change than it is to being a celebration of any society, past or present.

Avrom Fleishman
The English Historical Novel: Walter Scott to Virginia Woolf
(Baltimore: Johns Hopkins Univ. Pr., 1971), pp. 37, 49–50

MARY WOLLSTONECRAFT (GODWIN) SHELLEY

1797–1851

Born August 30 in London, the daughter of writers William Godwin and Mary Wollstonecraft, Mary Shelley determined early to be an author herself. When she eloped in 1814 with Percy Bysshe Shelley, she kept a journal jointly with Shelley, which was published as the *History of a Six Weeks' Tour through a Part of France, Switzerland, Germany and Holland* in 1817. Her best-known work, *Frankenstein*, was published in 1818. The Shelleys devoted their lives largely to writing and studying. In 1818 they settled in Italy. After Shelley's untimely death in 1822, Mary Shelley returned to England where she continued her career as novelist, essayist, short story writer, critic, and editor. She died on February 1, 1851.

W. H. Lyles, ed., *Mary Shelley: An Annotated Bibliography* (1975)

The Last Man deserves serious attention in any assessment of Mary Shelley's career. Indeed, although the novel is marred by overwriting and sentimentality (Mary's major literary vices) as well as by its excessive length, *The Last Man* is a book of genuine power. Less readable than *Valperga*, less intense and richly symbolic than *Frankenstein*, it easily surpasses, nonetheless, her three remaining novels and does seem, to me, to merit its current ranking of a firm second place (after *Frankenstein*) by virtue of a greater unity and a more substantial underlying conception than is found in *Valperga*. . . .

Mary Shelley, by virtue of her temperament and her experience, arrived at a psychic position which is strikingly similar to that reached by some of the greatest figures of the period. . . .

In short, in *The Last Man,* Mary Shelley, partly through the accident of temperament and experience, partly through the intention of design, undertook an artistic exploration of something far larger than a merely personal reaction to her own individual history. Furthermore, the prevalence of the theme of a "last man" in the literature of the period also suggests that Mary had touched on something much richer than a drawn-out lament for her own emotional isolation. In truth, by connecting the two themes of the isolated sensibility and the death of civilization, Mary created a total effect that is remarkably prophetic of the paradox of modern industrial societies. . . .

William A. Walling
Mary Shelley (New York: Twayne, 1972), pp. 73, 86–87

The worst distortion in the 1831 Introduction is the claim that although Shelley "incited" Mary in the composition of *Frankenstein*, and although he wrote the Preface to the first edition, "I certainly did not owe the suggestion of one incident, nor scarcely of one train of feeling, to my husband." . . . His assistance at every point in the book's manufacture was so extensive that one hardly knows whether to regard him as editor or minor collaborator. . . .

Like Rousseau and Godwin before her, Mary stresses the role of education in the liberation or enslavement of the personality. She apparently agrees with Locke that the mind is a blank slate at birth, and with the sceptics that sensory evidence can mislead the moral judgment. But *Frankenstein* does not survive as a "novel with a thesis." Rather it comes through to us, in Northrop Frye's words, as "a precursor . . . of the existential thriller, of such a book as Camus's *L'Etranger*." Its three concentric narrators, geographically, intellectually, and erotically cut off from the rest of mankind, deal with the world by means of a secret: the explorer's "secret of the magnet," the researcher's galvanic secret of life, and the Monster's pure embodiment of these secrets, together with his unique knowledge of what it is like to be born free of history. . . .

As well as foreshadowing the existential hero, Mary Shelley's and Godwin's characters have American cousins in the obsessed and claustrophobic heroes of Brockden Brown, Poe, Hawthorne, and Melville. Brockden Brown acknowledged his debt to Godwin, and it is not fortuitous that Melville read *Frankenstein* in 1849, two years before he published his own tale of a single-minded voyager, Ahab, chasing "round the Norway Maelstrom, and round perdition's flames" his own monstrous secret, "the monomaniac incarnation of all those malicious agencies which some deep men feel eating in them."

James Rieger
Introd., in Mary Shelley, *Frankenstein, or, The Modern Prometheus*, ed. James Rieger (Indianapolis: Bobbs-Merrill, 1974), pp. xvii–xviii, xxx–xxxi

The versatility of Mary Shelley's myth is due to the brilliance of her mind and the range of her learning, as well as to the influence of the circle in which she moved as a young writer. But *Frankenstein* was most original in its dramatization of dangerous oppositions through the struggle of a creator with monstrous creation. The sources of this Gothic conception, which still has power to "curdle the blood, and quicken the beatings of the heart," were surely the anxieties of a woman who, as daughter, mistress, and mother, was a bearer of death.

But more than mundane is Mary Shelley's concern with the emotions surrounding the parent-child and child-parent relationship. Here her intention to underline the birth myth in *Frankenstein* becomes most evident, quite apart from biographical evidence about its author. She provides an unusual thickening of the background of the tale with familial fact and fantasy, from the very opening of the story in the letters a brother addresses to his sister of whom he is excessively fond, because they are both orphans. There is Frankenstein's relationship to his doting parents, and his semi-incestuous love for an abandoned orphan girl brought up as his sister. There is the first of the monster's murder victims, Frankenstein's infant brother (precisely drawn, even to his name, after Mary Shelley's baby); and the innocent young girl wrongly executed for the infant's murder, who is also a victim of what Mary Shelley calls that "strange perversity," a mother's hatred. (Justine accepts guilt with docility: "I almost began to think that I was the monster that my confessor said I was. . . .") The abundant material in *Frankenstein* about the abnormal, or monstrous, manifestations of the child-parent tie justifies as much as does its famous monster Mary Shelley's reference to the novel as "my hideous progeny."

What Mary Shelley actually did in *Frankenstein* was to transform the standard Romantic matter of incest, infanticide, and patricide into a phantasmagoria of the nursery.

Ellen Moers
NYR (March 21, 1974), p. 28

As a writer of tales and stories, Mary Shelley surpassed many of her predecessors and contemporaries, because she avoided the explicit moralizing found in so many narratives in the late eighteenth and early nineteenth centuries. With the exception of "The Sisters of Albano," her short fiction successfully subordinates moral to theme and character. Like her husband, she disliked overtly didactic literature and preferred to familiarize her readers with beautiful idealisms of moral excellence (or, conversely, to teach the human heart by showing the effects of moral weakness). . . . She did in fact aspire to comfort her readers, and in doing so she idealized or, we might say, exaggerated the human condition. Her heroes and heroines are sometimes writ larger than life, but they never falsify the human experience. . . .

Mary Shelley would frequently idealize the circumstances of her narratives by a historical or Continental setting that removed her characters from the dull and sometimes painful realities of contemporary English life.

Less than one-fourth of her stories are set in England; and only one of these, "The Parvenue," realistically details the social plight of a young English woman torn between responsibilities to a rich husband and to her poor family. More characteristic are tales of passionate love and hate set in medieval Italy, sixteenth-century France, or contemporary Europe. In four of these stories, Mary Shelley uses a fantastic element to idealize her narratives even further. The Roman Valerius and the seventeenth-century Roger Dodsworth were both reanimated into contemporary life; the Mortal Immortal had attained the age of 323 when he narrated his tale; and in "Transformation," the hero and a misshapen dwarf exchange bodies. Yet in each of these cases, she subordinates the science-fictional element to a study in character that is designed to "exalt & soften" human sorrow.

It is also possible to read Mary Shelley's fictions as idealizations of her own life. Many of her heroines are orphans or at least alienated from one or both parents. . . . She has transformed personal experience into art, in accordance with the principle she explained while reviewing her father's novel *Cloudesley*: "the merely copying from our own hearts will no more form a first-rate work of art, than will the most exquisite representation of mountains, water, wood, and glorious clouds, form a good painting, if none of the rules of grouping or colouring are followed."

Charles E. Robinson
Introd., in Mary Shelley, *Collected Tales and Stories* (Baltimore: Johns Hopkins Univ. Pr., 1976), pp. xiv–xvi

Frankenstein, for all its exclusion of women, is—among other things—a parable of motherhood. . . . Her own mother, the feminist Mary Wollstonecraft, had set an example of simultaneous childcare and literary production; Mary Shelley's accomplishment is no less impressive, and its significance arouses our curiosity.

Briefly, I propose an approach to the novel through its organization, its narrative structure, in order to achieve a fresh perspective on its meaning for Mary Shelley—and for us. This will make it much easier to see the maternal imagery which runs through the story and to locate that aspect of the story's significance in the author's life. Further, it will free us somewhat from the controversy which has persisted from the very beginning over the author's status as a mere "passive reflection" of her circumstances, "her brain . . . magnetized" by Shelley. . . .

At that point in her life, Mary stood in the dual position of the monster and Frankenstein: looking backward, she was the abandoned, displaced child; looking forward, she was the new mother whose children might die or be the death of her. Either the outraged and murderous jealousy of the monster or the guilty destructiveness of Frankenstein suggests the aggressive and lethal side of the author's fear of "forwardness." It is as though to be involved in creation, let alone take the initiative in it, is to participate in a two-sided struggle where one party must die.

We cannot overlook the equation of forwardness and masculinity. Probably Mary could indulge as an adolescent in a limited amount of expression of some of her masculine identifications, though she was extremely defensive even then about any outright accusation of masculinity in her thinking (see her letter to Shelley for October 7, 1817). . . .

The spirit of stories within stories, or dreams within dreams, which pervades the novel is also restitutive and protective. The lost baby is found through the writing of a book that is constructed like a pregnancy, the feared experience of motherhood is repeated in the relative safety of authorship, the dead mother is resurrected—temporarily—within the heart of the story. Finally, the most curious aspect of all: the author, in looking for her mother, has in a sense found herself, for she has literally conceived of her own conception and thus becomes her own "hideous progeny."

Marc A. Rubenstein
SIR (Spring, 1976), pp. 165–66, 192–94

PERCY BYSSHE SHELLEY

1792–1822

All of Shelley's characteristic images appear in *The Revolt of Islam.* At the very beginning the history of mankind is allegorized as a struggle between an eagle and a serpent. The serpent, emblem of eternity, sheds its skin annually and thus became for revolutionaries, Shelley would have learned in Barruel, an emblem of revolution (IV, 349–350). Spring and renewal symbolism is concentrated in the episode where Laon senses renewed power and hope as he anticipates his reunion with Cythna. It is a pattern to be developed more richly later in the description of Prometheus and Asia. The revolution seems to have faltered, but when the lovers retreat to the home of autumn's dead leaves, some notion of the ritual spell of hope and renewal which lovers may invoke is suggested. Power, beauty, and knowledge were kindled by their relationship. . . .

The whole West-Wind complex of imagery is explored in *The Revolt of Islam.* In fact, the great ode might be described as an abstraction of the long poem, just as *Prometheus Unbound* is its symbolic and mythological counterpart. . . .

In the preface to his poem, Shelley outlined the revolutionary poetics. Like other men poets have active and passive faculties. Poets are partly shaped by their experience and environment, all of a particular age being subject to a "combination of circumstances" peculiar to their time, "though each is in a degree the author of the very influence by which his being is thus pervaded." Such passiveness, poets, allowing for their more highly developed sensitivity, have in common with all men. The true poet, however, having "a mind that has been nourished upon musical thoughts," can convert or transform his experience into images and harmonies capable of awakening in others sensations and ideas like his own. It was thus that Laon's poetry acted on Cythna's deep, aspiring, and sympathetic nature. The experiences and feelings recorded in his poetry came from a closeness to elemental nature, deep reading in rich mines of revolutionary lore, and his own shared love with Cythna. Laon's was the active, creative power. She was the profoundly receptive auditor able to sing and live those harmonies. . . . Thus can art and poetry rejuvenate a world of freedom, equality, and love.

Gerald McNiece
Shelley and the Revolutionary Idea (Cambridge, Mass.: Harvard Univ. Pr., 1969), pp. 196, 203

Shelley could face death and life with equal strength and courage because he had learned, after many trials and not a few errors, wherein his happiness lay: It was neither to be found in political panaceas, such as reform bills (though he would have welcomed the progressive democratization of England during the later nineteenth century), nor in an ideal antitype of his psyche embodied in another man or woman (though he highly valued true friendship); rather, his happiness lay in *words that praised* the social and personal ideals he had cherished so intensely during all his adult years.

In the life of the imagination, especially as that experience could be communicated to others through creative actions and gestures, through the plastic and performing arts, and most effectually through written words, Shelley saw the seeds of the values that could continually regenerate individual men and, at fortunate moments in human history, renovate entire societies. *Prometheus Unbound*, "A Defence of Poetry," *Epipsychidion, Adonais, Hellas*, and "The Triumph of Life" all say with one voice that the virtues of any living individual man are inspired, nurtured, and brought to fruition (or limited) by the imaginative ideals he holds—his personal vision of what a man ought to be. The *telos*, the goal of human life, thus lies within the best of the imaginative ideals available to men; and the greatest service one man can perform for his fellows is to augment and enhance those ideals.

If we were asked to evaluate Shelley's life and work, we could point to the practical effectiveness of his poetry and prose in the history of British political and social reform movements or to his pervading influence among great literary figures of the later nineteenth and the twentieth centuries—Tennyson, Browning, Rossetti, Swinburne, Meredith, Hardy, Shaw, Yeats, and (in spite of his early criticisms) T. S. Eliot. But a truer test, and one that Shelley himself would have approved, is the degree to which his imaginative mythic formulations have been diffused into the general cultural imagination. The figures of Prometheus, Queen Mab, Count Cenci and Beatrice, and such natural phenomena as Mont Blanc, the west wind, a cloud, or a skylark evoke in literate English-speaking people conceptions that are as vividly informed by Shelley's imagination as the characters of Falstaff, Richard III, Romeo and Juliet are by Shakespeare's, those of Comus, Adam and Eve, and Satan by Milton's, and the whole panoply of Canterbury pilgrimages by Chaucer's. . . . The measure of Shelley's success will remain . . . in the number of elements of public thought and discourse upon which he has placed the ineradicable stamp of his imagination.

Donald H. Reiman
Percy Bysshe Shelley (New York: Twayne, 1969), pp. 160–61

As a dramatist, Shelley is a great lyric poet, that he brings to his tragedy the innate sensibilities of a lyric poet. But that is not to say that [*The Cenci*] fails as a result. Rather it is to suggest why in basic terms *The Cenci* is not Shakespearean or Sophoclean and why, indeed, it is a unique work of art, forging its own rules and inhabiting its own world. Ernest Bates is correct in every point except his conclusion: one entire act of the play does not further the plot; two-thirds of the scenes are basically conversation rather than action; and the speeches are often long. But the play is still dramatic. It is true that three scenes, brief scenes at that, are barely adequate in this regard; but the other twelve are fully capable of holding the stage. That the play would profit from a few alterations and from cutting something less than a tenth of its lines indicates that Shelley was not always sure of his means, but it does not detract from the genuinely dramatic nature of the work.

The underlying structure of the tragedy is a unit of unshakable solidity from which no scene could be eliminated without undermining what is assembled with such disciplined austerity. . . . The fundamental dramatic nature of Shelley's play stems from the depth with which he grasped his subject and followed it to its philosophical rather than theatrical implications before setting the legend in dramatic form. No play in the English language deals with evil of this scope or this pronounced reality. . . .

On the deepest level Shelley is less interested in documenting cause and effect, the stuff of stage action, than he is in pursuing effects in the human mind, which he realizes in the form of a dramatic psychological tension. Despite its realism, *The Cenci* is cut from the same intellectual fabric as *Prometheus Unbound*, where every cause is its own effect, where the man who ceases to hate is suddenly free and she who asks when the hour of delivery is to come sees its instantaneous arrival.

Stuart Curran
Shelley's Cenci: Scorpions Ringed with Fire (Princeton, N.J.: Princeton Univ. Pr., 1970), pp. 274–76

It is only by taking *Prometheus Unbound* and *A Philosophical View of Reform* together that we interpret Demogorgon's final speech as a program of civil disobedience, based on the social psychology of unyielding patience. The drama attempts to give delight by showing how it works, and why, in a vision that exists irrefutably in its own language. . . . Shelley proposes by the drama to impel, through delight, a few readers who will impel a few more leaders who will impel the majority. He does not design the poem merely as "an astonishment," like the hieroglyphs on an obelisk whose meaning is lost; he tries to dissolve the manners, morals, and issues of his own day in the moving beauty of myth. The error of the critic would be to ignore the application and value of the myth for Shelley's own day.

In *Prometheus Unbound* Shelley avoided Coleridge's impasse and Keats's torment by carrying into his supreme work of imagination the agnosticism that had freed him from materialism, Cartesian dualism, hunger for certainty, and appeal to the reader's capacity for rational analysis. As the texture of his poetry thickened with symbols of the ideal, the stridency of his search for absolutes subsided. Violence, for example, was still a two-edged weapon to be used late, sparingly, and despondently, but it was not, in a just cause such as a revolution for national independence, an absolute evil. More than the other poets, Shelley could break new ground without giving up the old. He could insert a higher utilitarianism into mythic vision without any irritable reaching after God. Divinity, no more or less than the eternally best in and for man, would be the ultimate subject for choral hymning in a lyrical drama. The history of Shelley's reputation contains a remarkable testimony to his success. Although he has been charged with almost every other weakness man is capable of, he has not been charged with cynicism. His atheism had come to this: the inherited sin is Malthusian despair of reform; love is the effectual fulfillment of the law and the commandments; the duty of love exceeds any conceivable reliance on an external redeemer.

Carl Woodring
Politics in English Romantic Poetry (Cambridge, Mass.: Harvard Univ. Pr., 1970), pp. 309–10

Only after having explored the tragic actuality did Shelley then have the earned confidence to add the final celebrative act to his drama of optimism [*Prometheus Unbound*]. He has not abandoned his fundamental skeptical frame of mind; rather, instead of exposing his incertitude, he has internalized it in order that, on that fragile basis, he may take a stand and break free of what he called "the indolence of scepticism." In overtly skeptical poems like *Julian and Maddalo*, he explicitly engaged the actual and the ideal in indecisive debate; although he offered *Prometheus Unbound* and *The Cenci* as independent, self-sustaining works with confident postures, they represent, taken together, the antinomies of the skeptical contest as it was waged in Shelley's own mind, and in a very real sense they should be read against each other approximately as we read his hymns of Apollo and Pan. . . .

Skepticism alone proves inadequate for Shelley, for although it "destroys error and the roots of error," it also leaves a "vacancy" and can result in paralysis, since it arrives only at "negative truth." The ultimate function of Shelley's empirical skepticism and the probing incertitude of such poems as *Alastor* and *Julian and Maddalo*, which threaten to result in "the indolence of scepticism," is to clear the ground for a probabilism based on imagination and belief. . . .

This does not mean that Shelley would accept as real every capricious combination organized by the imagination. Not only are thoughts limited to perceptions and their combinations according to the laws of the mind, but in *The Necessity of Atheism* and ever afterward Shelley accepted Hume's doctrine that belief is a passion, not "an act of volition." It is necessary and involuntary, not capricious. In belief the mind is passive, unable to resist the persuasion of probability, which is "purely proportionate to the degrees of excitement," such as, progressively, conjecture, persuasion, and conviction. . . .

What the "mechanical philosophy" calls "true" is an external reality corresponding to the impressions received by the mind as it is supposedly "impelled or organized by the adhibition of events proceeding from what has been termed the mechanism of the material universe." But the "beautiful" is the imagination's most nearly perfect organization of phenomena according to the laws of the mind. A philosophy that overlooks the constitutive role of imagination and the confirming role of belief in determining the inclusive "universe" may supply us with a reality that is true in the empirical sense, but it also supplies us with a reality that is defective.

Earl R. Wasserman
Shelley: A Critical Reading (Baltimore: Johns Hopkins Univ. Pr., 1971), pp. 128, 151–52

In Ireland in 1812 [Shelley] had advocated building a large general organization around the issues of Catholic emancipation and the repeal of the Union Act, with a smaller group of "philanthropists" giving it guidance and focusing its ultimate sights on an egalitarian republic. In *Queen Mab* he had depicted the egalitarian society and stated that it was to be achieved by "the gradual paths of an aspiring change." A similar dual emphasis on the present and the future appears in his public letter on the Eaton case.

In 1817 his friendship with Hunt had brought him into contact with the reform movement. *A Proposal for Putting Reform to the Vote* was a "moderate" reform pamphlet of *The Examiner* type. Though it did not bring out his ultimate republican and egalitarian goals, he had not given them up, as *The Revolt of Islam*, written a few months later, adequately demonstrated. He simply did not wish in this tract to alienate reform readers. In examining any particular work by Shelley, one must take into account its purpose and the audience for which it was written.

A Philosophical View of Reform is wider in scope and appeal than the *Proposal for Putting Reform to the Vote*. The *Proposal* was on a specific topic; the *Philosophical View* is a general statement of reform policies. Nevertheless, it is a reform tract, not primarily an examination of history or economic theory, and if these matters were to be discussed—and Shelley obviously thought it important to discuss them in order to set the reform movement and its ideas in perspective—they had to be discussed as background. Shelley unfortunately never wrote a work in which he concentrated primarily on his general social theories. He did, however, succeed in working them into the fabric of his tract, and in so doing, he gave it a scope beyond that of any other reform tract, even Bentham's. He placed the present in the perspectives of history, and history in the perspectives of the future. . . .

This may seem a strange claim to make for Shelley, who was primarily a poet, not a political philosopher. But he was also a man of genius, writing, like Dante, in the sharp air of persecution and exile. Certainly among the political writers of the period there is no one who even approached him either for his sharp insights into the present or his vision of the future.

Kenneth Neill Cameron
Shelley: The Golden Years (Cambridge, Mass.:
Harvard Univ. Pr., 1974), pp. 148–49

That the field of astronomy provided a focus for Shelley's scientific interests, on the one hand, and for his melioristic beliefs, on the other, has long been recognized. His "Notes on *Queen Mab*" and the closely contemporary essay entitled *A Vindication of Natural Diet* not only abound with morsels of learning picked up from [Pierre-Simon] Laplace, Cabanis, and [Jean Sylvain] Bailly; but, as Earl Wasserman has shown, Shelley shared the mechanists' view that man's physical progress, his moral as well as biological evolution, was causally linked to a continuing process of cosmological change for the better. . . .

There is little need to stress the resemblance between [Leonhard]

Euler's geometrical construct, with its harmonious motions in Euclidian space, and Shelley's own imaginary creation of the multitudinous orb. The poet's description of "A sphere, which is as many thousand spheres," all on "a thousand sightless axles spinning," evokes so precisely Euler's idea as to make specific reference to the orb's "intense yet self-conflicting speed" as it rolls "with the force of self-destroying swiftness" (that is, the Earth's instantaneous axis) seem almost unnecessarily pointed. The concentricity of Shelley's design . . . at the same time repeats Laplace's own, of a structured progression of diminishing globes, so faithfully as to make the poet's indebtedness to the astronomer clear. Admittedly, Shelley's version contains details of a poetical order that are, scientifically speaking, gratuitous; yet, in combining Laplace's conception with Euler's—the static with the dynamic—Shelley makes each more vividly sensuous, adding the touch of music and color to an otherwise lifeless geometric abstraction. This in itself is a signal achievement; but what is more remarkable still is that the resulting conflation, further enriched with material borrowed from Milton and Dante, possesses a visionary integrity of its own. The symbol of the multitudinous orb has all the intellectual genesis, yet none of the actual attributes of a hybrid. It demonstrates Shelley's power to bring radically heterogeneous concepts into fertile imaginative conjunction, a power which (as "A Defence of Poetry" has it) "subdues to union under its light yoke, all irreconcilable things."

Thomas A. Reisner
K–SJ, Vol. 23 (1974), pp. 54–55, 58–59

Shelley's learned fusion of occidental and oriental mythic structures in *Prometheus Unbound* constitutes a complex extrapolation of the marriage of west and east symbolized by Prometheus and Asia. To the extent that they attain an archetypal stature, they contain multitudes, who are revealed in the receding vortices of mythic allusion. Yet, however much a universality composed solely of such traditional elaborations might satisfy a Peacock, to Shelley it would appear inadequate to the charge he had set himself. The strength of his own philosophical inclinations, not to mention the pressure of his irreligion, contributes to his gathering further ramifications to his drama. If all religions are essentially a single faith, it is necessary, in order to avoid mere ceremony on the one hand or mere superstition on the other, to distill from the myth its relevance to an actual human condition.

Shelley refuses the alternate options his generation posed: either the English tendency to subordinate foreign mythic structures to a single Christian orthodoxy, or that of the French to see them as imaginative flights unfortunately divorced from the natural laws they once preserved mnemonically. Both efforts deny the spiritual realities of human life, the first by limiting them to a single dogmatic standard, the second by reducing them to materiality. Once again, Shelley's endeavor is to unite rather than fragment: in its philosophical and psychological dimensions *Prometheus Unbound* does not deny the integrity of the mind nor of the world, but asserts that only in their balanced interaction can there be either mental health or truth. The skeptical model from which these attitudes take form is enunciated by Prometheus in describing the cave in which he and Asia will be united. . . .

That the phenomenal world assumes meaning through the organizational structures of the mind has a corollary: by changing the mental structures, one can alter the world. On Prometheus' shift of attitude, not only the drama, but the entire cosmos turns.

Stuart Curran
Shelley's Annus Mirabilis: The Maturing of an Epic Vision
(San Marino, Cal.: Huntington Library, 1975), pp. 95–96

I would suggest that [Rousseau's] sleep and rising in the valley [in "The Triumph of Life"] represent not birth but death, and that the subsequent experiences he recounts represent his symbolic reenactment, after death, of his mortal life. In Rousseau's oblivious sleep, this is to say, we see the sleep of death itself; in his rising, we see an awakening in death from this initial sleep to the bright promise of an afterlife, inversely analogous to a babe's awakening to the bright promise of life; and in his ruinous integration into Life's triumph, we see finally his spirit's progressive corruption and disillusionment in this afterlife, paralleling the fate it had already suffered in life. Hazlitt was speaking truer than he knew, I think, and truer than any later critic has recognized, when he wrote, "The poem entitled the 'Triumph of Life' is in fact a new and terrific Dance of Death . . ."

This reading of "The Triumph," while radically different from all earlier interpretations, finds both precedent and justification in Shelley's thought and work. In letters to Elizabeth Hitchener years before, Shelley had supposed that just as the intellect or soul is suspended in dreamless sleep, so may it be in death, and that "in a future existence it will lose all consciousness of having formerly lived elsewhere, and will begin life anew, possibly under a shape of which we have now no idea." And a few months previous he had expatiated on that "future state." . . . To be sure, these were the half-formed opinions of an immature philosopher, and Shelley was soon to retreat from them into a skeptical epistemology. Thereafter, he consistently acknowledged the impossibility of man's knowing anything about a future state. . . .

Just as Shelley blames Rousseau and the *Alastor*-Poet for similar failings, so in "The Triumph" as a whole does he visualize for all men the doom he had forecast in his Preface to the earlier poem. In *Alastor*, the assertion of this fate comes as something of an afterthought; in "The Triumph," however, it comprises both the beginning and ending of his vision as we have it, casting over the whole a shadow of the deepest pessimism and gloom.

John A. Hodgson
ELH (Winter, 1975), pp. 598–99, 614–15

In his recognition of the functions of translation for the translator, Shelley was unusual not only among translators but especially among the poets of his own day. For Shelley, translation was in part a propaedeutic, a poetic exercise which helped to ignite his creative faculties. As we have seen, many of the great translators have had an external motive to spur them to their work. Those whose motives were essentially personal, Cowper for instance, also had their eyes on the possible reading public. But few used translation for private purposes as systematically and as widely as Shelley. He translated from Latin, Greek, French, German, Italian, Spanish, and English. The authors included Pliny, Buffon, Aristotle, Spinoza, Plutarch, Tacitus, Plato, Virgil, Latini, Euripides, Bion, Moschus, Dante, Calvalcanti, Goethe, Calderón, Aeschylus, and Homer. He also projected translations from d'Holbach and Godwin, and he even rendered some of his work into Italian. . . .

For Shelley translation fulfilled a number of personal needs. It soothed him in time of distress. It tided him over periods barren of inspiration. It provided valuable poetic exercise. It gave him a framework for his poetry. Sometimes it offered direct inspiration. The importance of Shelley's translations is to be seen not only in the translations themselves, but also in much of his original work. In thus realizing the value of translation, Shelley was unique among the great original poets of his generation.

Timothy Webb
The Violet in the Crucible: Shelley and Translation (Oxford: Clarendon, 1976), pp. 48–50

ROBERT SOUTHEY

1774–1843

To attempt to read Southey's social and political writing as the expression of a writer devoted to the political positions of the ministerial party—an administration which literary historians usually call a Tory administration —is to do Southey a disservice and to misunderstand the various political groups which headed the British government during his lifetime. The changing conditions of the domestic and foreign scene—changes that no one could have foreseen—meant that individuals and government were necessarily shifting their sympathies. Southey was not a systematic political theorist, but he held certain views throughout his life and altered others as he grew older and feared some of the changes he saw coming. A constant thread throughout his career was a concern for humanity, a hatred for cruelty and injustice, and a sympathy for the poor and outcasts. . . . These humanitarian concerns led to his writing in favor of reforms in prisons and in the care of the mentally ill and towards the efforts of the Quakers who led in these two reforms.

Southey's early enthusiasm for the French Revolution was cooled by the turn of events in France, and he came to look upon Napoleon as the enemy of British freedom and security and a foe who must be defeated at all costs. From this belief came his support of the ministers who were directing the war and his willingness to write in aid of these policies in the *Edinburgh Annual Register* and the *Quarterly Review*, founded as they were to support the ministry against the pacifism and defeatism of some of the Whigs. Southey also supported the ministers in their opposition to any concessions to the Roman Catholics and to reforms in the process by which Members of Parliament were elected. But many of the reforms which he did recommend were viewed by the most conservative, whether Whig or Tory, as subversive of the constitution. . . .

His successes [as a poet] are far fewer than might have been expected and as his contemporaries—and he himself—predicted. The nagging question of the cause of this failure remains. Part of the reason is due to his truly amazing facility in composing verses and his unwillingness to give his poems the kind of ruthless revision and rewriting which they demanded. Part of this seeming carelessness was due to the pressure of writing for money and the difficulties of his personal life around 1800 when his poetic creativity was at its height, but a more significant cause was a reluctance to involve himself emotionally in the hard thought that must go into the writing of poetry. It was, for instance, easier to write a poem out of the materials of humble and rustic life than it was to exhaust himself—as Wordsworth often did—in seeking to penetrate all the implications of the chosen subject.

Kenneth Curry
Southey (London: Routledge & Kegan Paul, 1975),
pp. 75–76, 174

MARY WOLLSTONECRAFT

1759–1797

Born April 27 in London, Mary Wollstonecraft is now regarded as the progenitor of the modern movement for equal rights for women. Her writings include: *Thoughts on the Education of Daughters* (1781), *Vindication of the Rights of Men* (1790), and *A Vindication of the Rights of Woman* (1792). In 1797 she married the novelist-philosopher William Godwin, whose treatise *An Enquiry Concerning the Principles of Political Justice* (1793) and novel *Caleb Williams* (1794) demonstrate the same reformist political stance as the works of Mary Wollstonecraft. Mary Wollstonecraft died on September 10, 1797 from complications arising from the birth of Mary Wollstonecraft Godwin (who married Percy Bysshe Shelley).

Janet M. Todd, ed., *Mary Wollstonecraft: An Annotated Bibliography* (1976)

For Mary's purposes, indeed, the French Revolution was ideally timed. It burst upon her just as she was rounding out her apprenticeship to her new trade, just as she was seeking for a new creed and a broad outlet for her energies. Its spirit was ideally adapted to hers. As she had told Joseph Johnson, she was "not fond of groveling"; and at the moment she was glorying in her independence after years of bondage. Though the American Revolution had, in its time, seemed like the dawn of a new era, it had taken place in a remote country when Mary could hardly have comprehended its significance. But now freedom was coming to Europe, and Mary was old enough and wise enough to appreciate the meaning of the exciting events —and woman enough to be thrilled by them. Only a few months before, she had rejected her melancholy piety and tried to convince herself that reason could serve both as guide and as justification for human existence. But reason had proved cold comfort; it was, as she complained, "not a good bracer." The French Revolution, however, represented not *cold* reason, but reason in action, reason which recognized men's longings and tried to achieve them. The abstract rights of men, which she had heard so much about at Newington Green and at Johnson's dinner parties, were now about to be realized; and suddenly they made sense to her. Her whole life had been a struggle for just such rights. If all men could gain those rights, there would be an end to the tyranny and injustice which made life seem a thorny path. There would be no such discrepancies as she had seen between peasant and lord in Ireland. No nation would suffer in the grip of one man—perhaps a madman like George III, her own monarch. Instead, every man would be his own master; love would replace hatred; and heaven would reign on earth.

To Mary the Revolution must have seemed like a happy fusion of all that she had been taught to respect by her sage London friends, and all that she cherished by nature. It was Voltaire and Rousseau too, rationalism and enthusiasm; it appealed to her head and her heart, and for once she was not obliged to compromise between them. And so she, like many of her countrymen, looked hopefully to France as the great proving-ground. Once established there, freedom could easily be carried across to England and gradually spread throughout the world.

Ralph M. Wardle
Mary Wollstonecraft: A Critical Biography (Lincoln: Univ. Nebraska Pr., 1951), pp. 105–6

To understand [William] Godwin's appeal for Mary and the rapid development of their relationship, it must be remembered how much else they had in common. Both were reformers, but also gradualists who respected freedom, individual human dignity, and the power of reason. Both had come to a position of skepticism from deep religious commitment. Hard work, thought, and writing were at the center of their lives; they respected each other's need for privacy and the long hours of uninterrupted work they both required.

In addition, each brought the other something new. Godwin was touchingly grateful to Mary for opening up to him a whole new dimension of human experience. Passionate love and the deep affection which grew from it had a literally overwhelming effect on the "philosopher," who had previously underestimated (to put it mildly) the very nature of love between human beings. Judging by his discussion of "benevolence" in *Political Justice*, he had a good deal to learn. . . .

In the same work he had been profoundly critical of the institution of marriage. Not only did it often take place between people insufficiently acquainted with one another, but was "an affair of property, and the worst of all properties," a sentiment in which he antedated Karl Marx by more than half a century. But instead of recognizing, as Mary Wollstonecraft had, that marriage in its existing form too often debased the emotion on which it should be founded, Godwin denied the very existence of the emotion. He did not recognize love as something of value in itself. . . .

After Mary's death, Godwin made changes in successive editions of *Political Justice* which brought it into line with his own experience of marriage. He even projected a work whose aim would be to correct *Political Justice* in its failure to give "proper attention to the empire of feeling." The book was never written; instead, he wrote the novel *St. Leon*, which pays eloquent tribute to marriage as it could be and as he found it to be in his brief experience with Mary.

Eleanor Flexner
Mary Wollstonecraft (Baltimore: Penguin, 1973), pp. 230–32

While [Wollstonecraft] had written her polemical works and survived the Revolution, the English Jacobin novelists—Godwin, Thomas Holcroft, Robert Bage, Elizabeth Inchbald, Mary Hays, and others—had carried the novel into the thick of the political fray. In particular, her friend Mary Hays's *Memoirs of Emma Courtney* (1796) showed how philosophy and politics, feminism and autobiography, could all be transmuted into the form of popular fiction. In the hands of the English Jacobins, the "English Popular Novel" had become a serious literary kind, and Mary Wollstonecraft could not now but be "sensible how arduous a task it is to produce a truly excellent novel; and she roused her faculties to grapple with it" [J. M. S. Tompkins]. Now she attempted various forms, and rejected them, abandoned her usual manner of rapid but slovenly composition, and wrote and rewrote. When she died a year later she had still completed only a third of her novel [*The Wrongs of Women*] but she had learned that autobiographical fiction could be more objective by paradoxically being more personal. . . .

By extending the range of her "observations" on the condition of woman, and fusing them with her own "feelings and passions," she could unite her own experience with that of women everywhere, and still continue to explore all the varieties of autobiographical imagining through allegory and analogy, confession and compensation, fantasy, revenge, and reparation. It was not a classical shapely form, but it was romantically replete.

It was also constructed along the logical if inelegant lines of the typical English Jacobin novel. The militant purpose was outlined in a polemical preface: if like a sentimental or Romantic novelist the author "rather endeavoured to pourtray passions than manners," like an English Jacobin she also wished to exhibit "the misery and oppression, peculiar to women, that arise out of the partial laws and customs of society." Beside the Romantic interest in individual passions is the Enlightenment pursuit of the universal, "and the history ought rather to be considered, as of woman, than of an individual." Most interesting of all was the author's desire "to show the wrongs of different classes of women." If *Mary* had been a compendium of ideas and attitudes of the age of Sensibility, [*The Wrongs of Women*] was to epitomize the New Philosophy.

Gary Kelly
Introd., in Mary Wollstonecraft, *Mary, A Fiction and The Wrongs of Woman* (London: Oxford Univ. Pr., 1976), pp. xv–xvi

The strength of the social criticism in [*Letters Written during a Short Residence in Sweden, Norway, and Denmark*] is the strength of Mary

Wollstonecraft: she does not stop being a woman or a mother or a political radical as she observes. She is always the social meliorist, looking about her for signs of "my favorite subject of contemplation, the future improvement of the world" (Letter XII). She even seems oddly gratified to note that the countries she is visiting are in many ways backward, because this fact affirms her belief in social evolution, the progress of humankind. She had explained her position in *A Vindication of the Rights of Woman*: "Rousseau exerts himself to prove that all *was* right originally: a crowd of authors that all *is* now right: and I, that all will *be* right."

And of course here, as in her other work, the vehicle for social change is political equality and educational reform. The premise that all people should be treated as fully rational individuals, deserving of rights, underlies her fight for women's freedom as well as her argument for prison reform and her tolerance toward servants (she never progressed far enough to say that there need be no servants; they were always a given). Likewise a humane and sensible view of humanity fuels her arguments against capital punishment in Letter XIX, where she concludes that public executions, far from acting as a deterrent to crime, actually numbed the viewers to murder, making them more callous and therefore more apt to commit crimes themselves. And finally, even her long-range view of humanity is revealed when, three years before T. A. Malthus's first published observations about the exponential increase in population and the geometric increase in food supply, Wollstonecraft in Letter XI is concerned about "the state of man when the earth could no longer support him. Where was he to fly from universal famine?"

Carol H. Poston
Introd., in Mary Wollstonecraft, *Letters Written during a Short Residence in Sweden, Norway, and Denmark* (Lincoln: Univ. Nebraska Pr., 1976), pp. xv–xvi

Mary Wollstonecraft has not, on balance, been well served by her biographers. A variety of impedimenta, including personal and sexual prejudice, misunderstanding of her mind and personality, as well as rapidly shifting socio-historical tides, have combined to prevent a clear view of the woman and her work. The result has been to distort the achievement of one whom Godwin described as "inexpressibly the first of women." Perhaps there was in all her writings—polemical, fiction, letters—too personal a stamp, which marked her for easy misapprehension; or possibly that force of personality itself which so affected her contemporaries lost something vital in its transformation into the written word, so that the impression of a strong spirit became transmuted into an impaired reflection of its original. Starting with her first chronicler, the newly widowed Godwin who sought by his memorial to ensure for Mary the appreciation he thought was her right, and who so badly misread the audience, and Mary's impact on it, that *Memoirs of the Author of "A Vindication of the Rights of Woman"* aroused a reaction of unprecedented hostility, Mary's posthumous fortunes have been subject to dramatic extremes. The history of her reputation has been described by Jacob Bouten in an apparently little used, but important historical study, *Mary Wollstonecraft and the Beginnings of Female Emancipation in France and England* (Amsterdam, 1922). He defines three "distinctly marked phases" of, first, violent opprobrium; followed by a long period of oblivion; until, after the publication of Kegan Paul's study of Godwin and his circle, a series of efforts to rehabilitate and vindicate emerged.

Nevertheless, although a century has passed since Kegan Paul's work, and although the 1970's audience has so far been treated to five biographical enterprises . . . Mary's position as subject of both biographical and feminist studies remains problematical. Her thought continues to suffer a kind of dimunition, from being exploited out of its own context (and this notwithstanding Ralph Wardle's 1951 *Mary Wollstonecraft: A Critical Biography*, which is a model for locating an author in her cultural milieu, as is Bouten's earlier study). Her works have yet to receive the kind of scholarly editing and informed introduction which would situate her properly in *her* times for an intelligent reading in *our* times. The partial approach of her current biographers denies Mary Wollstonecraft her place in the history and ideology of her epoch, just as it deprives ours of the opportunity to realize the remarkable effort involved in the achievement of a woman refused the tools and discipline of an education which we take as our birthright.

Alice Green Fredman
K–SJ, Vol. 25 (1976), pp. 135–36

WILLIAM WORDSWORTH

1770–1850

Lyrical Ballads

The two poets who inaugurated a poetic revolution in the *Lyrical Ballads* of 1798 and 1800 left differing accounts of their intentions. . . . Both accounts made the *Lyrical Ballads* seem more planned, more formal in design and strategy, than they actually were. The truth is that they were rooted more in conflict than in harmony. The two poets shared many enthusiasms and dislikes, but their attempt at collaboration in 1797 brought out sharp differences of view between them. Out of these differences arose the experimental poems and the critical, sometimes polemical, essays that accompanied and followed them. Some of these poems appeared in the several editions of *Lyrical Ballads*, some did not. They cover a space of more than ten years, from "The Three Graves" of 1797 to "The White Doe" of 1807 and 1808 (roughly the span of Wordsworth's great decade). The critical disagreements that ran through these years reached a summing up in Coleridge's *Biographia Literaria* in 1817, where besides defining the dual purpose of the volumes, Coleridge pronounced Wordsworth's experiments—which "in a comparatively small number of poems he chose to try"—a failure. . . .

The newest notion about *Lyrical Ballads* is one of the most challenging. It is the notion that these poems were not after all original, but simply developed poetic modes widely prevalent in the 1790's. This notion sets aside—or ignores—a number of contemporary opinions. Wordsworth himself seemed to think his poems original, both when he discriminated them from "the popular Poetry of the day" in 1800 and when he reflected in 1815 how much they had altered English poetry and English taste. Coleridge thought some of them rather too original. Reviewers complained of their differences from poems they had learned to like. . . .

This notion has enough truth in it to require a special kind of refutation. I have tried to counter it by tracing the literary antecedents of Wordsworth's most experimental poems (mainly to [Gottfried August] Bürger in Germany, to Burns in Britain) and by showing how Wordsworth moved away from them in original directions.

Stephen Maxfield Parrish
The Art of the "Lyrical Ballads" (Cambridge, Mass.: Harvard Univ. Pr., 1973), pp. vii–x

Written within a few weeks of one another, these ballads [in *Lyrical Ballads*] show Wordsworth challenging the genre he has adopted—insisting first on writing with a definite "purpose," then on questioning the very basis of narrative convention, and finally subverting it altogether. The result is a genre capable not simply of expressing Wordsworth's vision, but of modifying and extending the reader's; offered "Such stores as silent thought can bring," we are shown how to "find/A tale in everything" ("Simon Lee," ll. 74, 75–76). The ballads of 1798 are not only technically exhilarating in their own right, but among Wordsworth's most effective statements about the aims and functions of his poetry. . . .

Coleridge wrote of Wordsworth that "without his depth of feeling and his imaginative power his *sense* would want its vital warmth and peculiarity; and without his strong sense, his *mysticism* would become *sickly*—mere fog, and dimness!" *Peter Bell* triumphantly expresses this balance. A manifesto for the Wordsworthian imagination, it also reveals "the loveliness and the wonders of the world before us"; its movement is both inward and outward, its values are personal but not solipsistic. The poem's special significance for *Lyrical Ballads* lies in bringing into the open the self-defining struggle for literary identity which is central to the volume. In *Peter Bell*, as in "Tintern Abbey," creative interaction with another poet makes Wordsworth most fully himself. In their different ways, the two poems are the culminating statement of poetic identity to come out of their period, and both affirm the creed of years to come—that restoration through the dual operation of nature and imagination which is to be Wordsworth's theme in *The Prelude*. *Lyrical Ballads* shows Wordsworth at once encountering tradition and freeing himself from it, as he had to do in order to achieve a permanently enduring poetry of his own.

Mary Jacobus
Tradition and Experiment in Wordsworth's "Lyrical Ballads" (1798) (Oxford: Clarendon, 1976), pp. 233–34, 272

Intimations Ode

Freud recognized sublimation as the highest human achievement, a recognition that allies him to Plato and to the entire moral traditions of both Judaism and Christianity. Freudian sublimation involves the yielding-up of more primordial for more refined modes of pleasure, which is to exalt the second chance above the first. Freud's poem, in the view of this book, is not severe enough, unlike the severe poems written by the creative lives of the strong poets. To equate emotional maturation with the discovery of acceptable substitutes may be pragmatic wisdom, particularly in the realm of Eros, but this is not the wisdom of the strong poets. The surrendered dream is not merely a phantasmagoria of endless gratification, but is the greatest of all human illusions, the vision of immortality. If Wordsworth's *Ode: Intimations of Immortality from Recollections of Earliest Childhood* possessed only the wisdom found also in Freud, then we could cease calling it "the Great Ode." Wordsworth too saw repetition or second chance as essential for development, and his ode admits that we can redirect our needs by substitution or sublimation. But the ode plangently also awakens into failure, and into the creative mind's protest against time's tyranny.

A Wordsworthian critic, even one as loyal to Wordsworth as Geoffrey Hartman, can insist upon clearly distinguishing between *priority*, as a concept from the natural order, and *authority*, from the spiritual order, but Wordsworth's ode declines to make this distinction. "By seeking to overcome priority," Hartman wisely says, "art fights nature on nature's own ground, and is bound to lose." The argument of this book is that strong poets are condemned to just this unwisdom; Wordsworth's Great Ode fights nature on nature's own ground, and suffers a great defeat, even as it retains its greater dream. That dream, in Wordsworth's ode, is shadowed by the anxiety of influence, due to the greatness of the precursor-poem, Milton's

"Lycidas," where the human refusal wholly to sublimate is even more rugged, despite the ostensible yielding to Christian teachings of sublimation.

Harold Bloom
The Anxiety of Influence: A Theory of Poetry (New York: Oxford Univ. Pr., 1973), pp. 9–10

The Prelude

Here, in short, is Wordsworth's conception of his poetic role and his great design [in *The Prelude*]. The author, though a "transitory Being," is the latest in the line of poets inspired by the "prophetic Spirit," and as such has been granted a "Vision" (lines 97–98) which sanctions his claim to outdo Milton's Christian story in the scope and audacious novelty of his subject. The vision is that of the awesome depths and height of the human mind, and of the power of that mind as in itself adequate, by consummating a holy marriage with the external universe, to create out of the world of all of us, in a quotidian and recurrent miracle, a new world which is the equivalent of paradise. . . .

If my explication of Wordsworth on imagination has been complicated, that is in part because—whether from the difficulty of what he had to say or from prudence in the way he chose to say it—Wordsworth's own account has been uncommonly abstruse. The immediate context, however, together with the overall pattern in *The Prelude* of insistent and coherent parallels with crucial passages in *Paradise Lost*, makes its tenor clear enough. The faculty of imagination is born, then goes underground, but only to rise "once more/With strength"; it is distinct from, yet "each in each" with, the intellectual love which is "the first and chief" and in which "we begin and end"; and it is also the indispensable mediator by which love manifests that it abounds over pain and apparent evil, by saving the poet from "a universe of death" and opening the way to an earthly paradise. It is apparent, then, that in Wordsworth's sustained myth of mind in its interchange with nature, the imagination plays a role equivalent to that of the Redeemer in Milton's providential plot. . . .

I do not mean to propose a strict correlation but only an overall functional parallel between Milton's sacred story of mankind and Wordsworth's secular account of the growth of an individual mind. . . . In this aspect Wordsworth's *Prelude* participates, however guardedly, in a major intellectual tendency of his age, and of ours.

M. H. Abrams
Natural Supernaturalism: Tradition and Revolution in Romantic Literature (New York: Norton, 1971), pp. 28, 119–20

Wordsworth's accounts of his seemingly "mystical" experiences, I shall maintain, contain within them indications of those psychic realities which are most often ignored in the criticism of his poetry. His accounts contain, too, traces of unconsciously remembered past experiences metaphorically associated with remembered experiences. Such memory traces are ordinarily unavailable to the memory as clear memories, and perhaps are only sometimes so available to the imagination with any clarity or consistency as they were for Wordsworth. But I think it is plain that the semblance of explanation, corresponding as it does to the poet's immediate *feeling* of his grasp on the matter he is presenting, is what makes possible for him the imaginative inclusion of unconscious memories in his significant recollections.

Wordsworth was aware of poetic statement as a kind of "modal proposition," a way of dealing declaratively, affirmatively, and generally with the possible, the necessary, the contingent, and the wishful in personal experience. He knew about "what we half-create and what perceive," but he seems to have trusted that the poetic representation of feeling would express the urgency of such activity in the self; and it is this activity—his attempt to take possession of his life by using the feeling of being possessed—that we value and study, if we respond to it. When Wordsworth speaks of fixing "the wavering balance of my mind," the reader is adverted to the perilous nature of such urgency: inactivity is not allowed to seem a simple alternative. The problem to be dealt with first is that of the relationship between expression and understanding as, on the one hand, it is managed by the poet within the poem, and, on the other, as it is interpreted by the reader.

Richard J. Onorato
The Character of the Poet: Wordsworth in "The Prelude"
(Princeton, N.J.: Princeton Univ. Pr., 1971), pp. 27–28

This struggle, the struggle of the religious confessant or the confessional poet, is linguistic in an especially intense manner. We have observed that, for the confessant, there is *no* guarantee of his salvation except the carefully maintained rectitude of his own confession, his own language. Throughout my reading of *The Prelude*, I concentrate upon the verbal texture of the poem, its own evolving sense of the proper language for poetic celebration, as one of its most intensely confessional aspects and also one of its most creative anticipations of later modes of thought and writing. A number of recent studies of Wordsworth have emphasized a more or less psychoanalytic approach to the poet: tracing the ways in which his emotional and intellectual problems shape the language of his poetry. But my interest here is in the ways language itself shapes consciousness, not the other way around. Whether we are speaking simply of language or of the rather specific linguistic sanctions of confessional rhetoric, we need to realize that the grammar of our experience, the verbal grid through which we receive and shape the world, goes far toward determining the nature of the experience itself. . . .

We have been tracing the history of Wordsworth's imagination as he reconstitutes that history in *The Prelude.* In the last chapter we discussed the basic plot of the poet's growth as his progressive enslavement to, and liberation from, an obsessively visual, allegorical, daemonic relationship to Nature—and therefore, of course, to his own experiences. This plot of liberation, furthermore, provided the liberated Wordsworth, the teller of his own tale, with a central, generative structure (fixation—blank desertion—release into vision) for confronting the worlds without and within him. Any confession tends to become a literal re-creation both of the confessant's self and of the world he inhabits. And Wordsworth's confession, with profound intuition of its own basic form, becomes a re-creation very like that of Genesis I, where the temporal order of God's constitution of the universe is also the rational order of the hierarchy of created things.

As we have seen, the point of transcendence in *The Prelude* is the Mount Snowdon episode in book 14. It is at this point that the two processes of liberation we have been tracing—historical and structural—unite in a final moment of exemplary vision, a final attainment of the language of poetic maturity. Wordsworth himself, very clearly, intends the episode to have just such summarizing power.

Frank D. McConnell
The Confessional Imagination: A Reading of Wordsworth's "Prelude" (Baltimore: Johns Hopkins Univ. Pr., 1974), pp. 8–9, 148

There are, I think, three recognizably distinct modes of Romanticism: the construction of new metaphysical, religious, and mythological redemptive explanations; the interiorization or subjectivization of redemptionism to the point at which redemptive explanations were reduced to intuitionism and eventually to hardly more than barely explicable feeling states; and finally the emergence of anti-redemptive, anti-explanatory, explanation, the emergence of a heuristic conception of explanation and the reduction of redemptive experience to feeling states of, at best, therapeutic or vacational value. In epistemological terms, these three mean an explanation which intellectually or mythologically or religiously resolves the distinction between subject and object; the subjective conviction of the fusion of subject and object (already available in Kant's *Critique of Judgment*); an acceptance of the irresolvable tensions between subject and object (in modern terms, the inaccessibility of the brain processes which lie between semiotic stimulus and response). . . .

Let me give a few examples of the results of what seems to be [M. H.] Abrams over-emphasis [in *Natural Supernaturalism*] upon secular redemptionism. Wordsworth, it seems to me, arrives at the end of *The Prelude* at an almost complete subjectivism of redemption, or at what might well be called, and often was, aesthetic redemptionism. (Hence the common Romantic failure for so long to distinguish between Nature and Art.) It is here, I suspect, that must be found the explanation for his failure to write the great philosophical poem he wanted to write and that Coleridge abused him for not writing. Coleridge wanted a full innovative redemption, a religious transformation of Christianity, a redemptive Christianity that was not really Christian. Wordsworth's interiorization of redemption had proceeded so far towards the reduction of redemptionism to a feeling state that it was impossible for him to construct an innovative redemptive scheme. On the other hand, the overwhelming cultural power and social redundancy of redemptive thinking made it impossible for him to proceed to an anti-redemptive position, even though his epistemology provided the foundation for it. Thus I believe that a careful study of his later work, especially the neglected and to me great poem *The Excursion*, can reveal that his adoption of Anglicanism was heuristic.

Morse Peckham
SIR, 13, 4 (1974), pp. 362–63

We may conceive two domains, an order of imagination or memory and an order of symbol or speech, though the content of these opposed domains ought to be educed from the analysis and not out of an hypothesis. *The Prelude* as a whole is an attempt to negotiate the strait leading from remembered images, and from the power of mind to which these images continue to testify, to capable speech. "I have seen such things—I see them still (memory)—and see moreover deeper into them, as if anew (imagination)—I therefore was and am a favored being (identity)—and I can speak (be a poet)." This argument, here abstractly reduced and overemphasized, presides over each rememoration in the poem, as if this poem were in fact a prelude, achieving its unforeseen finalities only under propaedeutic pretense. In a way the argument serves as "profoundest knowledge" to orient and occasion the "efficacious spirit" which is the poem itself. Moreover, the passage discernible in the project of *The Prelude* emerges with strange and almost literal insistence in the poem's crucial episodes and at the heart of its recurrent figures.

We use the notion of poetic imagination loosely to gloss over the mysterious gap between a power of perception and a power of articulation or composition. Keats says that "every man whose soul is not a clod/Hath visions, and would speak, if he had loved/And been well nurtured in his mother's tongue," but that can't possibly be true; a mute inglorious Milton is no Milton at all. At times it seems as if the Romantic poets (Blake, of course, apart) were engaged in a conspiracy of occultation concerning the

Word, as if to acknowledge that its enjoining power involved the betrayal of a dangerous secret.

The fact is that the passage from imagination to symbol was occluded for Wordsworth, and yet the essential moment of his greatest poetry is right in the midst of this occlusion. He halts or is halted right at the point where the image is eclipsed—where it is on the verge of turning into a "character" in a higher, nonvisual discourse. This moment—and it is an experience as well as a dialectical locus—is the sole province of what he calls "visionary power," and it is the very type of the sublime moment.

Thomas Weiskel
The Romantic Sublime (Baltimore: Johns Hopkins Univ. Pr., 1976), pp. 172–73

GENERAL

Wordsworth and Coleridge, especially Wordsworth, had, to an extent that they hardly realized themselves, inherited a recent (i.e., eighteenth-century) conception of a "natural society" which, for the first time in many centuries, had raised a central question about human identity. In the older myth, man was morally and intellectually separated from nature, hence his identity was primarily a social one, and the symbol of that social identity was . . . the city. In his evolution as a child of God, the city of God came first, then the garden of man as its suburb. Milton thinks of man's original nature in Eden as simple and pastoral but nevertheless civilized; Adam, for Milton, does not become the archetypal noble savage until after his fall. Rousseau had suggested that perhaps the anomalies and injustices of civilization were so great as to make one doubt whether this city-garden order is the right one or not. Perhaps man should seek an identity with nature first, not nature in its humanized form of a garden or park but simply nature as physical environment. After that, the genuine form of human society may have a chance to emerge. . . .

In Wordsworth also man first finds his identity in his relation to physical nature, in its rude or uncultivated form. In the older myth there were two levels of nature: an upper level of human nature, represented by the Garden of Eden and the Golden Age, which God had originally intended for man, and a lower level of physical nature, permeated by death, corruption, and, for man at least, sin, which man fell into. According to this construct, man is in the physical world but not of it, and only an elaborate social training, comprising education, law, morality, and religion, can help to raise him toward his proper level. In Wordsworth the existing social and educational structure is artificial, full of inert custom and hypocrisy. Nature is a better teacher than books, and one finds one's lost identity with nature in moments of feeling in which one is penetrated by the sense of nature's "huge and mighty forms." Thus already in Wordsworth it is the "pagan" or latent numinous powers in nature that man turns to. Wordsworth shook his head over the Hymn to Pan in the first book of Keats' *Endymion* and called it "a very pretty piece of paganism." But Wordsworth had done much, was probably the decisive influence, in making the Hymn to Pan possible, and Keats in his turn helped to create a new sensibility that ultimately led to the rebirth of Eros and Dionysus in Yeats and D. H. Lawrence.

Northrop Frye
A Study of English Romanticism (New York: Random House, 1969), pp. 18–20

As Wordsworth conceived it, the core of the imaginative process is "transformation." Whether it turns a stone into a sea beast, a doe into a patch of snow, a thornbush into a suffering outcast, or mist-covered peaks into the heaving backs of animals, imagination is a power that transforms, creating "new existences" from old. In this respect his theory is strikingly contemporary, for it seems to be a premise of modern abstract art—and indeed of modern poetry too—that natural objects are just so many indeterminate lumps of clay, which are not reproduced but rather reorganized and reshaped by the artist who uses them. . . .

It is the concept of life as change—or, more accurately, *interchange*—that drove Wordsworth beyond the picturesque poetry of his very early years, beyond the locodescriptive style of Gray, Thomson, and Joseph Warton into the subtle fluidity of poems like "Tintern Abbey." For Wordsworth even more than for the Augustans, poetry was an imitation of nature; but the nature it imitated was dynamic, not static. As he defines it in the concluding book of *The Prelude*, the task of the poet is to imitate the transformations wrought by nature herself. . . .

Between 1800 and 1815, "imagination" displaced "feeling" as the key term in Wordsworth's critical vocabulary. Feeling remained essential to the creative process, but it had to be "imaginative" feeling; it had to transform an object by conferring on it an emotive life of its own, as the unseen bird in "To the Cuckoo" is made to embody, movingly, the evanescent hopes of the poet's youth. And with this emphasis on imaginative transformation came the recognition that language, too, must feel the pressure of the creative act. The blind eruptions of feeling were no longer enough: if the poet expressed his imaginative power by transforming natural objects, he also expressed it by transforming "the real language of men." By 1815, Wordsworth clearly saw that the making of poetry could be nothing less than a conscious, deliberate, well-disciplined art.

James A. W. Heffernan
Wordsworth's Theory of Poetry: The Transforming Imagination (Ithaca, N.Y.: Cornell Univ. Pr., 1969), pp. 265–66, 268

Wordsworth's revolt against the star-symbol has various reasons: its trivialization in eighteenth-century poetry, a religiously inspired prudence, etc. To conventionalize it we can think of his distrust of personification, which it extends, or of English poetry's recurrent bouts of conscience vis-à-vis pagan myth. Yet we read Wordsworth unconscious much of the time of his place in the history of ideas or the polemical history of style. These histories, recovered, allow us to be articulate about his intentions but they describe his novelty rather than his originality. They remain external to his strong poetic presence.

Curiously strong, considering how little "glitter," or conventional texture, his poetry has. Many have suspected, therefore, that his imagery comes from a different loom. They have sought to discover the formula of its secret weave. It is equally inadequate, however—though far more interesting—to describe the diffusion of theme or image in Wordsworth, or the change from parallelistic to chiastic patterns in his metaphors. The only adequate rhetorical analysis is one that views his poems in terms of "mind in act," with the very temptation of symbolizing—that is, overcondensing, or turning contiguity (metonymy) into identity (metaphor)—as its subject. . . .

From Ben Jonson to Wordsworth, and from masque to ode, is too abrupt a jump. But it illumines an important difference between epochs, bridged in part by our previous, historically oriented sketch: a difference in structure of sensibility or mode of representation. Wordsworth's mind . . . loses itself only fractionally in the moon-moment. Its delight in other images is even more restrained: they remain as intransitive as the verbs, and alternate deliberately between sky and earth. Sight is segmented by them; and the serial impression they leave is of Wordsworth counting his blessings or storing them against the dying of all light. He is restrained because he is reflective; he is reflective because he is perplexed at nature's losing its immediacy. But the image of the moon challenges his restraint. With it the verses almost leap from perplexity into vision: the poet too would throw off all shadow, like heaven its clouds.

Yet the visionary personification that rises in him is simply the act of seeing—natural seeing—magnified. A personified moon makes the eyes of man personal again. Sight hovers on the edge of visionariness without passing over: "when the heavens are bare" is not an apocalyptic notation. Wordsworth's restraint is, as always, a restraint of vision. Though his eye leaps up, he subdues the star-symbol.

Geoffrey H. Hartman
in *New Perspectives on Coleridge and Wordsworth*, ed.
Geoffrey H. Hartman (New York: Columbia Univ. Pr., 1972),
pp. 102–3, 124–25

The Wordsworthian epiphany has two distinct though related forms. In one, spirit shows forth from Nature; the sudden revelation communicates to the poet a transcendent message which bears upon the comprehension of human existence or upon the direction his own life should take. An example of this kind of epiphany is Wordsworth's experience of the mountain dawn which dedicates him to the priesthood of the imagination. The other, less grandiose and more closely connected with Joyce's epiphanies, has as its locus and agent some unlikely person—a leech-gatherer, a bereft and deserted woman, an old man on the road—who, without intention, by something said or done, or not done, suddenly manifests the quality of his own particular being and thus implies the wonder of being in general. Lowness of social station, lowness even in a biological sense, is a necessary condition of the persons who provide Wordsworth's epiphanies: a man so old that he can scarcely move, a woman stupefied by despair, an idiot boy who says "Burr, burr, burr" and has no name for the moon. We wonder, indeed, whether people as marginal to developed life as these can be thought to partake of full humanity; yet this is of course why Wordsworth has chosen them, for what the epiphanies disclose is that these persons forcibly exist as human beings. . . .

To one of Wordsworth's epiphanies of authentic being Coleridge took strong exception—"The Idiot Boy," he said, is inevitably offensive to the sensibilities of the reader. This is an opinion with which we are at present less in agreement than we might once have been; yet the poem still provokes resistance in us. But when we admire it, as we should, we cannot fail to see that its offensiveness is part of its intention. That this is so suggests that authenticity is implicitly a polemical concept, fulfilling its nature by dealing aggressively with received and habitual opinion, aesthetic opinion in the first instance, social and political opinion in the next. One topic of its polemic, which has reference to both aesthetic and social opinion, is the error of the view that beauty is the highest quality to which art may aspire.

Something can be learned about the ideal of authenticity in its relation to beauty by calling to mind the artistic quality that is—or was—known as the sublime. The sublime and the authentic are certainly not equivalent, but they have one trait in common, a settled antagonism to beauty.

Lionel Trilling
Sincerity and Authenticity (Cambridge, Mass.: Harvard Univ. Pr., 1972), pp. 90–91, 94–95

The gradual emancipation of Wordsworth's deepest feelings from the temporal world has two profound effects on his art, both of which effectively reverse the direction of his earlier development. As he turns for hope from the objective world to the power and the immortal destiny of the mind, like Arnold, Tennyson and Yeats after him, the epistemology implied by his style gradually becomes idealistic. Instead of affirming the equality of objective and subjective powers, he progressively invests greater value in the mind's contribution to perception, and, in the years after 1804, in the creative and autonomous imagination. This aspect of his thought comes full circle in the Immortality Ode, where he finds "joy" and hope in the memory of an "abyss of idealism" that now testifies, in precise antithesis to its significance in his childhood, to the mind's hegemony over the sensible world and thus to its immortality. A corresponding change comes over the decorum that molds his style, which gradually ceases to embody a reverent imitation of "nature's shapes as she has made them," and instead relies upon language and art to dignify, elevate, and spiritualize the external world. In both respects Wordsworth surrenders his earlier protest against the "mighty stream of tendency" that throughout the eighteenth century had transferred the grounds of human hope from the outer to the inner world.

He does so, however, on behalf of the central commitment of his apprenticeship and his life, to man. His poetry remains "a motion of hope," undertaken in the light of truth. In his greatest later poems, the odes of 1804, *The Prelude*, the *Elegiac Stanzas*, and *The White Doe of Rylstone*, he succeeds in mastering the desire to escape an existence that had steadily grown more painful, and continues to devote his art to the task that Johnson regarded as the end of all writing, that of enabling man "better to enjoy life or better to endure it." His considered response in 1806 to the death of his brother a year earlier finds hope and the possibility of poetry in the role of a happy warrior who stands his ground in a darkened world. . . . Wordsworth remains what he was at the age of seventeen, when he bid farewell to Esthwaite, put the "flowery lays" of a pastoral fancy behind him, and for the first of many times dedicated his genius to the task of confronting, surviving, and ennobling the human condition, not as it might be, but as it is.

Paul D. Sheats
The Making of Wordsworth's Poetry, 1785–1788 (Cambridge, Mass.: Harvard Univ. Pr., 1973), pp. 250–51

In 1795, when Coleridge first encountered the poem, *Salisbury Plain* stood as a record of Wordsworth's earlier turbulent feelings, later recalled so vividly in *The Prelude*, about the war with France and the condition of England. In the story of the Female Vagrant, who loses her home through local tyranny, and her husband and children through war, Wordsworth created a powerful illustration for the homily he addresses to the statesmen of England on the corruption and oppression that are ravaging the nation.

The poem satisfied Wordsworth, however, for a very short time only, and in the autumn of 1795 he revised it extensively. The new poem was described to a friend who already knew *Salisbury Plain* as now "almost . . . another work," and so it is. In the second poem the poet as homilist has almost disappeared, and the Female Vagrant's story is subordinated to a more elaborately developed narrative that displays the torments of a good man driven by injustice to murder. . . .

Adventures on Salisbury Plain is both a continuation and a consummation of *Salisbury Plain*. It continues the social and political interests of the poem, and even extends them, but this continuing attack on the government of the country does not draw on any really new response to contemporary conditions. There were many good reasons why the attack should continue, and it is successful because the rhetoric of *Salisbury Plain* has been replaced by a fully dramatized presentation of the human calamities consequent upon war, but Wordsworth's interest was rapidly shifting from social and political phenomena to the more complex phenomena of human motives and behavior. . . . The poem now centers, not on the Female Vagrant or on the poet's declamations, but on the sailor, on his crime and subsequent life, and the new shape is determined only by the tension between various ways of looking at the man and at his deed. On the one hand Wordsworth is concerned with man in society, with the make-up and functioning of human loyalties, sanctions, and punishments. On the other he is concerned with man in solitude, with the agony such a man as the sailor suffers from his own sense that he has put himself beyond human love.

Stephen Gill
Introd., in *The Salisbury Plain Poems of William Wordsworth*, ed. Stephen Gill (Ithaca, N.Y.: Cornell Univ. Pr., 1975), pp. 3, 12

This opposition [between Freud and Wordsworth] derives, as I have said, from Freud's and Wordsworth's understanding of the nature of the universe, and it is at this profound level that one finds the closest association of Wordsworth and Constable. Superficially their landscapes are unalike; yet Constable's pictures do not yield much reward to Freudian analysis. In the ordinary terminology of criticism *The Haywain* shares with Wordsworth's barren scenes a certain simplicity. Indeed, the picture is so simple, and so simply charming, that a modern critic is inclined to wonder if it can be significant art. This simplicity, or accessibility, merits attention. In the "spots of time" passage [in *The Prelude*] Wordsworth deals with a familiar phenomenon, even though we have never had experiences identical with his, may never even have seen a northern moorland. But we all have childhood memories. Constable's scene is accessible in the same fashion. It looks ordinary and commonplace even today when few of us have actually seen such sights. It is familiar as a spot of time. . . .

I suggested in the first chapter that Wordsworthian and Freudian psychology are, in essentials, incompatible. My analyses have substantiated, I hope, the observation that the antagonism between modern and Romantic psychology rests upon antithetical cosmologies, the antithesis significantly determined by the special Romantic concern for a temporal continuity strange to our less historically oriented consciousness.

I conclude, therefore, by reaffirming my earlier observation: the nature in and the nature of Romantic art is obsolete. However we evaluate the configuration of competing alternatives the handbooks call Romanticism, for us it is an uncongenial point of view. If we insist on treating Romanticism as the beginning of the modern era, let us remember how long that era now has lasted, how far we stand from the origins of our civilization. This is the principal unity we find in the diversity of early nineteenth-century art: whatever Constable and Wordsworth may have shared, for us they are primarily though not exclusively linked by a common remoteness. However we may view the world today, we can no longer possess Romantic landscape vision. Therein lies both its irrelevance and its preciousness.

Karl Kroeber
Romantic Landscape Vision: Constable and Wordsworth
(Madison: Univ. Wisconsin Pr., 1975), pp. 14, 131

Wordsworth employs contrarieties in his poetry in the service of revealing us to ourselves. By involving our reader's mind dramatically in the experience of contrary thinking, he works to uncover for us primary characteristics of our own operations of mind. And it is by means of this anatomy of the mind that Wordsworth is ambitious of claiming his poetic fame. We recall Wordsworth's announcement in the "Prospectus" lines of his primary subject matter: it is "the Mind of Man" which Wordsworth claims as "my haunt, and the main regiòn of my song" ([*The Excursion*,] 40–41).

The implication of this announcement is important. A long-standing tradition in Wordsworth studies has held that Wordsworth is a philosopher of nature, or, more broadly still, of the transcendent nature of things. Given such familiar Wordsworth lines as "I felt the sentiment of Being spread/O'er all that moves, and all that seemeth still" (*Prelude*, II, 420–21), the older criticism thus tended to underscore "sentiment of Being," and then to position that phrase as a foundation-block in Wordsworth's presumed philosophy. But as Wordsworth's announcement of his subject matter implies, it is a mistake to read the poetry in this way. Wordsworth is not primarily interested in asserting or establishing the objective validity of the mind's perceptions. His concern is not with the mind's ability to discover which of its numerous and contrary perceptions is "true." Such a concern would prompt the poet to try to haunt regions somewhere between the mind and the object. But Wordsworth's haunting ground is the realm of mind alone. Wordsworth thinks he can gain his object by focusing simply on the mind's activity: *that* the mind perceives this or that (whether the perception be "true" to the objective nature of things or not); and *how* the mind goes about perceiving (whether that manner of perceiving be "correct" or not). Thus in our poetic text at hand, "I felt the sentiment of Being spread," it is not the objective phrase, "sentiment of Being," which demands primary attention, but rather the subjective assertion, "I felt." Wordsworth is not writing about Truths discovered, but rather about mental processes.

Some of the more recent Wordsworth scholarship has begun to recognize this distinction. But the old attitude toward Wordsworth dies very hard; and the notion of Wordsworth as a discoverer of truths tends to persist, exerting strong pressures upon the way present-day critics think about Wordsworth's poetry.

Lawrence J. Swingle
ELH (Summer, 1977), pp. 350–51

VICTORIAN LITERATURE

Wendell Stacy Johnson, editor

MATTHEW ARNOLD

1822–1888

> Kenneth Allott, ed., *The Poems of Matthew Arnold* (1965)
>
> R. H. Super, ed., *The Complete Prose Works of Matthew Arnold* (1960–77), 11 vols.

In his greatest prose work, *Culture and Anarchy*, Matthew Arnold examines each of what he considers the three classes of England to determine its fitness as a center of authority and a source of light. Each class in turn is found wanting, and Arnold then suggests that the nation rise above the notion of classes to the conception of a state. The state, as the corporate and collective "best self" of England, would have the power to restrain the excesses of each class and the intelligence to direct the strength of each class toward the proper modes of "expansion," that is, liberty.

As they appear in *Culture and Anarchy*, the three classes have undergone a process of simplification and heightening and acquired a symmetry of form. Within the work each class is matched part for part with the other classes; each has its virtues and defects, each has its virtuous mean and its dangerous excess. To give the abstraction an air of reality, Arnold names each of the means and excesses after a living member of the class being described. He dubs the classes "Barbarians," "Philistines," and "Populace," for these are the classes not as they exist but as they are transformed for a literary purpose, and new creatures need new names. Of course no description of a class has reality in any absolute sense, and Arnold is concerned to give his line drawings only enough of the semblance of reality that they may serve the purposes of the work. . . .

Of course Arnold's views of the three classes were not neat. They were the complicated and changing products of his complete experience with them, and these views are rooted in practical, specific affairs and issues. What these views were is important not only to an understanding of *Culture and Anarchy* but also to Arnold biography and to accurate judgments about Arnold's integrity and consistency. After 1880, for example, Arnold became interested in questions of practical politics and wrote about them at some length. In the course of these essays he expressed ideas that have been called reactionary. Whether Arnold had turned conservative in his last years or whether contemporary events made him overemphasize one aspect of his many-sided views is a question on which a history of Arnold's relationship to the classes may throw some light.

Patrick J. McCarthy
Matthew Arnold and the Three Classes (New York: Columbia Univ. Pr., 1964), pp. vii–viii

The position of Matthew Arnold as the most important English critic of the second half of the 19th century seems secure. His eminence is due not only to his literary criticism but also to his standing as a poet and general critic of English society and civilization. Today both in England and in the United States—especially in academic circles—his influence is still felt. It is rather the influence of his *Kulturphilosophie* than of his literary criticism, but among critics of the 20th century Irving Babbitt, T. S. Eliot, F. R. Leavis, and Lionel Trilling show marked affinities with his outlook. Arnold provides us with an apology for culture, a restatement of the Greek ideal of *paideia* modified by Christianity; he makes a defense of the study of the humanities against the growing encroachments of scientific and vocational training; he gives a satirical picture of the Anglo-Saxon middle classes: their Philistinism and their religion with its anti-aesthetic bias; he provides a defense of poetry and literature, a defense of the critical spirit and the exercise of criticism; and finally—though this part of his activity is most dated—he advocates an undogmatic religion. . . .

He attacks British provincialism and recommends an opening of doors to European, mainly French and German, winds of doctrine. It was and is a valuable plea, which must be seen in its historical setting. Arnold's ideal of "disinterestedness" must not be understood as Olympian aloofness or escape to the ivory tower. It is easy to show that Arnold himself was deeply absorbed in the problems of his age and was not above engaging in polemics and even losing his temper. But "disinterestedness" surely means for him something quite specific: a denial of immediate political and sectarian ends, a wide horizon, an absence of prejudice, serenity beyond the passions of the moment. . . .

Arnold also said important things about the theory of criticism. His point of view is not entirely consistent and may have shifted toward the end of his life. He often seems to have believed in a purely descriptive, interpretative criticism. "The judgment which almost insensibly forms itself . . . is the valuable one." The critic should "communicate fresh knowledge, and let his own judgment pass along with it"; he should be "a sort of companion and clue." Arnold even said: "I wish to decide nothing as of my own authority." . . .

Arnold's . . . certainty and authority are most boldly and memorably expressed in the series of essays devoted to the English romantic poets: the introductions to his anthologies of Wordsworth (1879) and Byron (1881) and to the selections from Gray and Keats in Humphry Ward's *English Poets* (1880). The actual ranking of the romantic poets was long settled in Arnold's mind; it is publicly announced in the Heine essay, but it is argued fully in the later essays. It is too well known to require more than the briefest summary: Wordsworth and, after him, Byron are the two greatest poets of the age; Keats—though falling short of actual accomplishment—is a great promise. Shelley and Coleridge are definitely inferior.

René Wellek
A History of Modern Criticism 1790–1950, Vol. IV
(New Haven, Conn.: Yale Univ. Pr., 1965), pp. 155–56, 177

Arnold imagined his scholar-gypsy as immortal because a literary artifact, "exempt from age/And living as thou liv'st on Glanvil's page," and he pictured a hunter on a tapestry in "Tristram and Iseult," forever alert, forever rooted in the greenwood, gazing out at the dead lovers in a bleak chamber. All such considerations of the power of art to arrest the moment (and they have been frequent in Victorian and modern literature, where one of the main themes of poetry is the nature of poetry itself) recall Keats's superb evocation of the youth and beauty frozen forever on the Grecian urn, the wild ecstasy that will not tire, the leaves that cannot fall.

Jerome H. Buckley
The Triumph of Time (Cambridge, Mass.: Harvard Univ. Pr., 1966), p. 144

The central feature of Arnold's world is a river which the poet unabashedly calls the River of Life or of Time. Characteristically, this river takes its rise in some cool glade on a high mountain, flows down through a gorge onto a hot and dusty plain, and then, after almost losing itself in the sands of the desert, empties at last into the full and glimmering sea. Needless to say, there are many variations upon this scene, and the one essential thing is that there should be three distinct regions which are separated from one another by some kind of "gorge." Borrowing phrases which Arnold himself employs, we may call these regions the Forest Glade, the Burning or Darkling Plain, and the Wide-Glimmering Sea. In the poem "The Future," which is Arnold's most straightforward exposition of the River, these regions are identified with the past, the present, and the future, and that is generally the case when the River denotes historic time. More frequently, however, it denotes the life of the individual, and then the three regions are childhood, maturity, and old age or death. Whichever they be, they invariably have the same character: the first is a period of joyous innocence when one lives in harmony with nature, the second a period of suffering when one is alone in a hostile world, and the third a period of peace in which suffering subsides into calm and then grows up into a new joy, the joy of active service in the world. . . .

The third phase of Arnold's myth, then, is the phase of reconciliation, first, with the self and then with the world. The river joins its various streams and then it merges with the sea. As a result, the transition to the third phase is not ordinarily dramatic. Rather it is a moment of inward illumination in which, thinking that we are still in a desert, we suddenly discover that we are not, but are in a path leading to the City of God or in an estuary leading to the sea. These two places represent the alternative goals of Arnold's myth, and as we have already noted, they have very different implications. The one is religious, the other naturalistic. The one is to be gained by effort, the other without any effort at all. The one appears to be a final goal, with the suggestion that once it has been reached life's journey is done. The other is not so much a goal as a stage in the world-process, the great cyclical movement which Arnold calls "the general life." For although to man's limited vision the sea is death, to his more extended vision it is the All, the vast continuum of nature into which all things flow and out of which they again return. Finally, corresponding to these two goals are two characters who inhabit the third phase of Arnold's world. They are called the Servants or Sons of God and the Children of the Second Birth.

A. Dwight Culler
Imaginative Reason (New Haven, Conn.: Yale Univ. Pr., 1966), pp. 3–4, 16

If we consider first what I would call the image of situation, it is apparent that Arnold practiced a kind of impressionism which looks back to the theories of Goethe and forward to Existential literature. Goethe, in a letter to Schiller, described his own need to find in external nature some *Anschauung*, or "thing seen," which would remove his art from the purely speculative level where, he felt, it perished, and give to his poetry a saving concreteness. On a relatively simple level Arnold builds his poems around aspects of contemporary life vividly realized as scenes, and so charged with significance that they come to represent a whole culture. . . .

The Grande Chartreuse and Dover Beach are features of a moral landscape, not symbols, but localities rich in associations which—for the reader as well as for the poet—provoke and convey the speculative thought.

But Arnold's finest achievement as a critical poet is his making intellectual activity dramatic. When his thought most fully expresses the sting of the real—in such poems as "The Strayed Reveller," "Resignation," or "The Buried Life"—we not only follow the exposition of an idea, but become aware of the process by which the poet perceives and realizes it. The poem recreates a moment of insight; its statement as a whole is an image of the poet's mind working on the materials of thought and perception. As I look back on the approaches I have made to Arnold's poetry, I see that a good deal of my comment devolves into an attempt to show how he made active the exposition of his ideas, how he gave a dramatic quality to his poems of statement. He did not always succeed as a poet: it is hard, he said, to be excellent. But in spite of the arid stretches and the early atrophy of his lyrical gifts, his poetic career represents something more grand than failure and less vulgar than success. It was Arnold's genuine and largely unheeded triumph to be one of the few poets in any language who could make a poem an active instrument of his vision, not merely the formulated result of his thought, but the means by which that thought assumed shape and life.

G. Robert Stange
Matthew Arnold: The Poet as Humanist (Princeton, N.J.: Princeton Univ. Pr., 1967), pp. 288, 290–91

Only in death can [Empedocles] . . . be redeemed, for only death can return him to his wholeness. Speaking now to the universe ("O ye elements!"), he is able at the last to "breathe free," and he leaps to his death triumphantly.

Aside from the character of Empedocles, Arnold employs another obvious device [in *Empedocles on Etna*] which embodies his own self-division: the contrast of poet and philosopher. We remember how, at the beginning of Act I, Callicles is shown alone enjoying the mountain morning. Act II, in contrast, opens on Empedocles' twilight view of Etna's "charr'd, blacken'd, melancholy waste." Unlike *Paracelsus*, where the two aspects of the poet's character were finally joined, no such union takes place in *Empedocles*. Perhaps a closer parallel is to be found in *Sordello*, which ends with the barefoot child singing as he races up the hill to "beat/ The lark, God's poet."

Empedocles made the irrevocable leap, but Arnold survived his crisis, saved undoubtedly by an ironic comprehension of his spiritual impasse. In the act of poetic composition he understood that the dialogue of the mind with itself can only be terminated in death. Without allowing himself "a hostile attitude" toward contemporary life, he would at the same time take care not to be "overwhelmed" (p. xxix) by it. This program, as set forth in the Preface, amounted to a *"volte-face,"* as E. D. H. Johnson calls it, in his poetic development. As it turned out, he paid a high price—poetry—for his spiritual health, and it is a great irony that the famed document prescribing a new course for that art should forecast his eventual farewell to the practice of it.

Masao Miyoshi
The Divided Self (New York: New York Univ. Pr., 1969), p. 199

I think Matthew Arnold will continue to speak to us in the last quarter of the twentieth century and quite probably in the deep forward and abysm of time after that too. His nineteenth-century crisis has become our norm: the "wandering between two worlds" seems less a diagnosis of the Victorian malaise than a statement of the human condition, and everyone who has taught "Dover Beach" will know the student's moved look of *recognition* when he encounters the ignorant armies' clash by night. Arnold's predictions were sometimes wrong; he assumed, for instance, the steady advance of rationalism and decline of supernaturalism. His poems still speak to us, but in ways he could not have imagined. He only heard, from the Sea of Faith, the melancholy long withdrawing roar. *We* hear a kind of threatening roar, an advancing tide of irrationalism, that surges about our bulwarks of Hellenism. And there are new Prisons of Puritanism, and new Prisons of inarticulateness. We find ourselves short of criticism, short of the power to discriminate and evaluate, short of "that tact which the study of letters alone can bestow."

This sounds like a call to return to Arnold's Essays, and I think in fact there is hardly an issue in *Culture and Anarchy, Literature and Dogma* that does not speak to the hour, in some way. But Arnold's career is peculiarly consistent, and the issues in the essays are virtually all adumbrated in the poetry. He found a method in the poems to work through to "making something" that embodies principles and concepts that were to be elaborated and exemplified at length in prose works. The poems remain for us perhaps the most telling and most functional embodiment of Arnoldian themes. Let me try to explain. If we are asked to say in brief what is the meaning of Callicles' songs, or their "function" in the context of *Empedocles on Etna*, or if we are asked to define the quest in "The Scholar-Gipsy" or to say what *is* the omen of the signal-elm in "Thyrsis," we find ourselves in some difficulties. These are not easy questions. "A piece of music," said Mendelssohn, "expresses not too vague a thought to be put into words, but too precise a thought." I think we can say that Arnold arrived at a poetic method, involving symbols that carry meaning too precise for discursive logic, for the limited spectrum of our literal speech. Hence the great challenge to commentary and explication in *Empedocles* and the two elegies. Some critics throw up their hands—the poems, in spite of lovely passages, are failures. But many who are convinced the poems are not failures have contributed valiantly to a significant body of critical literature on these poems. They have drawn from Arnold's prose for the later working out of some of the poetic symbols.

Ruth apRoberts
The Arnoldian (Fall, 1976), pp. 3–4

CHARLOTTE BRONTË
1816–1855

It is well known that Mrs. Gaskell, in her work published only two years after Charlotte's death, refrained from giving the Brussels period the significance which she knew from the letters shown her by M. Heger it had really possessed. Clement Shorter, writing forty years later, found it necessary to consider the position in more detail but rejected as unfounded the suggestion, largely due to the autobiographical interpretation of *Villette*, that she was in love with M. Heger. The publication in 1913 of her four letters to him naturally concentrated attention on the emotional drama. It was then generally recognised that the Brussels period was in fact of crucial importance and subsequent biographers have treated it in that light.

Its main interest, however, remained for most Brontë students on the emotional plane and its fertilising influence on Charlotte Brontë as an artist did not receive the attention it deserved. Mrs. Humphry Ward had already drawn attention to its significance in this respect in her admirable introductions to the Haworth edition of the novels. And Clement Shorter himself, in *The Brontës, Life and Letters* (1908), had stressed the importance of M. Heger's teaching for Charlotte Brontë's development as an author. But the publication of the letters in 1913 diverted attention from this aspect of the Brussels period, and Brontë critics since have not considered it in any detail, though some, in particular Phyllis Bentley and Kathleen Tillotson, have made very discerning comments.

To begin with, the stay in Brussels needs to be seen against a background which had prepared Charlotte Brontë to receive its impact. Her knowledge of French went back to childhood, and since childhood France had both attracted and repelled her. As the country of Napoleon, it was antipathetic to the worshipper of Wellington, but it had the attraction of all foreign countries for the creator of Angria, and its literature was connected in her mind with names like Mme de Staël, representative of the wider culture for which she longed. Brussels itself was as important for her intellectual and artistic maturation as for her emotional development. Some of her French essays have been reprinted from time to time in the *Brontë*

Society Transactions, but the total achievement they represent and the comments of M. Heger deserve a place in Brontë criticism they have not yet been accorded. Without knowledge of them it is impossible to understand the full meaning of Charlotte's declaration that she would have liked to write a book which would have been dedicated "à mon maître de littérature, au seul maître que j'ai jamais eu. . . ."

But it is the novels themselves that provide the ultimate criterion for the value of the Brussels experience to Charlotte Brontë as a creative artist. And here above all it has not been appreciated as it deserves. It did not awaken her genius, for that genius had already expressed itself in the Angrian cycle, begun in childhood and continued throughout adolescence. But it provided material peculiarly suitable for her creative powers to work on; it enlarged the scope of her vision, giving a new dimension to her delineation of character and milieu; it influenced her style, and no aspect of her art has been so underrated as the new and constructive use she made of French words and phrases in her narration and dialogue; and it strengthened the ties that linked her art with European culture, making her not only a great English novelist but one of the most eloquent representatives in nineteenth-century literature of the undying heritage of the Romantic movement.

Enid L. Duthie
The Foreign Vision of Charlotte Brontë (New York: Barnes & Noble, 1975), pp. xii–xiii

The years of professional success and growing fame gave [Charlotte Brontë] confidence which she had not known before. In the writing of *Villette* she had confronted her public and private selves. But there was still to be borne the effects of a lifetime of failed relationships. The neurotic interaction with a domineering father who had never loved her enough. Her own rejection of Branwell, essential to her growth but profoundly troubling. The tragic loss of her sisters—her feeling complicated by her recognition that she had always stood outside of their charmed circle, an awkward third, as they had stood outside the gates of Angria. And then the rejections of Heger and Smith; her frustrating indecision about James Taylor—his advances and withdrawals. There was only Nicholls's unquestioning devotion to balance thirty-eight years of humiliation and self-doubt. Indeed, the feelings which that devotion had begun to induce in her were sufficiently optimistic to illumine, however dimly, the dark and menacing psychic recesses that the past had slowly and painfully etched. In the growing tenderness of her relationship with Nicholls, "my dear boy," Brontë had begun to discover and trust the maternal principle in herself. But many doubts remained. Autonomy, defined in agony, was threatened everywhere. Her personal independence had not yet been truly won. Her professional freedom was still in question. In her writing and in her experience she had wrestled with the life-defeating forces of romantic mythology and personal history. She had described them. She had confronted them. But, Antaeus-like, they seemed to reappear—renewed by the social powers by which they had been formed.

Seven years earlier Brontë had given to Jane Eyre a dream which she herself had dreamt recurrently. Jane, we recall, is fleeing from the ruins of Thornfield in pursuit of Rochester. A strange child clings to her neck, almost strangling her in its terror. And as Jane scrambles up the rocks to watch her lover disappear beyond the hills, the baby falls from her arms and she awakens. The dream had been relevant to Jane's experience—to her anxieties and fears—as it had been and remained relevant to her author's. Brontë—like Jane—seems simultaneously to be child and mother. Her anxiety belongs to the helpless waif and the dependent wife. She fears the loss of the protective male, the loss of the child whom she must fail, the loss of herself—unable to assume the responsibilities of mature womanhood.

Helene Moglen
Charlotte Brontë: The Self Conceived (New York:
W. W. Norton, 1976), pp. 239–40

Valuable for us as readers 125 years later is the Brontës' urgency to explore the outer limits of experience, their cult of self. Even though Richard Chase (in "The Brontës: A Centennial Observance") tries to show that the Brontës "were essentially Victorian," nevertheless in both their males and females they explored existentially. The dialectic of a Brontë novel, as we suggested above, is almost always between that happy resolution (the refuge and lair) which Chase mentions and the unknown which lies outside the burrower's warm, safe hole. There are always other entrances to and exits from that Castle Keep. . . .

Most Brontë protagonists, male and female alike, are parent-less; if they do have families, the latter are foster or step. This is a condition we normally associate with Dickens, the archetypal novelist of the "wandering child." The Brontës, in fact, plumbed this theme more daringly, for while Dickens sought surrogate parents for his orphans, they more realistically confronted the consequences of what it is to be alone, isolated, and rejected. One need not attempt to match the Brontës against Dickens, but to demonstrate they faced the enormous consequences of such a theme—their basic theme—at a time when family inspired stability and moderation.

They moved, as did Dickens, into the interstices of society, and what they discovered was the terrible disorder of isolation. Like their other contemporaries, Carlyle, Ruskin, Arnold, but especially Carlyle, they forced their characters to seek deep within for their best selves, to grapple with the insanity that lies under the surface, to bring forth a new self, and to be transformed in the process. Perhaps our best example would be Lucy Snowe of *Villette*, whose icy name contrasts with the directionless passion of her nature. We recall that Harriet Martineau disagreed with Lucy's all-consuming greed for love, but Charlotte knew that the lack of love dislocated all other feelings and created an oceanic wave of illness and anguish.

Despite the frigid connotation of her name, Lucy attaches herself to a succession of males and females. Feeling herself drowning because she lacks love, family, support, connections of any kind—she always awaits that "beast in the jungle" to spring—she acts out her need in several conflicting ways.

Frederick R. Karl
in *The Victorian Experience*, ed. Richard Levine (Athens: Ohio Univ. Pr., 1976), pp. 146–47

EMILY BRONTË

1814–1848

Wuthering Heights inspired no school. Nobody has ever attempted to write a sequel. It stands alone in literature; complete and perfect, inspired to some extent by local legend and Byronic tradition; but in the main, it is a product of an imagination which does not need experience to shape it. It is a tale which gives one an overwhelming impression of passion, yet physical contact between Heathcliff and Catherine is actually rare. It is a tale which appeals with its sadism, yet it ends on a note of reflective tenderness.

Charlotte complained that certain portions disturbed her sleep, and was accused of affectation by Emily. Emily would assuredly lose no sleep over the scenes she had written. Such violence was a part of the Gondal world where she roamed freely, just as she strode across the moors at home. Her characters sprang from Gondal itself, and just as Catherine Earnshaw discovered that she *was* Heathcliff, so could Emily have cried out that she *was* Gondal. Her lovers were not twin souls, but possessed a single soul, so that to separate them was spiritually impossible. It was an agony of separation which Emily had endured during her mystical experiences and written about in some of her poetry.

The Victorians understood none of this. They dismissed *Wuthering Heights* as an early work by the author of *Jane Eyre*, and ignored or hissed it. Emily Brontë's poems and her novel were failures. According to Charlotte, she met the situation with cynical indifference. If Emily had craved public acclaim, she would never admit it. She had attempted to share the fruits of her genius with the world, but the world rejected them. It merely confirmed her intensely pessimistic view of human nature. Henceforth, she would trust nobody, rely on nobody. She referred to her work as "rubbish" and to her poems as "those rhymes," and if she was hurt by the public indifference nobody was allowed to guess the fact.

Maureen Peters
An Enigma of Brontës (New York: St. Martin's, 1974), pp. 128–29

ROBERT BROWNING

1812–1889

Roma King, Jr. et al, eds., *The Complete Works of Robert Browning* (1969–), 4 vols to date

William Irvine and Park Honan, *The Book, the Ring and the Poet* (1974)

Browning's theory of knowledge is based upon the concept of wholeness or order—the triple soul working in harmony to fulfill the divine plan. When one soul usurps the functions of another, order is disrupted and chaos ensues. Mind becomes evil only when body or spirit is atrophied through disuse or through abuse of intellect. In the harmonious functioning of the triple soul, man can find oneness with the divine purpose.

Life has a single supreme function: to test man's endurance and faith through frustration, evil, and doubt. Man is forbidden in this life to understand absolute truth, which lies beyond this world. The ultimate secrets of creation and God's inscrutable plan must not be seen by man directly, nor must he seek to tear the veil hiding the Absolute. To do so is to be guilty of hubris, the desire to become like God in knowledge and power. Life with its trials permits man to prefigure the infinite, but he can never in the flesh look steadily upon the white light of eternity. Life, this world, and all its mysteries are man's province, to study and love in wholeness and harmony. Man will never solve all the riddles of existence. But herein is precisely the test. The endless quest for truth, not absolute truth itself, is man's proper goal. Like the frog which jumps forever toward the wall, halving the distance with each leap, man is doomed never to arrive at the goal of final attainment; for if he did, life would cease to have meaning. Indeed, it would cease to be, for absolute knowledge and death are mysterious twins which man will meet in good time. Meanwhile, Browning affirmed, although ultimate knowledge is unattainable on earth, the quest for knowledge, like love and life itself, is essential to the development of the tripartite soul of man.

Norton B. Crowell
The Triple Soul: Browning's Theory of Knowledge (Albuquerque: Univ. New Mexico Pr., 1963), p. xiii

The circumstances of [Browning's] bringing up were certainly instrumental in developing that "clear consciousness/Of self, distinct from all its qualities" that the young man—with perplexity, pride, and dismay—recognized as central to his character. His problem was what to make of so energetic an ego.

In his poem *Pauline* (published 1833), where he first defined the problem as he understood it, Browning goes on to consider two further "elements" of his character that served as checks on his consuming selfhood. The first is his power of imagination and the second his yearning after God. His imagination is an "angel" to him that sustains "a soul with such desire/Confined to clay." ("Clay" is an obsessive word with Byron, and its use here reminds us that Browning's early poems—destroyed by their author—were supposed to be in the manner of Byron, whom Browning is recalling, along with Shelley, in *Pauline*. There is strong influence of Byron's "Dream.") It enables him to master his "dark past." But the imagination itself poses problems of direction and control which are solved by the premise of a divine Love which presents itself to him as goal and as surrounding presence. The forces united for the boy in the myths of ancient Greece, which enabled his ego to exercise itself heathfully in imaginings of godlike life, and these early experiences of integration remain to some extent normative for him. It is experience of this sort he wants to regain as he addresses himself in *Pauline* to more radical representatives of imagination and religion—Shelley and Christ.

George M. Ridenour
Introd., in *Selected Poetry of Browning*, ed. George M. Ridenour (New York: New American Library, 1966), p. viii

Difficulties of belief such as those presented by miracles or by conflicting versions of historical events are significant only insofar as they bear upon conduct. It is not so much what men believe as what they do, especially by way of responding to doubt, that is the crucial consideration. But, Guido's knotty argument [in *The Ring and the Book*] to the contrary notwithstanding, belief and action cannot be separated, for to Browning, the tireless activist, belief itself is a form of activity; action divorced from belief is sterile, and belief which neither occasions action nor results from it is meaningless.

This is the final statement of *The Ring and the Book.* Toward it all the poem's principal themes have pointed—the ceaseless conflict of testimony, the equally discrepant interpretations of character and motive, the constant reminders that appearance frequently is more plausible than reality and that language is oftener a vehicle of falsehood than of truth. The search for truth in the midst of deceit and illusion, for stability in the midst of flux, turns out to be the search for the principles of right conduct. In human affairs the pervasive curse of doubt can be countered only by the vigorous response of a soul inspired by Christian teaching.

Richard D. Altick and James F. Loucks
Browning's Roman Murder Story (Chicago: Univ. Chicago Pr., 1968), pp. 360–61

The importance of Browning in breaking down the barriers of literary *genres* cannot be overrated. Though apparently working in the opposite direction to the aesthetics of art for art's sake, he succeeded in bypassing them to arrive at the same conclusions to which they had been leading, an attitude toward poetry and art which is concerned with process, development, relations rather than with finality and completeness. What matters is no longer the end of the story but a series of revelations of its inner meanings at different moments of its development. . . . For Browning the short poem does not aim at defining once and for all a particular feeling, but at catching a fleeting state of mind with no sense of permanence or of finality. It is an attitude which was to be taken up and expressed as theory by the writers of the present century, not only by the novelists . . . but also by the poets: Ezra Pound, who acknowledged his debt to Browning (and who gave the title of *personae* to one of his earliest and best volumes of verse), and Eliot, whose major early works are dramatic monologues, although he was less willing to acknowledge his debt than Pound, possibly because Browning's reputation was at such a low ebb at the time.

Barbara Melchiori
Browning's Poetry of Reticence (Edinburgh: Oliver and Boyd, 1968), pp. 194–95

The distinctive feature of Browning's rhetoric is its dialectical temper, which forces the reader to discover the astonishing (and often disturbing) life of the ideas. We value Browning for the authority and brilliance, often the sheer excitement, of his thinking. Though this emphasis on rhetoric and "content" is especially helpful at a time when other elements of Browning's work are being stressed, I argue that the poet's doctrines are less important than the life represented and the values found along the way. The Victorian sage must use his doctrines for the sake of the discoveries that go with them, for the sake of what is formed in the progressive act of thinking.

The young Browning is one of the "subjective poets" who, according to his Introductory Essay to the *Letters of Shelley*, "seek the truth in their [own] soul[s]." In its extreme form, Browning calls subjective art "a deformity." Because "the world is not to be learned and thrown aside, but reverted to and relearned," Browning finds that as a subjective poet he must become his opposite; he must make the objective world an inseparable part of himself. In order to understand points of view other than his own, the poet has to play a series of roles and pretend to be what he is not.

W. David Shaw
The Dialectical Temper (Ithaca, N.Y.: Cornell Univ. Pr., 1968), p. 308

To see Guido [In *The Ring and the Book*] as saved is to justify the poem's design—to understand why Browning gave Guido two monologues and how the Pope's monologue leads into Guido's second. Once having understood the advances as well as the retreats in Guido's second monologue, we can surely expect him to return to at least his point of farthest advance. If Guido is not saved, then *The Ring and the Book* is absolutist in that it simply illustrates Guido's absolute evil and consigns him to an orthodox hell. To see Guido as saved is to understand the sense in which the poem is relativist—in that all limited points of view, all selves, are justified as part of God's scheme. Through being what they are intensely enough, they lead back to God. The relative is the index to an absolute reality that cannot be *known* through human institutions and judgments, but can at certain intense moments be felt.

Robert Langbaum
Victorian Poetry (Winter, 1972), p. 305

As Elizabeth [Barrett] was once, Pompilia [in *The Ring and the Book*] is imprisoned in a castle guarded by a watchful monster. As Browning once, Caponsacchi is confronted by a strict social code and even stricter scruples, which he defies to save a mortally threatened lady by flying south with her in a jolting carriage through Italian scenery. The priest's experience of feminine weakness on a journey is Robert's of Elizabeth, but the chasteness of the rescue suggests Robert's offer at one point during their courtship to "live as a brother" with his lady, if only he might be allowed to rescue her. Caponsacchi's love can burn all the more intensely in that it never will attain, and yet rise in conformity with Browning's doctrine of failure into a pure ozone where soul disinterestedly worships soul. The attributes of Caponsacchi's own soul are those of Browning's—enthusiasm, impulsiveness, chivalry, courage, and a rich capacity and an instant readiness to hate as well as love. If the pre-Pompilian priest, holding duchesses' hands and sipping mild refreshments in well-decorated chambers, is a fair prediction of what the poet is to become, the later priest is a picture of what he always was. For Caponsacchi—too—fervently trusts in action and just as fervently distrusts intellect. When he deliberates he is wrong (as when he delays in coming for Pompilia because he is lost in thought with Aquinas)—but when he answers his instinct without a thought for consequences, he is right. He exists rather as Browning did in order to feel intensely, and to expose the futility of most traditions and the corruption of most institutions—the Catholic Church in particular. Even his poignancy derives from an acutely felt bereavement:

> . . . My part
> Is done; i' the doing it, I pass away
> Out of the world. I want no more with earth.

Pompilia, in her turn, expresses the grandest illusion of Browning's life—his belief in the childlike innocence and divine goodness of Elizabeth. She is the priest's and the poet's *donna angelicata.* Her dark beauty, charity, articulateness, and perfect naïveté clearly derive from the middle-aged child Browning first saw at her father's house and last saw in the "young girl" who expired in his arms. As [William C.] DeVane has shown, the poem contains no fewer than thirty allusions to the twin and cognate myths enacted at Wimpole Street. Moreover its two great, central crises involve both a Perseus who carries off an Andromeda and a St. George who balks a dragon to save a virgin. As Caponsacchi snatches up a soul of purity from the beastly Guido, so at the last moment Pope Innocent slays Evil's sophistries to preserve Truth. The first crisis celebrates the decisive outward action of Browning's life, the second, most of its inward and mental action.

William Irvine and Park Honan
The Book, the Ring and the Poet (New York: McGraw-Hill, 1974), pp. 427–28

In his later work as in his earlier, Browning sought for the proper forms to embody the content of his intellect and imagination, that is, to express his idea of reality. He held no belief more firmly than that of growth and development; he insisted that life is not a having and a resting but a growing and a becoming, the organism being dead that ceases to change. And, of course, the man himself changed. Those critics, consequently, who hold that *The Ring and the Book* "is a definitive summing-up of Browning's philosophy of life" have, in my opinion, contributed to the confusion concerning Browning's later poetry. I do not wish to claim that his last thoughts were his best or that they more accurately represent the "real"

Browning. For the "real" Browning is the whole man, the poet who wrote the *Parleyings* as well as the poet who composed *Men and Women*. My point is that Browning's thoughts and feelings changed and, moreover, that as they changed so did his forms.

Clyde deL. Ryals
Browning's Later Poetry (Ithaca, N.Y.: Cornell Univ. Pr., 1975), p. 15

The self . . . amounts to the poems. Those who seek the poet's spirit will find it embodied in the objective constituents of his work.

"By the Fire-Side" is an especially lucid instance of the alternative to personal poetry Browning adopted as his major, but by no means invariable, mode. An analysis of the discrepancy between the facts as he experienced them and the events in the poem enables us to understand it as an enactment of Nietzsche's demand that the lyric poet must deal with his own emotions as aspects of an objective whole. It enables us to distinguish the man in the poem, who gives way to his will and desires, from the poet who wrote it, and to see that it cannot be read as if the speaker's happiness were its ultimate dimension. It emerges as the well-controlled work of a poetic consciousness which has performed the sacrifice of separating certain impressions from their personal associations, and setting them free to reverberate within the larger context of a mind's response to the mysterious promptings of the cosmos.

Jacob Korg
Victorian Poetry (Summer, 1971), pp. 157–58

In "My Last Duchess" and "The Bishop Orders his Tomb at St. Praxed's Church," as in Tennyson's "The Palace of Art," we see some of the highest attainments of Western culture perverted to diabolical ends. In a sense, the personae of all three poems may be regarded as representing the danger of moral decay situated at the very heart of the idea of civilization, the only antidote for which, once orthodox faith has lost its hold, is the Sympathy preached by the Romantics and their Victorian successors. It is worth recalling, in this respect, that Browning's Duke has two first cousins in later Victorian fiction—George Eliot's Grandcourt (*Daniel Deronda*) and Henry James's Gilbert Osmond (*The Portrait of a Lady*), another fastidious art collector. These are not merely three stereotypes: the emissary's interview with the Duke would have proceeded differently had he been dealing with either of the other two—just as the three heroines all have their individual personalities—but all three husbands eventually reveal themselves, through their treatment of their wives and their manipulation of others, to have been concealing a hard core of brutality beneath their polished, hyper-civilized exterior, while one at least—the cold, haughty

Grandcourt—is repeatedly described in imagery reducing him to an almost reptilian level. The implication in these works would seem to be that once an individual, a class, or a society has reached a certain point of over-refinement, the dark forces of human nature lurking underground threaten to wreak a terrible vengeance for their unnatural suppression. These works are thus part of the ongoing Victorian diagnosis of the disruptive forces menacing the fabric of Western society.

Joshua Adler
Victorian Poetry (Summer, 1977), pp. 226–27

THOMAS CARLYLE

1795–1881

By virtue of his acute embodiment of . . . dualities, Carlyle is peculiarly modern. He celebrates the dynamics of change, the possibilities of the new society, but he laments the loss of roots and fears the mechanization of man and a world governed by self interest and greed. He brings art adventurously into new areas, but in each area he futilely seeks some final note of ultimate authority to replace the stability of the religious finality he has lost. He strives for the rich public voice of a prophet who redefines what is enduring in the old traditions for a modern age, but in his very prophecy he embodies the problematic, the tentative, the doubtful, the negative, the skeptical and self-questioning, and even the futile. In both his style and the variety of his efforts, he seeks to encompass all the variety of modern existence, but the multiplicity of industrial society, the rapidity of change, and his own endless striking out into such varying directions frequently create a sense of restlessness, desperation, and incipient chaos. Even in his mythmaking of heroes, where his voice is most assertive, the tormented note shows through in the strident tone and the desperation of the social solutions.

Albert J. La Valley
Carlyle and the Idea of the Modern (New Haven, Conn.: Yale Univ. Pr., 1968), p. 3

Sartor Resartus is, in fact, a work of fiction, although it can only be regarded as a novel in a very special sense. Until the appearance of G. B. Tennyson's book, consideration of *Sartor* as a novel had almost inevitably led to misreading. Mr. Tennyson rightly argues, however, that if we accept a minimal definition of "novel" as "an extended piece of prose fiction," there is nothing to hinder acceptance of *Sartor* as a novel, especially as Carlyle himself called it a "Didactic novel." . . .

Sartor is a fiction whose form is not governed by the demands of either plot or character development. It is not concerned with verisimilitude, or with the construction of social modes or manners. Rather it is controlled thematically and by means of symbols and images; it is concerned exclusively with subjective states; and its aim is largely satirical and therefore didactic. . . . *Sartor* [is] a fiction belonging to the complex class of "confession-anatomy-romance" . . . the success of *Sartor* is largely the result of its fictions. I shall try to show that this suggests how powerful were the forces which went to the making of the novel as the supreme Victorian art (and which turned poetry so largely to the dramatic monologue and long narrative). These forces increasingly (though never entirely) lost their power with Carlyle, and for this reason *Sartor*'s success can help explain Carlyle's later failures.

George Levine
The Boundaries of Fiction (Princeton, N.J.: Princeton Univ. Pr., 1968), pp. 21–22

As rhetorical devices, neither Carlyle's single-minded assertiveness nor his repetitiveness are effective. Both of these habits of style suggest that he might have had a few misgivings about the simplistic diagnosis of his age put forth in the essay ["Signs of the Times"]. However, the irresistible current of his argument does not allow him pause to look at the thesis from new vantages. Too eager to judge, not quite critical enough to make the fine discrimination, he protests too much. The "desperado," which Matthew Arnold saw later on in Carlyle, is much too prominent in this essay.

At the frontier of fiction and life, Carlyle seems to have found the only way he could to document as he knew it the contemporary condition of man divided. If Carlyle fails as a novelist and fumbles as an essayist, he eminently succeeds in *Sartor Resartus* with its mixed bag of tricks. First, the double-faced Teufelsdröckhian mask, apocalyptic prophet one moment and comical eccentric the next, gives an elasticity to the handling of the argument that would not be available to an undisguised philosophical pronouncement. The "Reminiscences" chapter shows the advantages of this form over either novel or straightforward essay: The reader is warned against uncritical acceptance of each and every oracle; and whatever defects he might note in them he can attribute to Teufelsdröckh rather than to Carlyle—the author's personal endorsement of the professor not being expected at every point. Second, the device of the unidentified Editor, who transmits Teufelsdröckh's Philosophy of Clothes, adds to the effectiveness of the technique of indirection, for he too is not always a reliable narrator and commentator. Third, the presence of the false hero-worshiper, Hofrath Heuschrecke, still another narrator in the process of Carlylean expression, further complicates the irony without which Teufelsdröckh's beliefs would be mere assertions.

Masao Miyoshi
The Divided Self (New York: New York Univ. Pr., 1969), pp. 143–44

Carlyle's tone and manner is the least attractive side to him, and the least defensible. This seems a truism in spite of his defenders. Indeed to discuss and analyse such a style can be embarrassing because the weaknesses are so blatantly obvious. But since [David] DeLaura, in a note on Arnold's *Essay in Criticism*, writes that "here, Carlyle is treated as 'a man of great ability' suffering from a defect of style so notorious it need not, apparently, be specified" (p. 108, n. 21), it is clear that one cannot simply assume these defects to exist. It is even implied that the assumption is discreditable, or at least was in Arnold's case. Consequently, one feels at liberty to expand a little on the matter. I do not mean as it relates to simple matters of idiosyncratic grammar and the coining of unnecessary words, but to larger matters of emotional crudity and emotional bullying. The field seems to me to be too large to be fully comprehended in an essay, and too uninteresting for really extended treatment. It would seem sufficient to illustrate one or two common excesses, one important device, and to point to their effects. It would be absurd to suggest that in doing so the essence of Carlyle is thus fully and finally isolated. Rather, the aim is to draw attention sharply to elements in Carlyle that in any just account of his arguments and influence simply cannot be omitted, and yet these days often are omitted.

D. R. M. Wilkinson
PMLA (March, 1971), pp. 228–29

What Carlyle is struggling with [in *Sartor Resartus*] is a problem of integration, of identity, which he conceptualizes in terms of an integration of feeling, thought, and action—in terms, that is, of finding the thoughts appropriate to one's feeling and the action appropriate to one's thoughts. . . . Carlyle is very much a twentieth-century figure. . . .

Although Carlyle, unfortunately, does not make much progress in delineating the possibilities of action in the modern world, he does recognize that truly meaningful action must be a transcendence or a realization of thought. It must be action that somehow serves as an extension outward of man's mind into the historical realm in which we pass our lives. Just as thought without action is merely a self-indulgence that leads ultimately to the solipsism, so action without thought is brutality.

Philip Rosenberg
The Seventh Hero: Thomas Carlyle and the Theory of Radical Activism (Cambridge, Mass.: Harvard Univ. Pr., 1974), p. 54

LEWIS CARROLL

1832–1898

Lewis Carroll was aware of the extent to which people might live by, and perhaps run into dangers through, "an order . . . created from within and . . . co-extensive with the self." One name for that order is play. He never calls for the reinstitution of the gospel of work, but he would have liked to introduce an antidote to the destructive egoism that he himself portrays so damagingly (while so fetchingly) in the games of *Alice*, the sport of *Sylvie and Bruno*, and the hunt of the *Snark*. In the preface to *Sylvie and Bruno Concluded*, Carroll makes an appeal common enough for an inhabitant of a country and a century whose certainty of an "order outside and prior to the self" had been almost evolutionized and aestheticized away, although it is perhaps not quite the appeal one expects from the uncommon creator of the moral-less if not irreverent play worlds of the *Alices*; he calls for "the revival, in Society, of the waning spirit of reverence" (II, xxiii). Carroll espouses what can be called a gospel of amusement, or play. He shows us at the same time that not all in the gospel is holy.

Kathleen Blake
Play, Games, and Sport: The Literary Works of Lewis Carroll
(Ithaca, N.Y.: Cornell Univ. Pr., 1974), p. 212

Alice was the first and greatest of [Carroll's] love affairs with maidens, unformed women, little girls of nursery age, creatures in whose presence he lost his stammer, smelled the breeze across the cornfields of Daresbury and found the reality of Wonderland. His love life was as simple as that. He adored the image substantiated first in Alice Liddell, then in a succession, sometimes a plurality, of other child friends. This was the precious reality of his life, right up to its ascetic, overworked end at the age of sixty-six.

Where was the orgasm? Was there an orgasm? In his introduction to his *Pillow Problems* (seventy-two problems, chiefly in algebra, plane geometry or trigonometry) he wrote of nocturnal "unholy thoughts, which torture with their hateful presence the fancy that would fain be pure." Apart from this unsensational hint there is nothing in his writing, behaviour, or the witness of those who knew him, that his well-cared-for if sometimes under-fed body reached any climax of lust. This is not so very odd. Many die virgins. Many live with a love image without sexual desire. The man was unique in that the image provoked such poetic fantasies as *Alice* and the *Snark*. The man was also warm-blooded enough to enjoy the physical and tactile kiss-hug-cuddle of pre-pubescent girlhood. He was not deprived. He was prodigiously self-indulgent and always had what he wanted. Suggestions that he was a pervert or a "dirty old man" using child photography to further his carnal desires are as absurd as the fashionable theories that he was an acid head who climbed into Wonderland by way of the Caterpillar's mushroom. He was a singularly happy and contented man who enjoyed good health with a touch of hypochondria. Some have rated him epileptic, others have questioned his mental balance. All fail to prove their theories or to add much to the treasures of Wonderland. To a little girl who took his fancy his heart was open and communication was full and easy.

To the world at large he was a kindly man, quizzical, pedantic, extra alert because of his deafness and, as he got older, somewhat querulous and withdrawn. About his child friendships he was never secretive, indeed always explicit. He was totally self-centered. He knew, and got, what he wanted. He expected them to end with the end of childhood.

John Pudney
Lewis Carroll and His World (New York: Charles Scribner's Sons, 1976), pp. 67–69

Lewis Carroll has meant much to most of us. Some of us do not outgrow him. There are playful absurdities in his tales that tickle the logical mind. Now and again a passage of his can be aptly quoted in the course of some philosophical analysis, and the quotation sensibly leavens the lump. A posthumous new book of his after, lo, these eighty years is an event not to be lightly passed over.

Curiosity is twice piqued, in logico-philosophical minds, when the new book turns out to be *Symbolic Logic*. These minds were already cognizant of a Part 1, 1896, of 200 modest pages. It ran into four editions, as Lewis Carroll called them, in the space of ten months. Despite its austere title it was accessible to children, as it was meant to be. Parts 2 and 3 were already projected at that time, the one Advance and the other Transcendental. What is now newly before us is Part 2. Modern logic was little beyond its formative stage in Carroll's day, so the more romantic among us might look to his newly revealed Advanced Logic in hopes of finding historically interesting anticipations at least, and perhaps even new light on live topics. The editor of the volume, W. W. Bartley III, evinced and encouraged this romantic attitude on his advance publicity, which appeared as an article in the Scientific American.

Carroll worked on Part 2 up to his death in 1898. Much of it was typeset while the work was in progress. Professor Bartley has retrieved the galley proofs, running to 145 pages. He has eked this material out with twenty-eight pages from his own hand, sixteen pages from Carroll's notes and letters, and thirty pages of facsimiles, photographs, and humorous drawings from other sources. Part 2, thus synthesized, is just the second half of the volume that is now before us; for Bartley has also reprinted Part 1 and prefixed forty pages of editorial introduction. . . .

It is our admiration of Lewis Carroll's other works that lends interest to this one. That interest remains, and we can be grateful to Bartley for serving it. The volume also offers further gratification on its own account to all who respond to Lewis Carroll's magic touch. Those who are puzzle fanciers, in particular, can revel in the book for many long evenings.

W. V. Quine
TLS (August 26, 1977), pp. 1018–19

ARTHUR HUGH CLOUGH

1819–1861

Through its various personae, *Dipsychus* reflects many aspects of its author: the Dipsychus gripping his armchair for fear of sin or doctrinal error if he leaves it is Clough's neurasthenic aspect; Mephisto, who sees things as they are, reflects his healthy outgoing self; the poet, who is shown in the Prologue and Epilogue seeking to resolve the conflict between "the tender conscience and the world" in the unity of art, this is Clough the poet, of course; and the uncle, for whom the younger generation is "a sort of hobbadi-hoy cherub, too big to be innocent, and too simple for anything else"—and who is convinced in any case that "it's all Arnold's doing"—he is Clough's commonsense, rather conservative streak. Certainly, identifying Clough with his hero in a one-to-one relation is as absurd as calling Mr. Eliot "Prufrock." For one thing, Clough is remarkably saner and stronger than the enfeebled Dipsychus, and for another, much less robust than Mephisto. The poet's characteristic skepticism is as agonized as ever, but he has gained significantly in intellect, wit, and irony, and an enormously attractive humor, all of which have gone most noticeably into the blood and bones of Mephisto.

What Henry Sidgwick said of Clough in 1869, that he was "in a literal sense before his age," we see now was not exactly the case. In 1850, a good ten years before the full effect of the new spirit was felt, the cultural life of the nation was already in turmoil. The Oxford Movement was still adding members, when the Higher Criticism rose to challenge the foundations of Christian faith. Mary Ann Evans' translation of Strauss' *Leben Jesu* appeared in 1846; J. A. Froude's *Shadows of the Clouds* in 1847 and *Nemesis of Faith* in 1849, and Francis Newman's *The Soul* in 1849 and *Phases of Faith* in 1850. In 1848 Rossetti and his friends organized the Pre-Raphaelite Brotherhood, publishing *The Germ* to propagate their doctrines. A new style of sensibility began to form along with the new religious attitude, and the doubt troubling Clough was enervating many young Britons, among them Clough's best friend, Matthew Arnold. There were Europeans and Americans, too, infected by that sickness unto death: Melville's Bartleby would "prefer not" to be bothered with anything at all; for

Goncharov's Oblomov, there is nothing in the world to compare with the appeal of his warm bed, and he refuses to climb out; Baudelaire, meanwhile, drones on in his monotone, *c'est l'ennui, c'est l'ennui.*

The difference with Clough was that after a brilliant diagnosis of his spiritual malaise he pulled himself together, administering the simple but for that time radical therapy of laughing the symptoms away. Adam's longed-for "gaiety of soul" became Clough's own achievement, and the means by which *Dipsychus*—not at all the feeble *Hamlet* or mere inferior *Faust* that Arnold would have criticized—came into its own as a wise and worldly minor masterpiece.

Masao Miyoshi
The Divided Self (New York: New York Univ. Pr., 1969),
pp. 174–76

If the English Romantic poets sought to create an illusion of spontaneity and fluidity in their poetry in order to express their sense of liberation from the traditional forms of politics and morality, then perhaps an early Victorian poet like Arthur Hugh Clough sought to embody his Romantic inheritance of a liberated spirit in a new and more contemporary form. According to this interpretation, such a Victorian might find that his legacy of Romantic freedom was too burdensome a responsibility to carry on alone through the growing complexities of Victorian society; however, he would not reject his legacy, but rather he would seek to put it into a form that would define its limits and establish its relevance to his own time. It was this kind of problem that provoked Clough to ask whether Victorian poetry "could . . . not attempt to convert into beauty and thankfulness, or at least into some form and shape, some feeling, at any rate, of content—the actual, palpable things with which our every-day life is concerned?" . . .

One of Arthur Clough's own poems, " 'Blank Misgivings of a Creature Moving About in Worlds Not Realised,' " reflects this concern of the Victorian search for a form to embody a Romantic heritage of spontaneity and spiritual liberation. Clough's title line is taken from Wordsworth's "Ode: Intimations of Immortality," and very appropriately suggests his immediate debt of inspiration to the Romantics in general and to Wordsworth in particular. The irony of this inspiration is that for Wordsworth the "blank misgivings" of his childhood were cause for a "song of thanks and praise," while for Clough they are a source of moral and aesthetic anxiety. This irony is representative of Clough's response to his larger Romantic legacy of "spontaneous overflow," which was an aesthetic goal for Romantic poets but a difficult beginning for their Victorian heirs. . . .

The concluding stanza of " 'Blank Misgivings' " is a formal statement of that reanchorage of the soul in the body of the preceding stanzas. Consequently, this poem, which begins in an anxiety of spiritless passions, flees the pangs of conscience, and discovers the reality of spirit, is Arthur Clough's resolution of his aesthetic problem in finding a form to contain his Romantic legacy.

Richard D. McGhee
Victorian Poetry (Summer, 1969), pp. 105–6, 115

It is clear that the Clough who as late as 1852 found himself as alone as he had been as a schoolboy and youth (the Oxford years were only a partial respite) sought in Arnold an intensity and exclusiveness of friendship that Arnold, especially after his marriage, was unwilling to accord. The temperamental difference is evident even in the poetry of the two men: Arnold, exteriorly debonair and in some ways seemingly careless of the feelings of others, preserved an aloofness that was the echo of his own poetic self-admonition: " 'Thou hast been, shalt be, art, alone' "; whereas Clough, less secure in himself and attracted by the Olympian self-possession of Arnold, sought to base his life on a philosophy of "service" and community. I suggest, without benefit of explicit psychoanalytic theorizing, that this side of Clough's personality and character—his emotional dependence on Arnold, his general instability of temperament, his seeming inability to work out even a tentative intellectual position, and his reluctant coming to terms with the (to Arnold) ineluctable loneliness in life—was central in Arnold's judgment of the "loose screw" in Clough's organization. *Letters and Remains*, with its poignant revelation of the cruel emotional deprivations of Clough's boyhood years (partly thanks to Arnold's own father), as well as of his estrangement from his old associates after 1848, would have brought back the embarrassment and irritation which characterize so many of Arnold's letters to Clough, but now softened by a new remorse and a new pity.

David J. DeLaura
Victorian Poetry (Autumn, 1969), pp. 201–2

CHARLES DICKENS

1812–1870

Having claimed that never has Dickens enjoyed so high a critical reputation as today, we may venture further: we may affirm that some of the best contemporary criticism has been Dickens criticism. It is curious that Paul Elmer More should have declared that Dickens "will not bear analysis." Even although he would appear to place Dickens apart from the writers of his Great Tradition, F. R. Leavis is without doubt among the distinguished Dickens critics; nor is his approach confined to *Hard Times*, as is sometimes supposed. In the *Spectator* for January 1963 he went so far as to say: "I would without hesitation surrender the whole *oeuvre* of Flaubert for *Dombey and Son* or *Little Dorrit*." And we may agree with [Steven] Marcus that Leavis's analysis of Dickens's style is the best that has so far been made. Works such as Marcus's own *From Pickwick to Dombey* (1965), which is to be followed by a companion volume, J. Hillis Miller's *Charles Dickens: The World of His Novels* (1958), A. O. J. Cockshut's *The Imagination of Charles Dickens* (1961), K. J. Fielding's *Charles Dickens: A Critical Introduction* (1958), the extremely interesting study by Mark Spilka *Dickens and Kafka* (1963), and Monroe Engel's *Maturity of Dickens* (1959), the symposia *Dickens and His Readers* (1955), *The Dickens Critics* (1961), and *Dickens and the Twentieth Century* (1962), not to mention the works of continental scholars such as Sylvère Monod's *Dickens romancier* (1954), have underlined the unity of Dickens's work, his symbolism, and his poetic method. . . .

As to that work, it is so vast and many-sided, and retains to this day such vitality, as to be able to sustain the shock of the most bitter detraction, and equally to survive praise which is insidious in its one-sidedness. We may be confident that whatever men may be reading in another century, they will be reading Dickens: for his influence has become a necessary ingredient in our civilized life, and his gift was capacious enough to have satirized *in advance* the humbug, pretentiousness, and chicanery to which human nature is predisposed. For zest and gusto this endowment is without a parallel; no one "stops the show" like Dickens. It is because his art both "antedates" the novel and may well survive it; it is because he is at heart a traditional teller of tales and the inventor of a mythology concerning people larger than life, that his appeal remains perennial. His reputation both in his own country and abroad has long burst the narrow banks of "literature" and become part of everyday existence; and that is why he so well merits the title, conferred on him by *The Times* at his death, of the Great Commoner of English Letters.

E. W. F. Tomlin
Charles Dickens 1812–1870 (New York: Simon and Schuster, 1969), pp. 261, 263

It is with Sam Weller and Miss Wren . . . that we have the most exquisite bracketing of Dickens's career. From the very start, Dickens had an intuitive sense that the imagination alone can anchor our spirit in the drift of anonymity. First Sam Weller, with miraculous ease and finesse, and at the end Jenny Wren, wearied by pain and its remorseless threads of disillusionment, ratify this belief with adrenal and improving fancies. By the agency of imagination, and like no other characters in Dickens, they are empowered to know and understand—Sam through his "figurative" Wellerisms, Jenny through her "practical" visions—the ultimate anonymity of death itself. I will go back to Dick Swiveller now for one last parable. The imagination can be authenticated in Dickens's novels only when it makes an inward space for personality. Fictions that are no more than pretense merely close out the world and forestall its intimidations. But true fancy, as with Mr. Swiveller's "apartments," serves to pluralize reality. It builds alternative places in the mind, fictive chambers like Dickens's own expansive and colorful narrative (there is no better example) where new room is made for the imagination—spacious, airy, and gaily lit.

Garrett Stewart
Dickens and the Trials of the Imagination (Cambridge, Mass.: Harvard Univ. Pr., 1974), p. 227

With respect to the management of narrative . . . Dickens' procedure was more complicated and various than it has generally been credited with being. At times he very boldly experimented with mixed narrative modes, as in the alternate points-of-view of *Bleak House*, in which the burden of narration is divided between an omniscient narrator writing in a progressive present tense about one portion of the story, and Esther Summerson, a first-person narrator, whose autobiographical memoir is related in the past tense from a point in time long after the events she describes have transpired, and which concerns another portion of the story. More important, throughout his *oeuvre* Dickens was constantly shifting the ground upon which he stood as narrator in relation to the persons, things, and events he treats and in relation to his reader.

He often, of course, adopted the guise of omniscience, describing or narrating but editorializing all the while in order to control reader response, and maintaining a considerable distance between himself and the matters at hand. At other times, however, his imaginative identification with a character in a particular situation—Carker's flight from Dijon in *Dombey and Son* is a case in point—became so great that the presence of the narrator is extinguished by the dramatized workings of the consciousness of the personage. Or again, the imaginative hold on the narrator of a particular scene may be so strong—the death of Jo in *Bleak House* or of Paul Dombey will serve as illustrations—that all aesthetic distance is obliterated by Dickens' emotional involvement in it; and, like it or not, the scene is communicated to the reader in such compelling terms as to convince the reader of its total actuality in the mind of the author.

Sometimes, as in the burial of Nemo in *Bleak House*, the narrator may detach himself from the events recorded and take up the stance of his readers as a witness to occurrences over which he has no control, which are totally outside himself, but which elicit from him at length a powerful emotional and moral reaction. At other times, as in the coroners' inquest over Nemo's death, the narrator's presence disappears entirely behind scenario, and author and reader alike are thrust into the scene as neutral recorders of sense data. Very often in descriptive passages, the narrative voice assumes the stance of an alien consciousness who records without any informing comprehension the details of the most commonplace things, usually employing the techniques we would now associate with a moving camera eye; but no less frequently Dickens will indulge in all the patently artificial contrivances we recognize as belonging to farce comedy, burlesque, or parody. Occasionally he will indulge in a passionate exhortation to the reader, but these must be discriminated from outbursts which are directed to no one and which seem rather to be relief to the author's own feelings generated by the more or less autonomous creations of his own imagination, toward which he and reader alike stand as observers and respondents.

To prosecute such a catalogue further would serve no useful purpose beyond what has already been established: that Dickens' narrative procedure keeps in a continuous state of agitation all relations between reader, narrator, fiction and reality, indeed, that calls into question not only the reality-status of the fiction but the very nature of conventional notions of what is real. In a time like ours when "the new philosophy has cast all in doubt,"—not least those questions of personal identity with which Dickens' protagonists like Pip and Esther are so intimately involved—this novelist speaks with special pertinence and piquancy, and we see in him a precursor of the creators of Lafcadio and *The Stranger* [Gide and Camus]. Such an alienated, insecure vision of life can hardly be a matter of congratulation, for either ourselves or Dickens, but it enables us to hear his voice as one of our own.

William F. Axton
in *The Victorian Experience*, ed. Richard A. Levine (Athens: Ohio Univ. Pr., 1976), pp. 46–48

There are several reasons why the question of Dickens' religion is a vexed and difficult one. . . . One derives from a general reading of all his writings an impression that he thought Christianity true and important, uniquely important, but that almost all actual Christians were wrong, all churches were on the wrong track, because they had committed that very silly mistake, which, alas, was so common in the world, and was the cause of so many of its ills, of not taking Charles Dickens as their guide. Though Dickens disliked intensely most of the versions of Protestantism that came to his attention, he was at heart very Protestant, because he thought that his own response to Christ was uniquely right and self-authenticating, and that by its rightness it sufficiently demonstrated the wrongness of others.

Jane Vogel's *Allegory in Dickens* takes issue with those who treat the religion of Dickens as vestigial or merely conventional. And, on the whole, she seems to me justified in the arguments she uses to support it. She is right to lay stress on *The Life of Our Lord*, which Dickens wrote especially for his own children and refused to publish. (It remained unpublished until 1934.) A man whose every paragraph is saleable does not act in this way without being in earnest. She is right, too, to stress the very close relation that frequently exists between passages in the novels and biblical sources.

But all this leads on to more difficult questions. . . . What is the religious content of Dickens' strong and sincere feelings? And what, in an age so steeped in the Bible that it was the common possession of all, is the specific character of the use made of it by Dickens? It is not enough to show that Dickens knew the Bible well; so did Carlyle and Macaulay and George Eliot and Leslie Stephen and Newman and Pusey and literally millions of others. The fact tells us nothing about belief.

And then Dickens was so inconsistent. The man who took the trouble to write *The Life of Our Lord* for his children was also the man who hoped that his sons would not be chaste, because if they were, he should be inclined to worry about their health. A man of genius with a haunting imagination, an untrained intelligence and strong passions is unlikely to be consistent. The consequence is, and it is a most uncomfortable consequence for criticism, that almost impossibly rich and voluminous as Dickens is, he can only be taken as a whole. Anything true and important that can be said about him must take account of all his contradictions, must preserve a balanced judgment, and give due weight to exceptions without allowing that weight to be preponderant. . . .

Perhaps one cause of controversy and misunderstanding about the religion of Dickens is this. Those who belittle his religion are those who find his theology naïve and superficial, and perceive that the central Christian mysteries are mostly left out of his scheme. Those, like Mrs. Vogel, who emphasize and admire it are those who see that he was in earnest about it. And both have a fair point.

A. O. J. Cockshut
TLS (March 17, 1978), p. 308

GEORGE ELIOT

1819–1880

Gordon Haight, *George Eliot: A Biography* (1968)

George Eliot's dealing with this issue, the conversion of the woman novelist to the dominant sexual ethic, is . . . interesting. Her original intention in *Middlemarch* seems to have been almost suffragette, directly to resent the confinement of feminine intelligence. A generalization, for example, about "modes of education which make a woman's knowledge another name for motley ignorance" appears in the first edition and later disappears. But still, in fact, nothing is more essential to the final book (the first image of the whole which always re-enters the mind) than Dorothea Casaubon's tardy comprehension of her husband's mind. This is the novel's instant of irreversible dismay, like the cracking open of an old egg. Untrained clarity confronts professional moribundity, it recognizes the futility of a life's work. The prospect, then, of conjoined waste has a selfish terror about it, the first frantic sense of a cheat. But the novel resumes—to equate Casaubon and connubial duty, to translate the intelligence of his wife into a "self-forgetful ardour." The Casaubon branch of the book becomes an apotheosis of Dorothea. She is pampered as the prettiest in a long, long procession of girl martyrs to matrimony. . . .

To concur with the prevailing sexual opinions, even to George Eliot's extent—which was hardly more than to dramatize their difficulty—has since, in the best writing by women, grown obsolete. It is not that the opinions themselves have lost the attention, however reluctant, of those whom they describe. But the intellectual accommodation of these opinions, even in *Middlemarch*'s involuted mode, is no longer possible.

George Eliot's anger seems fortified by her objectivity, i.e., by her translation of the issue into "character" and "plot." When the novelist's concern shifts to self-examination, anger subsides into depression. . . . Beginning with Dorothy Richardson, the discontent with feminine stereotypes is not radically different from George Eliot's: what is different is the mode of expressing the dissociation. The newer impulse has been to discard preconception or prohibition by resorting to introspection alone.

Mary Ellmann
Thinking about Women (New York: Harcourt, Brace and World, 1968), pp. 192–93, 195–96

The concept of sainthood in *Middlemarch*, though of obvious importance, is more often discussed indirectly than directly. For example, when Joan Bennett suggests that the marriage of Dorothea Casaubon and Will Ladislaw is a necessary compromise, although the best possible under existing conditions, of Dorothea's ideals, she implies that both Dorothea and Will have been measured by a standard of goodness, and that Will has been found so markedly inferior to her as to be incongruous as a companion. When Professor [Gordon] Haight speaks of readers who feel that Dorothea should want someone else, he is touching upon essentially the same problem. The element of goodness in Dorothea's character, her aspiration for sainthood, seems to make it difficult to accept her second marriage as a credible choice. There is an important question that we should ask at this point: against whose conception of sainthood are the two characters being measured? In all likelihood, we would be forced to admit that the conception is our own, not that in the novel, and certainly not that of Dorothea. We tend to retain Dorothea's original conception of sainthood, the one which led her to marry Mr. Casaubon, because it carries all of the non-worldly, ascetic connotations which tradition has attached to the word. We fail to recognize that Dorothea herself transcends this narrow view by recognizing that she, unlike St. Teresa, will not find "her epos in the reform of a religious order" or in the vaguely abstract ideals which led her to marry Mr. Casaubon. The purpose of this paper, then, will be to show that Dorothea's conception of sainthood changes in the course of the novel from *attainment* of abstract ideals to *pursuit* of ideals which are defined in terms of human values in a physical world. . . .

In her movement from abstract ideals, which she felt had to be attained, toward sensuous reality, which she felt as an impulse, Dorothea arrives at a humanistic middle ground. In terms of her character this can be seen in the balancing of ascetic and sensuous tendencies, and in terms of her experience it is represented by her movement from Casaubon to Ladislaw. The fruitless marriage with Casaubon gives way to a fruitful one with Ladislaw, and while she dedicates her efforts to her husband's occupation in both cases, only in the second are those efforts meaningful in human terms. There she is working for social reform, not a pedantic compilation of antiquated facts.

It should also be pointed out that Dorothea's changing conception of sainthood does not violate the structure of the novel as a whole. [Richard] Lyons has noted that each of the major characters, to some extent, gradually comes to accept a religion of work modeled on that of Caleb Garth. Dorothea has always had a religion of work, but only after the death of Casaubon does her work become beneficial to mankind. Other interesting parallels open up. Both Dorothea and Fred Vincy lose a fortune and lower their social position in order to achieve a purpose in life. Dorothea, however, does so consciously while Fred does not. But even more important, the two approach from opposite directions: Dorothea is originally too far from sensuous reality while Fred is too much in it.

Robert F. Damm
The Victorian Newsletter (Spring, 1969), pp. 18, 22

To discuss George Eliot in connection with androgyny is almost to indulge in an act of supererogation. Perhaps no individual whose life has been passed in the cultural center of her time has so embodied the "masculine" and "feminine" impulses conjoined. George Eliot's extraordinary qualifications both of "masculine" strength of mind and "feminine" sensibility have perhaps never been combined to better purpose. . . . George Eliot, however, was courageous enough not to be deterred by the possibility that her talents could prove to be barriers depriving her of one role or another. She allowed both masculine and feminine traits to have sway within her personality. That she was destined to have her "masculine" intelligence constantly remarked upon was small enough price to pay for so rewarding a destiny as hers. No doubt had she not been loved by Lewes, had she not married Cross, had she not been able, as Lady Linton (who did not particularly care for her) said, to have married other men if she had chosen, she could have been safely dismissed as a "failed woman," who had traded her femininity for fame. Lewes, who protected her from so much else, saved her from this.

Yet her novels are androgynous in a very different way from Jane Austen's. She is far too sharply aware of the constraints upon females, of the lack of direct channels for their highest endeavors, to produce an actually androgynous character. Nor did she ever suggest the possible way in which a highly endowed woman might discover a destiny concordant with her talents. The destinies of all her heroines are, in great or small degree, constricted—nor was she ever to pretend or imagine otherwise. For Dorothea Brooke there was only a second-best marriage, and for the reader the knowledge that her influence would be "incalcuably diffusive." She was ever a brook, never a channel of "great name."

Yet George Eliot, while she believed, as did Shakespeare, in the diffusion of goodness through small acts, could not pretend that even the ideal marriage made possible correct action. . . . There lies, beneath the surface action, the suggestion that the separation of the sexes is somehow fundamentally connected with the impotence of society to hasten human progress. Dorothea's *moral sense*, at which Lydgate sneers, is precisely what he lacks. Yet by the time he realizes this, it is too late. That this moral sense appears to have been embodied in a woman, the least obviously influential figure in society, perhaps indicates George Eliot's understanding of society's moral weakness and her belief that its source is the grossly unequal influence available to the sexes. Metaphorically, androgyny would allow the return to society of the moral sense Lydgate patronizes.

Carolyn G. Heilbrun
Toward a Recognition of Androgyny (New York: Alfred A. Knopf, 1973), pp. 82–84

If *Middlemarch* seems ambiguous as to the possibility of effective social action in the contemporary world, *Daniel Deronda* is clear. Daniel finds a medium for his ardent and heroic action, the founding of a Jewish state in Palestine. He finds in his racial past not, like Maggie, bonds, but opportunities, a role, a social faith and order, and passional fulfillment as well. George Levine . . . finds Deronda's heroism and Mordecai's incompatible with George Eliot's vision, and Leslie Stephen, *George Eliot* (London: Macmillan, 1904), p. 189, finds Daniel's achievement inapplicable to our lives: "As we cannot all discover that we belong to the chosen people, and some of us might, even then, doubt the wisdom of the enterprise, one feels that Deronda's mode of solving his problem is not generally applicable." But George Eliot's vision does allow for the hero, not as one who tampers with history but whose career coincides with it, the right man in the right place. There was a Saint Theresa, after all. If there are unhistoric lives, there are also a few historic ones. Saints and heroes may be rare, the exception and not the rule of human life and lot, but that does not mean that they have not existed or cannot exist. Their lives are not meant to be "generally applicable." Our insignificant lives are the rule. But we can prepare for the heroes. That is why Gwendolen's story is related to Daniel's.

There is another reason as well. If our lives, our decisions, can make things a little better for those who follow, and if our words and deeds can prepare the social soil for heroic actions and achievement, the moral struggles of the inner and personal life are not only ingredients but microcosms of the battles on the national and world-wide scale. Though Gwendolen's ultimate moral vision shows her that her own life is only one among many, that she is but a speck in the universe, her history is important because each life is a microcosm. . . . The microcosmic personal battle and the macrocosmic humanity-wide battle is the same, the war between good and evil. . . .

War as an image of the struggle between good and evil and as a theater for heroic action did not seem so unsuitable to young veterans of World War II as it does for those of Vietnam. Eradication of slavery and its consequences, the founding of a Jewish state after Auschwitz did not seem either impossible dreams or unheroic acts. And the significance and relevance of diapers and doctoral degrees needed definition and reinforcement for those who had so recently felt themselves to have had a part, no matter how small a part, in a somewhat larger theater of operations. George Eliot's alternating microscopic and telescopic vision, her moving back and forth from the near to the far, has been spoken of fairly often, usually in imagistic or formalistic terms. A quarter century ago this systole-diastole was the functional heart of her work for us, more vital than *valvae*. Her stereoptic vision still illuminates. It can still serve as a corrective for the myopia of a decade like the 1950's or the short-lived hypermetropia of the 1960's.

Jerome Beaty
in *The Victorian Experience*, ed. Richard A. Levine (Athens: Ohio Univ. Pr., 1976), pp. 174–75

THOMAS HARDY

1840–1928

James Gibson, ed., *The Complete Poems of Thomas Hardy* (1976)
Irving Howe, *Thomas Hardy* (1968)

The poetic impulse is never absent from Hardy's fiction. But in the minor works it appears in isolated flashes and pulls against the narrative and dramatic impulses instead of creating a fruitful tension with them "to intensify the expression of things . . . so that the heart and inner meaning is made vividly visible" (*Life* [by Florence E. Hardy]). The great novels are memorable not only for plot but for the poetic-dramatic scenes that carry the inner meaning of the plot. In *The Return of the Native*, the gambling scene by glow-worm light on Egdon Heath, besides being crucial to plot development, is also a unit in the organic conflict of light and darkness, chance and control.

Reading one of the successful novels inspires poetic emotion. It has become a cliché of criticism to say that Hardy's novels are "poetic." The word needs closer definition to establish the factors which give Hardy's novels this quality, and to distinguish the poetry of a Hardy novel from the poetry of *Wuthering Heights* or *The Waves*. As David Cecil points out in *Hardy the Novelist*, "the English literary genius is, most characteristically, a poetic genius," which shows itself in other forms besides poetry. Cecil has made a study of the poetic aspects of Hardy's imagination. He defines the poetic imagination as "of a type that more often chooses verse as its mode of expression." Hardy was inspired by those aspects of experience which required the emotional and imaginative intensity of lyric, ballad and poetic drama. His vision of life was not primarily of man's relation to man, but of man's relation to the forces of ultimate reality. His characters live most fully not in the social encounters of Jane Austen's Bath or George Eliot's Middlemarch, but in the great emotional crises that express their heroic resistance to fate, the conflict of reason and instinct, or their harmonies and disharmonies with the natural world.

Jean Brooks
Thomas Hardy: The Poetic Structure (Ithaca, N.Y.: Cornell Univ. Pr., 1971), pp. 137–38

It is Hardy, so much the stonemason in his poetic imagination and so resistant to the temptations of the mythological and the mythopoeic, who can seem, more than Pound, the emblem and the exemplar in our time of what Pound meant by "the hard" in poetry. This is not how it is usually envisaged. He is thought of as a crepuscular poet, the voice of those half-lit hours in which phantoms and apparitions glimmer uncertainly at the edge of vision. But that is once again to mistake the process for the product; the poems as they lie on the page, or utter themselves from it, speak for themselves—they are dry, angular, hard-edged. Sometimes their angles are so sharp and so many that . . . they make us think of industrial metalwork rather than carved stone. And to that extent some poems are inferior to Hardy at his best. But between stone and metal, the distinction is not always important. Both can be images of authority, as they are, interchangeably, in the first line of Eliot's "Coriolan." . . . And the wish for the hard in art doubtlessly goes along with a wish for authority in public life. Hardy satisfies both demands, the one in fact, the other in fantasy.

Donald Davie
Thomas Hardy and British Poetry (New York: Oxford Univ. Pr., 1972), pp. 177–78

Hardy was aware of religious, intellectual, and social changes throughout his life. He treated these matters in his novels and expressed views so liberal that he was called "Hardy the Degenerate." He hoped for the future a better world than the one he lived in. If he could comment today, he would say, I think, that some conditions realize his hopes—for instance, young men like Jude can now attend a university—but that in other ways, time-tested standards have disintegrated.

What can our younger generation learn by reading Hardy thoughtfully? He phrased various mottoes that make sense and stick in the mind. He took one from Marcus Aurelius: "Be not perturbed; for all things are according to the nature of the universal." He stated another in the poem "In Tenebris II" as ". . . if way to the Better there be, it exacts a full look at the Worst." He supported strongly one basic moral principle, compassion (which he called "lovingkindness"), and extended it to all living creatures. He believed in the statement in the Gospels: do unto others as you would have them do unto you, for "this is the law and the prophets." Our confused world of the 1970s might well ponder these maxims, especially in the light of one phrased by the Spirit of the Years: "Old laws operate yet."

J. O. Bailey
in *Thomas Hardy and the Modern World*, ed. F. B. Pinion (Dorchester, England: Thomas Hardy Society, 1974), pp. 12–13

"Form alone *takes*, and holds and preserves, substance . . .": James's view of form is insistent on clarity and stability, finding its strength in the sharpness of the demarcation line to be drawn between the experience which goes into the creation and the created object itself. It is a notion which relies, at least tacitly, on a notion of a reality which is antecedent to form, and of which that form is a copy. In Hardy, we find a notion of form, which resides in the structuring power itself, rather than in that which is structured, a sense of form seen not as a result, a shape, more as a process, a direction, a verb rather than a noun. Where James finds his key term in structure, Hardy finds his in story. . . .

It is an image which identifies a central element in what Hardy called his "idiosyncratic mode of regard," so that the line to be drawn between man and man, man and nature is unusually fine. It goes on to suggest an idea of form antithetic to that which "preserves and holds," in that a web can be thought of more as something defining space than as an object; it is a provisional design flung across the vacancy of miscellaneous experience. Moreover, the web makes us think simultaneously of the spider and its weaving, of the creator and the act of creation, and in the end, this is the experience we have in reading Hardy's major novels: for he created a kind of fiction which enabled him to convey, at every stage in his career, and with a remarkable purity and directness, both what mattered to him as a total human being, and the dramatic sense of the way in which it mattered.

Ian Gregor
The Great Web: The Form of Hardy's Major Fiction (London: Faber and Faber, 1974), pp. 40–41

Sensuality of [a] gentle, feeling kind is present in all of Hardy's best poetry. Pater noted the sensuality of Wordsworth's best work; Hardy's poetry is often similar to Wordsworth's in this respect, and comes perhaps from his example or influence. Reading the "Apology" to *Late Lyrics and Earlier* one is tempted by all the allusions to Wordsworth to assume that Hardy's whole conception of poetry is founded there. He also quotes Arnold; but when he tries to write according to the Arnoldian theory, and apply "ideas" to "life," he usually fails both as a poet and as a thinker—as Arnold and Wordsworth also did, in like endeavors. When, however, he gives himself over directly, immediately, to the life, he writes with the clarity, insight, feeling, and understanding of a major poet, like Wordsworth, at his sensual and philosophical best.

One important line from Wordsworth which Hardy does not cite in the "Apology" is that which prescribes the use of "the language really used by men" in poetry, though that dictum is probably the most important thing Wordsworth could have said to Hardy as a poet. Only by speaking in such simple language can Hardy communicate; in any other tongue he hides his thoughts and feelings, disguises himself by disguising his voice, speaks bitterly and ironically, and removes himself from life. For Hardy "loving-kindness" and "fellow-feeling" are simple virtues, to be found in simple life; for Hardy the poet they require simple but deep thought, and simple but honest expression. Irony in Hardy's poetry too often means dishonesty, because it is the irony of withdrawal: a mask, a shield, an escape. The great poems, however, are not ironic in this way. Rather, they are entirely metaphoric, in the way that Hardy unites himself with their subjects, to find their experiences. And as always with metaphor, the result of this connection is new life.

Bert G. Hornback
Victorian Poetry (Spring, 1974), pp. 63–64

It often happens in Hardy's novels that a man who is perfectly contented in his own carefully built-up life suddenly meets a woman who completely destroys his peace of mind. It is Hardy's distinction to have provided something like a comprehensive theory to explain such phenomena. Why, he asks, does this kind of man like this kind of woman, when everyone around can see that it is a futile and pernicious choice? Pierre d'Exideuil cites Darwin and Schopenhauer to support his view that Hardy regarded the matching of pairs of opposites as somehow biologically determined by the needs of the species: "In order that this purpose of procreation may be perfectly realised, it is once more necessary, as with Darwin, that a given type of man should be united with a given type of woman . . . Almost in spite of themselves, the lovers defer to a regard for equilibrium."

The habitual mismatching, then, which causes ninety-nine per cent of the unhappiness in Hardy's novels, is required by the species. In point of fact, Hardy's stories support a number of different theories: sometimes people appear to require their own opposite, sometimes their own like. As we shall see, the subject is a little more complicated than d'Exideuil implies. Nevertheless, he has raised the right question: unhappiness in Hardy's world comes not from violating the natural order or from being weak-willed or just from being doomed from the start. It comes from the commitment of the self to others. Our understanding of Hardy's teleology, then, must begin with our attempt to unravel his complicated conception of the laws of human relationship.

Geoffrey Thurley
The Psychology of Hardy's Novels: The Nervous and the Statuesque (St. Lucia: Univ. Queensland Pr., 1975), p. 25

GERARD MANLEY HOPKINS

1844–1899

Bernard Bergonzi, *Gerard Manley Hopkins* (1977)

Even Browning, his tedious optimism and roughhousing aside, understands that poetry is a sacred game and that the game alone can justify the poet. Contentious and self-justifying, Browning's people direct their will at a hidden God. The poet is their advocate, caught in the same condition, and refuses to give the game away. He demands, yet does not preempt, judgment. His poetry builds up a sacrifice for which the consecrating fire must come from us or from above. Hopkins, though the purer talent, often appears narrow and idiosyncratic when placed beside him. We never forget, in Hopkins' poetry, that it is a priest speaking, and one more Roman than the Romans in his scruples as to what his religious order might allow. He does not even dare to follow where Ignatian meditation leads. Overcome by a "course of loathing and hopelessness which I have so often felt before, which made me fear madness, and led me to give up the practice of meditation," he can do no more (he says) than repeat: *Justus es, Domine, et rectum judicium tuum.* However authentic a suffering speaks in this, it is a passive suffering. Here is where vision or prophecy or scandal might have begun: where within his vocation a new vocation might have been born. Hopkins' acceptance of the Rule was so absolute that it did not permit him to be more than a pawn or servant in the sacred game he intuited. "Sheer plod makes plough down sillion shine." That shining remains his justification, when, in his poetry, he is challenged by an image of divine mastery akin to brute beauty, and when, so challenged, he becomes for a moment *magister ludi.*

Geoffrey Hartman
Introd., in *Hopkins: A Collection of Critical Essays* ed.
Geoffrey Hartman (Englewood Cliffs, N.J.: Prentice-Hall, 1966),
p. 13

Hopkins is neither perfect nor unique. Right as F. R. Leavis is in his perceptive essay defending the poet against the obtuseness of his friend and first editor, and against the normalizing of his verse by Sturge Moore, Leavis' response to genteel versifiers leads him to set the late Victorian Jesuit against the whole of his century in a way that exaggerates his eccentricity and probably overstates the case for his importance as an influence. Hopkins is said to bear "no relation to . . . any nineteenth-century poet," as there is "nothing approaching [his] imagery in subtlety and strength . . . in any other poet of the nineteenth century," and finally he is judged to be "the only influential poet of the Victorian age, and . . . the greatest." . . .

We may now be closer to making a fair estimate of Hopkins' place. We may be less in danger than before of reading him as a mere eccentric or an experimenter in poetry. . . . We may even have come to realize that he is more than a coterie poet or the poet of the Jesuits. The work of [Charles] Williams, [I. A.] Richards, [Gerald] Lahey, [W. H.] Gardner, [Jean-Georges] Ritz, [W. A. M.] Peters, [William] Empson, [David] Daiches, and [John] Pick, among others, should have helped to establish him as a most important Victorian writer. . . .

Hopkins perceives that the relations between self and nature are complex, that they seem to vary. The world outside can be the world of tempests, buffeting man and proving the weakness of his inscape as well as proving the strength of his soul. This is the hard seascape world of "The Deutschland." It can also represent, can shadow forth in its own nature, the higher Christlike nature of man, as the buffeting wind and the bird do in "The Windhover." At the same time, landscape nature represents in its ephemeral forms the parallel fragility and brevity of human shapes, of the wholly natural self, as it does in "Spring and Fall." Finally, the world's bonfire nature, which provides both stress and a source of knowledge and which, being both parabolically and physically like human nature, affects man directly, is given to be accepted and understood but also to be transcended. This is the sense of the "Heraclitean Fire." . . . Of course the poetry of Hopkins is almost all religious and is based on dogma. Its meaning, however, is as general and as psychologically valid, as it is dogmatic. We can fairly paraphrase to say Hopkins believes that the universe which a man lives in both threatens and teaches him, and that a man's personal value transcends the value of any objects in that universe; for whether or not he calls himself immortal, the meaning of his life outlasts his death.

Grasping the joy, the suffering, and the affirmation that Hopkins communicates in his art does not necessarily mean accepting his faith. The faith has no doubt helped him, in any case, to achieve an art often more lucid and consistent, often more rich and more intense, than that of his comparable contemporaries. But, Catholic and Victorian, he is still a strikingly individual voice expressing his own inscape and repeating no other's song. Hopkins is very much of his age in being self-conscious while he affirms the self, in being conscious of alienation from external nature while he compares and metaphorically identifies man and nature; but he is of his age, too, in being intentionally and peculiarly himself, with a style as unmistakably his own as Carlyle's, or Browning's, or Swinburne's. By declaring "myself I speak," he agrees with the Romantic (and Victorian) theory of art, and he declares himself a man of his century. In the latter half of this century he can be read and understood, surely, as one of the most impressive of that century's poets.

Wendell Stacy Johnson
Gerard Manley Hopkins: The Poet as Victorian (Ithaca, N.Y.: Cornell Univ. Pr., 1968), pp. 166–68, 171–73

"The Windhover" conveys one logically and poetically possible central meaning, and only one in which all the parts of the poem and all the images find a place. Belt buckles and buckles in armor are not part of it; they belong to some other poem; by some other poet, "in another country."

In the outline of its thought . . . "The Windhover" is simple, direct, and explicit. Its complexities lie, on the one hand, in the elaboration of the visual imagery interwoven with elaborately echoing patterns of sound, and, on the other, in the play between two counterpointed sets of opposites. The dominant pair is that of the material and the spiritual, which are expressly brought together by the dauphin-Son parallel and, more literally, by the primary theme of the poet's being stirred by one into more intense awareness of the other. Within the poem, however, these opposites are not in conflict; material beauty is seen wholly as a good, opening the heart to the incomparably higher good of Christ.

Of the second pair of opposites one is explicit and major, while the other appears only in shadowy, muted form. The opposition of beauty and terror (or pain), explicitly present in so much of Hopkins's writing, is present here only by implication. The two are not evenly balanced; they are not reconciled either, nor do they need to be. They are brought together in an uneasy harmony through the idea of power in the "mastery" of the bird and the "lovelier, more dangerous" fire of Christ. In "The Windhover" terror or pain is no more than an undertone, the habitually accompanying shadow of all life even at its happiest, reflected here only in one epithet of Christ; in the "gall" and the "gash" of coals against one another, which are only a means to the breaking forth of living beauty from outwardly inanimate matter (they may possibly also faintly suggest the self-hurt of self-sacrifice that results in spiritual brightness, but if so this is very faint indeed, for the inanimate coals are not even remotely personified and any hint of pain is extremely remote if present at all); possibly, but only just possibly, in the known predatory character as well as the daring mastery of the hawk and the poet's "hiding" heart. . . .

"The Windhover" . . . is not at all a poem of conflict or, as some have even thought, of renunciation and suffering. The faint, shadowy, unresolved suggestion of terror and pain merely gives an edge to the overriding spirit of breathless admiration. . . .

Richness of symbolic meaning cannot be had merely by reading into the poem a mechanical, dictionary-flavored ambiguity in *buckle*. For the interpretation of "The Windhover" at least, an inveterate commitment to irony and paradox is apt to defeat itself by producing only disjointed structure and discordant associations that destroy, by neutralizing, the resonance of the poem. Quite a good deal of the resonance of "The Windhover" derives from simplicity of theme, clarity of structure, and smoothness of movement. This is true even though the final effect is of an extremely complex poem.

Elisabeth W. Schneider
The Dragon in the Gate (Berkeley: Univ. California Pr., 1968), pp. 146, 156–58

["The Wreck of the Deutschland"] is certainly splendid, brilliant, emotionally charged; all of its strands are carefully interwoven, braided together, reeved in. It is an impressive poem, and despite its flaws of rhyme ("grubs in amber" Hopkins called them) and patches of flatness, the ode is a masterpiece. English literature, as Hopkins noted, "is not rich in odes." And "The Deutschland" 's music and sheer intellectual manipulation of images and wordplay are uncharacteristic of the traditional English ode (Ben Jonson, Andrew Marvell, Abraham Cowley, John Dryden, and Wordsworth come immediately to mind). So the accolade for England's finest ode is often given to Wordsworth for *Intimations of Immortality*. Certainly the music and movement, the serenity and tone of elevated celebration in that poem are more even-keeled and balanced than in "The Deutschland." And Hopkins knew that Wordsworth had touched on something here which was original and seminal to English literature itself.

But Hopkins' ode is, for all its grubs in amber, certainly equal to Wordsworth's. "The Wreck of the Deutschland" is unique: it is the one English ode to have captured the Pindaric spirit. Hopkins, like Pindar, is a metaphysical in his shaping power, for the most diverse and seemingly disparate subjects and ideas are interwoven, or better, welded into an artistic whole. Richmond Lattimore has said of Pindar's *Sixth Olympiad* that it "is exceptionally complicated; but the difficulties are met with triumphant, challenging, and almost perverse brilliance." This description fits Hopkins' ode just as well.

Paul L. Mariani
A Commentary on the Complete Poems of Gerald Manley Hopkins (Ithaca, N.Y.: Cornell Univ. Pr., 1970), pp. 72–73

The unconscious supposition that Hopkins was mostly excluded from the drama of the Victorian age has been quite natural, and until he had been presented to us for his own sake, it was even advisable. Hopkins's work was not published until the twentieth century and therefore contemporary poets instinctively claim him as a splendid colleague of immediate pertinence to themselves. He has thus been lifted out of his age as his own contemporaries have not. There has been no prior call for the particular act of historical imagination that would perceive Hopkins, first and foremost, walking and talking among other Victorians, as we think of Shakespeare in Renaissance London, Matthew Arnold in Victorian Oxford, or as Hopkins quite obviously saw himself. And then Hopkins's gnarled and tense prosodic style, usually so different on the surface from the more spacious and rhetorical prosody of his post-Romantic contemporaries, has blurred the Victorian voice behind the radical prosodist.

Perhaps Hopkins's conversion and his "unEnglish" vocation as a Jesuit priest have also deflected our attention from the fact that he was born in the "hungry forties" and died on the eve of the "yellow nineties," and that even as a Jesuit in exile, he took his past with him as all men do. But as twentieth-century scholars now admit, conversions, even conversions to Catholicism, were as common in Victorian England as conversions to agnosticism or to some latitudinarian faith. Each conversion was the response of a specific man at a specific time in his country's history, and it represents a way of dealing not only with crises of the self but crises in the society. And Hopkins's poems and prose are as full of these public crises as the works of Carlyle, Tennyson, Ruskin, Newman, or either of the Arnolds. His work reflects the anguish of religious strife, abuse of labour, the scandal of privileged cruelty, the horrors of rampant industrialism pouring its scum and smoke all over England, the search for personal and national prescriptions, and above all, the anatomy of mental suffering. . . . Like all serious Victorians he experienced the sensation of being crushed at times by private conflicts and public outrages. His fear for England . . . was a common fear, that she was wasting her spiritual patrimony. His desire for her was common also, that by adhering to the origins of her greatness, whether those origins were seen to have been in Periclean Athens or in a stable in Bethlehem, she might arrest the rot in her soil and in the hearts of her citizens.

Alison G. Sulloway
Gerard Manley Hopkins and the Victorian Temper (New York: Columbia Univ. Pr., 1972), pp. 5–6

["The Wreck of the Deutschland"] is a great love poem. Like all great love poetry, what moves us, what takes us, is the poem's celebration of the procession of adoring love. In the first part, it is the poet standing in the furnace of his heart aflame like a Romeo beneath Juliet's balcony. Hearing him exult and feeling him rejoice in his new love of God reminds us of the tenderness and sweetness of young love. Who would not desire to fall in love again for the first time? In the second part, we are surprised at the expansiveness of his feeling, how in his love's depth he can see the poor nuns and the terrible wreck as a love-drama, how he can feel with the tall nun standing in the freezing storm and calling out to her lover to come to rescue her for himself. For Hopkins, here was the Christian meaning of Creation, the Incarnation and the Eucharist; it was "the great sacrifice" in its triumphant progress to the end of time. This choosing was an act of love like his own, and in her heart and his was heard love's oldest and sweetest song. Young Hopkins, already in love, caught the inscape of the tall nun as the beauty of a new "virgin birth," and by it he came to know a new beauty of the Lord. Her loving act in his imagination put beauty in religion and certitude in art so that he felt free to write poetry about his love of God.

This is Hopkins at his best and most balanced, at his most beautiful and bountiful, "passion-plungèd" in his love for God.

In the end, "The Wreck of the Deutschland" is Gerard Manley Hopkins' new rendition of the Christian song of songs filling the air we breathe with grace and beauty. The poem is full of the language of the dearness, warmth, and sweetness of a lover. Its imagery abounds with the sighs and sights of love. Its rhythms are the love strokes of love's suitors. To read it is to hear love's whispers, to feel love's tenderness, and to experience love's promise. Whatever becomes of Christianity, however much the Christian contents of the poem have or will become a barrier to the appreciation of this poem, it remains available to every reader who can hear and feel the carol of a young heart beating with that shining new ecstasy of having fallen deeply in love for the first time.

David A. Downes
HQ (January, 1977), pp. 154–55

RUDYARD KIPLING

1865–1936

Four books on Kipling serve to underline our critical and moral difficulties in arriving at a common estimate of his worth. Vasant A. Shahane's book makes a careful defence of him, while Kingsley Amis elegantly glosses the dark spaces in Kipling's achievement with a seeming forthrightness which leaves the major literary issues untouched. Martin Fido faces his subject squarely in an impressive demonstration of committed criticism; and Philip Mason's study . . . is the only one to plunge deeper than usual into the novels and stories, revealing to us, to be sure, the glass and the shadow, though disappointingly little of the fire. . . .

Kipling was authoritarian, imperialistic, racist, and paternalistic. . . . Amis [*Rudyard Kipling and His World*, 1975] itemizes and answers the main objections against Kipling frankly and without fuss. . . . Amis concedes what he has to, and explains the rest by recourse to the times, or by an imperturbable damping down of awkward detail. . . .

Martin Fido [*Rudyard Kipling*, 1974] gives us a more full-blooded Kipling. His extended essay shows that the essentials of a good literary portrait need not be distorted, nor need the critic be condescending, even in an illustrated literary work designed for the general reader, about what might be thought to be embarrassing beliefs and attitudes in an author. . . .

As Vasant A. Shahane argues in his book *Rudyard Kipling: Activist and Artist* [1973], Kipling made a determined effort to "fuse into a totality the religious and the temporal aspects of life" (p. 26). Our difficulty is that Kipling, since he disliked intellectualizing, reached for this fusion intuitively. We are left to guess about a system of thought which gives unprecedented importance to the practical concerns of a certain group of people in both their relations with other people and with matters of the spirit. The difficulty is compounded when it involves explication in a multicultural context. Shahane brings us some of the way towards understanding the problem, although the reader is likely to be put off initially by his resort to terms like "alienation" and "existential suffering." . . .

Philip Mason's *Kipling: The Glass, the Shadow and the Fire* [1975] seeks to do justice to . . . diversity. Mason lays out the parts, as it were, for us to grasp both the complexity and the strength. Kipling is "different people in the same skin" (p. 12); in him are "a number of elements that had never been reconciled with each other nor even held in healthy tension within a mature personality" (pp. 25–26). This promising programme, however, is placed in jeopardy by Mason's unsatisfactory use of the metaphor of "levels of personality." The layers of Kipling's artistic personality are: first, the noisy defender of "the tribe to which he could never belong"; second, the brutal and insensitive dogmatist contemptuously dismissing some people from his consciousness altogether; and third, the tolerant and compassionate writer who shows how people somehow bear the burdens of practical living laid on them (p. 306). . . .

Without meaning to do it, Mason reduces Kipling's stature, and corroborates Fido's blunt labels for an important aspect of Kipling as the spokesman for Anglo-Indians and "the poet of the passenger liner." . . . Like Stevenson, Kipling was a wanderer in whom sojourns in foreign lands raised spectres which could only be kept at bay by the emphatic adoption of a conservative, authoritarian posture in relation to other countries, and by the fervent endorsement of those, like himself, who pressed on with the work of life to escape confrontation with their non-integrated selves.

Lloyd Fernando
Victorian Studies (Spring, 1977), pp. 303–7

THOMAS BABINGTON MACAULAY

1800–1859

The retreat into the past from his own excessive sensibility to pain and fear of uncertainty must surely have been part of Macaulay's impulse to the writing of history. But the impulse to write—because it was a retreat rather than an attempt to explore through the re-creative imagination some of the meanings of the experiences which frightened him—was also an impulse to self-censorship. What the public gentleman disapproved of, the historian could not sympathize with. Macaulay could not finally achieve the distance from his immediate experience which the writing of fiction allowed great writers. Always the gentleman with his defenses up, he could not expose himself to the possibility of pain or to the thought that his public might find in him a weakness he did not wish to reveal. Thus in his *History [of England from the Accession of James II]* he creates an imaginative world with great vividness but reinforces the prejudices of the moment. Sharing an enthusiasm for many of the qualities that made the novel popular, he lacked the capacity for self-surrender, for coping with the varieties of human possibility, which raised the great Victorian novels to the level of high art. Literature remained for him a retreat from life rather than the extension of it.

George Levine
The Boundaries of Fiction (Princeton, N.J.: Princeton Univ. Pr., 1968), p. 163

Like the fabled Ozymandias, Thomas Babington Macaulay confronts us with an enigmatic, larger-than-life presence. On the one hand, we look on that mighty figure and we despair of anyone ever duplicating his learning, his rectitude, his brilliance, his self-confidence, and his instantaneous success. On the other hand, we feel there is more in life than this complacent, optimistic, dogmatic spokesman for "the most enlightened generation of the most enlightened people that ever existed" ever dreamed of in a philosophy that held that the truth always lies between two absurd extremes. Jane Millgate's contribution to the Routledge Author Guides series [1973] is a serious attempt to shape this enigmatic Victorian presence into assimilable form for the nonspecialist reader. . . .

Judged in the light of the overall purpose of the Routledge series, *Macaulay* is never less than a competent and judicious study and it has, in addition, several important merits. It does not pretend to the comprehensiveness of John Clive's recent valuable study, but so far as it goes Professor Millgate's scholarship is both sound and carefully documented. . . .

I have only two reservations. In concentrating upon the quality of Macaulay's literary productions as literature, Professor Millgate leaves unclear their status as *history*. This, to be sure, is controversial territory, but it deserves attention even in an introductory volume. The nonspecialist reader may wish to consult the bibliographic essay of John Clive and Thomas Pinney, which touches perceptively on this matter, in the recent volume *Victorian Prose: A Guide to Research*, which apparently appeared too late to be included in Professor Millgate's bibliography. My other reservation has to do with what seems to me to be the book's failure to make Macaulay interesting. With a figure as haunted by intellectual inconsistencies and emotional ambivalence as Macaulay was—his curious evasions, for example, about Romanticism in general and about Byron in particular, or his extraordinary relationship with his sisters, one of whom felt obliged to expunge from Macaulay's own journals passages that express his feelings connected with that relationship—one would like to know what light the discipline of psychology might shed upon these matters. Professor Millgate alludes to them from time to time, but one wishes that she had explored this aspect of her subject in more detail. Nevertheless, this is a well-written, intelligent introduction to a man who was, if not a great thinker or writer, most certainly a remarkable and very influential Victorian.

William A. Madden
Victorian Studies (September, 1974), pp. 131–32

GEORGE MEREDITH

1828–1909

Readable people: here at the end of his career we are, I think, at the secret heart of Meredith's optimism as well as his desperate, pugnacious, and tricky focus on the reader of and in his novels. His faith is that reality is, with effort, *readable*; what he wants is to make of us all its *readers*, in the comprehensive, tough-minded sense in which he uses the word and construes the act of *reading*. His "readable people" are not only his characters, who can be read, but ideally his readers themselves, who are in a profounder sense read-able, able readers. And what enrages him even beyond the limits where the Comic Spirit wants to smile at authors, is that we will not be made to *read*. To read is to put together those arbitrary and meaningless characters into words, to build those crowding perceptions into conceptions, to find for that lengthening line of meaningless acts in a person or society the grammar and syntax that will allow you to read those mysterious discontinuous units as character.

For Meredith, reading is the name, not really the metaphor, for the primary human act of mind. When his Modern Novelist disdains Dame Gossip's "animation" as all act and no substance, all (one may say) fertilization and no incubation, he is really condemning her art as all alphabet and no words, and her supporters as hurried leafers through bright picture books, not readers at all. When he fancies himself spokesman for the future counterbalancing her nostalgic references to the past, when romance flashes living pictures before an audience sunk lovingly in "delicious dulness," when he speaks of these "days of a growing activity in the head," he is anticipating exactly that community of literacy called posterity . . . whose name is reader.

Judith Wilt
The Readable People of George Meredith (Princeton, N.J.: Princeton Univ. Pr., 1975), pp. 241–42

Meredith was clearly a forerunner of the twentieth-century novel. From the outset of his career, as we have seen, he was confident that "an audience will come to whom it will be given to see the elementary machinery at work; who, as it were, from some slight hint of the straws, will feel the winds of March when they do not blow." Eventually his expectation was fulfilled and his work received its full meed of praise. For approximately a generation, from 1880 to 1910, he was lauded as the greatest living novelist and exerted an immense influence on younger writers. Then an eclipse set in, and has continued until the present day.

I would be the first to acknowledge the defects in Meredith's novels—extravagance, ostentation, digressiveness, lack of proportion. But, though he often exasperates me, I find him to be, on the whole, the most vital, original, and consistently interesting English novelist of the past hundred years. He was the first to see clearly that a novel can be a work of literary art, meriting all the care for style and all the depth of suggestion that have always been expected of poetry. Necessarily, this meant that the best novels can be appreciated only by people with active minds and artistic sensitivity. Meredith's habit of making the first chapter of each novel more difficult to comprehend than anything that followed sprang from a sort of honesty that obliged him to discourage the wrong kind of reader. Oscar Wilde, a representative of the young authors who fell under Meredith's influence, called him "the one incomparable novelist we have now in England. . . . To him belongs philosophy in fiction. His people not merely live, they live in thought. One can see them from myriad points of view. They are suggestive. There is soul in them and around them. They are interpretative and symbolic. And he who made them, those wonderful quick-moving figures, made them for his own pleasure and has never asked the public what they wanted."

Forty years later than Wilde, J. B. Priestley said much the same thing: "He created for himself a new kind of novel, and thereby enlarged the scope of fiction. What he did was to make the art more mobile, more fluid. He bent and twisted the form to suit his own purposes. . . . So far as English fiction is concerned, there can be no doubt that the modern novel began with the publication of *Richard Feverel*."

Lionel Stevenson
in *The Victorian Experience*, ed. Richard A. Levine (Athens: Ohio Univ. Pr., 1976), pp. 200–201

JOHN STUART MILL

1806–1873

Although John Stuart Mill has been regarded as an unpoetic logician, his *Autobiography* is not a mere history of ideas but rather an imaginative construct portraying his life as a *commedia.* In the book, Mill journeys from a dark wood of unfeeling rationalism, through a purgatory of mental crisis and enlightenment, and finally into a realm of philosophic thought and action. Located at the center of this journey, two episodes—Mill's debate with [John] Roebuck and his friendship with [John] Sterling—crystallize the two major events of the *Autobiography*: Mill's break with his father's thought and his friendship with Harriet Taylor, a friendship in which both evolve into philosophers. Narrating this *commedia* is Mill's voice of a philosopher-thinker, one who has learned to cultivate deeply rooted feeling. In describing James Mill's character and educational methods, the *Autobiography* blends eulogy and irony to convey the paradox of his greatness and his inadequacy. To describe Harriet's influence, religious parallels are employed to establish her as the Beatrice of Mill's *commedia.* During the final chapter of the *Autobiography* Harriet dies and assumes a new life in which she continues to guide her lover toward philosophic perfection. . . .

A backward glance at the *Autobiography* . . . shows that Mill has traveled a path through three distinct realms corresponding somewhat to those of Dante's *Commedia.* As a child, Mill awakens in a dark wood of Benthamism: "I have no remembrance of the time." His childhood education is a sort of loveless *Inferno* where a heroic but inadequate father-guide introduces him to great knowledge and great sin. Mill's mental crisis serves as his *Purgatorio*, where he stands convicted of the Benthamist sin of neglecting feeling and where he learns from a series of guides (Wordsworth, Coleridge, et al.) how to purge himself of this sin. Having thus righted himself, Mill encounters the Beatrice of true philosophy in Harriet Taylor, who before and after her death leads him into the philosopher's *Paradiso* of an active life devoted to human betterment. As in Dante, Virgil disappears, but Beatrice endures.

Eugene R. August
Victorian Poetry (Summer, 1973), pp. 143, 161

WILLIAM MORRIS

1834–1896

The nineteenth century is the great epoch of history. From the vast millennia of Darwin's *Origin of Species* to the few decades of Mill's *Autobiography*, from the objective effort to reconstruct a dead past visible in [Theodor] Mommsen's *History of Rome* to the subjective attendance of Turner at the last rites of the "Fighting Téméraire," the ruling passion of the age was displayed in men's efforts to uncover the source, not of the Nile, but of the present. One form which that passion took was the creation of a band of artists who, in token of their reverence for the perspective of the past, took the name of "Pre-Raphaelite Brotherhood." Most of the group went on to become eminently respectable Victorian gentlemen; but among the people who gathered in their wake was one young man who never lost the simple conviction that contemporary life was ruled by an historical paradox which modern conventions struggled to ignore: "The past is past, though I cannot forget." . . .

The consequences of [the] distinction between history and fable are, for Morris, enormous. For thirty years Morris would play the role of teller of tales, recreating history in the subjective forms of art. He would be the first great historicist, welding the scattered fragments of the past embodied in the histories and myths of his predecessors into integral fables which resolve the dichotomy between past and present. "The past is past," and it is therefore always available for present recreation; "we cannot forget," and thus must always perform our individual acts of aesthetic recreation in order to avoid the tyranny of time. The ultimate theme of Morris' early work is not the individual personalities of an anonymous mason or a fabulous queen, but the artistic perspective which can transcend the historic individual and achieve the greater community of art.

Hartley S. Spatt
Victorian Poetry (Autumn–Winter, 1975), pp. 1, 10

William Morris' lifelong reforming aesthetic endeavors trace those mazy ways crisscrossing the landscape where art and life mingle, for he passionately believed, as he said in "The Aims of Art," "art is and must be, either in its abundance or its barrenness, in its sincerity or its hollowness, the expression of the society amongst which it exists." For this convinced socialist, change in the institutional framework of man's life, most basically a check upon the mindless and inhuman pace of industrialization and a recognition of the basic fellowship of man, had to precede any sure and sound establishment of a true art, an "Art of the People." Short of this social revolution Morris felt that even the most accomplished artistic achievements of individual genius lacked solid foundation; looking about the contemporary artistic scene he once commented that, "now such small scraps of it as are left are the result of individual and wasteful struggle, are retrospective and pessimistic." Faithful to his own assessment of those areas in contemporary society where aesthetic and widely relevant social concerns met and merged, Morris concentrated his greatest energies in the fields of book production and design of household goods, thus hoping to supply through modified industrial means an exemplary pattern for a daily life enlivened by art, based not on the dilettantism of an elite, but rather on the vigorous creative participation and enjoyment of the great mass of men. He realistically accepted the possibility that even his own carefully considered reformations, which drew their hope for future innovation from the best survivals cultivated from a better past, would one day be superseded and viewed as the constrained and severely limited transmitters of the integrative artistic impulse.

Barbara J. Bono
Victorian Poetry (Autumn–Winter, 1975), pp. 43–44

JOHN HENRY NEWMAN

1801–1890

His belief seems to me to have been the source of Newman's strength as a writer and a partial explanation of his superiority, as a writer, to Carlyle and to many of his more socially conscious contemporaries. The very qualities of his prose suggest a wide variety of possibilities, while Carlyle's prose, brilliant as it sometimes may be, tends to be regular in its eccentricity, tends to blur discriminations which for Newman were the source of all the world's charms. He could be freer because he was more confident, and more confident . . . because he was not constantly threatened.

George Levine
The Boundaries of Fiction (Princeton, N.J.: Princeton Univ. Pr., 1968), p. 214

With the exception of John Stuart Mill, all the great prose writers of the Victorian Age . . . were reared in one or another form of Christian belief. All set store by the cardinal Christian virtues of faith, hope, and charity. All were dedicated to what they would have agreed to call the life of the spirit. Yet only one man among them, John Henry Newman, lived and died an actual believer, giving assent not alone with his heart to Christian sentiment but also with his mind to Christian doctrine, making faith as it was confirmed by reason the very substance of his life.

It must be said at once that, except by reason of his genius, Newman was not singular among his fellow-countrymen at large. Throughout his lifetime religion was of vital importance to the English, not only as a public issue capable of arousing intense feelings but also as a power, although doubtless an ever less manifested one, in the lives of individuals. But for members of the intellectual class, although they might hold religion in elegiac esteem and be tenacious of its "values," it was not a living, imperative presence. It still touched but it did not shape their lives. It did not command their observance in acts of devotion nor their intellectual assent to its formularies of belief. Among the class of intellectuals, Newman stood preeminent for his intellectual abilities; none surpassed him in mental power; none equaled him in subtlety of thought. Yet to doctrines that his notable contemporaries could not suppose to come within the range of credibility he not only gave his eager assent but based upon that assent his hope of salvation.

Lionel Trilling and Harold Bloom
in *Victorian Prose and Poetry*, ed. Lionel Trilling and
Harold Bloom (New York: Oxford Univ. Pr., 1973), p. 108

WALTER PATER

1839–1894

Pater has magic, but nobody would call it natural magic; it is the result of the most labourious spells and incantations, it smells of the wizard's cave; nobody would claim for Pater natural abundance, spontaneity, ease. One would not even quite claim for him opulence, held back by an instinct of restraint, in the sense in which he himself claims that for Flaubert; in the richest passages one has the sense that the gold has been dug and smelted, the gems grubbed out of the earth and painfully polished. . . . And yet [George] Saintsbury perhaps convinces us that this almost excessive labour, of which we seem to feel the strain in the close and minute consideration that Pater's page demands, results in the end not merely in mannerism, not merely in artificiality, but in a high and difficult *art*, the strained but in the end adequate expression of the inner ardours of a noble and lonely soul, of an unsystematic and intermittently self-obfuscating but strikingly original and seminal mind. And, through the painful concentration on subtleties of rhythm, some chord of feeling is struck, new, strange, plangent, and individual, not like anything else in late nineteenth-century English literature. . . .

Pater's most interesting influence is that upon the prose of Yeats. It was an influence, of course, of ideas as well as of style: when Yeats talks in a poem of his early middle age about "the fascination of what's difficult" and of how this fascination is in danger of drying up his natural lyrical spontaneity, he might almost be commenting on Pater's essay on style, with its insistence on rejection and renunciation, on the avoidance of the otiose and facile. They were in the end unlike in temperament; Yeats in middle age became a masterful man of action and in spite of his shyness he was, even in youth, what he called himself in his speech of thanks when he received the Nobel Prize, a "very social man." Yet all high creation is germinated in solitude; and one central antithesis of Pater's essay on style, that between the necessary subjectivity of the literary artist and the necessity that he should grapple with objective truth if his style is to become "impersonal," can be seen as central also to Yeats's way of looking at life and art as a tension, a clash, a collision between mutually hostile, but individually inadequate and mutually complementary, opposites. Thoughts that were cloudy and vague in Pater, pregnancies and suggestiveness, became, as Mr. Ian Fletcher has suggested, hard and systematic in Yeats.

G. S. Fraser
in *The Art of Victorian Prose*, ed. George Levine and William Madden (New York, Oxford Univ. Pr., 1968), pp. 220–21

DANTE GABRIEL ROSSETTI

1828–1882

To call [as Harold Weatherby does] "the central weakness" in "The Blessed Damozel" "the problem of meaning in relationship to the reality or unreality of the supernatural" is to expose not a fault in Rossetti but a failure on the critic's part to understand what the poet was doing. "The Blessed Damozel" has nothing whatever to do with such a problem and to raise it is to ensure an oblique reading of the poem. Rossetti's ideal never admits a distinction between an order called nature and one called supernature. He uses a tradition which does make such a distinction because through it he can clarify his own very different ideas.

When critics say that Rossetti's artifice is unredeemed by an idea, or that it is beauty without any firm conceptual basis, one may be justifiably puzzled. Both Weatherby and [Graham] Hough make these charges, yet both also show that they understand at least the broad outlines of Rossetti's message. The point seems to be that they do not approve his message, that they consider it trivial, unprofound. But to see human sexual love as one of man's highest ideals, the value equivalent of a "supermundane" experience within a wholly non-transcendental frame of reference, does not seem to me either vague or trivial. The fact that Rossetti's Eros-Love must by its nature avoid any absolute fulfillments does not make it any less sublime (or actual) an experience nor his artistic rendering of it necessarily "confused."

On the point of craftsmanship, I think we have seen that the poetry achieves a careful integration of themes and techniques, at least in the works under discussion here. One cannot be as definite about the purely substantive issue. A sensibility more committed to moral and rational absolutes than to artistic ones will likely not think much of Rossetti's poetry. Rossetti will seem an aesthete because he places a higher value on images than on concepts. The heavy emphasis placed upon the thematic aspects of literature during the past four decades—the emphasis upon the sort of "interpretation" which Susan Sontag has recently declared "against"—helps to explain why Rossetti has been so long out of favor. Critics schooled in this method seek to define their absolutes not at the surface but below it, not in the apparition but the concept. Rossetti does not fare well in such a school because he forces the reader to attend to the surface, insists that the greatest significance lies there, unburied. He does not want deep readers, which is not to say that he does not demand intelligent ones.

If, then, Rossetti and his Pre-Raphaelite brothers (and sisters) cannot be fully recovered without some shift in current tastes and critical perspectives, at least we can clarify some of the issues. Rossetti's poetry is not vague, his imagery is not merely decorative, his themes are not manifestly trivial: insofar as these points have been substantiated by this discussion my purposes have been achieved.

Jerome J. McGann
Victorian Poetry (Spring, 1969), pp. 53–54

Rossetti is a difficult poet, not only because his art is deliberately committed to sustaining an intensity that precludes mere action, but because the intensity almost invariably is one of baffled passion. Though Rossetti's master was Keats, he was rightly associated with Shelley by Yeats, who observed that the genius of both poets "can hardly stir but to the rejection of Nature." Shelley, though skeptically accepting a pragmatic dualism of heart and head, quested for a monistic Absolute, but one of his own curious invention, neither Platonic nor Christian. Rossetti, a convinced sensualist, writes a naturalistic poetry that yet rejects natural forms, which is almost an impossibility. His lyrics and sonnets are set in a world that is at once phantasmagoria and nature, giving the effect of an artificial nature. His Blessed Damozel leans down to him from a Heaven where a woman's hair glistens "along her back . . . yellow like ripe corn." It is impossible, amid the forests and fountains in *The House of Life*, to decide whether we stand in the remembered natural world, or in some purgatorial realm heavier and more naturally luxurious than nature could ever have been. Rossetti's symbolic world is oppressive to the spirit, but this oppressiveness is his poetry's unique strength. He gives us neither a vision of nature, as Keats did, nor of a second nature, as Shelley rendered, but a surrealistic or fantastic blend of both, and since all are damned in his mixed realm, he gives us also a wholly oblique, and finally nihilistic, vision of judgment in which we cannot be saved through sensual fulfillment, and yet achieve no lasting release without it.

Lionel Trilling and Harold Bloom
in *Victorian Prose and Poetry*, ed. Lionel Trilling and
Harold Bloom (New York: Oxford Univ. Pr., 1973), pp. 616–17

JOHN RUSKIN

1819–1900

"Style," as I have just used the term, is a selection from among the infinite tonalities of language in accord with the matter at hand and the expectations of the audience. But the word has also a rarer and more elusive sense, which everything in this essay is an imperfect attempt to elucidate. I have in mind not an outward adaptation to the exigencies of subject and audience, but an inner manifestation: style as the incarnation of sensibility. Style of this kind has nothing whatever to do with levels of speech; it *is* speech, the unique voice of the writer, the felt presence that hovers over his pages and intones its way into our consciousness. We acknowledge its presence when we say of a very great writer that he "has genius" or is "immortal"; we know that his words, like the books which house them, cannot last forever. But he has succeeded in re-creating *himself*, not in the flesh, as we can do, but in the spirit, and his anima has miraculously passed into our own minds. In this ultimate sense, Ruskin is the greatest prose stylist in English.

Yet Ruskin has always been best known for his most mannered, conventionally stylish passages and less known for the works in which he most intensely lives. He is supposed to have become progressively unreadable; in fact, he was *always* solitary and eccentric, but as his hold on reality became more remote, his style became more and more intimate. In his later works he often seems to stand at an alien's distance from the world, but in almost frightening proximity to the reader. This effect of immediacy is in part due to Ruskin's lifelong labor to avoid all appearance of laboriousness; after a dazzling apprenticeship in which he delighted in making language do splits and somersaults, he discovered he could make it accomplish even more by standing it on its feet. In part the change in tone results from a shift in Ruskin's concerns. In the early volumes of *Modern Painters*, Ruskin focused his superb gifts of observation and articulation upon clouds, seas, and mountains. In middle life, however, the sense of divinity he had felt in nature began to fail him, and his interest shifted from the actual Alps to the mountains of his own mind. To scale those yet more perilous peaks, he perfected a subtler instrument of prose which registers the very pulsations of thought. Reading *Modern Painters* gives one, in Charlotte Brontë's phrase, a new sense, *sight*; reading Ruskin's later works expands one's awareness of consciousness itself.

John Rosenberg
in *The Art of Victorian Prose*, ed. George Levine and William Madden (New York: Oxford Univ. Pr., 1968), p. 179

In 1909 the Italian poet Emilio Marinetti issued his famous *Futurist Manifesto*. This flamboyant document, which totally repudiated the past and peremptorily demanded that art dedicate itself to an authentically modern sensibility based on recognition of the beauty and vitality of the machine, is generally regarded as the charter of Aesthetic Modernism, even of those movements of art upon which the Futurist principles had no direct influence. Some three years after the publication of the *Manifesto*, Marinetti gave a lecture in London on the Futurist program and in the course of it put a question to his audience which, he made plain, was crucial to any hope they might have of aesthetic salvation: "When, then," he asked in impatient disdain, "When, then, will you disencumber yourselves of the lymphatic ideology of your deplorable Ruskin?"

The question was shocking in its impiousness and it was doubtless heard with an appalled relief. By 1912 the educated English public was fatigued with Ruskin—he had said so much and had said it for so long, ever since 1843. By the pertinacity, passion, and brilliance of his teaching he had shaped the minds of three intellectual generations in their relation to art. No one had ever made art so momentous; in every sentence he wrote about it was the urgently communicated belief that created objects had a decisive bearing upon the moral and spiritual life and that one's preferences in pictures or buildings, or even household utensils, were indicative of one's relation to oneself, one's fellow men, and the universe. The theorists and practitioners of the new movements certainly held art to be no less momentous than Ruskin said it was, but, however diverse their aesthetic principles might be, they were at one in saying that such moral considerations as Ruskin adduced were irrelevant to the aesthetic experience, and, indeed, qualified art's chief claim to momentousness, its autonomy. Marinetti's English audience may not have been ready to accept the full challenge of the new art, but they had been prepared by their fellow countrymen Walter Pater and Oscar Wilde to acknowledge a growing impatience with Ruskin's overtly moralizing tone and with his insistence upon the necessity of maintaining a sensibility which was consonant with religious faith even while admitting that religion as a system of belief was not tenable. It was this sensibility that they found burdensome and in the assault that Marinetti made upon "their" Ruskin, which went to extremes of irreverence in its explanation of just why he was "deplorable," they heard the promise of liberation from it.

Lionel Trilling and Harold Bloom
in *Victorian Prose and Poetry*, ed. Lionel Trilling and
Harold Bloom (New York: Oxford Univ. Pr., 1973), pp. 154–55

By the autobiographical impulse Jay Fellows [in *The Failing Distance*] means "any desire for the emergence of the first person from a condition of voyeuristic invisibility, from an optical system without a sense of self, to a condition of density and opaqueness . . . beginning as a reflexive, spatial heresy of mirrors, as opposed to the orthodox space of windows, end[ing] in a triumph of tenses and memory, the triumph of a new sequence and a new distance that masters a recessional space that has failed" (p. ix). Fellows's idea is that throughout his writing, Ruskin was at pains to disguise a fundamental impulse to reveal and exhibit himself, and that *Praeterita* represents a consolidation of, or triumph over, the warring impulses of egotistical first person and reticent "annulled self." He tries to show this by examining the way Ruskin looks at things—as "Moral Retina," or "Camera Lucida" (Ruskin's phrases)—inferred from the language of Ruskinian texts. Particularly interesting are his elucidations of Ruskin's views on landscape painting, and of his use of parenthetical structures for both rhetorical and emotional reasons.

It is a question whether a critic can offer a valid phenomenological account of a writer's experience, as Fellows tries to do here; it may be that he can only give an account of his own experience of the writer's text. In any case, the success of such accounts depends on the reader's own assent to the critic's experience, not difficult when one is in the hands of the gentle Gaston Bachelard, or even of Georges Poulet (aided, perhaps, by unfamiliarity with many of Poulet's subjects), but difficult here because Fellows's account so often causes him to distort what one knows to be the historical context, the plain facts of Ruskin's life, and even the plain facts of human experience.

Diane Johnson
Victorian Studies (Winter, 1977), p. 202

ALGERNON CHARLES SWINBURNE

1837–1909

Swinburne is a poet not of natural objects but of natural energies—of winds and surging waters. His scale is macrocosmic, his focus less upon the small celandine than upon the spines of mountains, less upon things seen than forces felt. At times he is nearly a blind poet, all tongue and ear and touch. His poetry moves away from the art of painting and toward the art of music; after reading Swinburne one retains not an image but a tonality and a rhythm. . . .

That his most lifeless poetry is in all formal respects—meter, diction, and subject—virtually indistinguishable from his greatest poetry is one of the mysteries of his art. His genius is extraordinary above all for its *intermittency*; the verse-making engine spins constantly for half a century, but the surges of engaged power are sudden and unpredictable. Tennyson called him "a reed through which all things blow into music." Sometimes the melody carries; often it does not. Swinburne had a curious passion for monotony, which was undoubtedly linked to his love of bleak, monochromatic effects. . . .

One's final reservation toward Swinburne has to do with a certain arrested development. Wordsworth's genius flowers, then endlessly wanes: *Tintern Abbey* unfolds an organic evolution of growths, losses, and gains. Neither Swinburne nor his verse seems to undergo much change; a single note is struck early and held obsessively long. The reader wants a richer range of subject, more nuance of idea. Swinburne composes by compounding, not synthesizing. Too often, his method is merely quantitative: "I have added yet four more jets of boiling and gushing infamy to the perennial and poisonous fountain of Dolores." One wishes that his eccentric genius could have retained all its power while ridding itself of rigidity and repetitiveness. It did not, and the death of development in Swinburne may have been as large a loss to English poetry as the physical death of Keats.

John Rosenberg
Introd., in *Swinburne: Selected Poetry and Prose,*
ed. John Rosenberg (New York: Random House, 1968),
pp. vii, xxxiv

The "sad, shapeless horror increate" that was Swinburne criticism . . . has ceased, and Time—fulfilling itself in a manner that Swinburne, more than anyone else, made his personal note—has brought it as pasture to the sea. . . .

To a certain class, as Shelley wrote of "Epipsychidion," Swinburne's poetry will no doubt "ever remain incomprehensible, from a defect of a common organ of perception for the ideas of which it treats," but for others it seems clear that sensibility has shifted once more, as with Berlioz, Rodin, Gaudi, and that Swinburne can claim his own. . . .

We know there is such a thing as the "language of music," we know that the word *musical* applied to verse usually means nothing but "mellifluous," and, knowing these things, we ought to be able to learn whether there is, in fact, anything like musical structure in Swinburne's poetry. I, for one, though not musically trained or even informed, have no difficulty perceiving a kind of fugal pattern in (say) "When the hounds of spring," with repetitions and with modulations from tonic to dominant or from major to relative minor. Neither am I an art historian, but it is evident that both the poetry and prose of this connoisseur of Blake, amateur of the Uffizi and the Louvre, intimate of Rossetti, [Edward] Burne-Jones, Whistler, contain stores of wealth for the student of the visual arts—especially an iconographer (e.g., "The Triumph of Time," ll. 365ff., 381ff., "Hertha," ll. 116ff.).

[Georges] Lafourcade has told us something about his reading and even recorded the titles of books borrowed from the Taylorian Institute during fourteen months in 1859–60, but a trial dig undertaken some years ago suggested that there is very much more to be brought to light. Above all, his poetry cries out for the kind of annotation and explication that can exist only in a symbiotic relationship with historical research. When we have this, and have succeeded with some confidence in sorting out the *dii majores* and *dii minores* among his poems, we will see, I think, that Swinburne is neither one of the last romantics nor one of the first moderns. Like Yeats, he is both.

Cecil Y. Lang
Victorian Poetry (Spring–Summer, 1971),
pp. i, iii, v

Tristram of Lyonesse tells a tale already told by Arnold and by Richard Wagner, a tale that allows Swinburne to emphasize adultery and the literally "barren" life of the married woman. Tristram's marriage to the "other Iseult," in Swinburne's version, is not only a failure but is a "Maiden Marriage" (this is the title of his Part IV), one that is unconsummated. The "white-handed Iseult, maid and wife"—who is unlike the same character in Arnold's poem, who has children—curses Tristram and "his harlot," vowing revenge on them. But her frustration is less significant than that felt by the lovers themselves, a frustration that can be ended only in the peace of death. . . . The only true consummation of erotic passion is in death, a return to the unity of that great symbolic matrix.

It has been persuasively argued that Swinburne follows Blake in opposing a sort of pantheism to what he conceives of as the dualities of Christian theism, the dualities of soul and body, or heaven and earth, or eternity and time. . . .

"Eschatological monism" is a phrase that applies to Swinburne's poetry in a special sense: over and over, it seems that the end of passion, the end of conflict, indeed the end of all things, is not only a death but a merging into the night, the sea, the one. Swinburne's supposed advocacy of the flesh and of fleshly vices is really an insistence on the unity of life and an insistence that is ultimately anything but fleshly: it denies a dualism of body and spirit in order to assert that the body is really no single body but an abstraction, one which might as well be called spirit. Swinburne is the poetic spokesman for Carlyle's "Natural Supernaturalism," which is a kind of pantheism; nature is supernatural in that it is one, timeless, in some sense divine.

In many respects Swinburne's treatment of love and sexuality is strikingly unique. No other Victorian writer deals so openly with such aspects as homosexuality, masochism, and sadism. Yet it would be misleading to assert that Swinburne is atypical or a freak. His way of coping with sex, his sexual idealism or tendency to regard sexual passion as a virtually mystical passion for oneness—a passion can mean the destruction of a limited individual existence—is closely related to the responses of other artists, Victorian and modern, from Tennyson to Henry Miller and Norman Mailer, who either sublimate sexuality in pseudo religion or sublimate religion in pseudo sexuality, and for whom sexual experience is not the gratification of appetite or the demonstrating of erotic love for a specific person or the expression of a philoprogenitive urge.

Wendell Stacy Johnson
Sex and Marriage in Victorian Poetry (Ithaca, N.Y.: Cornell Univ. Pr., 1975), pp. 105–7

Despite its limitations, Philip Henderson's *Swinburne: Portrait of a Poet* (1974) brings us a step closer to the comprehensive modern biography so sorely lacking in Swinburne studies. Henderson rides no hobby-horse comparable to the flagellational one that distorted Jean Overton Fuller's account (1968); he also draws more extensively on the *Letters* and has a far surer feel for the intricacies of the mid-Victorian scene. But his reliance on previous biographers, extending back to Gosse, tends to trap him within the outlines of established biographical tradition and to commit him to the echoing of unexamined formulations. . . . Nor is there much of interest on the poems proper or on their relationship to Swinburne's imaginative world. The latter is hardly formulated in any consistent manner, and it is not clear that Henderson feels its absence from his account a difficulty. The result is a workman-like, largely exterior portrait that consolidates but fails sufficiently to probe its materials.

Robert A. Greenberg
Victorian Poetry (Autumn, 1976), p. 236

ALFRED, LORD TENNYSON

1809–1892

Christopher Ricks, ed., *The Poems of Tennyson* (1969)

In "Oenone" [Tennyson] made the defeat of reason an augury of the collapse of Troy. In *In Memoriam* he imagined a violence which spelled disaster,

The fortress crashes from on high,
The brute earth lightens to the sky,
And the great Aeon sinks in blood.

His "Lucretius" placed the suicide of the philosopher against the dissolution of the Republic, "the lust of blood/That makes a steaming slaughter-house of Rome," the Commonwealth, "which breaks/As I am breaking now!" And the late "Tiresias," designed to have relevance to contemporary England, warned of the imminent doom of Thebes.

But the *Idylls of the King,* above all, proved as a completed sequence the most trenchant and best sustained treatment of social decline in Victorian poetry. Having rapidly described the triumph of Camelot over the barbaric wilderness, the *Idylls* analyzes at length the forces of decadence that undermine the city-state: the failure of idealism, the substitution of self-interest for civic virtue, the decay of manners, the surrender of reason to sensuality (suggested by the omnipresent beast imagery). When a first generation has assured the basic security of the kingdom, a second begins to question the authority of the King, whose ideal standard must be taken on trust, and to follow the bad example of the Queen, whose adultery commits her to a life of miserable deception. For most of the knights the Grail quest is but an escape from immediate social responsibilities in an effort to achieve an unearned spiritual satisfaction, and the few who return to Camelot come back dejectedly to a crumbling city, "heaps of ruin, hornless unicorns,/Crack'd basilisks, and splinter'd cockatrices"; the culture that is not daily reaffirmed cannot long survive. Tristram, unabashed opportunist that he is, explains the logic of the late-comer who finds he has no need to pay more than lip-reverence to the faith upon which the civilization was originally built:

> "Fool, I came late, the heathen wars were o'er,
> The life had flown, we sware but by the shell. . . ."

The fair appearance for a while belies the essential emptiness; Camelot eventually falls, destroyed by what is false within. Though the settings of the separate Idylls reflect the cycle of the seasons, the implication of the poem as a whole is not that decadence must supplant cultural vigor as inevitably as autumn and winter follow summer. The fate of Camelot is not predestined; it depends on the will of the citizenry, the free decision to respond or not to the changing challenge of the time. The epilogue to the sequence makes this moral, as well as its application to Victorian Britain, only too explicit. . . .

Jerome H. Buckley
The Triumph of Time (Cambridge, Mass.: Harvard Univ. Pr., 1966), pp. 74–75

[The] tension between human instincts and the ideals of civilization is central to Tennyson's early lyrics as well as to the *Idylls*. "The Lady of Shalott" symbolically portrays an aesthetic psyche bound by the curse of her own perfection and destroyed—like Camelot in the *Idylls*—in the clash between rules "no man can keep" and her longing for the imperfect world of desire and Lancelot. She is, as Gerhard Joseph describes her in *Tennysonian Love*, "caught between two worlds to neither of which she can commit herself." Lancelot himself is torn by divided impulses in a somewhat different manner in the *Idylls*. Sir Galahad, although not portrayed in a social context as he is in "The Holy Grail," achieves his "strength of ten" only by renouncing the "kiss of love." "Sir Launcelot and Queen Guinevere" implies that an opposite abandonment to the kiss of love might cost a man "all his worldly worth." In all of his Arthurian writings Tennyson stresses the conflict between spirit and sense and the harm man can cause society and himself if he indulges in either sensual or spiritual extremes. In the *Idylls* Tennyson portrays this conflict as the mutual destruction of Guinevere's fantasy of a paradise with Lancelot and Arthur's dream of an Order that depends for its continuance upon the perfection of human conduct.

Although the *Idylls* is in part a hypothetical portrait of Victorian England with its high idealism, strict morality, and warring extremisms, Tennyson deliberately baffles any effort by the reader to localize the details of his poem regarding Arthurian sources, historical setting, philosophical school, or religious dogma. Tennyson presented his vision of the Order of the Round Table by drawing from an extremely large number of general materials—Anglo-Saxon social customs, bardic ideals, classical myths, Welsh myths, Victorian ethics, renaissance imagery, and many Arthurian legends. . . .

Tennyson makes Arthur's greatness most evident when the king appears in triumph in the beginning and when he passes in transcendent glory at the end. Otherwise he focusses on the Order itself as a mirror of Victorian society. King Arthur and his ideals provide a framework against which Tennyson judges his own milieu; his judgment is more adverse than complimentary. . . . Arthur's idealism reflects the need for a sustaining purpose in the Victorian era but also the sometimes foolish utopian hopes of the Victorians. Arthur's Order proves far less sound than he imagines. In his prose sketch of 1833 Tennyson described Camelot as the most beautiful mount in the world, "But all underneath it was hollow, . . . and there ran a prophecy that the mountain and the city on some wild morning would topple into the abyss and be no more." Such an explicit warning of doom no doubt proved too heavy-handed for use in the *Idylls*, but the ghost of Gawain in "The Passing of Arthur" shrills an echo of this early prophecy:

"Hollow, hollow all delight!" (line 33). Tennyson believed that his own society, like Arthur's Order, was deeply in trouble; and the *Idylls* was his greatest attempt to understand its problems.

J. Phillip Eggers
King Arthur's Laureate (New York: New York Univ. Pr., 1971), pp. 6–7, 20–21

Tennyson had all along felt, perhaps rather vaguely, that the divine was housed somehow in the person of Arthur Hallam and that the apparent contrarieties of nature could somehow be reconciled through faith in the spirit which lay behind them. It was not until the writing of *De Profundis,* however, that the divisibility–indivisibility of God from nature apparently suggested itself to him in panentheistic terms. The difference between Arthur Hallam as the personal form through which the persona of *In Memoriam* could contemplate celestial truths, as a being who in death fused with Christ, and an Arthur Hallam as both God and not God, is perhaps small. Tennyson's panentheism of the later poems, in other words, is rather an extension of his speculations on the material universe and the spirit behind it than a divergence from them. It is perhaps fortunate that Tennyson's theistic idealism had not become more systematic, however hypothetical, by 1850, or the lyricism of a long poem such as *In Memoriam* might have given way to exposition.

We have long regarded Tennyson as "Schoolmiss Alfred" or "Alfred Lawn Tennyson"; we have looked upon him as a mindless emotional poet, a diarist, at his best a lyrical poet of some genius but little intellect. We have accused him of shallow chauvinism or of playing the role of *sacer vates* for money or for vanity. And yet all of these responses to Tennyson seem to me to be in error, occasioned perhaps by the difficulty of looking upon the Victorian period with an unprejudiced eye. The Victorian world is now opening to us, however, and at a sufficient distance so that a more positive and more accurate judgment can be made. We can now see that Tennyson is one of many spokesmen for the age, but not in the narrow, complacent, or superficial way that we thought he was. He addresses the problems that were real for the Victorians and are real for us, and he addresses them in a thoughtful and often profound way, whether we agree with his responses or not. They are, of course, the responses of the artist, for like Hardy, who described his own art as "an endeavour to give shape and coherence to a series of seemings, or personal impressions," Tennyson is an artist, not a philosopher. But he is no less thoughtful and thought-provoking because his work is not philosophy, but art. If it is true that we cannot understand the present unless we understand the past, it is to our interest to seek to understand Tennyson. And for that, we need only listen to what he says.

Ward Hellstrom
On the Poems of Tennyson (Gainesville: University Presses of Florida, 1972), pp. 162–63

"Mind you put my 'Crossing the Bar' at the end of all editions of my poems." Hallam Tennyson had said: "That is the crown of your life's work." This is not to say that it is his greatest poem; but certainly, and without irony, it was a gift reserved for age, to set a crown upon his lifetime's effort. Its simple dignity is yet consonant with a fine patterning and subtle variety. The third line of each stanza, longer than the preceding line, swells into a release of feeling. But what saves this from self-indulgence, converting it rather to a religious indulgence or remission, is the immediate curbing effect of the stanza's shortened concluding line, reining and subduing the feeling. Two sentences, each two stanzas, each beginning with an exclamation which is vibrant rather than exclamatory and whose vibrations then die away; the poem itself "turns again home." The central stanzas incorporate rhymes which are disyllabic, but not as rhymes with each other; the first and last stanzas maintain only monosyllabic rhymes, and the concluding rhyme (*far* into *bar*) returns us to the first rhyme of the poem (*star* into *bar*). "Face to face": did Tennyson's mind go back to Arthur Hallam and to the manuscript of *In Memoriam*, the final two lines of its final section (CXXXI)?—"And come to look on those we loved/ And that which made us, face to face." And did his mind go even further back, moved by the deep reciprocity, to recall that it was Arthur Hallam, in a poem to Tennyson's sister Emily, who had glimpsed this distance: "Till our souls see each other face to face"?

One remembers what Hallam said about rhyme (which he called, with a paradoxical possibility apt to Tennyson, "the recurrence of termination"): "Rhyme has been said to contain in itself a constant appeal to Memory and Hope." *Star: bar/far: bar.* Once again, the poem turns again home, just as its last line returns to its title—to which it has now shown itself entitled. It is a perfect epitome of Tennyson's essential movement: a progress outward which is yet a circling home.

Christopher Ricks
Tennyson (New York: Macmillan, 1972), pp. 313–14

The *Idylls of the King* is one of the four or five indisputably great long poems in our language. Yet Tennyson's doom-laden prophecy of the fall of the West has been dismissed as a Victorian-Gothic fairy tale. So colossal a misreading bears witness to the power of the critical orthodoxy that for the past fifty years has obscured our perception of the Victorian poets in general and of Tennyson in particular.

The brilliantly biased essays of T. S. Eliot and the once-salutory fervors of F. R. Leavis in *New Bearings in English Poetry* (1932) have created a mythic literary country in which all of Victorian poetry figures as a Waste Land and the reader is rushed directly from Keats to Yeats to Eliot, with no stops on the way save for Gerard Manley Hopkins, who, Leavis contends, bears "no relation . . . to any nineteenth-century poet." Since Hopkins is clearly a fine poet, so the argument assumes, he cannot have been a Victorian and, by some chronological sleight of hand, he is translated whole into the twentieth century. The fault with this mythic map is that it bypasses one of the major English poets. Yet so great was the need of the first half of the twentieth century to free itself from the all-dominating voice of the greatest poet of the nineteenth century that the act of omission was achieved virtually without protest. . . .

The road leading back to Camelot passes through Byzantium and Eliot's *The Waste Land*. But the path will not be found until the bias of the modernist myth is broken. English poetry, so the orthodoxy holds, reached a dead-end with the Victorians. If it is to revive at all, it must develop, in Leavis' words, "along some other line than that running from the Romantics through Tennyson, Swinburne, *A Shropshire Lad*, and Rupert Brooke." Such a line, of course, never existed; Leavis has yoked the living to the dead and practices a kind of guilt by moribund association. He did not see, and Eliot as a practicing poet could not afford to see, that the great divide in English poetry occurred in 1798, with the publication of the *Lyrical Ballads*, and not between the death of Tennyson in 1892 and the appearance of *The Waste Land* in 1922. The ghost of Tennyson breathes everywhere in Eliot's verse. But until that ghost is seen full-face, Tennyson will remain virtually inaccessible to contemporary readers, "a Virgil among the Shades," as Eliot felicitously calls him, Eliot himself having consigned Tennyson to limbo. . . .

"Escapism" and "realism" in their profoundest meanings are not functions of time or place but of intensity of imaginative vision. No prima facie case can be made against the remoteness of King Arthur that cannot also be made against his colleague and neighbor, King Lear. Shakespeare turned from the Elizabethan marketplace to the blasted heaths of ancient Britain, and in so doing created a Waste Land at least as contemporary as T. S. Eliot's, or as Tennyson's blighted land of sand and thorns in "The Holy Grail," from which Eliot's in part derives.

John Rosenberg
The Fall of Camelot (Cambridge, Mass.:
Harvard Univ. Pr., 1973), pp. 2–3, 12

[Tennyson's] shifts in mood and emphasis reflect the poet's various attitudes toward Victorian society and the future; toward the hypocrisies, repressions, and distortions imposed on generous impulse by greedy mammonism; but also toward the apparently dangerous freeing of sexual desire that can overthrow the order of marriage and the order of the state. The appeal of marriage as an idea is deep and consistent in his poetry, but one asks why Tennyson so often observes or imagines its poignant failure here and now.

The tendency toward what we have called sexual idealism in Tennyson's work can lead to a rejection of the real, of the real woman and of real wedlock. When the poet tries to locate his spiritual ideal, not in the distant future toward which mankind can evolve, but in an imagined world of actual persons, the degree of actuality he achieves depends on the degree to which the ideal fails of realization. The idea of marriage means for Tennyson an escape from shadows and solipsism to the longed-for reconciliation of impulse and social order through a union of spirit and flesh, of the creative self and the responsive milieu, of woman and man.

But all these, including *woman* and *man*, are abstractions. When Tennyson writes of himself as woman or man, as the soul in "The Palace of Art" or the aged speaker in "Tithonus," the abstracted images, representing aspects of a whole personality, succeed. The poet's experience and imagination both, however, teach him that real women are not abstract soul or spirit; the resulting disillusion implies that he has a version of the "madonna-harlot" syndrome, the insistence on making *woman* either exalted or degraded. So this poet who begins by associating woman with spirit and who can even insist that women and men should become more alike, at last, in the mood of the *Idylls*, seems to fear the world, the flesh—and the woman. The feminine figure that was Soul in early Tennyson becomes corrupting Sense in the later Tennyson.

The frustrated and failed marriages in his poetry suggest that he finds in life not a union but a divorce, a conflict, of contrasting, complementary, and partial values—values, not people. But Tennyson is not always true in his abstracting and his allegorizing to his own profound imagination. In the *Idylls of the King* he accepts the painful actuality of divorce, the negation of his own temporal and redeeming idea, and he tries to make the divorce itself an ideal truth with a Carlylean denial of the flesh, the real world, and history. This paradoxical and doomed attempt helps to explain some flaws both small and large in the poetically impressive, often beautiful *Idylls*: the dimness of Arthur in "The Round Table," his priggishness here and there as he detaches himself from the flesh, and especially the contrast—indeed, a kind of divorce—between the central group of tales, about women and men, and the heroic frame tales that fail to explain or relate to the "Round

Table" world of difficult social bonds. Yet Tennyson's imagination triumphs over his avowed intentions: the *Idylls* demonstrate how a divorce of the very ideas of Soul and Sense can mean in human time only destruction and death. They demonstrate, finally, how sterile the total polarization of the sexes is, the Victorian and later tendency to define women and men essentially, not as persons in the traditional religious way, but in abstract sexual or antisexual ways: man as virile power *or* as Soul, as sheer "spiritual" subject; and woman as chastity personified *or* as Sense, as mere sexual object.

Wendell Stacy Johnson
Sex and Marriage in Victorian Poetry (Ithaca, N.Y.: Cornell Univ. Pr., 1975), pp. 183–84

Modern critics have tended lately to take Camelot as more than a correlative of private spiritual conflict. It is also an archetypal civilization: Alfred Lord Tennyson's *Idylls of the King* contains "an allegory of the collapse of society" [F. E. L. Priestley], a "cyclical view of history" [Jerome Hamilton Buckley], and the "doctrine regarding history as an organic growth" [Clyde de L. Ryals]; here "evolution has been tinged with Apocalypse" [John D. Rosenberg]. Accordingly, the older moral-ethical explanation for Camelot's fall—the individual moral fault, the "allowed sin" [Hallam Tennyson] which corrupted the order—is downplayed as simplistic. But on the other hand, no systematic historical explanation has been developed in its place. F. E. L. Priestley says that the "defection of Guinevere is by no means the sole, or perhaps the chief, cause" but then lists Vivien, Tristram, Mark, Modred, the powers of the wasteland, the Grail quest, and others as contributing factors. More recently, John D. Rosenberg has observed that "the causes of the catastrophe are multiple" and James R. Kincaid that "we have a multiplicity of reasons, all inadequate." So many reasons come down to no cause at all and, indeed, Kincaid concludes that "there are no resounding causes for the fall."

The central difficulty in explaining Tennyson's understanding of the historical process by which societies like Camelot fall is the difficulty of integrating the effects of individual freedom and historical necessity. Individuals are freely responsible for acts which injure society, but society collectively undergoes certain inevitable transformations which make it, as Ryals says, "like other organisms, . . . subject to decay." The intent of this essay is to offer both a thesis and a frame of reference for explaining Camelot's collapse. The central proposition (and somewhat of a commonplace in historical explanation) is an irony of history: that the state declines for the very absence of external opposition brought about during its successful ascent. The argument in brief is this: the state rises against severe opposition and bases itself, consequently, upon the most intense of natural passions, as these are in the process made subservient to the nobler passions. This is orthodox Christian "freedom." To the measure that the knights surrender themselves to and obey Arthur and the vows (their higher selves), Camelot assimilates and controls mere animal "freedom." The state continues to be vigorous as long as its necessarily warlike predisposition whets itself on external challenges to its development (challenge-and-response, in Toynbee's well-known dictum). Once it overcomes all challenges and stops growing, however, its active principle becomes objectified as mere custom (that "good custom" that "should corrupt the world") and the state, the vows, and Arthur alike become oppressive. Amid luxury and play, the will to perfection flags and the passions upon which the state was built are let loose to turn in upon the higher self. The result is sensuality, lassitude, and torment. On an historical level, Camelot begins to war against itself, ultimately destroyed fratricidally from within. In this process, the state transforms itself, not into something new, but into a dialectical opposite, whose form is determined by the very forces that made possible its inception. Such a description of Tennyson's historical system should not indicate an historical fatalism as much as a gloomy assessment of man's fallen condition, for (in another commonplace) man is free to expand indefinitely in history. However, with the loss of will in a "time of golden rest" ("Merlin and Vivien," l. 140), the next necessary stage is decline.

Henry Kozicki
Victorian Studies (Winter, 1977), pp. 141–42

WILLIAM MAKEPEACE THACKERAY

1811–1863

Thackeray's grand iconoclastic search has a rather unspectacular ending. Morally, a search for true values which begins with a ruthless exposure of untruths finds itself in the end with nothing left unrejected except . . . those whose delusion was first to be found wanting. Artistically, too, we must be disappointed. The search for a new narrative form seems to dissipate itself in a feeble sort of Idyll of the Hearth. . . .

Thackeray's depth and strength come from the tension between his perceptive . . . literal-minded criticism, and an exquisite regard and understanding of what he is destroying to dissect. He is constantly in pursuit of an excuse to retain myths he cannot let stand. His best work is certainly in the middle novels, *Vanity Fair* and *The Newcomes* especially, where the tension is most nicely maintained, where the puppeteer's strings never completely disappear. As Thackeray puts it, voicing a favorite dilemma, "I never know whether to pity or congratulate a man on coming to his senses." . . . The point is best made when the excellence of the illusion the narrator is dispelling is most evident.

Jack Rawlins
A Fiction That Is True (Berkeley:
Univ. California Pr., 1974), pp. 235–36

Thackeray was a Victorian who spent his working life defining his period. And he habitually defined it in terms of its relation to the past. The body of his novels is a kind of history of the development of his age—a "history familiar rather than heroic," as Esmond says, but a history nevertheless—and in its way as illuminating as histories more conventional. From *Henry Esmond* to *Philip* we are given little windows on scenes of the past: the Jacobite plottings of 1688, the American Revolution against a background of the Georgian age of scandal, the scramble for victory and status that is behind Waterloo and the Regency, the self-satisfied respectability of the Newcomes, and the dirty electioneering that was the prologue to the 1867 reform bill. They are Victorian windows, to be sure, as Thackeray's spectacles perched on his broken nose were adjusted to his personal vision; and so much the more they tell us about Thackeray's period, which defined itself, as other periods do, by reacting from the previous one. . . .

If one reads the body of Thackeray's major works in the order he wrote them, one finds oneself moving to and fro in historical chronology. *Vanity Fair* and *Pendennis* move forward; then we jump back with *Esmond*, forward with *The Newcomes*, back again for *The Virginians*, and again forward for *Philip. Denis Duval,* the novel he did not live to complete, would fit historically between *The Virginians* and *Vanity Fair*—still leaving space, as George Saintsbury reflected wistfully, for another novel to fill the gap between 1714, when *Esmond* ends, and 1755, when *The Virginians* begins. The chronological shifting is not unlike the progress within a single novel. At one point in *Vanity Fair* Thackeray explains, "Our history is destined in this chapter to go backwards and forwards in a very irresolute manner seemingly, and having conducted our story to to-morrow presently, we shall immediately again have occasion to step back to yesterday, so that the whole of the tale may get a hearing." "The whole of the tale" involves the reasons for this or that event, or attitude, or decision, and the reasons are to be found in the past. Chapter Fifty-two in *Pendennis* is called "Which accounts perhaps for Chapter Fifty-one," and it predictably reverses the chronology. This is a recurrent strategy. It is Thackeray's habit to be constantly accounting for things, to be finding the seeds of the present in the past. . . . A man is not himself merely, at a given age; he is his own youth, childhood, infancy, an accumulation of his bygone experience; more—he is his forebears and their values and allegiances, even if only to the extent that he is determined not to be like them. . . .

Thackeray, more than the other writers of the period, addresses himself to the very question of the relation of the present to the past. If he knew that experience is burning with a hard and gem-like flame, he also knew that the flame lives off something, and that to deny the past is as absurd as for the flame to reject the candle. Thackeray reminds us that, both personally and culturally, we are what we have been; that the past, though past, is always latent in the present.

Juliet McMaster
in *The Victorian Experience*, ed. Richard A. Levine
(Athens: Ohio Univ. Pr., 1976), pp. 49, 51–52, 86

ANTHONY TROLLOPE

1815–1882

In the theory of fiction this is a time of revolution: old orthodoxies and not-so-old orthodoxies are being thrown over, and there is much casting about for new criteria. Jamesian formalism has been frontally attacked by more than one operative, while symbolist interpreters are often finding themselves hoist on their own petards. A new kind of talk is heard, with a strange new vocabulary, "characters," "the sense of life"—"nature," even—as we search about for ways to support our approval of novels the old criticism could not defend. We have always known they were good, writers such as Tolstoi and Trollope, but it has been hard to say why.

One sector of the revolution concerns *style* in the novel. Philip Rahv, in a general manifesto, has asserted that the old orthodoxy fails because it tests fiction by the criteria of poetry, having deduced a "prosaics" from a poetics. One of the resultant errors, he says, is to consider "style as an essential activity of fiction." He makes an example of John Crowe Ransom "proving" that Jane Austen is a greater novelist than Tolstoi, on the basis of little snippets from each. One may sympathize with the problem of Ransom and the others: it is desirable to argue from an exhibit, and one cannot quote a whole novel. One can be more precise about sentences than about a panorama of life in three volumes. But Rahv's objection is valid. . . .

Novelists do not typically use words as poets do. The poem, asserts Rahv, is organized according to the structure of language, while the novel is organized according to the structure of the reality portrayed. This is why, he declares, the novel translates so well. . . .

Analyses of Trollope's style have, I believe, established its qualities. And I think it very significant that these three critics have concertedly overthrown the old *stylism* that Philip Rahv deplores. The plain, dull, flat style, the no-style style, has been declared to be a positive artistic advantage; in refusing to draw attention to itself it can the better display the reality of the content. I think we can now build on this achievement. We can now interest ourselves in what [David] Aitkin calls "the freight of moral implication," what [Geoffrey] Tillotson calls the "mastering of complexity," and what [Hugh Sykes] Davies calls "veering irony." However excellent the style is, it is still only the vehicle; in fiction, the medium is *not* the message. Let us turn to what Trollope calls "the wares he takes to market," or what Rahv calls "the structure of the reality portrayed." Let us try to understand the *translatable* virtues of this *translatable* genre.

Ruth apRoberts
The Victorian Newsletter (Spring, 1969), pp. 10–11, 13

OSCAR WILDE

1856–1900

In *The Unrecorded Life of Oscar Wilde* [1972] Rupert Croft-Cooke wishes not so much to present new materials concerning Wilde's life as to read available materials accurately and to identify many of the misconceptions and fabrications, most of which he traces to early biographers such as Robert Sherard and Frank Harris, that have been made part of the Wilde story. To achieve his end, Croft-Cooke relies largely on Wilde's letters, especially as they have been edited by Rupert Hart-Davis, and approaches his subject with worldly common sense rather than elaborate research and complex argument. . . .

[Martin] Fido's brief life [*Oscar Wilde*, 1974] as he himself acknowledges, has benefited from recent work on Wilde, including Croft-Cooke's biography. He is sympathetic to Wilde, though not uncritical, and he makes some intelligent observations. However, Fido's view that *hubris* is a central idea in understanding Wilde's personality does not take us very far, for the idea of *hubris* does not explain with sufficient psychological validity why Wilde needed to pose for the world at large as "haughty, supercilious, contemptuous, and indifferent to the feelings of mankind" (p. 8), while being extremely considerate and generous in his private life.

Christopher Nassaar's *Into the Demon Universe* [1974] explores the work that Wilde wrote from 1886 on, work that Nassaar believes makes Wilde the literary equal of major Victorian writers. . . .

Nassaar's strength lies in his refusal to sentimentalize Wilde. . . . In addition, he makes some illuminating connections between works by Wilde and works by nineteenth-century writers with whom Wilde is not ordinarily associated, such as Blake, Carlyle, and Hawthorne. Yet this study might have been more successful if it had been less schematic in some respects and more fully developed in others. Nassaar rightly argues in his interpretations of individual works that they pertain to the various artistic and intellectual movements of the nineteenth century, but he is much too rigid in the way in which he makes characters, events, and objects represent decadence, Ruskinian morality, Pre-Raphaelitism, and so forth.

That Wilde should have delighted in presenting the demon universe as triumphant in *Salome* and then cheerfully reverted to a prior, affirmative vision in *An Ideal Husband* and made light of the demon universe in *The Importance of Being Earnest* calls for an exploration of the reasons for this reaction. . . . Was it, after all, impossible for Wilde to sustain one point of view, or to find some way of reconciling opposed visions of life? If so, wasn't this ultimately a failure of art and intellect that makes Nassaar's evaluation of Wilde as one of the major Victorian writers questionable? . . .

One . . . realizes that despite the valuable work done in recent years on Wilde's life and writings there remains to be solved by both literary critics and biographers the central problem posed by Wilde: to come to terms with an artist whose works are deeply pervaded by his kaleidoscopic sense of all the different selves he wishes and needs to be.

John J. Pappas
Victorian Studies (December, 1974), pp. 243–44

AMERICAN LITERATURE

Ray C. Longtin, editor

LOUISA MAY ALCOTT

1832–1888

The fact that Louisa May Alcott—"The Children's Friend"—let down her literary hair and wrote blood-and-thunder thrillers in secret is in itself a disconcerting if titillating shock to readers in search of consistency. Like Dr. Johnson's dog that stood upon its hind legs, it is *per se* remarkable. Equally remarkable is the story of their discovery, an intriguing byway in literary detection. Most remarkable of all perhaps is the fact that these gory, gruesome novelettes—written anonymously or pseudonymously for the most part—were and still are extremely good: well paced, suspenseful, skillfully executed, and peopled with characters of flesh and blood. . . .

Her own anger at an unjust world she transformed into the anger of her heroines, who made of it a powerful weapon with which to challenge fate. The psychological insights of [her pseudonym] A. M. Barnard disclose the darker side of the character of Louisa May Alcott, and so her stories must appeal enormously to all who have been enthralled by the life and work of the author of *Little Women*. Since those same psychological insights reveal her as intensely modern, intensely if obliquely feminist, her stories must command an immediate response today.

Madeleine Stern
Introd., in *Behind a Mask: The Unknown Thrillers of Louisa May Alcott* (New York: William Morrow, 1975), pp. vii, xxviii

AMBROSE BIERCE

1842–1913?

Ambrose Bierce never acknowledged—and, in fact, explicitly denied—that error could be tolerated. But he was, of necessity, a writer for newspapers and popular magazines, and was confined by the conventions of literary journalism to forms which were familiar to his audience. Thus, at the heart of his work is a deep, unmediated conflict between his urge to attack, to utterly destroy the object of his humor, and the assumptions of the forms available to him, that wit should function as a gentle corrective of error. While his tone is always exacerbated and personal, defending the integrity of the head and assailing the excesses of the heart, the comic forms which he perforce used allowed for the heart's folly or the head's defeats. This is to say that there is a conflict in Bierce's work between attitudes which should produce wit and forms which must offer humor. "Nearly all Americans are humorous," he said; "if any are born witty heaven help them to emigrate! . . . Humor is tolerant, tender; its ridicule caresses. Wit stabs, begs pardon—and turns the weapon in the wound."

This conflict creates the primary tension in Bierce's style: the war between, on the one hand, his language—a language so savage that it is almost out of control, in which invective leads to vituperation and vituperation to frenzy; and, on the other hand, the forms he employs, whose tendency is to blunt, to efface, and to tolerate weakness. Indeed, the inert geniality of his forms becomes, itself, a prod which drives his diction to still greater fury, his images into more grotesque deformations. At times, he is willing, almost impelled, to allow his language to destroy the very forms which seek to hold them in check. For this reason, Bierce was never able to work in long forms. He hated the novel, and spoke of the work of Howells and James as "the offspring of mental incapacity wet-nursed by a conspiracy." But Bierce was incapable of controlling his language in the long, loose novel form. Even his longest stories are seldom more than a few pages, and his *Fantastic Fables* usually but a few lines long. All of his work is held together by the will, which knows that any opportunity for disruption, any flaw in the iron control, any lapse in logic, will allow the savage power of his language to break through the walls of form for a rampage of vituperative devastation.

Jay Martin
in *The Comic Imagination in American Literature*,
ed. Louis D. Rubin, Jr. (New Brunswick, N.J.:
Rutgers Univ. Pr., 1973), pp. 200–201

CHARLES BROCKDEN BROWN

1771–1810

Charles Brockden Brown may be called . . . a novelist of ideas, for all of his books reveal an intense intellectuality that must also have characterized the man. It is a mistake, however, to consider him closely akin to those novelists of ideas who flourished in England at the close of the eighteenth century. To a large extent, men like William Godwin, with whom Brown is often compared, were propagandists for their views, and David Lee Clark, a biographer of Brown, has made the mistake of assuming that Brown was the same. Nothing could be further from the truth. Brown's mind was a questioning one that could not be satisfied with too simple a view of man and society. Rather, he saw the human being as a marvelously complex creature who does not always know the springs that motivate his actions, and he developed his characters in terms of symbols that reveal their inner states. For this reason, some modern critics read Brown in Freudian terms. There is no question, of course, that Brown, like Hawthorne and Melville, saw deeply into the human mind and penetrated to areas that he himself may not have fully understood. But rather than read a twentieth-century psychology back into Brown, it is better, perhaps, simply to explore what he did in terms of the fictional means he had at his disposal.

Brown, after all, is a novelist and must be judged not so much in terms of the views he holds as the literary means he employs to give them expression. As an American writing fiction at the close of the eighteenth century, he had available to him only a handful of fictional forms, and of these only three were at all suited to his artistic ends: the sentimental romance, the Gothic tale, and the novel of purpose. Brown wrote in all three forms, but in each he included some elements from the others in such a way as to make classification of his novels difficult. Thus, although *Wieland* may surely be called a Gothic romance because of the mysterious events and episodes of terror it contains, it can also be seen, as Fred Lewis Pattee suggests in the introduction to his edition of *Wieland*, as a sentimental tale of seduction in the Richardson sense. If *Ormond* is in its basic structure just such a tale of seduction, it contains as well a number of Gothic incidents and strongly resembles too the novel of purpose. This is only to say, however, that Charles Brockden Brown was an individual artist who took the materials that came to him from the contemporary literary scene and shaped them to serve his own artistic ends.

Donald A. Ringe
in *Major Writers of Early American Literature*,
ed. Everett Emerson (Madison: Univ. Wisconsin Pr., 1972),
pp. 275–76

[Brown's] major novels are, indeed, characterized by a dark vision, by a world of terror, of "confusion, complication, misfortune and calamity" [William Hedges], but whereas this darkness may at first seem to stem from some malign external power, intelligence, or order, the ultimate locus of malignity is placed squarely in man and his society. In this Brown seems less like Edwards, Hawthorne, Melville, and Poe, with whom he is usually associated, than the darkness itself would suggest. Despite the emphasis on various kinds of compulsive behavior and despite the obviously catastrophic events surrounding them, Brown's characters seem less driven, less victims of fate than do so many of the figures in the works of America's other dark fictionists. In the plagues, the mountain lions, the shipwrecks, the bizarre coincidences, the dementia of Wieland, Clithero, and Edgar there is little of the human compelling force felt in Edward's God, Hawthorne's Satan, Melville's whale, Poe's maelstrom, or even Dreiser's Spencerian laws of nature.

A more natural comparison may be with William Dean Howells in *The Rise of Silas Lapham*, in which Silas' economic fall is felt to be the result of a melange of events, motives, and characters, to be a product of his own doing and of others, and in which at the end the moral meaning of all that has happened (except that Silas is a better man) remains a mystery. Thus, such a comparison, which might also be made with other late nineteenth-century writers—even James—who are concerned with society *and* morals, suggests precisely where the emphasis lies in Brown's work. He is certainly interested in psychology, including mysterious, subconscious forces, and there are many inexplicable vicissitudes in external events. But, what produces the moral blank is a rather close set of interpersonal involvements—for example, Carwin with the group at Mettingen, Craig and Ormond with Constantia, Clithero, Wiatte, Mrs. Lorimer, and Sarsefield with Edgar, Welbeck and the Hadwin group with Arthur—that come to represent the interactions of society in general. Society as it is embodied in institutions and mores is an important part of these novels, but it is society as it is embodied in interactions of central characters that I think is key.

John Cleman
EAL (Fall, 1975), p. 217

WILLIAM CULLEN BRYANT

1794–1878

Charles H. Brown, *William Cullen Bryant* (1971)

More than as a poet and editor, a defender of personal freedom, a fighter against corruption, a supporter of art, music, and literature, Bryant in the eyes of his contemporaries was the exemplar of the noble man. Almost every tribute—in the pulpit, in the press, in the resolutions of organizations—recognized that he was a man of character. The poet Edmund Clarence Stedman summed up this feeling of the country toward Bryant in an assessment of his life two days after his death: "He grew to be not only a citizen, journalist, thinker, poet, but the beautiful, serene, majestic ideal of a good and venerable man."

Charles H. Brown
William Cullen Bryant (New York: Scribners, 1971), p. 4

If his experiments were metrically successful, they often do not carry with them a corresponding weight of intellectual or emotional conviction. His sonnets, odes, and Spenserian stanzas satisfactorily solve their formal problems, but the results frequently are empty intellectual exercises. As for his use of the language and imagery of nature, he never fully realized the possibilities of the symbolic quality of language; his verses are never "organic." . . .

Still, we should accept Bryant for his strengths rather than criticize him for what he could not become. As an accurate observer of the flora and fauna of his own New England he remains unsurpassed and without precedent. . . .

Donald Barlow Stauffer
A Short History of American Poetry (New York: E. P. Dutton, 1974), p. 84

GEORGE WASHINGTON CABLE

1844–1925

Louis D. Rubin, Jr., *George W. Cable: The Life and Times of a Southern Heretic*, 1969

Cable has been underrated. Impressive novels and stories, important in the development of Southern and American fiction and full of unique insight into Southern and American experience, well worth reading in their own right as fiction, have gone unread and unappreciated. Of this there can be no doubt. Yet on the remorseless and absolute scale by which works of literature are tested and weighed, it must be said that Cable was a failure. He was and is a minor writer, important more for what he sought to do than for how well he did it. He wrote about the South and its people, white and black, as no one before him had ever done; he opened up areas of experience that had hitherto been ignored, exposed problems and attitudes that no one before him had been willing or able to delineate, including several that remain of compelling urgency in our own time. Some of the things he sought to reveal have yet to be better shown. Yet his artistry was inferior to his intentions, and his fiction, as fiction, never fulfilled the promise that it seemed to hold. . . .

Not until the 1950's did many people begin to read George W. Cable's work again. It was then, when the centennial of the Civil War in which Cable had fought as a Confederate cavalryman was drawing near, and the long-dormant conscience of the nation had at last awakened to the unfinished business of that war, that a Louisiana writer's remarks many decades ago about the Negro and what was being done to deprive him of the civil rights supposedly guaranteed him by the Constitution of the United States began to be remembered. Just as he had predicted in his last novel, the race issue had come round again, and with it a writer long out of fashion had come back into notice. Those who read his essays on the Negro question discovered that there was scarcely a single argument now being advanced against racial injustice that had not been made by Cable sixty years earlier. And with the scrutiny of his novels and stories that resulted, critics began to realize that long ago, in the heyday of the Genteel Tradition, there had been a Southern writer who alone in his time had broken through the trappings of local color and costume romance and sought to depict his native region in the rich daylight of reality. What William Faulkner, Thomas Wolfe, Robert Penn Warren, and the other writers of the twentieth-century South made into literary art of national and even international importance, George Washington Cable had, however imperfectly, first sketched.

Louis D. Rubin, Jr.
George W. Cable: The Life and Times of a Southern Heretic
(New York: Pegasus, 1969), pp. 274, 276–77

CHARLES W. CHESNUTT

1858–1932

Born June 20 in Cleveland, Ohio, he pursued a varied career as a teacher, newspaperman, and lawyer, becoming finally known as the "first Negro novelist." His early stories, collected in *The Conjure Woman* (1899), appeared to be an imitation of the Uncle Remus stories, but recent critics have found a sophisticated treatment of racial stereotypes in these tales. Dissatisfied with the results of this approach to racial problems, he turned to realistic portrayals of race prejudice in such works as *The Wife of His Youth and Other Stories of the Color Line* (1899); *The Marrow of Tradition* (1901) and *The Colonel's Dream* (1905). In 1928, he received the Spingarn gold medal award for his depiction of the struggles of the American Negro. He died November 15. An upsurge of serious critical interest in his work has occurred during the late 1960s and 1970s.

No standard edition of his works

J. Noel Heermance, *Charles W. Chesnutt: America's First Great Black Novelist* (1974)

Chesnutt's novels are not quite as well done as his short stories and occasionally seem forced or unreal, but each has the vitality that comes from honest grappling with life. . . .

Chesnutt's more ambitious works are too full of propaganda to be ultimately satisfying. One constantly feels that if he could do so well he could have done better. At the same time he always knew what he was about; his main plots are well in hand; and his work as a whole shows notable advance. In 1928 he was awarded the Spingarn Medal for his "pioneer work as a literary artist depicting the life and struggle of Americans of Negro descent."

Benjamin Brawley
The Negro Genius (New York: Dodd, Mead, 1937),
pp. 149, 151

Though it was generally known that Chesnutt was a Negro after the publication of *The Wife of His Youth* in 1899, he nevertheless continued to write occasional stories that gave no indication of his color. The satirical gem, "Baxter's Procustes," is the best known of these. But after a series of stories and novels dealing with the Negro and the color line and its problems, most of Chesnutt's objective stories seem forced and unnatural, wan and vigorless, mere water colors. For sheer accomplishment in work of this kind he never surpassed *The Conjure Woman*, and none of his later stories ever equaled the folk tale "The Gray Wolf's Ha'nt," that dark and cruel tragedy of jealousy and love. Nearly all the stories of this first collection are tragic with the fatal consequences of human actions and prejudices. It is not the weak pseudo-tragedy of propaganda, it is not pathos and tears in which Chesnutt deals—it is the fundamental stuff of life translated into the folk terms of a people who knew true tragedy.

Chesnutt's first volume proved two important points. It proved that the Negro could be made the subject of serious esthetic treatment without the interference of propaganda; and it proved that the Negro creative artist could submerge himself objectively in his material. It must not be thought, however, that the tradition of buffoonery was broken by *The Conjure Woman*. The buffoon had two faces. He grinned and danced and capered as a minstrel Sambo and in the stories of certain popular authors, while Joel Chandler Harris saw the other face, the blandly kind and childish smile, the improvident generosity and loyalty. But he was still a Negro, lazy, ignorant, dependent. Both faces showed him as a woefully inferior being, and that was the very core of the tradition. Like a Jewish actor in pre-Christian Rome, he might be the instrument of tragedy, but he was never tragic. Beneath the mask there grinned the Negro. . . .

Though in *The Marrow of Tradition* Chesnutt went as far back as [William Wells Brown's] *Clotelle* in mood and treatment, in his other works he brought Negro creative literature much further along. His early career was a great artistic success, for he did the one thing needful to the American Negro writer: he worked dangerous, habit-ridden material with passive calm and fearlessness. Considering more than the emotional factors that lay behind the American race problem, he exposed the Negro to critical analysis. Had he written a quarter of a century later his art would have gone far to solidify the frothy interest in the Negro aroused by [Carl Van Vechten's] *Nigger Heaven*, [Ronald Firbank's] *Prancing Nigger*, [DuBose Heyward's] *Porgy*, and the musical shows of Lew Leslie. No less can be said of him than has been already implied: he is the most solid representative of prose fiction that the Negro could boast before the 1920's and even now his work in its kind has not been equaled.

J. Saunders Redding
To Make a Poet Black (Chapel Hill:
Univ. North Carolina Pr., 1939), pp. 68–69, 76

[Chesnutt] indeed does deserve the honorable label of "Southern writer." I believe that he fits that label in terms of his biography, his concerns, his intentions, the things which influenced and motivated him most, his subject matter, and his writings themselves, especially his five books of fiction, and among them especially his three novels. Chesnutt was not a major writer, but why has he not been claimed by the South along with the many even less illustrious Southern writers who have been claimed, including some with fewer reasons to be called Southern than his? There are probably many answers to that question, but among them must certainly be his race and the realistic boldness of most of his subject matter in the eyes of much of the South, despite the benevolent intentions behind it. At any rate, the fact remains that he has been so ignored, except for an occasional inclusion here and there, and then usually only as one whose conjure stories show some North Carolina folklore and local-color—never with emphasis on his novels or whole career.

I have not put my emphasis on Chesnutt the leader in a national cause, the realistic writer per se, the outstanding American citizen, the delightful human being, all of which the record shows him to have been; but I have emphasized Chesnutt the Southern writer, which the record also shows him to have been. I believe that he was a Southern writer in the best sense of that term—one concerned for the South, and not one merely exploiting it. In that regard I know of the works of no other author which Chesnutt's works remind me of more than those of William Faulkner—not in quality, breadth of scope, or method, but in intention, concern, and boldness of theme. There is cause to, and we should, claim Chesnutt as a Southern writer—not to limit him, but to understand him even better. With welcome, we should allow him to come home again, to the South (which really fostered him), and to come not just for an occasional visit, but to stay.

Julian D. Mason, Jr.
MissQ (Spring, 1967), pp. 88–89

Chesnutt aimed to modify white minds to feel the equality of the black man, and with the conjure tales he developed a perfect vehicle for his artistic needs. Chesnutt's genius shows in the certainty of touch involved in the choice of Uncle Julius as his central character. Choosing a character so close to widely current pejorative stereotypes was a stroke as significant as [Richard] Wright's choice of Bigger Thomas, for only by confronting and thus destroying the stereotypes could the black artist hope to alter the public mind. Further, Uncle Julius resolves for Chesnutt the black artist's problem of creating a black character in a situation in which significant dramatic incident is possible. To demonstrate the equality of blacks and whites, a black character must be presented in dramatic conflict with whites in a situation which allows the black not only to survive but to succeed with dignity. . . .

The conjure story provided a subtle instrument which could portray with a terrifying accuracy and clarity the functioning of American racial life, but it offered no imaginative way out for either author or audience. The lesson of the white narrator—that whites are too blind to perceive the truth about race—may have suggested to Chestnutt that it was not enough to show race relations in action but that what was needed was an art which would outline explicitly the white misconceptions about blacks and the forces responsible for their formation and perpetuation. In any event, Chesnutt's concern shifted from working a subtle goopher on white minds to attacking specific social problems and clearly laying bare the mechanics and consequences of racism, and the conjure story ceased to be a useful vehicle. After *The Conjure Woman* was published Chestnutt gave full attention to the realistic fiction he had been working with throughout the 1890's.

If Americans were too blind for subtle methods, they were no more amenable to direct confrontation. White Americans would not allow themselves to perceive life from a black perspective, and Chesnutt's turn from the complex art of the conjure story was unavailing. Realism did give Chesnutt room to explore additional dimensions of racial life in America, but the ultimate irony is that his realistic fiction never achieved sharper insights than those of "Mars Jeems's Nightmare" and the early conjure stories, while losing their balance, control, and clarity. It is through the marvelously subtle conjure fiction, which transcends the nightmare of American racism in a near-tragic, near-comic lyricism, that Chesnutt works his most powerful goopher.

Richard E. Baldwin
AL (November, 1971), pp. 386, 397–98

As we come to see Chesnutt in perspective now, it becomes clear that his literary greatness lies on several different levels. He was, of course, the first Black author of profound and diversified short stories: from Southern conjure tales to Northern "Blue Vein" satire. He was also the first Black writer of significantly artistic novels, and was the first to be nationally acclaimed for his artistic craftsmanship. On his highest level, moreover, he partook of the eternal, cosmic artist: the Platonic searcher after Truth and Beauty and individual human dignity. More than a mere protester, more than a literary technician, Chesnutt was a craftsman and prophet combined. It is on this level that his artistic greatness ultimately lies.

At the same time, Chesnutt was no Greek god of flawless marble, as he is often portrayed; no literary Christ-figure of complete altruism and dedication to a social cause, who was finally crucified by the boorish rabble. Rather, he was a very human man, as well as a great social crusader and literary artist. Indeed, we have seen how he originally aspired to be an author largely because it was the easiest and quickest pathway in 1880 for fame and wealth in this country. For Chesnutt was human and American, and he early aspired to all the comfort, leisure, and independence that this country has symbolized to its people ever since Ben Franklin cradled those two clumsy loaves of bread under his arms and marched into Philadelphia on his way to London, Paris, and the hundred dollar bill.

Furthermore, not only were Chesnutt's early motives mixed in regard to his literary career, but his early feelings were equally mixed when it came to defining his "self" in social terms. Basically, Chesnutt did not think of himself as a Black man or Black writer. Instead, he dwelt in a double no-man's land: first, that of light skin color and "free issue" parentage, which made him too "uppity" for most local Blacks and too "dark" for the local whites; and second, that of a sensitive, intellectual nature, which set him off from every one in the nineteenth-century South, both Black and white. Hence he saw himself originally as a lonely isolattoe with no allegiance to any group or anything other than the strongly divergent artist-materialist drives within him and the higher Truths he saw around—and above—him.

What marks Chesnutt's greatness and interest then—in addition to his tremendous abilities as a writer and his profound, sensitive feeling for people—is the fact that he became a major artist, and saw the greatness in himself most clearly, when he found a cause far larger than himself to believe in and work for; and this ultimate sense of commitment in a man is, of course, crucial. His realization of himself as a committed social spokesman and crusader was not, somehow, what we would call a basically "racial" commitment. Rather, the "cosmic" Chesnutt saw the problems of discrimination, insensitivity, hatred, and violence on a higher, moral, universally human level—which is, ultimately, where the power of all great writers finally lies.

J. Noel Heermance
Charles W. Chestnutt: America's First Great Black Novelist
(Hamden, Conn.: Archon, 1974), pp. 236–37

KATE CHOPIN

1851–1904

Born Kate O'Flaherty, February 8, in St. Louis, she married a Creole businessman and spent several years moving among Creole circles in New Orleans and on a Louisiana plantation. Upon her husband's death in 1882 she returned to St. Louis, where she began writing children's tales and stories based on her New Orleans experiences. She gradually won recognition in national magazines for her local-color stories, collected in *Bayou Folk* (1894) and *A Night in Acadie* (1897). Her novel *At Fault* (1890) began to explore problems of marital relations, a theme that was extended in her powerful novel, *The Awakening* (1899). The frankness with which she explored feminine sexuality in this work aroused a storm of criticism and effectively ended her literary career. She died several years later, on August 22. In the 1960s and 1970s, with the growth of the feminist movement, there has been a revival of interest in her work and she has received serious critical attention.

Per Seyersted, ed., *The Complete Works of Kate Chopin* (1969), 2 vols.

Per Seyersted, *Kate Chopin: A Critical Biography* (1969)

Though she believed Cable's stories gave false impressions Kate Chopin never wrote anything deliberately to correct his work. Her short stories have added to the stock of our literature's artistic riches by their quality of vision and insight; they are sharply unique, with a particular subtlety all their own. Her fiction is more than an evocation of Creole and Acadian life. . . .

[Her works] describe not merely a special locality or a unique region, a forgotten village here and there, a segment of humanity off the beaten track, but also the spiritual forces which have created the humanity described and portrayed—faith and deeply rooted constancy, habits that accrue with passing generations, and custom that is as natural as life itself. With the exquisite restraint, gracious clarity of vision, and artistic force diffused throughout her work Kate Chopin's art attains the rank which is denied to even highly talented writers—the art of genius.

Her contributions to American letters should not be ignored. To consider that Kate Chopin may be forgotton is more remarkable than pleasing.

Donald S. Rankin
Kate Chopin and Her Creole Stories (Philadelphia: Univ. Pennsylvania Pr., 1932), p. 188

[Kate Chopin's] present literary rank is probably somewhere between Octave Thanet (Alice French) and Sarah Orne Jewett. In the fifty years after her death, she has provoked two articles and a doctoral dissertation on her life and work. Her own books are long out of print, and *The Awakening* is particularly hard to find. Their disappearance is not unusual; it is inevitable that much of a minor writer's work will be lost. What is unfortunate is that *The Awakening*, certainly Mrs. Chopin's best work, has been neglected almost from its publication.

The claim of the book upon the reader's attention is simple. It is a first-rate novel. The justification for urging its importance is that we have few enough novels of its stature. One could add that it is advanced in theme and technique over the novels of its day, and that it anticipates in many respects the modern novel. It could be claimed that it adds to American fiction an example of what Gide called the *roman pur*, a kind of novel not characteristic of American writing. One could offer the book as evidence that the regional writer can go beyond the limitations of regional material. But these matters aside, what recommends the novel is its general excellence.

Quite frankly, the book is about sex. Not only is it about sex, but the very texture of the writing is sensuous, if not sensual, from the first to the last. Even as late as 1932, Chopin's biographer, Daniel Rankin, seemed somewhat shocked by it. He paid his respects to the artistic excellence of the book, but he was troubled by "that insistent query—*cui bono*?" He called the novel "exotic in setting, morbid in theme, erotic in motivation." One questions the accuracy of these terms, and even more the moral disapproval implied in their usage. One regrets that Mr. Rankin did not emphasize that the book was amazingly honest, perceptive and moving. . . .

How Mrs. Chopin managed to create in ten years the substantial body of work she achieved is no less a mystery than the excellence of *The Awakening* itself. But, having added to American literature a novel uncommon in its kind as in its excellence, she deserves not to be forgotten. *The Awakening* deserves to be restored and to be given its place among novels worthy of preservation.

Kenneth Eble
WHR (Summer, 1956), pp. 262–63, 269

The Awakening was the most important piece of fiction about the sexual life of a woman written to date in America, and the first fully to face the fact that marriage, whether in point of fact it closed the range of a woman's sexual experiences or not, was but an episode in her continuous growth. It did not attack the institution of the family, but it rejected the family as the automatic equivalent of feminine self-fulfillment, and on the very eve of the twentieth century it raised the question of what woman was to do with the freedom she struggled toward. The Creole woman's acceptance of maternity as totally adequate to the capacities of her nature carried with it the complements of a fierce chastity, a frankness of speech on sexual matters, a mature ease among men, and a frank and unguilty pleasure in sensual indulgence. But this was not, ultimately, Edna Pontellier's birthright, and she knew it. She was an American woman, raised in the Protestant mistrust of the senses and in the detestation of sexual desire as the root of evil. As a result, the hidden act came for her to be equivalent to the hidden and true self, once her nature awakened in the open surroundings of Creole Louisiana. The new century was to provide just such an awakening for countless American women, and *The Awakening* spoke of painful times ahead on the road to fulfillment.

Kate Chopin sympathized with Edna, but she did not pity her. She rendered her story with a detachment akin to Flaubert's. . . . Edna Pontellier is trapped between her illusions and the conditions which society arbitrarily establishes to maintain itself, and she is made to pay. Whether girls should be educated free of illusions, if possible, whether society should change the conditions it imposes on women, or whether both are needed, the author does not say; the novel is about what happend to Edna Pontellier. . . .

In her own city of St. Louis the libraries refused to circulate the book, and the Fine Arts Club denied her membership because of it. Kate Chopin was not merely rejected; she was insulted. "She was broken-hearted," her son Felix said, and in the remaining five years of her life she produced only a few pieces, although her friends insisted that she still had a great deal to say.

Kate Chopin, a wise and worldly woman, had refined the craft of fiction in the nineties to the point where it could face her strong inner theme of the female rebellion and see it through to a superb creative work. *The Awakening* was also an awakening of the deepest powers in its author, but, like

Edna Pontellier, Kate Chopin learned that her society would not tolerate her questionings. Her tortured silence as the new century arrived was a loss to American letters of the order of the untimely deaths of Crane and Norris. She was alive when the twentieth century began, but she had been struck mute by a society fearful in the face of an uncertain dawn.

Larzer Ziff
The American 1890's: Life and Times of a Lost Generation
(New York: Viking, 1966), pp. 304–5

Mrs. Chopin had the vision, the originality and independence, and the sense of artistic form which are needed to give us the great novel. She also had remarkable courage. She hid her ambition and her goal somewhat, knowing that men do not readily accept what Mme. de Staël had called "superiority" in a progressive woman. But she was unable to keep her inclinations in check, and the tensions she felt between Paul [in "An Idle Fellow"] and Paula [in "Wiser than God"], between the dictates of the Biblical male and the urges of the female artist, resulted in unheard of illustrations of woman's spiritual and sensuous self-assertion. No wonder that she was shipwrecked, like another Margaret Fuller, with her cargo of iconoclastic views.

The great achievement of Kate Chopin was that she broke new ground in American literature. She was the first woman writer in her country to accept passion as a legitimate subject for serious, outspoken fiction. Revolting against tradition and authority; with a daring which we can hardly fathom today; with an uncompromising honesty and no trace of sensationalism, she undertook to give the unsparing truth about woman's submerged life. She was something of a pioneer in the amoral treatment of sexuality, of divorce, and of woman's urge for an existential authenticity. She is in many respects a modern writer, particularly in her awareness of the complexities of truth and the complications of freedom. With no desire to reform, but only to understand; with the clear conscience of the rebel, yet unembittered by society's massive lack of understanding, she arrived at her culminating achievements, *The Awakening* and "The Storm."

From "The Poor Girl" to her last novel she was praised for her artistry, but criticized for her subject matter. She obviously does not come near the breadth and stature of Dreiser, but among the American authors of second rank she occupies an important and distinctive position. In her best writings within her particular field, she not only equals Dreiser's courage, but shows an independence, a directness of purpose, a deep understanding, and a sensitive artistry which make them into minor masterpieces. With *The Awakening* and a handful of her stories, such as "Regret," "Athénaïse," and "The Storm," she deserves to be permanently included, not only in her country's literary history, but also in its body of living fiction.

Per Seyersted
Kate Chopin: A Critical Biography (Baton Rouge: Louisiana State Univ. Pr., 1969), pp. 198–99

[Kate Chopin] was feminine to the core, a wife, a mother, and a protester. But she was too complete a human being to be activist. Those who in her time were called bluestockings bored her: they chattered about books and rights and responsibilities. They formed themselves into organizations like that one in St. Louis in which T. S. Eliot's mother was a leader, which would "create and maintain an organized center . . . to promote the usefulness of its members" by, among other things, seeking out jobs for women and helping young girls who were in trouble because of misadventures with men. Mrs. Chopin resigned from that group after one year. The liberation she sought was only incidentally and symbolically sexual. That was something here to stay. It stood for and emphasized differences at the same time that it pointed toward one experience that men and women could share, in ecstasy leading toward joy or distress.

What she required was freedom of spirit: what was life but "a dash of love-light,/Some dreams and a touch of pain"? People were destined "To love a little then to die!/To live a little and never know why!" What sustained her was her comic sense, her winsome scepticism, her riotously nimble insight. Neither male nor female has sole right to the domain which she explored with humor and compassion. Truth rests, she said, "upon a shifting basis and is apt to be kaleidoscopic." There was a twinkle in her words which guaranteed that the nouns could as well be interchanged, one for the other, when she wrote that "women forever will whine and cry/And men forever must listen—and sigh."

Lewis Leary
SLJ (Fall, 1970), pp. 142–43

Had Kate Chopin lived to see the gradual relaxation of the prohibition of sexual themes in the next century, had her contemporary critics been more acute, or had her audience been more receptive to her explorations of feminine sexuality and psychology, there is no predicting what direction her talent might have taken. It is difficult to imagine a better novel from her pen than *The Awakening*, a better story than "The Storm," but the pattern of steady development during her brief career suggests that she would have improved upon even those performances. That she was not encouraged to undertake the task and that she died prematurely before belated encouragement might have been forthcoming in the form of national recognition, as it was, for instance, for the aging Dreiser, are facts to be lamented.

But it is seldom profitable to speculate on what might have been, particularly where so much wealth abounds. During the space of one remarkable decade, Kate Chopin permanently enriched American literature by the addition of two novels and almost one hundred short stories, together with occasional poems and pieces of criticism. One of those novels and at least a dozen of the stories rank high in the annals of American literature, even when judged by critical standards which they were not consciously built to meet. Nothing more could be asked of the woman who began by adopting Natchitoches Parish and New Orleans as her heart's home and the Creoles and Acadians as her people.

Robert Arner
Louisiana Studies (Spring, 1975), p. 139

It is difficult today to see why *The Awakening* was viewed as "shocking" in 1899. The woman's movement had been launched in 1848 at the Seneca Falls convention. Margaret Fuller's *Woman in the Nineteenth Century* had been published five years before that. The Shakers, the free lovers at Oneida, the Mormon polygamists and the intellectuals at New Harmony, Brook Farm and Modern Times had attempted to undermine the traditional family structure a half-century earlier, and Edward Bellamy's *Looking Backward*, which would revolutionize both the social and economic structures, assuming as a matter of course equality between the sexes, had been met a decade earlier not with shock, but with acclaim. Victoria Woodhull had come upon the stage as a "live" new woman in the 1870's and published her own newspaper, run her own brokerage office, advocated free love as well as women's rights from public platforms across the country, appeared before Congress and had even twice run for President of the United States. Not only that, but Edna Pontellier, in *The Awakening*, does not find an answer; like Zenobia [in Hawthorne's *Blithedale Romance*] a half-century earlier, she commits suicide. Her suicide, however, is different from Zenobia's. And Hawthorne's portrayal of sexuality is different from Chopin's—not because the end of the century was a more propitious time to write about sexuality and experiment with nontraditional sexual relationships between men and women. Hawthorne portrays Zenobia as a deviant; she is very unlike the ideal maiden whom Coverdale finally confesses he loves. Edna Pontellier is a respected member of society who awakens to herself as a sexual being. She has a real sexual identity, and her awareness of that identity is not damning, as is Zenobia's . . . it is an awakening. . . .

Edna's is not a noble death. The tone of that scene is set by the first word: "despondency." It is reinforced by such words as "antagonists," "slavery," "broken" and finally "exhaustion." It is a return to the womb of the sea, a return to the freedom of the blue-grass meadow, a choice to be a free child rather than a tortured mother-woman. Edna chooses to die because it is the one, the ultimate act of free will open to her through which she can elude those who would drag her down. In becoming one with the sea she is free. She has achieved a kind of rebirth. Edna Pontellier is not a tragic heroine; she is not a fairy-tale princess. She is a woman, a real woman living in a world which has no place for her.

Judith Fryer
The Faces of Eve: Women in the Nineteenth-Century American Novel (Oxford: Oxford Univ. Pr., 1976), pp. 206–7, 256–57

JAMES FENIMORE COOPER

1789–1851

Cooper retains stature despite literary imperfections so evident that they scarcely need rehearsing. He never found a form wholly adequate to portray his vision either of the glory or the downfall of his American dream. Nor, among all of Cooper's volumes, is there one that may be accounted among the greatest achievements of American literature. Filling out thirty-two novels to a prescribed length of five hundred pages had inevitable consequences: turgid prose, repetition, formlessness, cheap plotting, and lengthy stretches of empty words.

And yet Melville was right to insist that Cooper "possessed not the slightest weaknesses but those which are only noticeable as the almost infallible indices of pervading greatness." Cooper's achievement should ultimately be measured, not by post-Jamesian standards of novelistic art, but by the significance and integrity of his career as an American man of letters. To follow the development of his works is to experience an honest and significant conflict between political ideals and social preconceptions neither of which the author was willing to abandon. Cooper recognized that the responsibility for republican leadership should devolve upon men of principle, culture, and education. He also recognized that the egalitarian implications of democratic ideology would gradually deprive the republic of the men most qualified to guide it. Believing in the justice of a republican polity, Cooper feared that its helplessness before demagoguery would spell the end of the individual liberties by which republicanism was defined.

Like Tocqueville, Cooper understood the tendency of the American people to extend the meaning of equality from equality of political right into equality of condition. The anger that mars Cooper's later works is the artistic price exacted by his desire to clarify the distinction. In the heyday of Jacksonian democracy, Cooper insisted that a republican polity must maintain full equality of political rights without depriving society and government of those citizens, superior in merit, principle, and influence, who were necessary to sustain disinterested republican justice. Cooper had the moral courage necessary to argue publicly that a republic that cannot combine political equality with inequality of condition was doomed to failure.

John P. McWilliams
Political Justice in a Republic: James Fenimore Cooper's America
(Berkeley: Univ. California Pr., 1972), pp. 401–2

It is clear . . . that the career and myth of Natty Bumppo—and by implication, the career of his mythic ancestor, [John] Filson's [Daniel] Boone —has something to offer to civilized man, a set of values which is a result of long experience in the American wilderness. Supreme among these values is that of reverence for all life, which in Deerslayer's religion lies at the basis of all moral action. More significant is the fact that this value is derived from experience rather than from theory, for Deerslayer points out on a number of occasions his complete ignorance of the Bible. Moreover, the experience from which this basic principle has been derived is one that includes strife and violence, cruelty and hardship, loneliness and exile.

Innocence, in the idiom of the Boone-Bumppo myth, is the prerequisite for deriving moral value from the wilderness ordeal; and this innocence consists in a completely receptive, open state of mind, a naïveté and absence of preconception in one's approach to experience. Moral truth emerges only when the hero totally immerses himself in his wilderness environment, forgetting (however briefly) his other ties and even his concepts of the differences between man and god. Through this trusting immersion he discovers truths about himself and his world that were hitherto hidden to him; his discriminations are now more just, less the result of habit. In solitude and isolation his acts of war and hunting awaken him to his kinship with creation, to a sense of reality and of religious and social duty. His heart is cleansed of evil impulses, and his reason is clarified, strengthened, more dominant over his passions. This concept of the central drama of human experience is repeated throughout American literature and American culture, in the pietistic concept of conversion and the literary method of the Indian-war-personal-narrative tradition, as well as in Thoreau's experiment at Walden Pond and Whitman's journey through the jungle of "Myself." It is, at the same time, one of the universal themes of human literature.

Richard Slotkin
Regeneration through Violence (Middletown, Conn.:
Wesleyan Univ. Pr., 1973), pp. 506–7

Realizing, in the first novel of the [Leatherstocking] series, that the human social community, in its various forms, could not maintain a pastoral harmony, Cooper turned, instead, to the single individual—Natty Bumppo. But the precarious balance of independent, masculine activity and passive acceptance of nature's bounty proved impossible, and, with *The Prairie*, Cooper has Natty at first acknowledging his own complicity in the violation of nature's recesses and then disburdening himself of his guilt, in death. The fantasy of total gratification led, inevitably, to the spectre of incest, and that, Cooper realized, could not be permitted. It lasted but a few paragraphs in *The Deerslayer* before he pulled Natty back from manhood to sonhood. Only as son can he maintain the nondestructive, nonexploitive harmony he seeks; but the price, as Cooper tacitly acknowledged, is his adult sexuality and with it, much of what we know as civilized norms. Natty can never experience adult human relations within the social community; the pastoral impulse has led him back into the liquid embrace of nature's womb.

Just how aware Cooper was of the psychological substratum behind his vocabulary and landscape descriptions is open to debate; what cannot be dismissed, however, is the dramatic change in vocabulary that occurs in *The Deerslayer* and, before that, the psychological accuracy of the dream sequences and the labeling of Natty as "infantine" and "childlike" in *The Pathfinder*. Though initially Cooper was probably largely unaware of his character's scope and implications, he pursued his study of Natty until, gradually, he was able to make of "the pastoral design" in America what Leo Marx has called "a symbolic structure of thought and feeling, a landscape of mind in which the movement in physical space corresponds to a movement in consciousness." For, infantile and presexual as he is, Natty Bumppo remains, in many ways, an embodiment of The American Dream. A pastoral landscape still seems to beckon to us, calling us into state parks and our children to summer camps, urging us to withdraw from the current and go back to an initial moment of perfect peace, absolute harmony, and freedom from want, within a feminine and wholly gratifying natural world.

Annette Kolodny
The Lay of the Land: Metaphor as Experience and History in American Life and Letters (Chapel Hill: Univ. North Carolina Pr., 1975), pp. 114–15

The past [Cooper] allows us to reexperience is not only our own but also the nation's. The German critic Schiller wisely expanded the definition of pastoral beyond all specific literary forms and identified it as a state of mind, one which he said was universal: "All people who possess a history have a paradise, a state of innocence, a golden age; indeed, every human being has his paradise, his golden age, which he remembers with enthusiasm to the degree that he possesses something of the poetical in his nature." Cooper charges the nation's golden age with the reverie of his own remembered childhood and thereby accomplishes a vital intersection of public and private worlds. It is in this way that he created America's youth and made available to us what D. H. Lawrence called "the myth of America." . . .

Cooper gives to the American pastoral a quality of permanence. He thereby secures an ideal essential to our culture, a culture whose destiny is predicated on the possibilities of life in nature. Readers of all generations since Cooper's have undoubtedly found this ideal in his books, but for our own time he offers a particularly poignant aspect of the usable past. For if the American pastoral had been eroded by the second half of the nineteenth century, then surely it has been almost lost for us. Today, more than ever, we feel the need to be inspired by a timeless vision of simplicity and childhood wonder. As our own environment becomes increasingly threatened by spoliation and as our own "difficulty" becomes more acute, we can turn to Cooper to recover, perhaps to cultivate for the first time, a sense of the pastoral.

Daniel H. Peck
A World by Itself: The Pastoral Moment in Cooper's Fiction
(New Haven, Conn.: Yale Univ. Pr., 1977), pp. 189–90

STEPHEN CRANE

1871–1900

The Works of Stephen Crane, Univ. Pr. Virginia (in progress)

Crane's world is reality as he perceived it, externally amoral matter subject to chance upheavals of purposeless violence and therefore ultimately unknowable and forever beyond man's complete control; the mere fact that human life has to be lived in such a world places full responsibility for all moral values upon man alone, and thus the separation between the physical world and man's moral world is absolute. This perception . . . underlies everything Crane wrote. . . .

Crane's protagonists, from Uncle Jake to Timothy Lean, have freedom of the will to choose their own commitments from whatever alternatives their awareness of the particular situations they confront makes available to them. . . . Because Crane's adult characters possess this freedom they are without exception—honest or dishonest, aware or innocent—held morally responsible for whatever choices their actions imply that they have made; and the best people in this world, those who are both honest and aware of the human situation that man has to accept, also hold themselves personally responsible for their own shortcomings even if such weaknesses are unperceived or misunderstood by other men. And because the precarious human situation in the moral desert is at best difficult, no man escapes moral responsibility by simply doing nothing: failure to act in this situation is in itself an action freely chosen, and it is morally condemned. . . . Because the separation between man's moral world and external nature is absolute, Crane's characters are morally never subject to externality: human desires and intentions have to be carried out in the external world, and the ultimate success or failure of any human action is therefore contingent upon externals, but the moral value inherent in the choice of the action is not determined by externality. Morally, Crane's physically puny man is able to stand against the mountains and prevail.

Marston La France
A Reading of Stephen Crane
(Oxford: Clarendon, 1971), pp. 243–44

Throughout Crane's career—and increasingly after "The Open Boat"—he asserted in his writing an awareness of the risible yet maddening incoherence of the universe and man's need to apprehend and to understand it, of man's loss of role and his search for place and reason. It is this awareness, and not Crane's "naturalism" which best characterizes his vision.

For everywhere opposing this absurdity is a pressure for order, a pressure for apprehension and for understanding. The pressure is apparent from the very beginning in Crane's style, in his early painterly renderings, later in his dramatization of characters' emotions through the use of his impressionistic techniques, at the end in his increased use of vividly and intensely rendered expressionistic images. It is apparent also in Crane's early experiment in formalization of emotional response to color and in his later efforts at the composition of colors in nature. And it is apparent in his efforts at syntactic patterning, in his rhythmic arrangements, and in his verbal repetitions and refrains.

The pressure is also apparent in Crane's complex ironic relationships to his subjects. His irony was intense—so intense that it generates tonal discordances which damage, sometimes irreparably, certain of his works—and it was only in the final years that he gained a consistent control over that irony. But its object was always clear; Crane directed his irony at self-delusion, at the too easy acceptance of facile or self-serving explanations of reality—in short at refusals to see. . . .

It is pressure to see which remains the characteristic phenomenon of Steven Crane's prose writing. And the identification of the nature and the consequences of that pressure thus becomes one key, one means of access, to the central vision of this most available and at the same time this most obscure of the writers of his time. It is not only Crane's awareness of man's impulse to "walk barefoot into reality," but it is also his central vision of that reality and the intensity of the pressure that opposed it, which makes Stephen Crane one of the most intensely modern of the American writers of his century.

Milne Holton
Cylinder of Vision: The Fiction and Journalistic Writing of Stephen Crane (Baton Rouge: Louisiana State Univ. Pr., 1972), pp. 284–85

To apprehend how Crane effects [an] alteration of perspective and its subsequent—if only momentary—alteration of sensibility is to move close to that distinguishing habit of imagination which informs his best work. His virtue as a writer lies in the full attention given to the scene or mood at hand, no matter how it relates to common conceptions of experience. His is an effort to treat seriously and significantly every selected detail until that detail, or the scene of which it is a part, blossoms into a thing strange and new, often at the expense of a larger design or even of the dominant subject. He writes until one of those "short, terse epigrams struck off in the heat of composition," or a turn of phrase, or a surrealistic image, or even a striking word within a sentence, produces the desired aura of strangeness necessary to bend the reader's angle of vision. The reader now looks upon reality metamorphosed, a world in which tents can spring up "like strange plants" and campfires can dot the night "like red, peculiar blossoms." For Crane the "real thing" often seems not to be somewhere awaiting his discovery but rather a creation of his imagination, wrenched into existence. . . . It is this aspect of Crane's artistry that seems most often to astonish us into a search for words to describe his peculiar authority as a writer.

Frank Bergson
Stephen Crane's Artistry (New York: Columbia Univ. Pr., 1975), pp. x–xi

EMILY DICKINSON

1830–1886

[Emily Dickinson's] debt to her mother is of incalculable magnitude. For it is beyond question that Mrs. Dickinson unwittingly provided her daughter with the conditions necessary for the development of her peculiar gifts. Without such a mother Emily Dickinson could not have become the poet we know. It was Mrs. Dickinson's failure as a sufficiently loving and admirable developmental model that set in motion the series of psychological upheavals which were unmitigated misfortunes for Emily Dickinson *the woman.* These maturational impasses consigned her to a life of sexual bewilderment, anxiety, and frustration by impairing those processes of psychic growth which would have made the roles of wife and mother possible. With reference to Emily Dickinson *the artist*, one cannot speak of misfortunes at all. For, amazing as it may seem, Mrs. Dickinson's inadequacies, the sequence of internal conflicts to which they gave rise, and the final psychotic breakdowns all conspired in a unique way to make of Emily Dickinson a great and prolific poet.

John Cody
After Great Pain: The Inner Life of Emily Dickinson
(Cambridge, Mass.: Harvard Univ. Pr., 1971), pp. 484–85

"The Ear is the last Face. We hear after we see. Which to tell you first is still my Dismay." This is Emily Dickinson's statement to Thomas Wentworth Higginson. It is at the center of her poetic manifesto, which she incorporated at artful random into her letters to the man she acknowledged as her literary preceptor. . . . Since the material of verse begins with the written word, the poet's task of "shifting" that material necessarily involves bridging the gap between the written language and its life source, the spoken language. The marks of punctuation normally serve as one such bridge, symbolizing, in part at least, certain rhetorical patterns of speech. But for projective purposes of many twentieth-century poets (e. e. cummings serves as a particularly good example) the conventional system of punctuation has proved inadequate and has been supplemented by a strategic use of typography. A century ago such strategy would have been impossible for the poet composing in longhand. But for Emily Dickinson, whose concern with projection was equally as strong as that of any poet today, the standard elocutionary symbols of her day provided a means of accomplishing much the same purpose. . . .

Emily Dickinson's system employs some of the symbols of the nineteenth-century elocutionists and displays a good deal of the contemporary linguists' understanding of speech characteristics. But it is not meant to direct actual speech or to describe it scientifically, for it is essentially a poetic device, to be understood in those terms. In a sense her notations work upon the mind's ear in much the same way a poetic image works upon the mind's eye. Normally the image creates an impression of actual experience by attempting to define its essence in terms of a particular part. It does not describe the total experience because, of course, it could not. Working with and within the lines they punctuate, Emily Dickinson's notations register upon the mind's ear only those vocal intonations which are essential to define or particularize the tone of the lines. They are, then, not directions or descriptions of voice, but *impressions* of voice.

Edith Wylder
The Last Face: Emily Dickinson's Manuscripts
(Albuquerque: Univ. New Mexico Pr., 1971), pp. 1–2, 5

[A] number of stock notions should [be] laid to rest or so qualified as to lose the insistence they have often had in accounts of Emily Dickinson: that Amherst was no place for a poet to be born in; that she was the lone star in a colorless and insignificant family; that her home was either a prison to her spirit or, at the other extreme, a cozy retreat irradiated (after July 1, 1856) by the attentions of a loving confidante; that she lived apart from the passions and bitterness that plague the rest of humanity and, not knowing such things firsthand, made them up for the purposes of poetry; that a love tragedy is the only way of explaining her withdrawal from society . . . that she spent her day "meditating majestically among her flowers."

On the contrary, what should be emerging is a perceptive, critical, self-propelling person working hard in the midst of a busy town and busy family and taking the measure of both.

Richard B. Sewall
The Life of Emily Dickinson, Vol. I (New York:
Farrar, Straus & Giroux, 1974), pp. 235–36

JONATHAN EDWARDS

1703–1758

Edwards has created, in our modern term, a myth of reasonableness, and it is this that gives to his arguments the air of impeccable demonstration. Thus logic is poetry; it provides conclusive proofs, because it has also the power to suggest the world of which its proofs are true. Such an achievement is possible only to a writer of great genius. In reading Edwards we may disagree with his premises, we may protest against his conclusions, but we have to grant that that is the way he saw things. Even as we question the doctrine, we accept the vision.

It is as symbolist and student of symbolism that Edwards most clearly anticipates later American literature. He opens to the reader's mind the inspiriting possibility of an experience in which, as Emerson would write, "the world shall be to us an open book, and every form significant of its hidden life and final cause." Edwards' thought manifests the Puritan source of transcendentalism, and the relation between them is nowhere more apparent than in their common tendency to describe human error as a failure of perception. To the transcendentalists sin is inattention, a state of dullness, sluggishness, sleep. It is the failure to be aware of the symbolic meaning of things, and it is wrong as a refusal of life because it is a turning away from the deity that experience reveals. It is, in short, the condition of unresponsiveness which Edwards attributes to the unregenerate man.

But while the transcendentalists assume that anyone can rub his eyes, in Edwards' view the light of understanding is not given to all. This difference points to a more fundamental one between Edwards' theology and transcendentalism. In Edwards monism is balanced by dualism, as two sides of a true account, but in transcendentalist thought dualism is the difficulty to be overcome, the false appearance which in the highest states of consciousness is resolved by a vision of absolute unity. Thus to Emerson symbol is revelation: we may see God in the object if we try hard enough; while to Edwards symbols are but "Images or Shadows of Divine Things," and our power to see them is mysteriously given by a transcendent God, if given at all. Unlike Emerson, Edwards balances two views of symbol. He regards the symbol as continuous with its meaning, as Emerson argues, but he also regards it as markedly distinct. Edwards' healthy respect for the commonsense view of symbols as mere signs pointing to objects other than themselves follows from the fact that in his view meanings refer to a God entirely separate from the universe as well as immanent.

John F. Lynen
The Design of the Present: Essays on Time and Form in American Literature (New Haven, Conn.: Yale Univ. Pr., 1969), pp. 116–17

Whatever their content . . . [Edwards'] images are arranged in such a way as to deny the efficacy of human powers and the desirability of worldly goods. Complementing this process of denial is a cumulative emphasis on divine power and control. "Human wisdom," once held "in great repute," was diminished by the gospels; earthly princes are always powerless compared to God; and, in the most famous of the sermons, all mankind is emotionally reduced to the helplessness of an insect dangled on a thread; in his last sermon, earthly inheritances and earthly wealth are reduced from being comfortless to appearing actually dangerous in light of God's intended inheritance for his Saints. The threat of God's unleashed wrath or the horror of the imminent pit projects an anxious urgency; the listener at once desires and needs the salvation promised by the theology.

Understood in this context, the sermons reveal an intense awareness of the precariousness of Christian salvation and a deeply-felt obligation to make this insecurity obvious and meaningful to those who came to hear them. Doctrine and logical persuasion alone might not do the trick; Edwards was confronted with the challenge of making God manifest to "the common sort of people." For those "less used to much reasoning," he argued, "God commonly works this conviction by begetting in their minds a dreadful idea and notion of the punishment."

But, whether through threat or invitation, the result is essentially the same: the listener has either been frightened into religious awareness or else been presented, gently, with the futility of any other course.

The power of the sermons, however, lies not so much in the abstract theology as in the stylistic devices through which it has been experienced; and the images, as Perry Miller pointed out in "The Rhetoric of Sensation," effectively translate the mystery of the unknown and abstract to the accessible borders of immediate emotional experience. What we have typically, in each of Edwards' sermons, is an aggregate of images, contrasting, adding to, or alluding to one another in such a way as to *force* the listener to go through very specific and analyzable emotional responses.

Annette Kolodny
EAL (Fall, 1972), p. 181

[Edwards'] writings were an expression of the whole self, consisting of "knowing, esteeming, loving, rejoicing in, and praising God." The self should not remain merely passive, merely the recipient of light, but must actively participate in it through the use of the understanding and will: "A main difference between the intelligent and moral parts, and the rest of the world, lies in this, that the former are capable of knowing their creator, and the end for which he made them, and capable of actively complying with his design in their creation and promoting it; while other creatures cannot promote the design of their creation, only passively and eventually." In the "Dissertation" Edwards actively completes the circle wherein God first communicates externally His "internal glory to created understandings" and then, in turn, the recipient expresses himself, relating his "high esteem of God, love to God, and complacence and joy in God." Through his works Edwards contributes to mankind's upward ascent toward the Creator. In completing the circle he asserts his selfhood, a sense of selfhood now truly defined with regard to the reality of the divine Self. Devout expression—mental (thought), spoken (word), written (deed) in response to the divine communication evident in Scripture, the self, history, and nature—constitutes the true end of the regenerate self. Such devotion becomes the self's highest end, the only appropriate response to the "immediate communication between the Creator and [man,] this highest of creatures according to the order of being," just as "that nature in a tree, by which it puts forth buds, shoots out branches, and brings forth leaves and fruits, is a disposition that terminates in its own complete self." When it is aligned to the divine Will, when it actively participates in the ascent of all creation, the self possesses identity; in fact it then *is* indeed a self.

Whereas *Freedom of the Will* and *Original Sin* may be read as efforts to reduce man's illusion of free will and self-sufficiency, the "Dissertation" celebrates the discovery of genuine selfhood. God, to be sure, remains the alpha and omega of existence, the ultimate cause and effect. He "is the first author of their being and motion, so he is the last end." But the individual self of the saint does not suffocate within this boundary. Rather, it thrives because this larger dimension of expanded familial rings of meaning frees the self from the imprisoning constriction of subjective delusion. It is, as "The Justice of God in the Damnation of Sinners" makes clear, the wicked who are choked within the ring of perverse selfhood and who, paradoxically, find themselves outside the circle of God's city. Equally paradoxical is the fact that as his context of selfhood expands, the saint discerns God to be not only the outermost circle but also the inmost center of everything, especially of the self. Thus the saint is freed from himself—and this signifies an important distinction between Edwards' notion of the self and that of the antinomians—in order that he may discover who he truly is.

William J. Scheick
The Writings of Jonathan Edwards: Theme, Motif, and Style
(College Station: Texas A & M Univ. Pr., 1975), pp. 138–39

RALPH WALDO EMERSON

1803–1882

The Collected Works of Ralph Waldo Emerson, Harvard Univ. Pr. (in progress)

[Emerson] had perhaps the most seminal mind we have ever produced in this country. He believed that the development of the human soul was the ultimate end; that whatever stood in the way of the development and expression of that soul is vicious, however venerable or even sacred it may appear; and that unless life can be lived spontaneously and fully and gladly, there is no hope for the future of the world. It is not enough that God spoke to Moses; He must speak to me and to you. It is not enough that Shakespeare and Michelangelo created great art; you and I must create it also, and if we cannot do this ourselves, we must recognize its value in those of our contemporaries who can. . . .

He was a spiritual man, not because he despised the senses but because he wished to live a complete life. To his way of thinking, asceticism was not a satisfactory alternative to indulgence; both were bad. Any single fact, taken by itself, misleads; the libertine and St. Simeon Stylites were equally revolting to him. We were not made to breathe pure oxygen or to talk in blank verse or even to be always wise. The perfect man knew both poetry and mathematics, joined a hunger for beauty with a high devotional spirit, loved justice and produced beautiful manners. Our daily prayer should be to accord just measure to all that the universe contains. . . . Hence Emerson's ideal man was not pure spirit, but a balance between spirit and matter, reason and understanding.

Edward Wagenknecht
Ralph Waldo Emerson: Portrait of a Balanced Soul
(New York: Oxford Univ. Pr., 1974), pp. 225–27

Both in his Transcendental and in his Necessitarian phases, Emerson doesn't worry about ending in solipsism; he is only too happy to reach the transparency of solipsism whenever he can. He is very much Wittgenstein's Schopenhauerian solipsist who knows he is right in what he *means*, and who knows also that he is in error in what he *says*. The solipsism of Emerson's Transcendentalism issues finally in the supra-realism of the Necessitarianism of his last great book, the magnificent *The Conduct of Life*. Dialectical thinking in Emerson does not attempt to bring us back to the world of things and of other selves, but only to a world of language, and so its purpose is never to *negate* what is directly before us.

From a European perspective, probably, Emersonian thinking is not so much dialectical as it is plain crazy, and I suspect that even Blake would have judged Emerson to be asserting that "without negations there is no progression," a negation being for Blake opposed to a genuinely dialectical contrary. Yet Nietzsche, who could tolerate so few of his own contemporaries, delighted in Emerson, and seems to have understood Emerson very well. And I think Nietzsche particularly understood that Emerson had come to prophesy not a de-centering, as Nietzsche had, and as [Jacques] Derrida and [Paul] de Man are brilliantly accomplishing, but a peculiarly American *re-centering*, and with it an American mode of interpretation, one that we have begun—but only begun—to develop, from Whitman and [Charles S.] Peirce down to Stevens and Kenneth Burke; a mode that *is* intra-textual, but that stubbornly remains logocentric, and that still follows Emerson in valorizing eloquence, the inspired voice, *over* the scene of writing. Emerson, who said he unsettled all questions, first put literature into question for us, and now survives to question our questioners.

Harold Bloom
A Map of Misreading (New York:
Oxford Univ. Pr., 1975), p. 176

Emerson may not have fully practiced what he preached, but his importance lies in the fact that he did state the principles and begin the experiments. He stands, nervous and self-conscious in the role, as our teetotaling Bacchus, our New England and ministerial Pan. Moreover, his experiments were only a departure, heralding Whitman's free verse, Pound's and Williams' innovations with speech rhythms and breath units, E. E. Cummings' refashioning of syntax and punctuation and typography, Charles Olson's "projective verse" and Denise Levertov's organic form, the long lines and cumulative periods of Robinson Jeffers, William Everson and Allen Ginsberg. . . . Most of these poets came to view the poet as a special seer and all of them as a special perceiver. Their various explorations of ongoing form and emergent structure were grounded in the organic yet—in one way or another—transcendent process of nature. Along with other poets akin in inclination they comprise a distinct, perhaps distinctive, strain in the American poetic tradition. And Emerson is their source, more than some of them knew or wished to acknowledge and more than Emerson himself could have foreseen.

Albert Gelpi
The Tenth Muse (Cambridge, Mass.: Harvard Univ. Pr., 1975), p. 91

Community, friendship, love, grief, tragedy—these are all effectively absent from or effectively distorted in Emerson's vision, and together they encompass no insignificant slice of human experience. To admit that on these subjects Emerson really had nothing significant to say to us is certainly severely to qualify any claim that may be made for his greatness as a poet. But I suppose we do not demand of any poet, any artist, that he be equally strong on all subjects. Grant Emerson his subjects—especially the gods alone, with him alone—and he may still seem one of our major poets, despite his severe limitations, though not, in my opinion, what Frost would have him, our best. I call him "major" because, judging by Auden's twofold test, I find that he wrote a sufficiently large number of poems in distinguished verse and many beautiful prose-poems that "say something significant about a reality common to us all, but perceived from a unique perspective." What he said about the subjects on which he could think and feel and imagine well had "never been said before," to use Auden's words, partly because, as Santayana believed, they had never been said as well, partly because, to return to Auden, they convey perceptions gained from a unique perspective.

Though Emerson the poet could write well on many subjects, including the evils of politics and trade, he wrote best on what was closest to his heart, seeking out the traces in experience of the fugitive gods, to return to the words of Heidegger. . . . When he wrote on this subject in any of its aspects, affirmative as "Merlin" is, reflective as "Monadnoc" is, or cautionary as "The Titmouse" is, he often wrote strong, wholly memorable poems that say what had never been said before and that no poet had said better since. For him, staying on the track of the fugitive gods might require deflating humanism, as he does in "Limits" and "Water," or mocking the understanding, as he does in "Brahma," or reminding man of his mortality, as he does in "Hamatreya."

Hyatt H. Waggoner
Emerson as Poet (Princeton, N.J.: Princeton Univ. Pr., 1975), pp. 200–201

BENJAMIN FRANKLIN

1706–1790

The paradoxes which make Franklin so difficult to understand have their source in his manner of imagining the thinker's circumstances with reference to two standards—the limits of the thinker's view, on the one hand, and the rational orderliness of the reality of which it is a view, on the other. One must confront this ultimate fiction—this picture of the self—and thus it is Franklin the artist who matters most to those who would understand Franklin the historical personage. . . .

It is perhaps the greatest paradox of a paradoxical life that Franklin succeeded so well in his art that he has commonly been judged as if he were no artist at all. His critics, with a few rare and recent exceptions, have proceeded as if they were dealing with the real man, the historical figure. But if it is asked how they know of this personage, the answer is through the imaginative self-image he presents in the *Autobiography*. Much additional evidence is to be found in his other writings, of course, but such is the power of this book that there is no way to avoid interpreting the rest in the light of it, and even its omissions are, by the motives they suggest, almost as influential as the facts it includes. That we cannot avoid taking the Franklin we see in the *Autobiography* as the actual man is the surest proof of his literary achievement. As process is principle seen from within time, the process of Franklin's self-interpretation points toward the principle of his identity. We know Franklin as a way of seeing, but so coherent is the vision and so convincing the drama of its development that we feel we know the man himself. And which of us would say this opinion is false?

John F. Lynen
The Design of the Present: Essays on Time and Form in American Literature (New Haven, Conn.: Yale Univ. Pr., 1969), pp. 126–27, 148–49

Franklin spoke effectively from behind several masks. In "A Parable against Persecution" he so adroitly used a biblical style that some readers mistook his words for Scripture. When describing his experiments or inventions, he was straightforward and plain, whether the subject was an arrangement of balloons strapped about his shoulders to take weight off his gouty feet or a device by which short men might remove books or packages from a high shelf. His letters—on official business, to scientific associates, in friendly discourse, or of admonition and advice—were models, each of its kind. The inexhaustible energy, curiosity, and kindness of this multiple man are nowhere better revealed than in these letters which allow glimpses behind the familiar mask of doughty Ben Franklin to the intelligence and artistry that molded its features so well.

Like many men who glimpse truths which they find it wisest not directly to express, Franklin often spoke most effectively in banter. The indirection of humor could provide a defense against responsibility. Franklin's was the comic view—the world a stage, each man a player, often ridiculous, especially when he reached beyond what he could touch. Literature was of value when useful, but was at best an avocation. Writing that searched beneath or above levels of common sense was to be expected only of women, or perhaps of men too sickly for manly competition, or of clergymen from whom worldliness was not to be expected. Sensible men would use it as a prod or lever or, later, as a way toward wealth. It was often most expedient for them to speak from behind a pseudonymous mask, as Washington Irving and Samuel Clemens would speak.

Under Franklin's aegis, the ventriloquist writer invaded the new world. Humor such as his remained a hedge from behind which many who followed him would exploit the comic view. Dialect would become effective because it identified itself with the plain American, simple and wise, sly and forthright at the same time, himself a kind of comic mask. The cracker box, woodland stump, town meeting and camp meeting, lyceum and Chautauqua, the quiz show and panel discussion, good things all, became forums from which this plain American spoke or oracles to which he listened. He became a sturdy, likable, and dependable fellow, this plain American who is grave but seldom serious, a good man to have around in almost any emergency, just as Franklin was, who invented him.

Lewis Leary
in *The Comic Imagination in American Literature*,
ed. Louis D. Rubin, Jr. (New Brunswick, N.J.:
Rutgers Univ. Pr., 1973), pp. 46–47

PHILIP FRENEAU

1752–1832

Too much must not be made of Freneau. As a talented man he responded to the impulses of his time in the voice of his time, borrowing whatever was found useful in content or form. He argued in verse against the cutting of trees in cities, against the encroachment of commercial wharves; he pled the cause of the Negro, the American Indian, the debtor, the drunkard, and the abused army veteran; he championed Thomas Paine as well as Thomas Jefferson; he joined deistic societies; and he welcomed the writings of Swedenborg and, though cautiously, the advent of unitarianism. Wavering between extremes of passionate involvement and classical restraint, he has been found to be a primitivist sturdily convinced of the values of sympathy and national self-reliance, a patriot endowed with idealistic fervor and generous compassion, a brooding man dogged by personal adversity but serenely stoical in rational acceptance of his world, a humorist whose touch was not always light, a satirist of wide range and sharp-toothed striking power, but above all a lyricist haunted by a sense of the evanescence of beauty and the vacantness of death. To the historical scholar he becomes a convenient and quotable gauge. The convergence in him of familiar ideas and modes of expression render him a useful exemplar of the liberal or humane or democratic or patriotic convictions of an important time. The student of literature recognizes him as a transitional figure, grounded securely in the past and reaching tentatively toward the rewakening of sensibility called romanticism. Read carefully he may be discovered to be a poet who wrote a single poem in a variety of forms.

If Freneau did have but one effective note, and it of sadness at the frail duration of mortality, he sometimes struck that note remarkably well. His legacy may be four poems, or five, or perhaps six: each must make his own count. He was not, I think, "the father of American poetry," for in a strict sense he had no descendants. Poets who came after him looked to other models, and usually from abroad, so that it can be doubted whether the direction of literature in the United States would be in any important respect different without him. But he was there, isolated by war and his own limitations, a victim to his fancy and his fire: "To write was my sad destiny,/The worst of trades, we all agree." As a voice of his time, he shares the fate of time, but as a person who approached a mystery with wonder and stoic resignation he can survive until that mystery is explained.

Lewis Leary
in *Major Writers of Early American Literature*,
ed. Everett Emerson (Madison:
Univ. Wisconsin Pr., 1972), pp. 269–70

Still, for all its limitations, its awkwardnesses, its archaic diction, its proclivities for grandiose, overgeneralized statement, Freneau's poetry exposed that single tension that was to structure so much American literature to follow: the growing disillusionment with the pastoral possibility in conflict with a commitment to maintain that possibility—almost at any cost. And were we to look for a compendium of what constituted the threats to a pastoral America, we would not have to go beyond Freneau; from the first he struggled not only to describe a pastoral landscape appropriate to the New World experience, but, more important still, to delineate what one could or would actually do in the garden. Over and over again, he pitted his own delight in the passivity to be enjoyed within the luxuriously feminine ambiences of tropical islands against the various human urges toward mastery and progress, both political and agricultural, which he saw all around him—conflicts that [William Gilmore] Simms and Cooper would later convert to the uses of fiction. And finally, if reluctantly, he gave the lie to the myth that mankind had been reborn in the New World paradise; not so, declared Freneau, he had simply brought his European corruptions with him and, slowly but surely, was laying waste the garden.

Annette Kolodny
The Lay of the Land: Metaphor as Experience and History in American Life and Letters (Chapel Hill: Univ. North Carolina Pr., 1975), p. 51

Any judgment of Freneau's worth as a littérateur is difficult. He set in train no literary school; if his work influenced any later artists, they did not credit it. What influence his work had was chiefly exerted on his contemporaries and was felt not because of the artistry of the works, but because of their "gadfly" qualities. Today, we can criticize most of his works as imperfect, as somehow defective. We can see where, in this essay or that poem, he excelled himself and achieved art. But other writers have achieved art more consistently than Freneau did; in the history of literature, there are many better essayists and better poets.

But few in the history of American literature have contributed a total body of works so rich and so wide—so much a reflection of the life lived in his age. Freneau shows us the life lived by rich and poor; by stable-boy, slave, and president; by backwoodsman and city dweller. He records the great events of the day as well as the personal tragedies and triumphs. He writes in all the styles of the day, and he also mocks them when they violate his sense of decorum. He reflects the changing attitudes toward religion, and the various theories of the universe. He shows the discoveries of the new science, and he mocks it when it seems to exceed its bounds. Freneau's study is man in all his variety and complexity, and the totality of Freneau's works reflects back to us man's variety. This reflection is Freneau's value for us.

Mary Weatherspoon Bowden
Philip Freneau (Boston: Twayne, 1976), p. 173

MARGARET FULLER

1810–1850

It seems strange that such nineteenth-century middling names as Julia Ward Howe, Louisa May Alcott, Susan B. Anthony, are commonly remembered in the United States, while Margaret Fuller is not. Today she is known only to an intellectual elite—an elite so restricted that it includes few but students of American literature and occasional scholars in the general humanities. Vernon L. Parrington, in his *Main Currents in American Thought*, evaluated the Margaret Fuller matter precisely: "Misunderstood in her own time, caricatured by unfriendly critics, and with significant facts of her life suppressed by her friends by a chivalrous sense of loyalty, the real woman has been lost in a Margaret Fuller myth and later generations have come to under-estimate her powers and undervalue her work. Yet no other woman of her generation in America is so well worth recalling."

In the light of events in the second half of the twentieth century, it must be added that no other American woman of any generation is so well worth recalling—not for her sake, but for ours. Observed Charles A. Madison in *Critics and Crusaders*, "Her great intellectual vigor, her extraordinary generosity of spirit, and above all her passionate criticism of the parochialism and materialism about her, made her the effective leader of those who resented the restraints of their calvinistic environment and sought to enthrone the precious freedoms of civilized man. It is this championing of human rights, this abhorrence of oppression and inequality of any kind, that still endears her name to all lovers of liberty and democracy." . . .

Margaret's earlier rejections of Puritanism and Transcendentalism were of course significant forward steps philosophically; but perhaps the progression from nineteenth-century liberal to nineteenth-century radical was not so great as it might seem. Both, measured by today's brutal realities, were essentially romantic. The liberal was a gradualist; the radical wanted immediate action. Both believed, naïvely, in absolute goodness as an ethical norm, in progress as inevitable, and in "the People" as an abstraction. Yet toward the end of Margaret's European sojourn, she had parted company with romantic radicalism and was beginning to probe for both social and economic understanding. She never ceased to grow.

Joseph Jay Deiss
The Roman Years of Margaret Fuller (New York: Thomas Y. Crowell, 1969), pp. vi–viii

[Margaret Fuller's] espousal of the popular Roman cause is another manifestation of that desire for freedom which motivated her to write *Woman in the Nineteenth Century*. Were she to survey the Women's

Liberation Front today, she would certainly be heartened by the numbers of grass-roots clubs spread throughout the country and by their courage, enthusiasm, and persistence shown. Some advances, however great, might have seemed to her a long time in coming: the Nineteenth Amendment, which granted women the vote, was not passed until 1920; the Civil Rights Act of 1924 required various subsequent measures to secure salaries and opportunities for women equal to those of men. She would doubtless approve the broad reform program of the National Organization for Women in the fields of education, employment, child care centers, law and government. The eighteen thousand membership would certainly impress her, although the individualistic Margaret might find N.O.W. somewhat overorganized. She would, I believe, be gratified by the recent success of the National Women's Political Caucus in securing a greater proportion of women delegates to the National Democratic Convention and in getting the Mormon Jean Westwood elected chairman of the National Democratic Party. Some women like Bella Abzug and Betty Friedan Margaret might censure for choosing the wrong primary goals: "money, notoriety, or the badges of authority which men have appropriated to themselves." Certainly she would favor those who seek to work with rather than against, men. It is hard to imagine her using the term "male chauvinist pig."

Among the great women of our time whose achievement we would expect Margaret to applaud are Eleanor Roosevelt, unofficial world diplomat during her husband's presidency, and in her later years official representative to the United Nations; Clare Boothe Luce, diplomat, writer, and editor; the Negro Judge Juanita Kidd Stout of Philadelphia, who works efficiently with the men on her staff; Katherine Meyer Graham, publisher of *Newsweek* and *The Washington Post*; Dr. Rosa Lee Nemir, Professor of Pediatrics at the NYU School of Medicine; and Mary Bunting, who saw Radcliffe through the protest years and established a program for older women to renew their academic skills. These examples could, of course, be multiplied. Such women have not only surmounted barriers which Margaret found constricting to the sex but also have demonstrated faithfulness to their standards, unselfish service, and a heroism that was a treasured ideal of *Woman in the Nineteenth Century*. If one cannot assume that the twentieth-century woman has won complete emancipation, one can say that enough has been accomplished to justify the faith of that early and outspoken Women's Liberationist, Margaret Fuller Ossoli, in America as the seedbed of liberty for all.

Vivian C. Hopkins
ATQ (Spring, 1973), p. 34

BRET HARTE

1839–1902

Critics who write of Harte ignoring realism's "common vision" or of his "pimping for romanticism," or critics who regard his tales as "Easterns" which perjure the *real* experience of the West, sacrifice truth for a convenient oversimplification. Instead, Bret Harte should be credited with some significant literary accomplishments. Whether or not this one writer founded the local color movement may remain questionable; but it cannot be denied that he contributed a great deal to it. He also contributed to the realistic movement. Harte led the Nineteenth Century reading public into realizing that a well-crafted and moving story about a particular locale was more meaningful than a didactically moralistic or sticky-sweet romantic short story.

Often chided today for a lack of realism, in his own time Harte was frequently considered daringly realistic. . . . For all the sentimentality and disassociation from his subject, Harte wrote well about those local subversive types and their picturesque settings. And it is this aspect of the local color movement that such later authors as Willa Cather, John Steinbeck, William Faulkner and other greats found to be usable in their own writings.

The question still remains of why Harte's brand of local color was so popular in the late 1860's and for a generation thereafter. To me the best guess continues to be that local color arose out of ashes the Civil War left behind. Such primary sources as newspapers, letters, and travel books of the time point to a wide-spread national longing for reconciliation, a questioning of American identity and goals, a retreat to nostalgia and the past in the face of an uncharted and very likely perilous future. There seemed to be a national need for simplification, that pastoral desire to get back to our agrarian roots and rediscover the good and the true American nature. Bret Harte's local color parables provided fiction that was new, refreshing, and reassuring.

Patrick Morrow
WAL (Fall, 1973), pp. 129–30

NATHANIEL HAWTHORNE

1804–1864

The Centenary Edition of the Works of Nathaniel Hawthorne, Ohio State Univ. Pr. (in progress)

The images and symbols that Hawthorne attaches to the *personae* of his mythological tales are closely related to images which define character in his tales of experience. In broad outline, all of these images suggest that Hawthorne thought of two kinds of people; far from exemplifying the Head and Heart division so popular with criticism, his world contained one large and complex group associated with the daylight realm of sunshine, animal energy, and empirical things; and a second, equally complex group associated with the night realm of moonlight, imaginative energy, and spiritual reality. . . .

Stated in abstract terms, Hawthorne's basic myth is a quest to recognize the powers of both the sunlit and moonlit realms of experience, and to use both creatively in the mixed, human realm. Ideally, the cool vision of the night realm "marries" the benign warmth of the empirical world; only then does an individual or a society find its full self, its vision and power—its Heart. This fundamental action or conflict—as in the mythological formulations of Blake and W. B. Yeats—gives shape and coherence to Hawthorne's art. It enables him, moreover, to speak equally (and sometimes simultaneously) of the self, the society, and the artist—of *mythos, ethos,* and *dianoia.*

Hugo McPherson
Hawthorne as Myth-Maker: A Study in Imagination
(Toronto: Univ. Toronto Pr., 1969), pp. 214–16

Hawthorne's esthetic conscience was in direct opposition to his moral conscience. Instead of functioning in accordance with a simplistic set of antitheses it followed the sinuosities of the life process itself, transposed into the dimensions of art. The irreconcilable elements of his life, sources of distress on the everyday level, were made to balance and complement one another in the process of creation. The everyday personality was scattered, fragmented—the creative consciousness, male and female, active and passive, was one.

But this balance was a precarious one. Before long, the conditions that made it possible could no longer be met. As Hawthorne grew older, so he had more and more difficulty in making contact with the Oberon whose fertile imagination enabled him, without effort, to bring him into harmony with himself: a little peace, a little leisure, intense labor upon a page where all the anguish and love of one man's life were concentrated—these were enough to change the dimensions of being and reality, to transport them onto another level where everything was possible. The reign of impossibility began when the writer lost his power to deal with his own incompatible tendencies. Torn apart by his contradictions, Hawthorne tensed, tried to fight them, and was destroyed by them. Moreover, his physical and psychological nature as well as his creative nature had always proceeded by means of successive forward leaps and suddenly imposed halts. Such a rhythm is exhausting both for the physical constitution and for the mind. This would explain the premature wearing out of his athlete's constitution and the even more rapid exhaustion of a fecund talent. Yet that talent, at once powerful and precarious, seeking to consolidate its unstable equilibrium by yoking itself to other and antiesthetic tendencies, only to be finally devoured by them, that talent was nevertheless the living principle thanks to which Hawthorne, however much he may have lamented the fact, enjoyed the privilege of being himself. For the real Hawthorne, the only Hawthorne, was Oberon, the eternally youthful elf, ironic and ardent, tender and cruel, filled with equal wonder and despair by the ambiguity both of his inner self and of the reality he saw before him. It is rare indeed for a being so noble in appearance, and so gifted, to love himself so little, to sacrifice himself so totally to a prosaic double. Who would now remember the member of Brook Farm, the Salem customs inspector, or Consul Hawthorne, if it had not been for Oberon, the poet, the storyteller, the magician?

Jean Normand
Nathaniel Hawthorne: An Approach to an Analysis of Artistic Creation (Cleveland: Case-Western Reserve Univ., 1970), pp. 83–84

Running through all four of [Hawthorne's major] romances is the central dilemma of characters cut off from the main body of mortal men. In each work they must affirm sympathetic ties with the "procession of life," for that is the only sphere in which Hawthorne considers life real. Romantic individualism, for Hawthorne, is a deception—an interesting one perhaps, but still a deception. Hawthorne does not vary his attitude toward the importance of this dilemma. He attacks it from different angles, and he considers differing possibilities of the dilemma, but always it is there at the center of his work. Because he was so clear on the nature of his central dilemma, if not its solution, he could devote a large measure of his creative energy to the development of form.

I have traced a progression of experimentation with form beginning with *The Scarlet Letter* and ending with *The Marble Faun*. The progression does not imply "improvement," for surely all readers agree *The Scarlet Letter* is Hawthorne's masterpiece. It does show, however, the devotion to craft of the artist engaged in finding out the possibilities of his fictional method. It is this kind of devotion to craft that allowed Hawthorne to write *The Scarlet Letter* in the first place, and it is this kind of devotion that produced the other important advances in form we have looked at. Beginning with the raw materials of his era. Hawthorne moved to an astounding formal sophistication.

Toward the end of his career, Hawthorne tried and failed to write four more romances. . . .

The lesson of the failures is instructive because it directs us to the roots of Hawthorne's strength. Primarily he was a creator of forms and textures. Having arrived at a moral dilemma that he could be sure was overwhelmingly important, he was free to experiment with modes for treating the dilemma. He depended both on his sureness of the central conflict and on the stimulation of experimentation with form. Without these he could not go on. The romance theory which he assimilated from the unrealized claims of his contemporaries was uniquely suited to his interest in form. This theory makes the act of creating order one of the highest possible literary acts. Sure of his thematic nexus in his four major romances, Hawthorne devoted himself to the pursuit of form as the means of making life intelligible.

John Caldwell Stubbs
The Pursuit of Form: A Study of Hawthorne and the Romance
(Urbana: Univ. Illinois Pr., 1970), pp. 161, 164

What emerges when we try to analyze the narrative devices with which Hawthorne works is a kind of legerdemain, adroit, yet for the most part not beyond detection, and perhaps not really so greatly involved as some writers on Hawthrone have lately been insisting. But the legerdemain is realized in analysis; it does not intrude itself in ordinary reading. In the best tales the illusion is maintained, and the only requirement we need make of any narrative device or assumption is imaginative success. We are hardly aware of even the repeatedly used devices except in the artificiality of critical analysis; and the reason must be that the even tone and the pattern of the style—its care and calculation induce an acceptance.

But Hawthorne's narrative procedures only partly account for a peculiar quality of his work. Nor does this quality inhere solely in such passages as those commonly used as examples of his ambiguity, although they may serve to point it up. In the last chapter of *The Marble Faun* Hawthorne remarks, "The actual experience of even the most ordinary life is full of events that never explain themselves, either as regards their origin or their tendency." The sentence may have a special application to the romance, but it recognizes a quality which is in much of Hawthorne's fiction, and which (as it seems to me) is more impressively present in the early tales than in the later work. That quality is the realization, not so much of the complexity, as of the opaqueness of experience, a quality we know in our own. There is likely, therefore, to be a residue of mystery in Hawthorne's best tales which good criticism will always leave intact.

Just as in particular tales we must accept a residue of mystery as part of Hawthorne's realization of experience, so we must accept the difficulties in understanding his intention and his estimate of his work . . . He had some ideal, some measure of excellence for himself that his work in its entirety never fulfilled. The excellence he sought is not at all the excellence with which his critics invest him.

Neal Frank Doubleday
Hawthorne's Early Tales: A Critical Study
(Durham, N.C.: Duke Univ. Pr., 1972), pp. 250–51

Hawthorne's tales of the frontier employ the method of the personal narrative in its purest form. The hero's experience is always one of self-discovery and conversion, either from a sinner to a good man or from an innocent to a sinner. Although Hawthorne stresses the social virtues of fellow-love and domesticity, his heroes discover the importance of these values only through the confrontation of their isolated souls with a divine truth or reality. His vision of the wilderness is strongly influenced by that of the Puritans, as well as by the psychological theories of Romanticism. The wilderness is a screen on which the human mind and heart project images of secret guilts and desires. Because the wilderness is outside the realm of social order and convention, these desires become deeds and the dreams realities. True character emerges from the husk of social habit, to reveal the soul as either a white or a blasted ear. . . .

Hawthorne's tales are both critiques of and participation in the Puritan myth of the wilderness. Hawthorne sees that myth as a tale of man's fall and degeneration through the arbitrary grace of given experiences—not . . . as a myth of self-creation and self-renewal through the hunt. The hope of his protagonists is the captive's hope, that his ordeal will expiate his sin. It is not the hope of the hero that his trials will make him a king.

Richard Slotkin
Regeneration through Violence (Middletown, Conn.:
Wesleyan Univ. Pr., 1973), pp. 476–77

I find a controlling preoccupation, throughout all of Hawthorne's career, with defining a way of writing that could embody the imagination and justify it to a skeptical, practical-minded audience. In the greatly prolonged early period (1825–1849) and in the brief major phase (1850–1859), each work or group of works proceeds from this impulse but takes a different route toward fulfillment. As the weaknesses and shortcomings of a formulation manifested themselves in practice, Hawthorne shed it and tried another; or he corrected it; or he revised it.

For the first twenty-five years he worked under the influence of a commonsense attitude about imagination and the artist's place in society; he put forward very modest claims for literature and for himself as a literary man. With *The Scarlet Letter* he broke through to a much more aggressive position, one clearly linked to American and English romanticism; he describes his "conversion" in "The Custom-House." This romantic synthesis functioned throughout the 1850s and enabled him to write his major works; then it began to disintegrate. In his last phase he wavered between a return to earlier modes of conceptualizing and a push on toward another new formulation, literary realism. In the movement from common sense to romanticism to—potentially—realism, Hawthorne epitomized the history of fiction in nineteenth-century America.

Nina Baym
The Shape of Hawthorne's Career (Ithaca, N.Y.: Cornell Univ. Pr., 1976), pp. 8–9

OLIVER WENDELL HOLMES

1809–1894

Holmes did keep youthful and laughing and gay to the end. His humor was in many respects different from that of his contemporaries. It derived more from the jovial spirit of the coffee houses in Augustan England, or of convivial, aristocratic clubmen of any time, or from the epigrammatic wit of Horace at his frolicsome best than from the boisterous American frontier. It played more often on words than on vulgar risibilities. It was often bookishly intellectual. Though genial, it was perhaps at root snobbish, well-dressed, well-mannered, excellently contrived to delight a cultivated mind. He preferred, he said, above all others "the man who inherits family traditions and the cumulative humanities of at least four generations." He was fond beyond almost all besides of good talk, conversations which moved quickly, wittily over a variety of subjects. "What are the great faults of ordinary conversation among us?" he once asked. And he answered himself by explaining that "Want of ideas, want of words, want of manners are the principal ones." But in conversation, he especially disliked contentiouness. "Talking," he explained, "is like playing the harp: there is as much in laying the hand on the strings to stop the vibrations as in twanging them to bring out their music." . . .

So light and bright and good-natured was his humor that he made no enemies. His wit more often travelled delightfully over surfaces than penetrated to depths. His pinwheel mind darted exuberantly, hovering over serious thought as if afraid to alight. It was a native trait perhaps, the kind of comic coloration often taken on in self-defense, the rapier wit which pierces quickly to put an adversary off guard. He is closer to Washington Irving, whom he admired, than to Mark Twain, who puzzled and troubled him. But, if not in the main channel of American humor, Oliver Wendell

Holmes at least bubbles brightly through tributary streams which continue occasionally to refresh. He would, I think, have liked it that way.

Lewis Leary
in *The Comic Imagination in American Literature*,
ed. Louis D. Rubin, Jr. (New Brunswick, N.J.:
Rutgers Univ. Pr., 1973), pp. 123, 126

WILLIAM DEAN HOWELLS

1837–1920

A Selected Edition of William Dean Howells, Indiana Univ. Pr. (in progress)

Kenneth S. Lynn, *William Dean Howells: An American Life* (1971)

Despite the compassion and acceptance advocated in *The Vacation of the Kelwyns*, Howells' fiction does not generally or consistently illustrate the tradition of compassion as does that of Trollope or Hardy. Howells' sense of morality is generally too firm and too obtrusive. Often, as in *A Modern Instance* or *The Landlord at Lion's Head*, the morality fights against an interest in the descriptive presentation of individuals, relationships, and changes in society. Howells' loose ends, too, are less likely to be statements that all the issues of the novel cannot be reconciled, less likely to be admissions that the intellectual framework of the novel is not adequate to express all the issues of the novel, than are those of Trollope or Hardy. Rather, in Howells' a loose end is just that, failure to work the elements of the novel deeply enough. His form is less "open" than unfinished. As a result the fiction conveys a lack of tension, a kind of ease, an ultimate superficiality that is overcome only in *A Hazard of New Fortunes*—in its cohesive brilliance, its articulate point of view, its extensive characterization of a new America.

Howells' fiction contains some of the prerequisites for the fiction of compassion: a willingness to abandon fable or allegory, a questioning of morality, a deep interest in presenting man in combination with others and with his social environment. But the fiction is too much a collection of elements, too often fixed on the very moralities it questions, to belong entirely within the tradition of compassion. At the same time, the direction of Howells' fictional career, the gradual movement away from the firm system of moral judgment in *The Rise of Silas Lapham* to the suspension of judgment in *The Vacation of the Kelwyns*, along with the consistent avoidance of the romance and the consistent interest in human relationships, do point toward the tradition of compassion.

James Gindin
Harvest of a Quiet Eye: The Novel of Compassion
(Bloomington: Indiana Univ. Pr., 1971), pp. 112–13

Howells has suffered a decline in popularity for reasons not too difficult to understand. Many readers, particularly the young, are not really interested in the way Howells approached the issues that generated his art. The romance of money is dead; men who pursue wealth for its own sake are not our avowed culture heroes now; and our millionaires have abandoned conspicuous consumption for anonymity. Portraits of the domestic circle no longer entertain; families are hardly families any longer, in the old sense; and novels of family life, unless they are ethnic portraits of castrated sons, are no longer felt to reveal viable truths in the modern world. The dynamics of social ambition are apparently no longer taken very seriously, and at a time when we are all being adjured to "tune in, turn on, and drop out," the drama of social climbing is an anachronism to many young people. Upward social mobility and the old antagonisms of class are as real as ever. But since the thirties other social issues have concerned us. Accidents of the Zeitgeist thus have a way of seeming to render obsolete the social center of a writer's work.

Howells still deserves to be read, though, and read with affection. For few writers of his time brought to life so vividly the social experience of nineteenth-century America or dramatized so convincingly the problems of middle-class existence in fiction. Howells knew the East and the West, the city and country, the rich and the poor. He knew the range of their manners, their ambitions and values, their style and idiom. And his social awareness, matched by a notable psychological acumen, served him well in that most challenging of all the novelist's tasks—the creation of convincing characters, like Bartley Hubbard, Silas and Persis Lapham, Basil and Isabel March, Squire and Marcia Gaylord. These two preoccupations, character and manners, place his novels at the midpoint between sensibility and social history; they unify in themselves the extremes of self and society.

What makes Howells of particular interest to the student of the novel of manners in America is the considerable art with which he embodied the democratic social assumptions of the developing West in which he grew up. . . .

The fact is that few men of his time were more capable than Howells of representing accurately in fiction the social contradictions that characterized American life in the last quarter of the nineteenth century. He saw the spectacle of simple Westerners like himself thrown up against hypercivilized Boston snobs, of provincial country folk deracinated and struggling to find themselves in the developing cities, of the underworld of the laboring poor, and of the newly rich millionaires trying to crash polite society. He saw, in other words, a broad spectrum of social experience which could be brought into dramatic relief through the medium of the travel narrative and the social novel.

James W. Tuttleton
The Novel of Manners in America (Chapel Hill: Univ. North Carolina Pr., 1972), pp. 86–88

The ideals of realistic fiction which Howells zealously supported in his editorial and public roles were not merely applied at his convenience to his own work. Naturally some "motives" produced weightier, more complex novels than others, but all the work came from the same intelligence and the same sense of responsibility. It came, too, from the knowledge that honest work gives moral satisfaction and spiritual health. His industry in practicing his craft was both a need and a reward, as, he noted on [one] occasion, it should be for all men: "To be past the fear of want, that is an essential condition of happiness; but to be beyond the chance of work, which is the right and the duty of all, is the supreme misery, the very image of perdition."

So Howells worked almost to the end to express in his fiction the value of a "lenient, generous, and liberal life." He was a man whose understanding of human nature made him, in a broad sense, a humorist; whose experience with and reflection on the conditions in which human beings must function made him a meliorist; whose observations of human behavior made him a sceptical rationalist; and whose personal and vicarious experience of suffering and death and catastrophe as well as joy and love and success made him a hopeful agnostic. These attitudes expressed themselves in a fiction which was analytical rather than prescriptive, and which rejected the method and assumptions of satire, romanticism, and tragedy as the controlling principles in the representation of man's condition and fate. In short, this Howells was a realist.

George N. Bennett
The Realism of William Dean Howells: 1889–1920 (Nashville, Tenn.: Vanderbilt Univ. Pr., 1973), p. 249

WASHINGTON IRVING

1783–1859

The Complete Works of Washington Irving, Univ. Wisconsin Pr. (in progress)

In Irving's little narrative ["Rip Van Winkle"] the characteristic form of American fiction can be observed at the point of origin. Looking back from "Rip Van Winkle" or "The Legend of Sleepy Hollow," where the fable is even more elaborately conjured from the landscape, one can recognize the fictional process as an extension of the meditative process, as this is delineated in such a work as Anne Bradstreet's "Contemplations." Mistress Bradstreet finds the meaning of her immediate response to landscape by placing the moment within the predestined scheme of history which is God's will. Irving, by comparing epochs as different states of consciousness, develops a general view of the relations between them. But there is, of course, a great difference between the total history he attempts to formulate and Anne Bradstreet's, a difference which can be recognized by recollecting the change in viewpoint Franklin represents. Franklin well illustrates the transition from the view of history as a fixed and static design made known to man by revelation to the view of history as process. He retains the traditional premise of a total design, but assumes that it cannot be seen as such, since every human view, being one from the inside, is limited and relative to the moment. Thus history as it is known is incomplete, a continuous activity rather than an unchanging design. It is but a step from Franklin to Irving and not so large a stride from Irving to Faulkner, as the realization grows that "what really happened" in any given past moment is an event still to be completed.

John F. Lynen
The Design of the Present: Essays on Time and Form in American Literature (New Haven, Conn.: Yale Univ. Pr., 1969), pp. 166–67

Beginning in the late 1820's, after years of creating personae through whom he could gratify his own storyteller's instinct, Irving finally approached his readers *in propria persona*; but by then he had become a true historian—rescuing from oblivion first Columbus and old Spain, then Astoria and Captain Bonneville, then Goldsmith, then the ancient Islamic leaders, and climactically George Washington. His rare fictional efforts during these years were condescending and lacked imaginative commitment. Although not a scrupulously accurate historian by modern standards, he dedicated the last third of his life to the "great objects" of the past and attempted to render them useful to posterity.

In 1848, in an "Author's Apology" for new editions of *Knickerbocker's History of New York*, Irving confessed to "presumptious trespasses," some forty years earlier by "a young and inexperienced writer besotted with his own fancies." By then he had just one defense for his historian *manqué*: not that he was a successful comic character in one of the most imaginative and effectively sustained works of its day, not even that he influenced some of America's greatest short fiction, but only that he had "turned attention to that early provincial history and provoked research" (I, 3). The storyteller's work might be valuable and defensible *if* it stimulated valid historical activity.

Before the critics ambushed *Tales of a Traveller* in 1824, Irving had combined the historian and the storyteller in an innovative and arresting manner. Troubled, but resourceful, he had explored the relationship between writers and their material and created a persona caught between the conflicting roles: the historian *manqué*. Unfortunately, the new course he charted after 1824 precluded further fictional experimentation. Because the apologetic persona was inappropriate for the great man of letters, he adopted the historian's role and succeeded where Knickerbocker and Crayon had struggled and failed so entertainingly.

John C. Kemp
ATQ (Fall, 1974), pp. 18–19

HENRY JAMES

1843–1916

Leon Edel, *Henry James* (1953–72), 5 vols.

James was constitutionally incapable of belonging to the underworld of sex into which Oscar Wilde had drifted. These elements must be weighed in any consideration of James's intimate life. Somerset Maugham used to enjoy telling his friends of an alleged attempt by Hugh Walpole to violate the Master, and of James's passionate recoil—"I can't, I can't!" Since Maugham's feud with Walpole was notorious, we must regard the anecdote with suspicion; yet it may testify to an understandable reticence and even fear and anxiety in James. We may speculate endlessly on this theme, without discovering the answers. One thing is clear. The "heavy" [Hendrik] Andersen, whose brightness would fade so quickly, inspired feelings in Henry James akin to love—to a love such as Fenimore [Woolson] had had for him long before she ended her life in Venice. She had written of her loneliness and complained of the years that passed between their meetings as James now wrote to Andersen. She had known what it was to have the object of her love fail her, fail to recognize the depth of her feeling. This James would in due course learn from Hendrik.

Leon Edel
Henry James: The Treacherous Years
(Philadelphia: J. B. Lippincott, 1969), p. 316

Like his heroes, and more particularly like Strether [in *The Ambassadors*], whose progress is strikingly similar to his creator's, James crossed the water again to the "other side" after having had his share of experience. In France he had felt life burst out under the smiling surface with an intensity proportional to the force that attempted to subdue it. He had noticed that the revolutions there were bloodier than in less disciplined states, and that the adulterous relationships were more numerous than in non-Catholic communities. His actual immersion in a country where life claimed its rights louder than elsewhere had made him acutely aware of the tension between the expanding individual life and the contracting standards of society, between the powerful flow of life and the fixity of artistic forms, between the dynamism of his emotional needs and a static discipline imposed from outside.

This awareness constituted his experience, his "germ." All he wanted to do was to develop this intuition into something valuable and permanent. He could only do so by leaving the full light of experience and retiring into the quiet immunity of his creative imagination. Opening again in an upward spiral movement, James then detached himself from the constraining fixity of French society and from the narrow bonds of French realism. The movement was one of expansion back to the wide basis from which he had started, back to the freedom in which alone he could express himself. James's mature works, though they conform to a strict personal discipline, follow the same movement and are usually open to various interpretations. They do not pretend to give us any final solution to the questions they raise. Neither does James's literary career as a whole: *The Ivory Tower* remained unfinished, and we do not know whether Graham Fielder's aesthetic sensibility will ever be united to Rosanna Gaw's moral massiveness.

Both James's life and his literary career might be figured as a double spiral rooted at the one end of the American soil and in romanticism, contracting in its middle on contact with France and French naturalism and expanding again into the Anglo-Saxon world and into the twentieth century. The spiral—which also suggests the artist's indirect approach to reality—strikes me as an adequate symbol for Henry James.

Jeanne Delbaere-Garant
Henry James: The Vision of France
(Paris: "Les Belles Lettres," 1970), pp. 404–5

In a sense, James never outgrew, but merely developed, his tendency as a child to try to grasp the meaning of the external world through the picture: the controlled point of view and pictorial description in his fiction similarly give shape and coherence, helping to create the illusion that relations stop somewhere. The dualism in his mature response to art—his admiration for both the classical Renaissance and the painterly-picturesque styles—also has parallels in his fiction: both in the thematic conflict between the ideal and the real and in the tension, especially in the late work, between his desire to achieve formal balance and proportion and to represent shifting, indeterminate, ambient reality. He had much in common with the contemporary impressionists in technique and in thought but crucially differed from them in his formalism and traditionalism. He was closer in sensibility and in style to the mannerist Tintoretto, the Italian painter for whom he felt the deepest affinity. His experience with art, primarily with pictures, also carried over into his theory of fiction: the abundance of art terms in his works of criticism is indicative not merely of his feeling a lack of a vocabulary appropriate to a serious discussion of fiction as an art but also of a visual orientation leading him to conceive of fiction and painting as analogous in aim and form and even competitive in the rendering of appearances.

Viola Hopkins Winner
Henry James and the Visual Arts (Charlottesville: Univ. Pr. Virginia, 1970), pp. vii–viii

Though the garnering of experience remains a "value" throughout James's career, and though his heroes seek either an encounter with the great world or the knowledge of intimacy and passion, they want these things only as projected—and sometimes only as encountered—by the imagination. Once the innocent imagination is disillusioned, it tends to become suspicious, to become the imagination of disaster. Experience often is envisaged at first as ideal, and at last as sinister, corrupting, unreliable.

I suggest that this view of life underlies James's work from beginning to end, that his fiction exhibits a radical separation between actual, inadequate relations and ideal, impossible ones. The real experience of his heroes is the drama of their discovery of that separation, the drama of their illusions and their disillusionment; and this is a cerebral drama full of suffering and painful personal growth, but shared by no one else. Passion and intimacy are imagined, not encountered, by James's heroes, and it should be clear now that the protagonists in this respect imitate their creator, for in writing his fiction James, too, imagines but does not encounter these things. It is in this sense that, Edel notwithstanding, Henry James's life was his art, and that the intense but narrow experience in the one is paralleled by the intense but narrow experience in the other.

Philip M. Weinstein
Henry James and the Requirements of the Imagination (Cambridge, Mass.: Harvard Univ. Pr., 1971), pp. 199–200

Faced with a world in which the preposterous, the trivial, and the monstrous seem to rule, James, like our contemporary existential novelists, marshals comedy as a weapon against chaos and absurdity. If contemporary comedy is more radically wild and bizarre, and if a standard of value is much more clearly represented in James's works, the basic philosophical assumptions are similar. Both James and the contemporary novelists affirm the inviolable integrity of the creative spirit and insist upon the importance of the rare and strange and beautiful in even the smallest and most seemingly trivial gestures. . . .

Although the Jamesian hero, like the contemporary hero, often receives no material reward at the close of a novel, his spiritual reward is almost transcendent. The spirit of James's novels is not one of escape or evasion or repudiation of human behavior; it is one that delights in discovering the limitations of human life on earth, and, instead of being overwhelmed by this knowledge, uses it as a means of power. James's final comic vision is that of the potential consciousness and freedom of man coupled with an awareness of his innate limitations. The personal triumph of the individual Jamesian hero is capped by James's, if not always the hero's, recognition that he is superbly and ridiculously human. In the struggle between the forces that bring disintegration to the universe and those that hold it together, between what diminishes life and what expands and enhances it, James affirms the latter. . . .

James's comic forms reflect this affirmation. The heroes of the novels must preserve or create a society while the world seems to be collapsing around them. The protagonist originates in and is oriented toward society, and the insistence upon this fact is what ultimately gives James's comic view the edge over his tragic sense. The comic sense of life is one that constantly tries to expose life's imperfections and ugliness, not with the object of condemning life, but with the object of expressing it and making it acceptable. James's vision is of the possible fusion of life and art, of freedom and form, of the limitation and potential of man. Manners, form, art, and the novel itself are weapons *against* destruction and absurdity, and implements *for* preservation and creativity.

Ronald Wallace
Henry James and the Comic Form (Ann Arbor:
Univ. Michigan Pr., 1975), pp. 156–59

SARAH ORNE JEWETT

1849–1909

Miss Jewett's best fiction is precisely an escape from drama into the shell of self. Some of the characters in her best book [*The Country of the Pointed Firs*] need even a greater refuge than Dunnet Landing affords, the most extreme being Joanna who lives entirely alone on "Shell-heap Island." Indeed, one of the things the narrator particularly admires about

Dunnet Landing is its toleration of such voluntary hermitages. The narrator responds to such as the widower, Elijah Tilley, who would "rather tough it out alone" (106). For the narrator, as for Elijah, Dunnet Landing is a sufficient refuge, one in which they can be in a society yet preserve their most essential selves free from entangling alliances.

The small town, as Miss Jewett sees it, is closer to the private island than to the city. The town is an escape from the complications and emotional demands of the city, its distractions and artifices into a place of peace where private memories whether of joy or more often of grief can be clearly and simply defined and then hung onto as a basis for life as Elijah Tilley hangs onto his memories of his wife. Things *have* happened in Dunnet Landing, but it is the past happenings and relationships that sustain the characters. Nothing *does* happen in Miss Jewett's stories because the stories and their setting are an escape, not only from the distraction and confusion of life, but also from its immediacy and intensity. The escape from complication is, in truth, an escape from the less manageable forms of life itself.

Anthony Channell Hilfer
The Revolt from the Village, 1915–1930 (Chapel Hill: Univ. North Carolina Pr., 1969), pp. 14–15

SIDNEY LANIER

1842–1881

Edd Winfield Parks, *Sidney Lanier: The Man, the Poet, the Critic* (1968)

Any re-evaluation of Lanier as a poet might well start with his admitted weaknesses. These can be listed briefly: (1) a strong tendency toward moralizing and didacticism, sometimes combined with an excessive lushly-phrased sentimentalism, especially when these elements are not part of the texture of the poem, but are added on rather obtrusively; (2) a frequent use of over-fervid rhetoric as a substitute for imagination, as in the Sun-Bee passage in "Sunrise"; (3) a strained imagery that grew out of Lanier's desire to yoke together in one metaphor the concrete and the abstract; (4) the use of archaic words and constructions that, although characteristic of Lanier's thought, give a quaint, artificial character to many poems.

Such handicaps are severe. Yet they do not ruin, even if they do vitiate, his positive accomplishment. The best of the long poems have sufficient intellectual philosophical content and enough musical form to lift them above their inherent defects. At their best, they have also a strong sense of locale, derived from exact and sympathetic observation. . . . Yet it is as a religious poet that Lanier in his longer poems is at his best. All four are loosely constructed, and marred by rhetorical flourishes and illogical images. But the disordered though powerful "Sunrise" and the magnificent "Marshes of Glynn" express Lanier's mature religious belief: God is immanent, and he reveals himself to us through nature, in the ferns, the streams, the marsh, the trees, and the sun. . . .

It is a thin sheaf of authentic poetry that we can salvage from the occasional and the sentimental, but it remains an authentic one. Lanier never attained his goal of writing major poetry, but he wrote a small number of poems that have never received the recognition they deserved. He is one of our most vital and most interesting minor poets.

Edd Winfield Parks
Sidney Lanier: The Man, the Poet, the Critic
(Athens: Univ. Georgia Pr., 1968), pp. 68–69

Lanier's aggressive imagination, his musical sensitivity, and his ability to transform commonplace symbols into Transcendental experiences make a distinct force in and contribution to nineteenth-century American poetry. Against personal hazards, Lanier sought to impose his voice on an age that had beaten Melville, discarded Whitman, debased Emerson, co-opted Twain, and walled in Emily Dickinson. . . .

Lanier's creative compulsions have helped to form the modern tradition in poetry which derives from Baudelaire, Rimbaud, Verlaine, Mallarmé, and other French poets and which had been presaged by Poe and the English Romantic poets Coleridge, Shelley, and Keats. Lanier's contemporaries, Whitman, Tennyson, Swinburne, and Dante Rossetti, also shared some similarities with Symbolist poets. All were concerned with turning poetry toward more serious aims than either didactic sentiment or the personal effusions of sensitive plants. In his attempt to exploit the musicality of verse, Lanier certainly deserves a place with these writers. . . .

If Lanier's adherence to feeling were a retreat from reality, as it has been charged, he typified in this respect the South's need for psychological withdrawal and spiritual consolidation as it absorbed the nature of defeat. Lanier in a way began what some have called the "reconstruction of Southern literature" by his articulation of a belief in emotion that has become the dominant pattern of Southern literature.

Jack De Bellis
Sidney Lanier (New York: Twayne, 1972), pp. 148–49

JAMES RUSSELL LOWELL

1819–1891

Martin B. Duberman, *James Russell Lowell* (1966)

If we consider Lowell's criticism in relation to the works of modern critics, we find evidence besides his prophetic powers of his contemporaneity. His most striking affinity, of course, is with the New Humanists, particularly the followers of Irving Babbitt and Paul E. More who struggled most directly with critics who favored sensibility on the one hand and with sociologists who preached the inevitability of history on the other. Like the New Humanists, Lowell seems to accept the dualism of nature and culture, and finds the artist's main concern to be that world of ethical values that distinguishes man from the merely quantitative order of nature. Like them also, he is self-consciously Hellenic, believing in reason and grace and eschewing the wide-swinging alternatives of sensibility on the one hand and materialism on the other.

Yet, even among the New Humanists who most closely felt the affinity of Lowell—those, like Norman Foerster and Harry Hayden Clark, who specifically defended him against the jibes of dialectical critics—one senses almost as much Lowell's difference from their point of view as his similarity. To begin with, he is not opposed to Romanticism as they are: his essay on Rousseau, for all its strictures on the man personally, ends in a confession of admiration for his genius; his many critiques of sentimentality are modified by admiration for sentiment, for emotion in art, and one concludes that it is only the *habitual* use of sentiment, as a substitute for honest emotion, to which he is opposed. Perhaps more important, his consistent espousal of the need for roots in tradition and culture, particularly for archetypes and myth, caused his New Humanist defenders endless pain—indeed, led one of them to divide him, like Caesar's Gaul, *in partes tres*, so that his humanist self could be skimmed from his less pure nationalist and humanitarian self. The fact is that Lowell was at least as much a Romantic critic as he was a neohumanist, his taste leading him in one direction, his erudition and academic status leading him in the other. Indeed, it is, by and large, the *least* part of Lowell's criticism that is closest to the New Humanists: his style, his conscious superiority, his belief that he was at the center.

The better part of his criticism, his feeling for myth, his organicism, his catholicity of taste, align him with other schools of modern criticism. Many of his remarks on myth, tradition, and the artist's need for roots generally precede T. S. Eliot's ideas on these subjects, as collected in *The Sacred Wood* and elsewhere. His organicism and particularly his emphasis on the need for total design in art ally him with R. S. Crane and the Chicago critics generally. Perhaps strangest of all, his insistence on the need to experience a work of art fully and his unwillingness to attempt to explicate any part at the expense of the total experience, his absolute certainty that manner and matter in art are inextricably combined, find curious echoes in the writings of Susan Sontag and other recent critics who have reacted against the New Criticism and the assumption by the academic world that criticism is their province only.

Thus we see that Lowell is not entirely dead as a critic. At first glance his affirmation seems too tentative. He seems, when compared to modern critics—even those who agree with large parts of his theoretical criticism—to be something of a fuddy-duddy, to be embarrassingly old-fashioned. But if we persist in our examination of him, if we break through the formality of his presentation, particularly in the longer essays, he comes to seem remarkably contemporary. We discover that what seemed to have only an antiquarian interest was really written under conditions which still prevail, and his voice, which seems at first merely quaint, is one to which the modern reader ought still to listen.

Herbert F. Smith
Introd., in *Literary Criticism of James Russell Lowell*
(Lincoln: Univ. Nebraska Pr., 1969), pp. xxv–xxvii

HERMAN MELVILLE

1819–1891

The Writings of Herman Melville, Northwestern Univ. Pr. (in progress)

Melville explored the permutations of love to an extent unparalleled in nineteenth century American literature, portraying at one time or another, the heterosexual, the bisexual, the auto-erotic, the incestuous, the lustful, the sterile, the sexless, *et al.* These characterizations are not, of course, self-portraits—except in that imaginative sense which is, more properly, the concern of the speculative biographer than the literary critic—and they do not interest us for any confessional insights they may afford. Rather they interest us for their analogic truth: because the history of the quester's sexuality is directly related to his history in seeking the holy.

Most, though not all, of Melville's protagonists are questers, and although those who do quest are obviously individualized, almost all of them, consciously or unconsciously, seek a manifestation of the Sacred Reality and a version of sexual fulfillment. And since these two quests are collateral and since they are frequently unsuccessful, we should not be surprised that the questers bear common scars, common punishments for failure. On one hand, madness is the wound to the mind for those who hubristically seek God, and this is why at least ten questers—Captain Ahab is the foremost example—are mad, or rave, or are temporarily aberrant. It must be realized, however, that as Melville grew older, his protagonists grow saner; that is, with age, he came to realize that, despite the real nobility of questing, there was something fundamentally unhealthy about it as well, a sickness in seeking the impossible. His last protagonist, Billy Budd, who neither quests nor fears the death which must be, is, theoretically, the sanest of all.

Martin Leonard Pops
The Melville Archetype (Kent, Ohio:
Kent State Univ. Pr., 1970), pp. 4–5

Ceaselessly active in uncounted modes, the whale—and the world that he represents—is morally neutral [in *Moby-Dick*]. But to say that the world is neither good nor evil is not to say that the world cannot be, in specific instances, good *for man*, or evil *for man*. One must simply use the terms "good" and "evil" with the caution of the man who habitually refers to certain animals as "predators" while being ironically conscious that a "predator" is nothing more than a creature who wants something that human beings also want. Taken in this subtly qualified way, one may legitimately employ the terms "good" and "evil" in connection with Leviathan. We may, for example, perceive that the whale suffers as we suffer, is bound to necessity as we are bound—with a consequent increase in our sense of identity with that inscrutable *other* which is the world. This is good for us. We may humanize vast Leviathan, perceiving that his heart beats as ours beats, that he needs warmth as we need it, that he lives in the air as we also live, so that he becomes, alien though he is, Brother Whale—and such an imaginative shaping of external fact may precipitate a sense of brotherhood with things far more mysterious and terrible than *Physeter catodon*. This, too, is good for us. Conversely, we may contemplate those aspects of Leviathan which are evil for us: his juggernaut power, his insensate ponderosity, his incredible size, the blind, indifferent urgency of his processes—though it might be argued that to perceive and, through Leviathan, imaginatively apprehend and articulate these evils is itself good.

In all these instances we are, of course, using the mind as a lamp to illuminate and give moral coloration to the cosmic house in which we live. There is nothing wrong or misleading in this creative process, and for the best of all reasons: we can do nothing else and still be human. All that is necessary is that we never forget that our perceptions are, to an undefined degree, projections of ourselves. This is the tragedy of Ahab. He forgot, or never understood, that the image he saw in the world was in part an image of himself. But Ishmael knows the meaning of Narcissus, and never forgets it. Consequently, Ishmael never—despite his Christian background and

Ahab's temporary influence—really sees either the whale or the world as *antagonist*. He is part of the world, at one with it, and so cannot conceive of it as adversary. Here, perhaps, we touch on that meaning of *Moby-Dick* of most relevance to technological man in the latter half of the twentieth century. If we have debauched our air and polluted our streams it has been because, like Ahab, we have seen the world as a thing to be attacked and conquered. Like Ahab, Western Man has been tragically seduced by "all that serenity." Thanks almost entirely to Queequeg, Ishmael is able to offer us an alternative way of seeing things, is able to elevate a mere sailor's yarn to the level of what N. Scott Momaday has called a "vision quest," which he defines as a "quest after vision itself." *Moby-Dick*, at the deepest level, *is* a vision—a way of seeing things—and this may be its ultimate significance for a technological world now sick unto death.

Robert Zoellner
The Salt Sea Mastodon: A Reading of "Moby-Dick"
(Berkeley: Univ. California Pr., 1973), pp. 265–66

In Melville's habitual frame of reference of first and last causes, only a complete originative or teleological rationale of the supernatural can explain any individual being's behavior, for it takes place in the universal motivational context. But Melville can define in fictional action the mystery of one individual's motivation, just as classical science can define a body's motion by describing the complex of internal and external forces acting, but without providing a metaphysically adequate explanation why these forces exist at all. For the classical scientist qua scientist, the question of why in this sense is not pertinent; but for Melville as public artist and private man it clearly is. He designates it by the word "mystery." As a writer he is concerned both to define the mystery in the sense discussed above and, in his most ambitious works, above all to communicate its felt reality—in Wallace Stevens' famous words, to give not ideas about the thing but the thing itself. In order to perform this aesthetic substitution for an impossible explanation, Melville deploys the creative phenomena at his disposal—words in all their arrangements of tone, point of view, event, discourse, character, and image—in such a way that they heuristically direct our attention toward the noumenon yet suggest their own intrinsic "inadequacy" and so fall back; the result is that, having done their indicative but self-subordinating rhetorical work, the phenomena transmit a strong sense of the motive-in-itself.

Thoreau's inspired urging has a bearing here: "The volatile truth of our words should continually betray the inadequacy of the residual statement. Their truth is instantly *translated*; its literal monument alone remains." Plainly, my account may be capable of generalization beyond Melville's works; but each writer has his own method of "volatility." Melville's intense, evident desire for adequate explanation, his making the frustration of explanation a primary dramatic issue, and his exhaustive employment of discursive explication give his heuristic artistry an exceptional honest conviction and tensional power, as if the solid element of facticity resisted its own necessary translation. This clear sense of mystery, in Melville's signification of the term, is the very opposite of mystification, or obscurantism. The noumenal effect is heightened in "Benito Cereno," as in *Moby-Dick* and "Bartleby," by being punctuated by silence ("the only Voice of our God," according to *Pierre*): the tongueless whale, the refusal of Bartleby to state in "positive" terms what he desires, the soundless end of Babo. The noumenal is only present in the quickest perils of phenomena; motive is only present in action, to be defined there and nowhere else: "[Babo's] aspect seemed to say, since I cannot do deeds, I will not speak words." . . .

Warwick Wadlington
The Confidence Game in American Literature
(Princeton, N.J.: Princeton Univ. Pr., 1975), pp. 133–34

It is noteworthy how little his works have in common in subject or technique. It is difficult to think of another artist who produced in such quick succession works so fundamentally unlike one another as *Typee, Mardi, Moby-Dick, Pierre, Benito Cereno*, and *The Confidence-Man*. In devising techniques for his fiction he combines the conscious care of a dedicated craftsman with a remarkable tentativeness, a remarkable lack of commitment to his own achievements; he discards as readily as he invents. What we have just seen of his attitude toward creativity explains why this is so. Because each formulation seems to him to open up further vistas that require new formulations, he is always sailing on. His fictional techniques, like the hypotheses in his letters, are both brilliantly adequate and instantly obsolete.

Even within individual books Melville's methods change radically from beginning to end, and sometimes even from chapter to chapter. Like Lombardo [in *Mardi*], his wish to unleash his creative self urges him to write without plan. Having begun one sort of book he is often willing to throw that over in the middle and pursue an entirely new direction. In describing *Mardi* to its prospective publisher he tells how he become bored with "my narrative of *facts*" and so set to work composing another sort of novel. As a result *Mardi* "opens like a true narrative—like Omoo for example, on ship board—& the romance & poetry of the thing thence grow continually, till it becomes a story wild enough I assure you & with a meaning too." . . .

It is Melville's commitment to the unfolding of his vision as much as the cosmological dimension of his interests that makes his works such special cases within the general context of the novel. In particular it makes his works significantly different from Hawthorne's. Next to Melville's books, with their uncouth designs and their vigorous processes of self-shaping, Hawthorne's novels seem like models of deliberate and finished formal production.

Richard H. Brodhead
Hawthorne, Melville and the Novel (Chicago: Univ. Chicago Pr., 1976), pp. 124–25

FRANK NORRIS

1870–1902

Like most writers, Norris did not always practice what he preached. He advised the aspiring writer of fiction never to allow his message to become more important than the characters, yet message dominates some of his own fiction (especially his short stories). He protested loudly against the genteel tradition with its pink lace romance, but he was himself often sentimental and melodramatic in the worst Victorian fashion. Still, there was no basic contradiction at the center. Essentially all he wrote was of a single piece of brilliantly colored but rather coarsely woven fabric. Underlying all his other beliefs about writing was the conviction that "you can't *make* [it] come,—no digging it out—must be entirely a matter of instinct and if a man can be sure of his instinct, I think he has little to fear,—the rest he can work out of his own bowels and brains."

This instinctive feeling for his materials, a "sense of fiction," as he called it, he put much faith in. It made him impatient of slow, labored writing and tedious revision. He said that all the conscious artistry in the universe would not make a writer a great novelist if he did not possess the ability to feel sharply and to portray forcefully the drama of life. In actual practice he simply could not write unless he felt that instinctive push. Consequently, his work is rich for its exuberance, intensity, and drama, but it frequently lacks control and concentration, and it always lacks subtlety. He believed in force, not subtlety.

After the instinct came the bowels and brains. He did not by any means compose while in fits of inspirational ecstasy. Indeed, he was an avid researcher and systematizer. He had as little sympathy with the flighty, impressionistic writer as he did with the overly meticulous. With his temperament and outlook, it is not surprising that he was an apostle of creative fire, and like many another young Lochinvar, he might well have perished in the blaze had it not been for discipline, both in his personal life and in his writings.

William B. Dillingham
Frank Norris: Instinct and Art (Lincoln: Univ. Nebraska Pr., 1969), pp. 140–41

EDGAR ALLAN POE

1809–1849

The record presented here shows how Poe as a person was reduced to ruin by the New York literati and their sponsors, who used the occasion while he was defenseless to work out old grudges or new ones. What the record fails to show clearly enough is that Poe, up to the time he had written "The Literati" sketches, had achieved an unparalleled national reputation as a critic, whatever notoriety he earned in gaining that reputation; that, on the strength of "The Raven," he became famous as a poet, however parodied and mocked "The Raven" was; and that his narratives, widely if not invariably accepted as brilliant at home, were beginning to be acclaimed in England and France.

His encounters with [Thomas Dunn] English, [Hiram] Fuller, and company, however, brought his career to a grinding halt, for his personal reputation, smeared beyond recovery by his enemies, soured his literary reputation, so that his manuscripts often went begging for publication or he was forced, "anxious," as he says, "to get out of . . . pecuniary difficulties," to publish in a journal such as the Boston *Flag of Our Union*. . . .

In short, though totally committed to literature, Poe was almost literally starved out of the profession. The poverty and persecution he suffered, which exhausted his energies and drained his self-esteem—a self-esteem he vainly tried to recoup by efforts to establish his own magazine—led to his being found semiconscious on a street in Baltimore and to his death on 7 October 1849 at Washington College Hospital, having gone through a "state," to quote Arthur Hobson Quinn, "of utter despair and self-reproach" that "passed into a violent delirium."

Sidney P. Moss
Poe's Major Crisis: His Libel Suit and New York's Literary World
(Durham, N.C.: Duke Univ. Pr., 1970), pp. 217–19

Poe's created world is a series of containers, each of which is itself contained in a container, and so on, through an expanding series to the universe itself. One can trace the sequence upward from the heart and breath within the individual being, who is within walls (chamber, coffin, ships hold, house, school, palace) that are located in a region of earth located in a planetary system contained, in turn, within the universe itself. There the expansion ends. But at this point it is no longer expansion. The container and the contained theory tacitly recognizes discreteness, scale, separation; for each container is in some sense higher than what it contains, and consequently different. But *Eureka* changes all of that. *Eureka* transcends difference by affirming identity. By the end of the cosmogony it is no longer possible to say that the lower forms of existence are contained within the higher. Not even the universe is "in" God; rather, the universe *is* God. . . . Finally Poe's system folds in on itself. Having expanded all the way out to the divine, it then contracts to the human; the existence throughout the universe of perfect, unbroken continuity and perfect, unbroken identity is affirmed: man himself becomes God.

David Halliburton
Edgar Allan Poe: A Phenomenological View
(Princeton, N.J.: Princeton Univ. Pr., 1973), pp. 418–19

The contrast between the ideal and the demonic in Poe's works, between the serious and the comic, the Gothic and the satiric, and, thematically, between hope and despair, is a matter of balance achieved by the dynamic tension of opposite forces. The view of art and life informing both the tales and the poems, and to an extent the criticism, is that of skeptical dissembler and hoaxer who complexly, ambivalently, and ironically explored the fads of the Romantic Age. Flat statements or commitments in Poe are only seeming. Almost everything that Poe wrote is qualified by, indeed controlled by, a prevailing duplicity or irony in which the artist presents us with slyly insinuated mockery of both ourselves as readers and himself as writer. Irony was the device that allowed him both to contemplate his obsession with death, murder, torture, insanity, guilt, loss, and fear of total annihilation in a meaningless universe, and also to detach and protect himself from the obsession.

G. R. Thompson
Poe's Fiction: Romantic Irony in the Gothic Tales
(Madison: Univ. Wisconsin Pr., 1973), pp. 8–9

Poe had little confidence in democracy, human perfectibility, social reform, theories of progress and "natural goodness," nor did he indulge in early nineteenth century obsessions with countryside at the expense of the city. He preferred city life and despised the mob, was suspicious of anything which threatened the individual man (including female emancipation). He defended slavery as a property right, loathed any form of what he called "every-man-for-himself confederacy," and believed that there were "laws of *gradation* visibly impressed upon all things in both the moral and physical universes"; and that "Democracy is a very admirable form of government—for dogs." Poe as Virginian is an unreconstructed Southerner, without the sentimentality of Southern agrarian aristocratism. He was, however, more tolerant and liberal than reactionary and believed persistently in the elevation of society by education for "the heart and intellect fully developed." But like most individualistic liberals who fear revolutionary change, he was a bundle of contradictions.

Eric Mottram
in *Artful Thunder*, ed. Robert J. DeMott and Sanford E. Marovitz
(Kent, Ohio: Kent State Univ. Pr., 1975), p. 29

HARRIET BEECHER STOWE

1811–1896

Two main features of Mrs. Stowe's work . . . can be taken to typify what was generally expected and accepted in the fiction of her time. The first is that her novels are historical novels, in the tradition of Scott. The second and more important factor is the paramount importance of Byron. It was Byron, not Wordsworth, who mattered to Mrs. Stowe's contemporaries, and the reasons are extremely significant. We have tended to underestimate Byron's preeminence among nineteenth-century readers, specifically including the general or mass audience of the time, and the result has been a distortion of our understanding of the period. Because Mrs. Stowe was not a great original literary genius, because she often wrote carelessly and uncritically responded to the fashions of her day, she reflects those fashions clearly. This is not to say that Mrs. Stowe's fame rested on the literary opinions of the readers of *Godey's Lady's Book*. She was respected by a majority of educated critics and readers. She wrote in what we might call the mainstream of American fiction in the first half of the nineteenth century.

And then, with one stroke, she permanently discredited herself by her celebrated article, "The True Story of Lady Byron's Life." It was rash to make the revelations she made in that article, and in the book that followed it the next year [*Lady Byron Vindicated*], but Mrs. Stowe hoped to assist one in undeserved disgrace, Lady Byron, and also to help in the work of divine justice before which the magnificent poet's sins must eventually be confessed. It is not an exaggeration to say that, since she made that confession on Lord Byron's behalf, she has not, except by a handful of critics, been taken seriously as a writer. The article was written in the summer of 1869. It is time Mrs. Stowe's work was reconsidered.

Alice C. Crozier
The Novels of Harriet Beecher Stowe (New York:
Oxford Univ. Pr., 1969), pp. viii–ix

The emotional impact *Uncle Tom's Cabin* had on the North cannot be disputed, and its success ended the prohibition on publishing books on the subject of slavery. Following the appearance of *Uncle Tom's Cabin*, new novels dealing with slavery appeared and older ones, including [James

Kirke] Paulding's *Puritan and His Daughter*, [John Pendleton] Kennedy's *Swallow Barn*, [William Gilmore] Simms' *Woodcraft*, and [Richard] Hildreth's *The White Slave*, were published again. But despite the significance of *Uncle Tom's Cabin*, its portrayal of black people does not challenge white racism.

Uncle Tom's Cabin and *Dred* are Christianized, sentimentalized, sensationalized versions of [Hildreth's] *Archy Moore* and *The White Slave*. Character types, incidents, even names repeat from one to the other. But the Christian slave, who rebels in *Archy Moore*, patiently endures martyrdom in *Uncle Tom's Cabin*. The defiant rebel, lynched in *The White Slave*, in *Dred* becomes a mystic who never leads his insurrection. The relation between master and slave is shown as being based on hatred in *Archy Moore*, but *Uncle Tom's Cabin* shows love betrayed. *The White Slave* dramatizes the violence inherent in the slave system directed first against the black chattel and then engulfing an entire society, but in *Dred* the white reformist is the principal victim of brutality. *The White Slave* ends with a call for immediate abolition; *Uncle Tom's Cabin* concludes with a plea for colonization. Mrs. Stowe's mixture of antislavery and white supremacy had led her back to Jefferson's *Notes on Virginia*.

Working with the historical precedent of the Nat Turner revolt and with the literary precedents of *Archy Moore* and the slave narratives, Mrs. Stowe produced Uncle Tom. It is not surprising that, a few months after the book's publication, an ardent abolitionist should write, "I wonder not at the unprecedented popularity of *Uncle Tom's Cabin*. The conscience of this nation is lashed to madness by uncompromising antislavery. *Uncle Tom's Cabin* comes as a quietus, to some extent." With Mrs. Stowe's shift in emphasis from this world to the next, all is revealed as part of God's plan. The suffering endured under slavery is seen as morally beneficial to the savage African (who will ultimately Christianize the Dark Continent), and the sin of white America can be absolved merely by an extension of sympathy to the lowly. In the years that followed the publication of her sensational book, Mrs. Stowe warned that if the Southerner, unlike his black victim, would not heed Jesus' love, he must suffer His wrath at the hands of His chosen instrument: not black militants, but the Grand Army of the Republic. For Lyman Beecher's daughter, there were indeed two Christs.

Jean F. Yellin
The Intricate Knot: Black Figures in American Literature
(New York: New York Univ. Pr., 1972), pp. 146–47

EDWARD TAYLOR

1645–1729

If one considers the poetry of Edward Taylor in terms of the great body of verse in English, the conclusion is inescapable that its modern fame derives in great part from the historical fact that nobody else in America of his day produced verse of that quality, and the satisfaction to be derived from the discovery that, in a culture in which nearly every learned person wrote occasional and private verse, one such person, at least, wrote verse that lives beyond the occasion. But there can be small doubt that, in the larger English tradition, Taylor is a minor poet. Although the unevenness of his lines is explicable in terms of his method of syllabification rather than stress, and although the inconsistency of imagery is to be unified by a knowledge of the meditative process that gives the images connection rather than through an explicit consideration of the figures, the lines are no more fluent nor are the images more organic for such understandings. Writing without an audience, Taylor, well-read as he was, suffered the pattern that binds even the greatest primitive artists; although a development may be discernible, this development is not clearly from relative weakness to relative strength, but throughout his career he repeated certain weaknesses and repeated certain strengths. Writing regularly from 1682 to 1726, Taylor echoed tradition he had known in his native England more than fifty years earlier, and the rude voice of his poetry sounds frequently like that of an unfinished George Herbert, but never like Dryden or Pope. To say this is not to insist that good poetry must be in fashion, but it is to note that the greatest literature communicates beyond its time because it is rooted in the reality of its time. . . .

He stands as the greatest of American Puritan poets, but also as a Puritan whose verse is in significant ways unrepresentative of the main thrust of his culture. In contrast to Samuel Sewall, who was feebler in a strict literary sense, Taylor indicates the way in which Puritan belief can have a continued meaning for the individual in a changing world through that individual's retreat into the mystery of Christianity at its core. But in a broader sense, Sewall represents the way in which Puritanism can continue to have meaning for a people by adjusting to the shift in sensibility brought about by the shift in the economic world.

Larzer Ziff
Puritanism in America: New Culture in a New World
(New York: Viking, 1973), pp. 258–59

In his quest for saving identity amidst Puritan theological thought, psychological notions, and literary traditions, Taylor created the best poetry to emerge from seventeenth-century New England culture. It is generally true that we tend to recall or linger over certain striking, beautiful, even remarkable lines or stanzas rather than the somewhat sprawling entirety of the individual poems. Nevertheless, considered as a whole, the *Preparatory Meditations* still impresses us. We are moved less by any display of poetic pyrotechnics than by Taylor's unequivocal commitment to his inward quest for love, conversion, identity—for Being, eternal life. The intensity of his search redeems the times we are put off by some disproportion, starkness, impropriety or mismanagement; more often than not the reader is provoked to some deeper level of consent. We too are charmed by "The Lisping Child." We come to value the legacy of Edward Taylor's poetry for numerous reasons, not the least of which is its heartfelt, personal narrative of an ingrained faith and an unwavering devotion rarely possible for us today.

William J. Scheick
The Will and the Word: The Poetry of Edward Taylor
(Athens: Univ. Georgia Pr., 1974), pp. 167–68

Taylor's poems bespeak a vigorous, passionate, and learned mind shaping its apprehensions and speech without the chastening refinements which a sophisticated society of poets and readers would have bred in him: a society open to and assumed by both [George] Herbert and [Isaac] Watts. . . . Taylor wrote poetry more like an Anglican, but to that poetic tradition he brought a Puritan sensibility articulating his self-examination on the frontier eccentrically, crankily even, but always boldly. And in these accents we can hear the first intimations of a distinct poetic idiom, as the circumstances of the poet in America, almost surely without reflection or conscious intention on his part, began to separate him from the British tradition. Taylor's qualities suggest the advantages and difficulties of independence: honesty which lacks tact and finish, self-involvement which can snarl itself in knots and crotchets, fresh energy which can move into clumsiness, a complex personal idiom ready to sacrifice conventional clarity; and these are the characteristics which will mark the American strain as it splits away from the British.

Albert Gelpi
The Tenth Muse (Cambridge, Mass.:
Harvard Univ. Pr., 1975), p. 31

Though it is full of the desire for God and a life beyond this one, Taylor's poetry is a kind of humanistic poetry. Outdistanced in form and idea, untempted by enterprise and competition with the world, uninterested in the profanity of progress, and uncommitted to appearances, with verse Taylor cultivated the virtues of faith and hope. He was a poet who persevered in his religious thinking, preferring a quietude where things of the soul were alive. He managed without wisdom and without civilization, ridding himself of the superficial, the unreal, the useless, whenever he turned to writing his meditative verse. With his poetry he could reduce his needs to one: a simple faith that might cure him of fear and anxiety. The art of living was to the meditative Taylor a matter of preserving identity by turning inward against the grain of civilization. In his poems time stands still, he is not tied to time, really free of time by virtue of his faith. In the privacy of his meditating, renunciation gave him victory over meaninglessness. There is a Christian humanism here that is unusual.

Perhaps it is the privacy, more than anything else, that gives Taylor's meditative poetry the quality it has. Sure of what he was and what he was doing, he did not need praise. Though he desired approbation, as we shall see, he would not allow the world to be his judge. In his poetry he was a suppliant before only God. Not having to worry about saving his name, he could concern himself with saving his soul. This meant that he felt that in order to exist, one must produce. Detachment was the only solution—that is, achievement without fame—though this seems never to have reached the stage of the saintly, in whom the self-satisfaction of renunciation makes a kind of heroism. Steeped as he felt he was in the truth, there was not anything any man could bestow on him that he did not have already. He therefore did not need to publish his poems.

This does not mean, however, that Taylor did not pursue a destiny. To exploit one's capacities but without having one's merits recognized was to a Puritan like Taylor a definition of life itself. So it was with his poetry. His private, meditative poetry is itself therefore a paradigm of the Puritan's life in the world. Success and fulfillment belonged beyond this life; existing in the hope of recognition, as Taylor does through his poetry, signified something alive. His poetry therefore takes the form of prayers desiring to be appreciated on high, though without certainty of recognition. To Taylor there must have been both presumptuousness and power in such longing. His is a poetry of humility and hope.

Karl Keller
The Example of Edward Taylor (Amherst: Univ. Massachusetts Pr., 1975), pp. 6–7

HENRY DAVID THOREAU

1817–1862

Walter Harding, *The Days of Henry Thoreau: A Biography* (1965)

Like [Whitman's] "Song of Myself" and [Cooper's] Leatherstocking cycle, *Walden* is an attempt to achieve an American epic—a poem whose images and sequence will recapitulate the experiential and spiritual history of the New World as myth and as personal narrative. . . . So Thoreau in *Walden* goes, like Boone and Leatherstocking, into a wilderness of the material world and of the soul, seeking a primitive truth; he becomes acculturated to the woods; and he is finally able to bring down truths the way an Indian snatches scalps (to use his own metaphor). However, this thematic affinity with the backwoodsmen is offset by the awareness that the wilderness of Walden is second growth, really a back lot of civilization, in which Indians and larger predators are no longer even memories but myths. . . . Like the Matherian Puitans, he senses that his wilderness sojourn, which smacks of adventure, may also be seen as an exile, an imprisonment, a captivity; it is at least a sequestration. . . .

Thoreau's American epic is the epic of the captive, in which the adventuring impulse turns inward and becomes a moral and psychological struggle against the forces that imprison the body and against the torpor of mind and spirit that bind the soul to Satan or (to use a term more appropriate to Thoreau) to death and "deadness."

Richard Slotkin
Regeneration through Violence (Middletown, Conn.: Wesleyan Univ. Pr., 1973), pp. 537–38

The shifting, constant nature Thoreau investigated and described is a fit subject for his kind of mind—indeed, while it is recognizable to all of us as the Massachusetts we know, it also reflects his individual mind and corresponds with it. As it requires a flexible and changing approach, so the map of his mind is full of crooked bends. As it is diverse, so the ways he comes into relation with it are diverse. If he feels separate from it, the separation itself will take different forms and will stimulate him to adopt different strategies to deal with it. The meditative weed-killer of "The Bean-Field," the cloud-scaling idealist of "Saddleback," the disquieted observer of "The Shipwreck," and the frightened adventurer of "Ktaadn"—all are romantic personae trying to reach an accommodation with a separate nature. On the other hand, Thoreau's ability always to return to the thought of nature as a living, affectionate, and beautiful whole is a sign of his knowing how to adopt an obsession and abide by it.

Since Thoreau makes Concord and its wilder rural surroundings reflect him, his effort to understand and describe this landscape from many standpoints and even in contradictory ways is a peculiar, Thoreauvian method of being more fully, more comprehensively human. He is not content to express a fixed personality, but wants all the personal variety his perceptions will bring him. His version of nature is at once broad and subtle enough to provide a theatre for the varied tendencies of his mind. He has the courage and the intelligence to acknowledge both the natural man and the antinaturalist in himself. He cannot be the bittern or the fox, but he knows that something in him would be, and he is willing to experiment with that impulse. By refusing to deny the idea of nature, or any aspect of his sensuous experience of it, or any part of himself that would come in contact with it, he has given the romantic interpretation of nature a new experimental validity.

James McIntosh
Thoreau as Romantic Naturalist: His Shifting Stance toward Nature (Ithaca, N.Y.: Cornell Univ. Pr., 1974), pp. 301–2

The ecological wisdom of Thoreau is the direct result of his insight into the coinherence of reality. *Walden* is really an experiment in and demonstration of human ecology. His philosophy of holism or of an organic oneness differentiated through interdependent realities, is a rich and dynamic view of existence, but the most remarkable thing about it all is the complexity grasped does not atrophy the person's responsibilities but rather sharpens them in a heightening of individual action. It provides the needed corrective to that aggressively masculine determination to subject, conquer, and exploit nature that has brought the Western world to the brink of self-destruction. It communicates the certainty that nature awakens, heals, and renews the human spirit through sympathetic relationship rather than through domination. . . . What the ecological crisis of our day is plainly demonstrating to us, and what Thoreau so well anticipated, is that neighbor love needs to be expanded to include all creation, inanimate as well as animate.

William J. Wolf
Thoreau: Mystic, Prophet, Ecologist
(Philadelphia: United Church, 1974), pp. 177–78

MARK TWAIN

1835–1910

The Works of Mark Twain, Univ. California Pr. (in progress)

At the center of Mark Twain's consciousness as a novelist was a vision of an idealized relation between the individual and the community, in which an independent individual could freely challenge the community's values, disrupt its sense of order, and yet somehow retain his identity as a conventional member of it. An impossible ideal, no doubt, and fraught with tensions that Mark Twain could not ultimately control; yet it underlies the structures and themes of each novel he wrote up to and including *The Adventures of Huckleberry Finn*. It also exercised a compelling influence on the book that has lately been treated as the most important novel in the Mark Twain canon, *A Connecticut Yankee in King Arthur's Court*. . . .

But . . . *A Connecticut Yankee* fails because Mark Twain could no longer effect the stratagem central to the structural coherence of each of his previous novels, his protagonist's commitment to the community whose values and stability he paradoxically repudiates. . . .

In the development of Hank Morgan, Mark Twain faced the fact that the individual is in no sense the superior of the community he triumphs over—ostensibly in its best interests—and that the community, on the other hand, is an unworthy refuge for the individual.

But, in recognizing these tragic truths Mark Twain was not reconciled to the breakdown of the ideal relation he had so heavily relied upon, a fact which accounts not only for the total collapse of *A Connecticut Yankee*, but also in large part for the bitter, cynical fiction of the last two decades of his life.

Thomas Blues
Mark Twain and the Community (Lexington: Univ. Pr. Kentucky, 1970), pp. ix–xi

The central point of the present book is that Samuel Clemens was not a major talent frustrated at midpoint. Not in the least; not at all; not possibly so. And I think that we have more than amply refuted the old and recurrent thesis of Twain's "frustration," his "failure," his final "bitterness." On the contrary we have seen just how Clemens recovered his talent intact from the pit and quagmire of disaster. The whole point is that he surmounted the crisis of mid-life; he survived it and he transcended it.

He entered his mature and later periods of writing quite triumphantly indeed, with all his old powers enhanced, rather than broken or diminished, by his own central tragic experience; by his depth realization of life's pain and evil. He retained to the end the central source of his artistic virtue: that untouched spring of pagan, plenary, and edenic innocence, that full sense of joy and pleasure in life, which sprang up even more freely in his final decades—which came to a second and later flowering despite all those civilizational discontents which he, perhaps more than any other American writer, also felt so directly and personally at the center of his being.

It was only certain Twain critics, from the youthful Van Wyck Brooks, who came to change his mind, to Bernard DeVoto and Charles Neider and Justin Kaplan . . . who refused to acknowledge—or who were perhaps ignorant of—the value of his later writing. Mark Twain was more correct in his own estimate of that work, his joy in writing it, and yes, his pleasure in receiving the world's acclamation then (and yet again today) for having written it. The last periods of his writing were indeed younger in spirit if wiser in essence than much of his earlier and middle periods of work. *Huck*

Finn as his single great classic—what nonsense! His whole career was a classic. He was not merely the artist of American youth and the past; he was surely our most mature and wisest of artists whose acerbity and profundity alike were ringed about with the imperishable comic spirit. In his age he only became freer, bolder, more open and honest, more emancipated both socially and sexually, from the taboos of his epoch which, at base, his spirit had never accepted.

Maxwell Geismar
Mark Twain: An American Prophet
(Boston: Houghton Mifflin, 1970), pp. 535–36

Had [Twain] lived further south, the war might have caught him up in its magnitude—and God knows his father would have wanted it that way for him, once Virginia had been invaded—and left him trapped in the confusion and the shock of the defeated Confederacy. Instead he went West with his brother, became a humorist, and then came East, where he flung himself gleefully into the money-making frenzy of the Gilded Age, scheming to make millions with typesetting machines and kaolin compounds in much the same way that Tom Sawyer dreamed of pirate gold. But all the while the forces of his creative imagination held ferociously on, in hatred and in pride, to that faraway country of his youth. Again and again he sought in art to find in the play of his memory the order and meaning that would tell him who he was. In comedy he strove to articulate and resolve the tensions, incongruities, and contradictions that his restless self-scrutiny kept turning up. His great weapon was laughter. When finally it failed, he was left high and dry, dictating rambling memories to a secretary, along with furious but ineffective tirades against a hostile universe.

When we come to assess the place of Samuel L. Clemens in the story of southern literature, this much seems obvious. Clemens, as no one else in southern literature before the twentieth century, brought to bear upon the southern experience a critical scrutiny that enabled him to search below the surface pieties and loyalties and get at the underlying conflicts and tensions within the society. It seems safe to say that he saw these things so well because they were to be found within his own heart as well as in the life around him. No other southern writer came close to the liberation he achieved. He was able to do it for at least two reasons. The first was that by accident of time and place, he was jarred loose from the southern community in a way that none of the others were, with the social tensions involved therein present within his family and his society. The second reason, of course, was that he was Mark Twain.

He stands, with all his genius and his shortcomings, in a relationship to the society he knew that anticipates that of a generation of writers who came to literary maturity after the first world war. Not for decades after his time would there be other southern writers who would find themselves both tied to and dissociated from the southern community in something like the way he had been. When that day came, the twentieth century southern literary renascence would be under way.

Louis D. Rubin, Jr.
The Writer in the South: Studies in a Literary Community
(Athens: Univ. Georgia Pr., 1972), pp. 79–80

Throughout the nineteenth century [Twain] was able to channel his energies into creative impulses, to sublimate many of his resentments and his affections into literary use. His opinion of a betrayed trust might express itself with classic understatement in Jim's speech to Huck defining "trash" after the two outcasts are separated in the fog: "Dat truck dah is *trash;* en trash is what people is dat puts dirt on de head er dey fren's en makes 'em ashamed." His growing convictions about conscience as the all-controlling force in man's destiny could appear in fictional guise as Huck's famous debate in Chapter 31 of *Huckleberry Finn.* His political and economic ideas found an ideal method of expression in the tension between a nineteenth-century Yankee from Connecticut and the practices of the country ruled by Arthur. His own conflicting temperamental impulses were objectified in the twinning themes of *The Prince and the Pauper, Pudd'nhead Wilson*, and "Those Extraordinary Twins."

And even when the transmutations of his belief and his biases into art were less than successful, Mark Twain managed to capture in his literature the essential humanity of his own doubts and indecisions. Much of his literature was based on the honest, unsophisticated, and imperfect pose of a man who lived by his memory and whose craft was always basically autobiographical. He *was* the people's author and spokesman, as his publishers advertised him. He could dismiss plot (as in *Huckleberry Finn*), violate traditional forms (as in the autobiography), and fail to sustain his original intention (as in almost everything he wrote). The ability to recognize his own failures was often his strength with a demotic audience. Mark Twain simply "told himself" in his writings, and what he lost in structure and cohesiveness he gained in identification through honesty. [Albert Bigelow] Paine phrased the quality as aptly as anyone ever has: Mark Twain "reached the heart of the world . . . because he was so limitlessly human that every other human heart . . . responded to his touch."

Until 1900 Mark Twain managed to retain control over his universe, over his despair, pessimism, frustration, and insensitivity, by his artistic capacities. But when deaths, disloyalties, and his own old age dulled his creative instincts, when he outdistanced in tragedy his own ability to transmute fact into literature, he was crippled. When his vanity, fed by his court of worshippers, deflected his energies, he was adrift like the derelict ship he described in his poem. Something occurred which made the adversity and the conflicts no longer convertible into finished art. Age was itself a contributing factor. The death of his most sensitive critic was another. His ostentation, symbolized by his white suits and crimson Oxford robes, multiplied unchecked by constructive restrictions. His fear of isolation, his insomnia, his interminable games of billiards and only desultory literary activity were all the geriatric manifestations of a personality that had never been quite able to endure itself. And the junkyard of unfinished manuscripts and ill-conceived literary ideas was the most enduring testimony of the failure of Mark Twain to retain creative control over his world.

Hamlin Hill
Mark Twain: God's Fool (New York: Harper & Row, 1973), pp. 272–73

In justice to [Twain's] genius, which was grounded in ambivalence and confusion, we should shun the temptation to search out patterns of consistency where they do not exist. Any attempt to discover order in, or to impose it upon, Mark Twain's jumbled response to the issues of his time would distort the man and his achievement. He did not place tidy thought very high on his list of desiderata. Yet it is precisely in his response to black people and to the South that we find order emerging where we expected chaos. Having learned about the man's protean personality, we find that his feelings on race and region move in an intelligible direction: from Southerner to anti-Southerner to one who longed for a South he finally realized had never existed; from conscious bigot to unconscious bigot to one who became fully aware of his bigotry, fought it, and largely overcame it. For all the backing and filling that attended the Reconstruction of this Southerner, there is a clearly traceable movement away from the white South and toward the black race.

Arthur G. Pettit
Mark Twain and the South (Lexington: Univ. Pr. Kentucky, 1974), pp. 8–9

"The difference between the *almost right* word and the *right* word," Mark Twain affirmed "is really a large matter—'tis the difference between the lightning-bug and the lightning." Throughout his writing life he respected the search for the exact word as whole-heartedly as Gustave Flaubert, and he took as much pleasure in finding it as that other word-connoisseur, the New England poet Emily Dickinson. In fact, he learned so many right words from his reading and his listening to the talk of thousands of men and women, of every sort and condition, and he mastered so thoroughly the art of "sentencing" them (the word is Robert Frost's), that he became the prime mover and shaker in a revolution in the language of fiction, a "renewal of language," as Frost was to put it.

Just as Emerson had called for an American poet who spoke the language of the street, phrases strong as the oaths in a New England farmer's mouth, sentences that if cut "they bleed," and Whitman consciously answering the appeal created a new lingo for poetry, so Mark Twain responding to other appeals such as Southwestern humor created a new language for prose. Words in the mouth translated to the page with a skill that no one yet has properly measured—this is the base of his literary expression. His friend the Reverend Joseph Twichell, Howells, Ambrose Bierce, Paine (his official biographer), the thousands of Americans and Englishmen and Australians and Germans who flocked to hear Mark Twain in person, the continuing success of Hal Holbrook impersonating him and reciting his pieces with disarming simplicity—all attest to his astute use of a varied, rich, vital vocabulary. "The stately word" pleased his ear, but the colloquial word and phrase pleased it even more. He "caressed them all with his affectionate tongue," as his farmer John Backus caressed his words when naming cattle breeds. All the contrasting words fell then into place, serving nearly every kind of literary effect, permeated with "that fatal music of his voice."

William M. Gibson
The Art of Mark Twain (New York:
Oxford Univ. Pr., 1976), pp. 5–6

WALT WHITMAN

1819–1892

The Collected Writings of Walt Whitman, New York Univ. Pr. (in progress)

Gay Wilson Allen, *The Solitary Singer*, rev. ed. (1967)

[Whitman's] art centers in the child's relationship to the family: the infant's early dependency upon the mother, the loss (or death) of this relationship, the flight from the family in pursuit of a false concept of freedom, and the eventual return of the "prodigal son" and reconciliation. His poems are meditations on the anxieties of the search for identity and for a unifying principle in the seeming chaos of existence. Beyond their artistry, the successful poems operate upon the reader at an unconscious level because Whitman explores the psychic depths and evokes the traumas of Everyman. The reconciliation he seems to achieve satisfies the universal hunger for order and meaning. . . .

Only the steady vision of the great artist can take us to the abyss and at the same time renew our faith in ourselves and in life. Whitman does not so much ignore horrors or so-called evils as place them in perspective, perhaps in endurable perspective. He is no prophet, or if he is, he is the prophet of what alienated man can still achieve in the age of the dynamo. Nor is he a philosopher: when he thinks in prose he utters second-rate platitudes. But when he orders his feelings in his great poems, our response is visceral. For as the lonely poet of monologue, of the inner frontier, of love and death—of our anxieties—he refreshes our spirits, and our lives at least for a moment do not seem fractured and chaotic. Whitman is not a "cosmic" poet but—what is greater and perhaps rarer—the human poet of the human comedy. Art, almost alone in a world intent upon other pleasures, affirms the joys of existence as it defines the problems.

Edwin Haviland Miller
Walt Whitman's Poetry: A Psychological Journey
(New York: New York Univ. Pr., 1968), pp. 18–19, 223–24

The only mystery in the composition of *Leaves of Grass* was the mystery of the poetic imagination. In Whitman it flowered late, but it must have been innate. The perceptive reader may see signs of it in his early prose. The flowering, in my opinion, was not the result of an "illumination" or a love affair of whatever kind. It was more probably the gradual opening of latent faculties under the stimulation of his reading combined with a growing confidence in himself. . . . When he was ready to try his own hand at an American poem he had formed definite ideas about the character and speech of the person who would be its hero. That person must somehow represent the actual American of the nineteenth century and the ideal which he conceived to be latent in each person. He knew that if it was to be authentic, he must begin with himself, both as he was and as he would like to become as a type of the democratic American at his best. So he created the "I" of *Leaves of Grass* and tried to conform his outward life to that pattern.

Floyd Stovall
The Foreground of "Leaves of Grass"
(Charlottesville: Univ. Pr. Virginia, 1974), pp. 14–15

By means of linguistic symbolization Whitman moved between the internal and external worlds, each world informing and enriching the other; Whitman's ability to move back and forth afforded protection against the dangers of remaining too long in either world. The nature of these dangers is clear: to remain too long in the internal world is to risk madness; to avoid the interior altogether is to forgo any hope of integrating the two worlds and to be dependent on external whim and circumstance. When he began to write *Leaves of Grass*, Whitman adopted a device that enabled his ego to maintain sufficient flexibility to move back and forth between the internal and external worlds: he imagined himself writing for an ideal reader who would love and accept him unconditionally, acknowledge his genius and omnipotence, and affirm that the bard had reestablished, through poetry the psychologically archaic world of infantile security. . . . Whitman's ideal imaginary reader was modeled on the introjected imago of his mother. The relationship Whitman fantasized with his ideal reader was analogous to the patriarchal relationship the poet enjoyed with his brothers and sisters.

By reestablishing through poetic symbolization the crucial element of youthful security, Whitman could confront to an unusual extent the partly unconscious conflicts that determined the subject, method, and form of his poetry. These conflicts, which emerged in the fiction, became increasingly prominent in the poetry of 1855–1860. . . .

After 1860, Whitman's personal voice was withdrawn from most of his new poems. Five years after the third *Leaves of Grass,* the assassination of Lincoln called forth Whitman's personal voice to make a symbolic announcement that there would be no more confrontations with his unconscious self and that his conflicts would have to remain unresolved. The searching, doubting Whitman who had written the most remarkable poems of the nineteenth century gave way forever to the good gray poet.

Stephen A. Black
Whitman's Journeys into Chaos: A Psychoanalytic Study of the Poetic Process (Princeton, N.J.: Princeton Univ. Pr., 1975), pp. 44–45

Whitman is at once the greatest and the most repressed of American poets. If the surmise is correct that the poets invented all of the defenses, as well as all the tropes, then more is to be learned about why the repressed cannot wholly return by reading Whitman's *The Sleepers* than by reading Freud's essay "Repression." Freud thought that the repressed returns through a number of processes, but particularly through displacement, condensation and conversion. Whitman is a master of all three operations, but in him they converge, not to reverse repression, but to exalt repression into the American Sublime. . . .

Few writers reveal so well what repression truly defends against, and why repression is so close to the apotropaic function of representation, to the way in which poetry wards off destruction. What Whitman has repressed, *and goes on repressing,* now more strongly than ever, is the close association in him between the Primal Scene of Instruction (covenant with Emerson) and the Primal Scenes proper, Freud's *Urphantasie* and *Urszene* (refusal of covenant with Walter Whitman, Sr.). As the covenant with Emerson that begat the poetic self ebbs, so the rejected covenant with the actual father is accepted and made whole. Emersonian Self-Reliance freed Whitman from the totalizing afflictions of the family romance. Now the consequences of the poetic analogue of the family romance allow Whitman a reconciliation he never found while his father was alive. Imaginative loss quite literally is transformed into experiential gain, in a far more direct way than Wordsworth or Coleridge could have envisioned.

Harold Bloom
A Map of Misreading (New York:
Oxford Univ. Pr., 1975), pp. 178, 182

Whitman states from the outset that his words draw upon and conduct energies and lines of force that move above and below the fallible human ego, clinging as it does to the categories of reason and logic. Moreover, Whitman was far in advance of his time in anticipating later psychiatric discoveries that irrational impulses could not be sorted out into subrational and superrational. Whitman already saw that the id and the superego, to use Freud's labels, were not necessarily locked in conflict; if we did not fear and degrade the libido, if we did not elevate the superego into a stern moralist and intimidating judge, then we could see that the id and superego which create different kinds of problems for the ego are related, perhaps indistinguishable as manifestations of the Life-mystery which the individual ego must learn to acknowledge and assimilate and express. So in its diction, imagery and associational method Whitman's language is serving an exploratory function, releasing the nameless and striving to name it. And since naming is not just a later reflex of knowledge, but the coming to know, his poems are no residual analogues of an unanalytical and unanalyzable process; they are the process itself through which irrational forces break—from above, from below: who knows?—into the bright space of ego-consciousness, there to form the individual's gradual comprehension of his nature and capacities.

Albert Gelpi
The Tenth Muse (Cambridge, Mass.:
Harvard Univ. Pr., 1975), p. 165

JOHN GREENLEAF WHITTIER

1807–1892

Having struggled for years with the deep difficulties of his own life, Whittier at last found a way to fruitfully regard them, and *Snow-Bound* is the monument of this personal victory. No, it may be the dynamic image of the very process by which the victory itself was achieved. But there is another way in which we may regard it. It sets Whittier into relation to an obsessive and continuing theme in our literature, a theme that most powerfully appears in Cooper, Hawthorne, Melville, and Faulkner: what does the past mean to an American?

The underlying question is, of course, why a sense of the past should be necessary at all. Why in a country that was new—was all "future"—should the question have arisen at all? Cooper dealt with it in various dramatizations, most obviously in the figures of Hurry Harry and the old pirate in *Deerslayer* and that of the squatter in *The Prairie*, who are looters, exploiters, and spoilers of man and nature: none of these men has a sense of the pride and humility that history may inculcate. How close are these figures to those of Faulkner's world who have no past, or who would repudiate the past, who are outside history—for example, the Snopeses (descendants of bushwhackers who had no "side" in the Civil War), Popeye of *Sanctuary*, Jason and the girl Quentin of *The Sound and the Fury* (who repudiate the family and the past), and of course poor Joe Christmas of *Light in August*, whose story is the pathetic struggle of a man who, literally, has no past, who does not know who he is or his own reality. Whittier, too, understood the fate of the man who has no past—or who repudiates his past. This is his "worlding" of *Snow-Bound* (whom we may also take as an image of what the past might have been had the vainglorious dreams of his youth been realized), whom he calls to spread his hands before the warmth of the past in order to understand his own humanity, to catch the sweetness coming "he knows not where," and the "benediction of the air." . . .

Whittier, though without the scale and power of Cooper, Hawthorne, Melville, and Faulkner, and though he was singularly lacking in their sense of historical and philosophic irony, yet shared their deep intuition of what it meant to be an American. Further, he shared their intuitive capacity to see personal fate as an image for a general cultural and philosophic situation. His star belongs in their constellation. If it is less commanding than any of theirs, it yet shines with a clear and authentic light.

Robert Penn Warren
John Greenleaf Whittier: An Appraisal and a Selection
(Minneapolis: Univ. Minnesota Pr., 1971), pp. 56–57, 59

Whittier's achievement in his works devoted to legend is culturally important although the artistry of Hawthorne—even the sense of artistry itself—eluded him. American society was hungry for history to shield its naked exposure to an empty continent, a sense of the past that would people the village lanes with friendly shades and soften the raw landscape with human associations. It wanted what older nations had: the amiable jumbling in any locale of what had happened, and what was so convincingly written of as having happened that the distinctions blurred in a general sense of the native land being a homeland. This Whittier supplied. If Hawthorne's art was the finest product of the soil, Whittier's was the mulch without which such art cannot blossom.

Larzer Ziff
TLS (September 2, 1977), p. 1049

COPYRIGHT ACKNOWLEDGMENTS

The editor and publisher are grateful to individuals, literary agencies, periodicals, newspapers, and publishers for permission to include excerpts from copyrighted material. Every effort has been made to trace and acknowledge all copyright owners. If any acknowledgment has been inadvertently omitted, the necessary correction will be made in the next printing.

RICHARD D. ALTICK. From *Browning's Roman Murder Story.*

RUTH APROBERTS. From article on Trollope in *The Victorian Newsletter.*

ARCHON BOOKS. From J. Noel Heermance, *Charles W. Chesnutt: America's First Great Black Novelist*; Joseph Pequigney, "Marvell's 'Soul' Poetry" in Kenneth Friedenreich, ed. *Tercentenary Essays in Honor of Andrew Marvell*; Cynthia Griffin Wolff, *Samuel Richardson and the Eighteenth-Century Puritan Character.* Used by permission of the publisher (Hamden, Conn. Archon Books, The Shoe String Press, Inc.).

EDWARD ARNOLD. From essays by Inga-Stina Ewbank on Shakespeare; D. J. Palmer on Shakespeare in *Stratford-upon-Avon Studies*, Vol. 14 *Shakespearean Comedy*, ed. Russel Brown and Harris; T. J. B. Spencer on Milton in *Approaches to "Paradise Lost,"* C. A. Patrides, ed.

THE ARNOLDIAN. From article by Ruth apRoberts on Arnold.

THE ATHLONE PRESS OF THE UNIVERSITY OF LONDON. From essays by Norman E. Eliason on *Deor*, G. H. Russell on Chaucer in *Medieval Literature and Civilization*, D. A. Pearsall and R. A. Waldron, eds.; Margaret E. Goldsmith, *The Mode and Meaning of "Beowulf."*

DONALD D. AULT. From *Visionary Physics* (Blake).

BARNES & NOBLE (DIV. OF HARPER & ROW). From N. F. Blake, *Caxton: England's First Publisher*; Enid L. Duthie, *The Foreign Vision of Charlotte Brontë.*

BARRIE & JENKINS. From P. J. C. Field, *Romance and Chivalry* (Malory).

BASIC BOOKS INC. From J. H. Hexter, *The Vision of Politics on the Eve of the Reformation: More, Machiavelli, and Seyssel,* © 1973 by J. H. Hexter (More).

BELL & HYMAN. From Robert Latham's and William Matthews's Introduction to *The Diary of Samuel Pepys,* Vol. I, Robert Latham and William Matthews, eds.

ERNEST BENN LIMITED. From Nigel Alexander, "Intelligence in *The Duchess of Malfi*"; A. J. Smith, "The Power of *The White Devil,*" in *John Webster,* Brian Morris, ed.

N. F. BLAKE. From *Caxton: England's First Publisher.*

BLAKE STUDIES. From Hazard Adams, "Blake, *Jerusalem*, and Symbolic Form."

ROBERT J. BLANCH. From article on The Pearl-Poet in *Nottingham Mediaeval Studies.*

HAROLD BLOOM. From *The Ringers in the Tower* (Blake).

THE BOBBS-MERRILL COMPANY, INC. From James Rieger's Introduction to *Frankenstein* by Mary Shelley. Copyright © 1974 by the Bobbs-Merrill Company, Inc.; Louis D. Rubin, Jr., *George W. Cable.* Copyright © 1974 by Western Publishing Co.

BOLT & WATSON LTD. From Peter Hunter Blair, *The World of Bede.*

THE BRITISH ACADEMY. From lecture by Gordon Leff on Wycliff in *Proceedings of the British Academy.*

THE BRITISH COUNCIL. From Derek Pearsall, *Gower and Lydgate* in "Writers and Their Work" series, published for the British Council by Longman Group Ltd (1969). Distributors in the USA and Canada: Marshall Cavendish, Inc. (Gower).

RICHARD BRODHEAD. From *Hawthorne, Melville and the Novel* (Melville).

CURTIS BROWN, LTD. From Ellen Moers, "Female Gothic, The Monster's Mother" in *The New York Review of Books.* Copyright © 1974 by Ellen Moers. Reprinted by permission of Curtis Brown, Ltd., 575 Madison Avenue, New York, N.Y. 10021 (Mary Shelley).

BROWN UNIVERSITY PRESS. From Northrop Frye's essay in *William Blake: Essays for S. Foster Damon*, Alvin Rosenfeld, ed.; William V. Holtz, *Image and Immortality* (Sterne); Barbara Kiefer Lewalski, *Milton's Brief Epic*; Steven N. Zwicker, *Dryden's Political Poetry.*

CAMBRIDGE UNIVERSITY PRESS. From John Barrell, *The Idea of Landscape and the Sense of Place 1730–1840: An Approach to the Poetry of John Clare*; Stephen Booth's essay in *Reinterpretations of Elizabethan Drama*, Norman Rabkin, ed. (Shakespeare); Denis Donoghue, *Jonathan Swift: A Critical Introduction*; Donald Greene's essay in *Jane Austen: Bicentenary Essays*, John Halperin, ed.; John Anthony Harding, *Coleridge and the Idea of Love*; Howard Mills, *Peacock: His Circle and His Age*; Edward Pechter, *Dryden's Classical Theory of Literature*; Ian Robinson, *Chaucer's Prosody: A Study of the Middle English Verse Tradition*; Leo Salingar, *Shakespeare and the Traditions of Comedy*; Wilbur Sanders, *John Donne's Poetry*; A. C. Spearing, *The Gawain Poet.* From essays by Gerald Bonner on Bede; Kemp Malone on *Beowulf*; James Smith on *The Dream of the Rood* in *Anglo-Saxon England.* From William H. Matchett, "Some Dramatic Techniques in *The Winter's Tale*"; Albert Tricomi, "The Aesthetics of Mutilation in *Titus Andronicus*" in *Shakespeare Survey.*

CASE WESTERN RESERVE UNIVERSITY. From Jean Normand, *Nathaniel Hawthorne*, Derek Coltman, translator; John M. Steadman, "Passions Well Imitated" in *Calm of Mind*, Joseph A. Wittreich, Jr., ed. (Milton).

CHATTO AND WINDUS LTD. From Rosemary Freeman, "*The Faerie Queene*"*: A Critical Companion for Readers.* By permission of R. G. Freeman, Mrs. Diana Bevan, and Chatto and Windus Ltd. (Spenser); Paul Fussell, *Samuel Johnson and the Life of Writing.* By permission of Paul Fussell and Chatto and Windus Ltd.; Edward Lowbury et al., *Thomas Campion: Poet, Composer, Physician.* By permission of Edward Lowbury, Timothy Salter, Alison Young, and Chatto and Windus Ltd. Larzer Ziff, *The American 1890's*. By permission of Larzer Ziff and Chatto and Windus Ltd.

JOHN CLEMAN. From article on Brown in *Early American Literature*.

A. O. J. COCKSHUT. From article on Dickens in *TLS*.

COLUMBIA UNIVERSITY PRESS. From Frank Bergson, *Stephen Crane's Artistry*; Max Bluestone's essay on Marlowe in *Reinterpretation of Elizabethan Drama*, Norman Rabkin, ed.; Geoffrey H. Hartman's essay in *New Perspectives on Coleridge and Wordsworth*, Geoffrey H. Hartman, ed. (Wordsworth); Anthony Low, *The Blaze of Noon* (Milton); Patrick J. McCarthy, *Matthew Arnold and the Three Classes*; Alison G. Sulloway, *Gerard Manley Hopkins and the Victorian Temper*.

CORNELL UNIVERSITY PRESS. Reprinted from Nina Baym, *The Shape of Hawthorne's Career*; Kathleen Blake, *Play, Games, and Sport*. Copyright © 1974 by Cornell University (Carroll); Jean Brooks, *Thomas Hardy: The Poetic Structure*. Copyright © 1971 by Jean R. Brooks; John T. Clark, *Form and Frenzy in Swift's "Tale of a Tub*." Copyright © 1970 by Cornell University; Angus Fletcher, *The Transcendental Masque*. Copyright © 1971 by Cornell University (Milton); Thomas R. Frosch, *The Awakening of Albion*. Copyright © 1974 by Cornell University (Blake); Stephen Gill's Introduction to *The Salisbury Plain Poems of William Wordsworth*. Copyright © 1975 by Cornell University; James H. W. Heffernan, *Wordsworth's Theory of Poetry*; Robert D. Hume, *Dryden's Criticism*. Copyright © 1970 by Cornell University; Wendell Stacy Johnson, *Gerard Manley Hopkins: The Poet as Victorian*. Copyright © 1968 by Cornell University; Wendell Stacy Johnson, *Sex and Marriage in Victorian Poetry*. Copyright © 1975 by Cornell University (Swinburne, Tennyson); Mark Kinkead-Weekes, *Samuel Richardson*. Copyright © 1973 by Mark Kinkead-Weekes; Jon S. Lawry, *Sidney's Two Arcadias*. Copyright © 1972 by Cornell University; Paul L. Mariani, *A Commentary on the Complete Poems of Gerard Manley Hopkins*. Copyright © 1970 by Cornell University; James McIntosh, *Thoreau as Romantic Naturalist*. Copyright © 1974 by Cornell University; Reeve Parker, *Coleridge's Meditative Art*. Copyright © 1975 by Cornell University; Clyde deL. Ryals, *Browning's Later Poetry*. Copyright © 1975 by Cornell University; W. David Shaw, *The Dialectical Temper* (Browning). Used by permission of the publisher, Cornell University Press.

COWARD, MCCANN & GOEGHEGAN, INC. From Eleanor Flexner, *Mary Wollstonecraft*.

THOMAS Y. CROWELL. From Joseph J. Deiss, *The Roman Years of Margaret Fuller*. Copyright © 1969 by John Jay Deiss.

JOHN P. CUTTS. From *The Left Hand of God* (Marlowe).

J. M. DENT & SONS LTD. From Maurice Pollet, *John Skelton*.

ANDRÉ DEUTSCH LIMITED. From Ralph W. V. Elliot, *Chaucer's English*.

MORRIS DICKSTEIN. From *Keats and His Poetry*.

DODD, MEAD & COMPANY. From Benjamin Brawley, *The Negro Genius* (Chesnutt).

DOUBLEDAY. From David V. Erdman, *The Illuminated Blake*. Copyright © 1974 by David V. Erdman. Used by permission of Doubleday & Company, Inc.

DUKE UNIVERSITY PRESS. From article by Richard E. Baldwin on Chesnutt in *American Literature*. Copyright 1971 by Duke University Press; John Clubbe,

Victorian Forerunner: The Late Career of Thomas Hood. Copyright 1968 by Duke University Press; A. Lee Deneef, *"This Poetick Liturgie": Robert Herrick's Ceremonial Mode.* Copyright 1974 by Duke University Press; Neal Frank Doubleday, *Hawthorne's Early Tales: A Critical Study.* Copyright 1972 by Duke University Press; Sidney P. Moss, *Poe's Major Crisis: His Libel Suit and New York's Literary World.* Copyright 1970 by Duke University Press.

DUQUESNE UNIVERSITY PRESS. From article by David Lampe on Lydgate in *Annuale Mediaevali.*

DUTTON. From *Chaucer's Bawdy* by Thomas Ross. Copyright © 1972 by Thomas Ross. By permission of the publisher, E. P. Dutton; Donald Barlow Stauffer, *A Short History of American Poetry* (Bryant).

EARLY AMERICAN LITERATURE. From articles by John Cleman on Brown; Annette Kolodny on Edwards.

KENNETH EBLE. From article on Chopin in *The Western Humanities Review.*

GEORGE D. ECONOMOU. From *Geoffrey Chaucer.*

EDINBURGH UNIVERSITY PRESS. From Priscilla Bawcutt, *Gavin Douglas.*

PAUL ELEK LIMITED. From Jean Brooks, *Thomas Hardy: The Poetic Structure.*

ENGLISH LITERARY RENAISSANCE. From articles by A. R. Braunmuller on Greene; Donna B. Hamilton on Kyd; W. Speed Hill on Hooker; Richard A. Lanham on Sidney; Wayne A. Rebhorn on More; Peter Weltner on Lyly.

ESSAYS IN CRITICISM. From articles by John Bayley on Shakespeare; J. A. Burrow on Henryson; Raymond Southall on Wyatt; Robert M. Strozier on Ascham; T. F. Wharton on Marston.

EVANS BROTHERS LIMITED. From M. W. Grose and Deidre McKenna, *Old English Literature* (Alfred, *Anglo-Saxon Chronicle*).

FABER & FABER LTD. From Ian Gregor, *The Great Web* (Hardy).

DOROTHY M. FARR. From *Thomas Middleton and the Drama of Realism.*

FARRAR, STRAUS & GIROUX, INC. From Richard B. Sewall, *The Life of Emily Dickinson.*

FORDHAM UNIVERSITY PRESS. From articles by Louis Blenkner on The Pearl-Poet. Reprinted by permission of the publisher from *Traditio: Studies in Ancient and Medieval History, Thought, and Religion,* Vol. XXIV (1968) (New York: Fordham University Press, pp. 43–75 at 71–73; R. C. Marius on More. Reprinted by permission from *Traditio: Studies in Ancient and Medieval History, Thought, and Religion,* Volume XXIV (1968) (New York: Fordham University Press, 1968). Copyright © 1968 by Fordham University Press, pp. 379–407 at 404–405.

ALASTAIR FOWLER. From article on Douglas in *TLS.*

ROBERT WORTH FRANK, JR. From "*Troilus and Criseyde:* The Art of Amplification" in *Medieval and Folklore Studies,* J. Mandel and Bruce A. Rosenberg, eds. (Shakespeare).

ALICE GREEN FREDMAN. From "Recent Biographies of Mary Wollstonecraft" in *Keats-Shelley Journal.*

MAX GARTENBERG. From Maxwell Geismar, *Mark Twain.*

PROFESSOR RITCHIE GIRVAN'S EXECUTRY. From Ritchie Girvan, *"Beowulf" and the Seventh Century.*

SUZANNE GOSSETT. From "Masque Influence on the Dramaturgy of Beaumont and Fletcher" in *Modern Philology.*

G. K. HALL & CO. From Isabel St. John Bliss, *Edward Young*; Mary Weatherspoon Bowden, *Philip Freneau*; A. Russell Brooks, *James Boswell*; Nan Cooke Carpenter, *John Skelton*; Jack De Bellis, *Sidney Lanier*; Jack D. Durant, *Richard Brinsley Sheridan*; William N. Free, *William Cowper*; Donald Greene, *Samuel Johnson*; Lee A. Jacobus, *John Cleveland*; Ronald C. Johnson, *George Gascoigne*; Martin Kallich, *Horace Walpole*; Charles Moorman, *The Pearl-Poet*; Eugene B. Murray, *Ann Radcliffe*; Maximilian E. Novak, *William Congreve*; Donald H. Reiman, *Percy Bysshe Shelley*; Katherine M. Rogers, *William Wycherley*; William M. Ryan, *William Langland*; Robert Donald Spector, *Tobias George Smollett*; James G. Taaffe, *Abraham Cowley*; Ivan E. Taylor, *Samuel Pepys*; William A. Walling, *Mary Shelley*. Reprinted with the permission of Twayne Publishers, A Division of G. K. Hall & Co., Boston.

HARCOURT BRACE JOVANOVICH, INC. From *Thinking about Women* by Mary Ellmann. Copyright © 1968 by Mary Ellmann (Eliot); *Samuel Johnson and the Life of Writing* by Paul Fussell. Copyright © 1971 by Paul Fussell. Reprinted by permission of Harcourt Brace Jovanovich, Inc.

HARPER & ROW, PUBLISHERS, INC. From Hamlin Hill, *Mark Twain: God's Fool.* Copyright © 1973 by Hamlin Hill; © 1973 by Mark Twain Company.

PHILIP HARTH. From *Contexts of Dryden's Thought.*

HARVARD UNIVERSITY PRESS. From Robert Alter, *Fielding and the Nature of the Novel.* Copyright © 1968 by The President and Fellows of Harvard College; J. Robert Barth, S.J., *Coleridge and Christian Doctrine.* Copyright © 1969 by The President and Fellows of Harvard College; Walter Jackson Bate, *The Burden of the Past and the English Poet.* Copyright © 1970 by The President and Fellows of Harvard College; Larry D. Benson, *Malory's "Morte Darthur."* Copyright © 1976 by The President and Fellows of Harvard College; essays by Christopher Brookhouse on Chaucer; Anthony E. Franham on Gower; Edmund Reiss on Chaucer in *The Learned and the Lewed*, Larry D. Benson, ed. Copyright © 1974 by The President and Fellows of Harvard College; Jerome H. Buckley, *The Triumph of Time.* Copyright © 1966 by The President and Fellows of Harvard College (Arnold, Tennyson); Kenneth Neill Cameron *Shelley: The Golden Years.* Copyright © 1974 by The President and Fellows of Harvard College; essay by David Erdman on Byron in *Shelley and His Circle*, Kenneth Neill Cameron, ed. Copyright © 1970 by Carl and Lily Pforzheimer Foundation, Inc.; John Cody, *After Great Pain.* Copyright © 1971 by The President and Fellows of Harvard College (Dickinson); Anne Davidson Ferry, *Milton and the Miltonic Dryden.* Copyright © 1968 by The President and Fellows of Harvard College (Dryden); Albert Gelpi, *The Tenth Muse.* Copyright © 1975 by The President and Fellows of Harvard College (Emerson, Taylor, Whitman); Leslie A. Marchand's Introduction to *Byron's Letters and Journals.* Copyright © 1973 by The President and Fellows of Harvard College; Gerald McNiece, *Shelley and the Revolutionary Idea.* Copyright © 1969 by The

President and Fellows of Harvard College; Robert Ornstein, *A Kingdom for a Stage.* Copyright © 1972 by The President and Fellows of Harvard College (Shakespeare); Stephen Maxfield Parrish, *The Art of the "Lyrical Ballads."* Copyright © 1973 by The President and Fellows of Harvard College (Wordsworth); Donald H. Reiman's essay on Hunt in *Shelley and His Circle,* Donald H. Reiman, ed. Copyright © 1973 by The President and Fellows of Harvard College (Shelley); Mark Rose, *Shakespearean Design.* Copyright © 1972 by The President and Fellows of Harvard College; John Rosenberg, *The Fall of Camelot.* Copyright © 1973 by The President and Fellows of Harvard College (Tennyson); Philip Rosenberg, *The Seventh Hero.* Copyright © 1974 by The President and Fellows of Harvard College (Carlyle); Paul D. Sheats, *The Making of Wordsworth's Poetry, 1785–1788.* Copyright © 1973 by The President and Fellows of Harvard College; Patricia Meyer Spacks, *An Argument of Images.* Copyright © 1971 by The President and Fellows of Harvard College (Pope); Garrett Stewart, *Dickens and the Trials of the Imagination.* Copyright © 1974 by The President and Fellows of Harvard College; Jack Stillinger, *The Texts of Keats's Poems.* Copyright © 1974 by The President and Fellows of Harvard College; Lionel Trilling, *Sincerity and Authenticity.* Copyright © 1972 by The President and Fellows of Harvard College (Wordsworth); Helen Vendler, *The Poetry of George Herbert.* Copyright © 1975 by The President and Fellows of Harvard College; Philip M. Weinstein, *Henry James and the Requirements of the Imagination.* Copyright © 1971 by The President and Fellows of Harvard College; Carl Woodring, *Politics in English Romantic Poetry.* Copyright © 1970 by The President and Fellows of Harvard College (Shelley).

The Harvester Press Ltd. From Stephen Gill's Introduction to *The Salisbury Plain Poems of William Wordsworth*; William Keach, *Elizabethan Erotic Narratives* (Marlowe).

Carolyn G. Heilbrun. From *Toward a Recognition of Androgyny* (Eliot).

Heinemann Educational Books Ltd. From John Russell Brown, *Free Shakespeare*; John Preston, *The Created Self* (Sterne).

Ward Hellstrom. From *On the Poems of Tennyson.*

S. K. Heninger, Jr. From *Contemporary Thought on Spenser,* Richard Frushell, ed.

The Hopkins Quarterly. From article by David A. Downes on Hopkins.

Houghton Mifflin Company. From William B. Dillingham, *Frank Norris: Instinct and Art.* Copyright © 1969 by William B. Dillingham; Maxwell Geismar, *Mark Twain: An American Prophet.* Copyright © 1970 by Maxwell Geismar.

The Huntington. From Stuart Curran, *Shelley's Annus Mirabilis: The Maturing of an Epic Vision.* Reprinted by permission of the Henry E. Huntington Library and Art Gallery.

Indiana University Press. From Roy Battenhouse, *Shakespearean Tragedy*; James Gindin, *Harvest of a Quiet Eye* (Howells); Rainer Pineas, *Thomas More and Tudor Polemics.*

E. Anthony James. From *Daniel Defoe's Many Voices.*

The Johns Hopkins University Press. From Ralph Cohen, *The Unfolding of "The Seasons."* Copyright © 1970 by Ralph Cohen (Thomson); Alistair M. Duckworth, *The Improvement of the Estate.* Copyright © 1971 by Johns Hopkins University

(Austen); Avrom Fleishman, *The English Historical Novel.* Copyright © 1971 by The Johns Hopkins Press (Scott); Robert H. Hopkins, *The True Genius of Oliver Goldsmith.* Copyright © 1969 by The Johns Hopkins Press; J. Paul Hunter, *Occasional Form.* Copyright © 1975 by Johns Hopkins University Press (Fielding); Frank D. McConnell, *The Confessional Imagination.* Copyright © 1974 by Johns Hopkins University Press (Wordsworth); Charles E. Robinson's Introduction to Mary Shelley, *Collected Tales and Stories.* Copyright © 1976 by Johns Hopkins University Press; Raymond B. Waddington, *The Mind's Empire.* Copyright © 1974 by Johns Hopkins University Press. (Chapman); Earl R. Wasserman, *Shelley: A Critical Reading.* Copyright © 1971 by The Johns Hopkins Press; Thomas Weiskel, *The Romantic Sublime.* Copyright © 1974 by Johns Hopkins University Press (Wordsworth). From Patrick Grant, "Original Sin and the Fall of Man in Thomas Taherne"; Donald M. Greene, "Roger Ascham: The Perfect End of Shooting"; Joan Hartwig, "Feste's 'Whirligig' and the Comic Providence of Twelfth Night" (Shakespeare); John A. Hodgson, "The World's Mysterious Doom" (Shelley); Lawrence Swingle," Wordsworth's Contrarieties" in *English Literary History.* Copyright 1971, 1969, 1973, 1975, 1977 by The Johns Hopkins University Press.

EDGAR JOHNSON. From *Sir Walter Scott: The Great Unknown.*

KEATS-SHELLEY JOURNAL. From articles by Alice Green Fredman on Wollstonecraft; Thomas A. Reisner on Shelley.

THE KENT STATE UNIVERSITY PRESS. From Eric Mottram's essay on Poe in *Artful Thunder*, Robert J. DeMott and Sanford E. Marovitz, eds.; Martin Leonard Pops, *The Melville Archetype.*

ROBERT S. KNAPP. From "The Monarchy of Love in Lyly's Endimion" in *Modern Philology.*

ANNETTE KOLODNY. From "Imagery in the Sermons of Jonathan Edwards" in *Early American Literature.*

RICHARD LEVIN. From *The Multiple Plot in English Renaissance Drama* (Middleton, Tourneur).

LIBER. From Sven Bäckman, *This Singular Tale* (Goldsmith).

J. B. LIPPINCOTT COMPANY. From Leon Edel, *Henry James.* Copyright © 1962, 1969 by Leon Edel.

LIVERPOOL UNIVERSITY PRESS. From J. G. Nichols, *The Poetry of Sir Philip Sidney.*

LONGMAN GROUP LIMITED. From Bernard Blackstone, *Byron: A Survey.*

LOUISIANA STATE UNIVERSITY PRESS. From Lloyd Brown, *Bits of Irony* (Austen); Milne Holton, *Cylinder of Vision* (Crane).

MACMILLAN ADMINISTRATION (Basingstoke) Ltd. From Enid L. Duthie, *The Foreign Vision of Charlotte Brontë*; Stanley E. Fish, *Surprised by Sin* (Milton); T. Mc-Alindon, *Shakespeare and Decorum*; Christopher Ricks, *Tennyson.* Reprinted by permission of Macmillan, London and Basingstoke.

MACMILLAN PUBLISHING CO., INC. From Walter Jackson Bate, *Coleridge.* Copyright © 1968 by Macmillan Publishing Co., Inc.; Christopher Ricks, Tennyson. © 1972 by Macmillan Publishing Co., Inc. Reprinted with permission of Macmillan.

MANCHESTER UNIVERSITY PRESS. From Denton Fox's Introduction to Robert Henryson, *Testament of Cresseid*, Denton Fox, ed.; Michael Swanton's Introduction to *The Dream of the Rood*, Michael Swanton, ed.

JEROME J. MCGANN. From *"Don Juan" in Context* (Byron); *Fiery Dust* (Byron).

MCGRAW-HILL BOOK COMPANY. From William Irvine and Park Honan, *The Book, The Ring and the Poet*. Copyright © 1974. Used with permission of McGraw-Hill Book Company (Browning).

THE MEDIAEVAL ACADEMY OF AMERICA. From articles by Morton W. Bloomfield on *Beowulf*; D. S. Brewer on Chaucer; Edgar H. Duncan on Chaucer; Peggy Ann Knapp on Wyclif; Martin Stevens on The Gawain-Poet in *Speculum*.

MEDIUM AEVUM. From articles by Cecily Clark on The Gawain-Poet; Dorena Allen Wright on Henryson.

BARBARA ARNETT MELCHIORI. From *Browning's Poetry of Reticence*.

METHUEN & CO. LTD. From Pamela Gradon, *Form and Style in Early English Literature* (*The Seafarer, The Wanderer*); essays by D. W. Harding and by Barbara Hardy in *John Donne: Essays in Celebration*, A. J. Smith, ed.; Mark Kinkead-Weekes, *Samuel Richardson: Dramatic Novelist*; H. J. Oliver's Introduction to William Shakespeare, *The Merry Wives of Windsor*.

EDWIN H. MILLER. From *Walt Whitman's Poetry*.

EARL MINER. From *Dryden's Poetry*.

THE MISSISSIPPI QUARTERLY. From article by Julian D. Mason, Jr. on Chesnutt.

MODERN LANGUAGE ASSOCIATION OF AMERICA. From John M. Ganim, "Disorientation, Style, and Consciousness in *Sir Gawain and the Green Knight*," Copyright 1976 by The Modern Language Association of America; Thomas J. Garbaty, "The Degradation of Chaucer's 'Geffrey,'" Copyright 1974 by Modern Language Association of America; J. Schleusener, "History and Action in *Patience*." Copyright 1971 by The Modern Language Association (The Gawain-Poet); D. R. M. Wilkinson "Carlyle, Arnold, and Literary Justice." Copyright 1971 by The Modern Language Association of America (Carlyle); James I. Wimsatt, "Mediaeval and Modern in Chaucer's *Troilus and Criseyde*." Copyright 1977 by The Modern Language Association of America, in *PMLA*. Reprinted by permission of the Modern Language Association of America.

MODERN LANGUAGE QUARTERLY. From article by B. J. Layman on Tourneur.

THE MODERN LANGUAGE REVIEW. From article by Vincent F. Petronella on Shakespeare.

HELENE MOGLEN. From *Charlotte Brontë: The Self Conceived*; *The Philosophical Irony of Laurence Sterne*.

MOREANA. From article by Irma Ned Stevens on More.

WILLIAM MORROW & COMPANY, INC. From Madeleine Stern's Introduction to Louisa May Alcott, *Behind the Mask*.

MOSAIC. From article by Norma L. Hutman on *Beowulf* in *Mosaic: A Journal for Comparative Study of Literature and Ideas* published by the University of Manitoba Press, Volume IX, No. 1 (Fall 1975).

JOHN MURRAY. From Jerome J. McGann, "*Don Juan*" *in Context* (Byron); Gervase Mathew, *The Court of Richard II* (Shakespeare).

NEOPHILOLOGUS. From articles by N. A. Lee on *The Dream of the Rood*; G. A. Lester on Caedmon; L. Whitbread on *Deor*.

NEUPHILOLOGISCHE MITTEILUNGEN. From articles by Marcia A. Dalbey on Old English Literature; Katherine Proppe on Alfred; Robert Stepsis and Richard Rand on Cynewulf; F. H. Whitman on Old English Literature.

NEW AMERICAN LIBRARY, INC. From George M. Ridenour's Introduction to *Selected Poetry of Browning*, edited by George M. Ridenour. Copyright © 1966 by George M. Ridenour. Reprinted by arrangement with The New American Library, Inc. New York, N.Y.

NEW YORK UNIVERSITY PRESS. From Paul G. Ruggiers's essay in *Medieval Studies in Honor of Lillian Herlands Hornstein*, edited by Jess B. Bessinger and Robert Raymo, © 1976 by New York University (Chaucer); *King Arthur's Laureate* by Phillip Eggers, © 1971 by New York University (Tennyson); *The Divided Self* by Masao Miyoshi, © 1969 by New York University (Arnold, Carlyle, Clough); *The Intricate Knot* by Jean F. Yellin, © 1972 by New York University (Stowe).

NORTHERN ILLINOIS UNIVERSITY PRESS. Reprinted from *Literary Portraits in the Novels of Henry Fielding*, by Sean Shesgreen, copyright © 1972 by Northern Illinois University Press. By permission of the publisher.

NORTHWESTERN UNIVERSITY PRESS. From Ruth M. Amers, *The Fulfillment of the Scriptures* (Langland); Mary Carruthers, *The Search for St. Truth: A Study of Meaning in "Piers Plowman"* (Langland); Jeffry B. Spencer, *Heroic Nature* (Thomson).

W. W. NORTON & COMPANY, INC. From *Natural Supernaturalism: Tradition and Revolution in Romantic Literature* by M. H. Abrams, with the permission of W. W. Norton & Company, Inc. Copyright © 1971 by W. W. Norton & Company, Inc. (Wordsworth); *Charlotte Brontë: The Self Conceived* by Helene Moglen, with the permission of W. W. Norton & Company, Inc. Copyright © 1976 by Helene Moglen.

NOTTINGHAM MEDIAEVAL STUDIES. From article by Robert J. Blanch on The Pearl-Poet.

OHIO UNIVERSITY PRESS. From John A. Jones, *Pope's Couplet Art*; Charles G. Masington, *Christopher Marlowe's Tragic Vision: A Study in Damnation*; essays by William F. Axton on Dickens; Jerome Beaty on G. Eliot; Frederick Karl on C. Brontë, Juliet McMaster on Thackeray, Lionel Stevenson on Meredith in *The Victorian Experience*, Richard A. Levine, ed.

OLIVER & BOYD. From Dorothy M. Farr, *Thomas Middleton and the Drama of Realism*; Barbara Melchiori, *Browning's Poetry of Reticence*.

OSPREY PUBLISHING LIMITED. From N. F. Blake, *Caxton: England's First Publisher*.

OXFORD UNIVERSITY PRESS, NEW YORK. From *The Anxiety of Influence* by Harold Bloom. Copyright © 1973 by Oxford University Press, Inc. (Wordsworth); *A Map of Misreading* by Harold Bloom. Copyright © 1975 by Oxford University Press, Inc. (Emerson, Whitman); *The Novels of Harriet Beecher Stowe* by Alice C. Crozier. Copyright © 1969 by Oxford University Press, Inc.; *Thomas Hardy and British Poetry* by Donald Davie. Copyright © 1972 by Donald Davie; *The Art of Mark Twain* by William M. Gibson. Copyright © 1976 by Oxford University Press, Inc. *Victorian Prose and Poetry*, Lionel Trilling and Harold Bloom, eds, volume of *The Oxford Anthology of English Literature*, edited by Frank Kermode, John Hollander, et al. Copyright © 1973 by Oxford University Press, Inc. (Newman, Rossetti, Ruskin); essays by G. S. Fraser on Pater, John Rosenberg on Ruskin in *The Art of Victorian Prose* by George Levine and William Madden, eds. Copyright © 1968 by Oxford University Press, Inc.; Philip Stevick's essay in *Tobias Smollett: Bicentennial Essays Presented to Lewis M. Knapp*, G. S. Rousseau and P.-G. Bouce, eds. Copyright © 1971 by Oxford University Press, Inc.; *The Heirs of Donne and Jonson* by Joseph H. Summers. Copyright © 1970 by Oxford University Press, Inc. (Carew, Herrick); *Ralph Waldo Emerson* by Edward Wagenknecht. Copyright © 1974 by Oxford University Press, Inc. Reprinted by permission of Oxford University Press, Inc.

OXFORD UNIVERSITY PRESS, OXFORD. From Marilyn Butler, *Maria Edgeworth: A Literary Biography* © Oxford University Press, 1972; Marilyn Butler, *Jane Austen and the War of Ideas* © Oxford University Press, 1975; Kathleen Coburn, *The Self-Conscious Imagination: A Study of the Coleridge Notebooks* © Oxford University Press, 1974; Joos Daalder's Introduction to *Sir Thomas Wyatt: Collected Poems* © Oxford University Press, 1975; Margaret Anne Doddy, *A Natural Passion* © Oxford University Press, 1974 (Richardson); Ian Donaldson. *The World Upside-Down* © Oxford University Press, 1970 (Gay); T. C. Duncan Eaves and Ben D. Kimpel, *Samuel Richardson: A Biography* © Oxford University Press, 1971; Willard Farnham, *The Shakespearean Grotesque* © Oxford University Press, 1971; Judith Fryer, *The Faces of Eve* © Oxford University Press, 1976 (Chopin); David Gauthier, *The Logic of Leviathan* © Oxford University Press, 1969 (Hobbes); Harriet Hawkins, *Likenesses of Truth in Elizabethan and Restoration Drama* © Oxford University Press, 1972 (Congreve); Mary Jacobus, *Tradition and Experiment in Wordsworth's "Lyrical Ballads" (1798)* © Oxford University Press, 1976; Gwyn Jones, *Kings, Beasts and Heroes*, © Oxford University Press, 1972 (Beowulf); Gary Kelly's Introduction to Mary Wollstonecraft, *Mary, A Fiction and The Wrongs of Woman* © Oxford University Press, 1976; Karl Kroeber, *Styles in Fictional Structure* © 1971 by Princeton University Press (Austen); Marston La France, *A Reading of Stephen Crane* © Oxford University Press, 1971; F. R. Leavis's essay in *William Blake*, Morton D. Paley and Michael Phillips, eds. © Oxford University Press, 1973; Thomas McFarland, *Coleridge and the Pantheist Tradition* © Oxford University Press, 1969; Roy Park, *Hazlitt and the Spirit of the Age* © Oxford University Press, 1971; Mary R. Price, *Bede and Dunstan* © Oxford University Press, 1968 (Bede); John J. Richetti, *Defoe's Narratives* © Oxford University Press, 1975; Christopher Ricks, *Keats and Embarrassment* © Oxford University Press, 1974; Jean Robertson's Introduction to Sir Philip Sidney, *The Countess of Pembroke's Arcadia (The Old Arcadia)* © Oxford University Press, 1973; Murray Roston, *The Soul of Wit: A Study of John Donne* © Oxford University Press (1974); Samuel Schoenbaum, *Shakespeare's Lives* © Samuel Schoenbaum 1970; Timothy Webb, *The Violet in the Crucible: Shelley and Translation* © Oxford University Press, 1976. All excerpts reprinted by permission of Oxford University Press.

PAPERS ON LANGUAGE & LITERATURE. From articles by W. A. Davenport on *The Seafarer*; Kenneth Friedenreich on Marlowe; Ann Harleman Stewart on Riddles; Walter Scheps on Dunbar.

PENGUIN BOOKS LTD. From J. H. Hexter, *The Vision of Politics on the Eve of the Reformation: More, Machiavelli and Seyssel* (Allen Lane, 1973). Copyright © J. H. Hexter, 1973; J. B. Steane's Introduction to Thomas Nashe, *The Unfortunate Traveller, and Other Works*, J. B. Steane, ed. (Penguin English Library, 1972). Introduction © 1971 by J. B. Steane. Reprinted by permission of Penguin Books Ltd.

THE PENNSYLVANIA STATE UNIVERSITY PRESS. From articles by C. David Benson; Paul G. Ruggiers; Gloria K. Shapiro; A. Brooker Thro; Francis Lee Utley; Ann Chalmers Watts; Frank W. Whitman in *The Chaucer Review*; Rosalie L. Colie's essay in *Just So Much Honor*, Peter Amadeus Fiore, ed (Donne); Ralph Waterbury Condee, *Structure in Milton's Poetry from the Foundation to the Pinnacles.*

VINCENT F. PETRONELLA. From article on Shakespeare in *Modern Language Review.*

THE CARL AND LILY PFORZHEIMER FOUNDATION, INC. From essay by Donald H. Reiman in *Byron on the Continent.* Quoted by permission of The Carl H. Pforzheimer Library.

PHILOLOGICAL QUARTERLY. From article by Lee W. Patterson on Henryson.

PRENTICE-HALL, INC. From Donald K. Fry's Introduction to *The "Beowulf" Poet: A Collection of Critical Essays*, © 1968; A. Bartlett Giamatti, *Play of Double Sense*, © 1975 (Spenser); Geoffrey Hartman's Introduction to *Hopkins: A Collection of Critical Essays*, © 1966. Reprinted by permission of Prentice-Hall, Inc., Englewood Cliffs, New Jersey.

PRINCETON UNIVERSITY PRESS. From Ann E. Berthoff, *"The Resolved Soul": A Study of Marvell's Major Poems.* Copyright © 1970 by Princeton University Press; Stephen A. Black, *Whitman's Journey into Chaos: A Psychoanalytic Study of the Poetic Process.* Copyright © 1975 by Princeton University Press; William C. Carroll, *The Great Feast of Language in "Love's Labor Lost."* Copyright © 1976 by Princeton University Press (Shakespeare); Rosalie Colie, *Shakespeare's Living Art.* Copyright © 1974 by Princeton University Press; Rosalie L. Colie, *"My Echoing Song": Andrew Marvell's Poetry of Criticism.* Copyright © 1970 by Princeton University Press; Michael G. Cooke, *The Blind Man Traces the Circle: On the Patterns and Philosophy of Byron's Poetry.* Copyright © 1969 by Princeton University Press; Patrick Cullen, *Infernal Triad: The Flesh, the World, and the Devil in Spenser and Milton.* Copyright © 1974 by Princeton University Press (Milton); Stuart Curran, *Shelley's Cenci: Scorpions Ringed with Fire.* Copyright © 1970 by Princeton University Press; Leopold Damrosch, Jr., *Samuel Johnson and the Tragic Sense.* Copyright © 1972 by Princeton University Press; Howard Felperin, *Shakespearean Romance.* Copyright © 1972 by Princeton University Press, pp. 60–64 and 172–174; Jean H. Hagstrum's essay in *Blake's Visionary Forms Dramatic*, ed. by David V. Erdman and John E. Grant. Copyright © 1970 by Princeton University Press; David Halliburton, *Edgar Allan Poe: A Phenomenological View.* Copyright © 1973 by Princeton University Press; Karl Kroeber, *Styles in Fictional Structure: The Art of Jane Austen, Charlotte Brontë, George Eliot.* Copyright © 1971 by Princeton University Press (Austen); George Levine, *The Boundaries of Fiction: Carlyle, Macaulay, Newman.* Copyright © 1968 by Princeton University Press, pp. 21–22, 163 and 214 (Carlyle, Macaulay, Newman); Barbara Kiefer Lewalski, *Donne's "Anniversaries" and the Poetry of Praise: The Creation of a Symbolic Mode.* Copyright © 1973 by Princeton University Press; Isabel G. MacCaffrey, *Spenser's Allegory: The Anatomy of Imagination.* Copyright © 1976 by Princeton University Press; Earl Miner, *The Cavalier Mode from Jonson to Cotton.* Copyright © 1971 by Princeton University Press, pp. 66–67, 70, 192–93 (Herrick, Jonson); James Nohrnberg, *The Analogy of "The Faerie Queene."* Copyright © 1976 by Princeton University Press (Spenser); Richard J. Onorato, *The Character of the Poet: Wordsworth in "The Prelude."* Copyright © 1971 by Princeton University Press; Lewis Patton's Introduction in *The Collected Works of Samuel Taylor Coleridge*, ed. Kathleen Coburn and Bert Winer. Bollingen Series LXXV, Vol. 2, *The Watchman*, ed. Lewis Patton. Copyright © 1970 by Routledge and Kegan Paul; Robert M. Ryan, *Keats: The Religious Sense*. Copyright © 1973 by Princeton University Press; G. Robert Stange, *Matthew Arnold: The Poet as Humanist*. Copyright © 1967 by Princeton University Press. Irene Tayler, *Blake's Illustrations to the Poems of Gray*. Copyright © 1971 by Princeton University Press; Warwick Wadlington, *The Confidence Game in American Literature*. Copyright © 1975 by Princeton University Press (Melville); Hyatt H. Waggoner, *Emerson as Poet*. Copyright © 1975 by Princeton University Press; Judith Wilt, *The Readable People of George Meredith*. Copyright © 1975 by Princeton University Press. All reprinted by permission of Princeton University Press; selection by Michael G. Cooke on Byron also by permission of the *Keats-Shelley Journal*.

THE PSYCHOANALYTIC REVIEW. From Stephen A. Reid, "The Psychoanalytic Reading of *Troilus and Cressida* and *Measure for Measure*." Reprinted from *The Psychoanalytic Review*, vol. 57, No. 2, 1970, through the courtesy of the Editors and the Publisher, National Psychoanalytic Association for Psychoanalysis, New York, N.Y.

W. V. QUINE. From article on Carroll in *TLS*.

ESTHER C. QUINN. From essay in *Geoffrey Chaucer*, George D. Economou, ed.

MARTIN N. RAITIERE. From article on More in *Studies in the Renaissance*.

RANDOM HOUSE, INC. From *A Study of English Romanticism* by Northrop Frye. Copyright © 1968 by Random House, Inc. Reprinted by permission of Random House, Inc. (Wordsworth); *Toward a Recognition of Androgyny*, by Carolyn G. Heilbrun. Copyright © 1964, 1965, 1968, 1971, 1972, 1973 by Carolyn G. Heilbrun. Reprinted by permission of Alfred A. Knopf, Inc. (Eliot); *Swinburne: Selected Poetry and Prose*, by Algernon C. Swinburne, edited and introduction by John D. Rosenberg. Copyright © 1967, 1968 by John D. Rosenberg. Reprinted by permission of Random House, Inc.

THE REGENTS PRESS OF KANSAS. From Theodore Fenner, *Leigh Hunt and Opera Criticism*; Richard F. Hardin, *Michael Drayton and the Passing of Elizabethan England*; Ralph Wardle, *Mary Wollstonecraft: A Critical Biography*.

MAJA REID. From article by Stephen A. Reid on Shakespeare in *The Psychoanalytic Review*.

THOMAS REISNER. From "Some Scientific Models for Shelley's Multitudinous Orb," in *Keats-Shelley Journal*.

THE RENAISSANCE SOCIETY OF AMERICA. From article by Martin N. Raitiere on More in *Studies in the Renaissance*.

EDITIONS RODOPI N. V. From W. Anthony James, *Daniel Defoe's Many Voices*.

ROUTLEDGE & KEGAN PAUL LTD. From J. A. Burrow, *Ricardian Style* (Chaucer); Kenneth Curry, *Southey*; Carl Dawson, *His Fine Wit: A Study of Thomas Love Peacock*; Stanley B. Greenfield, *The Interpretation of Old English Poems* (*Beowulf*); John E. Jordan's Introduction to *De Quincey as Critic*, John E. Jordan, ed.; P. M. Kean, *"The Pearl": An Interpretation*; Andrea Kelly's essay on Landor in

The Latin Poetry of English Poets, J. W. Binns, ed.; John Norton-Smith, *Geoffrey Chaucer*; Derek Pearsall, *John Lydgate*; Derek Pearsall, *Old English and Middle English Poetry,* Vol. I of *The Routledge History of English Poetry* (Langland); Francis Yates, *Shakespeare's Last Plays: A New Approach.*

ROWAN AND LITTLEFIELD. From Ian Gregor, *The Great Web* (Hardy).

LOUIS D. RUBIN, JR. From Lewis Leary's and Jay Martin's essays in *The Comic Imagination in American Literature,* Louis D. Rubin, ed. (Bierce, Franklin, Holmes).

RUTGERS UNIVERSITY PRESS. From William Keach, *Elizabethan Erotic Narratives: Irony and Pathos in the Ovidian Poetry of Shakespeare, Marlowe, and Their Contemporaries.* Copyright © 1977 by Rutgers University, the State University of New Jersey. Reprinted by permission of the Rutgers University Press (Marlowe).

CHARLES SCRIBNER'S SONS. From Charles H. Brown, *William Cullen Bryant*; John Pudney, *Lewis Carroll and His World.*

PER SEYERSTED. From *Kate Chopin.*

SHAKESPEARE QUARTERLY. From articles by W. L. Godshalk and by Alvin B. Kernan.

SHAKESPEARE STUDIES. From articles by K. W. Evans; Michael West; Rose A. Zimbardo.

SHAMBHALA PUBLICATIONS, INC. *From Majesty and Magic in Shakespeare's Last Plays* by Frances A. Yates, pp. 47, 52–53. Copyright © 1975 by Frances A. Yates. Reprinted by special arrangement with Shambhala Publications, Inc., 1123 Spruce Street, Boulder, Colo. 80302.

SOUTHERN ILLINOIS UNIVERSITY PRESS. From John Gardner, *The Construction of Christian Poetry in Old English* (Caedmon, Cynewulf). Copyright © 1975 by Southern Illinois University Press. Reprinted by permission of Southern Illinois University Press.

THE SOUTHERN LITERARY JOURNAL. From article by Lewis Leary on Chopin.

SOUTHERN STUDIES. From article by Robert Arner on Chopin in *Louisiana Studies* (now: *Southern Studies*).

ST. MARTIN'S PRESS, INCORPORATED. From Peter Hunter Blair, *The World of Bede*; Maureen Peters, *An Enigma of Brontës* (E. Brontë); Mark Storey, *The Poetry of John Clare.*

JAMES STEPHENS. From *Francis Bacon and the Style of Science.*

STUDIES IN ENGLISH LITERATURE. From Philip J. Ayers, "Marston's *Antonio's Revenge:* The Morality of the Revenging Hero"; Ralph Berry, "Sexual Imagery in *Coriolanus*" (Shakespeare); John W. Blanpied, "'Art and Baleful Sorcery': The Counterconsciousness of *Henry VI, Part I*" (Shakespeare); A. P. Hogan, "*'Tis Pity She's a Whore:* The Overall Design" (Ford); Alexander Leggatt "Artistic Coherence in *The Unfortunate Traveller*" (Nashe); Waldo F. McNeir, "The Masks of Richard the Third" (Shakespeare); Michael Manheim, "The Construction of *The Shoemakers' Holiday*" (Dekker); Stella P. Revard, "The Design of Nature in Drayton's *Poly-Olbion.*"

STUDIES IN ROMANTICISM. From articles by Morse Peckham on Wordsworth; Marc A. Rubenstein on Mary Shelley. Reprinted by permission of the Trustees of Boston University.

STUDIES IN THE LITERARY IMAGINATION. From article by Richard Levin on Jonson.

SWETS PUBLISHING SERVICE. From articles by Larry S. Champion on Middleton in *English Studies.*

STUART M. TAVE. From *Some Words of Jane Austen.*

TEXAS A & M UNIVERSITY PRESS. From William J. Scheick, *The Writings of Jonathan Edwards: Theme, Motif, and Style.*

THAMES AND HUDSON LTD. From David Daiches, *Sir Walter Scott and His World*; John Pudney, *Lewis Carroll and His World.*

THOMAS HARDY SOCIETY LTD. From J. O. Bailey's essay in *Thomas Hardy and the Modern World*, F. B. Pinion, ed. Reprinted by permission of the Thomas Hardy Society Ltd., c/o Revd. J. M. C. Yates, Secretary, The Vicarage, Haselbury Plucknett, Crewkerne, Somerset, TA18 7PB.

THE TIMES LITERARY SUPPLEMENT. From articles by A. O. J. Cockshutt on Dickens; Alastair Fowler on Douglas; W. V. Quine on Carroll; Larzer Ziff on Whittier.

TRANSCENDENTAL BOOKS. From articles by Vivian C. Hopkins on Fuller; John C. Kemp on Irving in *American Transcendental Quarterly.*

UNITED CHURCH PRESS. From William J. Wolf, *Thoreau: Mystic, Prophet, Ecologist.* Copyright © 1974 United Church Press. Used by permission.

UNIVERSITÄT SALZBURG, INSTITUT FÜR ENGLISCHE SPRACHE UND LITERATUR. From Hoover H. Jordan, *Bolt Upright: The Life of Thomas Moore.*

UNIVERSITÉ DE LIÈGE. From Jeanne Delbaere-Garant, *Henry James: The Vision of France.* Bibliothèque de la Faculté de Philosophie et Lettres de l'Université de Liège. Fasc. CXCI. 1970.

UNIVERSITY OF CALIFORNIA PRESS. From Stanley E. Fish, *Self-Consuming Artifacts* (Bacon); Ruth A. Fox, *The Tangled Chain* (Burton); Rosemary Freeman, *"The Faerie Queene": A Companion for Readers* (Spenser); Dustin H. Griffin, *Satires against Man* (Rochester); Paul Jorgensen, *Our Naked Frailties* (Shakespeare); Richard A. Lanham, "*Tristram Shandy*" (Sterne); Richard Latham's and William Matthews's Introduction to *The Diary of Samuel Pepys*; John P. McWilliams, *Political Justice in a Republic* (Cooper); Jack Rawlins, *A Fiction That Is True* (Thackeray); Elisabeth Schneider, *The Dragon in the Gate* (Hopkins); William R. Siebenschuh; *Form and Purpose in Boswell's Biographical Works*; Anthony La Branche's essay on Daniel; Leonard Nathan's essay on Gascoigne in *The Rhetoric of Renaissance Poetry*, Thomas O. Sloan and Raymond B. Waddington, eds.; Harold E. Toliver, *Pastoral Forms and Attitudes* (Herbert, Marvell); Robert Zoellner, *The Salt Sea Mastadon* (Melville).

THE UNIVERSITY OF CHICAGO PRESS. From Richard D. Altick and James F. Loucks, *Browning's Roman Murder Stories.* Copyright © 1968 by The University of Chicago Press; Donald D. Ault, *Visionary Physics.* Copyright © 1974 by The University of Chicago (Blake); Harold Bloom, *The Ringers in the Tower.* Copyright © 1971 by The University of Chicago (Blake); Richard H. Brodhead, *Hawthorne, Melville and the Novel.* Copyright © 1973, 1976 by The University of Chicago

(Melville); Morris Dickstein, *Keats and His Poetry*. Copyright © 1971 by The University of Chicago; Philip Harth, *Contexts of Dryden's Thought*. Copyright © 1968 by The University of Chicago; Richard Levin, *The Multiple Plot in English Renaissance Drama*. Copyright © 1972 by The University of Chicago (Middleton, Tourneur); Jerome J. McGann, *"Don Juan" in Context*. Copyright © 1976 by The University of Chicago (Byron); Jerome J. McGann, *Fiery Dust*. Copyright © 1968 by The University of Chicago (Byron); James Stephens, *Francis Bacon and the Style of Science*. Copyright © 1975 by The University of Chicago; Stuart M. Tave, *Some Words of Jane Austen*. Copyright © 1973 by The University of Chicago; Douglas H. White, *Pope and the Context of Controversy*. Copyright © 1970 by The University of Chicago; from Suzanne Gossett, "Masque Influence on the Dramaturgy of Beaumont and Fletcher"; Robert S. Knapp, "The Monarchy of Love in Lyly's *Endimion*"; David Williams, "Patience" (Gawain-Poet) in *Modern Philology*. Copyright 1970, 1972, 1976 by The University of Chicago.

UNIVERSITY OF GEORGIA PRESS. From Larry S. Champion, *Shakespeare's Tragic Perspective*; Edd Winfield Parks, *Sidney Lanier: The Man, the Poet, the Critic*; Louis D. Rubin, Jr. *Mark Twain*; William J. Scheick, *The Will and the Word: The Poetry of Edward Taylor*.

THE UNIVERSITY OF ILLINOIS PRESS. From Jerome Mitchell, *Thomas Hoccleve*. Copyright © 1968 by Board of Trustees of University of Illinois; Ben Ross Schneider, Jr., *The Ethos of Restoration Comedy*. Copyright © 1971 by Board of Trustees of University of Illinois (Wycherley); Jack Stillinger, *The Hoodwinking of Madeline*. Copyright © 1971 by Board of Trustees of University of Illinois (Keats); John C. Stubbs, *The Pursuit of Form: A Study of Hawthorne and the Romance*. Copyright © 1970 by Board of Trustees of University of Illinois; from articles by B. K. Martin on Old English Literature; Claude J. Summers and Ted-Larry Pebworth on Vaughan; Mary C. Wilson Tietjen on *Beowulf* in *Journal of English and Germanic Philology*. Copyright 1969, 1975 by Board of Trustees of University of Illinois.

THE UNIVERSITY OF MASSACHUSETTS PRESS. Reprinted by permission of the University of Massachusetts Press, from *The Example of Edward Taylor* (copyright © 1975) by Karl Keller; *The Dialectics of Creation* (copyright © 1970) by Michael Lieb (Milton); " 'The Crown of Eloquence' " by Joseph A. Wittreich, Jr. in *Achievements of the Left Hand* (copyright © 1974), ed. Michael Lieb and John T. Shawcross (Milton).

UNIVERSITY OF MIAMI PRESS. From Michael Hurst, *Maria Edgeworth and the Public Scene*; Balachandra Rajan, *The Lofty Rhyme* (Milton).

THE UNIVERSITY OF MICHIGAN PRESS. From Ronald Wallace, *Henry James and the Comic Form*.

UNIVERSITY OF MINNESOTA PRESS. From Robert Penn Warren, *John Greenleaf Whittier: An Appraisal and a Selection*.

UNIVERSITY OF NEBRASKA PRESS. Reprinted from Carol H. Poston's Introduction to Mary Wollstonecraft, *Letters written during a Short Residence in Sweden, Norway, and Denmark*. Copyright © 1969 by University of Nebraska. Herbert F. Smith's Introduction to *Literary Criticism of James Russell Lowell*. Copyright © 1969 by University of Nebraska Press; Ralph M. Wardle, *Hazlitt*. Copyright © 1971 by University of Nebraska Press. By permission of University of Nebraska Press.

THE UNIVERSITY OF NEW MEXICO PRESS. From Norton B. Crowell, *The Triple Soul: Browning's Theory of Knowledge* (Albuquerque: University of New Mexico Press,

1963), p. xiii; Edith Wylder, *The Last Face: Emily Dickinson's Manuscripts* (Albuquerque: University of New Mexico Press, 1971), pp. 1, 2, 5.

THE UNIVERSITY OF NORTH CAROLINA PRESS. From Carol Jones Carlisle, *Shakespeare from the Greenroom*. Copyright © 1969 by The University of North Carolina Press; Anthony Channell Hilfer, *The Revolt from Village*. Copyright © 1969 by The University of North Carolina Press (Jewett); Annette Kolodny, *The Lay of the Land*. Copyright © 1975 by The University of North Carolina Press (Cooper, Freneau); Elizabeth Pochoda, *Arthurian Propaganda*. Copyright © 1971 by The University of North Carolina Press (Malory); J. Saunders Redding, *To Make a Poet Black*. Copyright 1939 by The University of North Carolina Press (Chesnutt); James W. Tuttleton, *The Novel of Manners in America*. Copyright © 1972 by The University of North Carolina Press (Howells); from articles by F. W. Brownlow on Skelton; Kenneth Friedenreich on Nashe; Carol McGinnis Kay on Kyd; Paul E. McLane on Skelton; Thomas R. Preston on Smollett in *Studies in Philology*. Copyright © 1968, 1973, 1975, 1977 by The University of North Carolina Press.

UNIVERSITY OF NOTRE DAME PRESS. From essay by Robert P. Creed on Widsith; James Doubleday on Cynewulf; John Gardner on *Beowulf* in *Anglo-Saxon Poetry*, Lewis E. Nicholson and Dolores Warwick Frese, eds. Copyright 1975, by the University of Notre Dame Press, Notre Dame, Indiana 46556.

UNIVERSITY OF PENNSYLVANIA PRESS. From Donald S. Rankin, *Kate Chopin and Her Creole Stories*.

UNIVERSITY OF PITTSBURGH PRESS. From Sherman H. Hawkins's essay in *Milton Studies* II; by permission of the University of Pittsburgh Press. © 1970 by the University of Pittsburgh Press; Roger B. Rollin's essay in *Milton Studies* V; by permission of the University of Pittsburgh Press. © 1973 by the University of Pittsburgh Press; *Masques of God: Form and Theme in the Poetry of Henry Vaughan* by James D. Simmonds, by permission of the University of Pittsburgh Press. © 1972 by the University of Pittsburgh Press.

UNIVERSITY OF QUEENSLAND PRESS. From Geoffrey Thurley, *The Psychology of Hardy's Novels*.

THE UNIVERSITY OF SOUTH CAROLINA PRESS. From articles by Lois A. Eben on Barbour; Ronald D. S. Jack on Dunbar; A. M. Kinghorn on Barbour; John McNamara on Henryson; Dolores L. Noll on Henryson; E. Allen Tilley on Dunbar in *Studies in Scottish Literature*. Copyright 1969, 1971, 1972, 1973 by G. Roff Roy.

THE UNIVERSITY OF TENNESSEE PRESS. From *Samuel Richardson: The Triumph of Craft* by Elizabeth Bergen Brophy. © 1974 by The University of Tennessee Press; *Structural Principles in Old English Poetry* by Neil D. Isaacs. © 1968 by The University of Tennessee Press (*The Wanderer* and *The Seafarer*).

UNIVERSITY OF TEXAS PRESS. From article by Raymond A. Anselment on Suckling in *Texas Studies in Literature and Language*; Thomas L. Ashton, *Byron's Hebrew Melodies*; John C. Pope's essay in *Studies in Language, Literature and Culture of the Middle Ages and Later*, Elmer Bagby Atwood and Archibald A. Hill, eds.; Truman Guy Steffan, *Lord Byron's "Cain": Twelve Essays and a Text with Variants and Annotations*.

UNIVERSITY OF TORONTO PRESS. From G. R. Hibbard's essay in *A Celebration of Ben Jonson*, Papers presented at the University of Toronto in 1972, Blissett, William et al, eds.; Nancy R. Lindheim's essay in *Some Facets of "King Lear,"* Rosalie

Colie, ed. (Shakespeare); Maynard Mack, *The Garden and the City* (Pope); Hugo McPherson, *Hawthorne as Myth-Maker: A Study in Imagination*; Irene Samuel's essay in *The Prison and the Pinnacle*, Balachandra Rajan, ed. (Milton).

THE UNIVERSITY OF WISCONSIN PRESS. From John E. Grant's essay on Blake in *Blake's Sublime Allegory*, Stuart Curran and Joseph Anthony Wittreich, Jr., eds., Karl Kroeber, *Romantic Landscape Vision: Constable and Wordsworth*; Lewis Leary's essay on Freneau; Donald A. Ringe's essay on Brown in *Major Writers of Early American Literature*, Everett Emerson, ed.; F. Anne Payne, *King Alfred and Boethius*; G. R. Thompson, *Poe's Fiction: Romantic Irony in the Gothic Tales*; Joan Webber, *The Eloquent "I"* (Milton); Joseph Anthony Wittreich, Jr., *Angel of Apocalypse* (Blake).

THE UNIVERSITY PRESS OF KENTUCKY. From Thomas Blues, *Mark Twain and the Community*. Copyright © 1970 by The University of Kentucky Press; Ira Konigsberg, *Samuel Richardson & the Dramatic Novel*. Copyright © 1968 by The University of Kentucky Press; Arthur G. Pettit, *Mark Twain and the South*. Copyright © 1974 by The University of Kentucky Press; Thomas A. Spragens, Jr., *The Politics of Motion*. Copyright © 1973 by The University of Kentucky Press (Hobbes). Used by permission of the publisher.

THE UNIVERSITY PRESS OF VIRGINIA. From Paul A. Magnuson, *Coleridge's Nightmare Poetry*; Floyd Stovall, *The Foreground of "Leaves of Grass"* (Whitman); Richard Waswo, *The Fatal Mirror* (Greville); Viola Hopkins Winner, *Henry James and the Visual Arts*.

THE UNIVERSITY PRESSES OF FLORIDA. From Ward Hellstrom, *On the Poems of Tennyson*. Copyright © 1972 by State of Florida; Helene Moglen, *The Philosophical Irony of Laurence Sterne*. Copyright © 1975 by The Board of Regents of the State of Florida.

VANDERBILT UNIVERSITY PRESS. From George N. Bennett, *The Realism of William Dean Howells, 1889–1920*.

THE VICTORIAN NEWSLETTER. From articles by Ruth apRoberts on Trollope; Robert F. Damm on Eliot.

VICTORIAN POETRY. From articles by Joshua Adler on Browning; Eugene R. August on Mill; Barbara J. Bono on Morris; David J. DeLaura on Clough; Robert A. Greenberg on Swinburne; Bert G. Hornback on Hardy; Jacob Korg on Browning; Cecil Y. Lang on Swinburne; Robert Langbaum on Browning; Jerome J. McGann on Rossetti; Richard D. McGhee on Clough; Hartley S. Spatt on Morris.

VICTORIAN STUDIES. From articles by Lloyd Fernando on Kipling; Diane Johnson on Ruskin; Henry Kozicki on Tennyson; William A. Madden on Macaulay; John J. Pappas on Wilde.

THE VIKING PRESS (VIKING PENGUIN INC.) From *The American 1890's* by Larzer Ziff. Copyright © Larzer Ziff, 1966 (Chopin); *Puritanism in America* by Larzer Ziff. Copyright © Larzer Ziff, 1973 (Taylor). All rights reserved. Reprinted by permission of Viking Penguin Inc.

A. WATKINS, INC. From William Irvine and Park Honan, *The Book, the Ring and the Poet* (Browning).

WEIDENFELD LIMITED. From E. W. F. Tomlin, *Charles Dickens*.

WESLEYAN UNIVERSITY PRESS. From Richard Slotkin, *Regeneration through Violence* (Cooper, Hawthorne, Thoreau).

WESTERN AMERICAN LITERATURE. From article by Patrick Morrow on Harte.

THE WESTERN HUMANITIES REVIEW. From article by Kenneth Eble on Chopin.

DOUGLAS H. WHITE. From *Pope and the Context of Controversy.*

DAVID WILLIAMS. From article on *Patience* in *Modern Philology.*

THE WORDSWORTH CIRCLE. From article by William A. Walling on Austen.

YALE UNIVERSITY PRESS. From Judith K. Anderson, *The Growth of a Personal Voice* (Langland); Anne T. Barbeau, *The Intellectual Design of Dryden's Heroic Plays*; Stephen Booth, *An Essay on Shakespeare's Sonnets*; Sanford Budick, *Dryden and the Abyss of Light*; A. Dwight Culler, *Imaginative Reason* (Arnold); Stuart A. Ende, *Keats and the Sublime*; Stephen J. Greenblatt, *Sir Walter Raleigh*; William H. Halewood, *The Poetry of Grace* (Herbert, Vaughan); Geoffrey Hartman, *The Fate of Reading* (Keats); Edward B. Irving, Jr. *A Reading of "Beowulf"*; Elizabeth D. Kirk, *The Dream of Thought of "Piers Plowman"* (Langland); Albert J. La Valley, *Carlyle and the Idea of the Modern*; Alvin A. Lee, *The Guest-Hall of Eden* (*Beowulf*); John F. Lynen, *The Design of the Present* (Edwards, Franklin, Irving); Carey McIntosh, *The Choice of Life* (Johnson); Alice S. Miskimin, *The Renaissance Chaucer*; Daniel H. Peck, *A World by Itself* (Cooper); Craig G. Thompson's Introduction to *The Complete Works of Thomas More*; David M. Vieth's Introduction to *The Complete Poems of John Wilmot, Earl of Rochester*; Ann Chalmers Watts, *The Lyre and the Harp* (Cynewulf); René Wellek, *A History of Modern Criticism* (Arnold); David P. Young, *The Heart's Forest* (Shakespeare); W. G. Zeeveld, *The Temper of Shakespeare's Thought.*

LARZER ZIFF. From article on Whittier in *TLS.*

CROSS-REFERENCE INDEX TO AUTHORS

Only significant references are included

INDEX TO CRITICS

Names of critics are cited on the pages given.